Gross National Product, Canada, 1870–1926
The Derivation of the Estimates

Gross National Product, Canada, 1870–1926
The Derivation of the Estimates

M.C. URQUHART

With chapters by A.G. Green, Thomas Rymes, Marion Steele and A.M. Sinclair, and contributions by D.M. McDougall and R.M. McInnis

McGill-Queen's University Press
Kingston & Montreal • London • Buffalo

Legal deposit first quarter 1993
Bibliothèque nationale du Québec

Printed in Canada on acid-free paper

This book has been published with the help of grants from
the Social Science Federation of Canada, using funds provided by the Social Sciences and Humanities Research
Council of Canada, and from Queen's University.

Material taken from Malcolm Urquhart, "New Estimates of
Gross National Product, Canada, 1870–1926: Some Implications for Canadian Development," and from John Dales'
comments on this article, originally published in *Long-Term
Factors in American Economic Growth*, edited by Stanley
L. Engerman and Robert E. Gallman, Studies in Income and
Wealth, vol. 51 (Chicago: The University of Chicago Press,
1986) © the National Bureau of Economic Research, appears
by permission of the University of Chicago Press.

Canadian Cataloguing in Publication Data

Urquhart, M.C. (Malcolm Charles)
   Gross National Product, Canada, 1870–1926: the Derivation
   of the Estimates
   Includes index.
   ISBN 0-7735-0942-9
   1. Gross National Product — Canada — History   I. Title
   HC120.I5077 1933   339.371   C92-090706-7

Contents

Preface

The emergence of this volume, *New Estimates of Gross National Product, Canada, 1870 to 1926: The Derivation of the Estimates*, marks the culmination of a project begun some fifteen years ago, on my initiative, as a collaborative undertaking of seven of us in academia. The importance of having series of national income data for the understanding of many economic matters had been long recognized. The official estimates of national income in Canada, developed, in the main, by a highly competent group at the Dominion Bureau of Statistics from 1945 onward, covered the period beginning in 1926. Estimates for years before 1926 were limited in scope: before the wartime years of 1939-45 Sydney Smith of the Dominion Bureau of Statistics had prepared national income estimates for 1919 and subsequent years; John Deutsch, subsequent to his work on national income with the Royal Commission on Dominion-Provincial Relations (reported in 1939), had prepared national income estimates for Canada for the years 1911 to 1920 (Canadian Journal of Economics and Political Science, 1940, p.538); O.J. Firestone had prepared estimates for the years beginning each decade from 1870 to 1920, preceding the decennial population census year, and a single series of annual constant dollar estimates from 1870 onward (plus 1867) (O.J. Firestone, *Canada's Economic Development 1867-1953*, Bowes and Bowes, London, 1958); a number of private estimates cited by Firestone had also appeared. These estimates had all served useful purposes but they had their limitations. There remained scope for a new set of annual national income estimates for Canada, for the years 1870 to 1926 based on both more extensive and more intensive investigations than had been done hitherto. The need can be no better put than was done by John Dales in this excerpt from his comments on the estimates when they were first given at a Conference on Research in Income and Wealth of the National Bureau of Economic Research at Williamsburg, Virginia in 1984.

> The new estimates constitute the second attempt to provide a comprehensive set of historical National Accounts for Canada; the first such estimates were prepared by O.J. Firestone some 30 years ago and published in his 1958 volume, *Canada's Economic Development, 1867-1953*. Since the two sets of numbers are bound to be compared I hope Urquhart will prepare a short account of the major differences between them and possible explanations for the differences. (McInnis provides a good commentary on the agricultural figures, perhaps the main source of these major differences.) The point would only be to satisfy our gross curiosity; the estimates differ in concept, construction, and especially in the amount of raw data that underlies them, and it would be pointless to attempt to reconcile them in any detailed way.
>
> Here I comment on the estimates from the point of view of their probable effect on research in Canadian economic history. In retrospect I find it rather surprising that

Firestone's estimates have stimulated so little research. Two reasons may be suggested. First, the Firestone figures were simply too skeletal, consisting essentially of estimates at census dates, with only a few annual series for large aggregates that represented interpolations made on a more or less mechanical basis between census years. Second, the worksheets of the people involved in the Firestone project were apparently never brought together in a safe repository, and over time they became lost. The result was that the scholarly community was faced with numbers that could be used to calculate decadal growth rates for a few major aggregates, but not for much else. More important, there was not much chance of fleshing out the skeleton by building on the raw data and attempting to improve the estimates, which is why improved estimates necessitated a whole new start.

If the Firestone estimates had a low research multiplier, I feel sure that the Urquhart estimates will greatly enrich the study of Canadian economic history. The main reason is their richness in detail. The GNP totals, for example, are built up from estimates for twenty sectors: agriculture, manufacturing, and six lesser commodity sectors; construction; transportation; residential rents; three government sectors; public education; three minor service sectors, and two large ones — trade, and personal and business services. Of these only the last two, constituting about 15 percent of the total, have had to be interpolated on a mechanical basic between census years; enough ancillary data have been found to develop annual series that can be used as interpolators for the other sectors. Moreover, the sectors are themselves constructed from subsectors: some 28 separate commodity series for agriculture, and 17 separate series for manufacturing. There is more than enough here to enrich scores of doctoral dissertations, and it is hard to think of any research in the field that will not benefit from this new material. Constant use, in turn, will act as a continuous testing of the data, and, when, anomalies appear, will lead to attempts to improve individual series. Our new numbers can confidently be expected to increase our research metabolism....

The product of our new project is then the new annual estimates of gross national product and related items for 1870 to 1926 contained herein along with a description of how the new estimates were obtained: the estimates themselves have been previously published. The various components of the estimates of gross domestic product, with particular reference to industrial subdivisions, are attributable to those engaged in the project as follows. Those for whom a University designation is not given individually are members of staff at Queen's University.

Alan Green was responsible for the income estimates in the transportation, communications, and electric light and power sector. This included estimates for the steam railways, the electric railways, the telegraph, the telephone, and the electric utilities, and the description of the derivation of his estimates given in Chapter 6.

Duncan McDougall prepared estimates of wage and salary payments and of outlays on goods and services of federal and provincial governments, in great detail for 1910 and in somewhat lesser detail for 1900, 1890, 1880, and 1870. I was responsible for estimates for provinces for 1920 and also for the interpolation of the yearly data between census years and between 1920 and 1926 when the official estimates begin. Duncan McDougall was also responsible for the preparation of the major part of the fisheries estimates; I did some work in reconciling the estimates at a point of junction of two series where the nature of the underlying data changed. I did the writeups on the preparation of both of these estimates.

Marvin McInnis and I developed the methodology of estimation of income for the agricultural sector in preparing an estimate for 1910. Marvin McInnis then wrote up the estimates for that year. I did the detailed direction of the preparation of the estimates for the full period, with some further consultation with Marvin McInnis, and I must bear the responsibility for their quality. I also did the detailed writeup on the preparation of the agricultural estimates.

Thomas Rymes, of Carleton University, prepared the income estimates for the finance, insurance, and real estate sector, and the description of the derivation of his estimates, all of which appears in Chapter 7. Prior work of Rymes was also of much use in preparation of the data on manufacturing.

Alasdair Sinclair, of Dalhousie University, prepared the balance of payments estimates and the description of their derivation given in Chapter 11.

Marion Steele, of the University of Guelph, prepared the estimates of residential rent, the estimates of capital formation through residential construction, and the descriptions of the derivation of her estimates which appear in Chapter 8.

I am responsible for the preparation of the remainder of the estimates and all of the remaining writeup as well as the coordination and direction of the whole project.

The fact that the work leading to the completion of this has been done by several authors and spread over many years, on a part-time basis on my part, has meant some difference in form among the chapters. It has remained our objective that each chapter and the work as a whole should avoid ambiguity and be readily comprehensible. The final arrangement of pages to fit a form for providing camera-ready copy for reproduction has been shaped by the need to keep the material in proper sequence.

We were assisted in our work at various times by many research assistants, among whom were David Arrowsmith, Merrit Cluff, Ann Green, Richard Huff, Marshall Lee, Gina Mathew, Rupendra Nath, Stephen Poloz, Leighton Reid, Rodney Schmidt, Joanne Stewart, Patrick Wilson, and Dennis Wrixon, and those to whom credit is given separately by T.K. Rymes and Marion Steele in their chapters. I wish also to thank Kim Roper for her heroic and splendidly accurate work in putting the material, all computer based, in a form for transfer directly to camera-ready copy for duplication. In addition, I wish especially to note the contribution of David Jones to the preparation of the estimates on manufactures: David Jones, who had been a senior member of the National Income Unit of Statistics Canada, spent one winter working especially on the data on manufactures and made a most valuable contribution to the manufactures estimates and some other figures.

The project is indebted to the University of Chicago Press for permission to reproduce parts of my paper "New Estimates of Gross National Product, Canada, 1870-1926: Some Implications for Canadian Development" contained in Stanley L. Engerman and Robert E. Gallman, *Long-Term Factors in American Economic Growth* published for the National Bureau of Economic Research by the University of Chicago Press, 1986. The material so reproduced in this volume comprises: Tables 1.1 to 1.13; pages 2 to 9; pages 47 to 51; pages 236 to 242. In some cases, there are slight modifications of the originally published material.

The project was supported by grants from the Killam Fund of the Canada Council and from the Social Sciences Research Council of Canada and by provision of working space, computer use, and other facilities by Queen's University. The cost of final editing and of formatting the material for camera-ready copy was a personal expense.

M.C. Urquhart

Chapter 1. The Project: Basic Methods and Sources; Basic Tables

M.C. URQUHART

This volume contains new estimates of Canada's gross national product and related measures for the years 1870 to 1926 and detailed descriptions of how these estimates were prepared. The final estimates themselves have appeared already in Stanley L. Engerman and Robert E. Gallman, *Long-Term Factors in American Economic Growth*, 1986, University of Chicago Press, Volume 51 in the National Bureau of Economic Research, Conference on Research in Income and Wealth Series under the title "New Estimates of Gross National Product, Canada, 1870-1926: Some Implications for Canadian Development" by M.C. Urquhart; the detailed descriptions of the way of preparing the estimates and the presentation of tables supplementary to them appear here for the first time. These detailed descriptions provide the means of assessment of the quality of the final product estimates and of their reconstruction or amendment; one would hope that they might also provide a springboard to the great amount of collateral work on the development of the Canadian economy that remains to be done.

In the process of the preparation of this extensive manuscript some minor errors in the original estimates were found. They were all small enough that the original estimates could have been left unchanged without any harm being done. However, it was deemed best to correct these errors to keep the credibility of the estimates on the highest plane, even though it meant very small changes in all gross national product totals and despite the burden of much work for little change. The changes from the original estimates of the values of gross national product in no case amount to as much as one per cent and are usually very much less. For those who are interested, the whereabouts of the changes are described in the appendix to this chapter.

The material of the volume is arranged in the following sequence. First, a general description of the method of estimation and identification of basic sources is given followed immediately by the basic tables of new data; some tables given in the Engerman-Gallman volume have been omitted since they are readily derivable from generally accessible data. Second, the detailed explanations of the derivation of the estimates are given: since the basic table of gross national product presents gross domestic product by industry, these detailed explanations are given on an industry by industry basis. At the end of many of the industry writeups, sets of supplementary tables of data for the industry appear. These latter tables are given because they were generated in the process of estimation of gross domestic product of the industry and may have some usefulness to research workers engaged on other projects — their derivation will be evident from the industry writeups.

Basic Methods and Sources

This note contains two parts. First, the method of estimation of gross domestic product (GDP) and gross national product (GNP) for the period 1870-1926 and the rationale for the use of this method are presented. Second, the major sources of data and their strengths and weaknesses are described.

There mainder of this note is taken almost unchanged from my paper in the Engerman-Gallman volume; the part on transportation and public utilities has been expanded slightly.

The Method of Estimation of GDP

There are three possible methods of estimating GDP or the closely related GNP which are not necessarily alternatives but which, in fact, often are just that, at least for the preparation of historical estimates. It is about the method appropriate for historical estimates that I shall speak, although I shall also make reference, at times, to current practice.

The Expenditure Method

One such method comprises the estimation of expenditure (actual and imputed) on final goods and services, on consumer commodities, on capital goods, on goods and services purchased by government, and on net purchases of goods and services by residents of foreign countries, to obtain GNP. It is then adjusted for net international income flows to obtain GDP. Practically all countries make estimates of such expenditure in their current preparation of their national accounts and, more important, make such estimates from data that are, for the most part, independent of those used to estimate GNP or GDP by alternative methods as well. However, most countries do not have the luxury of being able to make good historical estimates, from independent data, by both the expenditure method and either one or a combination of the two other methods that can be followed and consequently rely primarily on one method or another.

Many countries do not depend primarily on expenditure estimates for historical periods. However, the United States is one country that does. The historical GNP estimates for early years for the United States (before 1919) are based primarily on Kuznets's work; he obtained his estimates by use of the expenditure method. This method was reasonably appropriate for the United States since its census of manufactures obtained a large amount of commodity data from as early as 1869. These data made it possible to separate finished products from intermediate products and, in turn, along with such items as trade data, data on production of agricultural products, information on freight costs and on trade margins, and reports of government bodies, made possible the derivation of reasonably decent estimates for large components of the gross national expenditure.

This method was much less appropriate for Canada because her census of manufacturers did not report commodity data until 1917: only the value of output was reported. Hence it is much more difficult to separate production of intermediate products from final products and to divide the latter among consumer goods, capital goods, and goods sold to governments in Canada than in the United States. And we decided at an early stage not to use this method.

The Income Method

The second method of estimating GDP is to add together factor costs of production to obtain national income at factor cost, to further add on capital consumption allowances to obtain GDP at factor cost, and then, finally, if desired, to add indirect taxes less subsidies to obtain GDP at market prices. One can then, if one wishes, obtain GNP at market prices by subtracting factor incomes paid abroad and adding factor incomes received from abroad.

This factor income method is widely used currently to obtain most of the items of the factor income and GNP statements of the national accounts. Its use depends on the direct availability of data on, first, labour income and second, property income. Such data are now available in Canada and many other countries from personal and corporate income tax returns and from many surveys done by statistical agencies. However, in the historical period in which we are interested, before the widespread use of income taxes to obtain revenue, data on property income are not directly available, and while reports of wage data are somewhat better, even they may be incomplete. Hence many countries find the use of this method unsatisfactory for estimation of historical GNP. The United Kingdom is an exception: its continuous use of the income tax dates from 1842/43. There are few data for Canada to yield direct estimates of property income before the First World War — reports for the banks, insurance companies, and governments are exceptions — and so this method has for Canada only limited use for historical estimates.

The Value-Added Method

The third method involves obtaining estimates of GDP at factor cost by the value-added method and then deriving from them estimates of GNP by adding factor incomes received from abroad and subtracting factor incomes paid abroad. Basically, the value-added method of estimation involves subtracting nonfactor costs of production from gross value of production or gross sales on an industry basis in order to obtain gross value added by industry (that is, the sum of factor costs and depreciation). This is the method used even yet in the official estimates of agriculture income in Canada: a synthetic account is set up in which estimated nonfactor costs of farming items such as cost of feed, fertilizer, machinery operating costs, and farm taxes are subtracted from farm sales plus an imputation of income in kind for farm products consumed as final products on the farms on which they were produced.

This method is often the one most suited, at least for a first approach, to making historical estimates of GDP at factor costs for both the farm sector and the manufacturing sector, which are, by any measure and by a substantial margin, the two largest sectors in Canada throughout the period 1870-1926 and which are really dominant in the earlier part of this period. Other goods-producing industries such as mining, forestry, construction, and even the fisheries may be approached by the factor income method.

The Method Adopted

The method adopted in our project may best be given by a brief description of the procedure followed for selected industries, tedious as that procedure may be. Accordingly, I give now such an industry description.

Agriculture. Estimates for agriculture were made by the value-added method: the method is described more fully in the section of this volume that gives the estimates of income generated in agriculture. Here I just note that the main innovation is the direct estimation, in the first instance, of off-farm sales and farm consumption of farm products without its being necessary to deal with the presence of intermediate farm products that are used in further production in the farm sector itself. The only expenses that are relevant then are the costs of purchases from outside the farm sector.

Manufacturing. The value-added method is used: a general outline of the method is given in the section of this paper that deal with the manufacturing data. Basically, the method involves subtracting cost of materials, cost of fuel and electricity, and "miscellaneous" expenses (items like repair and maintenance expenditures, insurance, and office supplies) from gross value of production to obtain GDP at factor cost. The labour income component of GDP can be estimated directly from data collected in censuses of manufactures, and the property income emerges as a residual.

Mining. The value-added method is used for 1921-26 by use of Dominion Bureau of Statistics census of industry data. For 1870-1920 the estimates were made separately for each of five groups into which total mining was divided, namely: metallic mines; coal (further divided by province); asbestos; other nonmetallic minerals and fuels; and sand, gravel, and stone. For each of these, it was possible to get long annual series of gross value of production (GVP) running right back to 1886 for all minerals but coal and gold and for coal and gold themselves back to 1870. For the first four groups noted above we also had wage and salary costs for 1900, 1910, 1921-26, and for coal alone for 1917-18. The ratio of these wage and salary costs to GDP was constant for all of these aforementioned years. Estimates of annual wages and salaries were obtained by assuming that the ratios of wages and salaries to GVP, by groups, were the same before 1900 as in 1900 and that these ratios could be interpolated linearly between 1900 and 1910 and between 1910 and 1920 (with the exception of coal for which there were additional ratios for 1917 and 1918). Multiplication of gross values of products by these ratios then yielded estimates of wages and salaries.

In the absence of data before 1921, to permit a direct estimate of property income, an improvisation was necessary. Ratios of property income to labour income were available by groups for 1921-26, and for 1966 onward (Corporation Financial Statistics). Overall ratios for mining were also available from the *National Accounts* for 1926 onward. There was sufficient stability in these ratios through time to suggest that we might assume that such stable ratios existed prior to 1921 at the level of industry subdivision that we used.

A variation of the method was used for the sand, gravel, and stone subdivision, but it is not worth detaining us for the details at this point, particularly since this item was very small in early years.

After the above calculations were made, a small percentage was added to the whole series to take account of income of the self-employed. This percentage was based on data for the national accounts from 1926 onward.

Transportation and communication: the railways. For as far back as 1907 both wage and salary payments and property income are calculated from annual reports, submitted to the government, which are published. Prior to 1907 other methods were necessary, since the necessary data were not available in published reports. However, wage and salary data were available for a quite large sample of companies, in material housed in the national archives, for many years in the earlier period. By relating them to operating data one could obtain ratios that formed a basis for estimation of wages and salaries for all companies, since operating data were reported for all companies from 1875 onward. Property income was calculated from bond interest expenses — bonded indebtedness was fully known — and from reports of dividends paid in Poor's Manual of Railroads, an allowance being made for undistributed profits. These estimates can be taken as being quite reliable.

Information on other transportation, communication and electric power is given in the detailed writeup.

Finance, insurance, and real estate, excluding house rents. The estimates for finance and insurance were prepared predominantly by the income method. Insurance companies of all kinds have long had to report to the Federal Superintendent of Insurance for federally incorporated companies or to provincial counterparts for provincially incorporated companies. These reports contained the material from which estimates of both labour and property income could be made. Labour income included a large component of "commissions." It required summing of information for each company to obtain the aggregates.

The estimates for banks were also derived basically by the income method but with an added wrinkle. First, annual estimates of both wages and salaries and property income were obtained from records of two of the major banks made available by the banks themselves: for one of the banks both wage and salary income and property income were obtained directly from the bank statements; for the other bank wages and salaries were obtained directly but property income was obtained from the statements by the value-added method. GDP for the whole banking industry was obtained by multiplying the GDP for the two banks by the ratio of assets of all banks to the assets of the two banks.

Labour income of loan and mortgage companies and the real estate and brokerage sections of the "Finance, etc." industry was obtained by extrapolating estimates prepared by Statistics Canada (previously the Dominion Bureau of Statistics) for the 1920s backward, on the basis of assets of building societies and mortgage loan companies and of trust companies. The real estate and brokerage section extrapolation was tied into estimates of wage and salary income of real estate dealers and brokers for 1911 derived from wage and salary data obtained in the population census of 1911. The labour income of all of the financial operations described in this paragraph are a relatively small part of such income for the whole finance, insurance, and real estate industry.

Government: federal, provincial, municipal, public education. The main income item for all of the government components is salary and wage expense. Estimates of labour income for all of the government components are from annual reports that are reasonably complete for the federal and provincial governments and for education, and sufficiently good to permit passable estimates of municipal wages and salaries.

Miscellaneous service industries. These industries include wholesale and retail trade, business service, health and welfare, religion, recreation, other community services, and personal and domestic service. Labour income makes up a very large part of GDP in all of these industries. The estimation of labour income in all of these groups depends very heavily on the use of data collected in the population census on occupations of the gainfully occupied persons in all censuses from 1871 onward and on wages and salaries of every employed person in the censuses of 1901, 1911, 1921, and 1931. Labour income for the self-employed is imputed at rates that are derived from wages and salaries paid to hired workers. For census years before 1901, one obtains estimates of labour income by projecting wages and salary rates in 1900 by such items as average earnings in manufactures, reports of wages and salaries in Royal Commission reports and records of hearings (e.g., Royal Commission on the Relations of Labour and Capital in Canada; *Report*, 1889), reports of wage and salary rates in both agriculture and industry by the Ontario Bureau of Industries in the 1880s (and later for agriculture only), reported wage and salary rates for public servants and schoolteachers, and a considerable amount of other such information.

Residential rents. The new estimates of residential rents are much more firmly based than those available hitherto. The preparation of these estimates is best summarized in the words of Marion Steele, the author.

Estimates of residential rent in Canada 1871-1925 currently do not exist, except for those of Firestone (1958) for decade-ending years. In this note we present and describe new annual estimates for 1871-1930. The fundamentals of our estimation procedure are simple. First we estimate mean paid and imputed rent in 1931, using the Census data of that year. Next we estimate an index of mean rents back to 1870; this index is a patchwork of separate indexes which we estimate from sources as diverse as surveys carried out by Ontario Bureau of Industries in the 1880s and James Mavor's Toronto survey in the 1900s. Third, we estimate the stock of dwelling units by urbanization level — urban, rural non-farm, farm — and so derive gross rents by urbanization level. Finally we estimate deductions from gross rents: expenditure on repairs and maintenance and on fire insurance premiums.

Real Gross National Product

The current dollar values were deflated at a quite aggregate level to obtain estimates in constant dollars. The cost of living index, used to deflate all national expenditures except gross capital formation was, in part, a product of this project. The capital formation items were deflated at a more disaggragated level by indexes developed by Statistics Canada.

The cost of living index that was used to deflate the component of GNP (expenditure) that excluded gross fixed capital formation was prepared from three temporally distinct segments that were linked together at overlapping years.

The first segment, covering the years 1913-26, was a full-blown estimate prepared by the Dominion Bureau of Statistics. It appears as series K1 in Statcan, *Historical Statistics of Canada,* second edition.

The second segment, covering the years 1900-1913, was based on an index prepared by Gordon W. Bertram and Michael B. Percy which appeared in "Real Wage Trends in Canada, 1900-26: Some Provisional Estimates," *Canadian Journal of Economics* (May 1979). Bertram and Percy revised the federal Department of Labour's "Index Numbers of a Family Budget," which covered the years 1900, 1905, and 1909-26 (Urquhart M.C. Editor and K.A.H. Buckley, Assistant Editor, *Historical Statistics of Canada* (HSC), p.303) in two ways. First, they used an improved weighting system for aggregating the basic data, which were fully available. Second, they added a clothing component, prepared from mail-order catalogs of the T. Eaton company for the years 1900-13, to the existing Department of Labour components of food, fuel and light, and rent.

The Bertram-Percy index was used as given for the years which they covered from 1900 to 1913. It remained to fill in figures for the years 1901-4 and 1906-8, which they, following the Department of Labour, had not covered. The latter years were interpolated between 1900 and 1905 and 1905 and 1909, respectively, by use of the wholesale price index, excluding gold (HSC Series J34).

The third segment, covering the years 1870-1900, was based on a cost of living index for Kingston, Ontario, prepared by R.F.J. Barnett and appearing in his M.A. thesis at Queen's University, "A Study of Price Movements and the Cost of Living in Kingston, Ontario, for the Years 1865 to 1900" (1963). Barnett prepared his index by using newspaper material on prices supplemented by information obtained from good records of a food store that was in business throughout his period, similar types of records for a fuel company, and records of expenditures by the House of Industry (the poor house), which records were in the archives of the City of Kingston.

Barnett's weighting system used all available Canadian and United States data relevant to the period and, in addition, information on consumer expenditure patterns collected by the Ontario Bureau of Industries for the 1880s. It was quite good for what it covered. However, Barnett was able to cover only food and fuel and light, which made up a large part of the consumer budget of the time but omitted clothing and rent (as well as items like household furnishings, etc.).

Although it was not possible, at this time, to do anything about the omission of clothing, it was possible to make an improvisation for rent. In her work on estimating expenditure on residential housing, Marion Steele had prepared a construction cost index for housing. This index was used as a surrogate for an index of rents. Such a procedure is, of course, a makeshift measure. However, a check with United States rent data (the Rees-Long-Hoover data noted below) and United States construction cost indexes (United States *Historical Statistics, Colonial Times to 1970*, Series N138 and N139) showed a not unreasonable correspondence in the period from 1870 to 1900. And so a rental index component was added to Barnett's index, the weight given to rent being based on data for Kingston in the 1880s from the Ontario Bureau of Industries surveys of the time. (The actual weight was 0.2).

I believe that the resulting index for Kingston, although admittedly based on narrow regional data, reflects living cost movements considerably better than does a wholesale price index. It lacks a clothing component, which perhaps biases the index downward in the 1870s. However, at the same time the use of a construction cost index as a surrogate for rental rates may constitute a slight upward bias in the 1870s.

For readers to make their own judgements, I add Table 1.13 for comparing movements in our cost of living with a comparable one for the United States and with the DBS wholesale price index (HSC Series J34). The United States index is derived by linking together Rees's index for 1890-1900 (Albert Rees, *Real Wages in Manufacturing 1890-1914*, p.74) with Clarence Long's index for 1880-90 and Ethyl Hoover's index for 1860-80 (Clarence Long, *Wages and Earnings in the United States 1860-1890*, pp.156, 157). The United States index for 1870-78 is adjusted downward by the amount of the premium on gold in United States currency for that time. Concerning the DBS wholesale price index, I just note that an alternative index by H. Michell (HSC Series J1) shows considerably lower prices in the 1870s relative to 1900 prices and to 1880 prices than does the DBS wholesale price index of Table 1.13.

Major Sources of Data

It would take far too much space to even list all sources of data at this point. Hence only the most important ones will be covered. The sources of data are grouped into three classes: benchmark data sources, annual data sources, and occasional data sources.

Benchmark Data Sources

The data for some years are sometimes much more complete than those for adjacent years. These are the benchmark years. The main benchmark years for 1870-1926 are the decennial census years. The decennial census was taken in the first half of the second year of each decade. The production data collected in the census were for the preceding year. For example, the production data collected in the census of 1901 are for the year 1900. In the census years the following relevant special census data were obtained.

a) Census of manufactures for 1870, 1880, 1890, 1900, and 1910. (The annual census of manufactures began in 1917, and hence this census was separated from the decennial census.) Later I elaborate on these data.

b) Census of agriculture for each decennial census year from 1870 to 1980. Special data continued to be collected for decennial census years, even after the annual censuses of production in agriculture began. Quantities of products only were obtained in the censuses of 1870, 1880, and 1890. Quantities and values of products were collected in 1900 and later censuses. There was not much collected in the way of cost data until the census of 1920, and even then the information obtained was quite limited. Further information on these data is contained in the discussion of the agricultural data that are presented later.

c) A usable census of mineral products was taken with each of the decennial censuses of 1900 and 1910. Quantities and values of minerals produced were obtained. The numbers of persons employed and their wages or salaries were also obtained. There were no other costs data, but there was a description of plant and equipment.

d) A census of forest production was taken from 1870 onward to 1910, but it was of limited use until 1900, in which year it appears to have been quite complete. It covered only production on farms in 1910. There were no cost data.

e) The decennial census of population contained two valuable sources of data. First, from 1871 onward, in every census, the occupations of the gainfully occupied were obtained: the occupational data of the 1910 census were particularly valuable because they were classified on an industrial basis very much like the 1948 standard industrial classification. In addition to obtaining occupational data, the population censuses from 1901 to 1931 (and beyond) obtained records of remuneration in the form of wage or salary from every hired person in the population. Information on the number of weeks worked as well as age and sex characteristics were also obtained (on the same census form, of course). These data were tabulated according to occupational classifications that corresponded with those used for the gainfully occupied population.

Special mention must be made of the wage and occupational data for 1910. The tabulations by the census office for this year were much more elaborate than those for either 1900 or 1920. There was the additional fact that since the classification was like that of the 1948 standard industrial classification, it was possible to compare wages and salaries reported in the population census with those reported in the census of manufactures, in the census of mines, in reports of government bodies on the wage bill of the public service, in reports of teachers' wage bills in departmental reports, in reports of the railways on wages and salaries, and in other such reports. In general the correspondence was quite good. Such satisfactory correspondence gives one confidence in the reliability of the labour income data for other workers for whom there is ordinarily little information. Thus, it seemed appropriate to use these wage and salary data for such industries as trade (wholesale and retail), business service, recreation, domestic service, and other such groups for 1910. The year 1910 became in effect a benchmark year par excellence.

Annual Data Sources

The number of sources of relevant annual data is very large; only a small selection is mentioned here.

a) External trade data provide continuous annual series from Confederation onward. They are most important for the balance of payments. They have many other uses, of which I shall give only two examples. First, exports of wheat (quantity and value) help in the earlier years in the estimation of wheat production. Second, imports of raw cotton (and cotton thread) can be used as an interpolator between census years of value of production of the cotton textile industry.

b) Mineral production statistics, collected or assembled by the Geological Survey of Canada and successor bodies, are available on an annual basis for all minerals from 1886 onward; output of coal and gold is available annually back to 1870 from both provincial and federal government sources.

c) Agricultural field crop production data are available annually for Ontario from 1882 onward (Ontario Bureau of Industries); stocks of animals are available also for Ontario from 1882 onward and sales and slaughter are available from 1892; cheese production is available from 1882. Similar data are available from provincial sources for Manitoba from 1883, for New Brunswick from 1898, and for the Northwest Territories (Alberta and Saskatchewan) from 1898. From 1908 onward the federal Census and Statistics Office collected crop production data and data on numbers of animals annually for all but British Columbia, which was added in 1911; with the establishment of the Dominion Bureau of Statistics in 1918, annual production data on meat, dairy, and poultry products were added.

d) Government annual reports provide information on wages and salaries in the public service at all levels of government; they also provide expenditures on educational salaries for all provinces.

e) Government reports of excise and bounty data and on inspection services provide annual data on items such as pig iron production, tobacco products made, production of beer and spirits, production of petroleum products, and other items.

f) Forestry branches of the federal government collected annual output of sawmill products from 1908 onward.

g) Government bodies collected railway statistics annually from 1875 onward and banking and insurance company data from Confederation onward.

h) Price data are available from many sources right from 1867. Chief among these are the work of H. Michell in *Statistical Contributions to Economic History, Volume 2*, of Department of Labour, *Wholesale Prices 1890-1909* and subsequent annual volumes, and of DBS once it was established. The basis of much of this work was newspaper price quotations.

i) And then there are all the Dominion Bureau of Statistics data from 1917 onward in the census of industry, the census of agriculture, and so forth.

Occasional Data Sources

There were several occasional data sources:

a) Ontario Bureau of Industries Reports in the 1880s give a wide range of wage data for many occupations and also price data.

b) Some data came from commissions or committees of inquiry. Perhaps chief of these was the Report of the Inquiry into the Cost of Living (1915) of the Federal Department of Labour which was mainly Coats's work and which contains an enormous amount of data of many kinds.

c) Some data were collected on a nonrepetitive basis by government statistical agencies, for example, municipal financial data in the Statistical Yearbook of 1894, the predecessor of the Canada Year Book published by the Census and Statistics Office.

The basic tables follow, identified by their number in the N.B.E.R. volume.

Project Table No.	N.B.E.R. Volume Table No.
Table 1.1	2.1
1.2	2.2
1.3	2.3
1.4	2.4
1.5	2.7
1.6	2.9
1.7	2.10
1.8	2.11
1.9	2.14
1.10	2.15
1.11	2.16
1.12	2.17

Table 1.1. Gross National Product, Canada (thousands of dollars)

	1870	1871	1872	1873	1874	1875	1876	1877	1878	1879	1880	1881
Agriculture	143768	145003	146929	143742	153212	145436	137895	142897	132904	156784	156980	195031
Forestry (excluding agriculture)	5790	6960	7669	9175	9257	8184	7101	7244	6565	5911	5908	7923
Hunting and trapping	211	306	516	867	998	1047	1047	894	850	752	1019	1101
Fisheries	2921	3306	4249	4775	5186	4596	4936	5330	5868	6007	6540	6978
Mining	4431	5354	5507	5436	4762	6109	5906	5237	4736	5385	5289	5405
Manufacturing	76983	89406	98954	123997	107930	97479	84232	93173	83725	86996	103615	122923
Manufactured gas	399	505	641	744	778	813	848	562	534	825	719	847
Construction	20000	21000	26300	28700	32000	29000	22700	19500	17300	17400	20400	22400
Transportation	20000	22609	22014	23372	23777	19690	19849	19323	21454	21249	25001	27929
Electric light and power												
Communications												
Banking and finance	7000	8000	10000	10000	10000	8000	9000	9000	8000	9000	10000	12000
Residential rents	20756	21959	26609	28209	28769	27725	27123	26779	26515	26290	27275	28654
Federal government	4595	5268	6086	7989	7914	8689	8782	8474	8385	7723	7980	8404
Provincial government	1589	1756	2230	2548	3076	3058	2933	2890	2604	2607	2541	2704
Municipal services	3441	3587	3908	4202	4476	4748	4986	5340	5395	5482	5586	5711
Education, public	3480	3438	3978	4428	4800	5120	5355	5935	5900	6105	6198	6221
Universities	200	203	223	243	263	283	303	323	343	363	383	420
Wholesale and retail trade	21176										31976	
Community, business, and personal service	26454										34672	
Gross Domestic Product (old official basis)	363194	390509	422624	461000	460631	429876	399282	411581	386865	420140	452082	534715
Public revenues from resource royalties	1027	1120	1718	1451	1230	864	1040	999	807	862	1340	1871
GDP (new basis)	364221	391629	424342	462451	461861	430740	400322	412580	387672	421002	453422	536586
Less: net interest and dividends paid abroad	5412	4034	4991	5409	7039	8192	9079	9804	10047	11993	14286	14727
Gross National Product at factor cost	358809	387595	419351	457042	454822	422548	391243	402776	377625	409009	439136	521859
Indirect taxes, less subsidies	23715	24550	27029	29114	28456	27773	27967	28913	29268	32677	38236	42535
Gross National Product at market prices	382524	412145	446380	486156	483278	450321	419210	431689	406893	441686	477372	564394

Table 1.1. (continued)

	1882	1883	1884	1885	1886	1887	1888	1889	1890	1891	1892	1893
Agriculture	203075	183552	172201	163979	157312	175504	170750	177285	185723	189108	189499	181588
Forestry (excluding agriculture)	8940	9297	8685	8136	9343	9458	10170	10697	10933	11105	11422	11575
Hunting and trapping	798	745	924	1101	1130	1246	1280	1134	992	985	1013	1084
Fisheries	7459	7640	8044	8090	8385	8347	8143	8031	8279	8682	8668	9623
Mining	5740	5498	6065	6250	7500	8083	9155	10348	12350	14729	12285	14505
Manufacturing	142493	148958	132910	127817	133241	141622	148915	156984	171691	172454	165317	158575
Manufactured gas	769	906	950	1166	1281	1467	1361	1506	1705	1642	1715	1715
Construction	30000	34000	38000	25700	25500	30200	31600	34200	30100	31200	28600	26200
Transportation	29051	31301	31015	28672	32168	33604	36177	36320	40460	39840	42429	42234
Electric light and power						526	548	636	936	1012	1089	1166
Communications									745	855	921	1162
Banking and finance	13000	14000	14000	14000	15000	17000	18000	19000	18000	20000	22000	21000
Residential rents	31080	30687	30112	29689	28986	33892	35496	36580	37493	38724	41267	42442
Federal government	9240	10259	11091	12436	11249	11297	11250	11117	11416	11565	11818	12275
Provincial government	2882	3014	2984	3013	3186	3423	3451	3957	3904	4388	4119	4091
Municipal services	5904	6067	6205	6554	6788	6954	7766	8447	8635	9505	9202	9437
Education, public	6339	6580	6733	7045	7268	7152	7501	7663	7987	8285	8552	8479
Universities	456	493	530	566	603	640	676	713	749	786	804	821
Wholesale and retail trade									53052			
Community, business, and personal service									60143			
Gross Domestic Product (old official basis)	586379	582969	557811	528170	535226	585163	601984	630486	665293	680380	675107	659484
Public revenues from resource royalties	1982	1663	1379	1483	1675	2021	2739	2388	2080	2564	3649	3193
GDP (new basis)	588361	584632	559190	529653	536901	587184	604723	632874	667373	682944	678756	662677
Less: net interest and dividends paid abroad	15745	16846	17291	17961	22199	24817	24687	26920	29904	30313	31156	31951
Gross National Product at factor cost	572616	567786	541899	511692	514702	562367	580036	605954	637469	652631	647600	630726
Indirect taxes, less subsidies	42200	40221	40432	40463	44196	46434	49770	49561	49017	50253	51676	50257
Gross National Product at market prices	614816	608007	582331	552155	558898	608801	629806	655515	686486	702884	699276	680983

Table 1.1. (continued)

	1894	1895	1896	1897	1898	1899	1900	1901	1902	1903	1904
Agriculture	172555	167159	157150	186915	188867	200280	207754	243219	279778	266722	278332
Forestry (excluding agriculture)	10732	10973	12162	12697	12318	13020	13137	14439	14749	15109	15594
Hunting and trapping	1113	1119	1132	1046	1008	1084	1127	1143	1399	1508	1504
Fisheries	9790	9517	9809	10656	9625	10504	10649	12155	10640	11291	11454
Mining	14296	15010	16500	21126	28607	36481	47713	47922	44548	42201	40682
Manufacturing	145114	137998	138751	156082	169559	179188	200146	203941	243475	259771	254645
Manufactured gas	1728	1532	1366	1285	1255	1195	1309	1219	1238	1469	1755
Construction	21300	21100	20000	23300	30000	30400	32500	40900	46800	59100	67500
Transportation	42044	38658	43488	45107	52077	55589	62083	63794	73574	84534	86345
Electric light and power	1241	1320	1395	1471	1546	1625	1700	2124	2652	3234	4985
Communications	1162	1162	1162	1162	1512	1600	1818	2192	2548	2981	3429
Banking and finance	22000	22000	24000	25000	28000	32000	39000	41000	48000	57000	45000
Residential rents	44012	44544	46537	46138	49252	53288	60453	65529	68857	72380	77769
Federal government	12085	11397	11987	12631	14166	14107	15672	17259	17575	19456	23380
Provincial government	4334	4142	4523	4573	4687	4726	5240	5462	5872	6012	6146
Municipal services	9572	9443	9763	10295	10540	10725	11330	12419	13508	14825	16504
Education, public	9234	9280	9694	9737	9741	9939	10158	10687	11043	11662	12715
Universities	839	857	874	892	910	928	945	963	1126	1289	1452
Wholesale and retail trade							65553				
Community, business, and personal service							78914				
Gross Domestic Product (old official basis)	629471	609921	613372	684991	736994	788343	867201	945292	1068674	1120654	1147097
Public revenues from resource royalties	2353	2481	2341	3833	3849	4150	4740	4634	4878	5886	6300
GDP (new basis)	631824	612402	615713	688824	740843	792493	871941	949926	1073552	1126540	1153397
Less: net interest and dividends paid abroad	31380	29998	30499	31195	34450	35673	37120	39540	41493	42485	45765
Gross National Product at factor cost	600444	582404	585214	657629	706393	756820	834821	910386	1032059	1084055	1107632
Indirect taxes, less subsidies	49361	48985	53204	56315	59175	64631	66907	74694	81806	86907	93366
Gross National Product at market prices	649805	631389	638418	713944	765568	821451	901728	985080	1113865	1170962	1200998

13

Table 1.1. (continued)

	1905	1906	1907	1908	1909	1910	1911	1912	1913	1914	1915
Agriculture	303228	318203	353897	335004	401780	401404	468669	476105	515908	490146	684141
Forestry (excluding agriculture)	17263	19466	19795	18049	21187	22995	25066	25329	24341	24048	23453
Hunting and trapping	1611	1947	1812	1652	2276	2774	2641	3249	3683	2318	2823
Fisheries	14089	12961	12651	12356	14177	14359	16119	16059	16039	15409	17252
Mining	44686	49306	53077	52388	52979	61975	57026	75072	81903	74860	81724
Manufacturing	308439	363617	401828	349336	406284	452122	469566	516339	517791	447723	475178
Manufactured gas	1899	1679	2146	2141	1921	2078	2203	3181	3535	3042	1953
Construction	78500	91000	113100	113800	124100	158500	178200	215600	219600	172800	126500
Transportation	92760	108661	132799	131485	132869	153591	174855	207943	246670	222008	190025
Electric light and power	6023	6790	7660	8553	9512	9503	13786	16103	17995	20611	22080
Communications	4164	4860	8223	8807	9306	10401	11387	13467	15795	17507	17549
Banking and finance	56000	71000	77000	76000	75000	73000	92000	104000	125000	114000	93000
Residential rents	87312	96564	105533	115264	120417	132764	142948	162753	181142	182980	181795
Federal government	23934	18265	27448	30782	27759	32556	37194	42137	50515	79830	151371
Provincial government	6565	8288	10165	11628	13450	15465	17792	20904	22849	21050	20588
Municipal services	17458	19439	21078	23030	24722	27888	29838	34715	36692	40525	46275
Education, public	13435	14333	15387	17399	18976	20776	22229	25235	27274	30464	34428
Universities	1615	1779	1942	2105	2268	2431	2594	3088	3582	4075	4569
Wholesale and retail trade						204444					
Community, business, and personal service						148359					
Gross Domestic Product (old official basis)	1306322	1465254	1658996	1594001	1779522	1947385	2148425	2381856	2555675	2365768	2598050
Public revenues from resource royalties	5702	5677	7082	7267	6816	8653	9218	9202	9877	9874	7776
GDP (new basis)	1312024	1470931	1666078	1601268	1786338	1956038	2157643	2391058	2565552	2375642	2605826
Less: net interest and dividends paid abroad	49639	56030	60586	68628	77439	86239	105303	118759	141168	153271	173251
Gross National Product at factor cost	1262385	1414901	1605492	1532640	1708899	1869799	2052340	2272299	2424384	2222371	2432575
Indirect taxes, less subsidies	94545	107216	119341	118421	128577	152088	179874	219970	225237	224992	252469
Gross National Product at market prices	1356930	1522117	1724833	1651061	1837476	2021887	2232214	2492269	2649621	2447363	2685044

Table 1.1. (continued)

	1916	1917	1918	1919	1920	1921	1922	1923	1924	1925	1926
Agriculture	770523	933842	903200	947796	1029609	652988	706989	760975	768272	969926	911903
Forestry (excluding agriculture)	26208	37850	42285	49270	63740	37689	48229	46876	58588	66000	66000
Hunting and trapping	3666	5021	8188	12716	11536	9876	12376	11507	11159	10855	11807
Fisheries	19269	25593	29239	28042	25134	19118	21489	21480	22198	23919	27547
Mining	107252	117201	139388	113996	147166	115178	127971	136465	137769	132514	154000
Manufacturing	664054	960072	1084026	1042248	1271069	873027	865311	954824	899777	953898	1067402
Manufactured gas	3067	3653	3129	4660	6202	7558	8640	8811	6793	8759	9174
Construction	116300	122000	109700	148500	184600	175400	182400	215900	193900	198200	203200
Transportation	229617	260507	256400	334555	381516	347987	355327	363993	345071	368982	405179
Electric light and power	23861	27551	30858	32963	37353	39495	43718	46733	51635	59354	69877
Communications	20127	22503	25344	32031	31035	34156	34380	35418	37216	39815	46688
Banking and finance	104000	131000	132000	163000	221000	193000	169000	157000	168000	183000	209000
Residential rents	186371	203125	218207	242426	283216	314351	331245	344563	352049	357484	359551
Federal government	239223	264918	324396	172761	113350	98038	89769	87800	87632	91128	91954
Provincial government	19589	23135	25409	31316	39681	43758	49251	50666	49026	51564	50964
Municipal services	48725	50274	54540	58518	66621	76081	75599	75631	75941	75134	78671
Education, public	34491	36595	41168	47073	57043	68458	74549	77606	77443	79032	81111
Universities	5062	5556	6050	6543	7037	7335	7632	7930	8228	8526	8825
Wholesale and retail trade					439432						534000
Community, business, and personal service					303245						506000
Gross Domestic Product (old official basis)	3109946	3826514	4050354	4113906	4719585	3739336	3892035	4182305	4162772	4620233	4892853
Public revenues from resource royalties	7415	8048	8969	11612	14081	14978	13790	13175	15829	16974	18009
GDP (new basis)	3117361	3834562	4059323	4125518	4733666	3754314	3905825	4195480	4178601	4637207	4910862
Less: net interest and dividends paid abroad	172294	173505	176060	178467	186029	210928	225335	231279	241200	243394	208000
Gross National Product at factor cost	2945067	3661057	3883263	3947051	4547637	3543386	3680490	3964201	3937401	4393813	4702862
Indirect taxes, less subsidies	296627	330415	375364	427499	510708	502713	539181	572375	547796	578989	627000
Gross National Product at market prices	3241694	3991472	4258627	4374550	5058345	4046099	4219671	4536576	4485197	4972802	5329862

Table 1.2. Gross Fixed Capital Formation, Current Dollars (millions of dollars)

Year	Total Manufact- uring	Railway & Telegraph	Other Business	Housing Construc- tion	Total Private Business	Public Schools	Govern- ment Total	Grand Total
1870				23.2				60.0
1871	5.4	12.4	11.7	31.2	60.7	0.7	1.5	62.9
1872	6.1	27.0	13.2	27.5	73.8	1.3	2.8	77.9
1873	6.6	29.3	14.2	29.6	79.7	1.7	2.9	84.3
1874	6.6	25.3	15.2	35.3	82.4	2.1	8.0	92.5
1875	6.6	24.1	14.6	30.5	75.8	2.1	7.3	85.2
1876	6.1	15.3	14.2	23.8	59.4	1.7	9.0	70.1
1877	5.9	8.7	14.3	19.6	48.5	1.4	11.6	61.5
1878	5.6	6.4	14.2	17.4	43.6	1.3	10.4	55.3
1879	5.9	8.7	14.1	17.4	46.1	0.9	9.0	56.0
1880	8.9	14.1	14.7	20.6	58.3	0.9	6.9	66.1
1881	14.6	18.3	18.2	18.2	69.3	0.8	7.1	77.2
1882	19.7	44.0	22.1	14.3	100.1	1.0	5.7	106.8
1883	18.9	57.5	24.3	12.0	112.7	0.9	7.4	121.0
1884	14.1	72.5	20.0	14.4	121.0	0.9	8.0	129.9
1885	12.3	33.8	16.9	16.6	79.6	0.9	6.4	86.9
1886	12.5	23.7	18.1	22.7	77.0	1.0	7.5	85.5
1887	13.5	23.4	20.9	31.7	89.5	1.3	8.6	99.4
1888	14.1	20.7	25.8	38.2	98.8	1.5	5.6	105.9
1889	14.3	22.1	24.0	41.8	102.2	2.1	7.5	111.8
1890	13.8	15.3	21.8	39.7	90.6	1.8	6.2	98.6
1891	12.0	14.2	28.4	42.2	96.8	1.7	6.8	105.3
1892	11.8	12.0	26.8	39.2	89.8	1.5	6.1	97.4
1893	11.2	12.9	29.0	30.4	83.5	1.4	7.5	92.4
1894	10.5	8.8	21.8	22.2	63.3	1.4	10.2	74.9
1895	10.5	6.6	27.0	19.4	63.5	1.3	13.2	78.0
1896	12.6	7.4	25.3	20.2	65.5	1.1	7.2	73.8
1897	14.4	10.7	33.0	23.5	81.6	1.0	7.5	90.1
1898	19.1	18.6	42.4	26.9	107.0	1.4	10.1	118.5
1899	24.9	15.8	42.7	28.0	113.3	1.2	11.9	126.4
1900	30.2	18.7	51.4	25.6	125.9	1.3	13.0	140.2
1901	37.2	21.7	76.8	28.3	164.0	1.6	14.6	180.2
1902	42.8	24.3	90.1	32.8	191.0	1.6	16.0	208.6
1903	54.9	33.2	104.1	42.9	235.1	1.7	18.4	255.2
1904	55.5	37.6	105.6	54.5	253.2	2.3	21.6	277.1
1905	57.3	48.3	107.8	71.0	284.4	3.6	24.0	312.0
1906	61.4	63.4	128.3	83.9	337.0	4.1	18.6	359.7
1907	72.1	103.9	146.3	83.2	408.5	6.2	33.0	447.7
1908	70.0	103.0	137.7	78.2	388.9	7.1	42.0	438.0
1909	74.2	92.9	165.4	101.2	433.7	7.5	35.8	477.0
1910	97.9	109.5	204.1	131.0	542.5	9.1	45.3	596.9

Table 1.2. (continued)

Year	Total Manufact- uring	Railway & Telegraph	Other Business	Housing Construc- tion	Total Private Business	Public Schools	Govern- ment Total	Grand Total
1911	123.2	125.2	230.7	148.2	627.3	11.0	55.0	694.2
1912	155.8	157.0	282.1	171.0	765.9	14.8	69.4	850.1
1913	157.6	175.4	268.6	155.7	757.3	16.7	96.5	870.5
1914	108.7	126.6	197.0	108.6	540.9	18.9	100.5	660.3
1915	85.9	97.7	130.4	61.4	375.4	16.8	78.5	470.7
1916	135.0	49.0	190.6	60.2	434.8	11.6	54.5	500.9
1917	143.4	76.0	263.1	58.1	540.6	11.6	9.6	591.8
1918	100.4	86.5	247.8	59.1	493.8	10.7	44.9	549.4
1919	96.2	95.1	286.9	96.6	574.8	14.9	70.8	660.5
1920	152.1	115.5	335.9	127.3	730.8	20.7	87.7	839.2
1921	99.7	100.0	273.1	136.2	609.0	26.2	93.8	729.0
1922	92.1	50.5	227.7	180.9	551.2	27.6	90.7	669.5
1923	141.5	102.9	300.3	176.0	720.6	31.3	109.5	861.5
1924	136.7	83.1	252.6	164.0	636.4	22.1	102.9	761.4
1925	119.1	52.2	298.5	168.2	638.0	21.7	107.4	767.1
1926	129.8	84.3	304.0	184.2	702.3	19.7	84.4	806.4

Table 1.3.   Government Expenditure on Goods and Services (millions of dollars)

Year	Federal	Provincial	Municipal	Public Education	Total
1870	7.0	1.8	4.7	5.0	18.5
1871	8.9	2.9	4.9	5.0	21.7
1872	9.6	3.6	5.8	6.2	25.2
1873	12.5	4.0	6.2	7.1	29.8
1874	14.9	4.9	8.5	7.9	36.2
1875	14.6	4.9	8.6	8.3	36.4
1876	15.6	4.7	9.6	8.3	38.2
1877	13.9	4.7	10.9	8.7	38.2
1878	13.8	4.3	10.6	8.6	37.3
1879	13.2	4.3	10.0	8.5	36.0
1880	13.3	4.1	9.5	8.6	35.5
1881	14.3	4.2	9.6	8.5	36.6
1882	15.6	4.6	9.3	8.9	38.4
1883	20.8	5.0	10.2	9.0	45.0
1884	19.4	5.1	10.6	9.2	44.3
1885	32.4	5.1	10.5	9.6	57.6

Table 1.3.   (continued)

Year	Federal	Provincial	Municipal	Public Education	Total
1886	18.8	5.5	11.1	10.0	45.4
1887	21.7	6.1	11.8	10.0	49.6
1888	20.1	5.9	11.6	10.6	48.2
1889	17.9	7.1	13.0	11.3	49.3
1890	18.5	7.2	12.9	11.5	50.1
1891	20.7	7.6	14.0	11.8	54.1
1892	19.6	7.0	13.4	11.9	51.9
1893	20.8	7.0	14.2	11.7	53.7
1894	20.5	7.2	15.3	12.6	55.6
1895	19.8	6.8	16.2	12.6	55.4
1896	21.5	7.4	14.6	13.1	56.6
1897	22.3	7.4	15.4	13.0	58.1
1898	24.7	7.4	16.8	13.4	62.3
1899	25.7	7.4	17.7	13.5	64.3
1900	27.5	8.2	18.9	13.9	68.5
1901	32.1	8.5	20.9	14.8	76.3
1902	31.5	9.1	22.7	15.3	78.6
1903	41.8	9.3	25.2	16.1	92.4
1904	43.8	9.5	28.6	18.0	99.9
1905	46.3	10.2	30.6	20.2	107.3
1906	46.8	12.9	31.1	21.8	112.6
1907	53.0	16.3	38.9	25.2	133.4
1908	61.3	19.5	45.0	28.6	154.4
1909	56.6	22.3	44.6	31.0	154.5
1910	61.6	25.8	52.4	34.8	174.6
1911	74.8	30.5	58.2	39.4	202.9
1912	78.5	35.9	69.9	46.0	230.3
1913	101.2	40.1	82.9	50.4	274.6
1914	173.7	36.8	89.2	56.6	356.3
1915	257.5	33.2	89.1	59.4	439.2
1916	361.4	31.6	82.2	54.3	529.5
1917	361.1	36.6	79.2	53.9	530.8
1918	457.9	40.1	88.8	61.6	648.8
1919	515.9	51.7	104.8	73.1	745.5
1920	335.2	70.3	108.0	91.2	604.7
1921	281.1	76.0	118.6	110.9	586.6
1922	247.8	85.4	119.9	119.8	572.9
1923	188.0	85.6	127.0	127.3	527.9
1924	168.8	81.7	125.0	117.9	493.4
1925	174.0	85.1	128.9	119.4	507.4
1926	169.5	82.8	119.4	120.0	491.7

Table 1.4. Canada's Balance of International Payments (thousands of dollars)

	1870	1871	1872	1873	1874	1875	1876	1877	1878	1879	1880	1881
Credits												
Exports (adjusted)	66385	72981	81777	85609	80789	76781	76137	76080	74020	77470	90841	98782
Exports of gold coin and bullion	700	1600	3000	1200	1900	3100	2100	1600	2100	600	1800	1600
Freight	1328	1459	1636	1712	1616	1536	1523	1522	1480	1549	1817	1976
Tourist receipts	2100	2400	2600	3300	3300	3300	3300	3300	3300	4100	4100	4100
Migrants' capital (net)	804	1195	1466	2409	1303	688	419	711	790	2109	1723	612
Noncommercial remittance												
Insurance								4328				
Interest and dividends	850	1151	710	856	838	1173	975	973	858	1010	1116	1050
Total current	72167	80787	91189	95086	89746	86578	84453	88513	82548	86838	101397	108119
Capital (long term)	3394	13290	8019	22742	38509	14709	16303	10900	11414	14262	12358	25775
Capital (short term)		7350		289		3303	36	1913				
Net errors and omissions	25470	13519	35699	22443	17454	18267	10341	12200	14401	3719	6546	3210
Total current and capital	101031	114944	134907	140559	145709	122858	111133	113526	108363	104819	120300	137104
Debits												
Imports (adjusted)	81220	100267	115557	123169	121044	104679	93064	93785	85484	81698	93565	109819
Imports of gold coin and bullion												
Freight	5463	5957	7498	6985	7399	5579	4660	6141	5492	4772	4607	5699
Tourist payments	2400	2500	2600	2500	2400	2200	2200	2200	2400	2500	2700	2900
Migrants' capital												
Noncommercial remittance	553	658	785	835	755	696	666	624	583	541	550	688
Insurance	129	378	335	805	655	339	489		967	543	1067	303
Interest and dividends	6262	5185	5701	6265	7877	9364	10054	10777	10905	13003	15402	15777
Total current	96026	114944	132476	140559	140129	122858	111133	113527	105831	103057	117891	135186
Capital (short term)	5005		2431		5580				2532	1762	2409	1918
Total current and capital	101031	114944	134907	140559	145709	122858	111133	113527	108363	104819	120300	137104

Table 1.4. (continued)

	1882	1883	1884	1885	1886	1887	1888	1889	1890	1891	1892	1893
Credits												
Exports (adjusted)	98807	92548	87402	85252	86376	89085	88164	89868	94477	103388	111896	113806
Exports of gold coin and bullion	1500	1000	1200	400	2000	800		4800		1400		
Freight	1976	1851	1748	1705	1728	1782	1763	1797	1890	2068	2238	2276
Tourist receipts	4100	4100	4700	4700	4700	4700	4700	4900	4900	4900	4900	4900
Migrants' capital (net)	3935	4425	2130	494	1046	2219	1704	1270	336	2907	859	777
Noncommercial remittance												
Insurance												
Interest and dividends	1146	1175	1463	1211	1237	1358	1845	2440	2412	2023	2373	2771
Total current	111464	105099	98643	93762	97086	99944	98177	105076	104014	116686	122266	124530
Capital (long term)	10310	18704	23927	46870	35200	15632	66519	21334	22478	15048	28625	15921
Capital (short term)			5052					569				
Net errors and omissions	29450	32409	10754		10654	41087		32407	39975	41938	30207	35853
Total current and capital	151224	156212	138375	140632	142940	156663	164695	159386	166461	173671	181098	176304
Debits												
Imports (adjusted)	122777	120823	108387	101871	105090	108786	109684	115652	117435	119736	121689	117975
Imports of gold coin and bullion							1900		800		3300	1600
Freight	5676	6198	5130	4549	5693	5412	5561	6145	5701	5865	6072	6024
Tourist payments	3300	3200	3200	3200	3800	3800	3800	4100	4100	4100	4100	4300
Migrants' capital												
Noncommercial remittance	1179	1444	1946	1946	1869	1861	1987	2105	2028	1899	1662	1695
Insurance	817	763	958	1184	643	884	1451	2024	1735	984	793	363
Interest and dividends	16891	18021	18754	19172	23436	26175	26532	29360	32316	32336	33529	34722
Total current	150640	150449	138375	131922	140531	146918	150915	159386	164116	164918	171145	166680
Capital (short term)	584	5763		533	2409	9745	11900		2345	8753	9953	9624
Net errors and omissions				8177			1880					
Total current and capital	151224	156212	138375	140632	142940	156663	164695	159386	166461	173671	181098	176304

Table 1.4. (continued)

	1894	1895	1896	1897	1898	1899	1900	1901	1902	1903	1904
Credits											
Exports (adjusted)	111220	111004	122498	142958	152908	153399	168695	179216	198499	199704	188580
Exports of gold coin and bullion											6500
Freight	2224	2220	2450	2900	12900	22100	24800	21500	13700	6800	3772
Tourist receipts	4700	4700	4700	2859	3058	3068	3374	3584	3970	3994	12800
Migrants' capital (net)	11			4700	4500	9600	7000	8000	11000	10500	12326
Noncommercial remittance				39	2037	2385	5537	6915	13412	15264	
Insurance							1196	214			4799
Interest and dividends	3156	3351	3576	4024	4294	4506	4945	4831	5979	6110	5441
Total current	121311	121275	133224	157480	179697	195058	215547	224260	246560	242372	234217
Capital (long term)	31101	6568	10559	28036	16722		25350	33161	20367	30290	79091
Capital (short term)							2860			16723	
Net errors and omissions	10071	31627	29446		9388	42144		27737	22800	19914	32422
Total current and capital	162483	159470	173229	185516	205808	237202	243757	285158	289727	309299	345730
Debits											
Imports (adjusted)	109672	106921	111248	122538	144055	166632	180572	192136	213450	235037	246848
Imports of gold coin and bullion	600	300	2900								
Freight	6095	6397	6361	7649	10148	10983	11142	11068	11981	12410	12347
Tourist payments	4400	4500	5000	5300	5500	5300	4900	5400	6100	6000	6900
Migrants' capital		187	174								
Noncommercial remittance	1768	1514	1311	1352	1484	1800	2487	3484	4335	5640	7280
Insurance	556	666	952	404	565	46			3123	1616	
Interest and dividends	34536	33349	34075	35219	38744	40179	42065	44371	47472	48595	51206
Total current	157628	153834	162021	172462	200496	224940	241166	256459	286461	309299	324580
Capital (long term)	4855	5636	11208	6741	5312	1285			3266		21150
Capital (short term)						10977		28699			
Net errors and omissions				6313			2592				
Total current and capital	162483	159470	173229	185516	205808	237202	243757	285158	289727	309299	345730

Table 1.4. (continued)

	1905	1906	1907	1908	1909	1910	1911	1912	1913	1914	1915
Credits											
Exports (adjusted)	209015	239512	250527	251756	281116	285361	295366	348265	421392	442587	678205
Exports of gold coin and bullion	12500	3900	1400	5035	2700	5708	5907	11300	8428	22600	
Freight	4180	4790	5011		5622			6965		41100	70700
Tourist receipts	13300	16800	16200	19200	19600	24700	26200	29400	30500	29600	36600
Migrants' capital (net)	17191	18292	18258	9397	19825	26639	28023	24092	21366	28200	18300
Noncommercial remittance											
Insurance										3900	2000
Interest and dividends	6287	6918	6418	5545	9243	10587	9552	9690	9682	10400	9600
Total current	262474	290212	297814	290933	338106	352994	365049	429712	491368	578387	815405
Capital (long term)	108438	81306	69847	177045	185176	222072	172535	277868	326413	381836	28633
Capital (short term)		12514	21824			25886		182		21200	
War finance, external										24300	60400
Net errors and omissions	21	25215	71842	71577	5288		189348	164151	113384		90583
Total current and capital	370933	409246	461327	539555	528570	600952	726932	871913	931165	1005723	995021
Debits											
Imports (adjusted)	263513	303919	346256	307148	354317	429411	500023	631720	632593	521572	516370
Imports of gold coin and bullion				19100		4100			7400		9400
Freight	14521	15194	16080	13992	16131	18783	21800	32550	30160	80200	101000
Tourist payments	9400	12900	13400	15100	16600	21600	23882	29000	33200	35000	25000
Migrants' capital							25200				
Noncommercial remittance	9054	11624	17690	17029	19829	27014	36056	47483	55797	20100	11300
Canadian expeditionary force										5000	30000
Insurance	2734	2661	897	555	1409	874	1666	2711	2403	6100	5700
Interest and dividends	55926	62948	67004	74173	86682	96827	114855	128449	150850	163671	182851
Total current	355148	409246	461327	447096	494968	598609	723482	871913	912403	831643	881621
Capital (short term)	15785			92459	33602		3450		18762		113400
Net errors and omissions						2344				174080	
Total current and capital	370933	409246	461327	539555	528570	600952	726932	871913	931165	1005723	995021

Table 1.4. (continued)

	1916	1917	1918	1919	1920	1921	1922	1923	1924	1925	1926
Credits											
Exports (adjusted)	1039296	1462570	1336938	1300372	1265965	894290	918272	1042507	1075538	1270589	1272000
Exports of gold coin and bullion	14000		16300	15700	34200	42200		82200	4600	15100	30000
Freight	91700	84100	83800	86900	114400	84300	78500	89200	83000	86700	96000
Tourist receipts	53200	64400	66100	73000	64200	68300	78900	103300	117000	128500	152000
Migrants' capital (net)	19200	20000	21600	32200	40700	36300	31900	38000	37800	37800	
Noncommercial remittance											83000
Insurance	3600	6600	3200	2900	4800	4100	6500	8100	10500	15700	
Interest and dividends	14100	19300	18900	20000	20900	19200	13400	12300	12800	13500	32000
Total current	1235096	1656970	1546839	1531072	1545165	1148690	1127472	1375607	1341238	1567889	1665000
Capital (long term)	95823	55720	53570	57811	132745	50516	131453	117150	152563	55438	52300
Capital (short term)		10800			42400	144400	27000				
War finance, external					31000	27900	46800	63800	20700	1900	2300
Net errors and omissions	113097		69624	4450							
Total current and capital	1444015	1723489	1670031	1593332	1751310	1371507	1332725	1556557	1514501	1625227	1719600
Debits											
Imports (adjusted)	783825	958428	953372	1053065	1225783	890409	807417	891996	840267	915483	973000
Imports of gold coin and bullion		1700					45300				
Freight	145500	139000	144100	125600	170100	116500	94300	121400	99100	106400	105000
Tourist payments	29000	27000	30000	47000	48400	43300	40900	43900	49100	55900	99000
Migrants' capital	12300	18000	21200	12100	10000	23100	16900	8400	9400	20800	
Noncommercial remittance											
Canadian expeditionary force	100000	175000	170000	95000	20000	10600	9900	9900	14100	18600	121000
Insurance	5000	8300	8600	14800	19400						
Interest and dividends	186394	192805	194960	198467	206929	230128	238736	243579	254000	256894	240000
Total current	1262015	1520233	1522231	1546032	1700611	1314037	1253453	1319175	1265967	1374077	1538000
War finance, external	52600	113100	119300	25600							
Capital (short term)	129400		28500	21700				12700	15700	92800	51800
Net errors and omissions		90156			50699	57470	79273	224682	232834	158350	129800
Total current and capital	1444015	1723489	1670031	1593332	1751310	1371507	1332725	1556557	1514500	1625227	1719600

Table 1.5.   Total Gainfully Occupied and the Numbers Engaged in Agriculture, Census dates,1871 to 1921 (thousands of persons)

Year	Total Gainfully Occupied	Total Engaged in Agriculture	Proportion Engaged in Agriculture
1871	1130	579	0.5124
1881	1378	667	0.4803
1891	1606	744	0.4633
1901	1783	717	0.4021
1911	2724	958	0.3517
1921	3164	1041	0.3290
1931	3922	1128	0.2875

Table 1.6.   Gross National Product in Current and Constant Dollars and Real Gross National Product Per Capita, 1870 to 1926

Year	GNP in Current Market Prices ($MM)	GNP in Constant (1900) Prices ($MM)	Implicit Price Index 1900=100	Population in Thousands of Persons	Real GNP Per Capita in 1900 Dollars
1870	382.5	369.4	104	3625	102
1871	412.1	385.4	107	3689	104
1872	446.4	382.1	117	3754	102
1873	486.2	417.9	116	3826	109
1874	483.3	425.8	113	3895	109
1875	450.3	415.2	108	3954	105
1876	419.2	388.8	108	4009	97
1877	431.7	413.7	104	4064	102
1878	406.9	399.9	102	4120	97
1879	441.7	438.5	101	4185	105
1880	477.4	457.9	104	4255	108
1881	564.4	523.1	108	4325	121
1882	614.8	543.8	113	4375	124
1883	608.0	542.8	112	4430	123
1884	582.3	589.2	99	4487	131
1885	552.2	554.0	100	4537	122
1886	558.9	557.6	100	4580	122
1887	608.8	576.8	106	4626	125
1888	629.8	615.7	102	4678	132
1889	655.5	620.6	106	4729	131

Table 1.6. (continued)

Year	GNP in Current Market Prices ($MM)	GNP in Constant (1900) Prices ($MM)	Implicit Price Index 1900=100	Population in Thousands of Persons	Real GNP Per Capita in 1900 Dollars
1890	686.5	658.5	104	4779	138
1891	702.9	678.6	104	4833	140
1892	699.3	675.2	104	4883	138
1893	681.0	665.6	102	4931	135
1894	649.8	698.9	93	4979	140
1895	631.4	696.6	91	5026	139
1896	638.4	678.2	94	5074	134
1897	713.9	754.0	95	5122	147
1898	765.6	782.7	98	5175	151
1899	821.5	853.2	96	5235	163
1900	901.7	902.1	100	5301	170
1901	985.1	978.6	101	5371	182
1902	1113.9	1068.2	104	5494	194
1903	1171.0	1108.3	106	5651	196
1904	1201.0	1126.9	107	5827	193
1905	1356.9	1244.0	109	6002	207
1906	1522.1	1377.1	111	6097	226
1907	1724.8	1453.0	119	6411	227
1908	1651.1	1381.0	120	6625	208
1909	1837.5	1519.8	121	6800	224
1910	2021.9	1654.6	122	6988	237
1911	2232.2	1769.9	126	7207	246
1912	2492.3	1904.2	131	7389	258
1913	2649.6	1978.4	134	7632	259
1914	2447.4	1834.8	133	7869	233
1915	2685.0	1961.8	137	7981	246
1916	3241.7	2181.8	149	8001	273
1917	3991.5	2273.0	176	8060	282
1918	4258.6	2139.9	199	8148	263
1919	4374.6	1998.2	219	8311	240
1920	5058.3	1991.0	254	8556	233
1921	4046.1	1787.8	226	8788	203
1922	4219.7	2053.9	205	8919	230
1923	4536.6	2184.8	208	9010	242
1924	4485.2	2201.9	204	9143	241
1925	4972.8	2438.9	204	9294	262
1926	5329.9	2604.3	205	9451	276

Table 1.7.   Comparative Growth Rates of Canada and the United States (All growth rates in compound rates per cent per annum)

A. Population

	Canada	United States
1871-1880	1.6	2.3
1880-1890	1.2	2.3
1890-1900	1.0	1.9
1900-1910	2.8	2.0
1910-1920	2.0	1.4
1920-1925	1.7	1.7

B. Total Real Gross National Product

	Canada	United States
1871-1880	2.5	5.7
1880-1890	3.3	3.5
1890-1900	3.4	3.6
1900-1910	6.1	3.8
1910-1920	1.6	2.5
1920-1925	4.6	4.7

C. Real GNP per Capita

	Canada	United States
1871-1880	0.9	3.3
1880-1890	2.0	1.2
1890-1900	2.3	1.7
1900-1910	3.2	1.8
1910-1920	-0.4	1.1
1920-1925	2.9	2.9
1871-1890	1.5	2.2

Table 1.8.   Ratios of Selected Aggregate Expenditure Items to Gross National Product (both in current prices) and Terms of Trade

	Capital Formation/ GNP [1]	Capital Inflow/ GNP [2]	Implied Savings Ratio [3]	Exports/ GNP [4]	Govt. Spending/ GNP [5]	Export/ Import Prices [6]
1870	0.157	0.062	0.095	0.174	0.048	0.68
1871	0.153	0.083	0.070	0.177	0.053	0.66
1872	0.175	0.092	0.083	0.183	0.057	0.72
1873	0.173	0.094	0.079	0.176	0.061	0.76
1874	0.191	0.104	0.087	0.167	0.075	0.78
1875	0.189	0.081	0.108	0.171	0.081	0.82
1876	0.167	0.064	0.103	0.182	0.091	0.82
1877	0.142	0.058	0.084	0.176	0.088	0.89
1878	0.136	0.057	0.079	0.182	0.092	0.88
1879	0.127	0.037	0.090	0.175	0.082	0.86
1880	0.138	0.035	0.103	0.190	0.074	0.86
1881	0.137	0.048	0.089	0.175	0.065	0.91
1882	0.174	0.064	0.110	0.161	0.062	0.93
1883	0.199	0.075	0.124	0.152	0.074	0.92
1884	0.223	0.068	0.155	0.150	0.076	0.93
1885	0.157	0.069	0.088	0.154	0.104	0.95
1886	0.153	0.078	0.075	0.155	0.081	0.99
1887	0.163	0.077	0.086	0.146	0.081	1.06
1888	0.168	0.084	0.084	0.140	0.077	0.99
1889	0.171	0.083	0.088	0.137	0.075	1.01
1890	0.144	0.088	0.056	0.138	0.073	2.00
1891	0.150	0.069	0.081	0.147	0.077	1.05
1892	0.139	0.070	0.069	0.160	0.074	1.05
1893	0.136	0.062	0.074	0.167	0.079	1.08
1894	0.115	0.056	0.059	0.171	0.086	1.13
1895	0.124	0.052	0.072	0.176	0.088	2.06
1896	0.116	0.045	0.071	0.192	0.089	1.09
1897	0.126	0.021	0.105	0.200	0.081	1.09
1898	0.155	0.027	0.128	0.200	0.081	1.07
1899	0.154	0.036	0.118	0.187	0.078	1.00
1900	0.155	0.028	0.127	0.187	0.076	1.02
1901	0.183	0.033	0.150	0.182	0.077	1.06
1902	0.187	0.036	0.151	0.178	0.071	1.07
1903	0.218	0.057	0.161	0.171	0.079	1.05
1904	0.231	0.075	0.156	0.157	0.083	1.03
1905	0.230	0.068	0.162	0.154	0.079	1.05

Table 1.8.   (continued)

	Capital Formation/ GNP [1]	Capital Inflow/ GNP [2]	Implied Savings Ratio [3]	Exports/ GNP [4]	Govt. Spending/ GNP [5]	Export/ Import Prices [6]
1906	0.236	0.078	0.158	0.157	0.074	1.04
1907	0.260	0.095	0.165	0.145	0.077	1.06
1908	0.265	0.095	0.170	0.152	0.094	1.14
1909	0.260	0.085	0.175	0.153	0.084	1.14
1910	0.295	0.121	0.174	0.141	0.086	1.12
1911	0.311	0.161	0.150	0.132	0.091	1.13
1912	0.341	0.177	0.164	0.140	0.092	1.11
1913	0.329	0.159	0.170	0.159	0.104	1.04
1914	0.270	0.103	0.167	0.181	0.146	1.15
1915	0.175	0.025	0.150	0.253	0.164	1.24
1916	0.155	0.008	0.147	0.321	0.163	1.13
1917	0.148	-0.034	0.182	0.366	0.133	1.29
1918	0.129	-0.006	0.135	0.314	0.152	1.22
1919	0.151	0.003	0.148	0.297	0.170	1.18
1920	0.166	0.031	0.135	0.250	0.120	1.08
1921	0.180	0.041	0.139	0.221	0.145	1.06
1922	0.159	0.030	0.129	0.218	0.136	1.05
1923	0.190	-0.012	0.202	0.230	0.116	0.96
1924	0.170	-0.018	0.188	0.240	0.110	1.02
1925	0.154	-0.039	0.193	0.256	0.102	1.13
1926	0.151	-0.024	0.175	0.239	0.092	1.16

[1]   Ratio, gross fixed capital formation to current GNP (both in current prices).
[2]   Ratio, inflow of capital to GNP (current account balance to GNP)
[3]   Implied domestic savings ratio.
[4]   Ratio, exports of goods to GNP.
[5]   Ratio of government expenditure on goods and services to GNP.
[6]   Ratio of export prices to import prices 1899 = 1.

Table 1.9. Farm Revenue from Off-Farm Sales and Farm-Consumption (thousands of dollars)

	1870	1871	1872	1873	1874	1875	1876	1877	1878	1879	1880	1881
Wheat	22160	23979	25601	25088	20283	23564	25696	24361	25533	37181	32244	38437
Oats	3275	3215	3316	3521	4505	3680	3694	3638	2997	4993	4120	5874
Barley	3688	3981	3546	5089	6608	9414	5234	4824	5219	5057	7946	11379
Rye	163	124	134	143	152	99	67	269	382	665	801	1317
Hay	3125	3918	3463	3059	2859	2897	2649	2868	2774	2771	5178	4143
Vegetables	8558	11047	9597	8185	10705	7648	8553	10685	10566	11466	6586	13413
Potatoes	7463	10009	6704	5885	8507	5956	6717	8363	11652	10720	4684	13981
Hops	149	539	348	246	365	245	354	224	206	576	239	347
Flax seed	161	209	253	47	129	101	85	125	58	60	75	103
Tobacco	63	72	81	69	88	86	77	71	74	82	91	113
Flax fibre	112	115	86	113	164	165	182	98	46	95	67	85
Eggs	4579	4835	5414	5560	5168	5475	5347	5307	4241	5327	5386	6906
Maple sugar & syrup	1649	1709	1302	1673	1718	2324	1853	2101	2000	1345	1743	1581
Honey	351	355	264	336	336	445	348	385	358	233	292	290
Apples	2480	2988	3607	3058	3452	2566	3073	3615	2301	3265	2883	3742
Small fruit	1730	2064	2538	2131	2468	1881	2229	2583	1630	2334	1860	2235
Grapes	62	66	76	74	134	133	134	121	140	136	150	220
Orchard fruit	241	317	426	397	481	378	505	615	423	589	776	1325
Cattle & calves	32561	28751	29935	30233	24586	21866	21084	23332	22478	22324	23983	20998
Hogs	16175	11527	11718	11511	14141	15804	14502	12026	9213	10815	12176	16838
Sheep & lambs	4202	4642	4728	4177	3853	4821	3903	4078	4475	5439	5676	8308
Poultry	1383	1540	1686	1787	1501	1700	1716	1622	1289	1682	1805	2169
Cheese	2271	2663	3126	4638	4610	4304	4261	4514	3932	4278	6008	5925
Butter	12853	14053	12611	14387	19278	15858	16597	16684	12367	14307	18358	18727
Fluid milk	8700	8912	7988	9366	13196	11031	10006	10208	7811	9315	10892	11141
Horses	2586	2567	2371	2194	2087	2024	2115	2375	2336	2810	3094	4742
Seed, grass & clover	351	-15	-193	-216	-119	177	88	-56	-29	563	79	693
Wool	2272	3098	2814	2220	1985	2197	2214	2027	1919	2424	2248	2137
Forest products	16402	17621	20492	21896	20122	16765	15564	15842	15520	15892	17678	19739
Grand Total	159779	164914	164046	166867	173372	163615	158861	162917	151925	176757	177130	216921

Table 1.9. (continued)

	1882	1883	1884	1885	1886	1887	1888	1889	1890	1891	1892	1893
Wheat	33381	26223	21291	24088	26430	23340	26429	25484	26658	33720	26427	20725
Oats	4586	4279	4034	4911	4188	4203	4529	3895	5053	6316	6450	5087
Barley	7183	5819	5629	5659	5558	6562	7158	5089	3373	3272	1498	806
Rye	772	680	292	216	203	79	113	346	313	275	142	87
Hay	4035	3715	4469	4481	4169	4922	6472	4707	3667	5157	4771	5639
Vegetables	13252	14682	9619	10532	10085	13116	8614	12825	13094	9749	10948	12962
Potatoes	11261	11715	6848	9900	8845	14014	6783	11021	10703	7669	8845	9656
Hops	890	313	262	195	56	171	270	64	374	186	365	358
Flax seed	100	109	195	105	96	145	91	130	115	92	95	83
Tobacco	132	149	164	159	164	172	212	192	231	232	270	288
Flax fibre	108	73	59	49	78	80	121	175	181	112	124	268
Eggs	7927	9347	9231	8653	7496	8022	8490	8278	8501	8090	7199	8294
Maple sugar & syrup	1557	1409	1918	1629	1691	2184	1599	1744	1798	1678	1692	1604
Honey	312	302	447	403	441	601	459	527	565	409	398	371
Apples	4320	4311	3803	3230	3529	3485	3805	4283	5129	4114	5678	5183
Small fruit	1907	1921	1766	1791	2180	1804	1018	1251	1878	1901	2114	1533
Grapes	253	275	308	335	325	302	339	451	453	511	395	634
Orchard fruit	1676	1578	1862	2380	1495	1903	1232	1806	3053	1343	2148	1267
Cattle & calves	38135	34953	34307	28400	22828	25207	25595	24593	30443	31243	30504	30486
Hogs	17110	14111	13279	12263	12809	14889	15745	15398	13846	8929	14582	10285
Sheep & lambs	6312	7718	4617	4052	4146	4846	5313	6407	5423	5463	8095	6468
Poultry	2784	2980	2836	2955	1850	2066	2526	2748	2472	2038	1897	2438
Cheese	6822	7382	8279	6506	7154	8916	8814	9099	9032	11142	12621	14444
Butter	19235	18821	17799	15901	17150	19212	19389	18131	22257	26530	27177	27778
Fluid milk	12757	11553	11773	10480	10643	12360	12574	12787	14623	16528	16797	17061
Horses	5437	-2010	6209	4572	4162	6528	6592	9154	5634	5064	2746	316
Seed, grass & clover	7	-182	-133	-219	-251	-219	-510	-237	56	95	-233	145
Wool	2681	2361	2007	1563	1366	1374	1282	1631	1785	1709	1690	1719
Forest products	21315	21426	20408	19491	19781	18621	19715	20583	21046	21275	20978	21012
Grand Total	226260	206014	193591	184693	178680	198915	194782	202574	211769	214854	216425	207007

Table 1.9. (continued)

	1894	1895	1896	1897	1898	1899	1900	1901	1902	1903	1904
Wheat	18746	29715	22876	35754	26269	30505	28160	37127	45252	39026	49105
Oats	4076	3771	4170	5516	6168	5717	5912	7534	7213	6428	6268
Barley	1218	884	1000	496	754	1544	1650	1206	1227	1297	1423
Rye	108	106	129	498	223	321	402	298	346	195	211
Hay	4617	6922	4941	3740	3122	4788	5820	7929	7552	5958	5506
Vegetables	10868	8360	7559	13058	12275	12089	8428	13834	15519	19796	15743
Potatoes	9270	4095	6044	9562	9982	8748	5051	9879	13284	19882	14077
Hops	143	165	145	211	181	112	180	157	288	271	304
Flax seed	390	784	229	220	340	345	197	238	530	400	462
Tobacco	281	362	382	606	542	719	754	809	852	975	953
Flax fibre	151	128	304	38	75	196	235	143	175	271	410
Eggs	7291	7408	7465	6912	8218	9819	9848	9337	10550	10275	13753
Maple sugar & syrup	1497	1350	1511	1014	1352	2433	1427	1747	1761	1922	1807
Honey	369	362	390	303	301	364	356	411	401	370	361
Apples	4886	4868	4379	5854	6578	6606	5058	6271	7505	9057	7003
Small fruit	1542	1776	1357	1578	1367	1376	1408	1837	1627	1703	1498
Grapes	546	731	720	827	569	600	1166	1182	1249	1182	887
Orchard fruit	1320	697	925	1181	1005	1050	1805	1102	1034	1418	1350
Cattle & calves	24976	24047	23279	28718	32192	34578	36732	42722	51781	46816	47304
Hogs	19457	13577	13754	15949	19685	17835	17993	26944	32380	30739	30744
Sheep & lambs	6376	7516	4434	3559	4980	5331	5718	6037	5852	4971	3593
Poultry	2184	2357	2697	2354	2399	3103	3379	3622	3615	3465	3621
Cheese	13346	12576	13268	15699	14976	18528	19250	17994	22812	22056	18399
Butter	25562	23327	23511	23613	26187	23379	29586	31209	33531	33063	33274
Fluid milk	17326	15831	14288	14505	16580	16867	19083	17450	17899	18461	19089
Horses	-1035	30	1249	985	1552	4460	6563	6464	10041	-1894	14878
Seed, grass & clover	325	-254	-237	-87	304	-232	14	785	359	971	51
Wool	1655	1375	1445	1490	1432	2057	1609	1382	1534	1636	1730
Forest products	20147	20350	21065	21164	20700	20952	21604	22686	24128	25014	24848
Grand Total	197652	193229	183291	215330	220320	234201	239375	278350	320310	305738	318666

Table 1.9. (continued)

	1905	1906	1907	1908	1909	1910	1911	1912	1913	1914	1915
Wheat	56401	53547	70128	76691	119799	84584	124116	120913	137734	127468	298784
Oats	6811	7925	13131	8604	7626	8942	10272	9643	16716	16149	25515
Barley	1363	1420	2475	2523	2025	1939	3282	5564	6417	3635	5581
Rye	188	103	207	291	247	195	139	117	216	364	597
Hay	5754	6388	9276	7434	9709	8974	17573	12712	11273	13406	15144
Vegetables	18312	17134	20931	16707	15191	19918	21107	17512	21538	18463	26474
Potatoes	14467	15138	19278	16796	13411	18041	22108	16883	20152	19648	24458
Hops	157	227	132	112	311	290	519	374	348	214	170
Flax seed	599	968	1867	1415	2941	8472	25788	24846	15708	6552	8472
Tobacco	1054	1221	1352	1406	1597	1569	1242	669	1450	1020	801
Flax fibre	244	73	163	120	84	125	72	24	46	34	86
Eggs	12720	15690	18132	17807	21702	22310	27128	26984	32387	32346	31285
Maple sugar & syrup	1864	2926	2374	2232	2211	2514	2594	2598	2471	2678	3062
Honey	383	567	652	699	769	713	729	790	760	657	788
Apples	9599	7281	10053	7677	9734	7840	10291	9515	11200	7709	8328
Small fruit	2027	2179	2634	2196	1975	2467	2840	1809	2108	2255	2126
Grapes	1344	1384	1212	1215	1153	1217	823	857	1056	958	959
Orchard fruit	1248	1674	2739	1355	1984	1824	1786	709	1125	1045	701
Cattle & calves	48633	41582	41686	36809	44997	55761	63530	68968	74552	86110	93108
Hogs	30439	37426	30109	30643	38803	47606	46275	48438	59899	56676	52962
Sheep & lambs	4623	4129	5686	5102	4953	5218	6122	7412	6524	7230	7455
Poultry	3921	6979	4670	5633	6757	9016	9437	10978	11189	10879	10794
Cheese	22880	26525	22085	20078	20860	19997	20809	20755	19240	20010	26296
Butter	40906	40195	42766	48186	46825	50725	40670	50565	46763	45154	51320
Fluid milk	21907	22315	25881	29256	27601	25855	24005	30073	28238	29152	32482
Horses	10353	17954	20070	12570	23560	21107	15391	22764	29316	22823	13799
Seed, grass & clover	1011	-129	-208	-674	-203	564	-14	-714	-392	-1898	-2121
Wool	1961	1727	1748	1413	1506	1615	1472	1548	1945	2136	2967
Forest products	25612	30275	34076	30792	31765	33437	37969	38051	37549	41147	40888
Grand Total	346796	364836	405315	385101	459897	462846	538087	551367	597540	574030	783293

Table 1.9. (continued)

	1916	1917	1918	1919	1920	1921	1922	1923	1924	1925	1926
Wheat	280766	376802	275169	291538	383267	227439	307491	307525	291319	413771	386002
Oats	48549	38384	22295	31325	23152	15746	16547	18653	26143	20062	11532
Barley	8195	9022	9993	15861	10976	6323	7163	7312	21507	19085	21182
Rye	1491	1690	402	3360	4476	2445	5994	3467	7812	4326	5318
Hay	11470	12617	20465	19709	22493	16783	9622	10942	9676	10526	11428
Vegetables	32053	37444	41046	39899	46290	37283	29474	32067	36249	51206	41708
Potatoes	34254	44187	42556	46110	46676	36803	25648	29578	25190	66623	49421
Hops	216	80	81	206	455	311	142	329	235	279	318
Flax seed	17940	15261	16478	20175	14059	4506	8461	12174	19817	10542	8845
Tobacco	677	1265	2476	7564	12599	2252	4177	3833	3255	4924	4265
Flax fibre	277	370	827	1439	1298	167	331	185	400	109	28
Eggs	45799	52473	58132	73574	62682	55413	54827	56578	57712	50568	65196
Maple sugar & syrup	3263	4608	7261	8828	9376	4397	4188	5957	5991	5287	4896
Honey	831	984	1535	1492	1633	1392	1115	1189	1432	1540	1631
Apples	9073	8883	13476	15858	15016	18250	14842	14693	11847	10036	9619
Small fruit	2010	2521	3782	6105	6957	3235	3114	3051	2566	2385	2581
Grapes	1059	1359	1029	1761	2328	2812	3515	2742	1470	1750	720
Orchard fruit	1368	1461	2477	1890	4130	3394	2577	2886	1718	1463	2234
Cattle & calves	106691	124018	134806	106956	124546	45920	52198	61843	58488	75247	80375
Hogs	65234	73320	103446	111234	83357	63057	82013	75916	73068	109471	113929
Sheep & lambs	9960	15655	17739	16613	8957	8596	6276	8059	11315	9895	8592
Poultry	11552	14415	21309	19043	20389	23321	21488	20669	22154	23717	24391
Cheese	36278	39176	37774	45267	39240	28186	22682	28202	26199	37553	28851
Butter	57336	71057	82494	98805	108841	91342	79029	89690	91446	90232	94348
Fluid milk	38484	38768	54265	61501	72811	57158	47961	54343	52020	54921	59116
Horses	11932	22410	16859	-3155	20003	4879	-3297	3738	-1868	1623	-4369
Seed, grass & clover	-500	-422	1649	740	-447	-311	-223	772	-1009	1862	2084
Wool	3363	4435	5316	6755	3380	2092	2616	2651	3175	3409	3458
Forest products	38739	49884	63452	61666	67047	51408	50965	57421	60385	57698	54882
Grand Total	878373	1062140	1058603	1112130	1215992	814605	860947	916477	921742	1140127	1092593

Table 1.10. Farm Expenses of Production (thousands of dollars)

	1870	1871	1872	1873	1874	1875	1876	1877	1878	1879	1880	1881
Repairs, farm building	2965	3054	3047	3084	3258	3115	3006	3108	2880	3428	3401	3526
Repairs, machinery and implements	1402	1444	1441	1458	1540	1473	1422	1470	1362	1621	1608	1993
Tractor expenses												
Fertilizer expenses				22	14	22	29	24	24	3	2	4
Truck & auto expenses												
Mill feeds	1720	5176	2264	7984	4302	2652	5651	4234	3856	2844	2971	2640
Binder twine												
Blacksmithing	4313	4454	4596	4738	4879	5021	5163	5305	5446	5588	5730	5749
Miscellaneous	5609	5779	5767	5835	6163	5892	5691	5882	5451	6487	6435	7974
Total operating expenses	16011	19911	17117	23125	20160	18179	20966	20026	19021	19973	20151	21890

	1882	1883	1884	1885	1886	1887	1888	1889	1890	1891	1892	1893
Repairs, farm building	3651	3862	4057	4153	4247	4372	4505	4598	4651	4731	4813	4886
Repairs, machinery and implements	2076	1859	1734	1656	1600	1805	1750	1821	1901	1952	1959	1855
Tractor expenses												
Fertilizer expenses	5	4	6	5	8	14	16	13	37	43	61	38
Truck & auto expenses												
Mill feeds	3331	3589	2599	1978	2598	3141	3544	3853	3813	2875	3137	2897
Binder twine		242	484	727	969	1212	1454	1697	1939	1779	2217	1195
Blacksmithing	5815	5466	5571	5565	5540	5646	5759	6019	6098	6550	6899	7122
Miscellaneous	8305	7437	6936	6626	6402	7221	7000	7286	7604	7811	7837	7421
Total operating expenses	23185	22462	21390	20714	21368	23411	24032	25289	26046	25745	26926	25419

Table 1.10. (continued)

	1894	1895	1896	1897	1898	1899	1900	1901	1902	1903	1904
Repairs, farm building	4912	4951	4986	5061	5128	5229	5343	5962	6570	7190	7693
Repairs, machinery and implements	1788	1729	1639	1916	1970	2121	2187	2576	2939	2773	2900
Tractor expenses											
Fertilizer expenses	80	94	124	126	140	175	318	497	656	681	784
Truck & auto expenses											17
Mill feeds	2622	3840	3010	4351	5580	5213	3453	2743	4597	4626	4494
Binder twine	1335	1213	2252	1413	2585	3971	2171	3486	4017	2856	2559
Blacksmithing	7201	7320	7567	7842	8176	8720	9394	9560	9994	9792	10280
Miscellaneous	7155	6919	6559	7666	7881	8487	8751	10304	11756	11093	11603
Total operating expenses	25097	26070	26141	28379	31453	33921	31621	35131	40532	39016	40334

	1905	1906	1907	1908	1909	1910	1911	1912	1913	1914	1915
Repairs, farm building	8266	8917	9314	9907	10471	11123	11952	12531	12813	13209	13583
Repairs, machinery and implements	3151	3248	3651	3530	4224	4218	4918	5059	5593	5322	7393
Tractor expenses		1078	96	266	435	678	1452	3147	3704	3462	3922
Fertilizer expenses	998	48	1401	1390	1540	1696	2008	2965	2996	3090	4694
Truck & auto expenses	20	6208	40	76	102	204	586	1224	1504	1785	2499
Mill feeds	5297	2979	8880	7302	8764	9884	11442	11415	8780	12653	10741
Binder twine	2655	11166	1662	1487	3047	3660	3206	3233	6940	4896	7725
Blacksmithing	10574	12993	11763	12015	12630	13103	14175	15445	16922	18173	19016
Miscellaneous	12604		14607	14120	16899	16873	19674	20239	22373	21289	29574
Total operating expenses	43568	46633	51418	50097	58117	61442	69418	75262	81632	83884	99152

35

Table 1.10. (continued)

	1916	1917	1918	1919	1920	1921	1922	1923	1924	1925	1926
Repairs, farm building	14131	14551	16361	17959	18655	18302	18172	18171	18206	18093	18100
Repairs, machinery and implements	8347	9982	9825	10301	11484	7760	8200	8738	8731	10866	10404
Tractor expenses	4140	5956	8838	14650	21309	20510	20534	17580	18742	19154	24215
Fertilizer expenses	4990	5574	6316	2084	7120	6113	5710	5855	5945	5963	6182
Truck & auto expenses	3418	6938	10407	13085	18901	18391	18340	16860	19028	19896	25508
Mill feeds	9155	9364	27349	37400	26816	20648	19242	21940	18152	20638	24671
Binder twine	10508	14899	14729	5236	12334	16380	9892	11113	10707	14095	13353
Blacksmithing	19769	21101	22270	22408	23822	22465	21062	20289	19030	18028	16634
Miscellaneous	33389	39930	39303	41206	45938	31043	32802	34952	34924	43464	41619
Total operating expenses	107850	128298	155403	164334	186383	161617	153958	155502	153470	170201	180690

Table 1.11. Gross and Net Farm Revenue and Farm Gross Domestic Product (thousands of dollars)

	1870	1871	1872	1873	1874	1875	1876	1877	1878	1879	1880	1881
Gross farm revenue	159779	164914	164046	166867	173372	163615	158861	162917	151925	176757	177130	216921
Farm operating expenses	16011	19911	17117	23125	20160	18179	20966	20020	19021	19973	20151	21890
Farm GDP	143768	145003	146929	143742	153212	145436	137895	142897	132904	156784	156979	195031

	1882	1883	1884	1885	1886	1887	1888	1889	1890	1891	1892	1893
Gross farm revenue	226260	206014	193591	184693	178680	198915	194782	202574	211769	214854	216425	207007
Farm operating expenses	23185	22462	21390	20714	21368	23411	24032	25289	26046	25745	26926	25419
Farm GDP	203075	183552	172201	163979	157312	175504	170750	177285	185723	189108	189499	181588

	1894	1895	1896	1897	1898	1899	1900	1901	1902	1903	1904
Gross farm revenue	197652	193229	183291	215330	220320	234201	239375	278350	320310	305738	318666
Farm operating expenses	25097	26070	26141	28379	31453	33921	31621	35131	40532	39016	40334
Farm GDP	172555	167159	157150	186915	188867	200280	207754	243219	279778	266722	278332

38

Table 1.11. (continued)

	1905	1906	1907	1908	1909	1910	1911	1912	1913	1914	1915
Gross farm revenue	346796	364836	405315	385101	459897	462846	538087	551367	597540	574030	783293
Farm operating expenses	43568	46633	51418	50097	58117	61442	69418	75262	81632	83884	99152
Farm GDP	303228	318203	353897	335004	401780	401404	468669	476105	515908	490146	684141

	1916	1917	1918	1919	1920	1921	1922	1923	1924	1925	1926
Gross farm revenue	878373	1062140	1058603	1112130	1215992	814605	860947	916477	921742	1140127	1092593
Farm operating expenses	107850	128298	155403	164334	186383	161617	153958	155502	153470	170201	180690
Farm GDP	770523	933842	903200	947796	1029609	652988	706989	760975	768272	969926	911903

Table 1.12. Gross Domestic Product in Manufacturing at Factor Cost, by Industry, 1870-1926 (thousands of current dollars)

	1870	1871	1872	1873	1874	1875	1876	1877	1878	1879	1880	1881
Food and beverage	11263	12522	13697	14787	13179	12162	12022	14783	11967	12677	14413	16355
Tobacco and products	1014	1077	1150	1403	1693	1699	1665	1374	1021	982	1207	1421
Rubber products	112	141	168	199	222	146	123	171	141	153	243	390
Leather products	11717	13811	12632	10721	11137	8814	7314	9105	8428	9420	12825	14450
Textiles (ex. clothing)	2691	3751	3547	2710	2761	3047	2999	3248	3228	4314	5116	6021
Clothing	5386	7230	7664	7027	7052	6707	6270	6925	7120	8519	9373	10712
Wood products	16173	16743	16944	25499	24051	19937	15802	18960	15601	16776	22227	28488
Paper products	670	791	777	925	984	1044	1007	992	987	953	1035	1166
Printing and publishing	2270	2739	2930	3525	3880	4000	3816	3865	3906	3743	3579	4793
Iron and steel products	12803	16834	23698	34585	21633	21382	13459	14586	11813	10940	15485	18102
Transportation equipment	5943	5952	7104	13134	12883	9648	9978	9394	9844	7940	7105	9626
Non-ferrous metal products	770	882	992	1103	1212	1322	1429	1534	1640	1745	1849	1852
Electrical apparatus and supplies												
Non-metallic minerals	2398	2521	2642	2761	2876	2991	3102	3212	3320	3425	3528	3383
Petroleum and coal	1119	1352	1642	1822	601	1074	1822	1156	1055	1563	1308	1334
Chemical products	1560	1759	1908	1993	2128	1974	2024	2234	2166	2224	2332	2509
Miscellaneous industries	1094	1301	1459	1803	1638	1532	1400	1634	1488	1622	1990	2321
Total GDP	76983	89406	98954	123997	107930	97479	84232	93173	83725	86996	103615	122923

Table 1.12. (continued)

	1882	1883	1884	1885	1886	1887	1888	1889	1890	1891	1892	1893
Food and beverage	17739	17681	18077	16785	17028	18754	22768	24207	26232	27785	26170	23685
Tobacco and products	1556	1738	2118	1938	1586	1886	2102	2255	2713	2914	2881	2908
Rubber products	394	328	352	342	346	435	545	508	505	556	580	635
Leather products	14357	13347	13374	15502	16486	14468	12730	12102	14810	15073	14504	13378
Textiles (ex. clothing)	7836	7180	6293	6672	7150	7458	8159	9246	9380	9524	9840	9134
Clothing	13456	12583	11653	12520	13925	14099	15099	18288	19251	18739	19028	17811
Wood products	35098	39031	33868	30067	30925	31438	32256	32679	35035	35257	29452	29658
Paper products	1366	1625	1718	1768	1762	1936	2086	2236	2393	2581	2794	3017
Printing and publishing	5610	5244	4439	4496	4393	5309	6601	6391	5809	6199	7961	8222
Iron and steel products	22277	28292	21204	18669	19319	23810	23679	24652	27070	24780	24141	21615
Transportation equipment	11015	10215	9079	8276	8885	9844	10140	10305	11806	12178	12413	11868
Non-ferrous metal products	1942	1621	1164	1339	1943	1998	2458	3026	3337	4480	3394	3533
Electrical apparatus and supplies									416	435	461	520
Non-metallic minerals	3236	3085	2928	2769	2605	3032	3211	3798	5209	4209	4062	5285
Petroleum and coal	1064	1108	1036	1138	1127	1167	982	989	1020	1011	1090	1122
Chemical products	2902	3160	3140	3177	3323	3417	3366	3433	3596	3577	3532	3318
Miscellaneous industries	2645	2720	2467	2359	2438	2571	2733	2869	3109	3156	3014	2866
Total GDP	142493	148958	132910	127817	133241	141622	148915	156984	171691	172454	165317	158575

Table 1.12. (continued)

	1894	1895	1896	1897	1898	1899	1900	1901	1902	1903	1904
Food and beverage	22891	24050	24262	30203	30991	29327	33172	34653	37761	40929	43355
Tobacco and products	2884	2857	3185	4070	3937	3535	4012	4055	4343	4905	5332
Rubber products	588	663	818	1036	1269	1471	1516	1385	1421	1899	2450
Leather products	9859	12122	11361	17243	18719	17175	15863	17217	20889	20836	17535
Textiles (ex. clothing)	8014	7690	7360	9167	11036	12286	12825	13020	13599	13300	12454
Clothing	16451	16405	15816	16998	18751	20760	21669	23103	26223	28129	29024
Wood products	27959	23781	26109	27106	26126	29950	34024	33477	39258	44346	43470
Paper products	3287	3242	3254	3550	3831	4203	4752	4596	5471	5893	6299
Printing and publishing	6559	6574	7074	7298	7510	8035	8952	8955	9015	9521	10509
Iron and steel products	18994	14716	17801	14902	18684	20072	29077	23682	39683	39436	31718
Transportation equipment	11741	8855	6730	7732	9214	11045	10765	11833	15062	17303	16335
Non-ferrous metal products	3138	3162	3105	4113	5169	5682	6257	8316	8496	9489	11060
Electrical apparatus and supplies	587	634	714	792	1076	1269	1628	2190	2438	2607	3028
Non-metallic minerals	5319	6533	4454	4608	5271	5981	6329	7233	8064	8343	8229
Petroleum and coal	1168	1067	983	954	964	949	1075	1059	1135	1420	1791
Chemical products	3029	3090	3144	3338	3794	4123	4523	5404	6238	6769	7488
Miscellaneous industries	2646	2557	2581	2972	3197	3325	3707	3763	4379	4646	4568
Total GDP	145114	137998	138751	156082	169539	179188	200146	203941	243475	259771	254645

Table 1.12. (continued)

	1905	1906	1907	1908	1909	1910	1911	1912	1913	1914	1915
Food and beverage	48452	46528	50453	55998	61065	64767	64267	69030	66643	70857	82568
Tobacco and products	5703	5533	5910	7720	8430	8585	9430	9767	9735	10261	10327
Rubber products	2735	2983	3247	2629	3878	4497	5369	6749	5850	5964	8355
Leather products	21408	27282	19818	14197	25789	26746	30113	39097	27271	31448	26747
Textiles (ex. clothing)	13018	14323	13531	12156	14688	17894	14846	14984	15565	13678	17668
Clothing	32547	37089	38632	33675	43239	50605	45579	49244	50958	43019	47377
Wood products	49604	61148	67417	59614	66468	72168	78640	67843	62903	56641	56984
Paper products	7178	8449	9787	9985	11387	12388	11295	11240	12701	16320	18722
Printing and publishing	11086	11944	12266	13958	15667	15765	17282	18795	20559	20997	21006
Iron and steel products	50976	69246	87249	57338	68102	75808	78188	95780	103973	60352	72491
Transportation equipment	18565	23677	32452	27221	29415	31302	38919	44854	53299	43301	33281
Non-ferrous metal products	17401	20941	22341	18324	20240	24169	22760	28287	26281	20128	28364
Electrical apparatus and supplies	3782	4949	5789	6384	6778	7280	8471	7806	7633	7635	7181
Non-metallic minerals	9706	11699	12686	11199	11058	17076	19261	22384	23458	18831	14245
Petroleum and coal	2047	1827	2358	2379	2155	2355	2779	4494	5640	5531	4089
Chemical products	8828	9801	11097	10460	10852	12890	14670	17918	17637	16160	18926
Miscellaneous industries	5403	6198	6795	6099	7073	7827	7697	8067	7685	6600	6847
Total GDP	308439	363617	401828	349336	406284	452122	469566	516339	517791	447723	475178

Table 1.12. (continued)

	1916	1917	1918	1919	1920	1921	1922	1923	1924	1925	1926
Food and beverage	103300	144219	156916	169843	187062	152471	141002	143715	150220	156065	169158
Tobacco and products	11884	15997	20060	13957	19557	16646	18358	16960	16879	9779	12918
Rubber products	12744	17935	19665	22929	30558	18097	22236	24430	27188	32405	28366
Leather products	42026	39180	36692	43937	45462	36716	40818	38661	37228	35700	38795
Textiles (ex. clothing)	22932	36734	47618	54141	58872	46725	54141	54099	41450	41083	50047
Clothing	68874	80108	91133	107804	109493	83249	87978	89630	83364	84810	93436
Wood products	56703	85863	93048	107388	137470	87188	84079	101393	88223	87215	93509
Paper products	31507	47850	60691	74242	134378	71203	78066	92893	86010	94258	105444
Printing and publishing	26477	33403	32504	42105	54323	52162	52235	53007	53327	54537	58047
Iron and steel products	124805	185523	198134	158876	207531	125452	98746	132855	114033	124093	147981
Transportation equipment	37544	76866	106980	110800	111534	61432	58043	68923	61191	79775	95991
Non-ferrous metal products	41393	45321	35666	33352	36970	17595	21204	26784	26380	33445	34170
Electrical apparatus and supplies	10178	15909	12108	14707	22213	20141	18603	19744	26292	28506	32401
Non-metallic minerals	14918	17950	17792	19664	33494	25481	28856	29060	27932	28207	29365
Petroleum and coal	7621	10531	13169	14730	17208	10942	11553	4711	8254	8325	15129
Chemical products	41941	93829	124797	34433	39688	28061	29704	37941	35911	38497	43259
Miscellaneous industries	9207	12854	17053	19340	25256	19416	19689	20018	15895	17198	19387
Total GDP	664054	960072	1084026	1042248	1271069	872977	865311	954824	899777	953898	1067403

Table 1.13. Comparison of Barnett and Rees-Long-Hoover Cost of Living Indexes and Canadian Wholesale Price Index, 1871-1900 (Base of Index 1900=100)

Year	Barnett (Canadian)	Rees-Long-Hoover (U.S.)	DBS Wholesale Price Index	Year	Barnett (Canadian)	Rees-Long-Hoover (U.S.)	DBS Wholesale Price Index
1870	107	135	128	1886	103	111	100
1871	108	134	130	1887	109	112	102
1872	116	133	145	1888	105	112	106
1873	115	129	146	1889	107	109	106
1874	112	128	138	1890	105	108	108
1875	108	118	133	1891	105	108	108
1876	109	117	124	1892	105	108	100
1877	106	125	118	1893	104	107	101
1878	104	121	109	1894	95	102	95
1879	103	120	105	1895	91	100	93
1880	106	121	115	1896	95	100	90
1881	111	121	116	1897	96	99	91
1882	118	121	116	1898	100	99	95
1883	119	119	113	1899	97	99	97
1884	104	117	107	1900	100	100	100
1885	104	114	101				

Appendix to Chapter 1

The following are the changes in the estimates of data for this volume resulting from correction of errors.

1.   In agriculture farm revenue
rye	1870-1881
eggs	1916-1926
honey	1921-1926
apples	1921-1926
grapes	1870-1889
poultry	1921-1926
butter	1870-1889 and 1925-1926
wool	1920-1926
forest products	1875-1889
hogs	1870-1889

2.   In agriculture farm expenses fertilizer expenses 1900-1915

3   Community business and personal service census years
year 1880
year 1900

4.   Federal government
year 1912

These changes carried through to totals. No totals were affected significantly. The largest relative change is in the poultry data.

Should one wish it these corrected data may be compared with the originally published data.

Bibliography of Sources Cited in Chapter 1

Barnett, R.J.F., "A Study of Price Movements and the Cost of Living in Kingston, Ontario, for the years 1895 to 1900", M.A. thesis at Queen's University, 1963, in Queen's University Archives.

Bertram, Gordon W. and Michael B. Percy, "Real Wage Trends in Canada, 1900 to 1926: Some Provisional Estimates" in *Canadian Journal of Economics* (May, 1979).

Canada, Royal Commission on Labour and Capital, *Report*, 1889.

Dominion Bureau of Statistics (from 1971 onwards Statistics Canada), *National Accounts*, annual and periodical summaries, especially *National Income and Expenditure Accounts 1926-1974*, 3 volumes.

Engerman, Stanley L. and Robert E. Gallman, *Long-Term Factors in American Economic Growth*, 1986, University of Chicago Press, Volume 51 in the National Bureau of Economic Research, Conference on Research in Income and Wealth series.

Kuznets, Simon, *National Product Since 1869*, National Bureau of Economic Research, 1946.

Long, Clarence, *Wages and Earnings in the United States 1860-1890*, National Bureau of Economic Research, 1960.

Michell, H. "Statistics of Prices" in K.W. Taylor and H. Michell, *Statistical Contributions to Canadian Economic History*, Volume II (Macmillan of Canada, 1931).

Poor's Business Services, Dividend Record (see bibliography of Chapter 6 for references to Business Services).

Province of Ontario, Ontario Bureau of Industries, *Reports*, annual, 1883 to 1926.

Rees, Albert, *Real Wages in Manufacturing 1890-1914*, National Bureau of Economic Research, 1961.

United States, Bureau of the Census, *Historical Statistics of the United States, Colonial Times to 1970*.

Urquhart, M.C., Editor, and K.A.H. Buckley, Assistant Editor, *Historical Statistics of Canada*, 1965 (Macmillan of Canada and Cambridge University Press).

Chapter 2. Agriculture

M.C. URQUHART with acknowledgment
to R. MARVIN McINNIS

Gross Domestic Product in Agriculture, Canada, 1870-1926

Concept of Gross Domestic Product in Agriculture

The ultimate objective is to make an estimate of income originating in Canadian agriculture regardless of who receives this income. Thus it includes rent paid to nonresident owners of farms, interest paid to nonfarm holders of farm mortgages, and wages paid to hired farm labour, as well as all income from farm operations accruing from farm operations in Canada to the farmers themselves. Conversely, it does not include income accruing to Canadian farmers from sources outside of the farm sector of Canada, such as property income from nonfarm property or labour income received by farmers for work they have done outside of the farm sector. Gross income produced in Canadian agriculture is gross of capital consumed in agriculture production. Net income produced could be obtained by deducting capital consumption allowances from gross income produced but only gross income produced is estimated in this study.

Coverage

The income estimates provide only a total for all Canada. Geographically, they cover the provinces of New Brunswick, Nova Scotia, Ontario, Quebec, and Prince Edward Island for all years from 1870 to 1879, even though the latter province did not enter confederation until 1873; they cover all of present-day Canada, excluding Newfoundland, from 1880 to 1926.

The income estimates cover all activity that results in an output of agricultural products wherever it takes place. Thus, they include the feeding of animals on commercial feedlots as well as on farms. They cover production of all crops and especially fruits and vegetables on small lots. They cover the very considerable production of dairy and poultry products in villages, towns, and cities by nonfarmers, and they cover output of farm products consumed by farmers or owners of small lots themselves. Only the products of urban kitchen gardens are excluded.

The income is measured for each year from 1870 to 1926. The estimates for census years are particularly important since they are based on more complete data than those for other years. But, except for the 1870s, there are many production data for intercensal years.

Methodology

Two alternative methods, basically, are available for estimating agricultural income produced. The first method involves adding the value of consumption of farm-produced products by farm families (income in kind) to the value of off-farm sales of farm products for the whole agricultural sector and then subtracting the expenses of those nonfactor inputs that are purchased from off the farms to arrive at income produced on the farms themselves. The second method involves making estimates of the values of all products that are produced on farms, regardless of whether they are consumed by farm families themselves, used as intermediate commodities for use in further farm production (mainly feed crops), or sold off farms, and then subtracting the values of the intermediate products used for further farm production and also the expenses of off-farm purchases of nonfactor inputs, in order to arrive at income produced on the farms.

If marketing data (or information that serves the same purpose) can be obtained for the sale of farm products, the advantages lie with the first method. Its use eliminates the necessity to estimate the value of the intermediate farm products that are used for further farm production. The first method has been used by Statistics Canada for many years and is the basis on which the official statistics have been prepared for as far back as 1946.

The advantage of the second method, if market data are not available, is that agricultural statistics, once they are collected, have typically provided gross production data--that is, data on the total quantities of crops and other commodities produced regardless of whether they are sold off the farm or used on the farm for further production. If, then, some information can be obtained about the parts of gross farm production that are used as intermediate inputs, the second method may be better than the first. In the pre-World War II period the Dominion Bureau of Statistics had some such information, obtained from farmers, and used this second method.

A variant of the first method was used for two reasons. First, there is scarcely any information on the amounts of feed crops and other farm products that are used on the farms themselves for further farm production in the period before World War I. It would be very risky to assume that the ratio of intermediate products to the total gross output of all products was the same in the pre-World War I period as in the post-World War I period. The bulk of the intermediate products is made up of field crops, and the proportion of field crops that are used on the farms varies greatly between types of farms, especially between grain farms and livestock farms. Grain farms output grew much more rapidly than livestock farms output after 1900. Second, we have been able to find data that we believe permit us to make reasonably good estimates of the part of crops that is for off-farm disposal or for farm family consumption without getting involved in estimating the production of intermediate products in any major way.

The Estimation of Farm Output of Final Products

We now give the general method of arriving at off-farm disposal and farm family consumption of crops and other vegetable products, on the one hand, and livestock and dairy products on the other. The general practice, in almost every case, was to estimate the volume of such movements, first, and then to obtain a unit money value which permitted a valuation of total farm product, net of intermediate products.

The disposal of farm crop and vegetable products, net of intermediate products, is composed of human consumption (of both farm and nonfarm families), plus nonhuman off-farm uses in Canada, plus net exports (exports minus imports), plus increases (or minus decreases) of inventories. If we can estimate each of these for each product, we would have one way of estimating the volume of farm products produced, net of intermediate products. Let us deal with these in turn.

First, total human consumption of each product was calculated from estimates of per capita consumption and the numbers in the Canadian population. The numbers in the Canadian population are readily available on an annual basis throughout the whole period. Estimates of per capita consumption were arrived at in various ways, depending on the product. The way in which the per capita consumption estimates were obtained was specific to each product. It is sufficient at this point to note that it has been possible to obtain estimates in which one may have a considerable degree of confidence.

Second, nonhuman off-farm uses of field crops were calculated by a variety of methods, the chosen method being suited to the crop. The amounts of hay and oats sold to feed nonfarm horses were calculated by making estimates of consumption of each product per horse and of the number of off-farm horses. Barley used for malting could be obtained from excise figures; the consumption of grains for distillation was obtained in like manner. In some years the supply of flax fibre could be obtained from statements of raw materials used in scutching mills, and so forth. Fortunately, our decision to include commercial feedlots and nonfarm production of milk and poultry products in the agriculture sector eliminated the need to estimate the feeds that went from farms to these particular nonfarm uses.

Third, external trade data, both for exports and imports, were obtainable from the published trade returns for every fiscal year from 1870 onward. Usually the information was given in sufficient detail to provide information for individual commodities. However, in some cases, in the earlier years of our period, data were grouped in the source, and it was necessary to estimate individual commodities from the grouped data. The export figures used were those for Canadian products only, and the import figures were "imports for consumption"

Fourth, except for wheat, there are practically no crop data on inventories throughout the period. The lack of availability of inventories may affect the assignment of income to particular years. However, at this stage in Canadian development, carryovers at the end of crop years from one year to the next were probably rather small but, of course, insofar as minimum inventories, on the average, did increase, our estimates omit that part of the disposition of products that was directed toward the building up of inventories.

We also made use of whatever production data of field crops and fruits and vegetables were available. These production data, along with the trade data, for decennial census years often provided the basis of the estimates of human consumption in Canada, for census years, of those grains, fruits, or vegetables that were not intermediate products. Of course, a reconciliation of production and use data, where such is possible, provides the best ultimate check on reliability.

In some cases the production data alone provided the basis of the estimates. At the same time, the production data were of little help for those products for which a large part of the output is intermediate.

There was such diversity in the way that the farm prices, for valuing the farm products, were obtained that a general description of our method in short compass is not possible. The way in which individual prices were obtained was specific to each product.

Estimates of the value of products of livestock and poultry were obtained in a fashion similar to that of crops, with one difference. For all but the earliest decades of our period we had annual direct estimates of the production of crops and fruits and vegetables, for Ontario from

1882 onward, for Manitoba from 1885 onward, for Alberta and Saskatchewan from 1898 onward, for New Brunswick from 1898 onward, for all provinces except British Columbia from 1908 onward, and for British Columbia from 1911 onward. In the case of the provincial data on livestock we had estimates of the stocks of animals on farms for those periods described in the preceding sentence but, with one exception, not for off-farm disposition and farm family consumption. The exception was Ontario, for which many livestock sales and slaughter data were available from 1892 onward. Of course, the decennial census from 1870 provided production data as well as stocks for most livestock products. The nature of the data available meant that, for provinces other than Ontario and even for some of Ontario's products, in making our estimates for intercensal years, we had to infer production of livestock products from data on stocks of livestock and poultry. The availability of data on stocks of animals meant that we could take account of changes in inventories from year to year, a procedure that we could not follow in the case of crops.

The Estimation of Expenses of Off-Farm Purchases of Inputs

The expenses of off-farm purchases of inputs must be subtracted from the net value of products to obtain farm income produced. These purchases cover the acquisition of such items as tractor oil and grease, binder twine, blacksmithing, commercial fertilizers, fencing materials, harness and saddlery, and many other such items. Fortunately, many items that are expenses for an individual farm are only intermediate products for the agricultural sector as a whole, and our method of estimation is such that we do not have to estimate the quantities and values of these intermediate products. In addition, since we are interested in income originating in agriculture, we do not have to estimate the cost of hired labour, the interest paid on farm indebtedness and the rents of farmland.

These circumstances still leave a formidable list of expenses to be calculated. The data for their estimation are best at the end of our period and become increasingly less satisfactory as we go back in time. Luckily, expenses for off-farm purchases become relatively less important the further back we go. For example, there were no purchases of oil for farm tractors when there were no farm tractors or only steam tractors; these expenses increased more than in proportion to output as the use of farm tractors became increasingly widespread. Similarly, as the use of increasingly elaborate machinery grew with the passing of time, outlays on machinery parts and machine service grew. The introduction and spread of the use of binder twine, from about 1880 onward, added an element to off-farm costs that grew through the years. And one can add to the list readily. There were some elements of substitution, of course. For example, the interchangeable part probably replaced one element of the blacksmith's services. But these appear not to have been of great importance.

The quality of the estimates of farm expenses is best for the late years and less good the further back in time we go. They are sufficiently small in the earliest part of the period that even if the margin of error of their estimation is quite large it does not have an important effect on the estimates of income produced in agriculture.

Sources of Data

The details of the sources of data will emerge as we proceed; here we give only the general sources of information. These include: the decennial census reports for the Dominion together with the quinquennial reports for the Prairie Provinces; the reports of first the Census and Statistics Office (CSO, based initially in the Federal Department of Agriculture) and later the

Dominion Bureau of Statistics (DBS) on an annual basis from 1908 onward; provincial reports on agricultural production; the external trade reports; and finally, certain publications that give us prices.

From the agricultural censuses for 1870 onward, the data collected in the decennial census included the quantity of output of the main field crops and the larger types of livestock. In addition the numbers on farms, at a specific date, of the main types of livestock were obtained. No valuations of products were obtained until the census of 1900; from 1900 onward values as well as quantities produced and numbers and values of the inventory of livestock were obtained. The collection of data for some minor products was added in 1900.

The Census and Statistics Office collected annual data from 1908 onward on production and values of field crops, vegetables and fruit, and of numbers and values of the inventory of livestock (but not annual slaughter). For 1920 onward DBS made estimates of off-farm disappearance. Many of these data appear in a series, *Handbook of Agricultural Statistics*, in a number of volumes prepared by DBS after World War II.

Several provinces collected provincial data on an annual basis before the Dominion reporting system was set up in 1908. The Province of Ontario began the annual collection of data on the production of most field crops, of the numbers of livestock on farms, of capital invested in farms, and of prices of farm products in 1882; data collection on the sale or slaughter of farm animals was begun in 1892. The Province of Manitoba began the collection of considerable amounts of agricultural data in 1883, Alberta and Saskatchewan (initially the Western Territories) in 1898, and New Brunswick in 1898.

External trade data, both quantities and values, are available for every year from 1870 (and before) onward. Unit values of exports and imports may be calculated from these data.

In addition to the price or unit value data available from these just enumerated sources, there are two other general sources that give considerable agricultural price data. They are H. Michell in Taylor and Michell, *Statistical Contributions to Canadian Economic History*, volume 2 (Michell), and Department of Labour, *Wholesale Prices, Canada 1890-1909*, along with its successor annual publication, *Wholesale Prices*, which begins with 1911.

There were, in addition to these general sources of data, many other sources that apply to more limited periods or to specific agricultural products. We proceed now to examine the detail of the estimates.

FARM REVENUE FROM OFF-FARM SALES AND FARM CONSUMPTION

The following text describes, product by product, how estimates were made from the off-farm sales of farm products plus income in kind of farm families from personal consumption of farm products. The reader is referred to the bibliography at the end of this chapter for abbreviations of source titles.

Farm Revenue from Field Crops, Fruits, Vegetables and Eggs

Estimates of farm revenues from cereals, fruits and vegetables were, in large part, derived by first estimating quantities produced for non-farm uses and then valuing these quantities at current prices.

The production and use of agricultural data were generally estimated on a crop year basis which ran from July or August of year t to June or July of year t+1, depending on the crop. This meant that the production figures, reflecting the harvests of summer and autumn were for year t while the external trade figures were probably more largely for the year t+1. Further, insofar as consumption figures for a crop year were calculated within this project, they would be estimated from the populations of the year t+1. In our manuscript these crop years are recorded as for the year t, the year of production.

We now deal with these crops etc., item by item.

Wheat

Quantities of Net Off-Farm Disposition

We note, at once, that the annual volume of production, exports and imports, and the derived "apparent home consumption" (production plus imports minus exports) are available for the entire period on a crop year basis in Urquhart and Buckley, *Historical Statistics of Canada* (HSC) Series L139-146. However, the production data for the years between the 1871 and 1880 census are based, in large part, on calculated figures for apparent domestic consumption calculated on an assumption of use of 6.5 bushels per capita per annum for human consumption and for seed.

The calculations of volume, gross of seed requirements and cleaning, were made, period by period, as follows.

Crop years beginning 1870 to 1879

For this decade, the only directly obtained figure was one for 1870 from the census of 1871. The project estimate for each crop year was prepared by adding to net exports for the crop year, obtained from HSC Series L139-146, an estimate of human consumption in Canada which, in turn, was obtained by multiplying the population at April 1 following the harvest by an assumed annual human consumption of wheat of 5.5 bushels per capita. The human consumption figure of 5.5 bushels per capita was widely (and unquestionedly) accepted, by persons considering the matter, at all times throughout the period 1870 to 1926. The formula then for obtaining the net off-farm disposition of wheat in this period was human consumption plus exports minus imports.

Crop years beginning 1880 to 1907

For this period the net off-farm disposition of wheat was obtained for most years in essentially the same manner as for 1870-79 even though the computational methods differed: it was obtained by adding net exports to human consumption in Canada at 5.5 bushels per capita. However, there were variations from this method for a small number of years. This variation was possible because there were annual estimates of production in these years (HSC Series L139), which, aside from census years, were based on provincially collected data. In a small number of years, *viz.* 1893, 1896, 1897 and 1907, the estimates of wheat disposition, as calculated above, plus seed requirements exceeded the estimates of production. It was assumed for these years that the shortfall was made up from carryovers of wheat from the next earlier harvest. Hence an amount equivalent to the shortfall was attributed to the year of the next earlier harvest over and above the amount calculated from the earlier formula for that year.

It should be noted that in most years the estimated production exceeds our calculated off-farm disposition plus seed requirement. This excess was calculated for each year and designated in our working papers as non-merchantable wheat. Such wheat would be used on the farm for feeding purposes. We will return to this item later but just note, at this point, that when the Canadian census and statistics office began the regular annual countrywide collection of crop statistics in 1908 it provided an estimate of non-merchantable wheat with the 1909 crop. In the event, the ratios of the non-merchantable wheat to total production, obtainable from our estimates for 1880 to 1907 were of the same order as those derivable from the official estimates for 1908 onward.

Crop years beginning 1908 to 1925

Extensive data for this period have been published in DBS *Handbook of Agricultural Statistics, Part I, Field Crops* (HAS.I).

The net off-farm disposition of wheat was calculated province by province by the formula: production minus seed requirements minus cleaning loss minus non-merchantable wheat. These items, in turn, were obtained in the following ways.

Production: production by province for all years was available from HAS.I. These data had originally been published in Department of Agriculture, *Census and Statistics Monthly Bulletin* (CSM) and its successor *Monthly Bulletin of Agricultural Statistics* (MBAS). All production figures, except for 1910, were taken from the source. The 1910 figure was obtained by multiplying the decennial census figure for wheat acreage in 1910 by the HAS.I (CSM) average yield per acre for each province.

Seed requirements: seed requirements out of crop for year t were calculated at 1.75 bushels per acre for acreage sown in year t+1. The acreages sown, by province, were available in HAS.I.

Cleaning loss: cleaning loss was calculated at 3 percent of production.

Non-merchantable wheat (CSM): the proportion of wheat production that was non-merchantable was reported for each province in CSM and MBAS from 1909 onward. Since these data were not given in HAS.I, they had to be obtained from original sources. Except for 1908, the volume of non-merchantable wheat was calculated province by province from the production data and the proportion non-merchantable; there were no estimates for non-merchantable wheat in 1908. The 1908 figure for non-merchantable wheat was calculated by assuming, as was done for the period 1870 to 1907, that off-farm disposition was equal to 5.5 bushels per capita plus net exports and then subtracting this off-farm disposition plus seed requirements from the estimate of production to obtain a figure for non-merchantable wheat in 1908. This means, of course, that the 1908 figure for off-farm disposition was calculated in exactly the same way as was done for 1870 to 1907.

Prices for Valuing Wheat

Given our methodology, the price used was net price at the local grain elevator for prairie province wheat or the similar type of delivery point in the other provinces. In our period most farmers delivered their own wheat to the elevator; for the farmers who hired delivery services, these services were provided by other farmers and thus any income so-generated remained within the farm sector.

The way in which the prices were obtained is best explained separately for each of the two periods.

Prices for crops of 1908 (crop year 1908-09) to 1926 (crop year 1926-27)

Prices for these years for all provinces, except the prairie provinces, were obtained directly from HAS.I, and were used just as given there.

For prices of prairie wheat, HAS.I data were believed to be less appropriate since they were an unweighted crop year average price, whereas the delivery and sale of prairie grain was heavily concentrated in the first six months of the crop year, that is, from September to February. Thus, the crop of 1908 would be largely sold in the months September 1908 to February 1909. Consequently, an alternative source of prairie prices was used.

These alternative prairie prices were calculated in a number of steps.

Step 1. The closing monthly price on the Winnipeg grain exchange of No. 1 Northern wheat, basis in store Ft. William, was obtained for every month throughout the period. A simple average of these prices for September to February was calculated for each crop year. (An annual average price was also calculated in our project and a crop year average price was also available in HSC Series L98 but these series were not used.)

The basic sources of data were: for 1908-09 to 1916-17, "Grain Statistics" published as a part of the annual report of the Department of Trade and Commerce, usually as sessional paper 10d; and for 1917-18 to 1926-27, *Grain Trade of Canada*, an annual publication of DBS.

Step 2. Average closing prices at the end of November, basis in store Ft. William, for each grade of wheat for each year was obtained from "Grain Statistics" and *Grain Trade*. Similarly, the ratios of "inspected" wheat in each grade to all inspected wheat, for each crop year, were obtained from the same sources. A weighted average price for the close of November each year, the weights being the above-mentioned proportions of inspected wheat in each grade for the relevant calendar year, was calculated. (The "all other" grade category of wheat was given the same price as No. 3 Northern.) This calculation takes account of variation in the quality of crops from year to year.

Step 3. For each year the ratio of the simple average price of No. 1 Northern wheat for the months September to February to the closing price of No. 1 Northern at the end of November was calculated. This ratio was multiplied by the average closing November price for all grades to obtain an estimate of the average price for all grades from September to February. This step provided an average yearly price at Ft. William.

Step 4. Railway transport costs for each province to Ft. William were then calculated. The calculations were made first for the crop year 1909-10 from data in "Grain Statistics" giving rail rates from a very large number of prairie points to Ft. William. For Manitoba, a simple average was taken for all reported points on all three railways, the Canadian Pacific Railway (CPR), the Canadian Northern and the Grand Trunk Pacific (GTP); this average was 13 cents per cwt. or 7.8 cents per bushel. For Saskatchewan, first, simple averages were calculated separately for each railway for all reported points on the railway; second, these three average rates were combined giving the CPR a weight of 2 and each of the Canadian Northern and the GTP a rate of 1. The resultant rate for Saskatchewan was 19 cents per cwt. or 11.4 cents per bushel. For Alberta a simple average of all reported points on all railways gave 24.44 cents per cwt., rounded to 24.5 cents, or 14.7 cents per bushel. These rates were each adjusted from year to year on the basis of the Regina-Ft. William rate given in HSC Series L12. Actually, the rates were unchanged from 1908 to 1917 and from 1922 to 1926; the changes that took place occurred between 1917 and 1922.

A combined transport cost for all prairie wheat was then obtained for each year by weighting each provincial rate by the proportion of prairie grain produced in each province that year, the proportions being calculated from HAS.I production data. A transportation cost to Ft. William for each year was thus obtained.

Step 5. These transport costs were then subtracted from the average yearly price at Ft. William for all prairie wheat obtained in step 3. There was, in addition, a further subtraction of 3.4 cents per bushel from the Ft. William price made up of 1.5 cents spread between street and track, 1 cent commission and 0.88 cents (rounded to 0.9) handling charge. This step then yielded the price at which prairie wheat at the farm was valued.

Prices for crops of 1870 (1870-71) to 1907 (1907-08)

The method of obtaining prices differed among three sub-periods of this period.

From 1870-71 to 1879-80, the price used for all wheat was that for Ontario Winter No. 2 at Toronto, obtained from HSC Series L98. This tended to be slightly less than prices for the same period reported in the Ontario Bureau of Industries (OBI) *Report* for 1884.

For 1880-81 to 1889-90 a weighted price of Ontario and western wheat was used. The Ontario price was again Winter No. 2 at Toronto from HSC Series L98. The Manitoba price was calculated at the Ontario price less 8 cents per bushel and the North West Territories (Alberta and Saskatchewan) price at the Manitoba price less 7 cents per bushel. A single weighted price for all wheat was calculated by weighting prices by amounts produced in the relevant provinces. The weights for 1880-81 were obtained from the census. For 1882-83, to calculate the weights, Ontario's production was from the OBI Report; the western crop was calculated by subtracting from the whole country's total output, the Ontario output and an assumed output of 3.4 million bushels for Quebec and then dividing the western output at 0.9 for Manitoba and 0.1 for the North West Territories (NWT). For 1881-82, Manitoba and NWT outputs were calculated by linear interpolation between 1880-81 and 1882-83; the eastern crop was the difference between total production, HSC Series L139, and western production. For 1883-84 to 1889-90, Manitoba production was from provincial crop data and the NWT's production was calculated at 12 percent of the Manitoba crop, the proportion shown by the census data in both 1880-81 and 1890-91; the remainder of the country's output was attributed to production by eastern provinces.

For 1890-91 to 1907-08 the eastern price was obtained from annual reports of the OBI, which gave an average price in Ontario for the last six months of each calendar year; the Manitoba price was made equal to the eastern price less 7 cents for 1890-91 to 1900-01, 6 cents for 1901-02 and 1902-03 and 5 cents for 1903-04 to 1907-08; the NWT average price was made 7 cents less than the Manitoba price for 1890-91 to 1892-93 and 6 cents less than the Manitoba price for 1893-94 to 1907-08. The weights were production in Manitoba, NWT and eastern Canada. For 1890-91 to 1907-08 the production of Manitoba was obtained from provincial crop reports. The NWT production for 1898-99 to 1907-08 was likewise from provincial crop reports; for the years 1890-91 to 1897-98, the year 1894-95 figure was assumed equal to the 1890-91 census figure plus 40 percent of the difference between 1890-91 and 1898-99; linear interpolations were then taken for the years between 1890-91 and 1894-95 and the years between

1894-95 and 1898-99. For all years from 1890-91 to 1907-08, the eastern crop was taken as the Dominion total (HSC Series L139) minus the western crop.

The differentials in prices between Ontario, Manitoba and the NWT were based on the differentials that existed from 1908-09 onward as given in prices in HAS.I: 1903-04 to 1907-08 were exactly equal to the later differentials; the earlier differentials were adjusted by changes in freight charges given in HSC, p. 548.

The farm revenues from the sale of wheat were then calculated by multiplying the quantity of grain available for off-farm disposition by the farm prices as calculated above.

Oats

Quantities of Off-Farm Sales

Since the major part of the oats crop is used as a feedstuff for animals on farms, and thereby becomes an intermediate product in farm production, we can not use production figures as a measure of net farm revenues from outside agriculture from oat production. We must then devise alternative methods to estimate the off-farm sales of oats.

The major use of oats outside the agriculture sector itself, during the period of our interest was as feed for horses and cattle that were not located on farms, as human food and in net exports. The task then becomes one of making estimates for each of these parts.

Feed for Off-Farm Horses

The first step is to estimate the number of off-farm horses. The only direct estimates of off-farm horses, separate from farm horses, were obtained in the censuses of 1921 and 1931: they were 158,762 in number in the former year and 101,522 in the latter. Estimates for earlier census years must be obtained by inference from census records of the total number of all horses, farm and non-farm, recorded in the decennial censuses.

It is of particular importance to get the best estimate that we can for 1911 for the effects of motorization had scarcely begun by then. The numbers of off-farm horses in 1910 is placed at 180,000 derived as follows. The number of farm horses per 100 acres of improved farm land in 1921 was 4.87733. If the ratio of horses to improved farm land in 1911 had been the same as in 1921, the number of farm horses required in 1911 would have been 48,733,823 acres x 0.0487733 = 2,376,909 horses. This figure may be taken as an underestimate of farm requirements in 1911, because in 1921 there were 47,000 farm tractors to supplement the work of horses, while in 1911 the number of tractors, which is unknown, must have been small; if, as a guess, 40,000 horses were added to the 1911 farm requirement in compensation for the smaller number of tractors, the farm requirement would then fall short of the total of all horses in Canada (at 2,598,958 animals — Census 1911) to leave 180,000 horses for non-farm usage. This non-farm usage amounts to 6.9 per cent of the horse population in 1911.

For years before 1906 to 1910 and census years 1871, 1881, 1891 and 1901 the number of non-farm horses was assumed to be 6.9 per cent of the total horse population as reported in HSC Series L171; the data for 1871, which excludes Prince Edward Island (PEI), were supplemented by adding the number of horses in PEI obtained from its census. Estimates for the intervening years between pairs of the aforementioned census years and for 1902 to 1906 were made by linear interpolation. Estimates for 1912 to 1915 were obtained by changing the number of off-farm horses in 1911, 180,000 in number, in proportion to changes in the total number of horses in Canada as reported in the 1915 *Canada Year Book* (CYB), p.172. (These *Canada Year Book* numbers differ slightly from the HSC numbers but only by small amounts.) From 1916 to 1920, linear interpolation between 1915 and 1921; from 1922 to 1926 linear interpolation between 1921 and 1931.

The consumption of oats per non-farm horse was placed at 75 bushels per annum derived as follows. Bailey's *Cyclopedia Of Agriculture* places material requirements per 1,000 pounds of horse weight at 4,750 pounds of dry matter per year for a medium level work rate of which four-tenths is grain (oats in Canada). For an average horse-weight of 1,300 pounds, then, the oats requirement would be 1.3 x 0.4 x 4750 which amounts to 2,470 pounds of oats per year. At 34 pounds per bushel of oats this figure amounts to just over 72.5 bushels of oats which was rounded up to 75 bushels of oats per year.

Total off-farm sales of oats in bushels for non-farm horses were then obtained by multiplying the number of non-farm horses by 75.

Feed For Off-Farm Cattle

The procedure was much like that for horses. In both the 1921 and 1931 censuses the number of off-farm cattle were reported as follows:

Off-Farm Cattle

	1921	1931
Cows in milk or in calf, 2 years old & over	96,020	62,113
Number of other cattle not on farms	54,975	64,739
Total, all cattle	149,995	126,852

An estimate was made for other census years, 1871 to 1911, on the basis of the numbers of persons in incorporated centers of less than 1000 persons plus one-fifth of the number of persons living in incorporated centers of 1,000 to 4,999 persons. The relevant data follow.

	Pop. In Incorp. Centers Under 1,000 Persons	Pop. In Incorp. Centers of 1,000 to 4,999 Persons	Sum Cols. (1) + 1/5th of Col. (2)	No. of Non-Farm Cattle
	(1)	(2)	(3)	(4)
1871	74,973	196,000	114,173	33,000
1881	133,467	316,000	196,667	56,000
1891	96,493	427,310	181,955	51,500
1901	146,967	545,037	255,974	73,500
1911	264,519	652,084	394,936	112,500
1921	373,752	764,836	526,719	149,995
1931	409,797	830,742	575,945	126,852

Source: Column (1): For 1871 to 1901, HSC Series A18 (population in all incorporated centers) less series A20 (population in incorporated centers of 1000 or more persons calculated for 1871, 1881 using footnote values); 1901 to 1931, *Census of Canada*, 1951, Volume X, p.37. Column (2): *Census of Canada*, 1951, Volume X, p. 37 for 1891 to 1931, also in HSC Series A24, Page 15 with a minor difference for 1911; HSC p.15, footnote (3) for 1871 and 1881. Column (4): The number of non-farm milk cows for census years 1871 to 1911 was projected backward from 1921 on the basis of the data of column (3), the numbers being rounded to thousands; the number of "other cattle" was calculated as the same proportion of number of milk cows as in 1921, the figures being rounded to the nearest 500. The figures for all years were calculated by straight line interpolation between adjacent census years.

The consumption of oats per head of non-farm cattle was calculated from Bailey's *Cyclopedia Of Agriculture* at 8.04 bushels per head per annum, it being assumed that two thirds of the grain requirements were for oats.

Human Consumption of Oat Products

The human consumption of oatmeal and like oat products was placed at 14 pounds of oatmeal per year throughout. The number 16.5 pounds of oatmeal converts from one bushel (34 pounds) of oats. The consumption of oats per capita in bushels then was $14/16.5 = 0.08484848$ bushels of oats. Multiplication of this figure by the population (HSC Series A1) gave human consumption of oats.

The figure of 14 pounds of oatmeal per capita consumption was obtained from domestic disappearance of oatmeal and rolled oats. Subtraction of exports from mill production (DBS *Flour And Feed Mill Industry 1921*) and division by population yielded 12.4 pounds feed mill per capita in 1921. (Mill production was 212,115 (98 pound) bags of oatmeal and 1,419,362 (90 pound) bags of rolled oats, together making up 148,530 thousand pounds of product. Exports of these products amounted to 39,721 thousand pounds.)

The total off-farm disposition of oats, in bushels, is derived as the sum of off-farm horse and cattle oat consumption plus human consumption plus net exports. As usual, exports, throughout and imports (very small) from 1875-76 onward are available annually from DBS,

Trade of Canada (or variant, in name, thereof).

Prices for Valuing Oats

To obtain a money valuation of this off-farm disposition it was necessary to obtain a price per bushel at the farm for multiplication with the physical off-farm quantities. This valuation was done in two phases: for years 1870-71 to 1907-08; and for years 1908-09 to 1926-27.

The aggregate off-farm movement of oats was multiplied by a single price from 1870-71 to 1907-08. This single price was obtained from annual review or annual reports of the OBI (first volume for 1883, but 1884 volume substantially enlarged): the prices were quoted on a monthly basis for the last four months of each calendar year. For the period 1870-71 to 1883-84 the prices quoted were those of the Toronto produce market; for the period from 1884-85 onward the quoted prices were essentially farm prices. At the point of overlap it could be seen that Toronto produce market prices were about two cents per bushel above farm prices. Accordingly, the sum of two cents was subtracted from the Toronto produce market prices for 1870-71 to 1883-84. The price used for the annual price was the simple average of the monthly prices for September, October, November, and December each year.

From 1908-09 onward the valuation was done on a western (Manitoba to British Columbia) and eastern basis for while an average price is available (from Statistics Canada publications) for all Canada it applies to total production of oats and not to off-farm sales. The division of off-farm quantities between eastern and western Canada was done in two main steps. The share of western Canada of off-farm sales for horse, cattle and human consumption was calculated by splitting the totals for Canada in proportion to the shares of the urban population in eastern and western Canada. The data for urban populations by province, (1956 definition) were obtained from Census of Canada, 1956, *Analytical Report* Vol. III (1956 Census Bulletin 3-2, Table I): the proportions of the west in the total were calculated from census data for 1901, 1911, 1921 and 1931 and the proportions for intervening years were obtained by linear interpolation. To the western share of off-farm horse, cattle and human oat disposition was added the shipments of oats through Ft. William and Pt. Arthur (*Report on the Grain Trade of Canada*) to give a total for the west. The total for the east was then obtained by simply subtracting the total for the west from the grand total of off-farm disposition of oats as previously calculated. The price used for valuing the component for the western provinces came from HAS.I: it was a farm price for the three prairie provinces. The price used for calculating the component for eastern Canada was the OBI price as obtained from several volumes of OBI *Reports*; it was very similar, year by year, with the farm oat price in Ontario as given in the above-mentioned handbook.

In these ways, the calculations for income derived from final off-farm disposition of oats were obtained.

Barley

Total end product production of barley in agriculture was composed of human consumption of barley, the use of barley for making malt and net exports of barley. These measure the parts of barley production that were final products from the viewpoint of farmers; and although a major part of production of barley is for use as feed on the farm itself (an intermediate product) there was little off-farm sale for feeding horses and cattle and there were few off-farm hogs.

As for most grains the value of end product barley production was obtained by multiplying the quantity of end product barley by its price at the farm. We deal with the derivation of quantity first; then, with price; finally, with value as a product of quantity and price.

Quantities

Human consumption was measured by the domestic disappearance of pot and pearl barley. The figure for per capita consumption of pot and pearl barley was placed at 0.4 pounds based on the measure of such consumption annually for 1926-27 to 1930-31 as reported in DBS *Handbook of Agricultural Statistics, Part IV, Food Consumption in Canada, 1926-55* (HAS.IV). Now, since 20.5 pounds of pot or pearl barley is derived from one bushel (48 pounds) of grain barley the annual human consumption of grain barley was placed at one pound (48÷20.5 x 0.4). The number of bushels of barley grain going into human consumption, year by year, was obtained by dividing the number of persons in Canada, each consuming one pound of barley grain, by 48, the number of pounds per bushel of barley (population from HSC Series A1).

The use of barley for malting was obtained from Government of Canada reports on Inland Revenue (Report, Returns, Statistics of the Inland Revenue by Minister of Inland Revenue, annual, in Sessional Papers of Canada) which report the number of pounds of malt manufactured in Canada. Since, by measure, 36 pounds of malt constitute one bushel of malt and, in turn, one bushel of malt requires in input of one bushel of barley grain, the use of barley for malting, measured in bushels, was obtained simply by dividing the number of pounds of malt manufactured by the number 36.

Exports for all years and imports for 1875-76 onward of barley were obtained, as always, from the annual returns *Trade of Canada*. (Imports, which were small throughout, were not available for 1870-71 to 1874-75.) It was not necessary to deal with exports and imports of malt itself, since the inland revenue figures were for malt manufactured.

The total quantities of end product disposition of barley from farms was then the sum of human consumption plus use for malting plus net exports.

Prices

A single price was used to value all end product disposition for the years 1870-71 to 1904-05: from 1870-71 to 1883-84, the price used was the simple average of monthly prices in Toronto for September to December, as reported by the OBI, less two cents per bushel (Ontario Sessional Papers, Vol XVI, Part VII, OBI *Report* for 1884, p.90); from 1884-85 to 1904-05, the price used was the simple average of monthly prices from September to December for an average of several local markets as reported by the OBI. The two cent deduction in the 1870-71 to 1883-84 period was made because the Toronto price was two cents above the average of local prices in the years in which both were available.

From 1905-06 onward off-farm sales were split between east and west and an eastern and a western price were used to value the relevant component. We deal first with the way in which the division between eastern and western quantities were made. For all years from 1905-06 to 1926-27 the proportional division was made on the basis of total barley production in the prairie provinces for the west and total production in Ontario for the east. For 1905-06 and 1906-07 the western crop was obtained from the prairie census of 1906; the eastern crop was obtained from the OBI reports. The same ratio as obtained in 1906-07 was used for 1907-08 as data were lacking to make a direct estimate for this year. From 1908-09 to 1926-27 production in the Prairie Provinces and in Ontario, from which the ratios were derived, were obtained from HAS.I. The proportions so obtained were the following:

Proportional Division of Production

	East	West
1905-06	0.689	0.311
1906-07	0.575	0.425
1907-08	0.575	0.425
1908-09	0.48	0.52
1909-10	0.40	0.60
1910-11	0.54	0.46
1911-12	0.33	0.67
1912-13	0.32	0.68
1913-14	0.32	0.68
1914-15	0.42	0.58
1915-16	0.30	0.70
1916-17	0.18	0.82
1917-18	0.22	0.78
1918-19	0.34	0.66
1919-20	0.26	0.74
1920-21	0.29	0.71
1921-22	0.19	0.81
1922-23	0.21	0.79
1923-24	0.18	0.82
1924-25	0.17	0.83
1925-26	0.18	0.82
1926-27	0.15	0.85

The farm price for eastern barley from 1905-06 onward was obtained in two ways. For 1905-06 to 1908-09 the price used was the OBI price obtained in exactly the same manner, except for a slight variation in 1908-09, as for years from 1884-85 onward; for 1909-10 to 1926-27 the price used was the Ontario average farm price obtained from HAS.I.

The farm price for western barley from 1905-06 onward was also obtained in two ways. From 1908-09 to 1926-27 the price used was the average farm price for the Prairie Provinces obtained from HAS.I as in the case of Ontario; for 1905-06 to 1907-08, the price was derived from the Ft. William price for barley (HSC Series L100) multiplied by the average ratio of the average farm price from HAS.I (noted above) to the Ft. William price for the years 1908-09 to 1912-13.

The value of the end product (off-farm) disposition of barley was obtained by multiplying total quantity times price for 1870-71 to 1904-05 and by taking the sum of similarly calculated values for eastern and western barley from 1905-06 to 1926-27.

Rye

The farm end-product production of rye is calculated from human consumption, from use of rye grain in distillation of spirits and from net exports. Derivation of the farm value of this end-product is, as usual, obtained by multiplying end-product disposition by the farm price of the product. We will deal with the derivation of quantities, first, of prices, second, and finally values.

Quantities

Human consumption is obtained by multiplication of per capita consumption by population. The per capita consumption, throughout, was assumed to be the same as in every year from 1926-27 to 1930-31, *viz* 0.2 pounds of rye flour and meal per capita per annum (HAS.IV, p. 20). Multiplication of this figure by population gives human consumption of rye flour and meal. The equivalence between rye flour and rye grain is given at 5.7 bushels of rye grain being the equivalent of 196 pounds (one barrel) of rye flour (HAS.I). Hence, consumption in pounds then is multiplied by 5.7/196 to get conversion to bushels.

Rye used for distillation of spirits is obtained from reports of the Department of Internal Revenue of the Government of Canada where it is given in pounds of grain (Appendix A, first entry of each report). Pounds weight was converted to bushels at the rate of 56 pounds of grain per bushel.

The data on exports and imports of rye and rye flour are taken from *Trade of Canada*. Data for exports began in 1877-78 for rye grain and not until 1918-19 for rye flour; data for imports of rye grain and rye flour began in 1876-77. Grain trade was reported in bushels; flour trade was reported in barrels of flour (196 pounds per barrel) which convert to bushels of grain at the rate 5.7 bushels of rye grain equal to one barrel of flour.

Total end product disposition of rye grain is composed of human consumption, use for distillation and net exports.

Price

For 1870-71 to 1883-84 the price used was four cents less than the simple average of prices for September, October, November and December in the Toronto market for each year (the four cents represents the difference between prices in the Toronto market and in the local markets once the latter prices were available). Prices came from the *Report* of the OBI for 1884. For 1884-85 to 1908-09 the price was the average for September to December in local markets in Ontario as reported in OBI. For 1909-10 to 1926-27 the price was the average farm price as reported in HAS.I.

Hay

Off-farm disposition of hay is composed of provision of hay for consumption by off-farm horses, for consumption by off-farm cattle and for net exports. The value of the off-farm disposal of hay is obtained by multiplying the quantities sold off-farm by the farm price. The ways in which each of quantity and price are determined are dealt with separately.

Quantity

The quantity for each year is determined by the numbers of off-farm horses and of off-farm cattle and the amounts of hay consumed per animal for each category. An estimate of the numbers of off-farm horses and of off-farm cattle for each year and a description of the way in which the estimates are made is given in the part of this manuscript on oats. Consumption of off-farm hay per animal per annum was placed at 2.75 tons of hay per horse and 2 tons of hay per head of cattle. (For acreages to feed a horse and cattle-beast and for consumption of hay, Straus and Bean, U.S. Department of Agriculture, Technical Bulletin No. 703 Dec. 1940, *Gross Farm Income and Indices of Farm Products and Prices,* p.59; see also HAS.II.)

Exports of hay and imports of hay were obtained as usual from *Trade of Canada*: quantities were reported in tons. For the years 1870-71 to 1874-75, imports of hay and straw together were reported in packages of unknown size; an imputation of the amount of hay imported in these five years was made by assuming that the material was all hay and obtaining a quantity imported by dividing the value of imports by the unit price of exports.

Price

Prices were used in three different ways: from 1870-71 to 1884-85 price was the unit value of exports, calculated from *Trade of Canada*; from 1885-86 to 1907-08 price was a weighted average of the export unit value, with a weight of 0.4, and the OBI farm price with a weight of 0.6; from 1908-09 to 1926-27 the price was the DBS farm price for "Tame Hay, Canada" taken from HAS.I. It is worth pointing out that over the period 1885-86 to 1907-08 the average over all years of the weighted price used was almost identical with the average of the export unit values for the same years (though there were significant variances in particular years). It was the near coincidence of these averages that led to the choice of the export unit value as the price to be used in the period 1870-71 to 1885-86 before the OBI prices were available.

Vegetables Other Than Potatoes

This series was obtained by estimating the value of per capita consumption in 1910, extrapolating the value of aggregate consumption in 1910 in current prices to other years on the basis of population and a price index of prices of vegetables, and then subtracting net imports.

The value of consumption per capita in 1910 was obtained by dividing the value of the vegetables produced on farms by total population; value of vegetable production, *Census of Canada*, 1911, Vol. IV, p. 368, gives value of $18,806,544 divided by total population, 1910 HSC Series A1, of 6,988 thousand persons yields $2.69 per capita; in addition turnips of a value of $5,704,691 or $0.81 per capita were produced of which some part was most probably used for animal food; further there were net imports of value of $1 million, about $0.14 per capita. The value of consumption of "vegetables other than potatoes," taken at being $3 per capita in 1910, allows for some wastage or use as feed on farms.

The price index for vegetables was constructed from a price index for potatoes and a price index for apples equally weighted; there was no price index for "vegetables" as such available. The potato price index was constructed from three overlapping series as follows: from 1870 to 1890 (price in Toronto) from Michell, p.68; 1890 to 1908, Department of Labour, *Wholesale Prices*; for 1908 to 1926, HAS.I. The apple price index was derived from the unit value of exports of apples for 1884-85 to 1926 linked to the unit value of exports of green fruit for 1870-71 to 1884-85, all data of *Trade of Canada*.

The population series was from HSC Series A1.

The value of consumption in current prices for each year was then calculated by the formula: value of consumption of "other vegetables" in current prices = consumption per capita in 1910 ($3.00) x population x the price index (base 1910 = 1.00).

The value of net imports is obtained, year by year, from *Trade of Canada*. For the methods of separating out trade in potatoes, the years 1870-1875, from other vegetables see the notes on potatoes.

The value of production is the value of consumption less the value of net imports.

Potatoes

The basic method used, with some exception for the early 1870's, was to obtain the physical volume (in bushels) of human consumption in Canada to which was added exports and from which was subtracted imports in physical measure to obtain a measure of the volume of final farm production of potatoes. This physical volume was then valued at a farm price. (Data were calculated for a crop year eg. 1890-91 or 1910-11. Population for each of these years was for April 1 of the second year until 1900, eg. April 1891 and for June 1 of the second year in the crop year designation after 1900, e.g. June 1, 1911. Exports and imports were for the trade years of the year given. The production was assigned to the first year of the crop year designation e.g. crop year 1910-11 assigned to 1910. The rationale for this procedure is that the crop of one year is consumed over the following year.)

Quantity

Human consumption of potatoes in Canada was assumed to be five bushels (60 pounds per bushel) per capita throughout the period. This figure has been widely used as exemplified by MBAS, July 1922, p. 274; HSC Series L313; HAS.IV, p. 28; R.H. Coats, *Board of Inquiry into Cost of Living in Canada* Vol. III (King's Printer, 1915) p. 75. Volumes of exports and imports were obtained from *Trade of Canada* from 1876-77 onward.

Price

Prices at which the potatoes were valued were obtained as follows:

1908-09 to 1926-27: HAS.I

1890-91 to 1907-08: Department of Labour, *Wholesale Prices 1890-1909*, p.125, the link to the HAS.I prices for 1908 onward was obtained by taking the average of the ratios of the HAS prices to the *Wholesale Prices* prices for the years 1908-09, 1909-10, 1910-11 which gave a ratio of HAS prices to *Wholesale* prices at 0.856. The *Wholesale* prices were then multiplied by this factor to put them at the level of farm prices. The *Wholesale* price used for each year was the average of the prices for each of the four months from September to December.

1870-71 to 1889-90: Michell, p.68: these were wholesale prices in Toronto and were also multiplied by the adjusting factor 0.856 to obtain the farm price. The Michell prices also for each year were the average of the prices for each of the four months September to December.

The average of monthly prices for the four months September to December was used for the data of Michell and *Wholesale Prices* because it was felt that prices of the months immediately following harvest would reflect year to year movements better than year round monthly prices which include many months of low transactions. The link with the HAS.I prices at 1908-09 is made by using the ratio of the HAS price to the four month average *Wholesale* prices as the linking factor.

For the years 1870-71 to 1875-76 the quantities of exports and imports of potatoes were not available. Hence a slight variation of method was required. The domestic consumption of potatoes at five bushels per capita was valued by the Michell price as described above. In the foreign trade figures potatoes were included with other vegetables. Based on the relationship of potato imports to other vegetables from 1876-77 onward, the value of potato imports in 1870-71 to 1875-76 was taken at 25 per cent of the value of imports all vegetables. In the years from 1875-76 onward the values of potato exports were much larger than the values of exports of other vegetables but were quite variable from year to year compared with other vegetables. It was assumed that the value of exports of vegetables other than potatoes, at a value of $21,705 in 1875-76, was one thousand dollars less in each year than it was in the subsequent year as we moved back from 1875-76 (i.e. exports for 1874-75 were $20,705, for 1873-74 were $19,705, etc.). The values of potato exports were then calculated for 1870-71 to 1874-75 by subtracting these values of exports of all other vegetables from the total export values of all vegetables including potatoes as reported in the trade data. The value of production for final use for these years was then calculated by adding the values of net exports to the values of human consumption in Canada.

Note: The estimates of human consumption from the sources for the years following the 1920's were for weight at the household. There would be some wastage between the farm and the household.

Hops

The value of the hops crop was calculated by different methods for the time period 1870-71 to 1909-10 and the time period 1910-11 to 1926-27. The procedure for each period is given in turn.

Period 1870-71 to 1909-10

Basically, the estimates of the volume of hop production involved preparing an estimate of the domestic disappearance of hops and then subtracting the volume of imports and adding the volume of exports to obtain an estimate of Canadian production.

The estimates of domestic disappearance for census years were made from decennial census data and related trade data as follows:

	Production (lb.)	Exports of Canadian Produce (lb.)	Imports for Consumption (lb.)	Domestic Disappearance (lb.)	Population (000's)	Per Capita Consumption (lb.)	Per Capita Figure Used (lb.)
1870-71	1,711,789	39,589	193,923	1,866,123	3,625	.515	.300
1880-81	905,207	11,508	199,311	1,093,010	4,255	.257	.300
1890-91	1,126,230	265,152	606,465	1,466,943	4,779	.307	.307
1900-01	1,004,216	181,373	806,873	1,629,716	5,301	.307	.307
1910-11	1,208,450	156,679	945,625	1,997,396	6,988	.286	.286
1920-21	758,555	75,308	1,681,822	2,365,069	8,556	.277	.277

Sources: All production data from decennial census; trade data from *Trade of Canada* ; population from HSC Series A1.

The fourth column of data, domestic disappearance, is derived from the preceding three columns: exports were subtracted from production and imports added. Division by population (Column 5) gives statistical domestic disappearance as derived from the data. The figure for 1870-71 seemed anomalously high and that for 1880-81 perhaps anomalously low. Hence, since these early data are perhaps less reliable than the later data and, given the consistency of the per capita statistics from 1890 onward, it was decided to use a figure of domestic disappearance of 0.300 pounds per capita for each of 1870-71 and 1880-81 (Column 7). The year 1920-21 is included for comparative purposes.

The following steps in the estimate of production followed very simply. The per capita domestic disappearance was interpolated linearly between census years. Multiplication by population gave aggregate domestic disappearance. Subtraction of imports and addition of exports then yielded total production.

Value of production of hops was then obtained by multiplying the number of pounds of hops produced by the unit value of imports of hops. (Unit value of imports rather than exports was used both because imports usually greatly overshadowed exports and because export prices were more volatile than import prices.)

Period 1910-11 to 1926-27

Production data were from the decennial census of agriculture for 1910-11 and 1920-21. For other years they were obtained from data for British Columbia and Ontario. By 1910, hop production in nearly all provinces but British Columbia and Ontario had become of negligible size and even Ontario's production was small; by 1920 Ontario's production was less than 1200 pounds; conversely BC's production grew from 1900 onward and it was the only producer of any significance after 1920. For the intercensal years 1910-11 to 1920-21 the estimates for Ontario were made by straight line interpolation between 176,131 pounds in 1910-11 to 1,189 pounds in 1920-21; no entries were made for Ontario after 1920-21. The annual production estimates for BC were from production published in CYB 1924 p.368 and MBAS, March 1928, p. 92. (In the absence of a figure for 1918-19, the figure for that year is derived by linear interpolation between 1917-18 and 1919-20.)

The value of hops production for 1910 to 1926 was obtained in the same manner as for the preceding period: value was obtained as the product of quantity produced and the unit value of imported hops.

Flaxseed (As Distinct from Flax Fibre)

Receipts for flaxseed sale are rather small and relatively unimportant from 1870-71 until after 1900; they then grew substantially, especially from 1905 onward with production taking place mainly on the prairies (apparently often grown on newly broken land); the quantities became less in the 1920s.

The method of estimation of receipts from production and sale of flaxseed followed the common pattern of obtaining the volume of product for off-farm disposition and then multiplying this disposable product by a farm price.

Volume of Disposable Flaxseed

There is no significant farm use of flaxseed except for the quantities used as seed for the next year's crop. Therefore, the disposable volume of flaxseed amounts to production of flaxseed less seed stock for next year's crop and less wastage, if any.

The most basic source on the production of flaxseed is the decennial census of agriculture throughout — this source is particularly important as a primary source for this project for 1870-71, 1880-81, 1890-91 and 1900-01; from 1908-09 onward, annual production data are available for Canada and provinces from HAS.I; from 1891-92 on, Manitoba figures are available annually from Department of Agriculture Reports and particularly from Sessional Papers of Manitoba 1916, Paper Number 14, pp. 702-06; Saskatchewan data from 1902-03 onward, annually, Province of Saskatchewan, Annual Report of the Department of Agriculture, especially Report for 1905, p.11 and Report for 1913, p.108; Alberta data from 1902-03 onward, annually, Province of Alberta, Annual Report of Department of Agriculture, especially Report for 1906, p.101 and Report for 1913 pp.44-45; for 1905-06 Prairie Province census of 1906.

Quantities produced (in bushels) were obtained as follows for various years. (Note that 56 pounds of flaxseed comprise a bushel.)

Years 1870-71 to 1890-91: straight line interpolation between census data of 1870-71 to 1880-81 and 1880-81 to 1890-91. The amounts and values were relatively small in these years.

Years 1890-91 to 1900-01: for each of Ontario and Quebec, quantities produced were estimated by straight line interpolation between census data of 1890-91 and 1900-01 — these amounts were small; for Manitoba, annual production data from agriculture reports noted above — decennial census data used for census years.

Years 1900-01 to 1907-08: for Ontario and Quebec linear interpolation between census data of 1900-01 and 1910-11; for Manitoba, production for 1900-01 and 1905-06 was from the federal census of agriculture, the years 1902-03 to 1904-05 were interpolated between 1900-01 and 1905-06 on the basis of the movement of production data for the period reported by the Manitoba Department of Agriculture (see above), the data for 1906-07 to 1907-08 were from the Manitoba Department of Agriculture data; for Saskatchewan the data for years 1900-01 and 1905-06 are from the decennial census and quinquenniel census of the Prairies respectively, the data for years 1902-03 to 1904-05 and 1906-07 to 1907-08 are from Province of Saskatchewan Department of Agriculture figures, and data for 1901-02 are the average of 1900-01 and 1902-03; Alberta production was not large enough to be bothered with until 1908.

Years 1908-09 to 1926-27: all production data were from HAS.I (or total from HSC Series L133-134).

Seed Requirements for Planting

For years 1908-09 to 1926-27, the number of acres planted to flaxseed (HSC Series L133) multiplied by 0.65 bushels, the amount seeded per acre, gave total seed requirement.

For 1900-01 to 1907-08, an estimate of the number of acres seeded was derived by linear interpolation between the acreage of 1900-01 (census) and the acreages seeded in 1908-09 (HSC). These acreages were multiplied by 0.65 bushels per acre to obtain total seed requirements.

For 1890-91 to 1899-1900 an estimate of the number of acres seeded was obtained by linear interpolation between acres seeded in 1890-91 (census) and 1900-01 (census). Acreages were multiplied by 0.65 bushels seed requirement per acre.

For 1870-71 to 1889-90 there were no acreages available from the census of 1870-71 and

1880-81. The estimate of seed requirement for these years was obtained in two steps: first, the average ratio of seed used for planting to the total quantity produced was calculated for the years 1909-10 to 1918-19; this ratio, which was 0.0645 bushels of seed for planting for each bushel of flaxseed produced, was then multiplied by the total volume of flaxseed produced in each year to estimate the amount used for seed for planting.

Dockage and Wastage

For years 1908-09 to 1926-27 an allowance of six per cent of production was made for dockage and wastage: this procedure reflected the practice in the trade (e.g. in the grain elevator system) of subtracting dockage of waste material (weed, seed, etc.) from the weight of grain delivered which included the waste materials. Prior to 1908-09 the presence of waste in the grain delivered to the trade was probably reflected in the price quoted rather than in a formal deduction for dockage. (CSM 1913, p.313 gives 5 to 7 per cent as the usual loss.)

The volume of flaxseed available for off-farm disposal was calculated from production less requirement of seed for planting less dockage. Since in the calculation of values different prices were used for valuation of western flaxseed (that from the Prairie Provinces and British Columbia) and eastern flaxseed (Ontario, Quebec, etc.) for the years 1908-09 to 1926-27, the net product available for off-farm sale was calculated for the east and west separately. The use of flaxseed for planting was divided between east and west in proportion to the production in eastern and western provinces.

Prices

For 1870-71 to 1907-08 the price used for farm value was 80 percent of the export unit price (farm prices were approximately 80 percent of export unit values in the years 1908-09 to 1911-12); for certain years within this period for which no exports were recorded an export unit value was imputed from import unit values by use of ratios of export unit values to import unit values for years immediately adjacent to those for which the exports were missing. The years for which export unit values are imputed from import unit values are 1882-83, 1884-86; 1889-93, and 1902-03.

For 1908-09 to 1926-27 a western and an eastern price were used for the western (Prairie Provinces and B.C.) and eastern crop respectively.

The farm price for the western crop was calculated by subtracting from the Ft. William price freight and handling charges. The Ft. William price per bushel was calculated by taking an average of prices at Ft. William for the months of October, November (double weight), December and January following the harvest (Source: DBS *The Production and Distribution of Canadian Seeds, Part IV Flaxseed*). The freight and handling charges, per bushel, in cents, which were deducted from the Ft. William price were:

	Freight	Handling	Total
1908-09 to 1917-18	11.4	3.4	14.8
1918-19 to 1919-20	15.2	3.4	18.6
1920-21	20.6	3.4	24.0
1921-22	19.0	3.4	22.4
1922-23 to 1926-27	12.7	3.4	16.1

The price used for the Eastern crop was the HAS.I farm price for the prairies and British Columbia together.

Note: While some flaxseed was produced in Ontario and Quebec throughout the period from 1870 to 1926 the amounts were always relatively small; the substantial quantities were those produced on the prairie provinces after 1900: production in the prairie provinces is available on an annual basis for Manitoba from 1892, for Alberta and Saskatchewan from 1902. Therefore, for years in which the production of flaxseed was of significant amounts, production data are available annually.

About prices I am confident that there would have been a reason to use the procedure that was followed for the period from 1908-09 to 1926-27 in deriving a farm price rather than using the farm price given in HAS.I, but I have not put my hands on the note that would explain the reason.

Tobacco

The only data on production of tobacco before 1910-11 are the census figures. The census production figures are:

	Production (000 lbs.)
1870-71	1,596
1880-81	2,528
1890-91	4,278
1900-01	11,267
1910-11	17,632

From 1911-12 onward the data were collected annually in the federal government agricultural statistics program. Source of data: HSC Series L163, p.366. for census year data 1870-71 to 1910-11 and annually 1912-13 to 1926-27.

The annual data on production were obtained as follows.

1870-71 to 1890-91. The estimate of production was obtained by linear interpolation between each adjacent pair of census years, i.e. from 1870-71 to 1880-81 and from 1880-81 to 1890-91. The estimate for 1890-91 to 1900-01 were based on assigning one-third of the change to the years 1890-91 to 1895-96 and two-thirds of the change to the years between 1895-96 and 1900-01: linear interpolation was used in each of these sub-periods. The estimates for 1900-01 to 1910-11 were made by linear interpolation between census dates.

The estimate for 1911-12 was obtained as an average between 1910-11 and 1912-13.

The data were annual from the source for 1912-13 onward.

The price at which the crop was valued throughout was 0.4 of the import unit value of unmanufactured tobacco, data obtained from *Trade of Canada* throughout. The rationale for valuing the crop at 0.4 of the import unit value of unmanufactured tobacco was that this is the approximate ratio of the price of burley tobacco, an unmanufactured product (obtained from *Wholesale Prices in Canada*) to the unit import value.

Note: Strangely, data on tobacco production were obtained only in the decennial census until the census and statistics office began to collect the data annually with 1912-13. An attempt was made to use exports and imports plus an estimate of per capita consumption of tobacco but the data are not up to it. It is for this reason that resort was had to linear interpolation of production between census years in the early part of our period. The year to year movements of production are undoubtedly erratic; however, the growth between census years up to 1910-11 is sufficiently great that linear interpolation is not as capricious as it would be in an ungrowing industry.

Flax for Fibre

This is one of the least satisfactory series of the whole lot. Fortunately the amounts involved are not large.

The problems connected with obtaining decent estimates are of two sorts. First, it is not always clear at what stage of development the flax is measured, whether in green bulk from the fields, in which event the yields may be the order of two tons per acre, or in the flax fibre content of the crop, in which event the yields tend to be in the order of 200 to 300 pounds of flax fibre per acre. Second, census data are incomplete: some data were collected for 1870, 1880, 1890 and 1920 (and, indeed, in 1930 and later census years); there was not any information collected in the censuses of 1901 (for 1900) and 1911 (1910). There are annual production data for 1915 onward but this information came from the Central Experimental Farm in Ottawa and its data and especially their valuations do not correspond closely to the decennial census figures in years of overlap.

Some of the anomalies of the data follow.

Production of Flax Fibre (Census) (in lbs.)

1870	2,612,047
1880	2,056,353
1890	18,503,664

The external trade data and the data on scutching mills in the census of manufactures show no such change between 1880 and 1890. It seems probable that the data for 1870 and 1880 are measured in terms of flax fibre while those for 1890 are measured in weight of green crop.

A comparison of census and experimental farm data for 1920 show similar incompatibilities.

Flax Fibre Production, 1920

	Census Data	Experimental Farm Data
Acres sown	8,901	31,300
Production (lbs.)	2,807,918	7,440,000
Value of product ($)	430,410	5,952,000
Product per acre (lbs.)	315	190
Price ($)	0.15	0.80

Sources: Census data: *Census of Canada*, 1941, Vol VIII;
           Experimental farm data: MBAS, 1928, p.26.

An examination of the 1931 and 1941 census data does not help. From it we get:

Flax Fibre Production, 1930 and 1940

	1930	1940
Acres sown	1,639	17,757
Production (lbs.)	3,484,231	18,708,872
Value ($)	149,573	1,016,788
Production per acre	2,126	1,054
Price per lb. ($)	0.043	0.054

Productions of 315 pounds per acre in 1920 and 2,126 pounds in 1930 must reflect a measurement of the product at a different stage in the production process.

There are data also on the flax-dressing mills in the census of manufactures.

Flax Dressing Mills – Manufactures

Year	Value Of Materials Used ($)	Value of Finished Products ($)	No. Of Mills
1870	129,617	269,818	35
1880	220,704	431,062	33
1890	219,024	555,450	40
1900	136,224	338,176	31
1910	250,510	548,559	30
1915	496,275	1,116,002	11

Source: *Census of Manufactures*

In 1918, the product of the flax scutching mills (*Census of Manufacture 1918*) were as follows.

Product of Scutching Mills, 1918

	Quantity	Value ($)
Linen fibre (lbs.)	1,178,226	720,166
Flax tow (lbs.)	997,068	191,000
Flaxseed (bus.)	50,428	398,347
Other products, seed,straw etc.	--	562,780
Total		1,872,293

In view of the difficulty of finding anything on which to latch to obtain an estimate it was decided to use the value of exports of flax fibre as the measure of farm income. The 1916 experimental farm report (CSM, Jan. 1917, p.25) noted that 80 per cent of the flax fibre was exported. Export values would exceed farm values, of course, but flax fibre is only one of the products of the industry. The first feature leads to an overstatement of farm income, by export values, but the second feature leads to an understatement.

Hence: The value of exports of flax fibre is used as the measure of farm earnings from the production of flax fibre.

Eggs

The agricultural receipts from eggs, as from many other products, is calculated as the product of net quantity produced and price. Net product was 4 per cent less than gross product to allow for eggs used for hatching. It is to be noted that eggs produced both on farms and not on farms are included.

The Calculation of Production of Eggs

The calculation of net number of eggs produced was based on use of estimates of domestic disappearance of eggs for the years 1870-71 to 1880-81; the calculation was essentially based on the stock of hens and chickens and the production of eggs per hen and chicken for the years 1881-82 to 1926-27.

Production in the years 1881-82 to 1926-27 is considered first. The base year counts of the stock of hens and chickens were obtained from the decennial census onward from 1890-91, the first census in which the stock of hens and chickens was recorded, as follows:

Census Year	Stock of Hens and Chickens on Farms and Not on Farms
1890-91	12,696,701
1900-01	16,651,327
1910-11	29,773,457
1920-21	48,021,647

Stocks are for the time at which the census is actually taken. There were, in addition, the following basic data: stock of hens and chickens, annually, from 1881-82 onward to 1915-16 (and even later) for Ontario, data collected by OBI; stocks of hens and chickens on farms, annually from 1916 onward (HSC.II Series M369) data collected officially; census data for the prairie provinces collected in the quinquennial census of those provinces of 1906 and 1916; data for 1907 for all but the prairie provinces obtained in the census of agriculture of 1907 for such provinces.

The OBI data were used thus: (i) to extrapolate the number of hens and chickens in Canada from 1890-91 to 1881-82; (ii) to interpolate the number of hens and chickens for all Canada from 1891 to 1901 and for all provinces but the prairie provinces from 1901 to 1907, from 1907 to 1911 and from 1911 to 1916. The number of hens and chickens in all provinces but the prairie provinces in 1907 was obtained in the 1907 census of agriculture of such provinces. The 1916 stock figure for all provinces but the prairie provinces was obtained by multiplying the official figure of the number of hens and chickens on farms in all Canada in 1916 (HSC.II Series M369) by the ratio of the number of hens and chickens on farms and elsewhere than on farms to the number of chickens on farms only in 1921 (from the 1921 census) and by then subtracting from the resulting figure for all Canada for 1916 the number of hens and chickens in the prairie provinces in 1916 from the quinquennial 1916 census of the prairie provinces. The numbers of hen and chickens in the prairie provinces were interpolated linearly between 1901 and 1906, between 1906 and 1911 and between 1911 and 1916. The totals for all Canada for the years 1902 to 1910 inclusive and for 1912 to 1915 inclusive were obtained by adding the estimates for the prairie provinces to the estimates for the rest of the provinces.

A test of the representativeness of the OBI data for the Ontario figures as given in the census can be given for the census years by comparing the figures for Ontario of the OBI with those of the census of Canada for census years or the official estimate for 1916.

Ratio of Numbers of All Hens and Chickens in Ontario as Reported by OBI, to Numbers as Reported by the Census

Year	Ratio
1891	1.23
1901	1.19
1911	1.16
1916	1.23

The 1916 OBI reported figure was for all poultry. The number of hens and chickens was estimated by assuming that the ratio to all poultry was the same as in 1911.

It will be seen that the relationship of OBI coverage to census coverage of Ontario remains reasonably steady.

The stock of hens and chickens on farms and not on farms for 1916 to 1920 and 1922 to 1926 for each year was obtained by multiplying the number of hens and chickens on farms by the ratio of the number of chickens on farms and elsewhere than on farms to the number on farms as recorded for 1921 in the census of agriculture taken in 1921.

The production data of eggs per unit of the hen and chicken stock were derived from decennial census data. Egg production was first obtained in the 1901 census. The census data follow.

Year	Production of Eggs Per Unit of the Hen and Chicken Stock (dozens of eggs)
1900	5.05
1910	4.13
1920	3.48
1930	3.29

Note: For 1900, 1910, and 1930 this production per unit of the stock was obtained by dividing the total egg production of the year as reported in the census, which was for the calendar year immediately preceding the census year, by the stock of hens and chickens reported in the census as of April 1 of the census year itself until 1901 and June 1 of the census year thereafter. This procedure was followed for 1900 and 1910 because the census estimate of the stock of hens and chickens was the only firm estimate available and ordinarily stocks do not change by great amounts from year to year — the OBI data on stocks in Ontario show 1891 stocks slightly less than 1890 stocks, 1901 stocks about two percent more than 1900 stocks and 1911 stocks less than one-half of one per cent greater than 1910 stocks (and the official annual data show the stock of hens and chickens in 1931 only 1.3 per cent greater than that of 1930). For 1920, the egg production per unit of the stock was obtained by dividing the egg production reported in the census by the (official) stock on farms in 1920 augmented by the ratio of the numbers on farms and elsewhere to the number on farms only as reported for 1921 in the census of 1921 — the 1921 census stock figure was nearly 16 per cent greater than the officially estimated stock for 1920 (see HSC).

The probable effect of the change of census data from April 1 in 1901 to June 1 in 1911 is that in the former year, the spring hatch would be less complete than in the latter years and hence that the count of hens and chickens is made at a lower point in the seasonal stock standing in 1901 than in 1911. This effect, if it exists, would account for a part of the higher egg production per unit of the hen and chicken stock in 1901 than in 1911. It would affect the estimate of aggregate egg production only in the transition between 1901 and 1911.

Egg production per unit of stock was obtained by linear interpolation between census quantities for 1921 to 1926, for 1911 to 1919, and for 1901 to 1909; it was assumed that egg production was five dozen per unit in 1890 and was at linearly interpolated values for 1891 to 1899; it was assumed that egg production was uniformly at five dozen eggs per unit for 1881 to 1889.

For each year of the period 1881 to 1926 aggregate production of eggs was obtained by multiplication of the stock of hens and chickens by egg production per unit.

For the period 1870 to 1880 the domestic disappearance method of estimating egg consumption was used. The estimated per capita consumption per year for this period was obtained as the quotient of total production of eggs in 1881 (obtained by the method used for 1881 to 1926) divided by the population at October 1. This yielded a figure for consumption of 8.52 dozen eggs per capita per annum. Production for each year from 1870 to 1880 was calculated from domestic disappearance (population at October 1 multiplied by 8.52) plus exports minus imports.

The Calculation of Egg Prices

Different price series were used for different periods as follows: (i) for 1910 to 1926 the census unit values were almost interpolated and extrapolated by the import unit value. In census years import unit values were actually lower than the unit values of eggs derivable from census data: for 1910-11 the ratio of census (farm) unit values to unit value of imports was 1.038; for 1920-21, the like ratio was 1.030. The average of these two ratios is 1.034 and the price used annually for valuing eggs for the years 1911 to 1923 was the import unit value multiplied by the factor 1.034. (ii) For 1900-01 to 1910-11, the interpolator between the census unit values of eggs at the farm was the wholesale price index of storage eggs in Toronto obtained from the Department of Labour, *Wholesale Prices*: the ratio of census farm price to the wholesale price was 0.836 in 1910-11 and 0.873 in 1900-01; the ratios for intervening years were obtained by linear interpolation. (iii) For 1890-91 to 1899-1900, the Department of Labour wholesale price of storage eggs at Toronto (*ibid.*) was used to extrapolate the 1900-01 census unit value of eggs — the wholesale price for each year was multiplied by 0.873, the ratio of the census farm price in 1900-01 to the wholesale price in 1900-01. (The wholesale price and export unit values move in much the same way.) (iv) For 1870-71 to 1889-90, the wholesale price of fresh laid eggs in Toronto (Michell, p.78) was multiplied by 0.873, the 1900-01 ratio, to obtain the farm price for eggs. There was no overlap of the Michell figures with the Department of Labour figures; however, in 1916 when storage eggs and fresh laid eggs were both quoted, storage eggs were 34.304 cents per dozen in Toronto and fresh laid eggs were 34.9 per dozen.

Import valuations were reported in a changed form from 1924 onward and for 1924 to 1926 the import values were used to index the 1923 unit value — there were considerable other price data by that time to check on the validity of this procedure.

Maple Sugar and Syrup

The basic method of calculation was from 1870-71 to 1923-24 to estimate domestic disappearance for census years from census and foreign trade data, to interpolate domestic disappearance between census years or to estimate for years to 1923-24 and then obtain production by adding net exports; for 1924-25 to 1926-27, the production value estimates of DBS as published in MBAS were used. The production quantities so estimated were valued by a price per unit.

The Calculation of the Production of Maple Sugar

Production takes place in the form of either maple syrup (measured in gallons) as the final product sold to the consumer or as maple sugar derived from the sap (measured in lbs.). For statistical purposes the part sold as maple syrup is converted to sugar at the rate of one gallon of syrup is the equivalent of 10 lbs of sugar; in the earlier censuses the production was given only in terms of sugar.

Data for 1870 to 1923

Domestic disappearance of sugar equivalent per capita in base years was obtained by subtracting base year exports from base year production and adding imports. Exports varied from being quite small in the 1870s to as much as 15 per cent of production in some of the 1914-18 wartime years; imports were minuscule throughout.

The base years were the census years excluding 1901 until 1910-11 and then the average of the four years 1924-25 to 1927-28 for 1924. Until 1901 the census was taken on April 1 and the production reported was probably for the prior year since the sap production period can extend beyond April 1. The censuses of 1910-11 and 1920-21 were taken on June 1 and the production was no doubt for the year of the census itself.

The base year values are:

Base Year	Domestic Disappearance (lbs. per capita)
1870	4.70
1880	4.70
1890	5.13
1900	3.16 (not used for interpolation)
1911	3.77
1924-25	3.00

The interpolation values for domestic disappearance follow.

For 1871 to 1879:	4 lbs. per capita
For 1881 to 1889:	Linear interpolation between 4.71 in 1880 and 5.13 in 1890
For 1891 to 1899:	Linear interpolation between 5.13 in 1890 to 4 in 1900
For 1901 to 1909:	4 lbs. each year
For 1910:	3.9 lbs.
For 1911 to 1923:	Linear interpolation between 3.77 in 1911 and 3 lbs. for 1924
For 1900:	the census value of 3.16 was used
For 1921:	the census production was used.

Price

The price used was the export unit value per pound except for 1911 and 1921 when unit values of the census are used. This export unit value was consistently considerably below the wholesale price for strained honey. In 1911 and 1921 the export unit values were less than the unit values obtained in the census which were presumably farm unit values.

The rationale for not using the domestic disappearance figures derivable from the 1900-01 and 1920-21 censuses as base year figures is that each of these years appeared to be poor years — weather has a big effect on the catchable flow of sap from the maple trees. In particular, the figures of DBS for the 1920s after 1921, already cited, and the per capita consumption figures for 1926 to 1930 given in HAS.IV suggest a figure of about 3 lbs. per capita for the 1920s. In addition, the figure of 3.16 lbs for 1900 when there were few people in the west where there are not any maple trees seems inconsistent with the 1911 figures of 3.77 lbs. per capita when there was a much larger population in western Canada. Whether there might have been omission of syrup production in 1900, when only sugar is reported is conjectural: the same practice had been followed in earlier censuses.

Data for 1924 to 1926

For these years the values are those prepared by DBS (reported in MBAS, July, 1927 p.237). In these years, as well as in the census of 1921, the value of the maple syrup produced and sold substantially exceeded the value of the maple sugar.

Honey

The estimates for the entire period 1870 to 1926 were obtained from estimates of the quantity of honey produced multiplied by a price per unit of honey. (A very, very small amount of beeswax was taken account of in 1910 and 1920.)

The only really basic data on production of honey were those obtained in the decennial censuses. They reported amounts of honey produced that yielded the following production per capita.

	Production of Honey Per Capita (lbs.)
1870	0.547
1880	0.439
1890	0.892
1900	0.669
1910	0.858
1920	0.745

(In addition DBS started gathering data in the 1920s that appeared to have some limitations: a comment on these data will follow later.)

The principal other data that were available before 1920 were the external trade data — the amounts were small — and data giving the number of hives of bees reported by the OBI for 1892 to 1908; there were short term ups and downs in these last data but not a significant trend in numbers.

The procedure for estimating production was to interpolate per capita production linearly between adjacent census years for 1870 to 1930 and then to multiply the per capita production by population year by year.

The unit value per pound to the producer was obtained in the census for each of the years 1900, 1910 and 1920. The price per pound before 1900 was obtained by extrapolating the 1900 census unit value year by year to 1890 on the basis of the wholesale price index given in *Wholesale Prices 1890-1909* and from 1890 to 1870 on the basis of the maple sugar price index; the price between 1900 and 1910 was interpolated between unit values for each year also by use of the wholesale price index; interpolation between 1910 and 1920 was done by use of the wholesale price index from 1910 to 1919 and the export unit price from 1919 to 1920.

The prices used to value the production for 1921 to 1926 were the unit values of exports of nearest fiscal years for 1921 to 1924, the unit value of exports for calendar 1926 (from *Trade of Canada* for 1926, and an average of the 1926 and 1924 price for 1925. The unit value of exports of honey for fiscal 1920-21 was 0.249 dollars per pound; the unit value of census of

Canada production of honey and wax in 1920 was 0.253 dollars per pound. The export unit values are slightly below the MBAS values for common years: I believe them quite appropriate since the MBAS values may have been partly based on wholesale prices. Also, the export unit values are not unlike the wholesale prices before 1920-21.

Apples

The estimate of the final product value of the apple crop from 1870-71 to 1919-20 was essentially obtained by calculating a Canadian consumption of apples plus net exports and valuing the resulting quantity at a farm price; from 1920-21 to 1926-27 the estimates were derived from data of the Dominion Bureau of Statistics obtained directly from MBAS.

For the period 1870-71 to 1919-20 the estimate used for per capita domestic disappearance (i.e. per capita consumption) in Canada was 1.4 bushels for all but two years, namely 1890-91 and 1910-11 for which a figure of 1.25 bushels per capita was used (see below). This figure multiplied by the population (HSC Series A1) gave the estimate of total domestic consumption. From 1884-85 onward to 1919-20 the quantities of both exports and imports were available: accordingly for this period domestic production was taken to be domestic consumption plus net exports; farm receipts were then calculated by multiplying the domestic production by a farm price. The farm price used was calculated by multiplying the unit value of exports by 0.67 to obtain an estimate of price at the farm.

For the years 1870-71 to 1883-84 all of the quantities of exports and imports were not available in the trade data and so a slightly different procedure was used; within this period a different procedure was used for years 1870-71 to 1878-79 and the years 1879-80 to 1883-84. For both of these sub-periods, domestic consumption was calculated at 1.4 bushels per capita as in the later period. For the years 1879-80 to 1883-84 it was possible to get an estimate of net exports as follows. OBI reported exports of green fruit of all kinds in barrels (*OBI Reports* 1883, p.102, 1885, p.69); in addition, there were data to show that the ratio of the value of green apple exports to the value of all green fruit exports in 1884-85 was $602,000 apples ÷ $635,240 total fruit (*Trade of Canada* 1884-85, p.726). The number of barrels of apples exported was estimated for each year by multiplication of the number of barrels of all green fruit exported by the above ratio. Imports of apples were available in the official Canadian trade data in barrels of green apples and pounds of dried apples. Dried apples are converted to green apple equivalents by a ratio of 10:1 (a barrel of green apples comprises three bushels; a bushel of apples weighs 45 lbs). Net exports of apples for 1878-79 to 1884-85 were, as usual, obtained by exports minus imports. Addition of net exports to domestic consumption yielded a quantitative measure of production which when multiplied by a price per unit yielded the measure of revenue from final sales of apples that was required for each year from 1879-80 to 1883-84, in the same fashion as for 1884-85 to 1919-20.

For the years 1870-71 to 1878-79 the treatment of external trade had to be different mainly because the import data were different: apple imports were no longer given separately. The only available relevant data were the values of exports and of imports of green fruit. However, an estimate of the value of apple exports in the total for each year was made by assuming the ratio of apples to the total was the same as for a year early in the period when the data were first available: thus based on 1888-89 trade data in which the ratio of apple values to values of all green fruit, including a small category that was not separated until 1888-89, was 1,532,390 ÷ 1,627,818 = 0.9414, it was estimated that the same ratio applied to export values of green fruits for 1870-71 to 1878-79; by a similar process, the ratio of the value of apple imports to all green fruit imports was determined from the 1880-81 trade data at 47,815 ÷ 382,020 = 0.1252 and the values of apple imports for 1870-71 to 1878-79 were estimated by calculating apple import values at this same proportion of green fruit imports values for each year from 1870-71 to 1878-79. Net export values were then calculated by subtracting import values from export values for each year. Net farm receipts from external trade were then calculated at two-thirds (0.67) of these net export values to allow for the difference between trade prices and farm prices. To those annual sums were added domestic consumption valued at farm prices to obtain net farm receipts from apple production.

Export unit values which provided the basis for calculating a farm price were derivable from the Canadian trade data explicitly from 1884-85 onward. Prior to 1884-85 exports of apples were lumped with other green fruit, the whole measured in barrels. Since apples comprised nearly all of the exports of green fruit, the unit value of exports of green fruit were accepted as a measure of the unit value of apples from 1870-71 to 1884-85. The farm price of apples was then taken to be two-thirds of the export unit value of apples from 1870-71 to 1919-20.

The Basis of the Estimate of Per Capita Consumption and the Farm Price

The per capita consumption estimate of 1.4 bushels of apples was based on what was regarded as two reliable years, 1920 and 1921, in which data were obtained from the decennial census of agriculture for both acreages and yields for 1920 and acreages for 1921; yields for 1921 came from separate surveys, of course. The relevant data are:

	1920	1921
Production (bushels)	17,485,896	16,103,100
Net exports (bushels)	3,469,795	6,040,081
Domestic Disappearance (bushels)	14,016,101	10,063,019
Population	8,556,000	8,778,000
Domestic Disappearance per capita (bushels)	1.64	1.15

Other measures of apple consumption measured as above are the following:

Year	Domestic Disappearance Per Capita (bushels of 45 lbs)
1870-71	1.74
1880-81	2.86
1890-91	1.26
1900-01	2.94
1910-11	1.24
1922	1.28

Apple consumption appeared to decline after 1922; after 1937-38 apple consumption per capita was estimated at 35 pounds (HAS.VI, p.21).

The upshot was that domestic disappearance of 1.4 bushels per capita was used for 1870-71 to 1920-21 with the exception of the single years 1890-91 and 1910-11 for which a domestic disappearance of 1.25 bushels per capital was used since it jibes with census production estimates. The 1880-81 and the 1900-01 census based estimates seem particularly out of line.

Evidence for using 0.667 of the export unit value as the farm price: (i) Quotations in the Canadian Farmer's Sun; (ii) in one report of the OBI the relationship of the street price to the market price; (iii) in 1910 the unit price from the census is $0.74; export unit value is $1.12.

The estimates for 1920-21 to 1926-27 were made in a different way. Estimates of production of apples (measured in barrels of apples initially) on an annual basis were obtained from the Dominion Bureau of Statistics publications MBAS: the 1920-21 figure is that of the 1921 *Census of Agriculture*; the figures for later years were the final estimates as the initially published figures were usually revised.

Prices for Monetary Evaluation

The same publications also gave prices for apples, but, aside from 1920-21 which was a farm price derived from the 1921 Census, the prices for 1921-22 to 1925-26 were described as market prices (presumably wholesale) which were substantially above farm prices. The basis of pricing was changed in 1926: the first price published for 1926 (MBAS 1927, p.28) was $5.38 per barrel, a market price; a revised price for 1926, described as a price received by growers at shipping points (MBAS, 1928, p.86) was $3.28, still later at $3.24, per barrel. In fact, a new annual DBS publication in 1927, *Annual Statistics of Fruits and Floriculture, 1927*, had the following statement, p.3: "In previous years valuations have been based on wholesale prices. This year, in conformity with the valuations of the products of other branches of the agricultural industry, valuations have been based on the prices reported to have been received by the growers at shipping points." The revised growers' price of $3.24 per barrel for 1926 was 60 per cent of the original market price of $5.38 per barrel for 1926. The growers' price was then calculated as 60 per cent of the reported market or wholesale price for 1922 to 1925. The "market" price for 1921 seemed particularly out of line with regard to the census farm price for 1920 and the movement of the export market price. Consequently a growers' value for it was taken as the average growers' value, at 60 per cent of wholesale price, for all years 1921 to 1926. These procedures led to use of the following growers' prices for apples from 1920 to 1926.

Year	Growers' Price Per Barrel (dollars)	
1920	2.58	(census figure)
1921	3.40	
1922	2.94	
1923	3.27	
1924	3.51	
1925	3.41	
1926	3.24	

A barrel is 3 bushels of 45 pounds each.

Small Fruit (Berries, i.e., strawberries, raspberries, etc.)

The description of the preparation of the apple estimates should be read before reading the material of this section. There is much in common in the manner of estimation of revenue from apples and from small fruit.

By far the largest part of the small fruits is comprised of strawberries and raspberries.

Basically, the method of estimation was as follows. For years from 1870-71 to 1920-21 an estimate of domestic disappearance in pounds of fruit was made on the basis of multiplication of estimated consumption per head of 4 pounds of berries by population. From 1870-71 to 1879-80 this domestic disappearance was valued by use of a farm price per pound and then the value of net imports was subtracted to obtain an estimate of farm revenue from production. For 1880-81 to 1920-21 imports of fruit in pounds was subtracted from domestic disappearance to get farm production. This farm production was then valued at a farm price per pound. In this period, 1879-80 to 1920-21, no account was taken of exports of small fruit since they were so small. For 1921-22 to 1926-27 the production of small fruit in pounds was estimated by DBS and reported in the *Monthly Review of Business Statistics*; these DBS estimates provide also values of products.

The estimate of domestic consumption of berries of four pounds per capita was derived from estimates of domestic disappearance in 1900, 1910 and 1920 (census data); in 1921 to 1926 (MBAS); and in HAS.IV, p.21.

Domestic Disappearance
(lbs. per capita)

Year	Domestic Disappearance	Year	Domestic Disappearance
1900	5.3	1921	3.2
1910	6.1	1922	3.2
1920	4.2	1923	2.7
		1924	2.3
		1925	2.0
		1926	2.9

Source: 1900, 1910, 1920: *Census of Canada*,
1921 to 1926: MBAS for production;
All years: *Trade of Canada* for imports.
The production data are given in quarts which are converted to pounds at 1.25 pounds per quart.

The HAS.IV domestic disappearance data for 1937-38 to 1955-56 imply on the average just about 4 lbs. consumption per capita.

If one examined decennial census year estimates only, one would perhaps arrive at a figure of consumption per capita of five pounds. However, it must be remembered that data on small fruit production were first collected in the census of 1900 and were perhaps not well collected until 1920; in particular, the unit of measurement for recording strawberry and raspberry production in 1910 only was the "box" (used only in this year) which may well have caused problems both of the recording in the field and conversion into pounds. In addition the data for the years 1921 to 1926 are all much below the census figures. In the conflicting evidence the 1920 consumption figure rounded to 4 lbs. has been used. It is possible that this figure may be low for pre World War I years.

The price used for evaluation of production from 1880-81 to 1920-21 was the unit value of imports. For comparative purposes we note that the unit value of production on the farm according to the 1920-21 census was 21 cents per pound whereas the unit value of imports was 22 cents per pound. In the prewar period use of the unit value of imports as the farmers price may be a bit on the high side. Since the estimates of per capita consumption in the prewar period may be on the low side, the two biases, indeed if they are as such, are fortunately offsetting.

The values of production for the years 1921-22 to 1926-27 are those obtained from the MBAS. They are described in the MBAS as being in market prices which suggests that they exceed farm prices. The comparative unit value of imports and MBAS values, in cents per pound, follow.

Comparison of Import Unit Values
with MBAS Unit Prices, 1920 to 1926
(All unit values or prices in dollars per pound)

Year	Import Unit Values	MBAS Prices
1920	0.22	0.21 (census)
1921	0.19	0.13
1922	0.13	0.14
1923	0.15	0.16
1924	0.15	0.16
1925	0.19	0.15
1926	0.17	0.11

For 1870-71 to 1879-80 the unit value of imports was estimated by extrapolating the unit value of imports back from 1880-81, the first year it was available, on the basis of the unit value of apples for these years. The domestic disappearance was then valued at this price. From this valuation the value of net imports was then subtracted to obtain the net value of production.

Net imports could not be obtained directly since before 1880-81 neither exports nor imports of small fruits were separated from all green fruits. Import values were estimated by assuming that throughout the 1870s the ratio of the value of small berry imports to the value of all imports of green fruits was the same as in 1880-81: the ratio was $24,855 \div 382,020 = 0.0651$. Export values were estimated by use of the assumption that the ratio of export values of small berries to total fruit exports was the same as in 1888-89, the first year of complete segregation of berry exports: the ratio was $75,754 \div 1,627,818 = 0.0465$.

Grapes

For 1870-71 to 1919-20 the value of grape production was calculated as the product of quantity produced multiplied by price; for 1920-21 the values were as obtained in the census and for 1921-22 to 1926-27 the quantities and values were those provided by DBS.

Production

The data for grape production are very sparse. From 1870-71 to 1920-21 the only production data available are those for the decennial census years; from 1921-22 onward DBS published estimates annually. These data follow.

Census Year	Production of Grapes (in lbs.)	Year	Production of Grapes (in lbs.)
1870-71	1,126,402	1921-22	46,872,308
1880-81	3,896,508	1922-23	70,308,462
1890-81	12,252,336	1923-24	42,185,077
1900-01	24,302,634	1924-25	24,500,000
1910-11	32,898,438	1925-26	25,000,000
1920-21	33,232,315	1926-27	24,000,000

In the absence of any other information on production from 1870-71 to 1920-21 an estimate of production for intercensal years was made by linear interpolation between adjacent pairs of census years. This procedure is probably more realistic of what happened for the decades of high growth, when growth itself may dominate fluctuations; it is probably less realistic in decades of low growth, such as the decade 1910-21 when annual fluctuations could easily outweigh growth.

Prices

Price data have three major sources. First, for 1890-91 to 1917-18, the price used was the wholesale price for grapes from the Department of Labour publication *Wholesale Prices*. The Department of Labour price is for a 6 quart basket which is the equivalent of 7.5 pounds by weight. The 1920-21 price is the unit value obtained in the census of agriculture for 1920-21. There was not a published price for grapes for 1918-19 and 1919-20; prices for these years were obtained by using the price of raisins (DBS *Prices and Price Indexes*, 1913-24, p.37) as an interpolator between prices for 1917-18 and prices for 1920-21. Second, for 1876-77 to 1889-90 a unit value of imports, calculated from the external trade data derived from sessional papers *Trade of Canada* and its predecessor, Trade and Navigation, could be used, after adjustment, to provide an estimate of farm price. The unit values of imports and the wholesale prices of grapes for the ten years 1890 to 1899 are given below: the ratios of Department of Labour wholesale prices to import unit values was, on the average, 0.55 for these 10 years. Hence for the years 1876-77 to 1889-90 the grapes were valued at the import unit values, multiplied by 0.55. A calendar year price was calculated as an average of adjoining trade years. Third, the wholesale price of raisins from Michell was used to extrapolate a farm price from 1877 to 1870.

Comparison of Import Unit Values and
Wholesale Market Prices, 1890 to 1899

	Unit Value of Imports (cents per lb.)	Wholesale Price (cents per lb.)	Ratio: Wholesale Price to Unit Value of Imports
1890	7.94	3.7	0.47
1891	7.34	3.8	0.52
1892	5.95	2.7	0.45
1893	7.05	4.0	0.57
1894	5.25	3.2	0.61
1895	5.74	4.0	0.70
1896	5.84	3.7	0.63
1897	6.21	4.0	0.64
1898	5.56	2.6	0.47
1899	6.13	2.6	0.42

The price for 1920-21 was that of the census and hence was the price on the farm. The DBS prices used for valuation after 1920-21 were said to be local market prices.

Orchard Fruit

The orchard fruit estimates for 1870 to 1919 were made by estimating quantities produced and then multiplying by an estimated price; the 1920 to 1926 estimates were DBS estimates of product values.

"Orchard fruit" includes peaches, pears, plums, apricots and cherries. (Apples have been dealt with separately.)

Quantities Produced, 1870-71 to 1919-20

Since external trade data for orchard fruits were not available for 1870-71 to 1880-81, the production of all fruits for that decade was obtained by straight line interpolation between 1870-71 and 1880-81, both census years for which production was available.

The quantities produced for years 1880-81 to 1919-20 were obtained by estimating domestic disappearance and subtracting the quantity of imports. The domestic disappearance of all the orchard fruits together (measured in bushels) was obtained in 1880-81, 1890-91 and 1910-11 by adding imports of major orchard fruits to production as reported in the censuses for those years. (There were small discrepancies, among years, of the content of the imports so added.) No exports were recorded in the trade data. The per capita domestic disappearance of all orchard fruit, rounded, was:

1880-81	0.19 bushels per capita
1890-91	0.22 bushels per capita
1910-11	0.29 bushels per capita

Domestic disappearance per capita between these years was calculated by simple linear interpolation. The data for 1900-01 were not used for obtaining a base-year value since they would yield a domestic disappearance of 0.39 bushels per capita; this value was used for 1900-01 itself since it was reasonable to envisage exceptional years, but domestic disappearance per capita for other years between 1890-91 and 1910-11 was obtained by linear interpolation between these two years. For the years between 1910-11 and 1920-21, the 1910-11 per capita consumption figure was used for 1911-12; for 1912-13 to 1919-20 the per capita domestic disappearance figure used was 0.25 bushels per capita, the DBS per capita consumption figure for Canada after 1927-28 of 0.25 bushels as reported in HAS.IV, p.21. (The 1920-21 census of agriculture production figure per capita was not used for base-year purposes since it was unusually much higher than the figures for the years immediately following 1920-21 and for the census years of 1930-31.)

The aggregate domestic disappearance for each year from 1880-81 to 1919-20 was then calculated by multiplying per capita domestic disappearance by population.

Imports of orchard fruits were estimated from foreign trade data. These trade data for peaches and cherries were reported throughout the years from 1880-81 to 1919-20; the reporting of imports of other orchard fruits separately was erratic over the years. Consequently some improvisation was necessary. Only in 1917-18 were all of imports of peaches, pears, plums, quinces and apricots estimated separately; in that year the imports of all these four fruits together in bushels were 3.138 times the imports of peaches alone. The imports of all fruits in other years were then estimated by multiplying the imports of peaches by this ratio of all fruit imports to peaches — the partial separate data for fruit imports other than peaches that were available for other years suggested that this method of estimating all four fruit imports was reasonably satisfactory or in other words that peach imports were about one third of all imports of orchard fruits (excluding cherries) throughout the years 1880-81 to 1919-20.

Domestic production for 1880-81 to 1920-21 was then calculated by subtracting imports from domestic disappearance (note that there were no exports). Imports ran up to as much as one-third of domestic disappearance from 1910-11 to 1919-20; imports in the 1880s tended to be less than 10 per cent of domestic disappearance, rising slightly above that percentage only in the last two years of the decade.

Prices, 1870-71 to 1919-20

The next step was to calculate a price series for 1870-71 to 1919-20. A composite unit value per bushel of undifferentiated orchard fruits was calculated from the 1910-11 census of agriculture production data: it was $0.96 per bushel. This series was extrapolated, yearly, forward to 1919-20 and backward to 1879-80 by the unit value of imported peaches; the price was then carried back from 1879-80 to 1870-71 by use of the price of apples which was linked to the peach price at 1879-80.

The Estimates for 1920-21 to 1926-27

The estimates for these years were those of DBS published in various copies of MBAS (1924, p.32; 1926, p.21; 1927, p.28; 1928, p.87). The data for 1920-21 were taken from the decennial census of agriculture returns and reflected prices on the farms; the 1921 to 1925 prices were said to be prices in local markets which meant that values given were higher than actual farm receipts; by 1927 the prices used were clearly reported as prices on the farm and it seems probable that this was also the case in 1926. Thus the values in 1921-22 to 1925-26 are probably somewhat inflated.

Net Farm Revenue from Animals and Poultry

The estimates of revenue from livestock or poultry and products were derived from two components, first, the net off-farm disposition of livestock and products, including consumption in kind by farmers, and second, the net change in farm stocks of animals or poultry. Inclusion of the latter is justified because stocks of animals or poultry are quite large relative to annual production and changes in these stocks are both important in size and measurable. (Changes in carryover stocks of grains were not included in net revenues from grains because the means of measuring such changes were poor — the changes in values in carryover grain stocks would be much smaller relatively than the changes in values of livestock and poultry inventories).

The values of livestock products were obtained usually as the product of a quantity produced multiplied by a unit value, just as was done for most of the grain and vegetable products.

We now deal with these animal products, item by item.

Cattle

First, the method used to derive the livestock estimates, without elaboration of sources of data, will be described. Then the sources and uses of data will be given. (It should be recalled that census of agriculture production data are for the calendar year preceding the year in which the census was actually taken.) One matter of definition is necessary immediately. The term "cattle" will be used to contain both adult cattle and calves. If data apply only to adult cattle the term "adult" will be used.

Method of Estimation

Different methods of estimation of income from cattle were used for the period 1870 to 1889 and the period 1890 to 1926. For both periods estimates of the total stock of cattle on an annual basis were the starting series. From these annual estimates of cattle stock, inventory change attributed to Canadian production on an annual basis could be obtained simply by taking first differences of the cattle stock figures and subtracting imports of live cattle, all of whom were presumed to be for additions to herds. The rest of the procedure differed between the two periods.

Period 1870 to 1889

After the cattle inventory and changes therein were obtained, the steps were:

(a)   Per capita consumption of (i) beef and (ii) veal were calculated from census data for 1870, 1880 and 1890 as follows.

	1870	1880	1890
Per capita consumption of beef (in lbs.)	40.27	45.47	55.28
Per capita consumption of veal (in lbs.)	4.13	4.74	6.52

Per capita consumption for years between adjacent census years was calculated by simple linear interpolation between census years.

(b)   Total consumption per year for each of beef and veal were estimated by multiplying population for each year by per capita consumptions.

(c)   (i) Numbers of cattle exported and imported, each year, were obtained; (ii) imports of salted beef and dressed carcasses and exports of salted beef and beef tongues, all measured in pounds, avoirdupois, each year, were obtained.

(d)   Sales and slaughter of Canadian produced adult cattle, measured in number of beasts, were calculated by (i) attributing the proportion 0.667 of the number of live cattle-beasts exported as adult cattle for years 1870 to 1876, the proportion 0.750 of live exports for 1877, and, the proportion 0.800 of live exports for 1878 to 1889, and (ii) adding thereto the adult cattle-beast equivalent number (calculated at 500 pounds avoirdupois of dressed meat per beast) of domestic consumption of beef plus exports of meat less imports of meat.

Sales and slaughter of Canadian produced calves, measured by number of calves, were calculated by (i) attributing the proportion 0.333 of the number of cattle-beasts exported as calves for 1870 to 1876, the proportion of 0.250 for 1877 and the proportion 0.20 for 1878 to 1889 and (ii) adding thereto the calf equivalent number at 100 pounds avoirdupois of dressed meat per calf of Canadian consumption of veal.

Additions to inventory of cattle, obtained directly by first differences of the cattle stock, were reduced by imports of live cattle to obtain changes in inventory arising from domestic production. (In the method of treatment used it was assumed that all cattle imported alive were added to the stock. They had not been taken account of in the prior calculations of domestic consumption.)

(e)   Total value of net cattle production was obtained for each year by summing: (i) the product of the total number of cattle and calves together produced in Canada for sales and slaughter by an average value per unit of such sales and slaughter, and (ii) the product of the change in stock inventory net of imports of live cattle by a value per unit of the cattle stock.

Period 1890 to 1920: after the cattle inventory and the changes therein were obtained the steps were:

(a)   (i) A ratio of sales and slaughter for domestic consumption or for net export to stocks of cattle for the year is determined.

(ii) This ratio is multiplied by the cattle stock to give total number of sales and slaughter of cattle for domestic consumption or net export.

(b)   (i) An average value per cattle-beast of sales and slaughter is obtained for each year and multiplied by the number sold or slaughtered to get an aggregate value.

(ii) An average value for each animal in inventory change is determined. It is multiplied by the change in inventory to give a value of change in inventory.

(iii) The two foregoing estimates are added together to give a total value of production.

Period 1921 to 1926: as in earlier years, changes in cattle inventories were obtained by taking first differences of the cattle stock. Thereafter the procedure was:

(a)   Estimated farm output of cattle and calves were obtained directly from Dominion Bureau of Statistics data.

(b)   (i) Estimated output of cattle and calves for sales or slaughter was multiplied by an average price per unit of such production to give total value of production for sales and slaughter.

(ii) Changes in inventory were multiplied by an inventory price per unit to give a total value of inventory change.

(iii) The two preceding quantities were added together to give a total value of production.

Sources of Data

(a)   The stock of cattle and calves. The totals for Canada were obtained by adding together the totals by province. For the basic census years, the numbers of the stock of cattle were obtained from the decennial census. The stock data were for the actual date at which the census was taken, *viz.* April 1 for 1871, 1881, 1891 and 1901, and June 1 for 1911 and 1921; however, the production data were for the year before the census year. Accordingly, the production data of the census were related to the stock data of the same census: hence the production data of year t were related to the stock data of year t+1. In the tables both were put in the column for the year t. The interpolation or extrapolation was done differently for each province, as follows, for 1870 to 1920.

(i) Ontario: For census years attributed to the preceding year, the figures were as obtained in the decennial census.

(α) for 1871 to 1879: linear interpolation between 1870 and 1880 done at the aggregate of all Canada.

(β) for 1881 to 1889, 1891 to 1899 and 1901 to 1904: OBI actual recorded figure, and for 1905 the Statcan HAS.VI (see below). (For census years the OBI figures corresponded closely with the Census of Canada figures.)

(γ) for 1905 to 1926: see the total for Canada.

(ii) Quebec: for census years: the Census of Canada; for 1905: Statcan HAS.VI

(α) for 1871 to 1879: linear interpolation between 1870 to 1880 done at the Canada aggregate level.

(β) for 1881 to 1905: for 1881, straight line interpolation between 1880 and 1890; for 1882 to 1889, 1891 to 1899, and 1901 to 1904, interpolation done using the OBI figures as interpolators.

(γ) for 1905 to 1926: see the total for Canada.

(iii) Maritime provinces and British Columbia: for census years, the Census of Canada.

(α) P.E.I. added to census of Canada for 1871 (1870).

(β) for Maritime provinces and B.C. for all intercensal years before 1906 (1905) the annual estimates were obtained by straight line interpolation between census years and HAS.VI data for 1906 (1905); B.C. data begin only in 1880.

(γ) for 1905 to 1926: see the total for Canada.

(iv) Manitoba: Manitoba data begin with 1880. For census years (production years): from the Census of Canada.

(α) for 1881 to 1889: straight line interpolation between census year data;

(β) for 1891 and 1892: linear interpolation between 1890 and 1900; 1893 to 1899 and 1901 to 1905 (1906) interpolation done by Manitoba annual stock data, collected by the Province of Manitoba beginning with production for 1892 (published in sessional papers of Manitoba, especially Manitoba Sessional Papers of 1912, Sessional Paper No.2, pp. 164-5.)

(γ) for 1905 to 1926: see the total for Canada.

(v) Alberta and Saskatchewan together: The data begin with 1880. For census years: from the Census of Canada.

(α) for 1881 to 1889: straight line interpolation between census year data.

(β) for 1891 to 1899: the same method was used as for Manitoba, using the Manitoba data for interpolation for 1893 to 1899.

(γ) for 1901 to 1905: the Manitoba year data were used to interpolate for Saskatchewan and Alberta individually. The stock for each province for 1905 (1906) was obtained in the quinquennial census of the prairie provinces taken in 1906. The division of the stock series for the North-West Territories obtained in the Census of 1901 between what became Alberta and Saskatchewan is given in the *Census of Agriculture, 1941*. See HAS.VI, p.10 fn. (1).

(vi) For original data at the Canada level

(α) 1871 to 1879: Interpolation was done on a straight line basis, at the level for all Canada, between the census figures for 1870 (1871) and 1880 (1881). The cattle stock for Prince Edward Island was added to the 1870 data; Manitoba and B.C. and the Territories were included in 1880.

(β) 1905 (1905-6) to 1926 (1926-27). The data were from Statcan, HAS.VI, p.9 except for 1920 (census of 1921) which is from the 1921 census of agriculture and includes cattle not on farms as well as on farms.

(vii) Note about imports of live cattle

It was presumed that imports of live cattle were additions to herds. Numbers of live cattle imported were obtained from the official *Trade of Canada* figures for every year.

(b) Other data sources. For 1870 to 1889

(i) Population figures were from HSC Series A1. Since these figures were for April 1, the actual population figures used for year t was the average of population of April 1, year t and of April 1, year t+1. (Note that the population of Prince Edward Island is included from the beginning.)

(ii) Per capita domestic disappearance of beef and of veal were derived from census data for 1870, 1880 and 1890.

The censuses of agriculture for 1870-71, 1880-81 and 1890-91 report a figure for number of cattle "killed or sold." In this project, it was deemed that the reported numbers covered farm slaughter and net off-farm sales and that sales of feeders from one cattleman to another were not included. Support for this review came from three sources. First, from the beginning in 1870-71 the census schedule on which the data were collected specified the farm disposition of cattle by the wording "Cattle killed or sold for slaughter or export"; like wording was used for sheep and swine. Second, in the 1900-01 census and most later censuses the numbers reported were for animals "killed or sold for slaughter or export" and therefore did not include interfarm feeder sales. A comparison of the ratio of the sales and slaughter numbers used in this project to the stock of cattle in census years does not suggest that the pre-1900 ratios (except possibly in 1890/91) are high; the ratio of net production, i.e., sales and slaughter plus inventory change, to stock does not change this impression. See the data in the following table. Third, our data give a higher per capita sales and slaughter number from 1900 onward than before 1900. The main item contradictory to the above view lies in the OBI data implying a larger rise in sales and slaughter of cattle in Ontario between 1890 and 1900 than do the decennial census data; the 1900 census suggests that some home-slaughtered cattle might have been missed in the 1901 census; however, it is possible that the census figure for 1890 had included some feeder cattle.

Data on Cattle, Stocks and Production, Census Years

	1870-71	1880-81	1890-91	1900-01	1910-11	1920-21
Stock of cattle (000)	2,687	3,515	4,121	5,576	6,526	8,519
Sales and slaughter (000)	533	657	964	1,260	1,648	2,144
Ratio to stock	0.198	0.187	0.234	0.226	0.253	0.252
Net production* (000)	616	732	1,067	1,474	1,659	2,510
Ratio to stock	0.229	0.208	0.259	0.264	0.254	0.295
Population (000)	3,689	4,325	4,833	5,371	7,207	8,788
Net sales and slaughter of animals per capita	0.144	0.152	0.199	0.235	0.229	0.244
Production of animals per capita	0.167	0.169	0.221	0.274	0.230	0.286

* Net production is sales and slaughter plus change in stock.

It was assumed that one third of the animals killed or sold for slaughter or export were calves and two thirds were adult animals. (There is much support for this decision in data from 1920 onward in HAS.VI; and the census data for earlier years are sufficient to show that changes in the proportion of dairy cattle in the total would not be important in affecting the composition of cattle output during the whole period from 1870 to 1926.)

The relevant exports and imports of cattle and beef products to be associated with census years were those recorded in the official *Trade of Canada* figures for the trade year ending June 30 of the year following that to which census production data applied. For purposes of calculating domestic consumption of beef and veal, it was necessary to make an estimate of how the single figure given for live cattle exports would be divided between adult cattle and calves. For making these calculations it was estimated that for 1870 one-third of the cattle exports were calves, for 1880 one quarter of the cattle exports were calves and for 1890 five per cent of the exports were calves. (The different proportions of calves in exports in the three census years involved is explained by the proportions of live cattle exports going to the United States and the United Kingdom. Unit export values showing low unit export values to the United States and high unit export values to Great Britain indicate that exports of calves went to the United States and that exports to the United Kingdom were adults; the trade data for 1890-91 were quite unusual in composition.)

For each of 1870, 1880 and 1890 (census years) per capita consumption of veal in Canada, in pounds, was calculated by subtracting the number of calves exported from the total number of calves killed or sold for slaughter or export to obtain domestic consumption and then calculating the aggregate number of pounds of veal consumed in Canada by attributing 100 lbs. of veal to each calf. For each of these three census years the per capita consumption of beef was estimated by (α) subtracting the number of adult cattle exported from the total number of adult cattle killed or sold for slaughter or export, (β) converting the resultant number of cattle into pounds of beef at 500 pounds of beef per adult cattle-beast, (γ) subtracting beef exports in pounds and adding beef imports in pounds. (In 1870 and 1880 it is assumed that one tenth of the exports and imports of preserved meats are beef exports and imports — most of the preserved meats are pork products.) These calculations lead to measures of domestic disappearance of beef and veal. Per capita consumption of each of beef and veal were then obtained for 1870, 1880 an 1890 by dividing domestic disappearance by related measures of population.

(iii) Estimates of the aggregate numbers of cattle and calves killed or sold for slaughter or exports for intercensal years were then calculated as follows:

(α) as already noted, per capita domestic disappearance estimates for beef and veal for years between census years were calculated by linear interpolation between census years;

(β) aggregate domestic disappearances of beef and veal were obtained by multiplying the domestic disappearance per capita by population for each year;

(γ) exports of beef products were added and imports of beef products were subtracted (Note that there are no exports or imports of veal as such.);

(δ) the resulting figures, measured in pounds, are converted to numbers of animals by division of the beef figures by 500 (the weight in pounds of an adult cattle-beast carcass) and the veal figures by 100 (the weight in pounds of a calf carcass);

(ϵ) The numbers of each of cattle and calves killed or sold for slaughter or export were then obtained by adding the numbers of each exported live, to the relevant category (since only one figure is reported for live bovine exports the divisions of the export figures between cattle and calves were calculated by placing the proportion of calves at 0.333 for 1871-76, at 0.250 for 1877 and at 0.20 for 1878-79 and for 1881-1889). The resultant estimates were totalled to obtain an estimate of the combined total of cattle and calves killed each year or sold for slaughter or export.

(iv) The valuation of the sales and slaughter numbers (as well as of changes in inventory) will be dealt with for the whole period as a unit after the sources of production data for the years 1890-91 to 1920-21 and for 1921-22 to 1926-27 have been given.

For 1890-91 to 1920-21. Estimates of Sales and Slaughter

Estimates of animals (adults and calves together) killed or sold for slaughter or export were obtained by multiplying the estimate of the aggregate cattle stock in each year by an estimated ratio of animals killed or sold for slaughter or exports to the aggregate stock. This ratio was estimated as follows:

(v) Estimates for each of 1890-91, 1900-01, 1910-11 and 1920-21 were obtained basically from data from the census of agriculture taken in conjunction with the population census.

(α) In 1890-91, the aggregate number of cattle and calves killed or sold for slaughter or export was 957,737, being the data for the year 1890 from *Census of Canada, Agriculture*; the 1890-91 census stock figure of 4,120,586 cattle and calves was for April 1, 1891 and our estimate for 1890 was originally 3,993,644 cattle and calves (later amended to 4,017,433). These data yield a ratio of sales and slaughter to stock (original figure) of 0.240 for 1890 (or 0.238 to the amended figures).

(β) In 1900-01: according to the opinion of the census takers, in 1901 the numbers slaughtered on farms were underreported. An estimate for 1901 was obtained by use of the Ontario sales and slaughter data obtained from OBI. For the year 1910-11 the Census of Canada ratio of sales and slaughter to total stock in 1911 for the Province of Ontario was 1.043 of the similar ratio of the OBI for 1910-11. If the OBI similar ratio for 1900-01 is adjusted upward by 1.043 to obtain a comparable census estimate, it yields a ratio 1.134 times the actual ratio reported in the census of 1901. The figure for animals killed or sold for sales or slaughter were adjusted upward by this ratio (1.134) to take care of the undercoverage; the resultant figure as a ratio of total cattle stock in 1900 was 0.235. (Note that this ratio is just slightly below the similar ratio (0.240 or 0.238) for all Canada in 1890; for Ontario, the adjusted census ratio of sales and slaughter in 1900 is 0.254 of stock in 1901 as compared with a similar ratio for Ontario for 1890-91 from the Canadian census of 0.274; note also that the census count of sales and slaughter for Ontario in 1910-11 for the calculations used here was obtained by valuing the farm slaughtered animals, reported only in total value in the census, at the same value per head as the unit value of the animals sold.)

(γ) For 1910-11, two calculations from reported figures were required. First, the numbers of cattle sold as well as sales values were reported; only the value of animals slaughtered on farms were reported. Consequently to obtain a total number killed on farms or sold it was necessary to estimate the numbers slaughtered on farms. The estimate was made as follows. Unit values of farm slaughtered animals in 1920, in which census data were available, were 0.771 of unit values of sales of animals. It was assumed that the same ratio prevailed in 1910 and the numbers of cattle slaughtered on farms was estimated by dividing the reported aggregate value of farm slaughter by a unit value equal to 0.771 of the unit value of cattle sold. The addition of farm slaughter plus sales yielded a figure for total sales and slaughter. Second, it is stated explicitly in the 1910 census of agriculture that the sales figure includes all cattle sold whether for slaughter or export or sold to other farmers (as feeders or for stock). One has to wait until the 1930 census of agriculture to get a measure of this interfarm sale. In that year farm purchases from other farms are recorded. These purchases as a proportion of total sales and slaughter, including that portion of the interfarm sale that is for feeders and not for long term additions to stock, amounted to 16 per cent of those total sales and slaughter. In the absence of other relevant data, this estimate of interfarm feeder sales was used to adjust the 1911 data; the disposition of farm cattle in the form of farm slaughter or farm sales in 1910 was reduced in numbers by 16 per cent to take account of the interfarm sales. This yielded a figure for farm slaughter and off-farm sales, in 1910, that amounted to 0.253 of the stock of cattle (and calves). It should be pointed out before this section is left that the proportion of sales and slaughter to stock for Ontario increased substantially between 1900-01 and 1910-11 according to both the OBI data and the Census of Canada data: there is not significant inconsistency even before the adjustment for 1900-01 undercoverage is made.

(δ) For 1920-21 the data reported for both numbers and value are (i) sales of cattle raised on the farms from which they were sold and (ii) farm slaughter of cattle raised on the farm on which the slaughter took place. These data leave out interfarm sales which are not reported. The sum of these two items plus an additional 45,000 estimated sales from off-farm (less than one acre) establishments yield a figure for sales and slaughter which is 0.263 of the stock of cattle in 1920 (which it should be noted is not the stock reported in the census, which is for 1921).

(ε) The ratios for years 1891 to 1899, 1901 to 1909 and 1911 to 1919

Fortunately, OBI obtained data on both sales and slaughter of cattle and stocks of cattle annually from 1891-92 onward and ratios of Ontario sales and slaughter to cattle stocks could be calculated for every year from 1891-92 to 1920-21 and later. (Ontario accounted for more than half cattle sales and slaughter in 1900-01 and still about 40 per cent of sales and slaughter in 1920-21.) The ratios for all Canada for intercensal years were then determined as follows.

The all-Canada ratio for 1891-92 was assumed to be the same as that of the census year 1890-91 (the ratio was 0.240); the all-Canada ratios for 1892-93 to 1899-1900 were interpolated between the vales for 1891-92 and 1900-01 using the Ontario OBI ratios as interpolators. (The computational procedure was to assume that the all-Canada ratios for these years departed from a linear trend of the ratio from 1891-92 to 1900-01 in the same proportion that the Ontario OBI actual ratios departed from a calculation of a linear trend of OBI ratios from data for the years 1891-92 and 1900-01.)

The interpolation of the all-Canada ratios between the values for the census years 1900-01 and 1910-11 and between census years 1910-11 and 1920-21 was done in exactly the same manner as for the period 1891-92 to 1900-01: the annual OBI ratios were used as interpolators for each of these intercensal decades.

For 1921-22 to 1926-27. Estimates of Sales and Slaughter

Estimates of sales and slaughter for each year of this period came from Statcan HAS.VI, pp. 34-35. Cattle and calves are given separately.

Unit Values

Total production was made up of sales and slaughter of Canadian produced cattle and changes in cattle stock but no use was made of the total as such. Separate unit values were used to value sales and slaughter of cattle and changes in cattle stocks. The unit values of stocks of animals were below the unit value of sales and slaughter. In 1920 (1921 census) the unit value of the cattle slaughtered on farms on which they were raised was the proportion 0.771 of the unit value of livestock sold off the farms on which they were raised.

Cattle unit values, 1910

The first census of agriculture in which sales and slaughter values for cattle livestock were obtained was that of 1911 in which the sales and slaughter pertained to 1910. Numbers of cattle sold off farms include both adult cattle and calves and an aggregate value was given for the receipts from the sales; for animals slaughtered on farms an aggregate value only was given and to get an estimate of the numbers slaughtered on farms, the unit value of off-farms sales as multiplied by 0.771, the 1920 ratio, to get a unit value for farm-slaughtered cattle and the census aggregate value of farm slaughtered animals was divided by this derived unit value of farm slaughtered animals to yield a total number of farm slaughtered animals. The results were the following for 1910.

	Number	Aggregate Value ($)
Cattle sold	1,752,792	60,438,593
Cattle slaughtered on farms (no. estimated)	210,337	5,594,961
All cattle sold and farm-slaughtered	1,963,129	66,033,554

Unit value of all sales and farm slaughter = $33.64

The unit value of the stock of cattle in 1910 was obtained by multiplying the unit value of sales and slaughter for that year by the ratio of the unit stock price to unit sales and slaughter price from OBI 1910 data for Ontario.

The derivation was from OBI Stock unit value ÷ OBI Sales etc. unit value x Unit value of Canadian sales = 32.57 ÷ 38.57 x 33.64 = 28.39. This figure was used rather than the unit stock value of $30.01 of the decennial census since the latter figure was for unit value of stock in 1911.

Cattle Unit Values 1870-71 to 1909-10, and 1911-12 to 1919-20

All unit values were obtained by using the 1910 unit values for sales and slaughter and for stocks as base year prices. Prices for other years were then obtained by using index numbers of prices to extrapolate the 1910 prices. The derivation of the index numbers was the following.

Unit values of sales and slaughter for Ontario (as well as unit values of stocks) were available annually from 1891 onward: these data were obtained from OBI and were published in its annual reports until 1918 and by the Department of Agriculture, Report of Statistics Branch from 1919 onward, all of which can be found in Ontario Sessional Papers; there is a lag of one year in presentation of data. (See especially Ontario Department of Agriculture *Report of Statistics Branch, 1927* — Sessional Paper No. 22.) These reports were for a year ending June 30 until 1918 and then June 15. Stocks of animals were reported as of July 1 and June 15. Thus the report for year t gave stocks at July 1 of year t plus sales and slaughter for the year ended June 30 of year t. In our calculations the sales and slaughter for year ending June 30 of year t were attributed to calendar year t-1 in the belief that more sales and slaughter take place in the second half of a calendar year than in the first half. (Crop statistics in year t's report were for calendar year t-1.)

Wholesale prices of prime export steers were available for all years. Sources: 1870 to

1889, Michell, p.70; 1890 to 1926, DBS *Livestock and Animal Products, 1940* p.26 (Cat. 23-303).

Cattle, Western Butchers (Winnipeg) from Department of Labor *Wholesale Prices 1890-1909 et seq.* were available and used for 1900 to 1910.

An index of prices of cattle, base 1910, was then calculated as follows:

For 1870 to 1891 the wholesale price at Toronto only was used.

For 1891 to 1900, the weighted index was derived from the OBI livestock sales price, carrying weight 66 two-thirds per cent, and the wholesale price index of steers at Toronto, weight 33 one-third per cent. The linking was done at 1891.

For 1900 to 1910 a weighted index comprised of 50 per cent weight for OBI livestock prices, 25 per cent for choice steers at Toronto and 25 per cent for western butchers cattle at Winnipeg. Linking was done at 1900.

For 1910 to 1919 only the OBI price of sales and slaughter of Ontario livestock was used. The reason that the wholesale price index of export steers was not used was that it moved erratically and departed quite widely from the OBI series.

For 1920 separate calculations were needed. The OBI unit value reported for 1920 as used in the project was much below that for 1919 because, in fact, it was for the year ended June 30, 1921 and prices had fallen sharply by the end of calendar 1920. The Canadian Census of Agriculture for 1920-21 (taken in June 1921) reported sales and slaughter data for animals killed or sold on farms on which raised, which yielded a unit value of $44.26. It was believed that the latter unit vale was too low in that it did not include data for feeder cattle sold from a different farm than where they were raised and these cattle are the high-priced ones. The procedure used was to extrapolate the unit value for 1919 (derived above) by the ratio of the export price per unit of Toronto steers in 1920 over the export price in 1919. This procedure yielded a value of $50.77 from the calculations 12.89÷13.06, the ratio of export prices, multiplied by $51.44 the unit price of sales and slaughter in 1919.

It will be noted that unit values of stocks of cattle were extrapolated from 1910 both backward and forward, by the same index as that used for unit values of sales and slaughter. This meant that the unit values for stocks bore the same ratio to unit values of sales and slaughter throughout.

A different procedure could have been used since OBI obtained data from which unit values of stocks as well as unit values of sales and slaughter could have been derived. However, the reporting of stock values involves subjective judgements that yield data which are unlikely to be as accurate as market data. A check between our calculations and Census of Canada data for unit values of stock yields the following comparison.

Ratio of 1911 unit value of stock to 1901 unit
value, from the Census of Canada   1.358

Ratio of 1911 unit value of stock to 1901 unit
value of stock, this project   1.345

It can be seen that the results are very close.

Cattle Unit Values 1921 to 1926

There were problems in obtaining unit values here. Unfortunately, the OBI unit valuations for this period are available only for 1921 (1921-22), 1922 and 1924 after which they are no longer available. Further, as already noted, the Census of Canada figures (at decennial census dates) for values of cattle sold or slaughtered from farms on which raised in 1920 and 1930 are low — the 1930 census unit value is considerably below that used by DBS in calculating farm income as given in HAS.II. A check with the agriculture division of DBS confirmed that in official calculations of farm income for 1926 onward, the numbers of cattle sold and slaughtered on farms would have been the figure given in HAS.VI which is the figure we used for each year from 1921 onward. We therefore got a unit value for 1926 by taking as the total value of cattle and calves disposed of from farms by net sales and slaughter the HAS figure and taking as the total value to farmers of these sales and slaughter of 84.2 million dollars for net off-farm sales and 4.0 million dollars for farm slaughtered cattle (being one fifth of $20.1 million farm revenue reported for farm slaughter of animals — the other four fifths being for hogs). Income figures are from HAS.II *Farm Income* pp. 48 and 68. A unit value for sales and slaughter in 1926 was calculated as the quotient of aggregate value of sales and slaughter divided by the number of cattle involved. This gave a unit value for 1926 of $43.56 per beast. Unit values for 1921 to 1925 were then obtained by using the wholesale price of choice steers in Toronto (see earlier reference) as the interpolator between the unit values for 1920 and 1926 for cattle disposal in the form of net sales and slaughter. This procedure yielded much the same values as would have been obtained by using OBI prices for the three years for which the latter were available. Unit values of stocks of cattle were taken as the proportion of unit values of sales etc. as in earlier years (*viz.* ratio 0.844). (This gave unit values for stock that were very similar to those obtained by dividing annual stock values by annual stocks of cattle (HSC Series L311-314)).

Hogs

The method of estimation of income from swine was very much like that used for cattle. Critical data were: the stock of hogs on an annual basis; the ratio of sales and slaughter plus inventory change to total stock from 1891/92 onward and per capita consumption of pork products from 1870-71 to 1890-91; annual unit values of hogs sold or slaughtered net and annual unit values of the stock of swine. Owing to the similarity of the method of income estimation to that used for cattle, which is described in detail in the section on cattle, the description of the method of estimation of income from hogs will be rather cursory. Note that until 1910-11, and for several years later, Ontario accounted for more that half the stock of hogs and much more than half in earlier years.

Estimation of Stock of Hogs on an Annual Basis

For 1870-71 to 1880-81

For all provinces together, including P.E.I. in 1870-71 (but not Manitoba which was negligible then), a straight line interpolation between the decennial census numbers of 1870-71 and 1880-81 was used to get estimates for the intervening years: the census stocks are for April 1 of 1871 and 1881. The census data show an actual decline in stocks from 1870-71 (1,418,597 head) to 1880-81 (1,207,619 head). This may well reflect the fall in unit values of cattle relative to unit values of hogs in this decade and the substantial growth in the stock of cattle in the decade.

For 1880-81 to 1890-91

The maritime provinces intercensal years were derived by linear interpolation between number of head reported in the census of agriculture: 140,524 for April 1, 1881; and 141,622 head for April 1, 1891.

Manitoba, territories (Alberta and Saskatchewan) and British Columbia, were done individually by straight line interpolation between census years, April 1, 1881 and April 1, 1891.

Ontario: Census of Canada for 1880-81 and 1890-91. OBI for intervening years (from Ontario Sessional Papers, 1926 "Annual Report of the Statistics Branch" of the Ontario Department of Agriculture). The OBI count and the decennial Census of Canada counts for census years are the following:

Stock of Hogs
(number)

	1891	1901	1911
Census of Canada*	1,121,396	1,562,696	1,887,451
OBI (June)	1,156,315	1,491,885	1,744,983

* April for 1891 and 1901, June for 1911

Quebec: Census of Canada data for April 1, 1881 and April 1, 1891. Interpolation was done using Ontario data as interpolator. (See Cattle for details of method.)

For 1890-91 to 1900-01

For all provinces, Census of Canada data for 1891 (April 1) and 1901 (April 1). Interpolation between census years as follows: the Maritime Provinces — straight line interpolation from 141,622 head in 1890-91 to 145,175 head in 1900-01; Quebec — interpolated between census values by use of the OBI data as interpolators; Ontario — OBI figures; Manitoba — Estimates for 1892 and 1893 were derived by straight line interpolation between decennial census figures; interpolation between 1893 and the decennial census figure for 1901 was done by using the stock figures collected by the Government of Manitoba as interpolators; Saskatchewan and Alberta — Interpolation between census years was done by using the Manitoba figures as interpolators; British Columbia — straight line interpolation from 1890-91 to 1900-01.

For 1900-01 to 1905-06

Estimates for 1905-06, i.e. 1906 values, to be used for interpolation purposes were derived as follows: the Maritime Provinces — The figure for 1906 is from HAS.VI; Quebec — also from HAS.VI; Ontario — OBI figure; Prairie Provinces — Quincennial Census of Agriculture for the provinces; British Columbia — straight line interpolation between decennial census figures for 1900-01 and 1910-11. Note that these figures do not add to the HAS.VI total for 1905-06 since the Ontario and British Columbia figures differ from HAS.VI figures; the total we actually use for 1905-06 is the HAS.VI total.

Interpolation between 1900-01 to 1905-06 is derived as follows: Maritimes and British Columbia — straight line interpolation in each case; Quebec — interpolation using Ontario OBI figures as interpolator; Ontario — OBI figures; Manitoba — Manitoba provincial figures as interpolator between 1900-01 and 1905-06; Saskatchewan and Alberta — Manitoba figures used as interpolator.

For 1905-06 to 1926-27: We use the official figures from HAS.VI, p.52.

Note the following: (1) Census of Canada figures from 1870-71 to 1901-02 are for a day around April 1; for 1910-11 onward the decennial census figures are for a day around June 1. All OBI data are for a day in June. (2) HAS figure for 1921 is farm figure only (from decennial census) — there was an additional 80,000 approximately in "elsewhere than farm" sites; however, the figures for 1910-11 and earlier census figures include the pig stock on farms and elsewhere. We accepted the HAS figures as given. (3) The Statistics Canada data for stock at June 1 and at December 1 from 1931 onward suggest that there is not a seasonal pattern, over the year, of the stock of pigs.

Estimation of Sales and Slaughter

The method of estimation differed among three periods as follows: 1870-71 to 1890-91; 1891-92 to 1920-21; 1921-22 to 1926-27.

Period 1870-71 to 1890-91

The method used was essentially the same as that used for cattle for the same period. A full description of the method is given in the cattle section and so only the rudiments are given here. Essentially the method is: (a) to calculate consumption per capita for the census years, 1870, 1880 and 1890 from census data on production, and export and import data. These calculations led to a per capita consumption of pork of 54.2 pounds in 1870, 44.3 pounds in 1880 and 54.8 pounds in 1890; (b) attribute a per capita consumption of pork to intercensal years by straight line interpolation between census years; (c) reverse the initial process to obtain intercensal year estimates by multiplying population by per capita consumption to obtain domestic disappearance and then adjust for exports and imports.

The numbers as ordinarily calculated from census data and trade data follow.

	1870	1880	1890
Number of head disposed of for slaughter or export (includes PEI) Census no.	1,251,176	1,302,503	1,791,104
Add imports of live animals, no.	+ 855	+ 2,463	+ 1,099
Subtract exports of live animals, no.	− 11,187	− 2,819	− 334
Domestic disappearance of live animals, no.	1,240,844	1,302,147	1,791,869
Domestic disappearance of live hogs in dressed carcass equivalent at 154 lbs. dressed weight per carcass, lbs.	191,089,976	200,530,630	275,947,820
Add imports dressed meat, lbs	+ 4,795,611	+ 18,809,487	+ 14,751,502
Subtract exports dressed meat, lbs	− 17,185,238	− 12,142,534	− 7,669,658
Domestic disappearance, all forms, dressed weight equivalent, lbs.	178,700,349	207,197,583	283,029,669
Population at April 1 (000 persons)	3,625	4,255	4,779
Domestic disappearance per capita hog weight in dressed form, lbs.	49.2	48.7	59.2

However, as noted earlier, there is some doubt about the coverage of the sales and slaughter figures of the decennial census before 1900. In particular, it looks as if the 1871 census figure may reflect a substantial under-reporting. Some light is thrown on the matter by comparing the sales and slaughter figures and the stock figures. One might expect stock figures to be more accurately reported than sales and slaughter because they reflect easily made counts of numbers at the date at which the census is taken; sales and slaughter, on the other hand, take place throughout the year. A comparison of sales and slaughter with stocks as reported in the decennial census may be seen in the following table.

Swine, Sales and Slaughter
and Stocks, Canada, Decennial Census
1870-71 to 1900-01

Census Year	Stock of Swine (no.)	Sales and Slaughter (no.)	Ratio Sales and Slaughter to Stock at Census Date	Ratio Change in Stock in Census Year to Stock at Census Date
1870-71 (includes P.E.I.)	1,418,597	1,251,176	0.882	0
1880-81	1,207,619	1,302,503	1.079	-0.018
1890-91	1,733,850	1,791,104	1.033	-0.018
1900-01	2,394,628	2,555,413	1.067	-0.103

Among the impressions one gets from these data, the most notable is that the 1870 level of sales and slaughter appears to be abnormally low: while the stock of swine was substantially higher in 1870-71 than in 1880-81, the sales and slaughter figure was actually increased from 1870-71 to 1880-81; the ratio of sales and slaughter to stock in 1870-71 is much below the like ratio for each of the three succeeding censuses. In addition, the net production of hogs (i.e. the sum of sales and slaughter plus inventory change) as a ratio to stock was considerably lower in 1900-01 than in 1880-81 and 1890-91.

The ratio of sales and slaughter of hogs and of inventory change to stock in census years in the data of our project were as follows.

Year	Ratio Sales and Slaughter to Stock at Year's End	Ratio of Inventory Change in Year to Stock at Year's End
1870-71	0.965	0
1880-81	1.079	-0.018
1890-91	1.033	-0.018

The rationale for the choice of these values for the parameters is the following. For 1880-81, and 1890-91, the parameter values are those derived directly from census data: they reflect per capita consumption of pork products of 48.7 pounds in 1880, and 59.2 pounds in 1890. The parameter value of 0.965 for the ratio of sales and slaughter of hogs to stock in 1870-71 is based on a per capita domestic disappearance of pork products of 54.2 pounds in the year. This figure is halfway between the actual reported values which yields per capita consumption of pork products of 49.2 pounds in 1870-71 and 59.2 pounds in 1890-91. Further, later censuses yield higher estimates of per capita domestic disappearance: the 1901 census yields a figure of nearly 70 pounds per capita. Only 1880-81 shows a lower per capita domestic disappearance (although not a lower ratio of sales and slaughter to stock) and that phenomenon can be explained by the expansion in the consumption of beef in 1880-81 which was promoted by the fall of beef prices relative to pork prices. The 1900 census personnel believed some farm slaughter was probably unreported in 1900 and the same could certainly have been true of the 1870 census. The total production, of course, was the number of head disposed of for slaughter or export plus the change in inventory.

Period 1891-92 to 1920-21

The estimates for this period were made by first multiplying the stock of hogs by a ratio of sales and slaughter plus inventory change to obtain an estimate of the numbers of pigs that were produced in Canada each year. The ratio for each year was obtained from data for Ontario. OBI obtained and reported full data on both stocks each year (in June) and all sales and slaughter for Ontario producers. The ratios for year t were obtained by adding to sales and slaughter in each year the change in inventory from year t to year t+1 and taking the resultant total as a proportion of stock in year t. An alternative could have been to take just sales and slaughter as a proportion of stock and then total production could be derived by adding to the derived sales and slaughter estimates the changes in stock. However, it was believed that sales and slaughter and changes in stock were not entirely unrelated: one might expect sales and slaughter to be higher when stocks are drawn down than when they are unchanged or building. The OBI sales and slaughter figures included sales of feeders from one farmer to another and sales of breeding stock from one farmer to another. Data from the 1931 census and other DBS data suggest that about 15 per cent of sales are for these intrafarm sales. Accordingly, the estimates of production first obtained were reduced by 15 per cent to take account of the intrafarm sales.

For later purposes (for evaluation in money) the estimates of farm disposition of pigs were divided between disposition of pigs for off-farm sales for slaughter or export (including therein farm slaughter of hogs) and changes in inventories. The latter were derived directly from the stock data; the former was then obtained as a residual in the estimation process.

Period 1921-22 to 1926-27

Farm output for slaughter or export: source HAS.VI, p.65. Change in inventory obtained from annual stock figures.

Unit Values of Hogs

The prices used were unit values for a hog. Prices quoted in papers are more likely so much per hundred weight (or some like standard measure).

Unit values 1891-92 to 1920-21

Unit values of sales and slaughter for 1892 to 1920 were, for all except the last year, those obtained from the OBI reports on values of sales and slaughter and numbers of hogs sold or slaughtered. The OBI year for reporting sales and slaughter was from June to June and therefore to obtain a calendar year unit value an average of the unit value for the year ending in June of year t and the unit value for the year ending in June of year t+1 was used for the calendar year t; the unit value used for calendar 1920 was that derived from the Census of Canada: that unit value was $27.51 compared with a unit value of $25.41 derived from averaging the OBI unit values for 1919-20 and 1920-21.

The unit value of the stock of hogs used for valuing the change in the stock inventory for 1892 to 1920 was simply the unit value of stock derived from the quotient of total value of the stock divided by the number in the stock as reported in the OBI data for June of each year; the unit value for 1921 was that obtained from the Census of Canada: that unit value was $10.84 compared with $12.28 from the OBI data.

Unit values for 1921-22 to 1926-27

For valuing sales and slaughter: for 1921-22 to 1926-27 the wholesale price (per cwt.) of hogs in Toronto was multiplied by the average of the ratio of the unit price of hogs (per hog) from OBI data to the wholesale price of hogs (per cwt.) in Toronto, the ratio being 1.643.
   This gave the following unit values per hog, and the comparable OBI values.

	1921	1922	1923	1924	1925	1926
Project derived unit values $	19.26	20.75	17.31	16.31	23.20	24.17
OBI unit values $	20.42	19.95	NA*	18.52*	NA	NA

* A single year value for June 1924 to June 1925 (which explains why it is above the project calendar year values for 1924): there were not any unit values for 1923-24; NA — not available.

For valuing changes in stock: for each year from 1921-22 to 1926-27 the unit price for stock was obtained by multiplying the unit price for sales and slaughter by the average ratio of the OBI unit value of stock to the project unit value for sales and slaughter for the years 1910-11 to 1924-25: the ratio was 0.675.

Unit values for 1870-72 to 1891-92

The procedure followed was much like that for the years 1921-22 to 1926-27. The OBI unit values were not available prior to 1891-92; nor were there any unit values from the decennial census.
   The derivation of a unit value per hog for sales for each year of this period was derived as follows: first, an average ratio of the OBI unit price per hog for sales and slaughter to the wholesale price of hogs per cwt. in the Toronto market for the 15 years 1892-93 to 1906-07 was calculated, the resultant average ratio being 1.688, there being no trend and not a wide variance in the annual ratios from which the average was calculated; second, the wholesale price of hogs per cwt. at Toronto for 1870 to 1891 (obtained from Michell, 1870 to 1889 and *Wholesale Prices*, 1890 onward) was multiplied by this ratio on a year by year basis to yield the unit values that were used to evaluate sales for slaughter and export from 1870 to 1891.
   The derivation of a unit value per hog for stock (and changes in stock) for the period was as follows: first, an average ratio of the OBI unit value of the stock of hogs to the unit value of hogs sold or slaughtered based on project unit value for sales and slaughter (derived from OBI data) was calculated for the fifteen years 1891-92 to 1905-06, the resultant ratio being

0.669, there being small variance in the year to year annual ratios and little or no trend; second, the unit value of sales and slaughter as derived above was multiplied by this ratio on a year to year basis to calculate the unit value of the stock for each year from 1871 to 1891.

Aggregate Values of Farm Slaughter and Sales for Slaughter or Export, Entire Period 1870 to 1926

This aggregate value for each year was obtained as the sum of the aggregate value of farm slaughter and sales for slaughter or export and the aggregate value of changes in inventory. These values were calculated as the product of quantity and unit value for sales and slaughter and for changes in stock.

Sheep

The method of estimation was a variant of that used for cattle. Basically, for all years, the method involved getting estimates of the annual changes in inventory and the annual number of the aggregate of farm slaughter plus off-farm sales for slaughter or export and then valuing the resultant figures, by multiplication, by a unit value for each year. To obtain the data for changes in stock, it was necessary to estimate the stock of sheep on a year to year basis.

Estimates of Stock of Sheep and Lambs

The estimates of total stock are used only to obtain an estimate of inventory change. One problem in the estimation of the stock of sheep and lambs is that the numbers vary enormously between seasons owing to the lambing season being in the early part of the year and the slaughter of lambs (and sheep) taking place late in the year. The June numbers taken in the censuses from 1906 onward are probably approximately the maximum for the year since the lambing season is over by then. The censuses of 1871 to 1901 were taken at April 1 and the lambing season would not be over by then but the actual proportion of the lambing after April 1 is not known. However, the count of sheep at April 1 is undoubtedly below that for June 1.

For the foregoing reasons, an estimate of the stock of sheep for each of 1870, 1880, 1890 and 1900 was obtained by inference from the census of Canada figure for sales and slaughter as follows. From data in HAS.VI, the annual output (farm slaughter plus sales for slaughter or export) of sheep and lambs, in numbers, was related to the stock at June 1 of the same year, for 1920 to 1940, account being taken also of the change in the stock from year to year. The calculations yielded a ratio (a median value with small dispersion) of production, as defined above, plus inventory change to the stock of sheep of 0.46. The stock numbers then for June of 1870, 1880, 1890, and 1900 were estimated by dividing the numbers for slaughter plus sales for slaughter or export from the decennial census for the appropriate year by the factor 0.46. This yielded the following estimates:

Estimates of Stock (000's of sheep)

	1870	1880	1890	1900
Project estimate of stock at June 1	3,385.7	3,253.2	3,183.0	2,918.0
Census estimate of stock at April 1 of following year	3,155.5	3,048.7	2,563.8	2,510.0
P.E.I. (1871)	147.4			

The census stock for June 1, 1906, taken from HAS.VI, was 2,543.0 thousand.

It will be noted that: (1) the project stock in 1870 is almost like that of the decennial census, especially if P.E.I. is included; the project stock in 1881 is fairly close but is slightly above the census value, the latter of which is to be expected for June 1; the project figure for June 1, 1890 and 1900 are considerably above the census figure for April 1 of the following year in each case. It is possible that the project estimates for 1890 and 1900 are too high. However, it is worth noting that OBI figures for numbers in Ontario in June, decline from 1,915,303 head in 1882 to 1,693,751 head in 1891 (1,339,695 in 1890), and are back at 1,761,799 in 1901 (1,797,213 in 1900). In addition, the OBI count declined from 1,797,213 in 1900 (1,761,799 in 1901) to 1,304,809 head in 1906, which decline corresponds to the change in the project estimate for Canada of 2,918.0 thousand head in 1900 and 2,534.0 thousand head in 1906. In any event there were not large changes in stock over the period from 1870 to 1906 and hence the additions to stock, which are a part of aggregate output, are negligible on an average annual basis. However, the year to year variations as shown by OBI data were considerable in both directions.

The annual data between census years and up to 1906 were derived as follows: (i) for 1870 to 1880: straight line interpolation; (ii) for 1880 to 1890: 1881 only, straight line interpolation between 1880 and 1890; 1882 to 1890 OBI annual stocks used as the interpolator between our data for all Canada; (iii) for 1890 to 1900: 1891 straight line interpolation between 1890 and 1900; 1892 to 1900, interpolator was size of stock in Ontario as estimated by dividing annual data for number sold or slaughtered by 0.46 rather than using the stock as reported by OBI; (iv) for 1900 to 1906: used same figure for 1901 as for 1900; 1901 to 1906 interpolated using Ontario estimate of stock as derived in same manner as for 1892 to 1900, i.e. by dividing the figure for numbers sold or slaughtered by 0.46.

For 1906 to 1927, the annual stock data for 1906 to 1927 are obtained from HAS.VI.

The change in stock is just taken as the first differences. It is worth noting that over the whole period this change in stock is small, from 3,385,717 in 1870 to 2,829,700 in 1927. The average change per year over these 56 years is negligible (a decline of 9,929 head per annum).

Production for Slaughter or Sale for Slaughter or Export

Different procedures were used for 1870 to 1890, 1891 to 1905 and 1906 to 1926.

Period 1870-71 to 1890-91

There are no annual sales and slaughter data before 1891-92 (OBI data begin then). For these two decades production for slaughter plus sales for slaughter or export is available, decennial census, for 1870, 1880, and 1890. From these data, plus foreign trade data, domestic consumption per capita for each of these years was determined as follows:

	1870*	1880	1890
Sales and slaughter,(no.)	1,557,430	1,496,465	1,464,172
Less exports live sheep and lambs	− 313,613	− 354,155	− 299,357
Plus live imports	+ 86	+ 9,007	+ 45,067
Domestic slaughter (no.)	1,243,903	1,151,317	1,209,892
Domestic slaughter dressed weight @43 lbs. per carcass (lbs.)	53,487,829	49,506,631	52,025,356
Less exports of mutton, (lbs.)	− 459,338	− 173,398	− 291,991
Plus imports of mutton, (lbs.)	+ 8,951	+ 32,582	+ 6,388
Domestic dis-appearance lamb and mutton, (lbs.)	53,019,540	49,365,815	51,739,753
Population, Oct. 1.	3,453,761	4,275,000	4,806,000
Per capita consumption, (lbs. of meat)	15.35	11.55	10.77

* Note that for 1870 the domestic disappearance per capita was calculated from data for Ontario, Quebec, New Brunswick and Nova Scotia only; in the final estimates for 1870, the same per capita consumption was attributed to P.E.I., Manitoba, British Columbia and the Territories.

The dressed weight of 43 pounds per carcass was derived from HSC, p.373, data for the 1920s.

Per capita consumption of lamb and mutton for intercensal years was calculated by straight line interpolation between adjacent pairs of census years.

The estimates of sales and slaughter for intercensal years were then made by the exactly opposite procedure to that used to estimate domestic disappearance of lamb and mutton per capita in census years: population of Canada for each year was multiplied by per capita consumption of mutton and lamb; imports of meat were subtracted and exports added; the resultant figure in dressed carcass weight in pounds was converted into number of sheep and lambs by division by 43 pounds (carcass weight); live imports were subtracted and live exports were added. The result was the estimate of the number of sheep or lambs slaughtered or sold for slaughter or export in each year. In fact, numbers exported were quite large.

Period 1890-91 to 1920-21

For 1890-91 to 1920-21 the anchor years were the census years. Two adjustments were needed: for 1920-21; and for 1910-11. The 1920-21 adjustment was merely to infer the same ratio of sales and slaughter to stock for the small off-farm numbers of sheep as for the farm numbers; in 1910-11, sales numbers and values were given but only the value of sheep slaughtered on farms was reported and numbers were estimated by assuming the same unit value for these farm slaughtered sheep as for the sold sheep and the resultant estimates for total sales and slaughter were reduced by 8.86 percent to eliminate feeder sales (feeder ratio derived from 1931 census). Note that in 1920 (census data) the unit value per head of sales was $8.66 and unit value of farm slaughter was $8.76: this fact gives some credibility to the use of the same unit value for sales and for farm slaughter in the 1910 data.

The resultant figures of sales and slaughter for each of the census years follow.

	1890	1900	1910	1920
Numbers killed or sold for slaughter or export	1,464,172	1,342,288	999,801	1,219,319

Interpolation between each pair of census years in this span from 1890 to 1920 was done by using the OBI data on sales and slaughter as interpolators. The OBI data in turn needed some manipulation. It appeared that the number reported for each year from 1891-92 to 1894-95 probably was for off-farm sales only and did not include farm-killed animals. The OBI sales figures for these years were adjusted upward by 17.04 per cent, which was the average of the farm slaughter to off-farm sales in the 1910 census (15.59 percent) and the 1920 census (18.48 percent).   An estimated OBI figure for farm slaughter and sales in 1890-91 was obtained as follows: the ratio of off-farm sales to stock was 0.31 for each of the years 1891-92, 1893-94 and 1894-95 and was 0.32 for 1892-93; it was assumed that the comparable ratio of 0.31 would hold also for 1890-91; adjustment upward for farm slaughter would lead to a ratio of total sales and slaughter to stock of 0.362824 (1.1704 x 0.31); this ratio was then multiplied by the stock in 1890-91 to give a figure for aggregate sales and slaughter in 1890-91 (year ending June, 1891) which approximates in time the Census of Canada year. (Most lambs are slaughtered before the end of the calendar year.)

Period 1921-22 to 1926-27

The sales and slaughter figures were the official estimates reported in HAS.VI.

Unit Values

For 1891-92 to 1926-27

The price per animal used was the OBI unit value of farm sales and slaughter (except for years 1906-07, 1923-24, 1925-26 and 1926-27 — note that the OBI price is available for 1924-25). The unit value of stocks in the OBI data was usually close and often quite close to the unit value of sales and slaughter. For the years 1906-07, 1923-24, 1925-26 and 1926-27, the wholesale price of sheep in Toronto (quoted by the hundred weight) was used as an interpolator or extrapolator from the OBI unit values per animal; these wholesale prices came from the Department of Labour, *Wholesale Prices 1890-1909* and DBS, *Prices and Price Indexes*.

For 1870-71 to 1890-91

The export unit values of sheep, per head, multiplied by the factor 0.9845 was used for each year. Export unit values were derived from *Trade of Canada* data, of course. The factor 0.9845 was the average ratio of the OBI unit value of sales to the export unit value for the years 1891-92 to 1905-06.

The OBI unit value for 1920 may be a bit on the low side as it is really the value for the year ending June 1921 and prices fell quite rapidly from mid-1920 onward. At the same time the slaughter of lambs takes place late each calendar year and rather than trying to make a special adjustment, the OBI figure was used (the OBI unit value for sales was $7.22; the decennial census unit value was $8.66).

Total Farm Value of Farm Production

For each year, the change in stock was added to the figure for net farm sales and slaughter. The resultant figure was multiplied by the unit value of sales and slaughter for the year.

Poultry

This section measures the value of the sales and slaughter of poultry plus the value of the change in the stock of poultry.

Both of the above measures require data on the stock of poultry annually. From these stocks the sales and slaughter and the changes in inventory can be estimated. These measures of physical quantities must then be valued. The steps necessary for the achievement of the measurement of values are described in order.

The Stock of Poultry and Sales and Slaughter

The stock of poultry includes, in addition to hens and chickens, the numbers of turkeys, geese, ducks and a negligible miscellaneous group. The stock of hens and chickens is already available in the estimates of egg production for the years 1881-82 to 1926-27; they are estimated for the years 1870-71 to 1880-81 by dividing the annual egg production, from the section on eggs, by an estimate of the number of eggs produced per unit of the hen and chicken stock — the estimate of egg production, in dozens, is divided by output per unit of hen and chicken stock of five dozen eggs (see Egg section).

The stock of poultry is derived from the stock of hens and chickens. The ratios of the stock of all poultry to the stock of hens and chickens in the decennial censuses follow.

Census Year	Ratio of Stock of All poultry to Hen and Chicken Stock on Farms and Elsewhere
1891	1.111
1901	1.076
1911	1.068
1921	1.048
1931	1.060

These ratios were interpolated in linear fashion between 1891 and 1901, 1901 and 1911, 1911 and 1921; the ratio was extrapolated to 1926 at the same annual rate of change as between 1911 and 1921 to give a value of 1.036 in 1926; the ratio was extrapolated from 1891 to 1871 in linear fashion at the same rate of change per annum as between 1901 and 1891 to give a value of 1.181 in 1871. (One might question the procedure for the 1920s in light of the 1930 ratio but there were not data to show when turning points came between 1921 and 1931: the data of Series M369 to 372 of HSC.II, available after our work was done, which pertain only to farms, yield a figure of 1.070 for 1926; the similar ratio, farms only, for 1921 was 1.054).

The numbers of birds either sold or slaughtered were obtained in the censuses from 1901 onward. The ratios of the numbers of poultry sold or slaughtered in census years follow.

Ratios of Numbers of Poultry Sold or Slaughtered
to Stock of Poultry at the Census Date

Census Date	Ratio
1900	0.394
1910	0.367
1920	(0.353) see text
1930	0.338

The actual value of the ratio of numbers of poultry sold or slaughtered in 1920 to the numbers at the census date was 0.269. This ratio is much too low for interpolating purposes owing to the fact that the stock of poultry in 1921 was more than 15 per cent higher than that of 1920: a large part of the output of 1920 went to building stock. What was done was to use a ratio of 0.353 for 1920, halfway between the 1910 and 1930 ratios, for purposes of providing a benchmark for 1920 for interpolation purposes; the actual figure used for the 1920 sales and slaughter was, of course, the census figure for 1920.

The ratios of sales and slaughter numbers to stocks of poultry for intercensal years after 1900 and for all years before 1900 were obtained in three separate ways. For 1900 to 1910, 1910 to 1920 and 1920 to 1924, the annual sales and slaughter ratios for poultry for Ontario, obtained from data collected by OBI, were used to interpolate the countrywide census ratios for 1910, 1920 and 1930 and the 1925 and 1926 ratios were obtained by simple linear interpolation between the 1920 and 1930 census values; the OBI ratios for 1891 to 1900 were used to extrapolate the Canada wide Census ratio for 1900 annually back to 1891; a ratio of 0.333, a simple average of the previously calculated ratios for 1891 to 1895, was used for all years from 1890 backward to 1870.

The actual numbers of sales and slaughter of poultry were then obtained for each year by multiplying the stock of poultry by the ratios of the numbers sold or slaughtered to the stock in each year. The actual change in the size of stock year by year was obtained simply by taking first differences in the stock series.

The Unit Values Of Poultry

The next step was to obtain a value per unit of sales and slaughter of poultry and a value per unit of the stock of poultry. The following are the census unit values of sales and slaughter, which apply to the years preceding the actual census dates, and of the stock which apply to the census dates themselves.

Year	Unit Value Sales and Slaughter Poultry ($)	Unit Value Stock of Poultry at Census Date ($)
1900-01	—	0.319
1910-11	0.684	0.461
1920-21	1.192	0.631

There are in addition annual unit values for sales and slaughter of poultry for the Province of Ontario, from 1891-92 to 1924-25 (1923-24 excepted) and unit values of stocks of poultry from 1891-92 right through 1926-27. (There were also wholesale prices in Montreal of fowls and turkeys from 1890 onward from *Wholesale Prices* which could be used as a casual check on the farm price sources noted above.)

The Census unit values were accepted for the years to which they applied. The estimates of the annual data for the entire period were made in five ways: first, from 1910 to 1920, the OBI unit values for sales and slaughter or for the stock of poultry were used to interpolate between the 1910 and 1920 Census of Canada unit values for sales and slaughter and for stocks; second, the 1920 census unit value of sales and slaughter was extrapolated through to 1926 by the wholesale prices of poultry in Toronto (from HSC Series L106) and the unit values of stock of poultry were extrapolated from the decennial census value of 1921 to 1926 by the OBI annual unit value of stocks data; third, the unit price for sales and slaughter was extrapolated annually from 1910 to 1900 on the basis of the OBI unit value of sales and was then extrapolated from 1900 to 1870 by the unit values of egg production (obtained from the section on estimation of income from egg production); fourth, the unit value of the stock of poultry was interpolated between the Census of Canada unit values of stocks for 1900 and 1910 by the OBI annual unit value series; finally, the census unit value of stock for 1900 was extrapolated on an annual basis back to 1870 by use of the series of egg unit values from the section on eggs. (Two qualities of the data are noted: between 1891 and 1900, for which years the OBI data are available, the movement of egg prices was very similar to the movement of OBI unit values for both stocks and sales and slaughter, which last two were very similar; the index of the wholesale prices of fowl in Toronto moved in almost identical fashion with the index of the OBI sales and slaughter unit values which were available until the year 1924-25.)

The values of production of poultry were then obtained, year by year, by multiplying the changes in the stock of poultry by the unit value of poultry, multiplying the number of birds sold or slaughtered by the unit values of sales and slaughter and then summing the two.

Dairy Products

The farm segment of the dairy industry comprises the production of fluid milk. The production of dairy products is comprised of three components derivative from milk production viz.: (i) fluid milk itself used for farm or non-farm human consumption; (ii) butter, farm and creamery produced; (iii) cheese, almost entirely factory produced. Of these components, butter has been by far the largest user of fluid milk.

As in many other cases, the farm value of dairy products is derived by multiplying quantities produced by price.

The proportionate distribution of the entire use of fluid milk in 1920 and 1926 is given below. It is based on official figures.

Proportionate Disposition of all Milk

	1920	1926
Farm butter	0.220	0.180
Creamery butter	0.238	0.308
Cheddar cheese	0.152	0.143
Fluid sales *	0.143	0.141
Farm consumption by persons	0.140	0.152
All other**	0.107	0.076

Source: Based on data in HSC, p.374 (also HAS.II)

* Includes milk equivalent of cream sales for fluid use. ** Includes milk for concentrated products and for ice cream and farm fed milk (the latter accounting for 0.079 of all milk in 1920).

The method of obtaining estimates of the various quantities of milk produced for the period 1870 to 1920 was: to make estimates of per capita consumption for each of butter, cheese and fluid milk (the latter including an allowance for ice cream and concentrated milk products both of which were relatively small until the 1920s); to get Canadian consumption of each product by multiplication of per capita values by population; to then obtain production estimates by adding exports to domestic use and subtracting imports therefrom. It is worth noting at this juncture that by far the larger part of the cheddar cheese was exported; quite substantial amounts of butter were also exported in several periods; fluid milk, itself, did not enter into the external trade.

The basic per capita consumption estimates were obtained in the decennial censuses for census years. For the most part, the estimates of per capita consumption of various components for intercensal years were obtained by straight line interpolation of the per capita figures for the bracketing census years.

The external trade data were available for every year.

The quantities of milk products produced as final products, for years 1920 to 1926, were DBS estimates, published in HSC, pp.374 and 375.

The estimates of the various per capita Canadian consumption figures for the census years were as follows.

Per Capita Consumption of Dairy Products, Canada

	1870	1880	1890	1900	1910	1920
Butter consumption (in lbs. of butter)	16.6	24.7	23.5	23.4	28.1	24.0
Cheese consumption (in lbs. of cheese)	3	3	3	3	3	3
Fluid milk consumption (in lbs. of milk)	300	320	340	360	370	370

It is to be noted that the official figures are based on the premises that one pound of butter requires 23.4 pounds of milk for its production and one pound of cheese requires 11.2 pounds of milk.

Cheese consumed domestically is not a large user of milk; the very large exports of cheese do require large quantities of milk.

We shall deal with the estimates of the various components of milk in the order: first, butter, on account of its dominance of milk use, then cheese, and, finally, fluid milk for human consumption.

Butter

Production of farm butter (sometimes called dairy butter) was reported in every census from 1870-71 onward. Production of creamery butter (including that produced in mixed cheese and creamery factories) measured in pounds of butter was collected also in the censuses for 1920, 1910 and 1900. Value of production of butter factories was also obtained in the censuses of manufactures for 1880 and 1890: an approximate quantity for production can be derived since the unit value of butter produced was available from other sources. We point out that, at least from 1893 onward, OBI collected statistics of creamery factories, although its writers complained on occasion that there were quite a number of unreported creameries.

Since considerable amounts of butter are exported (and fully reported) the estimate procedures were as follows.

First, per capita consumption of butter in Canada was calculated for each census year from estimates of total production, exports and imports, yielding the following results.

Year	Per Capita Consumption of Butter (lbs)	Year	Per Capita Consumption of Butter (lbs.)
1870	16.6	1920	24.0
1880	20.4	1921	26.8
1890	23.5	1922	27.2
1900	23.4	1923	29.1
1910	28.1	1924	28.5
1920	24.0	1925	28.4
		1926	29.4

Source: From HSC.

This butter could have been converted to a milk equivalent at 23.4 lbs. of milk per pound of butter, but such was not done as it was more convenient to obtain a value for the milk used in butter production directly from the butter production figures. The calculation of the per capita consumption figures for 1900, 1910 and 1920 was quite straight-forward from production data (census) plus foreign trade data. The calculations for 1870, 1880 and 1890 were somewhat more speculative. The farm butter production was reported in the census for each year. The values of creamery production produced in butter factories were available in the censuses of industry for 1880 and 1890 and an estimate of creamery production of butter was made by attributing a price of $0.20 per pound of butter in 1890 and 17.6 cents per pound of butter in 1880 to derive a quantity produced from the values. (Creamery production was small in both 1880 and 1890). There is no record of creameries or butter factories at all in the 1870 census and it is probable that they were so few as to be negligible at that time. (The 1901 census has a discussion of the times at which creameries and cheese factories began and that discussion confirms the view that butter factories were almost absent in 1870; some cheese factories also produced butter.)

Per capita consumption for each intercensal year between 1870 and 1910 was obtained by straight line interpolation between the census year values; for the decade 1910 to 1920, the per capita consumption was placed at 28.0 lbs. for 1911 to 1914, at 26.0 lbs for 1915 and 24 lbs (wartime years) for 1916 to 1919; per capita consumption of butter for 1920 to 1926 was taken from HSC, p.380, Series L310.

The population figures for obtaining national consumption of butter were from HSC Series A1.

The external trade in butter is based ultimately on *Trade of Canada* annual reports for fiscal years ending in the year following the calendar year for which data are given.

Cheese

Throughout the entire period the cheese market is characterized by the fact that net exports exceeded domestic consumption of cheese for all but the first year (1870) and for most years by very large amounts: for instance, in 1900, total production is above 221 million lbs., exports 196 million lbs. and domestic consumption 25 million lbs. Owing to the fact that cheese is aged (by as much as 3 years) production of a given year may be reflected in exports of immediately succeeding years (although most of the exported cheese is probably aged abroad). Nevertheless, the complete annual data on cheese exports and imports provides direct information on a major part of the production of this sector.

The data for 1870 to 1914 and 1915 to 1926 were obtained by different means.

The estimates of cheese production for 1870 to 1914 were based on two components, domestic consumption and net exports, except for the years 1900, 1907 and 1910 for which years production was based on on Census of Canada data.   The figure for per capita domestic consumption of cheese was set at three pounds per capita throughout the period and total domestic consumption was derived by multiplication of this per capita consumption by population numbers.   The net exports relevant to year t were taken as the recorded net exports for the trade year ending in year t+1.   (Trade years ended June 30 until 1906 and March 31 from 1907 onward.)   Imports were relatively very small compared with exports.   The figure of three pounds per capita consumption was derived from production and trade data — factory production less net exports divided by population — for various combinations of years as follows:

	Per Capita Consumption (lbs. of factory cheese)
Average 1900, 1907, 1910, 1920	2.95
Average 1900, 1907, 1910 and 1915 to 1921	2.96
Average 1900, 1907, 1910 and 1915 to 1926	3.13

While the figure for 1900, derived as above, was 4.75 lbs. per capita, that for 1907 was 2.44 lbs. and for 1910, 2.70 lbs.   The figures for a particular year, of course, may be subject to measurement problems in the imperfect matching of production and trade data: the high 1900 figure may be explained, in part, as a statistical artifact of that sort, since it is so much higher than the figure for 1907, 1910 and every year but one for 1915 to 1921; at the same time it is possible that cheese consumption in the newly settled west was lower than that of the older provinces but such an effect would be of limited size in 1907.   The one trend that does seem apparent is the increase in per capita consumption from 1922 to 1926 which carried over into later years.   In any event it was our best judgement that a uniform per capita consumption figure of three pounds was the best measure to use for each year from 1870 to 1914 in which years its use was a part of the method of estimation and this figure would also take account of the small amount of farm-produced cheese.

For the years from 1915 to 1928 production data were taken directly from official sources — the Canadian Statistical service obtained the data annually from 1915 onward.   These annual data are given in HSC Series L256.   The official sources are cited therein.

Fluid Milk

The third component of final use of milk products is fluid milk used for human consumption or for providing liquid cream (other than that used for butter) a relatively small item.

The per capita consumption figures adopted for these calculations for census years follow.

Year	Per Capita Consumption of Fluid Milk (pounds per person per annum)
1870	300
1880	320
1890	340
1900	360
1910	370
1920	370

Source: For 1920: HSC Series L306 gives per capita consumption of fluid milk in 1920 at 362.8 pounds: this is obtained by dividing "fluid sales" (Series L249) plus "farm home – consumed" (L251) by population (Series A1) at 8,556,000. The figure of 370 allows something for ice cream (Series L247) at 10.6 pounds per capita. For 1911: Total quantity of milk produced (1911 census) at 9,807 million pounds less factory use of milk = 6,902 million pounds leaves 2,905 million pounds of which about 10 percent will be farm fed and wasted leaving 2,615 million pounds for fluid milk consumption = 374 pounds per capita. 1900 and earlier: Total production of milk in pounds for 1900 (reported in the 1911 census of agriculture (Census 1911, Agriculture, p. LXXXVIII) is obviously too low — it implies per capita consumption of fluid milk of 211 pounds per person.

There are alternative checks on the projects dairy products data. The number of milk cows on farms at the time of taking of the census is available for every census. The production of the milk equivalent of butter (23.4 pounds of milk per pound of butter) and of cheese (11.2 pounds of milk per pound of cheese) added to the consumption of fluid milk yields the following production for these uses per milk cow. Comparable figures for total U.S. production of milk per cow are given back to 1889 which is as far back as the full data go (*U.S. Historical Statistics*, p.523).

Production Per Milk Cow
(pounds of milk)

Year	Canada	Year	U.S., All Milk
1870	2,454		
1880	2,827		
1890	3,122	1889	3,047
1900	3,427	1899	3,883
1910	3,587	1909	3,344
1920	3,169	1919	3,116

The Canadian figures look reasonable compared with the U.S. figures: the Canadian figure for 1880 is probably too high on account of the overestimate of factory butter; the U.S. figure for 1899 looks quite out of line.

A further check is provided by overall per capita domestic disappearance of these three products in the U.S. and Canada.

Per Capita Consumption of Dairy Products
(pounds of product per annum)

Year	Canada			U.S.		
	Fluid Milk	Butter	Cheese	Fluid Milk	Butter	Cheese
1870	300	16.6	3		10.7	3.2
1880	320	20.4	3		15.5	2.7
1890	340	23.5	3		18.2	3.8
1900	360	23.4	3	315	20.1	3.7
1910	370	28.1	3	348	18.3	4.3
1920	370	24.0	3	337	14.9	4.0

Source for U.S. (*U.S. Historical Statistics* p.330)

Note that consumption of lard in the U.S. is quite high, which may account for some of the difference in butter consumption.

The per capita consumption of milk was interpolated linearly between each pair of adjacent census years for years 1870 to 1920. The per capita consumption values for 1921 to 1926 are official estimates taken from HSC p.380.

There were not any exports or imports of fluid milk.

Prices of Dairy Products

There were nominally three farm unit values (prices) for dairy produce: *viz.* milk for butter; milk for cheese; fluid milk, for farm consumption or off-farm use in other forms. In fact only two separate prices were used: one for farm-made butter and milk products sold for creamery butter was also used for fluid milk sales; a second price was used for milk in cheese making. These prices were obtained separately as follows.

The Farm Price of Dairy (farm-made) Butter

A unit value on the farm of "dairy" butter was obtained in the censuses of 1911 and 1921 for each of the years 1910 and 1920. These values were 22.1 cents a pound of butter in 1910 and 48.5 cents per pound in 1920 (Census, 1921, Vol. IV *Agriculture* p. cvii). The wholesale price of dairy butter in Toronto in 1910 was 23.25 cents per pound and in 1920 was 52.5 cents per pound, a much inflated value, (the Ontario farm unit value of dairy butter in 1920 was 50.3 cents per pound). In view of this evidence, the price used to evaluate dairy butter, at the farm throughout was taken to be equal to one cent per pound less than the wholesale price in Toronto of dairy butter. (Source: 1890 to 1913 and later, *Wholesale Prices; Prices and Price Indexes, 1913-1926*, p.54; 1870 to 1889, H. Michell. Now a pound of butter requires about 23 pounds of milk (we used 23.4 pounds of milk per pound of butter — the figure used by DBS). The value of this butter at the farm per pound of milk content then was 1.0 cents per pound of milk in 1910 and 2.24 cents per pound of milk in 1920. And the farm unit value of milk per pound as reported in the censuses of agriculture in 1910 and 1920 were 10.5 cents and 22.2 cents per pound of milk, respectively. It looks as though dairy butter was selling at prices that just covered the value of the milk content, the implication being that the use of the by-products of dairy butter production, the skim milk, and buttermilk, for farm feed provided the recompense for the work of making the farm butter. The milk used for all butter then was valued at the same price as that used for farm butter as much of the creamery butter would have been made from purchases of cream from farmers, with there again being a skim-milk by-product.

Unit Values. Milk Used for Butter

The final product values at farms of dairy products in the form of butter or of dairy products sold to creameries to make butter was measured simply as the product of the quantity of butter in all forms and our estimate of price at the farm of farm butter as derived above. (Creamery butter prices ran at prices up to 20 percent above dairy butter prices.)

Unit Value of Fluid Milk at the Farm

Since the farm unit value of dairy butter just seemed to cover the milk cost of the butter, the unit value at the farm of fluid milk was made equal to the value of the milk used for butter and was obtained by dividing the price at the farm per pound of dairy butter by the factor 23.4 (the number of pounds of milk required to make a pound of butter) to yield a unit value per pound of fluid milk.

The Valuation of Milk Sold for Cheese Production

The estimates of the value of milk used for production of cheese in cheese factories for all years from 1870 to 1926 were made directly from the unit value of cheese rather than first converting cheese to milk and then valuing the milk.

The actual calculation of the farm value of milk used for cheese was obtained by subtracting 1.5 cents per pound of cheese from the unit value per pound of cheese of exports thereof to derive an estimate of the farm value of the milk used in the production of one pound of cheese. The multiplication of the number of pounds of cheese produced per year by this estimate of the farm value of the milk required to produce one pound of cheese provides the estimate of farm receipts for the production of milk for factory cheese.

There were several supporting data for the use of this method of valuation. First, correspondence between export unit values of cheese and wholesale prices is very close — export unit values tend to be slightly below wholesale prices at Montreal. (Wholesale prices from *Wholesale Prices*). Second, the unit values of exports of cheese correspond very closely with unit values at cheese factories as reported by the OBI (See OBI, 1901, p.64 for a long run — also earlier and later volumes) — the export unit values are perhaps ever so slightly above unit values at cheese factories. Third, census of industry reports show cost of materials ranging upward to seven-eighths of the value of the cheese produced. Fourth, the OBI from as early as 1883 onward obtained data on milk used by cheese factories and from 1894 onward amounts paid to "patrons" along with a unit price for milk purchased from patrons.

As an example, the following comparisons for the period 1893 to 1900 are reassuring: (From OBI *Report*, 1901). In making comparisons, it should be remembered that somewhere in the neighbourhood of 11 pounds of milk are used to produce one pound of cheese. (The DBS official figure for post-1918 is 11.4 pounds of milk per pound of cheese; the OBI ratio of milk used to cheese produced, varied slightly from year to year around, say, 10.65 pounds of milk per pound of cheese.)

Year	Value at the Factory of Cheese Per Pound (in cents)	Amount Paid to Patrons for Milk Necessary to Produce One Pound of Cheese (in cents)
1893	9.68	NA
1894	9.70	8.15
1895	7.88	6.34
1896	8.28	6.74
1897	8.53	7.06
1898	8.00	6.57
1899	9.83	8.65
1900	10.19	9.07
1901	9.09	7.98
1902	10.08	8.95
1903	10.41	9.30
1904	8.33	7.04
1905	10.56	9.46

NA — not available

Source: OBI *Report*, 1901, p.14, *Report*, 1906, p.44. The amount paid to patrons for milk requirements per pound of cheese was derived from the cost per pound of milk and the number of pounds of milk per pound of cheese, both of which are given in the table up to 1900 and could be calculated from the data for later years.

It may be seen that with the export price being slightly above the factory price the subtraction of 1.5 cents per pound from the export unit value approximates quite closely the price received by patrons.

Horses

Farm income from the production of horses is derived as a product of the net production of horses and a unit value of horses for each year.

Farm production was calculated as the sum of the annual net change in inventory of horses — inventory change for year t was calculated as the stock for year t+1 minus stock in year t — plus off-farm sales for nonfarm use, plus net exports. The method of estimation for each of these, in turn, follows.

Stock of Horses and Changes in Inventory

A Note on the Statcan Numbers for the Horse Stock

The coverage of nonfarm horses in the census data requires attention. Although in most censuses before 1921 the numbers of horses given is labelled as being those on farms, it seems highly likely that the reported number includes a large part, if not all, of the nonfarm horses. In 1901, a separation is made between farms and lots and there are quite large numbers (166,978 head) on the lots. All of the censuses from 1871 to 1911 give number of horses broken down by quite a large number of local divisions, counties or census divisions, including cities, and, in one case, by city wards. Usually a division by age is also given, such as horses under three years old, as well as three year olds and up. The data given for cities record considerable numbers of adult horses, three year olds and up, but very few young horses indeed, the latter feature contrasting strongly with data for non-urban areas. For example, in 1901, Toronto centre had 773 horses three years and older and only 5 head under three years, while for the whole country there were 1,150,938 horses three years and older and 259,577 under three years of age; in 1891, Toronto city had 7,269 horses over three years old and 132 horses three years old and under compared with, for all Canada, 1,068,584 horses over three years old and 401,988 who were three years and under. It seems most likely that the horses reported for cities are for dray or carriage purposes, an inference supported by the near absence of young horses. In the census of 1921, the total stock of horses in the country is divided between those on farms and those elsewhere than on farms: there were 158,742 horses elsewhere.

It is not clear what is covered in the horse stock figures given in HAS.VI. The series is labelled "Horses: Numbers on Farms at June 1, ... 1871-1973" yet the figures used for census years for 1871 to 1911 are the census values, described above: consequently, these census year data include many if not all of the nonfarm horses. On the other hand, the 1921 data in HAS.VI are for horses on farms only. The foregoing situation makes interpretation of the annual figures in the HAS.VI which are available from 1906 onward difficult. One would presume that the numbers given for 1906 to 1910 are at the same level of comprehensiveness as the census figures for 1901 and 1911; the figures for 1912 to 1920 in HAS.VI must undergo a change from the more comprehensive coverage of horse numbers in the 1911 census to the farms-only number of the 1921 census but there is no indication of how or when the transition took place; one may safely presume that the HAS.VI numbers for 1922 to 1926 inclusive are only for horses on farms. (Incidentally, the censuses were taken at April 1 from 1871 to 1901 and the count of horses was taken at that date.)

Estimation of Stock of Horses for 1871 to 1906

For these years the estimates of the annual stock of horses were made on a province by province basis. For all provinces, the data of the census of Canada for census years were used; in 1871 the number of horses in Prince Edward Island, obtained from its census, was included in the total for Canada. The data for 1905-06 and 1906-07 were obtained by use of HAS.VI (See also HSC, p.367). The interpolation was done in the following way.

1870-71 to 1880-81

For all provinces, the stocks in the intercensal years were calculated on a straight line basis between 1871 and 1881 and they were extrapolated to 1870 on the same basis.

1881 to 1906

For Ontario, from 1881 to 1906, interpolation between census years and from 1901 to 1906 was done basically by using the OBI horse count as interpolator. The OBI count for Ontario was obtained annually from 1882 onward for a date in June. The 1882 figure, obtained through the schools, appeared low in view of the count for later years and it became necessary to extrapolate the OBI numbers of horses from 1883 onward back to 1881 to overlap with the census: this extrapolation was done on the basis of the trend in numbers from 1883 to 1891. From 1881 to 1891 and from 1891 to 1901 and 1901 to 1907 the method of using the interpolator was like that already described for cattle — it was assumed that the numbers of horses departed from straight line interpolation between the census values for census years and 1907 in the same proportion that the OBI actual data departed from a straight line interpolation of the OBI data between each of these pairs of base years, i.e. 1881, 1891, 1901 and 1907. While the year 1907 was used for interpolation for the years 1902 to 1905, the actual figure for Ontario from HAS.VI was used for 1906. The year 1907 was used for interpolation purposes because it corresponded to the year for the stock in the western census of 1906, taken in 1907.

The comparative census and OBI base year data follow:

Number of Horses in Ontario
(thousands of horses)

	1891	1901	1907
Census of Canada	771.8	721.1	764.5 (HAS)
OBI	678.5	620.3	725.7

For each of New Brunswick, Nova Scotia, Prince Edward Island and Quebec, calculated individually, the OBI data were used to interpolate between census of Canada data for census years and for 1906-07 for each province.

Data for Manitoba from 1891 onward played the same part for the western provinces that the OBI figures had for the eastern provinces. Before 1891, linear interpolation of census data was used: Manitoba had a census of agriculture in 1886 and straight line interpolations was used between the Census of Canada data for 1881 and 1886 and again between 1886 and the Census of Canada figure for Manitoba in 1891. The estimates for British Columbia and for the Territories (Alberta, Saskatchewan, *et al*) for 1881 to 1891 were obtained by linear interpolation of Census of Canada figures for the two years.

Manitoba had an estimate of the stock of horses from 1893 onward; a figure on a comparable basis for 1891 was estimated by assuming that the horse population (Manitoba count basis) changed in the same proportion as the acreage in wheat, oats, and barley crops between 1891 and 1893. (The acreage in 1891 was 0.8087 of that in 1893.) The horse population in 1892 was then taken as half way between 1891 and 1893. The Province of Manitoba data on the horse stock, extended to 1891 as just described, were then used as an interpolator between the Census of Canada data for Manitoba, the Territories and British Columbia, for 1891 and 1901 and, 1901 and the 1907 HAS figure which was the figure obtained in taking the western census for 1906, taken in 1907. The HAS figures were used for 1906.

The Census of Canada and the Province of Manitoba figures compare as follows.

Number of Horses on Farms in Manitoba

	1891	1901	1907
Census, Canada	86,735	163,867	228,700 (HAS)
Province, Manitoba	76,622 (est.)	141,080	173,212

Estimation of the Stock of Horses Annually, 1906 to 1927

These estimates were taken from HAS.VI.

The 1911 figure in HAS.VI is that of the census of 1911. The 1921 figure in the HAS.VI is for horses on farms, from the 1921 census; however, we used a figure for all horses from the 1921 census, which was our only departure from the *Handbook* series.

Change in Stock Inventory

The net change in inventory of horses was calculated, for each year, from the stock data. The net change in the stock inventory assigned to year t was obtained as the remainder of the stock in the t+1 less the stock in year t; since there was not a stock figure for 1870 the change in inventory for 1870 was assumed to be of the same size as the yearly change between 1871 and 1881. As noted above, the change in nonfarm stock is probably largely covered in the so-called "farm" stock until 1911. Between 1911 and 1921 our estimates are that the nonfarm stock declined and continued to decline in the 1920s: these changes will not be included in the project figures but they are not large in number.

Farm Sales of Horses for Off-Farm Use in Canada

The method of estimation of the off-farm stock of horses in Canada is given in the section on oats.

The changes in nonfarm inventory, of which account is taken, are those that were covered in the total stock of so-called farm horses. No further allowances for changes in the nonfarm horse stock were made.

However, a portion of the nonfarm stock that dies each year has to be replaced and the replacement is largely done from farm-raised horses. It is assumed that the working life of a horse is such that ten per cent of the nonfarm stock has to be replaced each year. (This assumes a working life of approximately 10 years or a little less.) Hence sales of farmers to nonfarm owners were taken to be equal to 10 percent of the nonfarm stock.

Net Exports of Horses

Numbers of horses exported and imported and hence net exports were obtained from the usual *Trade of Canada* annual reports. In later years (the 1920s) a category called imports for exhibition was included.

Total net farm production then became the sum of the above three categories, *viz.*, additions to inventory, sales for off-farm use in Canada and net exports. (Actually from 1898-99 to 1913-14 and from 1919-20 to 1926-27 imports exceeded exports in number, in many years substantially.)

Unit Values of Horses Sold Off Farms

In this section, first, a description will be given of the way the unit values were obtained and, second, a critique of these values will be given.

The period 1891 to 1920 is dealt with first. Unit values of the stock of horse could be obtained from each census year for the date of the taking of the census, *viz.*, 1901, 1911, and 1921. The unit value of horses sold from farms on which raised were available from the 1921 census (for sales in calendar 1920). The unit value of sales of all horses, including all intra-farm sector sales, were obtained in the census of Canada for 1911 but were not used in project calculations since it is not known to what extent all farms sales were representative of off-farm sales. Rather, a unit off-farm sales value was calculated for 1910 and 1900 as the product of the census stock unit value at the time of taking of the census multiplied by the ratio of the off-farm sales unit value in 1920 to the stock unit value at June 1, 1921, both from the 1921 census. (The foregoing ratio was 1.0527.) The unit values follow.

Stock and Off-farm Sales Unit Values
1900-01, 1910-11, 1920-21

	1900	1910	1920
Unit value of stock at census date ($)	74.98	146.95	121.54
Unit value off-farm sales ($)	(78.93)	(154.69)	127.94

Bracketed figures are calculated.

The interpolator between 1900 to 1910 and between 1910 to 1920 and extrapolator from 1900 to 1891 was the unit value of sales of horses recorded annually for Ontario by OBI: these were all sales including inter-farm sales. The OBI stock count (and value) were taken in June of each year and the annual sales data were for the 12 months immediately preceding the date of the stock count i.e. from June to June.

The interpolation-extrapolation was done as follows. The ratio of the census unit value of sales to OBI unit values of sales were calculated for 1900, 1910 and 1920. The ratios were of census unit values to OBI unit values for the average of the two years that each extend six months into the census year, e.g. the ratio of the census unit value for 1920 to the average of the OBI unit value for 1919-20 and 1920-21. The resulting ratios follow.

Ratios: Census Sales Unit Value
to OBI Sales Unit Value

	1900	1910	1920
Ratio	0.9601	1.089	0.962

These ratios were interpolated linearly for intervening years between pairs of years above and extrapolated from 1900 to 1891 at the single ratio 0.96. Multiplication of these ratios by the OBI unit selling value for the OBI year ending in June of the following year yielded the unit value used for valuation of sales, in the given year. This procedure gave unit values for 1891 to 1920.

For 1921 to 1926, farm unit values of the stock of horses (for June of the year following) were multiplied by 1.053, the ratio of the census unit value of sales for 1920 to the census unit value of stock in June, 1921 (source of data for 1921 to 1926, HAS.VI, p. 100).

For 1870 to 1890 the unit values for sales were obtained by multiplying the export unit value by 0.6766, the average ratio for several years in the period from 1891 onward of the unit value of sales, as previously calculated to the unit value of exports. Exports of horses were quite substantial from 1890 to 1900 at which time they were beginning to decline.

Value of Production of Horses

The value of production of horses was calculated by multiplying the farm production of horses as noted above (inventory change plus sales of horses for nonfarm use plus net exports) by the unit values per year.

An Evaluation of the Unit Value Data

There can be argument about the unit values that should be used for the valuation of horses. A good argument could probably be made just to use the OBI sales unit values or to use them as a stringer for the 1920 unit values of off-farm sales from the Canadian census. The project method for 1910 may appear to give a too high unit value for that year. The following comparisons are perhaps relevant in making a judgement.

Census: Sales unit values for 1920 ÷ Stock unit value at June, 1921 = 1.053
OBI: Sales unit value for year ending June, 1921 ÷ Stock unit value in June, 1921 = 1.165
OBI Sales unit values: Year ending June, 1911 ÷ Year ending June, 1921 = 1.163
OBI Stock unit values: June 1, 1911 ÷ June, 1921 = 1.285
DBS Stock figure: June 1, 1911 ÷ June 1, 1921 = 1.209
Project sales unit value: Year 1910 ÷ Year 1920 = 1.3164

In defence of the prices used for 1910-11 it seems probable that there were considerably larger proportions of colts in 1910-11 when the horse population was growing rapidly than in 1920-21 when it was relatively static. These larger numbers would be present in stocks and affect stock values as well as in a sales figure that includes all sales. The OBI figures included all sales, including inter-farm sales, and probably included considerable proportions of the colts. It is not likely that there would be many colts in the off-farms sales. Colts sales values would be considerably less than those for adult horses.

The 1900 and 1920 figures seem to be pretty much consistent one with the other.

Seeds, Grass and Clover

Since the sale of seeds within the agricultural sector is merely a transfer within agriculture and since the non-agricultural sale of these products in Canada is negligibly small, the measure of the off-farm receipts for these products was simply the value of net exports (exports less imports). The problem then became one of obtaining the correct data for the components covered in this category.

Exports: The value of exports was obtained from the trade categories as follows: for 1870-71 to 1887-88, the value of exports of this category were obtained by subtracting the value of flaxseed exported from the figures given for total seeds; for 1888-89 to 1926-27, the value of exports was obtained as the sum of the entries for "clover" seeds, "grass" seeds and "seeds n.e.s.".

Sources of all data: reports in *Trade of Canada*, annual reports — also available in some issues of CYB.

Imports: Value of imports of this category was calculated as the value of total seed imports less flaxseed, less aromatic, non-edible and crude seeds less bulbous roots.

Sources of all data were the individual reports in *Trade of Canada*.

Note: It is to be noted that in many years, the value of seed imports exceeded the value of exports. When such was the case the entry in the revenue side of the farming operations was negative. For a relatively small item such as this category, it was thought best to leave all of the entries in either the revenue or the expenses rather than putting the data in the revenue side when export values exceed import values and in the expenses side when the value of imports exceeded export values.

Wool

The method of measuring income received by agriculture for wool was the multiplication of an estimate of the physical value of wool production by a unit value, for each year for the entire period.

Estimation of the Quantity of Wool Produced

The base year estimates of the quantity of wool produced was reported in the census for every census year as follows:

Year	Production in Pounds
1870-71	11,592,123
1880-81	11,300,736
1890-91	10,031,970
1900-01	10,657,597
1910-11	6,933,955
1920-21	11,338,268
1930-31	12,794,634

Interpolation, or in the case of the 1920's extrapolation was done in three different ways for different periods. From 1870-71 to 1881-82 production was estimated by linear interpolation between the census years 1870-71 to 1880-81 and extrapolation by the same yearly change to 1881-82 — Prince Edward Island production was included in 1870-71 output; from 1881-82 to 1910-11, annual production data for Ontario, obtained by OBI and published in its annual statistical publication were used to interpolate Canadian production between 1881-82 and 1890-91, 1890-91 and 1900-01 and between 1900-01 and 1910-11; from 1910-11 to 1920-21, the average production of wool per unit of the stock of sheep and lambs was interpolated linearly between 3.088 pounds of wool per beast in 1910-11 to 3.567 pounds per beast in 1920-21 and the resulting production per year was multiplied by the number of sheep and lambs (HAS.VI, p.80); for 1920-21 to 1926-27, the DBS data on production were used (*ibid.*, p.116).

Prices

The price used for valuing the wool crop for the years 1870 to 1919 was the import unit value derived from the record of the very large imports. The import unit value compares with the unit value of product as reported in the census as follows.

Year	Census Unit Value ($/lb.)	Import Unit Value ($/lb.)	Export Unit Price ($/lb.)	Wholesale Price (Washed Wool) ($/lb.)
1900-01	.177	.151	.179	.177
1910-11	.231	.233	.215	.214
1920-21	.298	.548	.297	
1921-22	--	.251	.233	

The import and export values are for the fiscal year ending June 1 for 1900-01 and April 1 for 1910-11 and 1920-21 whereas the census unit value is presumably for the calendar year. The great divergence is in the import unit value for 1920-21: this divergence must be explained in the difference in timing of contracting exports and imports and timing of valuing of the census year product.

DBS produced conflicting sets of price figures. Its data in MBAS 1923 p.472 give considerably higher prices than does *Prices and Price Indexes, 1913-1926*, pp. 58-59 and likewise MBAS, 1917. Further, the "average farm price per pound" given in HAS.VI, p.116 for the period 1920 to 1965 gives average farm prices for 1920 at about two-thirds the census unit value for the year, though only slightly below for 1930.

In the light of all the above circumstances, the prices for 1920 to 1926 were derived as follows: the price for 1920 was the unit value for 1920 reported in the census of 1921; prices for the years 1921 to 1926 were obtained by indexing the unit value of the census for 1920 by the prices given in HAS.VI.

Forest Products

See the general section on forestry in Chapter 3.

FARM EXPENSES

The reader is referred to the statement at the beginning of the section on agriculture for a general statement concerning the approach to measuring expenses.

A description of the way in which farm expenses were calculated will be given, item by item, according to the categories of expenses given in Table 1.10 of the published estimates. These items follow in order.

Repairs to Farm Buildings

The estimates of costs of repairs to farm buildings were made by first obtaining estimates for each year of the values of farm buildings in Canada and then multiplying these values, year by year, by an estimate of the ratio of repair expenses to the values of buildings. The derivation of estimates of farm building values is described first.

Values of Farm Buildings

Values of farm buildings were estimated separately with some variation in method for each of the following periods:

> 1870-71 to 1879-80
> 1880-81 to 1899-1900
> 1900-01 to 1909-10
> 1910-11 to 1920-21
> 1921-22 to 1926-27

Years are reported in the form "t"-"t+1" where "t" is the year to which production of agricultural products applies and "t+1" is the year in which the value of farm buildings is measured. This procedure is followed because, in a census year, the census is taken at April 1 (until 1901) or June 1 (after 1901): the value of buildings applies to the census date itself; the values of farm production is taken for the calendar year preceding the census date. Thus census data for 1900-01 give building values at April 1, 1901 and production of crop and livestock products in 1900.

The crucial or base years are the census years. Values of farm buildings were first collected in the census of Canada for 1900-01: they were collected for the province of Ontario on an annual basis as early as 1882-83.

(i) Decade 1870-71 to 1879-80

There were not census data on value of farm buildings for 1870-71 and not any direct values for other years of this decade. To make an estimate for each year of this decade, the 1880-81 value of farm buildings (derivation described in the descriptions of estimates for 1880-81 to 1899-1900) was extrapolated back to 1870-71 on a yearly basis by an index of the value of gross farm income. This index had the following values:

Year	Index	Year	Index
1870-71	0.872	1875-76	0.916
1871-72	0.898	1876-77	0.884
1872-73	0.896	1877-78	0.914
1873-74	0.907	1878-79	0.847
1874-75	0.958	1879-80	1.008
		1880-81	1.000

Value of buildings in 1880-81 $ 251,935,746.

(ii) Decades 1880-81 to 1899-1900

Basic data were: the values of farm buildings, at April 1, 1901, available on a provincial basis, obtained in the federal 1900-01 census; the values of farm buildings in Ontario on an annual basis from 1882-83 to 1900-01 obtained and published by OBI; acreages of land under crops by province.

The OBI estimates were extrapolated from 1882-83 to 1880-81 in two steps: the increment in farm building values between 1882-83 and 1890-91 was divided by 8 to provide a notional average increment for each of the eight years; this average increment was then subtracted from the figure for 1882-83 to obtain an estimate for 1881-82 and a like amount was subtracted again to get an estimate for 1880-81. The relevant figures for Ontario are:

Year	Value of Farm Buildings	
1890-91	$191,268,327	Actual OBI figure
1882-83	163,030,675	Actual OBI figure
1881-82	159,500,969	extrapolated
1880-81	155,971,262	extrapolated

The annual series for Ontario is derived very simply. The Canadian census of 1901 reported the value of farm buildings in Ontario at $211,206,905 compared with the OBI estimate for the same date of $226,575,278. It was decided to use the Canadian census value for 1901 since it was the only source for farm building values in the other provinces as well. The series of values then used for Ontario for 1880-81 to 1899-1900 was obtained by multiplying the OBI figure for each year by the ratio (211,206,905) ÷ (226,575,228), being the ratio of Canadian census value of buildings in 1900-01 to the corresponding OBI value for the same year.

The estimation of values of farm buildings in all other provinces required a little more complicated procedure as follows. First, the value of buildings per acre of land under crops was calculated for Ontario for 1881 and 1891 from OBI data and for 1901 from Census of Canada (found in HSC, p.352; see also Census, 1921 VII, various pages). (The OBI acreage under crops in 1881 was calculated by simple linear extrapolation of the acreages in 1891 and in 1882.) Second, the value of buildings per acre of land under crops was calculated for all provinces, other than Ontario, as a group for 1901 from Census of Canada data (HSC p.352 and Census of Canada). The Ontario value of buildings per acre of land under crop was $22.135 and the value of buildings per acre of land under crop for all other provinces as a group was $15.803 in 1901. It was assumed that the value of buildings per acre of land under crop for all provinces other than Ontario in 1891 and 1881 bore the same ratio to the Ontario value of buildings as in 1901: in other words the building values per acre of land under crops for all provinces but Ontario was obtained for 1881 and 1891 by multiplying the Ontario values by (15,803)÷(22,135). The aggregate values of farm buildings for all provinces but Ontario for 1880-81 and 1890-91 were then obtained by multiplying the relevant acreage under crops for these years (HSC p.352) by the estimated values of farm buildings per acre. Estimates of farm buildings values for all provinces other than Ontario were made by linear interpolation between the census years 1880-81 to 1890-91 and 1890-91 to 1900-01.

The total values of farm buildings for all Canada were then obtained as a simple sum of the values for Ontario and values for all other provinces. Aggregate values of Ontario farm buildings were consistently larger than the totals for all other provinces.

(iii) Decade 1900-01 to 1910-11

The estimates of values of buildings in this decade were obtained quite simply. Census of Canada data (obtained from Census of 1931, Vol. VIII, p.4) gave the values of farm buildings in all Canada in 1900-01 and 1910-11 as follows.

Census Year	Value of Farm Buildings, All Canada
1900-01	$395,815,143
1910-11	823,951,767

The first step, but not the final one, was to interpolate values for intervening years linearly. The second step was to use the OBI data on farm building values for every year in the period 1900-01 to 1910-11 as a indicator of the extent to which the change (growth) of the farm buildings in Ontario departed from a linear path between the end years: the procedure was to get annual values between the two end (census) years on a straight linear interpolation and then to calculate the ratio of the values of farm buildings as actually obtained by OBI for each year to the values obtained by straight line interpolation. These ratios were:

Ratio of Actual Building Values to Linearly
Interpolated Values, Ontario

Year	Ratio	Year	Ratio
1900-01	1.000	1905-06	1.004
1901-02	1.007	1906-07	1.012
1902-03	1.011	1907-08	0.992
1903-04	1.016	1908-09	0.994
1904-05	1.005	1909-10	0.993
		1910-11	1.000

As may be seen the departures of the Ontario data from linearity is very small.

The third step was to multiply the linearly interpolated values for all Canada by the foregoing ratios, year by year, to obtain estimates of values of farm buildings in each year for all Canada. This process amounts to using the OBI data for Ontario as the interpolator between census years for all Canada.

(iv) Decade 1910-11 to 1920-21

The procedure was similar, in principle, to that used for 1900-01 to 1910-11 but slight variations were made. An agricultural census of the prairie provinces, taken in 1916, provided values of farm buildings for these provinces in 1915-16. The procedure followed then was: first, for the prairie provinces linear interpolations were made between the census values for 1910-11 and 1915-16 and similarly linear interpolations were made between census values for 1915-16 and 1920-21; second, linear interpolations of values for all the other provinces of Canada were made between the census years 1910-11 and 1920-21; third, the OBI annual data for Ontario were used to calculate ratios of actual values in Ontario to linearly interpolated values between 1910-11 and 1915-16 and between 1915-16 and 1920-21. Finally, the interpolated values for the prairie provinces and all other provinces in Canada were multiplied by these ratios and the two components were then added together to give totals year by year for all Canada. The procedures used for this decade departed from those used for 1900-01 to 1910-11 mainly in the use of the quinquennial agricultural censuses of the prairies to provide the census data for the prairie provinces in 1915-16.

The OBI ratios of actual farm values to linearly interpolated OBI values in this decade follow.

Ratios of OBI Actual Data to Linearly
Interpolated Data by 5-year Periods

Year	Ratio
1910-11	1.000
1911-12	1.029
1912-13	1.035
1913-14	1.017
1914-15	1.009
1915-16	1.000
1916-17	0.968
1917-18	0.932
1918-19	0.985
1919-20	1.018
1920-21	1.000

(v) The years 1920-21 to 1926-27

As in the preceding decade full agricultural censuses for all Canada were taken in 1920-21 and 1930-31 and an agricultural census of the prairie provinces was also taken in 1926. For the prairie provinces building values were linearly interpolated, first, between census data for 1920-21 and for 1925-26 and 1926-27 was obtained by linear interpolation between census values of 1925-26 and 1930-31. For the remaining provinces of Canada a linear interpolation between census data for 1920-21 and 1930-31 was first made. The Ontario Bureau of Industries only collected annual data of values of farm buildings until 1924. These OBI figures, then, could be used only to correct for departures from linear trend between the years 1920-21 and 1924-5 for both the region of the prairie provinces and the region of all other provinces. The values of farm buildings used for 1924-25 in the prairies were the linearly interpolated values between 1920-21 and 1925-26 and those used for 1926-27 were from the linear interpolation between 1925-26 and 1930-31. The values of farm building for provinces other than the prairie provinces for 1924-25 to 1926-27 were the linearly interpolated values between 1920-21 and 1930-31. Fortunately, there was little change in the values of farm buildings in this decade.

The annual repair costs for buildings were placed at 1.35 percent of the value of the buildings. This figure was obtained from a DBS mimeographed paper "Outline of Sources and Concepts etc." prepared by W.G. Morris dated February, 1963. The farm management group at the University of Saskatchewan used 1 percent of the value of farm buildings for the cost of repairs (College of Agriculture, University of Saskatchewan, *Agricultural Extension Bulletin No. 64* "Studies of Probable Net Farm Revenues for the Principal Soil Types of Saskatchewan on the Basis of Their Past Production", contributed by the Department of Farm Management, March, 1935). See also the DBS 1958 farm expenditure survey for information on this matter.

Repairs to Farm Machinery

Repairs to farm machinery were estimated at one percent (1%) of gross farm revenue from off-farm sales and farm-consumption, exclusive of income from forest-products. (Slight amendments to the estimates of farm revenues were made after these machinery repair estimates were calculated but the changes of revenue estimates were so small that the farm machinery repair estimates were not recalculated.) It remains to explain the justification for using this one percent figure.

The sources of information on machinery and machinery repair costs follow.

(i)   The value of farm machinery for all Canada, by province, was obtained in each decennial census from 1901 onward and for the prairie provinces in the prairie censuses taken in 1916 and in 1926. From these data estimates were made for the value of farm implements on farms in all years from 1870 onward by use of the same method as that used for farm buildings, which has been described, already, in the preceding section of these notes.

(ii)   In the preparation of the national income estimates for 1926 to 1937, by the staff of the Rowell-Sirois Royal Commission, data on sales of farm machinery repair parts by the 10 largest companies doing about 90 percent of the Canadian farm implement business were obtained by questionnaire from each company for each year. (Royal Commission on Dominion-Provincial Relations, *Report, Appendix 4, National Income* (Rowell-Sirois))

(iii)   Farm managements studies for Saskatchewan, between 1926 and 1933, by the Department of Farm Management of the College of Agriculture of the University of Saskatchewan provided data on machinery repair costs as well as blacksmithing costs for Saskatchewan farms which data were published in University of Saskatchewan, College of Agriculture, *Agricultural Extension Bulletin No. 64* (March, 1935).

(iv)   The official Statistics Canada estimates for 1926 onward give estimates of machinery repair costs plus blacksmithing, which appear to be based in considerable measure on the data described in sources (ii) and (iii) *supra*.

(v)   The availability of the value of farm equipment on farms in Ontario, annually, for 1882 onward to 1924, in Reports of the OBI has been implied already in the first category of source material described above.

There were three reasons for calculating machinery repair costs from gross farm income (excluding forest products) rather than from estimates of the value of farm machinery. (i) There are no data for costs of farm machinery repairs before 1926. Therefore one must rely on the data from 1926 onward from the Rowell-Sirois estimates and the official figures of DBS along with what can be gleaned from the Saskatchewan farm management data. In any event, neither Rowell-Sirois nor the official DBS estimates made any use of the estimates of the value of the stock of farm machinery in making estimates of repair costs. (ii) Another reason for having some reservation about using estimates of the value of the stock of machinery for deriving estimates of machinery repair costs is that it is not clear whether census estimates of farm machinery values are based on original cost or replacement cost — it might be expected that the latter would be a better extrapolator than the former but we do not have much information on this matter. (iii) A third reason for basing repair costs on gross agricultural income is that, even given the above reservations, it appears that the estimates of the value of the stock of farm machinery that we have reflects a relatively stable ratio of such values to agricultural income. These ratios follow.

Ratio of Estimated Value of Stock
of Farm Implements to Value of
Gross Agricultural Product

Year	Ratio
1880-81	0.50
1890-91	0.49
1900-01	0.50
1910-11	0.57
1920-21	0.57
1926	0.60

Given the changes in prices throughout this period, the above ratios reflect considerable stability and insufficient change to cause one to be disturbed by using gross farm product as an extrapolator of farm machinery expenses. If there is a bias in the procedure it would be to making estimates for the early years that are relatively too high compared with later years; but the bias, if there is one, would not be large.

The basis for using 1% (one percent) of gross farm revenue from off-farm sales plus farm-consumption of farm products, exclusive of income from forest products, as the estimate of expenditure on farm machinery repair rests entirely on data for 1926 onward. As noted above, the Rowell-Sirois national income estimation procedures resulted in a good estimate, from direct survey of farm machinery companies, of the sale of parts to farmers; at the same time, the Rowell-Sirois project made estimates of farm expenses for blacksmiths' services. By these estimates, these two categories of expenditure were about equal in magnitude. Statistics Canada (DBS) in its estimates for 1926 to 1949 combined these two items into one category and produced estimates that were very similar to the sum of the Rowell-Sirois for implement repairs and blacksmithing. The ratio of the Statcan estimates for the combined category to their measure of Realized Gross Income in Agriculture follow.

Ratio of Machinery Plus Blacksmith Expenses to Realized
Gross Farm Income, in Percentages

Years For Which an Average is Taken	Ratio
1926-30	1.52
1931-35	2.14
1936-40	2.09
1941-45	1.91
1946-49	2.09

Since, in the Rowell-Sirois estimates, machinery parts and blacksmiths expenses were about equal in size the machinery parts costs ran at about one percent of gross farm receipts in this period. (It will be noted that the ratio of these expenses to farm income was somewhat lower in the period of relatively good farm income in the 1920s than in the later period. It should also be pointed out that the figure for gross farm realized income that we used for 1926 was about 82 percent of the Statcan figure which included some inter-farm sales.)

Our estimates for blacksmith expenses are dealt with below.

Tractor Expenses

Tractor expenses are relevant only for the years 1907 to 1926.

Tractor expenses were estimated from three components which were: tractor expenses as calculated by DBS for 1926 (taken from HAS.II); an estimate of the number of tractors on farms for each year from 1907 to 1926; an estimate of the movements of prices of tractor fuel from year to year, 1907 to 1926. The technique used was: first, each of the number of tractors on farms and tractor fuel prices was put into index form with a common base year; second, these two indexes were combined into a single index by simple multiplication which meant giving each component equal weight; third, the single joint index was used to extrapolate the 1926 Statcan estimate of tractor expenses for 1926 backward to each year. It remains to describe the origin of each of the tractor number series and the fuel price series.

The numbers of tractors on farms came from two main sources: for the years 1920 to 1926, they came from HSC Series No. L318 — these data had been obtained from unpublished estimates by DBS; for 1907 to 1920, the estimates were obtained by subtracting a number equivalent to the number of tractor engines imported each year from the numbers in the stock of tractors at the end of the relevant year — the process involved working backward year by year from 1920 and the source of the data on imports were the annual reports *Trade of Canada* contained in the sessional papers of Canada.

The price series also came from two sources. For the period 1913 to 1926 the wholesale price index of petroleum products was used: Source: *Prices and Price Indexes* 1913-29, p.84 (or 1913-28 or 1913-27). For the period before 1913, the price of gasoline, converted into an index, was used: source, for 1907 to 1912-13, Board of Inquiry into the Cost of Living. *Report* Vol. II (1915), p.56, for 1913-14, *Wholesale Prices, 1914*, p.163.

Year	Number of Tractors on Farms	Wholesale Price of Petroleum Products 1913 = 100	Year	Number of Tractors on Farms	Wholesale Price of Petroleum Products 1913 = 100
1907	452	83.7	1917	18,288	114.4
1908	1,152	83.7	1918	25,129	123.7
1909	1,754	86.2	1919	40,236	128.1
1910	2,970	81.3	1920	47,456	157.8
1911	5,140	98.9	1921	51,832	139.2
1912	8,997	123.2	1922	55,914	129.2
1913	13,021	100.0	1923	57,428	107.6
1914	14,181	85.9	1924	60,015	109.8
1915	14,658	93.9	1925	65,480	102.9
1916	15,496	93.9	1926	75,482	112.8

Fertilizer Expenses

Fertilizer expenses were calculated from series on (i) value of product produced in Canada, (ii) imports of fertilizers, and (iii) exports of fertilizers. For the years 1870 to 1919 the farm use of fertilizers were calculated from the formula domestic production plus imports less exports all calculated in value terms; for the years 1920 to 1926 estimates were made by interpolation of farm expenditures between the beginning and ending year for each of which there was an official estimate of farm expenditure on fertilizer. It remains to deal with sources for each for these periods separately.

Period 1870 to 1919

(i) Domestic production

The first record of domestic production of fertilizer appears in the census of manufactures for 1890 where it appears in the small value of $20,000. The smallness of this figure was taken as justification for the assumption that domestic production began in 1890. The only other directly available estimates of domestic production of fertilizers were those provided in the censuses of manufactures for 1900 and 1910 and a figure was derivable, as will be explained below from the 1920 census. The specific sources of the estimates of value of production for the census years were: 1890 — Census of Manufactures, 1890 p. 149; 1900 — Census of Manufactures, 1900 p. 356-7; 1910 — Census of Manufactures, 1910 p. 5; 1920 — Census of Agriculture, 1920 p. 30 for farm expenditure on fertilizer, production being estimated by subtracting imports from farm expenditure and adding exports.

Estimates of value of production of fertilizers for intercensal years were obtained by straight line interpolation between adjacent pairs of census years.

(ii) Imports of fertilizers

Values of imports of fertilizers were obtained for each year from *Trade of Canada* publications as follows: for 1873 to 1914 — from *Trade of Canada, 1916, Part I,* p.422. Fertilizer is only recorded separately from 1873-74 onward: imports were small in 1873-74 and have been left at zero before then; for 1914-15 to 1918-19 — *Trade of Canada 1920*: imports p. 867, exports p.1302; for 1919-20 to 1920-21 — *Trade of Canada 1922*: imports pp. 1059-1060.

(iii) Exports of fertilizer

Values of exports of fertilizer were available from 1889-90 onward and being very small in that year were placed at zero before 1889-90; for 1889-90 to 1914-15 — *Trade of Canada 1916, Part I,* p.620 (one category only); for 1915-16 to 1918-19 — *Trade of Canada 1920*, page 1302; for 1919-20 to 1920-21 — *Trade of Canada 1922*: exports, p.1597.

Given these data the value of farm use of fertilizer was obtained by adding value of imports to value of production and subtracting value of exports. The data were used as they appeared in the source.

Period 1920-21 to 1926-27

For the period 1920-21 to 1926-27 a quite different technique was used.

The value of fertilizer used on farms was available for 1926 from official estimates in HAS.II, p.75. The value of fertilizer used on farms in 1920 was obtained from Census of Canada 1921, Vol. *Agriculture*, p.30.

The fertilizer expense figures for each of 1920 and 1926 were then deflated by the wholesale price index (base 1913) for chemicals and chemical products (*Prices and Price Indexes* 1913-26, p.84); a straight line interpolation was then made between these real values for 1920 and 1926 for intervening years; the whole series for 1920 to 1926 was then reflated by the same price index for chemicals and chemical products to get current dollar values for 1920 to 1926.

It should be noted that the category "fertilizers" in the import classification included nitrates of soda, sulphate of ammonia, and marinated and sulphated potash, from 1915-1916 onward but not before that year. Imports of nitrates of soda grew from 1900 onward to become an important item; the sulphate of ammonia and marinated and sulphated potash items were quite small and not important in themselves. These three categories of excluded items were added to the fertilizer category for 1900 to 1914. Before 1900 nitrates of soda were included in a large catch-all group and cannot be identified separately; this treatment probably reflected the smallness of this item at the time. In any event, nothing was added to the import category "fertilizers" before 1900: the excluded amounts are most probably insignificantly small.

It should also be noted that an estimate of the value at farm prices of domestically produced fertilizers in Canada in 1920, obtained by taking the value of farm purchases of fertilizer (from Census of Agriculture, 1920) then subtracting imports and adding exports yielded a figure of $7,685 thousand; the actual figure for GVP for "fertilizers" from the Census of Manufactures in 1920, was $3,788 thousand. This suggests that a considerable mark up on Census of Manufactures production values in 1910, 1900 and 1890 might have been desired. However, there is no basis on which to guess what the mark up should be. And the issue is not important, in any event as the Census of Manufactures GVP for fertilizers in 1910 was only $644 thousand in 1910, $100 thousand in 1900 and $20 thousand in 1890.

Truck and Auto Expenses

There were three main components to the estimation of truck and auto expenses on farms. First, a series of the number of automobiles plus trucks was obtained for each year from 1904 to 1926. Second, a price index for petroleum products for each year was obtained. Third, the official (DBS) estimate of farm auto and truck expenses for 1926 was obtained and then extrapolated back to preceding years by a combined index of the number of farm auto and truck vehicles and the price index of petroleum products. Each of these components is described in turn.

Numbers of Autos and Trucks on Farms

The numbers of automobile and truck registrations in Canada are available for all years in HSC Series S222-235. Numbers of autos and of trucks are given separately for all Canada; numbers of auto and truck registrations in combination are also given for each province for each year. It remained to estimate the numbers of these registrations that were for farm vehicles. The numbers of auto and trucks on farms, by province, were available: for all provinces in 1921

(Census of Canada Vol. V, *Agriculture*, p.58); for the Prairie provinces in 1926 (HSC Series L330 and L334); for all provinces individually, in 1931 (Census of Canada, 1931, Vol. VIII *Agriculture*, pp.xvi and 1xvii). The census data apply to June 1 of the year in which the census was taken. Total numbers of registrations, of auto and trucks, and the numbers on farms along with the calculated proportions on farms at June 1, 1921 follow.

Total Registrations and Numbers
of Autos and Trucks on Farms,
by Province, 1921

Province	Total Registrations of Autos and Trucks	Numbers of Autos and Trucks on Farms	Proportion on Farms
Prince Edward Is.	1,750	687	0.393
Nova Scotia	14,050	3,464	0.247
New Brunswick	13,460	4,111	0.305
Quebec	54,670	10,072	0.184
Ontario	206,521	61,145	0.296
Manitoba	40,336	16,645	0.413
Saskatchewan	61,184	36,098	0.590
Alberta	39,852	20,616	0.517
British Columbia	32,900	4,184	0.127
3 Prairie Prov.	141, 372	73,359	0.519
Canada	464,800	157,022	0.338

The procedures for estimating the numbers of autos and trucks on farms for others years differed between the prairie provinces and all other provinces.

The procedure for the prairie provinces was done in two parts.

Period 1921 to 1926: for 1926 for all three prairie provinces together, farm autos and trucks amounted to 48.9 percent of total provincial registrations of the same; the percentage at June 1, 1921 for all three prairie provinces of 51.9 percent was actually used for 1920; the percentage of farm autos and trucks used for 1921 to 1926 was derived by linear interpolation between the figure for 1921 and the figure for 1926 (in fact I believe the percentages were shifted backwards by one year so that they were applied to the years 1920 to 1925 — a figure for 1926 was then obtained by interpolating between the "misplaced" 1925 figure and the 1931 ratio, from the 1931 agricultural census, yielding a ratio for 1926 of 0.503. Fortunately the year to year changes were sufficiently slight that this misplacement of years did not matter much.).

Period 1920 backward: calculations for all three prairie provinces together were made by using the ratio of farm registrations to total registrations of 51.9 percent, the ratio for 1921.

The procedure for obtaining annual time series for all provinces but the prairies was to multiply the number of registrations of autos and trucks by the ratio of farm autos and trucks to the total registrations in 1921 on a province by province basis.

The totals of farm autos and trucks for Canada were then obtained by simple summation of the prairie total and the total for all other provinces.

A Price Series for Petroleum Products

The price index used was that for petroleum products, 1913 to 1926, and for gasoline, 1904 to 1913. The sources are given in the section on tractor expenses. We could have used the price index for gasoline for 1913 to 1926 but it is not greatly different than that for petroleum products.

The Value Series

The official estimate of farm auto and truck expenses for 1926 is 25,508 thousand dollars (HAS.II, p.75). This figure was extrapolated back to earlier years on the basis of a combined index of the number of autos and trucks on farms and the cost of petroleum.

Mill Feeds and Corn

The mill feed expenses were estimated from two components, *viz.*, (i) the value of the bran, shorts and middlings that were a by-product of the flour mills, (ii) the value of net purchases of corn by farmers. The estimation of each of these, in turn, is described.

The Value of Wheat Milling By-products

The wheat flour milling process yields wheat flour, used for human consumption and by-products of wheat grain which are bran, shorts, middlings, and cream of wheat. The wheat flour and cream of wheat were used for human consumption in Canada or for export. Some small portion of the bran was used for human consumption but most of the bran, middlings and shorts were used as animal food on farms. Its value therefore became an expense of farm production and must enter our calculations of farm costs since the entire value of wheat used for flour production had been included as a part of gross farm income; the rather small use of bran for human consumption and the small proportion of by-products in the form of cream of wheat were ignored.

The estimation of the money cost of these wheat by-products used on farms was made by multiplication of an estimate of physical quantity by its unit value. These were derived as follows.

The estimate of the farm use of by-products involved a number steps. First, an estimate of the number of bushels of wheat was obtained from estimated use of wheat to produce flour for domestic consumption plus exports of flour. Wheat milled for production of flour for domestic use was calculated by multiplying population each year by 5.5 bushels per head — see the justification for this consumption per head figure in the section on wheat production. Wheat used to produce flour for export was calculated from the recorded exports of flour from year to year, recorded in *Trade of Canada*: exported flour was reported in barrels of 196 pounds each. Each bushel of wheat (60 lbs. in weight) produces 44.2 lbs. of flour and 15.8 lbs. of by-products. Hence, production of 196 lbs of flour would involve the milling of 4.4344 bushels of wheat and the use of wheat for milling export flour could be calculated accordingly from the flour exports. The addition of the wheat used to mill export flour to that used for the production of domestically consumed flour yielded the figures for total use of wheat in flour milling, measured in bushels — imports of wheat flour were not significant. Total production of by-products of the Canadian wheat milling industry were then obtained by use of the figure of 15.8 lbs of by-products per bushel of wheat. Exports of bran, middlings and shorts were subtracted from the production total to yield the estimate of the amount of by-products used in Canada, which, it was assumed, was all used on farms.

These by-products were valued at the export unit value of the bran, middlings and shorts, obtained from *Trade of Canada*.

The Value of Corn Purchased for Farm Use

Canadian farms produced some corn both for ripe cobs and for ensilage. However, in most years, production of ripe corn was not sufficient to meet farm feed requirements and some foreign corn was purchased for farm use. It was necessary to estimate the value of this net farm purchase. The value estimate was obtained, as was done so commonly, as the product of a net physical quantity purchased and the price at which it was purchased.

The estimate of the quantity of corn grain purchased for use on farms was obtained essentially by subtracting from net imports of corn each year an estimate of the off-farm use of corn. The off-farm use of corn grain was comprised of corn used for distillation, corn used for human consumption in the form of corn flour and meal, and corn used for starch, glucose and breakfast foods.

Exports and imports of corn were obtained from *Trade of Canada*: they predominantly took the form of corn as grain, which was recorded in bushels of corn; there were small amounts of exports and somewhat larger imports of corn as flour and meal which were converted from barrels of flour to bushels of corn at the rate of one barrel of flour corresponds to 5.92 bushels of corn (conversion factors from Canada Department of Agriculture, *Weights and Conversion Factors for Canadian Agricultural Products* Publication 1155, September 1962).

Domestic use of corn for distillation was obtained from *Annual Reports* of the Department of Inland Revenue. Through misapprehension originally that these data are not available from 1870-1880, when, in fact, they are, and through failure to correct these data when other corrections were made, values of corn used for distillation were omitted in the years 1870-1880. In fact, the value of corn used for distillation averaged 500 thousand dollars per year in this decade, and farm costs of corn were overstated by this amount in the 1870s. In view of the smallness of this amount and the fact that further correction involved substantial recalculation of other data, no further change was made.

Corn flour and meal for human consumption was estimated at 3 lbs. per capita per annum: this figure was calculated from HAS.IV for the years from 1926 onward. This figure multiplied by population and converted to bushels off corn (56 lbs. per bushel) provides the figure for each year for this series.

For domestic use of corn for production of starch, glucose and breakfast foods, annual consumption per capita was placed at one-third of a bushel of corn for each year and the total figure for each year for this category followed multiplying this figure by the population for the year. (A research assistant's note refers to the figure of one-third bushel per capita per annum as coming from calculations which I had made from which I had left instructions for the use of that measure. I have not been able to locate these instructions and calculations, a situation that happened very rarely indeed. I would expect that they were made on the basis of information from DBS *The Starch and Glucose Industry* annual reports from the early 1920s in which both the output and the inputs are given quantitatively for the industry, including the inputs of corn.)

Farm purchases of corn were then obtained by subtracting the measure of off-farm uses of corn, i.e. the sum of the three off-farm uses noted above, from net imports of corn: in all years from 1902 onward and in a majority of years before 1900 the net imports of corn exceeded off-farm uses which mean that Canadian farms were net purchasers of corn in those years; however, in some years before 1902 net imports of corn were less than off-farm uses which meant that Canadian farms were net sellers of corn in those years. Rather than transferring these proceeds of net sales of corn by Canadian farms to the measures of receipts of farmers they were treated as negative expenses: that procedure meant that in these years the net values of sales of corn from farms were subtracted from the other items of expense in this category (the value of purchases of the bran shorts and middling) to yield the final estimate of outlay for this whole category.

The net farm purchases of corn (negative in a few years) were measured first in quantities of kernel corn. This corn was then valued at the unit price of the imports of kernel corn calculated from annual data of Canadian imports obtained from *Trade of Canada*.

The farm expenses for this whole category then were the sums of outlay on mill feeds plus the farm outlays on purchases of corn.

Binder Twine

Binder twine farm expenses were obtained by calculating domestic supply from Canadian production plus imports less exports and then valuing this domestic supply at an estimate of farm cost per unit.

The data for the derivation of binder twine expenses came from the three different sources for three different periods. These will be dealt with in turn.

Period 1919 to 1926

The DBS manufacturing industry publication *The Cordage Rope and Twine Industry* provided the data for production, exports and imports, both for quantity and value for each year in this period. For the years 1923 to 1926 the consumption in Canada (virtually farm consumption) valued at wholesale prices was directly available from DBS *The Textile Industries of Canada in the Decade 1917-1926* p. 138. For years 1919 to 1922, the annual production, both quantity and value, was taken from *The Cordage, Rope and Twine Industry* reports of DBS; quantities and values of imports and exports of Canada were from *Trade of Canada* for the fiscal year ending March 31, closest coincident to the calendar year. Domestic consumption at wholesale prices was, annually, value of production plus value of imports less value of exports. This consumption figure at wholesale prices was marked up 25 percent to obtain cost to the farmers, as had been done in the preparation of the Rowell-Sirois cost estimates for 1926 to 1936.

Period 1904 to 1918

In these years, (except for 1907) domestic production of binder twine was obtained from reports of the inspector of binder twine of the Department of Trade and Commerce. These data were in annual reports of the Department of Trade and Commerce (Sessional Papers of Canada, no. 10 back to 1917 and then no. 10c) and were reported in tons or pounds. The data related to calendar years back to 1913, fiscal years ending march 31 back to 1907 and fiscal years ending June 30 theretofore. We did not have data for the fiscal year ending March 31, 1908, and estimated it as the average of the two immediately adjacent fiscal years. These fiscal year data were used for the calendar year with which they most nearly coincided. These production data were valued at the unit value of imports. Domestic consumption at wholesale prices was obtained by adding value of imports to value of production and subtracting value of exports, all data in the sources being fiscal year data.

A mark-up of 25 percent was added to the value of domestic consumption at wholesale prices to get costs to the farmers.

Period 1882 to 1903

Production data for binder twine were not available before 1904; however, the quantity of undressed hemp imported, the raw material for making binder twine, was available in the foreign trade reports. This series of quantity of imports of undressed hemp was used to extrapolate the 1904 figure for production of binder twine back to 1890 on an annual basis. As in the next later period, this production series was valued, year by year, at unit import prices. To it was added the value of imports of binder twine less the value of exports both obtained from the annual foreign trade data. A mark-up of 25 percent to obtain farm cost was added.

The only direct data before 1890 were the imports of undressed hemp: in this circumstance the cost of binder twine to farmers was reduced in linear fashion from the 1890 figure to zero in 1882 which latter corresponds roughly with the introduction of the twine binder, although it should be remembered that some twine was used for hand tying before the advent of the twine binder.

Imports of hemp, undressed, are available, under that specific description, as far back as 1879-80 (and for two years prior thereto under the heading "hemp and tow, undressed") as follows:

Hemp, Undressed

Fiscal Year Ending June 30	Quantity (cwt. lbs.)	Value ($)
1890-91	128,748	864,597
1889-90	97,004	774,587
1888-89	160,188	1,214,088
1887-88	148,045	1,045,925
1886-87	89,973	535,759
1885-86	101,097	522,421
1884-85	89,180	535,351
1883-84	72,221	497,915
1882-83	74,604	630,488
1881-82	57,785	484,475
1880-81	N.A.	323,283
1879-80	90,434	362,774

Hemp and Tow Undressed

1878-79	3,960	21,247
1877-78	29,350	166,582

These data suggest a bit different pattern than our projection from 1890 gives. However, we must keep in mind that the twine binder was only introduced into the United States in 1880 and took some time to spread — see Leo Rogin, *The Introduction of Farm Machinery* etc...)

Blacksmithing

Blacksmiths' services were a substantial element of farm costs throughout this period. The work done by blacksmiths included the shoeing of horses, the sharpening of ploughshares, the repair of machinery parts and the like.

The critical values of blacksmith expenses were those for the census years. Accordingly, the derivation of farm blacksmith expenses for those years will be described first.

Different methods were used for the census years 1870, 1880 and 1890 than for the census years 1900, 1910, 1920 and 1930: the census of manufacturers covered all blacksmith shops, regardless of numbers engaged in 1870, 1880 and 1890; they covered only shops employing more than four persons in 1900 and 1910; they did not belong to the census of manufactures proper in 1920 and 1930.

The Estimates for 1870, 1880 and 1890

For these three census years it was assumed that the blacksmith shops, most of which were small, were divided between providing services to farmers and non-farmers in the same proportions of rural to urban population. The definition of rural and urban used was the 1941 definition and the actual numbers of population in each category were taken from HSC Series A18-19. In this definition all incorporated municipal centers were classified as being urban and unincorporated were classified as rural: the proportions rural were 0.804 in 1870-71, 0.743 in 1880-81, and 0.682 in 1890-91. The gross value of product of the blacksmithing industry was then divided between rural and urban in these same proportions and all the income of the rural blacksmith was attributed to farm sales. Hence, the rural blacksmith GVP became the farm expenses for blacksmiths' services. Two characteristics of the blacksmith industry manufactures should be noted: first, the great majority of the blacksmith shops were small, in many cases, single man shops; second, there were considerable numbers of blacksmiths employed in other industries such as mining, construction, iron and steel manufactures, and the like.

The Estimates for 1900, 1910, 1920 and 1930

Since the census of industry did not cover blacksmith shops fully, or even substantially, from 1900 onwards, an alternative method of estimation was necessary. The method followed was to estimate the number of own account (self-employed) blacksmiths for each of these census years (on the assumption that these were the blacksmiths doing work for farmers, and that they were one-man shops), to value the labour services of these own-account blacksmiths at a going wage rate for blacksmiths, and to apply a mark-up figure to the resultant wage component to obtain the costs to the farmers. Each of these will be examined in turn.

The numbers of own accounts in each census were calculated from the census of occupations, which gave the number of gainfully occupied in the census year. The numbers follow.

	1900	1910	1920	1930
Total gainfully occupied				
Blacksmiths	17,426			
Apprentices and helpers	1,192			
Total	18,618	16,660	18,891	15,902
Number of wage earners				
Blacksmiths	9,493			9,350
Apprentices	580			
Total	10,073			
Number of own-accounts	8,545	8,712	8,621	6,552

Sources:
1900:   Census of 1901, Census Bulletin No. I *Wage Earners by Occupation* p.15, Bulletin No. XI *Occupations of the People* p.7
1910:   Printout from 1911 Census microfiche provided by Statistics Canada of occupational and wage data not published.
1920:   Census of Canada, 1921 Vol. *Occupations* p.86 ff. for additions from industry allocations for number gainfully occupied. I could not find the worksheet that David Jones used to calculate the self employed which was done by subtracting wage-earners from total (as in 1900). The wage earners had to be estimated as the 1920 census only recorded such data for centers of over 30,000 persons. The figure of 8,621 for self-employed corresponds quite well with Jones' figure of 9,267 for self employed plus some apprentices and no-pays.
1930:   Census of Canada, 1931, Vol. V, p.120; Vol. III, Table 40, p.66, Table 50, p.558 ff., p.562.

In 1901 and 1920 there were not specific designations of own accounts in the census but approximations of the number were obtained by subtracting the number designated as wage earners from the total number of gainfully occupied blacksmiths as recorded from the occupational classification of persons in the 1901 and the 1921 censuses; in each of 1911 and 1931 there was a designation of own account workers derivable directly from the individual returns, tabulated appropriately, of course, and these were the figures used for these census years.

The value of the services of these own accounts to farmers were then obtained in two steps. First, an aggregate ordinary labour income for these own accounts as a group was calculated for each year. The average earnings of wage-earners reporting wages follow.

Year	Average Earnings of Wage Earners Reporting Wages (dollars per year)
1900	413
1910	565
1920	1,038
1930	679

The aggregate ordinary labour income was a product of the number of own account blacksmiths and the above average earnings. These aggregate ordinary wage data for each year were then marked up to give a figure for the cost of blacksmiths services to the farmer. The basis for the mark up was the average relationship between the aggregate wage bill and the gross value of the product in the 1870, 1880 and 1890 censuses of manufacturers: these years were used because it was only in these censuses of manufactures that blacksmithing as a whole was covered. The average for these three census years yielded a ratio of GVP to wages and salaries of 2.6621 and this was the markup ratio used. For comparison a very small coverage of hand-traders covering only businesses with five or more employees in the 1900 census (75 employees only) gave a ratio of 1.849 and in the 1910 census (118 employees) gave a ratio of 2.877; in addition, the much fuller coverage of blacksmiths of the "hand trades" in the censuses of manufacturers 1917, 1918, 1919 and 1921 (between 4,000 and 5,000 employees each year) yielded an average ratio of GVP to wages and salaries of 2.293. Thus the blow-up figure we used for each census year from 1900 to 1930 may be a bit on the high scale (moreso in the later than the earlier years). However, these figures do not include machine shop charges which are included in the official statistics from 1926 onward.

Interpolations Between Census Years

Interpolations between census years were done by using the movements of the annual measures of the stock of horses on farms: these measures of the stock of horses are described in the section of these notes on horses. The method is best explained by following its steps. First, linear interpolations, year by year, of blacksmith expenses were run for each decade including the decade of the 1920s. Second, linear interpolations between census years, year by year, of the stock of horses on farms were run for each decade. Third, the ratio of the actual stock of horses to linearly calculated stock of horses for each year was calculated. Finally, the linearly calculated annual values for blacksmith expenses were multiplied by these ratios. The rationale for using the stock of horses as an interpolator is that, first, part blacksmith expenses arises from the shoeing of horses, and, second, at the time covered by our estimates the size of the horse stock reflected the amount of farm machinery in use — one large blacksmithing item was the sharpening of plough shares.

Miscellaneous Expenses

Miscellaneous expenses were calculated at four percent of Gross Farm Income excluding income from forest products.

This figure of four percent is derived as follows.

A comparison of the project operating expenses and the operating expenses of HAS.II implied that the expenses of the project so far did not include the "miscellaneous expenses" of HAS nor that part of "other crop" expenses that was in excess of binder twine costs. The "miscellaneous" expenses of HAS were described as "fencing, custom work, and other supplies and services not previously specified"; the "other crop" expenses were described as "pesticide, nursery stock, containers, seed and twine" (p.75).

For the years 1926 to 1930 then the following calculations were made.

"Realized Gross Income" for each year, 1926 to 1930 from HAS.II p.28, was reduced by 13 percent to reflect the fact that the project estimate of gross farm income (excluding forestry) in 1926 was 13 percent less than HAS realized gross income in the same year. The main reason for the discrepancy between the two estimates was that the official figures of gross farm income include some sales within the farm sector; the project estimates of gross farm income do not include any farm sales of products that ultimately go as inputs to other farmers.

The sum of "miscellaneous expenses" for each year and "other crop" expenses (from HAS.II p.75) less binder twine expenses was obtained. The binder twine expenses subtracted for 1926 were the project estimate and for 1927 to 1930 were from the estimates of the Royal Commission on Dominion-Provincial Relations in their publication *National Income* p.61.

The average ratio of these expenses to farm income (excluding forest products) was 3.7 percent which was rounded to four percent. It was thus that the four percent used in calculating the miscellaneous farm expenses was obtained.

Bibliography of Sources Cited in Chapter 2

Since reference is made to some sources of data many times, it is desirable to use shortened titles in referring to them in the text; where reference is made infrequently, a shortened form has not been used. In this bibliography those bodies of information to which reference is made repeatedly are given first in their full citation and with the shortened form; those bodies of, information which are not used in shortened form then follow.

The nature of the source data is illuminated by a knowledge of the evolution of the central statistics office in Canada. A census office, newly constructed on each occasion within the Department of Agriculture, was responsible for taking each of the censuses of 1871, 1881, 1891, and 1901 and for publishing the tabulated data (the census included a census of agriculture). This office, as the Census and Statistics Office, was made permanent in 1905: it was transferred to the Department of Trade and Commerce in 1912, expanded into the Dominion Bureau of Statistics in 1918, and was renamed Statistics Canada in 1971. It was the main statistical agency of the federal government but some other government bodies, in the course of their administrative duties, also collected and published relevant data. These federal statistics bodies are referred to in shortened form terms.

The federal publications to which references are made in this body are all published by the federal government as publisher; like provincial publications are published by provincial governments as publishers. Dates of publication are self-evident if not given.

Government statistical agencies and abbreviated form:

CSO: Canada, Census and Statistics Office
DBS: Canada, Dominion Bureau of Statistics
Statcan: Canada, Statistics Canada
OBI: Ontario, Ontario Bureau of Industries

Abbreviated references and abbreviated form government statistical agency publications:

Census and Statistics Office:

CSM   *Census and Statistics Monthly* from 1908 to 1917
MBAS   *Monthly Bulletin of Agricultural Statistics* (replacing the CSM in 1917 and being carried on by DBS when it was formed).

Dominion Bureau of Statistics, 1918 to 1971 (becoming Statistics Canada):

The Dominion Bureau of Statistics published several reference papers providing useful historical data. Some of these reference papers were republished, usually just bringing annual series up to date. The copy that is cited is that which was generally used in this project. Since all federal government documents are published by a government printing office, that fact is not repeated with each publication.

HAS.I   *Handbook of Agricultural Statistics, Part I: Field Crops, 1908-62* (also 1908-58 and 1921-74)
HAS.II   *Handbook of Agricultural Statistics, Part II: Farm Income, 1926-65* (also 1926-57)

HAS.IV   *Handbook of Agricultural Statistics, Part IV: Food Consumption, 1926-55*
HAS.VI   *Handbook of Agricultural Statistics, Part VI: Livestock and Animal Products, 1871-1965* (also 1871-1973 — identical paging; adds 8 more years of data)
CYB   *Canada Year Book*, annual since 1905, by CSO and DBS; previously the *Statistical Year Book*, annual, Department of Agriculture.

Ontario Bureau of Industries:

OBI *Report*   *Ontario Bureau of Industries Reports*, Annual 1883 to 1926, published as a separate report until 1918 then succeeded by the annual Report of the Statistics Branch of the Department of Agriculture; report appears also in Ontario Sessional Papers.

Other abbreviated frequently used references:

HSC   M.C. Urquhart, Editor, and K.A.H. Buckley, Assistant Editor, *Historical Statistics of Canada*, 1965, Macmillan and Cambridge University Press.
HSC.II   Second Edition, 1983, by Statcan, referred to rather infrequently and designated HSC.II.
Michell   H. Michell, *Statistics of Prices*, in K.W. Taylor and H. Michell, *Statistical Contributions to Canadian Economic History*, Macmillan, 1931.

Unabbreviated references

Central Statistical Office and Dominion Bureau of Statistics, *Census of Canada*, periodic, several volumes each census, frequently cited by volume.
Dominion Bureau of Statistics; *Prices and Price Indexes*, first issue 1918-1922, then 1913-1923 and annually.
Dominion Bureau of Statistics; *Flour and Feed Mill Industry*, 1921.
Dominion Bureau of Statistics; *Grain Trade of Canada*, annual beginning with 1917-18, Department of Trade and Commerce, Canada.
Department of Labour, Canada, *Wholesale Prices in Canada, 1890-1909*; Department of Labour, Canada, *Wholesale Prices Canada*, annual, 1910 to 1917.
Canada, Board of Inquiry into the Cost of Living in Canada, Canada, *Report, Volume II*, 1915.
Canada, Royal Commission on Dominion-Provincial Relations, *Report, Appendix 4, National Income* (1939), known conventionally as the Rowell-Sirois Commission, named for the two chairmen.
United States, Bureau of Census, *Historical Statistics of the United States Colonial Times to 1970*.
University of Saskatchewan, College of Agriculture, Department of Farm Management, *Agricultural Extension Bulletin No. 64*.
L.H. Bailey, *Cyclopedia of American Agriculture*, 4 volumes, Macmillan, New York and London, 1907-1909.
Leo Rogin, *The Introduction of Farm Machinery in its Relation to the Productivity of Labor in the Agriculture of the United States During the Nineteenth Century*, University of California Press, (Publications in Economics – University of California), 1931.

Agriculture Supplementary Tables

The following tables give data on agricultural products that lie behind the estimates of farm revenue from agricultural products appearing in Table 1.9.

Table 2.1 Wheat
2.2 Oats
2.3 Barley
2.4 Rye
2.5 Hay
2.6 Vegetables
2.7 Potatoes
2.8 Hops
2.9 Flaxseed
2.10 Tobacco
2.11 Eggs
2.12 Maple Sugar and Syrup
2.13 Honey

Table 2.14 Apples
2.15 Small Fruit
2.16 Grapes
2.17 Orchard Fruit
2.18 Cattle
2.19 Hogs
2.10 Sheep and Lambs
2.21 Poultry
2.22 Dairy Products
2.23 Horses
2.24 Seeds, Grass and
Clover
2.25 Wool

Table 2.1. Wheat

Year	Wheat Available for Sale (000 bu.)	Year	Wheat Available for Sale (000 bu.)	Average Farm Price: Prairies (¢/bu.)
1870	17449	1900	44000	
1871	19817	1901	60864	
1872	20481	1902	69618	
1873	20734	1903	55751	
1874	20283	1904	53375	
1875	22442	1905	80574	
1876	18894	1906	83667	
1877	22146	1907	81544	
1878	26597	1908	90525	83.09
1879	30476	1909	139096	84.08
1880	27325	1910	111865	73.01
1881	28900	1911	175591	68.57
1882	31197	1912	180280	64.91
1883	23624	1913	198230	67.64
1884	25048	1914	119321	106.37
1885	29375	1915	335863	88.42
1886	32630	1916	189938	147.20
1887	29175	1917	185622	201.92
1888	25911	1918	136226	200.24
1889	26272	1919	144722	192.73
1890	29620	1920	204572	186.57
1891	37055	1921	240049	93.42
1892	39444	1922	339691	89.37
1893	37009	1923	401889	75.37
1894	36757	1924	205850	142.89
1895	46430	1925	332810	124.19
1896	34144	1926	336589	113.86
1897	48316			
1898	42369			
1899	49202			

Note: Average unit value for Canada may be obtained by dividing farm revenue from wheat by quantity of wheat available for sale.

148

Table 2.2. Oats

Year	Net Exports (000 bu.)	Off-farm Horses (no.)	Total Off-farm Disposition (000 bu.)	Eastern Price (¢/bu.)	Canada Price (¢/bu.)	Western Price (¢/bu.)
1870	542.0	59483	8398.6		39.00	
1871	486.0	60842	8518.2		37.75	
1872	629.5	62201	8843.1		37.50	
1873	998.1	63559	9390.7		37.50	
1874	2989.8	64918	11552.9		39.00	
1875	2016.0	66277	10746.2		34.25	
1876	1224.7	67636	10121.9		36.50	
1877	2215.7	68995	11280.8		32.25	
1878	1463.0	70353	10703.6		28.00	
1879	5828.3	71712	15248.8		32.75	
1880	3480.6	73071	13080.9		31.50	
1881	4652.4	75914	14504.8		40.50	
1882	1577.2	78757	11685.7		39.25	
1883	1949.2	81600	12315.7		34.75	
1884	2862.3	84443	13480.8		29.93	
1885	4936.7	87286	15801.4		31.08	
1886	2584.5	90129	13697.8		30.58	
1887	694.9	92972	12062.0		34.85	
1888	813.8	95815	12433.7		36.43	
1889	1220.6	98658	13092.6		29.75	
1890	303.3	101499	12430.5		40.65	
1891	7589.0	102237	19831.7		31.85	
1892	9074.6	102975	21431.1		30.10	
1893	3679.4	103713	16149.6		31.50	
1894	1654.7	104451	14237.8		28.63	
1895	2048.9	105189	14745.8		25.58	
1896	8272.7	105927	21083.3		19.78	
1897	11776.3	106665	24704.9		22.33	
1898	11493.4	107403	24546.0		25.13	
1899	8473.9	108141	21655.5		26.40	

Table 2.2. (continued)

Year	Net Exports (000 bu.)	Off-farm Horses (no.)	Total Off-farm Disposition (000 bu.)	Eastern Price (¢/bu.)	Canada Price (¢/bu.)	Western Price (¢/bu.)
1900	9646.2	108879	22960.3		25.75	
1901	5954.5	114193	19802.9		38.05	
1902	9200.7	119507	23612.1		30.55	
1903	7062.2	124821	22052.9		29.15	
1904	3848.5	130135	19417.6		32.28	
1905	4205.3	135447	20284.8		33.58	
1906	6157.4	145314	23274.7		34.05	
1907	8966.1	155112	27031.2		48.58	
1908	7221.0	160563	25874.7	40.3		30
1909	7788.0	170982	27414.0	39.5		27
1910	7799.0	180000	28318.5	35.0		31
1911	11444.0	186687	32649.6	44.2		30
1912	14825.0	198728	37170.0	38.6		24
1913	36475.0	204395	59484.8	36.9		25
1914	11592.0	207748	34970.0	49.5		44
1915	53972.0	199580	76784.5	39.5		32
1916	67047.0	191412	89327.1	66.0		46
1917	31731.0	183244	53503.3	77.9		63
1918	8975.0	175076	30303.2	75.0		71
1919	17057.0	166908	38110.6	97.7		69
1920	30994.0	158742	51562.1	58.2		42
1921	29440.0	153020	49671.5	50.4		25
1922	25469.0	147298	45329.9	43.5		30
1923	43116.0	141576	62642.0	45.4		25
1924	36803.0	135854	56009.4	54.2		44
1925	34749.0	130132	53640.9	45.2		34
1926	6601.0	124410	25202.9	51.8		41

Table 2.3. Barley

Year	Net Exports (000 bu.)	Total Off-Farm Disposition (000 bu.)	Year	Net Exports (000 bu.)	Total Off-Farm Disposition (000 bu.)	Western Price (¢/bu.)	Eastern Price (¢/bu.)
1870	4833.0	5832	1900	2380.6	4273		
1871	5606.3	6865	1901	448.5	2587		
1872	4346.9	5653	1902	944.4	2909		
1873	3748.3	4713	1903	1056.6	3081		
1874	5419.1	6641	1904	1040.1	3258		
1875	10134.1	11659	1905	877.0	3507	29.99	42.88
1876	6071.0	7245	1906	1195.6	3543	33.4	45.05
1877	6965.2	8391	1907	1981.6	4886	39.3	59.08
1878	5340.7	6714	1908	2826.3	5618	38	52.4
1879	7225.6	8951	1909	1879.9	4541	37	56
1880	8783.6	10739	1910	1040.0	3970	44	53
1881	11579.0	13629	1911	2642.0	6012	47	70
1882	8800.8	11268	1912	9389.0	12844	35	61
1883	7752.2	9386	1913	12294.0	16173	32	56
1884	9082.8	10553	1914	2813.0	6310	53	64
1885	8546.1	9981	1915	8851.0	11075	48	56
1886	9451.9	11067	1916	7870.0	10226	76	99
1887	9364.1	10969	1917	6552.0	8587	102	116
1888	9941.4	11720	1918	8270.0	10471	90	106
1889	9963.4	11849	1919	10869.0	13478	113	131
1890	4892.1	6465	1920	10815.0	14132	71	94
1891	5201.2	6877	1921	12419.0	14792	38	63
1892	2038.5	3639	1922	13842.0	16442	40	57
1893	594.1	2016	1923	15394.0	18513	35	60
1894	1697.8	3015	1924	27772.0	31689	66	77
1895	789.2	2365	1925	34171.0	37585	47	68
1896	1808.2	3246	1926	38766.0	42238	47	68
1897	435.1	1806					
1898	235.2	2039					
1899	2151.6	3970					

Table 2.4. Rye

Year	Net Exports (bu.)	Price (¢/bu.)	Year	Net Exports (bu.)	Price (¢/bu.)
1870		65.25	1900	678790	47.68
1871		62.25	1901	393725	50.2
1872		61	1902	462539	48.83
1873		63.75	1903	86505	48.63
1874		66.25	1904	6587	57.85
1875		60.75	1905	-34442	56.7
1876	-76637	56	1906	-47578	60.98
1877	258269	57.25	1907	-5260	69.25
1878	564099	49	1908	162043	69.7
1879	951086	59.50	1909	87099	73
1880	869535	77.75	1910	47299	67
1881	1279422	88	1911	-28592	76
1882	1047188	58.25	1912	-90053	72
1883	872363	59.25	1913	8309	66
1884	286703	59.15	1914	144922	83
1885	170085	54.23	1915	606014	77
1886	119066	50.65	1916	1111021	111
1887	-76314	50.33	1917	870858	162
1888	-108783	60.85	1918	188430	150
1889	434223	49.45	1919	2313158	141
1890	338114	53.98	1920	3238973	133
1891	219604	73.48	1921	3180503	72
1892	56653	54.33	1922	10104882	58
1893	60775	45.27	1923	6811938	49
1894	60096	44.27	1924	7503222	99
1895	-4627	44.6	1925	5341225	77
1896	212181	34.7	1926	6474147	77
1897	1131651	39.9			
1898	317821	43.55			
1899	467575	50.68			

Note: Off-farm disposition may be obtained by dividing farm revenue from rye by the price.

Table 2.5. Hay

Year	Hay Consumed Off-farm Horses (tons)	Hay Consumed Off-farm Cattle (tons)	Exports (tons)	Imports (tons)	Price ($/ton)
1870	163578	66000	23487	190	12.36
1871	167316	70600	50827	218	13.58
1872	171053	75200	36385	1524	12.32
1873	174787	79800	26725	2406	10.97
1874	178525	84400	20758	1987	10.15
1875	182262	89000	33520	2674	9.59
1876	185999	93600	29575	1485	8.61
1877	189736	98200	17269	2585	9.48
1878	193471	102800	11704	681	9.03
1879	197208	107400	64444	993	7.53
1880	200945	112000	168381	501	10.77
1881	208764	111100	90647	253	10.10
1882	216582	110200	93740	1012	9.62
1883	224400	109300	108461	865	8.42
1884	232218	108400	134939	1128	9.42
1885	240037	107500	93944	814	10.17
1886	247855	106600	76843	542	9.68
1887	255673	105700	93269	978	10.85
1888	263491	104800	91480	1025	14.11
1889	271310	103900	115162	5093	9.70
1890	279122	103000	65083	533	8.21
1891	281152	107400	84926	1153	10.92
1892	283181	111800	151881	1494	8.75
1893	285211	116200	276806	2043	8.34
1894	287240	120600	199072	1796	7.63
1895	289270	125000	214640	3001	11.06
1896	291299	129400	113754	4204	9.32
1897	293329	133800	37091	6334	8.17
1898	295358	138200	62428	5739	6.37
1899	297388	142600	175416	6218	7.86

Table 2.5. (continued)

Year	Hay Consumed Off-farm Horses (tons)	Hay Consumed Off-farm Cattle (tons)	Exports (tons)	Imports (tons)	Price ($/ton)
1900	299417	147000	252977	6519	8.40
1901	314031	154800	434585	8397	8.86
1902	328644	162600	450053	7737	8.09
1903	343258	170400	219874	8613	8.22
1904	357871	178200	151563	8665	8.11
1905	372479	186000	206714	7014	7.59
1906	399614	193800	112778	6416	9.13
1907	426558	201600	63472	11538	13.64
1908	441548	209400	55884	8061	10.64
1909	470201	217200	191098	7680	11.14
1910	495000	225000	326132	12247	8.68
1911	513389	232500	784864	19721	11.63
1912	546502	240000	394208	36472	11.11
1913	562086	247500	191515	19923	11.49
1914	571307	255000	131875	16078	14.23
1915	548845	262500	255407	9881	14.33
1916	526383	270000	198914	4748	11.58
1917	503921	277500	440368	2686	10.35
1918	481459	285000	492208	9273	16.38
1919	458997	292500	218561	20212	20.75
1920	436541	299990	179398	50789	26.00
1921	420805	295362	31287	28999	23.36
1922	405070	290734	58300	37040	13.42
1923	389334	286106	332293	13870	11.01
1924	373599	281478	225403	10282	11.12
1925	357863	276850	368787	8510	10.58
1926	342128	272222	321733	5464	12.28

Table 2.6. Vegetables

Year	Net Imports ($)	Price Index (1910=1)	Year	Net Imports ($)	Price Index (1910=1)
1870	16596	0.7885	1900	158802	0.54
1871	20550	1.0001	1901	22519	0.86
1872	15851	0.8536	1902	303662	0.96
1873	27490	0.7155	1903	377766	1.19
1874	46332	0.9201	1904	513349	0.93
1875	44696	0.6486	1905	413599	1.04
1876	-8098	0.7105	1906	241584	0.95
1877	36383	0.8794	1907	609063	1.12
1878	31125	0.8574	1908	583610	0.87
1879	46176	0.9170	1909	720196	0.78
1880	21615	0.5177	1910	1045005	1.00
1881	-82821	1.0274	1911	1810717	1.06
1882	65576	1.0147	1912	2437940	0.90
1883	58522	1.1092	1913	2502451	1.05
1884	71928	0.72	1914	1627610	0.85
1885	83797	0.78	1915	-855365	1.07
1886	82176	0.74	1916	110242	1.34
1887	67960	0.95	1917	1727321	1.62
1888	86788	0.62	1918	1485792	1.74
1889	84198	0.91	1919	2237249	1.69
1890	95786	0.92	1920	2478541	1.90
1891	109899	0.68	1921	2262665	1.50
1892	38397	0.75	1922	2633710	1.20
1893	55259	0.88	1923	2531234	1.28
1894	35668	0.73	1924	2424928	1.41
1895	83564	0.56	1925	2605363	1.93
1896	51973	0.50	1926	2805386	1.57
1897	156431	0.86			
1898	144034	0.80			
1899	159915	0.78			

Table 2.7. Potatoes

Year	Total Off-farm Disposition (000 bu.)	Net Exports (000 bu.)	Price ($/bu.)	Year	Total Off-farm Disposition (000 bu.)	Net Exports (000 bu.)	Price ($/bu.)
1870	(18894.0)	(450.0)	0.395	1900	27606.2	751.2	0.183
1871	(18849.0)	(81.0)	0.531	1901	28719.3	1249.3	0.344
1872	(19488.0)	(359.0)	0.344	1902	28508.5	253.5	0.466
1873	(20505.0)	(1034.0)	0.287	1903	31164.0	2029.0	0.638
1874	(20016.0)	(247.0)	0.425	1904	30209.6	199.6	0.466
1875	(20259.0)	(215.0)	0.294	1905	31520.5	1035.5	0.459
1876	23406.8	3086.8	0.287	1906	32485.8	430.8	0.466
1877	21612.0	1012.0	0.387	1907	33587.0	462.0	0.574
1878	23539.6	2614.6	0.495	1908	35434.2	1434.2	0.474
1879	22665.5	1390.5	0.473	1909	36644.3	1704.3	0.366
1880	23900.5	2275.5	0.196	1910	36669.3	634.3	0.492
1881	25653.3	3778.3	0.545	1911	37220.0	275.0	0.594
1882	24535.2	2385.2	0.459	1912	38546.2	386.2	0.438
1883	23017.5	582.5	0.509	1913	40960.0	1565.0	0.492
1884	23295.7	610.7	0.294	1914	40428.2	523.2	0.486
1885	25064.8	2164.8	0.395	1915	40361.1	356.1	0.606
1886	24638.0	1508.0	0.359	1916	42604.6	2304.6	0.804
1887	26048.4	2658.4	0.538	1917	43577.1	2837.1	1.014
1888	24577.7	932.7	0.276	1918	43514.3	1959.3	0.978
1889	25221.7	1326.7	0.437	1919	48639.7	5859.7	0.948
1890	27800.3	3635.3	0.385	1920	48021.5	4081.5	0.972
1891	24901.9	486.9	0.308	1921	47921.0	3326.0	0.768
1892	25714.5	1059.5	0.344	1922	47498.0	2448.0	0.540
1893	25889.3	994.3	0.373	1923	48330.9	2615.9	0.612
1894	26411.8	1281.8	0.351	1924	49392.8	2922.8	0.510
1895	25923.6	553.6	0.158	1925	53902.7	6647.7	1.236
1896	26279.4	669.4	0.230	1926	56034.0	7849.0	0.882
1897	27243.3	1368.3	0.351				
1898	26763.6	588.6	0.373				
1899	27084.1	579.1	0.323				

Note: For 1870 to 1875 the net export quantities were obtained by assigning net export values the same price as domestic consumption.

Table 2.8. Hops

Year	Production (000 lb.)	Net Exports (000 lb.)	Price ($/lb.)	Year	Production (000 lb.)	Net Exports (000 lb.)	Price ($/lb.)
1870	933.2	-154.3	0.16	1900	1001.9	-625.5	0.18
1871	1459.3	352.6	0.37	1901	925.0	-712.6	0.17
1872	1339.8	213.6	0.26	1902	1109.6	-553.9	0.26
1873	879.1	-268.7	0.28	1903	970.7	-728.5	0.28
1874	1142.3	-26.2	0.32	1904	1051.1	-688.8	0.29
1875	1226.3	40.1	0.20	1905	831.6	-948.6	0.19
1876	1143.4	-59.3	0.31	1906	1082.9	-712.7	0.21
1877	1245.8	26.6	0.18	1907	736.3	-1138.3	0.18
1878	1217.6	-18.4	0.17	1908	751.3	-1172.0	0.15
1879	1516.0	260.5	0.38	1909	1246.6	-713.1	0.25
1880	1087.7	-188.8	0.22	1910	1208.5		0.24
1881	1287.4	-13.1	0.27	1911	1180.3		0.44
1882	1156.9	-161.7	0.77	1912	1171.0		0.32
1883	1044.0	-294.2	0.30	1913	1161.7		0.30
1884	1143.2	-215.3	0.23	1914	1074.1		0.20
1885	1223.3	-153.4	0.16	1915	949.2		0.18
1886	297.4	-1095.5	0.19	1916	1205.5		0.18
1887	952.5	-457.7	0.18	1917	323.4		0.25
1888	902.2	-527.0	0.30	1918	339.8		0.24
1889	355.7	-1092.3	0.18	1919	356.1		0.58
1890	961.0	-506.2	0.39	1920	758.6		0.60
1891	718.1	-765.7	0.26	1921	864.3		0.36
1892	1259.3	-239.8	0.29	1922	680.9		0.21
1893	1281.7	-232.1	0.28	1923	999.8		0.33
1894	895.5	-633.1	0.16	1924	813.2		0.29
1895	1100.3	-442.6	0.15	1925	848.2		0.33
1896	1036.0	-521.7	0.14	1926	966.4		0.33
1897	1174.7	-397.8	0.18				
1898	954.0	-634.7	0.19				
1899	748.0	-859.1	0.15				

Table 2.9. Flaxseed

Year	Total Net Production (bu.)	Price ($/bu.)	Western Production (bu.)	Eastern Production (bu.)	Western Price ($/bu.)	Price ($/bu.)	Eastern Price ($/bu.)
1870	110389	1.464					
1871	109453	1.912					
1872	108705	2.328					
1873	107863	0.44					
1874	107021	1.208					
1875	106179	0.952					
1876	105337	0.816					
1877	104495	1.20					
1878	103653	0.568	1328129				
1879	102811	0.584	1989870				
1880	101969	0.744	3810886				
1881	104682	0.992	14010666				
1882	107395	0.94	23541946				
1883	110108	0.992	15020701				
1884	112821	1.73	5660623				
1885	115534	0.91	4987092				
1886	118247	0.816	7418438				
1887	120960	1.200	5063769				
1888	123673	0.736	4859700				
1889	126386	1.03	4254527				
1890	128366	0.90	6460408				
1891	115532	0.80	2819494				
1892	119853	0.80	4269394				
1893	200255	0.416	6261566				
1894	248108	0.872	8599394				
1895	1362770	0.576	4907122				
1896	337866	0.680	4985903				
1897	324866	0.832					
1898	425337	0.800					
1899	378566	0.912					
1900	157439					1.256	
1901	268965					0.888	
1902	447005					1.187	
1903	562673					0.712	
1904	378147					1.224	
1905	635338					0.944	
1906	1017295					0.952	
1907	1703898					1.096	
1908				--	1.066		0.97
1909				--	1.478		1.25
1910				89714	2.174		2.09
1911				127241	1.827		1.50
1912				142104	1.05		0.90
1913				151724	1.036		0.97
1914				74557	1.144		1.03
1915				55468	1.682		1.51
1916				44779	2.406		2.04
1917				87573	2.968		2.65
1918				234325	3.24		3.13
1919				195815	4.552		4.13
1920				347187	2.072		1.94
1921				117479	1.538		1.44
1922				91580	1.945		1.72
1923				82473	1.921		1.77
1924				104446	2.281		1.94
1925				125824	2.101		1.85
1926				101754	1.741		1.62

Note: Net production is Canadian production net of seed requirements.

158

Table 2.10. Tobacco

Year	Domestic Production (lb.)	Price ($/lb.)	Year	Domestic Production (lb.)	Price ($/lb.)
1870	1596000	0.040	1900	11267000	0.067
1871	1689200	0.043	1901	11903500	0.068
1872	1782400	0.046	1902	12540000	0.068
1873	1875600	0.037	1903	13176500	0.074
1874	1968800	0.045	1904	13813000	0.069
1875	2062000	0.042	1905	14449500	0.073
1876	2155200	0.036	1906	15086000	0.081
1877	2248400	0.032	1907	15722500	0.086
1878	2341600	0.032	1908	16359000	0.086
1879	2434800	0.034	1909	16995500	0.094
1880	2528000	0.036	1910	17632000	0.089
1881	2703000	0.042	1911	12066000	0.103
1882	2878000	0.046	1912	6500000	0.103
1883	3053000	0.049	1913	12500000	0.116
1884	3228000	0.051	1914	10000000	0.102
1885	3403000	0.047	1915	9000000	0.089
1886	3578000	0.046	1916	5943000	0.114
1887	3753000	0.046	1917	8495000	0.149
1888	3928000	0.054	1918	14232000	0.174
1889	4103000	0.047	1919	33770000	0.224
1890	4278000	0.054	1920	48088000	0.262
1891	4739274	0.049	1921	13249000	0.170
1892	5200548	0.052	1922	25948000	0.161
1893	5661822	0.051	1923	21297000	0.180
1894	6123096	0.046	1924	18711000	0.174
1895	6584370	0.055	1925	29141000	0.169
1896	7506918	0.051	1926	28824000	0.148
1897	8429466	0.072			
1898	9352014	0.058			
1899	10274562	0.070			

Table 2.11. Eggs

Year	Total Production (000 doz.)	Price ($/doz.)	OBI Stock of Hens & Chickens (000)	Year	Total Production (000 doz.)	Price ($/doz.)	OBI Stock of Hens & Chickens (000)
1870	34144.1	0.1397		1900	84089.3	0.1220	8124.0
1871	35174.1	0.1432		1901	85167.1	0.1142	8300.3
1872	35902.9	0.1571		1902	85191.0	0.1290	8359.8
1873	37272.5	0.1554		1903	83619.0	0.1280	8244.0
1874	36926.4	0.1458		1904	86095.9	0.1664	8590.0
1875	37773.9	0.1510		1905	89715.4	0.1477	9087.9
1876	39393.3	0.1414		1906	113267.9	0.1443	11937.6
1877	40094.4	0.1379		1907	108992.2	0.1733	10921.9
1878	40792.8	0.1083		1908	110742.6	0.1675	10745.0
1879	42360.5	0.1310		1909	116712.4	0.1937	11104.8
1880	45578.5	0.1231		1910	122964.4	0.1890	11532.8
1881	47358.7	0.1519	4508.7	1911	127693.4	0.2213	11586.2
1882	52564.3	0.1571	5000.6	1912	134080.5	0.2171	11924.6
1883	55230.7	0.1763	5251.9	1913	141872.3	0.2378	12419.2
1884	57071.7	0.1685	5431.6	1914	146813.9	0.2295	12636.4
1885	62594.7	0.1440	5952.4	1915	151505.7	0.2151	12825.2
1886	58849.2	0.1327	5600.7	1916	148850.5	0.3205	
1887	56309.9	0.1484	5356.6	1917	150163.1	0.3640	
1888	57579.5	0.1536	5478.4	1918	150933.0	0.4012	
1889	62531.3	0.1379	5949.4	1919	156025.0	0.4912	
1890	63483.5	0.1395	6039.9	1920	144599.6	0.4520	
1891	63033.7	0.1337	6005.3	1921	166154.7	0.3474	
1892	63180.8	0.1187	6036.4	1922	182871.8	0.3123	
1893	67184.2	0.1286	6425.2	1923	188112.0	0.3133	
1894	69169.6	0.1098	6636.2	1924	191884.4	0.3133	
1895	69086.5	0.1117	6626.9	1925	192172.9	0.2741	
1896	74207.7	0.1048	7135.4	1926	195207.6	0.3479	
1897	79034.5	0.0911	7605.7				
1898	78177.9	0.1095	7536.2				
1899	80860.8	0.1265	7794.3				

Note: OBI is the Ontario Bureau of Industries
        The farm net revenue from eggs is 4 per cent less than the product of price and production (see text).

Table 2.12. Maple Sugar and Syrup

Year	Production (lb. of sugar)	Exports (lb.)	Imports (lb.)	Price ($/lb.)
1870	17276054			0.0955
1871	17662651	18851		0.0968
1872	18015923	33723		0.0723
1873	18314117	7617		0.0914
1874	18602303	18503		0.0924
1875	18852808	10508		0.1233
1876	19126852	26052		0.0969
1877	19371207	7207		0.1085
1878	19671388	1888		0.1017
1879	20117832	119332		0.0669
1880	20556049			0.0848
1881	21059032	277782		0.0751
1882	21389362	169662		0.0728
1883	22063558	391348		0.0639
1884	22106894	11704		0.0868
1885	22638755	150955		0.0720
1886	23114231	215531		0.0732
1887	23543692	200472		0.0928
1888	24197024	410154		0.0661
1889	24464701	235171		0.0713
1890	25088274			0.0717
1891	25272384	774373		0.0664
1892	24920138	738514		0.0679
1893	24306800	452411		0.0660
1894	23654174	142725	179	0.0633
1895	24077583	918022	3249	0.0561
1896	23282886	491559	11817	0.0649
1897	22945222	512351	21454	0.0437
1898	23167358	1141019	96771	0.0584
1899	22488880	785371	99504	0.1082
1900	17804825			0.0802
1901	23112123	1220838	84715	0.0756
1902	25268464	2758979	94515	0.0697
1903	25102137	1873954	79817	0.0766
1904	25933917	1975887	49970	0.0697
1905	27055154	2719151	51997	0.0689
1906	27435381	1802901	11520	0.0837
1907	29347543	2862301	14758	0.0809
1908	28731946	1542939	10993	0.0777
1909	29724160	1779767	7607	0.0744
1910	29508389	1412311	11222	0.0852
1911	28514150			0.0910
1912	28581651	1193095	24634	0.0909
1913	29811101	1977393	23092	0.0829
1914	29789112	1524066	20564	0.0899
1915	29965569	1800795	8156	0.1022
1916	30676656	2920192	7006	0.1064
1917	31138881	3660859	6578	0.1480
1918	32146496	4772866	3650	0.2259
1919	31519183	4097824	4941	0.2801
1920	35827416	8111773	5797	0.2617
1921	24702781			0.1780
1922	30616098	2797077	8259	0.1368
1923	30413350	2849090	6340	0.1959
1924	29092375			
1925	27217192			
1926	24603003			

Note: Data are given in terms of sugar equivalent (see text).

Table 2.13. Honey

Year	Production (lb.)	Price ($/lb.)	Year	Production (lb.)	Price ($/lb.)
1870	1999300	0.176	1900	3569567	0.100
1871	1994992	0.178	1901	3737904	0.110
1872	1989750	0.133	1902	3940111	0.102
1873	1988415	0.169	1903	4166514	0.089
1874	1978200	0.170	1904	4406675	0.082
1875	1963126	0.227	1905	4622200	0.083
1876	1945834	0.179	1906	4890628	0.116
1877	1927332	0.200	1907	5220918	0.125
1878	1914533	0.187	1908	5504660	0.127
1879	1899000	0.123	1909	5784066	0.133
1880	1875745	0.156	1910	6089784	0.117
1881	2105400	0.138	1911	6181406	0.118
1882	2333590	0.134	1912	6271685	0.126
1883	2563925	0.118	1913	6390944	0.119
1884	2797440	0.160	1914	6447090	0.102
1885	3036294	0.133	1915	6408782	0.123
1886	3272733	0.135	1916	6344490	0.131
1887	3516912	0.171	1917	6313016	0.156
1888	3767904	0.122	1918	6320640	0.243
1889	4026638	0.131	1919	6376104	0.234
1890	4285970	0.132	1920	6461450	0.253
1891	4226460	0.097	1921	6498836	0.173
1892	4156229	0.096	1922	6472730	0.116
1893	4087875	0.091	1923	6453747	0.106
1894	4017409	0.092	1924	6453300	0.111
1895	3944050	0.092	1925	6457997	0.105
1896	3864284	0.101	1926	6461288	0.099
1897	3789664	0.080			
1898	3716370	0.081			
1899	3640188	0.100			

Table 2.14. Apples

Year	Net Exports ($)	Net Exports (bu.)	Farm Price ($/bu.)	Year	Net Exports (bu.)	Farm Price ($/bu.)
1870	44547		0.48	1900	2902069	0.49
1871	148056		0.55	1901	1841535	0.67
1872	86227		0.67	1902	4612615	0.61
1873	58965		0.56	1903	6241180	0.64
1874	71299		0.62	1904	4348957	0.56
1875	74989		0.45	1905	4396732	0.75
1876	-13035		0.55	1906	3600475	0.60
1877	31429		0.63	1907	6257481	0.66
1878	-5549		0.40	1908	4194496	0.57
1879		302363	0.53	1909	6437836	0.61
1880		748476	0.43	1910	1719018	0.75
1881		511037	0.57	1911	5045051	0.68
1882		47330	0.70	1912	3648839	0.68
1883		-453537	0.75	1913	3143523	0.81
1884		510609	0.56	1914	3515638	0.53
1885		521159	0.47	1915	1074045	0.68
1886		1096795	0.47	1916	582368	0.77
1887		1100204	0.46	1917	-1073510	0.87
1888		2099043	0.44	1918	625101	1.12
1889		765467	0.58	1919	3048596	1.08
1890		1460967	0.69	1920	3469795	0.86
1891		1987234	0.47	1921	6040081	1.13
1892		4298493	0.51	1922	3696726	0.98
1893		1071154	0.65	1923	4456158	1.09
1894		3425329	0.47	1924	3801499	1.17
1895		1814533	0.55	1925	4429708	1.14
1896		6167694	0.33	1926	2619816	1.08
1897		1699337	0.66			
1898		4936598	0.54			
1899		3681746	0.60			

Note: Off-farm disposition may be obtained by dividing farm revenue from apples by the price.

Table 2.15. Small Fruit

Year	Net Imports ($)	Imports (lb.)	Unit Value of Imports ($/lb.)	Year	Imports (lb.)	Unit Value of Imports ($/lb.)	Production (lb.)
1870	9022		0.12	1900	1079274	0.07	
1871	1510		0.14	1901	1064251	0.09	
1872	13927		0.17	1902	1067035	0.08	
1873	11057		0.14	1903	1305528	0.08	
1874	24011		0.16	1904	1902277	0.07	
1875	16777		0.12	1905	1484833	0.09	
1876	15659		0.14	1906	175115	0.09	
1877	17882		0.16	1907	1696115	0.11	
1878	17479		0.10	1908	2097849	0.09	
1879	8699		0.14	1909	2503594	0.08	
1880		106418	0.11	1910	3272636	0.10	
1881		100340	0.13	1911	3000833	0.11	
1882		161565	0.11	1912	6939470	0.08	
1883		254758	0.11	1913	7104745	0.09	
1884		282998	0.10	1914	6457356	0.09	
1885		231378	0.10	1915	5336597	0.08	
1886		150419	0.12	1916	6868647	0.08	
1887		454882	0.10	1917	7024965	0.10	
1888		1742272	0.06	1918	5574338	0.14	
1889		1043752	0.07	1919	4171468	0.21	
1890		334871	0.10	1920	2599785	0.22	
1891		319412	0.10	1921		(0.13)	25754675
1892		312541	0.11	1922		(0.14)	22234343
1893		556993	0.08	1923		(0.16)	19595925
1894		630944	0.08	1924		(0.16)	15580563
1895		361620	0.09	1925		(0.15)	15608750
1896		902690	0.07	1926		(0.11)	23348125
1897		756675	0.08				
1898		1162389	0.07				
1899		1270509	0.07				

Note: From 1921 onwards the entries for price are rounded unit values of production.

Table 2.16. Grapes

Year	Production (000 lb.)	Price ($/lb.)	Year	Production (000 lb.)	Price ($/lb.)
1870	1126.4	0.055	1900	24302.6	0.048
1871	1403.4	0.047	1901	25162.2	0.047
1872	1680.4	0.045	1902	26021.8	0.048
1873	1957.4	0.038	1903	26881.4	0.044
1874	2234.4	0.060	1904	27741.0	0.032
1875	2511.5	0.053	1905	28600.5	0.047
1876	2788.5	0.048	1906	29460.1	0.047
1877	3065.5	0.0395	1907	30319.7	0.040
1878	3342.5	0.0420	1908	31179.3	0.039
1879	3619.5	0.0375	1909	32038.9	0.036
1880	3896.5	0.0385	1910	32898.4	0.037
1881	4732.1	0.0465	1911	32935.5	0.025
1882	5567.7	0.0455	1912	32972.6	0.026
1883	6403.3	0.0430	1913	33009.7	0.032
1884	7238.8	0.0425	1914	33046.8	0.029
1885	8074.4	0.0415	1915	33083.9	0.029
1886	8910.0	0.0365	1916	33121.0	0.032
1887	9745.6	0.0310	1917	33158.1	0.041
1888	10581.2	0.0320	1918	33195.2	0.031
1889	11416.7	0.0395	1919	33232.3	0.053
1890	12252.3	0.037	1920	33269.4	0.07
1891	13457.4	0.038	1921	46872.3	0.05
1892	14662.4	0.027	1922	70308.5	0.05
1893	15867.4	0.040	1923	42185.1	0.06
1894	17072.5	0.032	1924	24500.0	0.06
1895	18277.5	0.040	1925	25000.0	0.07
1896	19482.5	0.037	1926	24000.0	0.03
1897	20687.5	0.040			
1898	21892.6	0.026			
1899	23097.6	0.026			

Table 2.17. Orchard Fruit

Year	Domestic Production (000 bu.)	Domestic Disappearance (000 bu.)	Unit Value ($/bu.)
1870	359		0.673
1871	407		0.779
1872	455		0.936
1873	504		0.789
1874	552		0.873
1875	600		0.631
1876	648		0.779
1877	697		0.883
1878	745		0.568
1879	793		0.747
1880	841	--	0.924
1881	794	831	1.671
1882	828	886	2.027
1883	808	897	1.956
1884	846	907	2.204
1885	918	962	2.596
1886	896	971	1.671
1887	941	982	2.027
1888	829	1040	1.494
1889	927	1051	1.956
1890	1063	--	2.88
1891	987	1123	1.351
1892	1064	1134	2.027
1893	1024	1145	1.244
1894	1130	1206	1.173
1895	976	1218	0.924
1896	1091	1229	0.853
1897	1194	1294	0.996
1898	1142	1309	0.889
1899	1192	1325	0.889

Year	Domestic Production (000 bu.)	Domestic Disappearance (000 bu.)	Unit Value ($/bu.)
1900	2040	--	0.889
1901	1203	1428	0.924
1902	1281	1469	0.818
1903	1439	1573	0.996
1904	1419	1621	0.96
1905	1422	1646	0.889
1906	1575	1795	1.067
1907	1617	1855	1.707
1908	1497	1904	0.924
1909	1719	2027	1.173
1910	1940	--	0.96
1911	1570	2143	1.173
1912	974	1908	0.818
1913	1186	1970	1.031
1914	1177	1995	0.96
1915	1162	2000	0.64
1916	1285	2015	1.102
1917	1174	2037	1.315
1918	1438	2078	1.778
1919	1292	2139	1.600
1920	2892		2.88
1921	1621		1.351
1922	1688		2.027
1923	1215		1.244
1924	691		1.173
1925	510		0.924
1926	1109		0.853

Note: The unit value series covers prices of orchard fruits, excluding cherries; the value series of the main tables does reflect values of cherries. Therefore, the value series can not be obtained by multiplication of production quantities of this table by the price series.

Table 2.18. Cattle

Year	Total Stock of Cattle (no.)	Sales and Slaughter (000 head)	Unit Value: Inventory Change ($)	Unit Value: Sales and Slaughter ($)	Year	Total Stock of Cattle (no.)	Sales and Slaughter (000 head)	Unit Value: Inventory Change ($)	Unit Value: Sales and Slaughter ($)
1870	2687274	533	45.57	53.99	1900	5576451	1260	21.52	25.50
1871	2770046	486	43.69	51.77	1901	5877994	1372	22.17	26.27
1872	2852817	503	44.29	52.48	1902	6286417	1481	23.93	28.36
1873	2935589	541	42.07	49.85	1903	6534444	1502	23.08	27.35
1874	3018360	547	33.87	40.13	1904	6865190	1444	23.17	27.45
1875	3101132	548	30.15	35.73	1905	7201598	1490	23.14	27.42
1876	3183903	564	28.39	33.64	1906	7153400	1556	23.17	27.45
1877	3266675	586	30.21	35.79	1907	6997000	1595	24.05	28.49
1878	3349446	610	28.02	33.20	1908	6651300	1588	23.96	28.39
1879	3432218	632	26.94	31.92	1909	6515100	1603	25.52	30.24
1880	3514989	657	28.11	33.30	1910	6526083	1648	28.39	33.64
1881	3435844	680	29.33	34.75	1911	6685500	1665	29.81	35.32
1882	3839066	706	31.26	37.04	1912	6855100	1752	30.72	36.40
1883	4001436	750	33.59	39.80	1913	6911400	1865	32.90	38.99
1884	4088034	832	32.42	38.42	1914	7221200	1825	34.83	41.28
1885	4160516	806	27.74	32.87	1915	7498900	1870	37.33	44.24
1886	4060838	854	25.47	30.18	1916	7789600	1957	40.88	48.44
1887	4041880	864	25.13	29.77	1917	8251000	2041	43.07	51.03
1888	3998393	888	25.41	30.11	1918	8485000	2385	44.06	52.21
1889	4017433	887	23.05	27.32	1919	8153700	2359	43.41	51.44
1890	4120586	964	24.44	28.96	1920	8519484	2144	42.85	50.77
1891	4298917	989	23.14	27.42	1921	8267300	1674	26.53	31.43
1892	4405909	1040	22.77	26.98	1922	7975100	1865	27.23	32.26
1893	4563771	991	22.88	27.11	1923	8135400	1773	27.35	32.41
1894	4662739	926	20.87	24.73	1924	7976700	1865	28.51	33.78
1895	4796648	961	18.91	22.40	1925	7817600	2023	33.62	39.84
1896	4858366	1103	17.01	20.15	1926	7603900	2026	36.76	43.56
1897	4952966	1210	18.79	22.27					
1898	5108331	1204	20.36	24.12					
1899	5362904	1180	20.92	24.79					

Note: Total net production of cattle comprises sales and slaughter and change in inventory.

Table 2.19. Hogs

Year	Total Stock of Hogs (no.)	Sales and Slaughter (000 head)	Unit Value: Inventory Change ($)	Unit Value: Sales and Slaughter ($)
1870	1418597	1368	7.91	11.82
1871	1397499	1291	6.04	9.03
1872	1376401	1475	5.37	8.02
1873	1355304	1308	5.95	8.90
1874	1334206	1237	7.73	11.56
1875	1313108	1298	8.28	12.37
1876	1292010	1325	7.40	11.06
1877	1270912	1262	6.45	9.64
1878	1249815	1280	4.87	7.28
1879	1218717	1300	5.63	8.41
1880	1207619	1303	6.32	9.45
1881	1415486	1343	7.60	11.36
1882	1486856	1350	8.19	12.24
1883	1491445	1402	6.72	10.04
1884	1352612	1452	6.54	9.77
1885	1400135	1497	5.37	8.02
1886	1358434	1609	5.42	8.10
1887	1336531	1607	6.26	9.35
1888	1356272	1584	6.60	9.86
1889	1763274	1653	5.35	8.00
1890	1733850	1790	5.23	7.82
1891	1573202	1206	5.50	8.14
1892	1598839	1477	5.80	9.77
1893	1790801	879	6.83	10.21
1894	1980366	1987	5.47	9.27
1895	1957751	1674	5.12	8.18
1896	1979154	1834	5.08	7.44
1897	2412700	1864	5.31	7.32
1898	2836685	2332	5.17	7.50
1899	2596757	2511	5.42	7.62

Table 2.19. (continued)

Year	Total Stock of Hogs (no.)	Sales and Slaughter (000 head)	Unit Value: Inventory Change ($)	Unit Value: Sales and Slaughter ($)
1900	2353828	2353	6.23	8.29
1901	2675672	2607	6.68	9.51
1902	3141843	2857	6.59	10.26
1903	3335738	2875	6.43	10.26
1904	3250144	3142	6.44	9.96
1905	3378800	2965	7.02	9.96
1906	3701100	3474	6.92	10.13
1907	3545900	3071	6.67	10.14
1908	3286600	3108	7.18	10.46
1909	3304000	3321	8.50	11.64
1910	3634800	3534	8.36	12.69
1911	3683800	3575	8.31	12.83
1912	3683300	3667	9.51	13.21
1913	3640100	4173	10.14	14.46
1914	3464500	3864	9.93	15.12
1915	3561800	3351	10.83	15.49
1916	3292400	3875	12.89	17.73
1917	3676900	3184	18.80	20.76
1918	3623000	4192	19.62	24.93
1919	3151900	4139	19.98	29.15
1920	3324300	2962	10.84	27.51
1921	3493200	3160	13.00	19.26
1922	3985600	3620	14.01	20.75
1923	4594300	3975	11.68	17.31
1924	4009100	4740	11.01	16.31
1925	4036700	4700	15.65	23.20
1926	4301500	4535	16.31	24.17

Table 2.20. Sheep and Lambs

Year	Stock of Sheep and Lambs (no.)	Sales and Slaughter (000 head)	OBI Sales and Slaughter (no.)	Price ($)
1870	3385717	1630		2.60
1871	3372464	1654		2.83
1872	3359211	1600		2.98
1873	3345957	1532		2.75
1874	3332704	1501		2.59
1875	3319451	1379		3.53
1876	3306198	1438		2.74
1877	3292945	1449		2.84
1878	3279691	1493		3.16
1879	3266438	1563		3.51
1880	3253185	1497		3.81
1881	3246165	1468		3.88
1882	3919365	1466		4.43
1883	3878549	1458		4.89
1884	3966878	1482		3.70
1885	3732977	1516		3.24
1886	3467949	1599		3.53
1887	3043842	1563		3.18
1888	3005202	1510		3.46
1889	3030503	1462		3.97
1890	3182983	1465	614534	3.77
1891	3156486	1564	674073	4.58
1892	2785691	1628	721244	4.52
1893	2948318	1588	721488	4.14
1894	2923147	1587	740061	3.93
1895	2958985	1600	766896	3.45
1896	3538084	1493	732872	3.46
1897	3327233	1318	664239	3.70
1898	2971010	1287	665238	3.95
1899	2944514	1491	790058	3.64
1900	2918017	1342	729148	4.26
1901	2918017	1357	732994	4.24
1902	2985165	1355	727850	4.22
1903	3017131	1287	687144	4.22
1904	2908448	1138	603736	4.28
1905	2610149	1090	574416	4.52
1906	2543000	1070	559868	4.71
1907	2350100	1051	545320	5.26
1908	2380300	1036	533441	5.19
1909	2327000	1006	512909	5.36
1910	2245600	1000	505015	5.62
1911	2174300	1069	531957	5.74
1912	2171500	1090	534311	5.92
1913	2333300	1060	512066	6.29
1914	2310300	1028	489320	6.72
1915	2358600	1012	475406	7.55
1916	2333900	1001	463576	9.15
1917	2421900	982	449268	13.08
1918	2636400	1016	458952	13.35
1919	2948700	1107	493694	12.42
1920	3179100		537087	7.22
1921	3200467			7.03
1922	3045300			7.63
1923	2600906			7.07
1924	2498800			8.70
1925	2628400			7.19
1926	2829700			6.60

Note: OBI is the Ontario Bureau of Industries

Table 2.21. Poultry

Year	Stock of Poultry (000 Birds)	Sales and Slaughter (000 Birds)	Unit Value: Sales and Slaughter ($/Bird)	Unit Value: Inventory Change ($/Bird)	Year	Stock of Poultry (000 Birds)	Sales and Slaughter (000 Birds)	Unit Value: Sales and Slaughter ($/Bird)	Unit Value: Inventory Change ($/Bird)
1870	8064.8	2685.6	0.515	0.365	1900	17922.7	7063.6	0.450	0.319
1871	8287.0	2759.6	0.528	0.375	1901	18458.6	7494.2	0.460	0.327
1872	8430.0	2807.2	0.580	0.411	1902	18787.5	7608.9	0.461	0.327
1873	8729.2	2906.8	0.573	0.406	1903	18827.4	7455.7	0.463	0.346
1874	8618.6	2870.0	0.538	0.381	1904	19739.5	7007.5	0.470	0.360
1875	8793.7	2928.3	0.557	0.395	1905	20953.1	7249.8	0.478	0.376
1876	9139.3	3043.4	0.522	0.370	1906	26957.7	9138.7	0.518	0.374
1877	9277.9	3089.5	0.509	0.360	1907	26444.8	8726.8	0.557	0.371
1878	9406.8	3132.5	0.400	0.283	1908	27492.9	9292.6	0.564	0.374
1879	9742.9	3244.4	0.483	0.343	1909	29565.3	9520.0	0.614	0.440
1880	10446.6	3478.7	0.454	0.322	1910	31793.3	11681.1	0.684	0.461
1881	10826.2	3605.1	0.560	0.397	1911	33445.0	12842.9	0.678	0.442
1882	11974.2	3987.4	0.580	0.411	1912	35665.4	14551.5	0.685	0.455
1883	12548.4	4178.6	0.650	0.461	1913	38240.7	14875.6	0.675	0.446
1884	12921.0	4302.7	0.621	0.441	1914	40212.6	15321.0	0.655	0.428
1885	14133.9	4706.6	0.531	0.376	1915	42071.6	15356.2	0.652	0.421
1886	13241.1	4409.3	0.490	0.347	1916	43090.3	16158.9	0.686	0.459
1887	12635.9	4207.8	0.547	0.388	1917	44067.5	16877.8	0.823	0.537
1888	12874.8	4287.3	0.567	0.402	1918	46236.1	17754.7	1.119	0.665
1889	13944.5	4643.5	0.509	0.360	1919	43629.2	16666.3	1.254	0.712
1890	14105.1	4697.0	0.514	0.365	1920	50325.2	13560.3	1.192	0.631
1891	13940.4	4251.8	0.493	0.350	1921	55605.7	17404.6	1.167	0.574
1892	13922.5	4343.8	0.438	0.310	1922	57423.6	18088.4	1.134	0.537
1893	14735.0	4567.9	0.474	0.336	1923	58806.9	19465.1	1.025	0.518
1894	15115.4	5124.1	0.405	0.287	1924	59130.1	20518.2	1.072	0.493
1895	15026.0	5785.0	0.412	0.292	1925	60305.2	20865.6	1.111	0.455
1896	16080.8	6223.3	0.387	0.274	1926	61545.5	21233.2	1.124	0.423
1897	17045.7	6324.0	0.336	0.238					
1898	16798.9	6114.8	0.404	0.286					
1899	17293.0	6294.7	0.467	0.331					

Table 2.22. Dairy Products

Year	Price of Fluid Milk ($/lb.)	Net Exports of Cheese (000 lb.)	Price of Cheese ($/lb.)	Net Exports of Butter (000 lb.)	Price of Butter ($/lb.)
1870	.008	8205.0	.119	15433.3	.170
1871	.008	16390.4	.097	19064.6	.172
1872	.007	19383.0	.102	15153.7	.157
1873	.008	23924.0	.131	12056.4	.180
1874	.011	32222.0	.105	9083.0	.242
1875	.009	34920.8	.092	12109.1	.186
1876	.008	35848.7	.089	14511.0	.184
1877	.008	37965.8	.090	12895.1	.183
1878	.006	46327.8	.067	14211.5	.130
1879	.007	40261.9	.081	18408.5	.140
1880	.008	49172.6	.097	17505.1	.176
1881	.008	50729.6	.093	15048.9	.179
1882	.009	57936.8	.096	7700.9	.193
1883	.008	69651.2	.089	7793.8	.184
1884	.008	79562.0	.089	6986.4	.171
1885	.007	78023.2	.071	4343.5	.153
1886	.007	73507.7	.082	5239.2	.160
1887	.008	84105.4	.091	4266.8	.177
1888	.008	88452.6	.086	1286.7	.179
1889	.008	94132.6	.084	1570.3	.163
1890	.009	106095.8	.075	3443.4	.19229
1891	.010	118145.7	.084	5489.9	.22291
1892	.010	133830.3	.085	6811.6	.22375
1893	.010	154820.7	.085	4831.9	.23041
1894	.010	145857.4	.083	3375.6	.21270
1895	.009	164583.1	.070	5599.8	.18895
1896	.008	164071.1	.074	11085.2	.18083
1897	.008	196579.9	.074	10880.3	.18041
1898	.009	189628.6	.073	19566.2	.18604
1899	.009	185683.3	.092	24084.4	.19354

Table 2.22. (continued)

Year	Price of Fluid Milk ($/lb.)	Net Exports of Cheese (000 lb.)	Price of Cheese ($/lb.)	Net Exports of Butter (000 lb.)	Price of Butter ($/lb.)
1900	.010	195639.9	.091	15188.9	.21250
1901	.009	200677.0	.083	27197.0	.20083
1902	.009	228813.1	.093	33589.2	.20041
1903	.009	233678.8	.088	24087.5	.20125
1904	.009	215420.6	.079	31350.9	.18625
1905	.010	215465.9	.098	33888.1	.21708
1906	.010	225059.5	.109	17802.4	.22625
1907	.011	189120.0	.106	4048.8	.24416
1908	.012	164323.0	.109	5396.7	.26000
1909	.011	180176.1	.104	4221.8	.24375
1910	.010	181029.1	.099	1915.3	.25583
1911	.009	162531.5	.113	4969.8	.19670
1912	.011	153720.6	.118	-7160.9	.25317
1913	.010	142966.2	.116	-6088.5	.22525
1914	.010	136439.2	.125	-4097.6	.20855
1915	.011	167989.8	.143	-868.6	.24836
1916	.013	179948.2	.188	6993.1	.2881
1917	.013	169187.5	.201	4492.1	.359
1918	.018	152034.1	.216	11720.1	.398
1919	.020	126033.1	.272	17214.7	.456
1920	.023	133069.3	.263	5997.8	.515
1921	.017	132972.4	.175	2351.7	.384
1922	.014	113632.4	.167	18227.0	.303
1923	.015	115088.7	.186	12090.9	.327
1924	.014	122418.7	.175	24303.7	.321
1925	.014	141654.7	.212	16274.8	.322
1926	.015	135325.4	.168	2688.1	.3363

Table 2.23. Horses

Year	Stock of Off-farm Horses (No.)	Total Stock Horses (No.)	Exports of Horses (No.)	Imports of Horses (No.)	Unit Value ($/head)
1870	59483	862072	15293	293	63.59
1871	60842	881801	11997	351	68.55
1872	62201	901529	8782	1359	71.05
1873	63559	921258	5399	794	71.50
1874	64918	940986	4382	1225	71.13
1875	66277	960715	4299	1577	69.62
1876	67636	980444	8306	1465	63.47
1877	68995	1000172	14179	1724	60.78
1878	70353	1019901	16629	1677	56.02
1879	71712	1039629	21393	1032	59.47
1880	73071	1059358	21993	992	64.42
1881	73071	1097010	20920	2862	75.25
1882	75914	1144382	13019	3919	84.88
1883	78757	1107402	11595	3788	94.41
1884	81600	1160050	11978	2084	87.82
1885	84443	1189846	16525	2761	87.93
1886	87286	1215644	18779	2394	81.75
1887	90129	1270216	20397	3921	81.54
1888	92972	1327925	17767	5027	82.67
1889	95815	1420094	16550	2644	79.15
1890	98658	1470572	11658	3495	82.25
1891	101501	1509858	11063	2623	87.50
1892	102237	1522801	13219	2171	80.27
1893	102975	1509912	8734	1857	73.80
1894	103713	1469962	14744	1797	62.26
1895	104451	1441045	21852	2860	58.58
1896	105189	1438018	17993	4518	59.58
1897	105927	1441771	14349	12900	62.40
1898	106665	1456732	12384	15115	67.80
1899	107403	1507038	10053	12104	75.60

Table 2.23. (continued)

Year	Stock of Off-farm Horses (No.)	Total Stock Horses (No.)	Exports of Horses (No.)	Imports of Horses (No.)	Unit Value ($/head)
1900	108141	1577493	7609	9070	82.24
1901	108879	1643533	12687	18280	90.62
1902	114193	1756623	3878	30510	102.59
1903	119507	1756377	2395	31666	107.85
1904	124821	1877736	2659	12448	119.94
1905	130135	1963100	2794	17822	124.22
1906	135449	2105600	2115	17406	127.56
1907	145314	2247900	2270	5824	130.94
1908	155112	2327100	2028	4725	136.62
1909	160563	2477600	2762	8702	146.69
1910	170982	2599000	2781	10040	160.83
1911	180000	2694100	1816	22614	166.75
1912	186687	2826800	2156	19925	170.39
1913	198728	2992200	3568	8099	162.20
1914	204395	3115000	10414	3352	151.55
1915	207748	3167300	26818	1715	140.56
1916	199580	3209800	25277	2375	139.79
1917	191412	3346400	16468	7523	136.08
1918	183244	3445000	10457	3606	136.21
1919	175076	3404500	3889	4181	135.53
1920	166908	3553322	3626	5404	122.17
1921	158742	3502822	2251	5154	76.87
1922	153020	3442322	1863	5597	67.39
1923	147298	3485522	2447	4905	67.39
1924	141576	3449922	1429	5698	72.66
1925	135854	3462222	1413	5886	75.82
1926	130132	3398622	2017	6025	80.03

Table 2.24. Seed, Grass and Clover

Year	Exports ($)	Imports ($)	Year	Exports ($)	Imports ($)
1870	438343	87025	1900	603591	617717
1871	74519	90199	1901	1308359	523291
1872	6383	199453	1902	919172	559461
1873	3831	219953	1903	1426521	455389
1874	45225	165028	1904	598675	546933
1875	312568	135182	1905	1475141	463167
1876	281028	192063	1906	552508	682222
1877	203235	260039	1907	963825	1172617
1878	186211	216055	1908	605128	1279344
1879	567457	4423	1909	960321	1164195
1880	190599	111497	1910	1914761	1350496
1881	913179	219767	1911	1157781	1172697
1882	207052	199894	1912	908157	1622818
1883	80464	273139	1913	1259669	1652411
1884	116267	250207	1914	450078	2348135
1885	140025	359153	1915	407356	2258579
1886	96690	348444	1916	1270739	1771152
1887	162939	382895	1917	1403845	1826420
1888	168252	678387	1918	3516233	1866785
1889	182200	419957	1919	4519716	3779327
1890	321184	264304	1920	2236576	2684347
1891	458137	362688	1921	2178987	2490730
1892	227543	461232	1922	2189190	2412338
1893	537217	392021	1923	3023797	2251066
1894	849326	523674	1924	3445730	2436177
1895	426460	681205	1925	3909090	2046687
1896	372239	610181	1926	4011409	1927344
1897	410849	498555			
1898	732208	427446			
1899	322310	554476			

Table 2.25. Wool

Year	Ontario Wool Production (lb.)	Price ($/lb.)	Year	Ontario Wool Production (lb.)	Price ($/lb.)
1870		0.196	1900	5834097	0.151
1871		0.268	1901	5690673	0.133
1872		0.244	1902	5419900	0.155
1873		0.193	1903	4972042	0.180
1874		0.173	1904	4634922	0.204
1875		0.192	1905	4543981	0.236
1876		0.194	1906	4347246	0.217
1877		0.178	1907	4150510	0.230
1878		0.169	1908	4218475	0.183
1879		0.214	1909	4010300	0.205
1880		0.199	1910	3780798	0.233
1881	5746185	0.191	1911		0.216
1882	6608418	0.210	1912		0.224
1883	6511918	0.189	1913		0.258
1884	6086866	0.173	1914		0.282
1885	5547867	0.149	1915		0.378
1886	4658249	0.156	1916		0.427
1887	4691027	0.157	1917		0.535
1888	4588896	0.151	1918		0.581
1889	4574700	0.194	1919		0.651
1890	5498141	0.178	1920		0.298
1891	5643706	0.166	1921		0.184
1892	5896891	0.157	1922		0.241
1893	6235036	0.151	1923		0.284
1894	6214811	0.146	1924		0.355
1895	5581387	0.135	1925		0.355
1896	5139984	0.154	1926		0.326
1897	5104686	0.160			
1898	5525122	0.142			
1899	5805921	0.196			

Note: The implied wool production can be obtained by dividing the revenue from wool production by the price.

Chapter 3. Non-Agricultural Primary Industries

M.C. URQUHART with acknowledgment

to DUNCAN McDOUGALL

Gross Domestic Product in Non-Agricultural Primary Industries, 1870-1926

FORESTRY

Methodology

The general method of calculating income produced in non-farm production of forest products and in farm production can be presented in terms of the steps taken in arriving at the income data.

The first step was to derive estimates of the physical production of various forest products in total and the division of the totals, in every case, between farm and non-farm production. The categories of production, each estimated separately were (i) logs and bolts for sawmill and shingle mill use, (ii) pulpwood, (iii) railway ties, (iv) squared timber exports, (v) firewood, (vi) all other products as a group.

That part of production belonging to the farm was valued at farm prices and the resulting sum was included as a part of farm receipts in just the same way that other farm products were included.

Calculation of non-farm income produced involved a number of further steps. First, the volumes of non-farm products of various kinds were all converted into equivalent cubic feet of standing timber in order to be able to get a single aggregate measure of volume of non-farm forest production. Second, a wage cost per thousand cubic feet of standing timber was calculated and then used to obtain a wage bill for obtaining the primary forest products. Third, the wage bill was marked up to add in non-wage factor costs. In order to tie in with the official statistics in 1926 the public resource royalties (stumpages) were calculated separately.

We proceed now to the derivation of the measures of production.

(i) Logs and Bolts

For 1910 to 1926

For 1910 to 1926 the basic annual data for the estimation of saw log and bolt production were the output of lumber and shingles of Canadian saw, lath and shingle mills, estimated annually from mailed questionnaire to sawmills by the Forestry Branch of the federal Department of the Interior from 1908 to 1916 and by the Dominion Bureau of Statistics from 1917 onward, and exports and imports of logs and bolts. The measure of the output of lumber in thousands of feet board measure (Mfbm) was also used as the measure of the volume of standing timber from which the lumber was produced. This period may be further subdivided into periods 1910 to 1921 and 1922 to 1926. DBS itself produced estimates of primary log and bolt production for 1922 to 1926 and these estimates were taken directly from the DBS publication *Canadian Forestry Statistics Revised 1959, p.20.* For the years 1910 to 1921 the procedure was: estimates of output of lumber measured in fbm were obtained from *ibid.* pp. 32-33; output of shingles, measured in thousands (called squares) was obtained from the *Canada Year Book 1927-28, p.309* — it is also available in DBS publications *The Lumber Industry*; the measure of shingles was converted from squares to fbm by the formula one square of shingles is the equivalent of 135.68 feet board measure (source of the conversion factor DBS *Sawmills* from 1960 to 1964 and partially 1965 and 1966, in which publications the fact that inputs of bolts to produce shingles are measured in feet board measure rather than in cords, can be used to check the conversion factor used here which is based on quantities of shingles and lumber that can be produced with a given amount of labour); the sum of these two series then yielded an equivalent of the measure of log input into the production of lumber, shingles and lath (the latter being in considerable measure a by-product obtained from sawmill waste); exports of logs were added; imports of logs were subtracted. The result was the measure of production of logs for lumber, shingles and other minor products, in Canada.

Note: I am indebted to Mr. Pat Martin of Statcan for the knowledge that information obtained by Statcan from some logging companies around 1970 was to the effect that from six to 10 squares of shingles could be obtained from 1000 feet board measure (log measure) of *merchantable* timber, depending on the quality of the logs — an average of eight squares per 1000 feet board measure would yield an equivalent of 125 feet board measure of *merchantable* timber per square of shingles. The use of the figure 135.68 feet board measure of *standing* timber per square is reasonably in line with this estimate from Mr. Martin.

A check can be made of the estimate of log production obtained in this way for 1910 against an estimate made from data of the 1910 census of manufactures as follows.

Cost of material used in saw and shingle mills ($000)	56,208.6
Cost of logs at 90% of cost of materials ($000)	50,587.7
Unit value of saw logs (from farm production) per Mfbm ($)	10.72
Volume of logs consumed in mills (line 2 ÷ line 3), Mfbm	4,719,000
Add exports of logs, Mfbm	121,645
Total	4,840,645
Subtract imports of logs, Mfbm	69,778
Production of logs in Canada, Mfbm	4,770,867

By coincidence the estimate of log production for 1910 from the method used for all years from 1910 to 1921 was 4,771,704 Mfbm, an almost identical figure.

For 1900

We deal with 1900 next since there was a complete census of forest products in that year providing both quantities and prices. The census estimate of production was accepted because it was supported by calculations from alternative data as follows. In what follows the "saw mill" industry always includes saw mills proper, shingle mills, lath mills insofar as they are distinct, etc.

Estimated cost of materials (1900 census of manufactures, adjusted for omission of small saw mills) ($000)	30,496.9
Cost of logs only at 95% of materials ($000)	28,972.1
Unit cost * of saw logs (census) per Mfbm ($)	8.147
Volume of logs consumed in thousands feet board measure and equivalently the volume of lumber produced = 28,972,100 ÷ 8.147 =	3,556,165
Add exports of logs, calendar year basis, Mfbm	113,094
Total	3,669,259
Subtract imports of logs calendar year basis, Mfbm	42,283
Remainder: Estimated production, Mfbm	3,626,976
Production logs from 1900 census of forestry, Mfbm: this figure was adopted for 1900	3,656,963
Volume of logs consumed in saw mills (production less net export of logs), Mfbm	3,586,152

*The export unit value for calendar 1900 was $8.131

If the above figures are accepted, there were 1,619,438 Mfbm of lumber available for building construction in Canada, (production of 3,556,165 Mfbm less net calendar year exports of 1,936,727 Mfbm) valued at 384.3 million of 1971 dollars or 4,214 Mfbm for each million of 1971 dollars of construction. This is almost twice the 2,117 Mfbm that was calculated from an average for the years 1910 to 1916 and 1920 to 1926 of the ratio of the domestic supply of lumber in Mfbm to each million dollars worth of building construction measured in 1971 dollars, i.e. the average availability of 2,117 Mfbm of lumber of each million of 1971 dollars of construction. The measure of building construction for 1900 at 384.3 million of 1971 dollars is for new construction only. In addition, there would be other uses of lumber which in a year of low building activity, such as 1900, might almost match the building use: large amounts of lumber were used at that time in railway box cars, wagons and other such uses in addition to repair usage. (The sources of the data on construction are given in Chapter 5 on construction; the source gave data in 1971 dollars as well as current dollars.)

For 1890

Values of logs were not obtained in the censuses of forest products before 1900 and so a unit value is not derivable from that source. Further, while there is a unit value for logs exported, the volume of logs exported was small and its composition among species of wood changed substantially, so that use of a unit export value to make an estimate of the volume of logs used in saw mills from census cost of material would be questionable.

Given these circumstances, the method used was to chain the 1890 value of log production to that for 1900 on the basis of combined changes in the net volume of lumber exports and the volume of building construction, adjusted for exports and imports of logs themselves. The actual data used follow.

Building construction 1890 (millions of $1971)	387.6
Lumber etc. used @ 2,117 Mfbm	
per million building construction in $1971, Mfbm	820,549
Net exports of lumber and similar products, Mfbm	1,527,690
Partial estimate of lumber etc. produced, in Canada, Mfbm	2,348,239
Building construction 1900 (millions of $1971)	384.3
Lumber used in construction @ 2,117 Mfbm	
per million building construction in $1971, Mfbm	813,563
Net exports of lumber and similar products, Mfbm	1,936,727
Partial estimate of lumber produced in Canada	2,750,290
Final estimate of production of lumber in 1890 using above partial estimates for indexing the 1900 final estimate of saw mill use of logs, (2,348,239 ÷ 2,750,290 x 3,586,152) Mfbm	3,061,911
This figure measures the standing timber used for saw mills in Canada, Mfbm	3,061,911
Add net export of logs, (104,497 − 81,546) Mfbm	22,951
Log production in Canada Mfbm	3,084,862

This is the project estimate.

The figure of 2,117 Mfbm per million 1971 dollars construction is the figure derived from the construction data of a period of large new construction. If the figure of 4,214 Mfbm for each million of building construction measured in $1971 implied in the 1900 estimate were used to measure lumber used in building construction in 1890 the result would be:

Use of lumber for construction	
4,214 x 387.6 Mfbm	1,633,346
Plus net exports of lumber, Mfbm	1,527,690
Total volume of logs used in lumber production, Mfbm	3,161,036
Plus net export of logs, Mfbm	22,951
Total volume of logs produced, Mfbm	3,183,987

This is about 3.2 percent higher than the project estimate. However, it is difficult to put a measure on the meaning of the above-mentioned 1900 figure of 4,214 Mfbm for each unit of building construction worth one million 1971 dollars.

Accordingly the figure we use for log production in 1890 is 3,084,862 Mfbm.

Cost of materials of saw mills in 1890 was $28,030,600 and if we take 90% of this as the cost of logs the implication is that the unit cost of the logs was $8.18 per Mfbm.

For 1880

The 1880 figure was chained to the 1900 figure in nearly the same way as for 1890 except that gross values of exports of lumber were used in the chaining rather than net exports. The procedure follows.

Use of lumber in construction @ 2,117 Mfbm for $1 million construction measured in 1971 $

1900:	Construction $384.3 million $ 1971 x 2,117 Mfbm	813,563
	Gross exports of lumber, Mfbm	2,041,558
	Total, Mfbm	2,855,121
1880:	Construction $212.9 million $ 1971 x 2,117 Mfbm	450,709
	Gross exports of lumber, Mfbm	1,365,455
	Total, Mfbm	1,816,164

Estimate of lumber production 1880 using above
quantities for indexing to 1900 lumber production.
1,816,164 ÷ 2,855,121 x 3,586,152 = 2,281,178 Mfbm

Then logs used in saw mills, Mfbm	2,281,178
Add exports of logs, Mfbm	35,939
Sub-total, Mfbm	2,317,117
Subtract imports of logs, Mfbm	61,238
Production of logs in Canada, Mfbm	2,255,879

This is the project estimate of saw log production.

Checks

We can check what such a measure implies about the unit price of the logs used in saw mills as valued in the census of manufactures for 1880. The cost of materials used in saw mills in 1880 was 21,207.2 thousand dollars.

If we take 90 percent of this as the cost of logs we have log cost of $19,086,500 and as the unit cost of logs, $8.46 Mfbm. This appears to be high relative to the 1900 price of $8.147 and relative to such prices as the export prices of logs as a group. For example, the export unit values of the very small quantities of logs exported were $4.56 per M.ft. in calendar 1880 compared with $6.76 in calendar 1890 and $8.13 in calendar 1900. For the decade from 1890 to 1900, for which export unit values of logs are available by species, unit values in Mfbm of certain individual species behaved as follows: pine rose from $8.34 in 1890 to $9.46 in 1900; spruce rose from $5.79 in 1890 to $6.89 in 1900; oak actually fell from $19.05 in 1890 to $15.59 in 1900. The log prices vary greatly among different species and it is not at all clear how the composition of log exports compares with that of domestic usage of logs. Certainly, among log products, the production and sale of spruce products, relatively low-priced products, grew substantially relative to the quantity of pine, a high-priced product.

Other comparative data between 1880 and 1900 are more reassuring. For example the unit price of firewood exported, per cord, was $2.04 in 1880, $2.12 in 1890 and $1.90 in 1900 (calendar years in each case). Similarly, there was not great change in the export unit values of either pine deals or spruce deals, each taken separately, between calendar 1885 and calendar 1900 — they are not available separately before fiscal 1885 — or of the export unit values of the pine and spruce combined between calendar 1880 and calendar 1883 or fiscal 1884. In addition, the ratio of GVP of saw mills in 1880 to GVP of 1900 is 0.618 while the ratio of the project estimate of lumber production in Canada in 1880 to the estimate for 1900 is 0.636: relative export unit value of lumber seems to have changed very little but it should be kept in mind that the proportion of spruce in the total increased as time passed.

For 1870

The 1870 figure was chained to the 1900 figure in exactly the same way as for 1880. The procedure follows.

Use of lumber in construction at 2,117 Mfbm per $1 million building construction in 1971 $

1870:	237.3 million $ 1971 x 2,117, Mfbm	502,364
	Gross exports of lumber, Mfbm	1,271,380
	Total use of lumber, Mfbm	1,773,744

Estimate of 1870 lumber production by indexing to 1900 lumber production
(1,773,744 ÷ 2,855,121) x 3,586,152 Mfbm =   2,227,897

We use this figure without adjustment for import or export of logs, as imports of logs are not given in the trade data and exports are very small.

Interpolation between census years 1870 to 1910

Interpolation between base years 1870 to 1910 was done basically by use of a measure based on the export of lumber products plus lumber used for building construction. Exports of lumber products were obtained on a year to year basis from *Trade of Canada*: several categories of exports had to be added together and the data were converted from a fiscal year to a calendar year basis: net exports of lumber were used for 1890 to 1910; gross exports of lumber were used for 1870 to 1890. Lumber used in building construction was calculated by multiplying the volume of building construction measured in $ 1971 (obtained from the project estimates for the construction industry) by a factor of 2,117 Mfbm per million dollars worth of construction measured in $1971. The sum of the number of board feet of lumber disposed of in exports and in building construction then became the interpolator for the consumption of logs and bolts in Canadian mills. The procedure was to calculate the ratio of the estimated mill consumption of logs in each base year to the interpolator for the particular year, to interpolate this ratio linearly between base years and then to multiply the elements of the resultant series by the interpolator for the year involved. Exports of logs obtained from *Trade of Canada* were then added to mill consumption of logs, year by year, for all years; imports of logs were then subtracted for years 1880 to 1910 — imports were not available before 1880 and were negligibly small.

The ratios of the mill consumption of logs to the values of the interpolator were as follows, for base years.

Year		Ratio
1870		1.256
1880		1.256
1890	comparable with 1880	1.280
1890	comparable with 1900	1.304
1900		1.304
1910		1.022

The similarities of the ratios for 1870 and 1880 and again for 1890 (compared with 1900) and 1900 follows from the way in which the base year estimates for 1870, 1880 and 1890 were made.

(ii) Pulpwood Production

Pulpwood is measured in cords.

For 1908 to 1926

Official estimates (DBS) are available for 1908 to 1926. They were built up from data on exports plus data on consumption of pulpwood in Canadian mills. The latter were obtained by survey. They were obtained from DBS *The Pulp and Paper Industry*, 1926, p.29 and *ibid.* 1927, p.29.

Estimates for census years 1880 and 1890 were devised in much the same way as the official figures for 1908 onward. The figure for 1900 was taken directly from the census of forestry.

For 1900

The census of forestry in the decennial census covered all forestry activity. The census figure of 668,034 cords of pulpwood harvested for 1900, valued at $2,168,509, was accepted. The following check against this number was made by use of the census of manufactures and export data.

The census of manufactures material costs for 1900 were:

Total value of product of woodpulp mfg. industry		$ 4,246,781
Cost of materials:	in crude form	1,167,866
	in partly mfgd. form	296,221
Total cost of materials		1,466,087

Division of the value of the crude material by the unit value per cord of pulpwood from the census yields, as an estimate of pulpwood input

Pulpwood input of mills, 1900   1,167,866 ÷ 3.246 =   359,786 cords

Exports of pulpwood were given in value only.
Division of average value of pulpwood exports for fiscal 1900 and 1901 by the price 3.246 yields as estimate calendar year export

Exports of pulpwood, calendar 1900	354,250 cords
The sum of the domestic use plus foreign exports thus amounts to	714,036 cords

This figure is sufficiently close to the census of forest production figure that the latter was accepted.

The production figure for 1900 is then   668,034 cords

For 1890

The decennial census of 1891 forestry statistics gives production of pulpwood in 1890 at 261,155 cords.
A check using the census of manufactures figures and exports yields the following:

Value of all material inputs of pulpwood mills 1890	$ 469,845
Value of crude material inputs at 80% of total material inputs (see 1900 division)	375,876
Value of exports, calendar year estimate	134,502
Total value of pulpwood	$ 510,378

The forestry estimate of production for 1890 did not have a value and exports were given in value only, hence there were not data therein to get a unit value of pulpwood directly. A price for pulpwood in 1890 was obtained by extrapolating the unit value of pulpwood for 1900 to 1890 on the basis of the unit value of spruce logs exported.
The estimated unit values of spruce logs exported for calendar 1900 was $6.89 per Mfbm and for calendar 1890 was $5.79 per Mfbm.
The unit value of pulpwood in 1900 was $3.246 per cord and chaining by the unit value

of pulpwood logs exported would yield a unit value of $2.728 per cord for pulpwood in 1890. Unfortunately, owing to an error, a price of $3.122 was used in 1890. Dividing the value of exports and domestically used pulpwood by $3.122 yields

Quantity of pulpwood produced: 510,378 ÷ 3.122 = 163,478 cords

This is the figure that was used for 1890 — the forestry census figure of 261,100 cords is too high as were the other census of forestry figures for this year.

(Had the correct price of pulpwood for 1890 been used the estimate of pulpwood produced would have been, quantity of pulpwood produced = 510,378 ÷ 2.728 = 187,089 cords: this quantity is still much below the 261,100 cords estimate of the census of forestry which is 40 percent greater. Fortunately, a shortfall of 24,000 cords represents a quite small part of total forest production with a value of 65 thousand dollars. Since the quantities involved were so small and revision would have involved much recalculation, the original estimates was allowed to stand.)

For 1880

Pulpwood was not reported separately in the forestry census of 1880. Pulpwood exports were not shown separately but, in any event, were probably negligibly small (inferred from the trend of exports from 1890 onward). Therefore, the estimate for 1880 was based entirely on the use of pulpwood logs in pulpmills in 1880 from the census of manufactures.

Value of materials used in pulp mills 1880	$ 137,068
Value of crude material inputs at 80% of total (see the 1900 data)	$ 109,654

The price per cord of pulpwood was chained from 1890 to 1880 by use of the unit value of spruce log exports. The unit value of exports of spruce logs per M feet in calendar 1880 was $3.385; $5.79 per M feet for 1890. The chaining gave the price of pulpwood per cord in 1880 as follows: price 1880 = (3.385 ÷ 5.79) x 3.122 = $1.83. The pulpwood consumption in Canadian pulp mills then equals 109,654 ÷ 1.83 = 59,920 cords.

(The error in 1890 led to an understatement of mill consumption of 9,000 cords in 1880.)

We used the figure of 59,920 cords as the forest production of pulpwood in 1880.

Modes of Interpolation

For 1870 to 1880 — see 1880 to 1890

For 1880 to 1890

A linear interpolation was made between 1880 and 1890, there being no base for interpolation. For years before 1880 it was assumed that the absolute annual increments were the same as those of the 1880s; this meant that pulpwood production disappeared in 1875.

For 1890 to 1900

Exports of pulpwood were used as the interpolator. The procedure follows.

Only the value of exports of pulpwood were available in the trade data. A unit value of exports of pulpwood was estimated for each year by using the unit value of exports of spruce logs to extrapolate back to 1890 the unit value of pulpwood in 1900 obtained from the census of forestry data. Estimates for each year of the quantity of exports were obtained by dividing the value of pulpwood estimates by the estimated price of pulpwood. The ratio of total production (in cords) to exports (in cords) was calculated for each of 1890 and 1900. This ratio was then linearly interpolated between 1890 and 1900 and multiplication of these ratios by the volumes of exports for years 1891 to 1899 yielded the estimates of pulpwood production for these years.

For 1900 to 1908

In principle, the same method as for 1890 to 1900 was used for interpolation between 1900 and 1908 but the detail of the steps were somewhat different.

From 1904 to 1908 the quantity as well as the value of pulpwood exports was given so these quantities were obtained directly. Between 1900 and 1904 the unit value of pulpwood exports was obtained by use of the unit value of exports of spruce logs as an interpolator of the unit value of cordwood, between the unit value of cordwood in 1900, from the census of forestry, and the unit value of pulpwood exports in 1904, from the trade data. The physical volume of cordwood exports for 1900 to 1903 was obtained by dividing the value of exports of pulpwood by the unit values just obtained. The physical volume of exports was then used as an interpolator between 1900 and 1908 in exactly the same fashion as was done for 1890 to 1900.

(iii) Railway Ties

The estimates for railway ties were made in different fashion for three discrete periods, 1870 to 1907, 1908 to 1920, 1921 to 1926.

For 1870 to 1907

The estimates for 1870 to 1907 were built up from two components, tie use for replacement and repair, and tie use for building new rail lines. I deal with these in turn.

Tie Use for Replacement and Repair

The number of ties purchased by the railways for replacement and repair are available in *Railway Statistics* for railway year ending June, 1907 and each year from 1911 to 1921 (the year changes from a year ending June 30 to a calendar year in 1919). If these numbers are divided by total track mileage at June 30 we get the number of replacement ties per mile for each year. The average number for the above years was 214 ties per mile of all track including double track and yard track. However, before 1907 good figures are available only for first main track. For the five railway years 1907 to 1911, all track mileage is about 25 percent above mileage of first main track (See HSC Series S77-80). If one relates the replacement ties to the number of miles of first main track, one would then multiply the 214 ties per mile of all track by 1.25 to get number of replacement ties per mile of first main track. Such a multiplication yields a figure of 266 ties per mile of first main track and since that figure is only an approximation, I actually used the figure of 250 ties per mile of first main track as the measure of replacement. The total number of ties bought for replacement then was estimated for 1870 to 1907 by multiplying the miles of first main track (available in HSC series S28) at June 30 each year by 250.

Ties Used for New Construction

Miles of first main track are available for June 30 of each year from 1870 to 1907 (HSC Series S28). The item net miles of track added between June and June each railway year was obtained by taking first differences. I have it on the authority of Professor J.L. McDougall of Queen's University, an authority on railway matters, that on first main track there was a tie for each 22 inches — the ties would not be quite as close in subsidiary tracks — and, if one accepts the estimate that secondary track of one quarter the mileage of first main track would be constructed, on the average, then the estimate of total use of ties in construction of new track would be obtained by multiplying construction of first main track by 1.25 and then using a measure of one tie per two feet of new line of all kinds or 2,640 ties per mile of new line of all kinds.

Railway ties produced in Canada are then obtained by adding exports of ties (from *Trade of Canada*) to use of ties by steam railways for all years from 1870 to 1907 and subtracting imports for years 1894 to 1907; imports of ties were not reported separately before 1894. Production of railway ties is one case where the census figure for 1900 was not used — it could have achieved the census figure only if there had been most unusual accumulation of inventory and one would not want to incorporate unusual inventory behaviour into base year figures.

For 1908 to 1921

Numbers and values of ties bought (and average unit values) for replacement and repair were obtained from *Railway Statistics* for 1907 and 1911 to 1921; numbers for 1908, 1909, 1910 were obtained by linear interpolation between 1907 and 1911 and price per tie was obtained likewise.

Numbers of ties used for new construction were estimated in much the same manner as for the years 1870 to 1907 with only slight variation of process. One difference was that miles of all track were available for this period (HSC Series S77-80) and accordingly, estimates of net additions of mileage of all types of track were obtained by taking first differences, year by year. Track mileage constructed was multiplied by 2,640, (the number of ties to the mile) to give total ties used in construction (J.L. McDougall believed that 2,640 ties to the mile was an appropriate figure to use since while there were 22 inches per tie for first main track there would be somewhat sparser use of ties for siding, yard track etc.). Exports of ties were added and imports subtracted: for many years for exports and for all years, until 1919, for imports only values were given and numbers were calculated by division of the value figures by cost per tie to the railways which was available from their data on purchased ties.

The initial estimates were on a railway and trade year basis of June to June until 1919. The data for these years were converted to a calendar year basis by the usual method.

For 1922 to 1926

Production figures for railway ties, in Canada, are given in *Operations in the Woods, Revised Estimates, 1959* (p.28 ff.). The numbers given for 1922 to 1925 include all ties, both hewn and sawn; from 1926 onward the data are for hewn ties only. Since sawn ties are already included in the sawmill industry they should not be included again with hewn ties. Sawn ties can be obtained from DBS *The Lumber Industry*, various issues, usually in Table C, for years from 1922 onward. For 1922 to 1925, sawn ties, thus obtained were subtracted from the total of all ties noted above, to yield a figure for hewn ties.

Note: Some ties were sawn from quite early times and hence were the product of the saw mills. There may be some duplication in data on production of the forest if some logs from which ties are produced are included as a part of input of the saw mill industry as well as being counted separately. I believe that this should not be a problem with our data since prior to 1922 we have only used the output of lumber as being indicative of the input of saw logs. It must be taken account of, however, once DBS estimates of production of forests are available, beginning in 1922.

(iv) Squared Timber Exported

Tonnages of squared timber exported, classified by species of wood, are available in *Trade of Canada* (Sessional Papers, 1915 Paper Number 25) for fiscal years 1868 to 1913. These data were converted to cubic feet of standing timber at a rate of 100 cubic feet of standing timber per ton of squared timber. (Exports of squared timber are available for 1913 in both tons of squared timber, 52,912 tons, and in Mfbm, 24,161 Mfbm. The latter multiplied by the conversion rate of lumber to cubic feet, at 219 cubic feet per Mfbm yields, 5,291,259 cubic feet, rounded to 5,291 thousand cubic feet).

Quantities of squared timber exported were not published for 1914 to 1919 and had to be calculated from data for values of squared timber exported. Quantities in Mfbm and values were available from *Trade of Canada* data for each of 1913 and 1920 (fiscal years); for each of these two years a unit value was calculated and unit values for the intervening years were obtained by using the unit value of exports of planks and boards, which was calculable, as interpolator. The quantities exported in 1914 to 1919 were then derived by dividing the value figures of squared timber exports by the unit values.

From 1920 onward quantities exported in Mfbm were available in *Trade of Canada*.

(v) Production of Firewood: Farm and Non-Farm

The basic source of data for this particular forest product was the decennial census. From 1870 to 1900 there was a separate schedule for forest products and presumably all of forest product production was covered. From 1910 onward the decennial census only obtained records of production of forest products on farms; non-farm production was not covered in the census.

Of all of these censuses only three could be regarded as reasonably basically quite useful, namely, the censuses for 1900, 1920 and 1930 and some use could be made of the 1910 census reports of farm production. Checks with material on use of forest products suggest that the census data before 1900 are unreliable and they were not used.

The properties of the four censuses of which some use was made were the following. The censuses of 1920 and 1930 gave total production of firewood on farms, by province (and by much finer subdivisions), divided between the part sold and the part used on farms; the 1910 census gives figures for total farm production with considerable geographic detail but does not give information on what part was sold; the 1900 census provides data on both farm and non-farm production of firewood together, with geographic detail, but does not report farm and non-farm production separately.

There was very limited information on non-farm production of firewood in 1920 and 1930. DBS reports on primary production of forest products from 1917 onward, reported annually in *Operations in the Woods* and like publications, contained estimates of very small amounts of non-farm production and although DBS published what were supposed to be revised estimates of total production of firewood from 1926 to 1930, the estimates of quantities from 1920 onward appeared to be roughly the agricultural census figure for 1920 augmented annually by modest increments until 1931; there was then a big drop in reported production in 1932 which undoubtedly reflected not a real drop but just the availability of the new census of 1931 data on farm production of firewood in 1930. Given this circumstance, an estimate of non-farm production of firewood for 1920 was made by using data on production of firewood on crown lands of Canada, Quebec, Ontario and New Brunswick, reported by the relevant government department at about 160,000 cords, supplemented by some data on production on private limits from reports on primary forest operation in annual reports on lumber mill production from 1917 to 1924 (an amount of about 30,000 cords in 1920). To make some allowance for non-farm production in British Columbia and on other private limits, the estimate for non-farm production was rounded up to 300,000 cords in total for 1920; non-farm production was arbitrarily estimated at 150,000 cords in 1930, that being one-half the 1920 figure.

The 1900 census data for production of primary forest products other than firewood checked out quite well with data on use of such forest products and it was decided to accept the 1900 census firewood production figure as the correct measure of all production of firewood.

There were no data to provide a direct estimate of the non-farm production of firewood in 1910.

Given the above background, the estimate of the volume of production of firewood on farms and off-farms was calculated as follows. First, an estimate was made of the countrywide consumption of firewood for census years and since the volume of firewood entering into international trade was sufficiently small to be ignored the estimate of total consumption also provided the figure for total production. The data for 1920 and 1900 were especially critical and those for 1930 were also of considerable importance. Consumption of firewood was calculated in two parts, farm consumption and all the rest which for convenience of interpolation was attributed to non-farm rural household consumption.

The relevant data for making the calculations for 1920 and 1930 follow.

Firewood Used on Farms From
Farm Production, 1920 and 1930
(firewood measured in cords)

Region	1920			1930		
	No. of Farms	Total Consumption	Consumption Per Farm	No. of Farms	Total Consumption	Consumption Per Farm
Maritimes	97,788	921,644	9.42	86,334	929,275	9.01
Quebec	137,619	2,668,280	19.39	135,957	3,064,838	16.95
Ontario	198,053	2,481,360	12.53	192,174	2,307,018	10.06
Prairies	255,657	1,015,304	3.97	288,079	1,604,903	4.88
B.C.	21,973	137,674	6.26	26,079	180,568	5.46
Canada	711,090	7,224,212	10.16	728,623	6,563,337	9.01

Sources: Census of Canada, 1921 and 1931, *Agriculture*, for firewood production; HSC for number of farms.

Production of Firewood on Farms
and Elsewhere, 1920 and 1930
(firewood measured in cords)

Region	1920			1930		
	No. of Farms	Total Consumption	Consumption Per Farm	No. of Farms	Total Consumption	Consumption Per Farm
Maritimes	97,788	1,026,542	10.50	86,334	929,275	10.76
Quebec	137,619	3,303,436	24.00	135,957	3,064,838	22.54
Ontario	198,053	2,855,675	14.42	192,174	2,307,018	12.00
Prairies	255,657	1,169,807	4.58	288,079	1,604,903	5.57
B.C.	21,793	173,966	7.92	26,079	180,568	6.92
Canada, farm	711,090	8,529,426	11.99	728,623	8,086,602	11.10
Canada, non-farm		300,000			150,000	
Canada, Total		8,829,426			8,236,602	
less:						
Farm consumption		7,224,212			6,563,337	
Non-farm consumption		1,605,214			1,673,265	
Number of non-farm rural homes, Canada		268,700			328,300	
Average consumption per non-farm rural house		5.97			5.10 (5.04 *)	

Sources: same as previous table

* Note: Owing to an error of transposition in original worksheets (the figure 8,086,602 had been written 8,068,602) the figure used for consumption per non-farm rural houses was 5.04 cords rather than 5.10 cords. The consequence of the error was relatively small and the original calculations have been left unchanged.

Interpolation between 1920 and 1930 was done by first, interpolating consumption of firewood per farm on a countrywide basis linearly between 1920 and 1930 and consumption per non-farm rural house linearly between 1920 and 1930, and then multiplying the interpolated figures for each year by the relevant number of farm houses or non-farm rural houses. For the interpolation between base years, Marion Steele's figures for farm households and non-farm households, in her work on housing for this project, were used. It should be noted that her figures for farm households in census years differ from those that we use to make census year estimates of consumption and production but that circumstances does not create any problem since Marion Steele's figures are consistent within themselves.

The procedure was somewhat different for census years before 1920. Farm consumption of firewood was calculated by attributing to each earlier census year the same consumption per farm for each of the five regions in Canada as in 1920 and multiplying these figures by the number of occupied farms (HSC) in each of the regions. Non-farm consumption estimates were made in two steps. First, since the census figure for all production of firewood, farm and non-farm, in 1900 was accepted, the non-farm rural aggregate consumption could be calculated as just the difference between total production and farm consumption. Division by the number of non-farm rural houses in 1900 (Marion Steele's figure) gave a figure of 10.85 cords per household for the 213,900 non-farm rural households. For estimation of 1910 non-farm rural consumption an average of such consumption per household for 1900 and 1920 was used (yielding a figure of 8.41 cords per non-farm rural household) and total consumption was derived as the product of the number of non-farm rural households and the consumption per household of such households. For census years before 1900 the figure of 10.85 cords per non-farm rural household, the 1900 figure,was used and multiplied in each instance by the number of non-farm rural households to give aggregate non-farm rural consumption. For interpolation between census years, farm consumption was obtained by interpolating Canada wide consumption of firewood per farm linearly between census years and then multiplying by the number of farms (Marion Steele's data) for each year. Non-farm rural aggregate consumption was obtained in like manner between 1900 and 1920; before 1900 the figure of 10.85 cords consumption per non-farm rural house was used for every year and the aggregate obtained by multiplying that figure by the number of non-farm rural houses. Total consumption of all firewood in Canada, and equivalently total production, is the sum of farm and non-farm rural consumption.

It is necessary, of course, to divide total firewood production between farm and non-farm. This division is already done for 1920 and 1930. In addition, farm production is available by region, from the census of 1910, and the non-farm rural production is merely the difference between total production and farm production. For census years before 1910 an estimation procedure was necessary. The figures used for averages of farm production in 1900, for each of the five regions separately, were the averages of the 1910 and 1920 figures as shown next.

Average Production Per Farm
(in cords)

	1920	1910	1900: Average of 1920 and 1910
Maritime provinces	10.50	9.74	10.12
Quebec	24.00	19.21	21.61
Ontario	14.42	12.18	13.30
Prairie Provinces	4.58	1.46	3.02
British Columbia	7.92	8.04	7.98

The average production figures per farm for each region, as derived for 1900, were also used to calculate the output of firewood on farms for each region, for censuses of 1870, 1880 and 1890.

Division of Forest Products into Farm and Non-Farm Components

This division was heavily dependent on the censuses of farm products and of forestry for 1910, 1920 and 1930. The proportions of farm production to total production, by volume, was the following for these years. The absolute amounts produced on farms were obtained from the census data for these years and the proportions for farms was just obtained by taking the ratios of the absolute amounts produced on farms to total national production from all sources. There was one special case: in 1920 the census of forest products in agriculture had quantities of log products designated by "number" of logs, a completely unsatisfactory measure; the quantity of farm production of logs in 1920 was estimated by dividing the census value of farm production of logs by a price per Mfbm of logs which is described in the section on valuation of farm logs below.

Proportions of Productions of Forest Products on
Farms to Total Production, Census Years

	1910	1920	1930
Logs and bolts	0.271802	0.115034	0.057047
Pulpwood	0.436023	0.292688	0.148036
Firewood	(0.740618)	(0.966023)	(0.981749)
Railway ties	0.335091	0.143809	0.151689
Squared timber	Nil	Nil	Nil

There were small amounts of other products that were dealt with separately. The total production of each product was divided between farm and non-farm as follows:

(i) **Logs and Bolts:** 1870 to 1909: farm product was placed at 0.271802 of the total for each year, which was the 1910 ratio. 1910 to 1920: farm produced ratios were linearly interpolated between 1910 and 1920. 1920 to 1930: farm produced ratios were linearly interpolated between 1920 and 1930.

(ii) **Pulpwood Production:** 1870 to 1909: the farm production ratio for every year was placed at 0.44 based on the 1910 ratio. 1910 to 1920: the ratios were linearly interpolated between census year ratios. 1920 to 1930: the ratios were linearly interpolated between census year ratios.

(iii) **Firewood Production:** The method of division has been described already: it differs somewhat from the log and pulpwood methods.

(iv) **Railway Tie Production:** 1870 to 1909: the farm production ratio for every year was placed at 0.34 based on the 1910 ratio. 1910 to 1920: the ratios were interpolated linearly between adjacent census years. 1920 to 1930: the ratios were interpolated linearly between adjacent census years.

(v) **Squared Timber:** All of the squared timber is attributed to the non-farm sector.

(vi) **All Other Wood Products:** The procedure for dealing with other woods products will be dealt with separately for farm and non-farm production at the time of aggregation of the components of output for each of these sectors.

AGGREGATION OF PRODUCTION OF FOREST PRODUCTS

There are not sufficiently good records of "Principal Statistics" of the primary forest products industry to permit the calculation of gross domestic product at factor cost in the same manner as for manufacturing when costs of non-factor inputs are subtracted from gross product values to obtained gross domestic product values. In these circumstances, it was decided to aggregate non-farm forestry product production into a single measure for each year and to estimate the gross domestic product at factor cost for the non-farm sector from this aggregate measure; in the case of farm production of forest products, all that was necessary was the calculation of the value of net off-farm disposition of forest products plus farm consumption of firewood. The non-farm and farm aggregation will be dealt with in turn. In addition, the modes of estimation in both farm and non-farm sectors differed between the periods 1870 to 1920 and 1921 to 1926.

Non-Farm Gross Domestic Product

We deal with non-farm from 1870 to 1920 first.
    DBS and Statcan have long had factors for converting primary forest products into equivalent measures of cubic feet of standing timber for the purpose of obtaining measures of forest products as a whole. These conversion factors used herein were as follows:

Logs	Mfbm	= 219 cubic feet of standing timber
Pulpwood	1 cord	= 117 cubic feet of standing timber
Firewood	1 cord	= 95 cubic feet of standing timber
Railway ties	1 tie	= 12 cubic feet of standing timber
Squared timber	Mfbm	= 219 cubic feet of standing timber
	or 1 ton	= 100 cubic feet of standing timber

These conversion factors can be found in early volumes of DBS *Operations in the Woods* or more specifically in *Operations in the Woods 1940-53*.

(It should be noted that in the 1940s DBS shifted to converting forest products into cubic feet of merchantable timber, which use somewhat smaller conversion factors into cubic feet.)

By use of the conversion factors, all quantities of non-farm forest products falling into the five categories, logs, pulpwood, firewood, ties and squared timber were translated into cubic feet of standing timber and totals, in cubic feet, were calculated for each year by summation for the years 1870 to 1920; years 1921 to 1926 were treated differently as described below. The resulting totals for 1870 to 1920 were increased by two percent to take account of other forest products such as poles etc. The amount, two percent, was derived from the reports of *Operations in the Woods* for the years 1920 to 1924 and data from the census of forestry for 1900.
    The remaining steps were to estimate the factor costs of production of this product. Factor costs were calculated in two parts, wage costs and all other factor costs.
    Wage costs per thousand cubic feet of forest products were calculated for each year of 1920 to 1924 from data on output of forest products and labour costs collected and published in *Operations in the Woods* for those years. Labour costs were then indexed backward from the 1920 figure to 1901 by use of an index of wage rates in the logging industry (HSC Series D2); from 1901 to 1889 by an index of the wage rate of common wages in the Ottawa area (HSC

Series D488) linked at 1901; from 1889 to 1884 on the basis of Ontario Bureau of Industries reports on labourer's wages per hour (HSC, p.93); and from 1884 to 1870 on the wholesale price of wood and wood products (HSC Series J39).

The labour costs in 1920, which are the key to labour costs for prior years were derived as follows: for Canada as a whole; for British Columbia; and for Canada excluding British Columbia.

First, a word about the data for 1920 is in order. The data on the logging industry were published as an adjunct to the DBS *Report on the Lumber Industry*, for that period. The information was collected from about 900 businesses, many of whom were connected with saw mills. Many small logging operations were not covered but the coverage was quite high: the quantities of individual products, which were given separately, were converted to cubic feet, and as will be seen from the data below, the production coverage of the survey amounted to more than two-thirds of full production of the country. Numbers of persons employed in production, clerical and management functions were obtained and the corresponding wage bill was given. The data were available by province but in this report only the information for B.C. and the rest of Canada separately will be given.

It should be noted, parenthetically, that the principal statistics for the logging industry include very large amounts for purchased materials. This characteristic of the industry arises because much work is contracted out or sub-contracted by the primary logging concerns. The data collected in *Woods Operations* is based partly on surveys of operations (including employment and wages) of the sub-contractors or secondary contractors as well as the primary contractors.

The relevant information from *Operations in the Woods* 1920 follows.

Production in cubic feet of standing timber cut, 1920

Canada (000 cubic feet)	1,039,103
British Columbia (000 cubic feet)	354,535
Canada excluding B.C. (000 cu feet)	684,568

Total wage and salary bill

Canada	$ 39,813,373
British Columbia	13,004,612
Canada excluding B.C.	$ 26,808,761

Salary and wage cost per thousand cubic feet of standing timber

Canada	$ 38.3151
British Columbia	36.6808
Canada excluding B.C.	39.1616

It may be seen that the cost per thousand cubic feet is much the same in both British Columbia and the rest of Canada. This is so because while B.C. has a much larger output per worker it also has a much higher wage rate. The data, all of them tied in directly with the foregoing quantities, are:

Number of wage and salary earners, 1920

Canada	37,484
British Columbia	8,132
Canada excluding B.C.	29,352

Output per worker in cubic feet

Canada	27,721
British Columbia	43,598
Canada excluding B.C.	23,323

Average wage or salary per employee, in dollars

Canada	1,062.14
British Columbia	1,599.19
Canada excluding B.C.	913.35

One gets the same results for the other years of 1921 to 1924 for which the same data are available: that is, the labour costs per thousand cubic feet of standing timber for B.C. and the rest of Canada are quite similar.

Since we are going to obtain labour costs per unit of output for earlier years by indexing labour costs from 1920 backwards by using an index of wage rates it is worth seeing how such an indexing would compare with direct estimation of labour costs for 1921 to 1924. The comparison follows.

Comparison of Directly Estimated and Indexed
Labour Costs 1920 to 1924, Canada Totals.
(costs in dollars per thousand cubic
feet of standing timber)

	Labour Costs Derived From Industry Data	Labour Costs Indexed to 1920
1920	$ 38.3151	38.3151
1921	25.4618	27.5008
1922	29.6599	21.3960
1923	24.4359	25.1171
1924	28.3245	28.4892

In only 1922 was the difference really significant. The 1922 data are featured by a large surge in output in B.C. accompanied by a substantial increase in wage outlays per employee.

The inferences that one may draw from the data are that, while there might be some gain from breaking down production between British Columbia and the rest of Canada in running the labour costs per thousand cubic feet back, the gain would be marginal and, given that the basic cost data are not completely comprehensive and do have margins of error, the use of data on an all-Canada basis appears to be justified and that is what was done.

To complete the calculations of labour costs for 1920 the cost per thousand cubic feet of standing timber was multiplied by the estimate of total number of cubic feet of non-farm standing timber cut in 1920. That estimate is 1,482,397 thousand cubic feet of timber (note: the coverage of 1,039,103 thousand cubic feet in the data above, obtained from the *Operations in the Woods* report for 1920). At a labour cost of $38.3151 per M. cu. feet the labour cost component becomes $56,789,189 and this sum is adjusted upward by one percent to $57,366,000 to account for quite small absence in the labour cost data of *Operations in the Woods* 1920 of some, but by no means all, of self-employed and owned managers labour income. (I have not been able to put my hands on my note concerning this one percent undercoverage; however, I suggest that the curious person look at the *Operations in the Woods* component of the *Lumber Industry* for 1920 for a description of the coverage of the wage and salary data.)

I shall return to non-labour factors later but shall just note at this point that it is assumed that labour costs make up 0.9 of all gross factor costs, excluding net rents of the publicly owned forest resource. The use of this figure was based upon data of the official national accounts from 1926 to 1930 as follows.

Data for the Forestry Industry from
Canadian National Income and Expenditure Accounts

Year	Wages and Salaries ($ Million)	GDP ($ Million)	Wages and Salaries as a Proportion of GDP
1926	59	66	0.894
1927	61	69	0.884
1928	65	72	0.903
1929	69	78	0.885
1930	53	61	0.869
		Average =	0.887

In addition to this non-labour income, there is the forest rent which is included with indirect taxes for this period in the official accounts and is included with "public revenue from resource royalties" in Table 2.1 of our data: the most considerable part of this item in our data for 1870 to 1920 is royalties on forest products.

In retrospect, I probably should have placed the proportion of wages to gross domestic product less publicly owned resource rents at 0.85 instead of 0.90, but the actual choice inevitably involves matters of judgement.

The estimates for 1921 to 1926 were made on a different and possibly less satisfactory basis than those for 1920 and prior years. One advantage in this period is that there are official estimates of production of forestry products, though one would have wished more description of how the estimates were made. A disadvantage is that the estimates of total production of firewood are considerably too high (see the discussion of estimates for firewood); a second disadvantage was that the measure of production of logs in agriculture in 1920 was an improvised one (see above). In these circumstances, an improvisation was followed. The productions of logs and bolts, of pulpwood and of railway ties were all attributed to the non-farm sector entirely and after conversion to cubic feet of standing timber and aggregation were raised by three percent to take account of the omission of production of other forest products.

This meant that of the total production of forest products attributed to the non-farm sector, the proportions in terms of number of cubic feet of standing timber cut, were as follows:

Year	Total Volume of Forest Products Produced, in Cubic Feet of Standing Timber (000 cu.ft)	Number of Cubic Feet Produced in Non-Farm Sector (000 cu.ft)	Percentage Non-Farm
1920	(2,610.2)	(1,482.4)	56.8
1921	2,234.4	1,293.3	57.9
1922	2,377.8	1,420.8	59.8
1923	2,671.1	1,676.2	62.8
1924	2,808.5	1,807.3	64.4
1925	2,839.1	1,791.2	63.1
1926	2,838.1	1,814.9	63.9

Sources: Columns (1) and (2) 1921 to 1926 from *Operations in the Woods, Revised Estimates etc.* (Statcan Catalogue 25-501) Table I; 1920 data from the previously described data for 1920 in the description of the processes from 1870 to 1920.

Had the proportion of non-farm forest harvesting of all forestry production been calculated by the same procedure as for 1870 to 1920 it would have been 61.2 percent in 1926 which is close to the figure of 63.9 percent that is obtained by alternative method.

Labour costs per thousand cubic feet of standing timber felled for 1921 to 1924 were obtained from *Operations in the Woods* for these years in the same manner as described for 1920 earlier in this manuscript. They were multiplied by the number of cubic feet of non-farm timber felled in each year to obtain the total wage bill; as before the non-wage component of GDP was placed at 0.10 of total GDP or one-ninth of the total wage bill.

Unfortunately, the *Operations in the Woods* data of DBS for 1925 and 1926 did not contain data from which labour costs could be calculated. For those two years, in which almost identical values of forest products were produced (*Operations in the Woods 1940-1953 etc*, p.29) the GDP was entered at that given in the official figures for 1926, viz. $66 million.

These valuations for 1925 and 1926 are probably higher than would have been obtained had the same data been available for them as for the years 1921 to 1924 - they are therefore probably a bit out of line with the estimates for 1921 to 1924. The break in the series between 1924 and 1925, insofar as there is one, is more a result of the official estimates being too high for output of forest products that we measure rather than the figures before 1925 and especially from 1920 back being too low. The official estimates coverage for 1926 *et seq.* is greater than ours since "Forestry includes establishments engaged in forest patrol, fire inspection, fire fighting, forest nurseries, reforestation and other forestry services whether conducted by government organizations or commercial enterprises" (Statcan, *National Income and Expenditure Accounts 1926-1974, Volume 3*, p.291); our estimates include only production of forestry products.

I shall assess the quality of the estimates after having dealt with output of forest products in agriculture.

Value of Output of Forestry Products in Agriculture

For 1870 to 1920

The way in which the physical output of farms of saw logs and bolts, pulpwood, railway ties and firewood were estimated has been described already. It remains to explain how these outputs were valued.

The values per unit of the above were obtained predominantly from decennial census data for 1900, 1910 and 1920. The prices per unit for these years were as follows:

Price Per Designated Unit
of Farm Forest Output
(in dollars per unit)

	1900	1910	1920
Logs and bolts (per Mfbm)	8.147	10.721	21.323
Pulpwood (per cord)	3.246	4.388	13.007
Firewood (per cord)	1.645	2.1469	4.3143
Railway ties (per tie)	0.173	0.2643	0.592

Sources: 1901: All unit values, Census 1901, *Forestry* p. lxxii. 1910 and 1921: unit values for pulpwood, firewood and railway ties from Census of Agriculture, 1921 p. lxxii; for 1910, unit value of logs from Census (Agriculture) 1911, Vol. 5., p. vi, and Table 2; for 1920, unit value of logs derived by dividing total cost of logs and bolts for sawmills in 1920 from *The Lumber Industry 1920*, p.31, by our estimate of output (and input) of logs in saw and shingle mills. This unit value seems low compared to the unit export price. However, the unit value from *Operations in the Woods 1940-1953 etc.*, p.28 is $20.209 and from "materials used" in DBS *The Lumber Industry* 1920 p.31 is $21.204; on the other hand, the unit value of logs produced from the *Operations in the Woods* part of *The Lumber Industry 1920*, p.42 for 1920 was $25.898, although that has been revised downward, as quoted, in DBS *Operations in the Woods 1940-1953 etc.*

Interpolators between 1900 and 1910 and 1910 and 1920 and extrapolators to 1870 were as follows:

Logs and Bolts: The interpolator was the unit value of exports of all logs, calendar year basis, calculated from official trade data published annually as *Trade of Canada* or by like designation.

Pulpwood: 1908 to 1920, DBS *The Pulp and Paper Industry*, 1926, p.29 (also *op.cit, 1927* p.29); 1904 to 1908, unit values per cord, pulpwood blocks (*Trade of Canada* 1915, p.540); 1900 to 1904, straight line between 1900 and 1904; 1890 to 1900, unit value of spruce logs exported per Mfbm (*Trade of Canada*); 1875 to 1890, unit value of exports of all logs, as used in the log and bolt products section (our own data).

Railway Ties: 1874 to 1920, the interpolator-extrapolator was the unit value of exports of ties, obtained from *Trade of Canada* e.g. Sessional Papers of 1915, sessional paper 10; Sessional Papers of 1913, sessional paper #10; DBS *Trade of Canada*, various years from 1917 onward; from 1914 to 1919, quantities, and hence unit prices, could not be obtained from trade data and for these years the unit values of planks and boards was used as an interpolator of railway tie unit values between the unit values available from the trade data for (fiscal) 1913 and 1920. Fiscal year values were accepted as reflecting the unit proceeds of the producers for the preceding calendar year: for example, the unit value for fiscal 1905 (the year ending in June 1905) was taken as indicative of the unit value of ties produced in 1904; the delay between the production and marketing of hand-hewn ties provides some justification of this practice.

1870 to 1874, the unit values of exports of logs and bolts was used as the extrapolator from 1874 to 1870.

Firewood: 1870 to 1920, the unit value of firewood exported was used as the interpolator-extrapolator throughout. Unit values were calendar year values. (In the procedure, the export unit values for 1900 backward to 1887 were scaled down by the factor 0.8644 since the unit value per cord from the 1901 census was $1.645 and the unit value per cord from the export data was $1.903; from 1886 back to 1870 the unit price of exports was not scaled down but just used as it came from the trade data. (I have not put my hand on the reason for the change in procedures between 1887 and 1886 but I am sure that there would have been a valid reason — it may have resulted from a change in composition of exports between soft and hard woods but this latter is conjecture — I have not really dug into the pile of material to find the reason.)

All Farm Products: 1920 to 1926, for reasons noted earlier, e.g. the imprecision of the 1920 data for farm production of logs, but more importantly, the availability of official figures on total value of forest products from 1920 to 1926 and official estimates of the value of farm production of forest products in 1920 and 1926, a different method of estimation of farm production between 1920 and 1926 was used. The procedure followed was first, to calculate the ratio of the value of farm production to total forest products production for each of 1920 and 1926; second, to interpolate this ratio linearly between 1920 and 1926; third, to multiply the value of total production of forest products for each year from 1921 to 1925 by the ratio of the value of farm production to that of total production and thus to obtain the value of farm production of forest products. The data are presented in the following table.

Estimate of Farm Income From Forest Products, 1920 to 1926 (thousands of dollars)

Year	Total Value of Forest Products	Value of Farm Forest Products	Ratio of Farm Value to Total Value
1920	213,941	67,047	0.3134
1921	168,054	51,408	0.3059
1922	170,850	50,965	0.2983
1923	197,459	57,421	0.2908
1924	213,147	60,385	0.2833
1925	209,277	57,698	0.2757
1926	204,599	54,882	0.2682

Sources: Column (1): from Statcan *Canadian Forestry Statistics* 1959 and *Operations in the Woods, Revised Estimates 1940-1953 etc.*
Column (2): 1920 from the project estimate described above. 1926 from DBS *Handbook of Agricultural Statistics, Part II, 1926-1957.*

Some Tests of Reliability of the Data

Some reliability tests of the data have been made already. A further three tests will be helpful.

One such test involves use of the 1911 census of population data on wage earners and gainfully occupied persons which are given here. The occupational classification in this census was very similar to the standard industrial classification of 1948 and everyone was classified to an industry (occupation) — there was not a residual group.

Calculation of Total Labour Earnings, Forestry,
1910, from 1911 Census Data on Persons

	Wage Earners For Whom Wages Reported	Earnings ($)	Average Earnings ($)	Number Gainfully Occupied	Implied Total Earnings If All Gainfully Occupied Employed ($)
		Males			
Tree and log contractors	406	282,500	696	1,943	1,352,328
Lumber camp employees	22,730	10,766,000	474	24,648	11,683,152
Riverdrivers	2,096	862,700	412	2,326	958,312
Timber workers /woodmen	11,587	5,126,200	442	13,741	6,073,525
Office employees	--			243	112,508
Total male	36,819	17,047,900	463	42,901	20,179,833

Multiplying at the aggregate level gives 463 x 42,901 = $19,863,163

		Females			
Lumber camp	18	9,300	517		
Timber workers	1	600	600		
Forestry	1	600	600		
Total female	20	10,500	525	13	6,825

Grand total if all gainfully occupied earned the same wage as reported wage earners is $20,186,648.

Sources: Wage data from Population Census 1911, microfilm tapes 11006 p.3654 and 3787. Gainfully occupied numbers from Census 1911, Vol. VI *Occupations*, p.32.

This compares with wage payments of $20,695,000 in the estimates that we used, calculated from quite independent data. The average number of weeks worked was 39 weeks for the wage-earners, in total and being almost the same for all classes of wage earners. Possible shortcoming of this test is that some workers in non-farm forestry may actually have been farmers who worked in non-farm forestry jobs in the winter but were reported as farmers or casual labourers who did not designate an industry; conversely, some of the numbers included among the gainfully occupied in forestry but not reporting a wage income may actually have only worked short time, or possibly not at all. In a work designed to produce a consistent and exhaustive assignment of the work force by industry for census years 1911 to 1961, McInnis places 42,917 workers in forestry, which exceeds our number of gainfully occupied by only three persons.   (Marvin McInnis, *A Consistent Industrial Classification of Canadian Work Force Statistics.*)

The like data for 1900 are perhaps less reliable than in 1911. Only total numbers of wage earners and gainfully occupied will be given in this case. Data on wage-earners and gainfully occupied were published in bulletins for the 1901 census. The wage-earner bulletin reported 16,438 male wage-earners reporting wages for total earnings of $5,014,821, an average of $305.07 per wage earner for an average period of 9.28 months of work; the same bulletin reported total wage earners, including those who did not give their wages, at 17,806 person which, if valued at $305.07 per worker, would yield earnings of $5,432,076. The bulletin giving the gainfully occupied reported 17,113 males as the number in forestry, which it can be seen, is less than the total wage earners reported above and further calculation would not be of help. The wage bill that is derived here is about half of the project estimate for 1900. My estimate is that the personal census wage data were not as good for 1900 as for 1910. I just note as one matter that the census average earnings per year for 1910 ($463) are slightly more than 50 percent higher than the census average earnings for 1900 ($305.07); the wage index places the 1910 wage rate at just 30 percent higher than the 1900 wage rate.

Like data were also collected in the 1920 personal census with the following result.

Category of Occupation	Number of Employees Reporting Wages	Aggregate Earnings	Average Earnings Per Employee	Number Designated As Gainfully Occupied	Computed Earnings of the Gainfully Occupied
		Males			
Managers, superintendents	1,319	2,158,920	276.30	4,449	1,229,259
Foresters, timber cruiser	205	229,653	1,120.26	234	262,141
Inspectors etc.	602	694,204	1,153.16	626	721,878
River drivers	1,486	1,097,337	738.45	1,506	1,112,106
Shantymen	31,259	23,112,579	733.06	32,379	23,735,749
Office employees			735.00	614	451,290
		Females			
Office employees			735.00	7	5,145
Totals				39,815	$26,517,528

Sources: Wage data: microfilm tapes from DBS giving unpublished wage and earnings data. Gainfully occupied data: Census of Canada, 1921, Vol. IV *Occupations.*

This wage bill total is considerably less than the $57,366,000 calculated from alternative data including industry data. One would expect it to be somewhat smaller for a number of reasons. For one matter, the wage data collected in the census of persons are for June 1, 1920 to May 31, 1921 while the industry data (and project data) are for calendar 1920. The wage bill for the census year ending May 31, 1921 would be smaller than that for the calendar year for two reasons: first, wage rates in forestry fell drastically between 1920 and 1921, although, unfortunately, there are not the monthly data available to show how much change had taken place by May 31, 1921; second, levels of employment were considerably lower in 1921 than in 1920 and, while the foregoing calculations are based on the number of "gainfully occupied" as reported by individuals themselves, that number might well be smaller at early June 1921 then in 1920. For another matter, there were 91,511 male labourers unassigned to an industry in the whole occupational distribution. (In this regard, McInnis has placed the labour force in forestry in the 1921 census at 40,026 workers which is only slightly above our figure for the number gainfully occupied.) Yet again, lumber camp workers received some free room and board, which most likely was not reported as part of a wage by the individual workers in the census of persons but may have been included, in some measure, as part of the wage bill by companies. I would judge that the foregoing matters might explain a substantial part of the shortfall of the census wage bill below our calculations. At the same time, they do not suggest that our estimate of the wage bill in forestry in 1920 requires any upward revision.

I add one final table showing the total gross domestic product of forestry for farm and non-farm production together, along with royalty receipts of governments.

Total Gross Domestic Product at
Factor Cost of Forestry, Census Years
(thousands of dollars)

	1870	1880	1890	1900	1910	1920	1926
Non-farm excluding public timber receipts	5,790	5,908	10,933	13,137	22,995	63,740	66,000
Agricultural forestry	16,402	17,749	21,046	21,604	33,437	67,047	54,882
Public resource royalties	1,027	1,340	2,080	4,740	8,653	14,081	18,009
Total	23,219	2,080	34,059	39,481	65,085	144,868	138,891

It should be noted that the agricultural forestry income has not had any specific farm expenses charged against it. Insofar as there have been such expenses, they are included in the general farm expenses in the calculation of agricultural GDP. The agricultural income from forest products is of course included in agriculture in the industrial distribution of gross domestic product at factor cost.

FUR PRODUCTION: WILDLIFE

In the official statistics fur production (excluding fur farms) is presented along with the fisheries. On inquiry from the project, Statistics Canada made available some background worksheets on each of fisheries and fur: the worksheets on fur included the basis of estimation of gross domestic product 1926-1938.

The basic raw data available are the following: from 1919-20 onward into the 1940s, the value of fur pelt production for years ended June 30, reported in DBS *The Fur Production of Canada*, annual; from 1920 onwards the sale of pelts from fur farms for calendar years reported in DBS *The Fur Farming Industry;* exports of raw furs of Canadian origin, volume and value, from 1868 onward in *Trade of Canada*; imports of furs, annual, in *Trade of Canada*.

The method of estimation was by simple procedures, separately for each of two periods.

Period 1920 to 1926

For these years the value of wildlife furs produced was calculated by subtracting value of furs produced on fur farms (*The Fur Farming Industry*) from the aggregate value of all furs produced (*The Fur Production of Canada*). DBS, in its estimates for 1926 to 1938 (and later), in effect, estimated all expenses of production at 25 percent of the value of wild fur production, leaving 75% of value of wild fur production as gross domestic product. The same method was used in the project. Gross domestic product was obtained by multiplying the value of wildlife furs produced by 0.75. (In the Statcan working papers this item was called a "net" income but there was no entry for depreciation so it was also a gross income.)

Period 1870 to 1920

The values of exports of raw furs are the extrapolator prior to 1920. The values of exports of raw furs, which are given for fiscal years in the source, were converted to calendar years by the usual method of appropriately weighting the data of the two fiscal years that bracket the calendar year: these data were available for every year from 1870 onwards. For these years before 1920, an estimate of the value of wildlife pelt production was obtained by multiplying the value of exports by the factor 0.9. This factor was obtained by taking the average of the ratios of total value of production of fur pelts (excluding seal pelt production) to value of exports of raw furs (including seal pelts which are negligibly small) for the years 1920-21 to 1937-38: this average ratio was 0.9013 which was rounded to 0.9. There was not a need to remove fur farm production before 1920 since it was very small prior to the 1920s: value of fur farm pelts was 2.6 percent of value of all pelts in 1920.

An estimate of gross domestic product was then obtained by multiplying the estimate of the value of wildlife pelt production by the factor 0.75 as had been done in the official estimates and in the project estimates for 1920-26.

I believe that these estimates are not too bad. The one area of concern is that the value of imports (which was never negligible) varied considerably relative to the value of exports. From 1870 onward for several years import values were considerably less than exports values; they then gradually rose to match and then exceed export values frequently in the period 1900 to 1913; they fell to less than half export values in the war and remained at those levels or less for most of the post war years to the end of the 1930s, being measured in ratios of more than 50 percent of export values for four years in the late 1920s. The reason for concern is that although the project used only export values of Canadian pelts in the calculation of gross domestic product there must have been some consumption of fur pelts in Canada. Presumably a larger part of this consumption would have been catered to by Canadian produced furs when imports were low than when they were high. If there is a problem connected with these phenomena it applies especially to the period 1900 to 1913. However, a comforting part of the picture is that the ratio of production values to export values remained fairly stable in the period 1920 to 1938, for which years we have independent measures of both, and these ratios did not appear to be affected, in any great measure, by relatively high or low levels of import values.

FISHERIES

Duncan McDougall was responsible for the major part of the fisheries estimates: see acknowledgement in the preface. This write-up was done by M.C. Urquhart.

The primary source material for the fisheries came from the two main sources; viz.: Department of Marine and Fisheries, Canada, *Annual Report, Fisheries* for the period 1870 to 1917; Dominion Bureau of Statistics, *Fisheries Statistics of Canada*, (annual) for 1917 to 1926. Many of these data appear in *Historical Statistics of Canada*. Fisheries data were collected through the fisheries officers of the Department of Marine and Fisheries and published annually by the Department from Confederation to the fiscal year ending March 31, 1917; the Dominion Bureau of Statistics took over the collection and publication of the fisheries data for 1917 onward. Other sources of data will be given as the discussion proceeds.

A great deal of effort was put into investigation of various sources of data, such as Census of Canada data, and choice of methodology.

Since the methodology was simple, we begin by explaining more or less the bare details of how the estimates for fisheries gross domestic product were made. The one comprehensive measure of fisheries output, available for the whole period, was the "market value of fisheries products": this included the value of fish, whole or filleted in fresh or frozen form, plus the value of canned and cured fish and the value of reduction (fish oil and meal) products. A better measure of the output of the primary industry only is given by the "value of fish landed" but these data are available only from 1911 onward, first for just the sea fisheries and then from 1917 onward for sea and inland fisheries. Therefore, to retain continuity throughout the whole period, the series on the "market value of fisheries product" was used to derive estimates of wages and salaries and entrepreneurial income.

That the "market value of fisheries products" rather fairly reflects the "value of fish landed" may be seen from the ratio of the latter to the former during the period of overlap, which ratios follow:

Ratio of Value of Fish Landings to
Value of Fisheries Products

Year	Ratio	Year	Ratio
1911	0.5257 *	1921	0.6634
1912	0.5137 *	1922	0.6601
1913	0.5021 *	1923	0.6218
1914	0.6440 *	1924	0.6145
1915	0.6082 *	1925	0.6260
1916	0.5458 *	1926	0.6268
1917	0.5320 *	1927	0.6570
----		1928	0.6130
1917	0.5984	1929	0.6297
1918	0.5391 *	1930	0.6226
1919	0.6682		
1920	0.6350		

Source data: *Historical Statistics of Canada*, Series M1 and M69. The data for 1911 to the first entry for 1917 are for fiscal years ending in the year given; the data for the second entry for 1917 onward are for calendar years.

* In these years the value of fish landings are for sea fish only for 1911 to fiscal 1917 and also for the Quebec and New Brunswick component in 1918.

In addition to these ratios, the composition of the aggregate of the "market value of fisheries products" throws some light on whether this aggregate is an approximate guide to the value of fish landings or not. While the project did not do a formal analysis of this composition, two casually observed features are the following: a main feature of the changes onward from 1881 (the first year for which the composition is available) is the decline in the salted and pickled component share and the rise in the share in canned form; the part sold fresh in whole or filleted form approximated 35 percent of the aggregate from the mid 1880s onward, when the data probably became more precise than they had been earlier.

So much for the measures of output. The same statistic gathering process that obtained data on market value of fisheries products also gathered data on number of persons engaged in primary fishing and the value of the capital equipment used in the primary fisheries. Unfortunately, a great many of the "persons engaged" were part time workers and it was hard to determine how many were part time and what part time meant. Accordingly, a judgement was made that the method of determining labour income and income of the self employed that was used, and is described below, was better than an attempt to estimate labour income directly from the recorded numbers of persons engaged in primary fishing. On the other hand, the measures of the value of capital equipment, subdivided into large vessels, boats, nets and seines, and other primary fishing capital goods, appeared to be sufficiently good to be used, at least, for the measurement of depreciation on this equipment. The estimation of wages and salaries plus entrepreneurial income (including net property income) was calculated as one item; depreciation of capital goods was calculated as another item. This format was used partly because it corresponded to the way the official statistics were estimated for 1926 onward.

Statistics Canada very kindly made available a worksheet showing the official calculation of net income in fisheries for the years 1926 to 1938. The Statcan calculation involved subtracting wages, depreciation and repair of boats and vessels, fuel costs and miscellaneous expenses (a relatively small item) from the value of fish landed to obtain a residual which is essentially income of unincorporated business and property income. The measure of gross domestic product is obtained from these data by adding together income of unincorporated business and property income, wages and salaries, and depreciation of capital equipment. A description of the Statcan methodology can be found in Statistics Canada: *National Income and Expenditure Accounts, Volume 3* (1975).

The data for 1926-29 were the following:

Fisheries Income and Gross Domestic Product
(millions of dollars)

	1926	1927	1928	1929
Value of fish landed	35.3	32.5	33.7	33.7
less:				
Wages	6.7	6.2	6.4	6.4
Depreciation of nets and traps	6.5	6.8	6.6	7.3
Boats and vessels —				
depreciation and repair	2.9	3.3	3.3	3.5
Fuel	3.6	3.6	3.6	3.6
Miscellaneous	0.4	0.3	0.3	0.3
Residual	15.2	12.3	13.5	12.6

Source: Data obtained from Statcan

From these data for 1926 alone the gross domestic product would have been $31.3 million equal to 6.7 + 15.2 + 9.4 and like figures could be derived from the other years.

As noted above, the product series that runs right back to 1870 is the "market value of fisheries products" rather than "value of fish landed". In the project estimates the wages and salaries plus net entrepreneurial income, as a single sum, were calculated right back to 1870 from the relationship of this item, as obtained from the Statcan data, to market value of fish products in the years 1926-1929. The relevant ratios for 1926 to 1929 are:

Ratio of Wages Plus Entrepreneurial and
Property Income to Market Value

Year	Ratio
1926	0.3883
1927	0.3737
1928	0.3612
1929	0.3551
Average 1926-29	0.3695

This item, wages plus entrepreneurial and net property income, then was calculated for

1870 to 1926 by multiplying the market value of fish products by the factor 0.37. This formula was used for 1926, as for all other years, rather than using the slightly higher actual figure (which was used, of course, in calculating the ratio).

The other item entering gross domestic product is depreciation. It was calculated from the value of capital items used in the fishery. These values were collected by the Fisheries Department from 1878 onward. These data gave values of vessels, boats and nets separately and an "all other capital" which included canneries as well as docks, wharves, ice houses etc.

The values of vessels (larger craft) and boats (smaller craft) were obtained from Fisheries and DBS reports as originally recorded. In the preparation of the first edition of *Historical Statistics* the Economics Service of the Department of Fisheries compiled, for the same years, a series measuring the aggregate value of capital goods used in primary fishing operations which included vessels, boats and fishing gear of all kinds such as nets, lines, lobster traps etc., just called "gear" from here on (HSC Series M49). A series on gear by itself was obtained as the difference between the HSC aggregate value and the value of vessels and boats. In addition, DBS included freezers and ice houses, piers and wharves and small fish houses as a part of the capital of the primary fisheries in its national product calculations and the project followed suit. DBS collected these data from 1917 onward, in a bit more distinct form than had been done previously, and published them. (They were actually calculated for 1917 onward by subtracting the value of capital in primary fishing, from HSC Series M49, from aggregate value of all fisheries capital, including canneries etc., to provide an estimate of fisheries capital in land form; the capital in canneries, given in *Fisheries Statistics* from 1917 onward was then subtracted to leave the value of wharves, piers, ice houses, etc. which are treated as a part of primary capital.) It was not possible to get an estimate of these primary fishery land forms — the wharves, smoke houses etc. — in this way before 1917. Hence, an estimate was made by calculating an average ratio of value of land capital in this form to the value of gear for the years 1920 to 1926 and multiplying the value of gear for years before 1917 by this ratio to make the estimate of primary land capital. The data from which this ratio was calculated follows.

Year	Value of Gear of All Kinds ($000)	Value of Primary Capital in Land Forms ($000)	Ratio: Primary Capital in Land Forms to Gear
1920	10,045	3,672	0.3656
1921	9,001	3,549	0.3943
1922	8,795	3,252	0.3698
1923	8,560	3,022	0.3530
1924	8,476	3,231	0.3812
1925	9,196	3,026	0.3291
1926	9,800	3,165	0.3230

Average ratio for 1920-26 = 0.3594

Note: the data for 1917 to 1919 were not used in the calculation of this ratio since some items, e.g. docks and wharves, freezers and ice houses, were reported at much higher values in 1917-1919 than from 1920 onward.

The result of these calculations was that the project had a series on capital values of vessels, of boats, of gear, and of other primary fishery capital goods in land forms, valued at market prices.

The rates of depreciation on these capital forms were:

Type of Capital Goods	Depreciation Rates (percent per annum)
Vessels	6 2/3
Boats	10
Gear	50
Primary land capital	15

Source: Information provided by Statistics Canada

Total depreciation of capital goods was then calculated by multiplying the value of capital equipment in different forms by the depreciation rates and summing the results for all capital forms.

The gross domestic product for the years 1880 to 1926 was then obtained for each year as the sum of the wage income and entrepreneurial and property income and the depreciation of primary fishing capital.

Capital values were not available before 1878 and those for 1878 and 1879 might be termed exploratory. The depreciation for 1870 to 1879 was estimated as being equal to 20% of the wage income plus entrepreneurial and net property income. The 20% ratio is derived from the similar ratios of the data that the project has for 1880-82 and 1884-86.

I feel reasonably happy about these estimates. The wages plus entrepreneurial income for 1910 check reasonably well with estimates made from decennial census data on wages and on gainfully occupied persons for that year, supplemented by fisheries statistics data on the number employed.

MINING

The scope of the mining industry will be apparent from the nature of the constituent components, for each of which estimates were made and the industry totals then derived as sums of the components. Those components were: (i) metallic mines; (ii) coal mines; (iii) asbestos mines; (iv) non-metallic minerals and fuels, other than coal and asbestos; (v) structural materials.

There were three major sources of data and a few minor sources. The major sources were: DBS *Annual Report on the Mineral Production of Canada, 1921 to 1939;* DBS *Coal Statistics For Canada 1919, 1920, 1921* (for calendar years) and annually thereafter; DBS *Canadian Mineral Statistics 1886-1956; Mining Events 1604-1956* (Reference Paper No. 68), a single document; the minor sources will be identified on the appropriate occasion in what follows.

The methodology, determined by the nature of the available data, was relatively simple.

For the years 1921 to 1926 quite comprehensive annual data for each of the five components of the industry, noted above, were available in *Mineral Production of Canada* and *Coal Statistics* including gross value of product, wages and salaries, cost of fuel and electricity and miscellaneous expenses. (The data for 1925 and especially 1926 were less full than for 1921 to 1924 and so the data for 1921 to 1924 or 1921 to 1925 were used to get some of the important ratios for calculations for years before 1921.) Subtraction of cost of fuel and electricity and relevant miscellaneous expenses from gross value of product (GVP) yielded a measure of gross domestic product (GDP). Data on wages and salary were available in the same source and an average ratio of wages and salaries to GDP was calculated for each component.

The financial data available before the 1920s were: gross value of product for each category, on an annual basis, in *Canadian Mineral Statistics 1886-1956*; and for 1900 and 1910 in the relevant census, gross value of product and wages and salaries. Ratios of wages and salaries to gross value of product were determined for each year in which both were available and by interpolation and extrapolation of these ratios to other years an estimate of wages and salaries was obtained by multiplying each year's GVP by the ratio for that year. For the first four categories (thus excluding construction materials) for the years before 1921 gross domestic product was estimated by assuming a ratio of GDP to wages and salaries, equivalent to the average for 1921 to 1926 adapted to be consistent with the data of DBS *Corporation Financial Statistics, 1965 et seq.*, and thus obtaining GDP from the wage and salary series; a modification of the method was used for the construction materials component and will be described when we deal in detail with that component.

Such detail as seems appropriate for each component now follows.

Metallic Mines

Period 1921 to 1926

The source *Mineral Production of Canada* includes non-ferrous smelting in this group but the data for this item are given separately and are not included in this mining group since they are a part of manufacturing.

Salaries and wages, cost of fuel and electricity, and gross value of product are available in the source for all years; miscellaneous expenses were available for 1921 to 1924 but not for 1925 and 1926. These miscellaneous expenses were quite large, since they included all material and other purchases, except fuel and power; they also included royalties and some government taxes which are properly a part of income generated in the mining industry.

Gross domestic product for this metals component for these years was obtained by subtracting cost of fuel and electricity and miscellaneous expenses from gross value of product. But first, some work on the miscellaneous expense estimates was necessary. In 1921 and 1922, cost of purchased power had been included with miscellaneous expenses but in subsequent years was included appropriately with fuel and power expenses; these purchased power costs were transferred from miscellaneous expenses to fuel and power in 1921 and 1922. The average ratio of miscellaneous expenses thus measured to GVP for 1921 to 1924 was about 22 percent and this factor was used to estimate miscellaneous expenses in 1925 and 1926, years in which such expenses had not been reported. One further adjustment was still necessary. These miscellaneous expenses, as reported, included royalties and taxes which are really a part of mining gross domestic product. These royalties and taxes were shown separately from other miscellaneous expenses in the source for 1921 only; comparable detail was again available only from 1969 onward in the report of financial statistics of metal mines in Statistics Canada, *Corporate*

Financial Statistics. Data from these statistics for 1969 to 1976 plus the data for 1921 led to an estimate that the royalty and other items of an income nature, included in the miscellaneous expenses, amounted to approximately four percent of GVP. An amount equivalent to four percent of GVP was subtracted from the miscellaneous expenses.

With these manipulations done gross domestic product in metal mines was calculated from gross value of product less costs of fuel and electricity and miscellaneous expenses. For its use for earlier year estimates, the ratio of wages and salaries to gross domestic product in these years was calculated yielding the results shown in the section on 1870 to 1920 below.

Period 1870 to 1920

The annual series to which all else was attached was the gross value of product: the source was *Canadian Mineral Statistics 1886-1956.* The data on production given therein were collected by the Geologic Survey of Canada or the Department of Mines of Canada. The series for value of product for all metal mines extended back to 1886. The series was extrapolated from 1886 to 1870 on the basis of gold produced in Canada (DBS *Historic Tables of the Mineral Production of Canada* (1948) p.35) which in 1886 accounted for just over two-thirds of mineral product.

The ratios of wages and salaries to gross value of production, geologic survey basis, were derived from estimates for three base years, 1920, 1910 and 1900. The ratio for 1920 at 0.2150 was the average ratio derived from the ratios of wages and salaries in 1921 to 1925, from *Mineral Production of Canada*, to the gross value of metallic mineral production as collected by the geologic survey. (Data for 1926 were not used on this occasion since the geologic survey changed its method of valuation from value of refined metal equivalents in the world market to value actually received in Canada.) The data are:

Year	Wages and Salaries ($mm)	Gross Value of Product, Geologic Survey ($mm)	Ratio of Wages and Salaries to GVP
1921	11.83	49.34	0.2398
1922	13.32	61.79	0.2156
1923	17.86	83.76	0.2132
1924	21.56	102.06	0.2112
1925	24.16	116.95	0.2066
1926	(26.45)	(115.09)	(0.2298)

Chosen ratio of wages and salaries to
GVP Geologic Survey basis for 1920   0.2150

The ratios for 1910 and 1900 were obtained from the censuses of mining in 1910 and 1900. In each case, the data for smelters were omitted because they were already included in manufacturing. The ratios of wages and salaries to GVP were 0.1732 in 1910 and 0.2900 (rounded from 0.2892) in 1900. The reason for the relatively high ratio in 1900 is that the base metals were relatively underdeveloped then and lode gold production, which has a high ratio of wages to GVP, was large. By 1910 the composition of mineral production, as well as the scale, had changed dramatically. Nickel copper ores and silver cobalt ores had become very large, accounting for more than half total metallic mines production: they each had very low ratios of wages and salaries to GVP in 1910. The nature of the change can be seen from the following data.

Salaries and Wages and Gross Value of Product,
Metal Mines, 1900 and 1910

	1900		1910	
	Salaries and Wages ($)	Gross Value of Product ($)	Salaries and Wages ($)	Gross Value of Product ($)
Copper ore	1,053,973	3,339,674	46,787	59,782
Gold ore, lode or vein	2,525,735	4,587,854	704,089	1,590,541
Copper gold ore	---	---	2,220,941	9,881,483
Gold Placer	321,794	584,880	1,767,218	4,711,301
Nickel-copper	752,237	1,181,811	1,011,964	10,275,079
Pyrites	---	---	142,806	328,648
Silver ore	122,108	199,451	---	---
Silver-cobalt ore	---	---	2,980,150	17,901,228
Silver-lead ore	1,533,278	3,369,878	926,912	1,889,496
Manganese	13,406	61,080	10,374,513	46,637,558
Iron ore	271,691	607,000	573,646	2,693,989
Chromium iron ore	15,044	20,300	---	---
Total (including smelting)	6,609,266	13,951,928	10,374,513	49,331,547
Less: nonferrous smelters		1,331,503		1,523,100
iron smelter	---		286,823	
Mining salaries and wages	5,277,763		8,564,590	

Sources: *Census of Canada 1901*, Vol II, Table LVIII.
          Census of Canada 1911, Vol V. *Mineral Production* Table XVII.

Geologic survey GVP 1900 ex. Yukon gold. $18,246,807 *(Canadian Mineral Statistics, 1886-1956)*

Geologic survey GVP 1910 — $49,438,873 *(Canadian Mineral Statistics 1886-1956)*

The ratios of wages to GVP for 1911 to 1919 were obtained by linear interpolation between 1910 and 1920, and the ratios for 1901 to 1909 by linear interpolation between 1900 and 1910. Since gold mining production made up two-thirds of metallic mine GVP in 1886, the ratio of wages and salaries to GVP was placed at 0.35; the ratios for years from 1887 to 1899 were obtained by linear interpolation between those for 1886 and 1900; the ratios for 1870 to 1885 were kept constant at 0.35.

Multiplication of GVP by these ratios, year by year, provided estimates of wages before 1921.

There remained the final step of deriving gross domestic product (as distinct from gross value of product) for years before 1921. A singe ratio of 0.40 of wages and salaries to gross domestic product was used for every year from 1870 to 1920. This ratio was derived from data for 1921 to 1926, which permitted direct estimates of gross domestic product for those years, supplemented by data from DBS *Corporate Financial Statistics*, annual from 1969 onwards. The ratios for individual years from 1921 to 1926 together with gross domestic product itself follow.

Year	Ratio of Wages and Salaries to Gross Domestic Product	Gross Domestic Product ($000)
1921	0.5388	21,948
1922	0.4047	32,910
1923	0.5025	35,548
1924	0.4234	50,908
1925	0.4081	54,205
1926	0.4161	63,558

The ratio for 1921 is abnormal — there was a substantial fall in value of output and profits in that year. Data for 1900 (census 1901) are consistent with a ratio of 0.40 in that year.

The ratios of wages and salaries to gross domestic product, derived from DBS *Corporate Financial Statistics* are:

Year	Ratio of Wages and Salaries to Gross Domestic Product
1969	0.3676
1970	0.3677
1971	0.4795
1973	0.3419
1974	0.3579
1975	0.4962
1976	0.5193

The gross domestic product, 1870 to 1920 was then obtained by dividing total wages and salaries each year by the ratio 0.40.

Coal Mining

The estimates of gross domestic product in coal mining were obtained in much the same way as for metallic mines. Exactly the same source documents were used but, in addition, there was an annual publication of DBS *Coal Statistics for Canada* covering the calendar year 1921 and onward and a DBS *Report on the Coal Trade of Canada* covering the fiscal years 1917-18 and 1918-19. Since the methodology is the same as for the metallic minerals, the description of what was done with coal mines will be less elaborate than that given for the metallic minerals.

Estimates of wages and salaries in coal mining were done on a province by province basis. The reason for this province by province approach was that the ratios of wages and salaries to GVP were very different among the provinces. Three provinces, Nova Scotia, Alberta and British Columbia, produced the predominant part of Canadian production; lesser amounts were produced by Saskatchewan and New Brunswick. The extent of the differences in the ratios will emerge as we proceed. In the following we again distinguish between the two periods, 1921 to 1926 and 1870 to 1920.

Period 1921 to 1926

Gross domestic product was calculated directly from the principal statistics of the coal mining industry, obtained from *Mineral Production of Canada* various years in the 1920s to 1930.

As had been done in the metallic minerals group, gross domestic product was obtained essentially by subtracting non-factor costs from gross value of product. The non-factor costs were first, costs of fuel and power and second, "miscellaneous" expenses after removal of factor costs such as royalties and direct taxes. The calculations involved in both of these categories of expenditures were of exactly the same kind as in metallic mines to which reference may be made if further detail is required.

Period 1870 to 1920

Again, the basic principles of calculation of gross domestic product were the same as in metallic minerals. The original relevant data that we have for all years is gross value of product and data on wages and salaries as well as gross value of product for 1900, 1910, 1917, 1918 and 1921 to 1926. From the years for which wage and salary data are available estimates of the ratios of wages and salaries to gross value of product are made. These ratios are then extrapolated or interpolated for other years and multiplied by the relevant gross value of product for each year to provide an estimate of wages and salaries for the year. The gross domestic product is then inferred from these wages and salaries.

The coal mining industry was unique among the five mining categories in that the wage and salary series were calculated separately for each of the five producing provinces of Canada and then added together to provide a Canadian total.

The wage and salary ratios to GVP calculated from the basic data were as follows.

Ratio of Wages and Salaries to Unadjusted GDP

Year	Ratio	Year	Ratio
1921	0.84	1924	0.91
1922	0.81	1925	0.94
1923	0.89	1926	0.83

Ratios of Wages and Salaries to Gross
Value of Production, By Province

Year	Nova Scotia	British Columbia	Alberta	New Brunswick	Saskat- chewan
1900	0.49869	0.72107	0.61580	(0.64704)	(0.41545)
1910	0.53483	0.67348	0.60276	(0.31305)	(0.59997)
1917	0.54252	0.70870	0.62489		
1918	0.63906	0.69076	0.64557		
1921	0.52949	0.71879	0.66846	0.60598	0.71678
1922	0.53613	0.67998	0.62486	0.57662	0.62067
1923	0.59439	0.70126	0.65557	0.68197	0.69706
1924	0.59940	0.75936	0.66183	0.69560	0.64166
1925	0.73760	0.67850	0.62319	0.73085	0.63942
1926	0.56045	0.67031	0.60589	0.69635	0.64978
1927	0.61410	0.68970	0.61589	0.70168	0.63656
1928	0.72703	0.68415	0.62281	0.69295	0.65171
1929	0.70700	0.66221	0.63700	0.65310	0.60479
1930	0.73923	0.67865	0.63531	0.66033	0.56358

For both Saskatchewan and New Brunswick the 1900 scale of operation was too small to yield reliable ratios and even in 1910, outputs in both cases were still small. Therefore data for these years, presented in brackets, are purely to complete the information from decennial census data. Alberta production essentially begins in 1886.

The ratios actually used to estimate wages and salaries for 1870 to 1920, derived from the foregoing, now follow.

Nova Scotia	1870-1916, 1919, 1920, ratio 0.53340; 1917, ratio 0.54252; 1918, ratio 0.63906
British Columbia	1870-1916, 1919, 1920, ratio 0.69364; 1917, ratio 0.70870; 1918, ratio 0.69076
Alberta	1886-1916, 1919, 1920 ratio 0.63126; 1917, ratio 0.62489; 1918, ratio 0.64557
New Brunswick	1900-1920, ratio 0.60 *
Saskatchewan	1900-1920, ratio 0.64220

* The ratios for New Brunswick of 1921 and 1922 seemed most relevant for earlier years since ratios for 1917 and 1918 were approximately 0.50.

The relative importance of each province in 1921 is shown by the gross value of output.

Gross Value of Coal
Output, 1921 ($000)

Nova Scotia	27,782
British Columbia	15,677
Alberta	27,247
New Brunswick	921
Saskatchewan	823

The series on gross value of product, by province, for 1886 to 1920 are found in DBS *Canadian Mineral Statistics 1886-1956*. Only Nova Scotia and British Columbia had coal production before that date. The GVP data for these two provinces from 1870 to 1885 were obtained from DBS *Coal Statistics of Canada* 1929, pages 36 and 83.

The wage and salary bills on an annual basis were obtained, province by province, by multiplying GVP's by the wage and salaries ratios and then adding the provincial wage bills together to obtained a wage bill for Canada.

The Ratio of Wage and Salaries to Gross Domestic Product

The final step of obtaining gross domestic product from the wage and salary series remains. It was done by use of an estimate of the ratio of gross domestic product to wages and salaries. One source of information is the ratio for 1921 to 1926, for which years, it will be remembered, the gross domestic product was estimated directly; a second source of information lies in the annual publications of Statcan, *Corporate Financial Statistics* 1969 and succeeding years. The ratios from each of these sources are now given.

Ratio of Wages and Salaries to Gross Domestic Product, 1921 to 1928,
From Project Calculations Based on *Mineral Production of Canada*

Year	Ratio	Year	Ratio
1921	0.8456	1925	0.9020
1922	0.8100	1926	0.7953
1923	0.8851	1927	0.8396
1924	0.8754	1928	0.9059

Ratio of Wages and Salaries to Gross
Domestic Product, Statcan *Corporate* Data

Year	Ratio	Year	Ratio	Year	Ratio
1965	0.7670	1970	0.6154	1976	0.3507
1966	0.5455	1971	0.6190	1977	0.3865
1967	0.7248	1973	0.5564	1978	0.3552
1968	0.7553	1974	0.4758	1979	0.4354
1969	0.7801	1975	0.3306		

Source: derived from *Corporate Financial Statistics*

The very large differences between these two sets of data raise some questions. But a prior consideration is the relevance of 1965-79 corporate data. Concerning them there is no doubt but that they, coming as they do from tax returns, reflect a higher accuracy of measurement of the underlying data than do the DBS production data of the 1920s but the question of how well coal mining in the 1960s and 1970s reflects the conditions of coal mining in the 1920s and earlier must be examined. Our judgement was that the data of the sixties and seventies were quite relevant for the performance of the industry in the 1920s. If this judgement is accepted, it becomes necessary to choose between the high ratios of wages to GDP, as derived from the industry statistics of the 1920s and the much lower ratios of the corporate data of the '60s and '70s.

The ratio chosen as applying to all years for the industry as a whole from 1920 back to 1870 was that wages and salaries comprised 0.70 of gross domestic product. This ratio is considerably lower than the ratios of the industry data of the twenties. Its choice is rationalized on two grounds. First, DBS estimated that in 1926 "miscellaneous" expenses included $3 million of capital outlay charged to current expenses; second, there may have been some charges for depletion in miscellaneous expenses. Neither of these items is considered as an expense item for national accounting purposes. Hence GDP as measured from industry data in the 1920s is too low. (In fact, we make a correction for this understatement for the years 1921 to 1926 when we finally sum up for the mining industry as a whole.) We have taken it that the corporate financial data of the 1960s reflect the relationship of wages and salaries to GDP better than the industry data.

Asbestos

The estimates for asbestos were done very much like those for the metallic mines. Accordingly, the description hereat will be brief. As in the other sections the estimation processes differed between the periods 1921-26 and 1870-1920.

Period 1921 to 1926

The basic data came from DBS *Mineral Production of Canada* (e.g. report for 1926 p.23). In it gross value of production, cost of fuel and electricity, and wages and salaries were reported for all years: "miscellaneous expenses", which included cost of materials and were very large, were available only for 1921 to 1923. (Full data were also available for 1920 — in *Mineral Production in Canada 1921*, pp. 180, 183 — but it was a year of volatility and the data appeared to leave something to be desired in accuracy and so, except for wages and salaries and some exploratory excursions, were not used.) The pattern of ratio of miscellaneous expenses to GVP in 1921 to 1923 did not appear to be sufficiently regular to hazard a guess for a ratio for 1924 to 1926. In these circumstances, the gross domestic product for 1921 to 1923 was obtained by subtracting cost of fuel and miscellaneous expenses, adjusted to exclude royalties, direct taxes etc., from gross value of product; a similar calculation was made for the exploratory data for 1920. From these data a ratio of average wages and salaries to GDP was calculated. The estimates of GDP for 1924 to 1926 were then made by assuming wages and salaries were 0.88 of the GDP, a ratio derived from the data of the four immediately proceeding years. (I am not entirely happy about these estimates for 1924 to 1926 but our best judgement, in not very good circumstances, was used.)

Period 1870 to 1920

As with the metallic mines, an estimate of a wage and salary series was made by inference from the gross value of product which was available in the source material: the gross value of product for 1886 to 1920 was taken from *Canadian Mineral Statistics 1886-1956*; the gross value of product for 1879-1885 was taken from *The Statistical Year Book of Canada 1894* (p.514).

The ratios of wages and salaries to GVP were derived from *Mineral Production of Canada* and the censuses of 1900 and 1910 for which years both wages and salaries and gross value of production were available. The actual wages and salaries for 1900 and 1910 were taken from *Census of Canada 1901*, Vol II, p.1xvi and from the 1911 *Census of Canada Vol. V*, p. xxxi, p. 90 and for 1920 from *Mineral Production of Canada*. The directly calculated ratios to be used for interpolation and extrapolation follow.

Year	Ratios of Wages and Salaries to Gross Value of Production
1900	0.5365
1910	0.4467
(1920)	(0.3221)
1921	0.5416
1922	0.4649
1923	0.4795
1924	0.4437
1925	0.3334
1926	0.3509

On the basis of these data, the ratios actually used were:

Period:	1870-1899	1901-1909	1911-1919
Ratio:	0.50	0.495 to 0.455 *	0.45

* Linear interpolation between 0.50 in 1900 and 0.45 in 1910

While the wages and salary bill for 1920 from *Mineral Production* was used, the ratio calculated from the actual data for that year was ignored since 1920 was such an unusual year with high inflation.

The multiplication of the foregoing ratios by the gross value of production along with the directly observed wages for 1900, 1910 and 1920 provided the wage and salary series for the whole period 1870 to 1920.

The gross domestic product for all years from 1870 to 1920 was calculated by using a ratio of wages and salaries to GDP of 0.60. The choice of this ratio comes from the GDP directly calculated from the 1921 to 1926 *Mineral Production* data modified by the data derived from *Corporation Statistics*. The ratios from the *Mineral Production* data follow.

Year	Ratio of Wages and Salaries to Gross Domestic Product
1921	1.2835
1922	0.9208
1923	0.8239
(1924)	(0.7692)
(1925)	(0.5651)
(1926)	(0.5950)

The 1924 to 1926 figures are bracketed since it was necessary to estimate the "miscellaneous" expenses in deriving the estimate of property income and hence the GDP. In any event, the *Corporation Statistics* data give a somewhat different picture of this ratio as they have for the other mining sectors. Unfortunately, the *Corporation Statistics* data are not given for the asbestos mines group by itself: asbestos is included with non-metal mining of which it comprises a considerable part. Ratios for five years for non-metal mining follow.

Year	Ratios of Wages and Salaries to Gross Domestic Product For Non-Metal Mining (*Corporation Statistics*)
1965	0.3040
1966	0.2726
1968	0.4508
1971	0.4561
1972	0.4343

These *Corporation Statistics* ratios for all non-metal excluding fuels are undoubtedly lower than those for asbestos by itself as will be seen from the next section of these notes on non-metal mining. Nevertheless, they do suggest that the ratios are somewhat lower than the data for 1921 to 1924 show. It was in this light that the ratio of 0.60 was chosen as the ratio of wages and salaries to GDP for the asbestos industry for all years from 1870 to 1920.

The mechanics of deriving the GDP from the wages and salaries was simply to divide the wages and salary bill each year by 0.60.

Non-Metallic Minerals Excluding Coal and Asbestos

The estimates for this group are constructed much like those for asbestos and metallic minerals.

The group that makes up the non-metallic mines in the annual reports on mining, covered in DBS *Mineral Production of Canada*, annual from 1921 onward, includes coal, natural gas, crude petroleum and asbestos as well as 26 other non-metallic minerals (1923 report). Coal mining and asbestos mining have been dealt with already and the coal mining and asbestos mining data were extracted from the commodity detail of this group. The mechanics of obtaining the data of *Mineral Production of Canada* for 1921 to 1926 was to subtract the data, item by item, on production of coal and crude asbestos from the corresponding totals that were given for the non-metallic mineral group. It is important to note that this group includes natural gas and crude petroleum production: thus, it is not necessary to dealt with them separately.

To make the coverage the same for the years from 1870 to 1920 the data (gross value of product) of the category "non-metallic minerals" in *Canadian Mineral Statistics* were augmented by addition of the data for natural gas and crude petroleum, which were given separately in the source. This procedure gave the same industry coverage in the years 1870 to 1920 as in the years 1921 to 1926.

The estimates of gross domestic product were made separately for each of the periods 1921 to 1926 and 1870 to 1920.

Period 1921 to 1926

The procedures here were so similar to those of metallic minerals and metals that they merit only a cursory statement. In general, gross domestic product was calculated by subtracting fuel expenses and that grab-bag "miscellaneous" expenses from gross value of product. A number of adaptations of data were required. First, for 1921 and 1922 an estimate cost of purchased power was shifted from miscellaneous expenses to cost of fuel and electricity. Second, a ratio of miscellaneous expenses to GVP was calculated from the data for 1921, 1922 and 1923 for which years such expenses were given in the data — the average ratio, from which the individual ratios varied little, was 0.27. Multiplication of the GVP in 1924, 1925 and 1926 by this ratio yielded estimates of miscellaneous expenses for each of these years thus filling the corresponding gap in the data for these years. Third, the miscellaneous expenses for all years were reduced by an amount equivalent to 0.04 of GVP to remove payments of interest, royalties and direct taxes from the miscellaneous expenses. With these adaptations of the data the GDP was then calculated by the method noted above.

Period 1870 to 1920

The basic original data available were annual measures of gross value of product of the non-metallic minerals. The source of such data for 1886 to 1920 was *Canadian Minerals Statistics 1886-1956*. To obtain consistency with the 1921-26 data, the following manipulation of the source material was necessary: since, in the source, the non-metallic mineral category included asbestos but did not include natural gas or crude petroleum it was necessary to subtract the values of asbestos from the recorded total for non-metallic minerals and to add values for natural gas and crude petroleum.

For years 1870 to 1885, the 1886 GVP for the group was extrapolated backward on the basis of the production of crude petroleum and its value. The volume of production of crude petroleum in thousands of barrels was taken from *Historical Statistics of Canada*, Series N174; a measure of price that in effect provided an index of petroleum prices was obtained from Michell on prices in K.W. Taylor and H. Michell, *Statistical Contributions to Canadian Economic History*, p.83. A combination of these two series, which, in effect, was an index of the value of crude petroleum, was then used to extrapolate the gross value of non-metallic minerals, excluding coal and asbestos, from 1886 back to 1870, year by year. (A small bit of detailed manipulation that was necessary is not worth elaboration.)

The next step was to calculate wages and salaries and then, from them, gross domestic product. For the years 1921 to 1926, the ratios of wages and salaries to gross value of product were the following:

Year	Ratio of Wages and Salaries to Gross Value of Product
1921	0.3013
1922	0.2598
1923	0.2942
1924	0.3336
1925	0.2840
1926	0.3271

The average of these is 0.3065 which was rounded to 0.31. (The mining data for 1910, from the census of 1911, yielded a ratio of 0.3434.)

Wages and salaries for 1870 to 1920 were then determined as the product of gross value of product and the wage and salary ratio of 0.31.

Gross domestic product was then calculated on the basis of wages and salaries bearing a ratio of 0.425 to gross domestic product: this ratio was equal to the average of the ratios for each year from 1921 to 1926; as may be seen from the data on asbestos it was not inconsistent with the somewhat broad corporation financial data result for 1968-1972, though it was above the ratios for 1965 and 1966. Gross domestic product was then calculated as the quotient of wages and salaries divided by 0.425.

Structural Materials

The coverage herein, in this category is limited to the production of sand and gravel and the crude stone materials, limestone, sandstone, granite, marble and slate. Both of the main sources, *Mineral Products of Canada* and *Canadian Mineral Statistics*, include in this category such other products as clay products, cement, and lime which are manufactured and hence are already included with manufactures; accordingly, they are not included in this mineral section.

As with the other categories of minerals, different methods are used for the periods 1921-1926 and 1870 to 1920.

Period 1921 to 1926

The procedures were almost the same as in the other sections. The basic data came from *Mineral Production of Canada*. (The GVP from *Canadian Mineral Statistics* was identical with that of *Mineral Production* in these years.) As usual, GDP for 1921 to 1924 was obtained by subtracting costs of fuel and electricity and "miscellaneous expenses", which includes costs of materials etc., from gross value of product. The same calculations were made for 1925 and 1926: in these two years, it was necessary to estimate "miscellaneous expenses", which was done by attributing to them the same ratio to GVP as the average for 1923 and 1924. The result for 1925 and 1926 yielded almost the same ratio for each year of GDP to GVP as the almost fixed ratio of GDP to GVP for the years 1922 to 1924. Owing to the fact that the miscellaneous expenses for 1925 and 1926 had been estimated, the final estimate for GDP in 1925 and 1926 was made by making GDP equal to 0.825 of GVP — the results were so close to the direct calculations above, that either figure for each year could have been used. The ratio of GDP to GVP of 0.825 was derived from the almost identical ratios for each of 1922, 1923 and 1924.

Period 1870 to 1920

Although this period is labelled as beginning in 1870 our data, in fact, are available only from 1886 onward: the category, construction materials, accounted for a gross domestic product of less than 0.75 million dollars in 1886, about 10 percent of mining, and its omission before that year is of minor consequence.

Annual wages and salaries were calculated for this period although, as will be explained later, they were not used to estimate gross domestic product. As usual, wages and salaries were calculated as a proportion of gross value of product except in 1920, for which year the wages and salaries were given in *Mineral Products of Canada, 1922* (pp.203, 205). Those proportions, determined from the production data for 1920 to 1926, and the data of the decennial censuses of 1900 and 1910 were as follows:

Year	Ratio of Wages and Salaries to GVP
1886 to 1899	0.59
1901 to 1909	Linear interpolation between 0.59 in 1900 and 0.39 in 1910
1911 to 1919	0.39

The wages and salaries for 1900 and 1910 were the actual figures obtained in the census for each year. The ratio of wages and salaries to GVP rose markedly before 1910 because sand and gravel, an important item in railway building, was a much smaller part of the total in 1900 and earlier years and the said sand and gravel had a very low ratio of wages and salaries to GVP: hence, its reduction in size leads to a rise in the wage ratio for the whole category.

The GVP series for the years 1886 to 1920 were obtained from *Canadian Mineral Statistics 1886-1956*. The sand and gravel component of this series before 1912 includes only exports in the source: the series for sand and gravel for 1886 to 1911 was adjusted by multiplying the value of exports for each of these years by the average ratio of value of total production to value of exports in 1912, 1913 and 1914.

It was not appropriate for this structural materials category to derive gross domestic product from wages and salaries by treating wages as a constant proportion of gross domestic product as determined from later data — the change in the ratio of wages to GVP made this method unsuitable. Rather, gross domestic product was calculated directly from gross value of product for all years 1886 to 1920. The ratio of gross domestic product to gross value of product of 0.835 (noted above) for later years (after 1921) was adopted as the appropriate ratio for all years 1886 to 1920. The gross domestic product was calculated then by multiplying gross value of product by the factor 0.835. (Note that the ratio 0.825 had been used for 1925 and 1926.) The ratio of gross domestic product to gross value of product in these structural materials is high because there is little outlay on purchased materials.

Totals for All Mining

The totals of wages and salaries and of gross domestic product were then obtained by first adding the like items of each of the components and then adjusting these totals for understatement. The adjustments differed between the years 1921 to 1926 and the years 1870 to 1920 for reasons that one would expect from what has been written already.

The Adjustments of Gross Domestic Product 1921 to 1926

The project 1921 to 1926 data overlapped with the official data, i.e. DBS-Statcan data, in 1926. The project and official gross domestic products compare as follows:

<table>
<tr><td></td><td>Gross Domestic Product,
Mining</td></tr>
<tr><td>Official estimate</td><td>$ 154,000,000</td></tr>
<tr><td>Project estimate</td><td>122,048,900</td></tr>
<tr><td>Ratio of official estimate
to project estimate</td><td>1.2618</td></tr>
</table>

This ratio was used to adjust all of the project estimates of gross domestic product upward for the years 1921 to 1926. The reasons that this adjustment was upward and was as large as it was were twofold. First, certain head office salaries and supplementary labour income, included in the official figures, were not included in the project source figures for 1921 to 1926. (See the note on 1870 to 1920.) Second, the implied property income component of gross domestic product derived from *Mineral Production of Canada* for 1921 to 1926 appears to be considerably too low. It was for these reasons that resort had been had to the ratio of wages to gross domestic product in the *Corporation Financial Statistics 1965 et seq.* in making estimates of gross domestic product for years 1870 to 1920.

The project wages and salaries were also less than the official wages and salaries, although to a much lesser extent and reflecting only the absence of head office statistics and rather small elements of supplementary labour income in the *Mineral Production of Canada* data from which the project data were derived. Since the adjustment factor for wages was the same throughout the whole period from 1870 to 1926, it will be dealt with in the description of the adjustments for 1870 to 1920, which follows immediately.

Adjustments of Gross Domestic Product 1870 to 1920 and of Wages and Salaries 1870 to 1926

To make this adjustment, calculations were made of what the 1926 gross domestic product would have been had that same method of estimation been used as that used, in fact, for the 1870 to 1920 period. The results of this calculation were compared with the official estimates.

The calculations follow.

	Project Wages and Salaries, 1926 ($)	Ratio of Wages and Salaries to Gross Domestic Product	Inferred Gross Domestic Product, 1926 ($)
Metallic minerals	26,448,860	0.40	66,122,150
Coal	35,841,196	0.70	51,201,709
Asbestos	3,544,097	0.60	5,906,828
Non-Metallic minerals ex. coal and asbestos	4,993,961	0.425	11,750,496
Structural materials	5,320,950		10,694,102 *
Total, Project method of 1870-1920	76,149,064		145,675,285
Add official head office and supplementary labour income	5,003,452		5,003,452
Add official capital outlay charged to current expense	--		3,000,000
Project totals adjusted	$ 81,152,516		$ 153,678,737

Wage and salary adjustment factor = 81,152,516 ÷ 76,149,064 = 1.0657060

Gross domestic product adjustment factor = 153,678,737 ÷ 145,675,285 = 1.05940356

* GDP = 0.835 x GVP

The project adjusted figure of $153,678,737 for gross domestic product in 1926 compares with the official national accounts figure of $154 million; similarly, the project adjusted wage and salary estimate for 1926 is within $1 million of the official figure. This method of calculation of gross domestic product, then, with the adjustment for the omissions of head office wages and salaries and excluded supplementary labour income and also for the capital outlay charged to current expense, from the source data used by the project, gives an estimate that corresponds almost exactly with the official estimates in 1926. A check of the 1921 estimates of gross domestic product by using the 1870 to 1920 method against the method from *Mineral Production of Canada* yields a 3.6% higher estimate for the 1870-1920 method. In the light of these checks, the project initial estimates of gross domestic product for 1870 to 1920 were multiplied by the gross domestic product adjustment factor 1.05940356 to obtain the final project estimate of gross domestic product. The initial project estimates of wages and salaries were multiplied by the wage and salary adjustment factor 1.0657060 for all years, 1870 to 1926, to get the final project estimate of wage and salaries.

It should be noted that the project wages and salaries for 1921 to 1926 (before adjustment) came directly from the source document, *Mineral Production of Canada*.

Bibliography of Sources Cited in Chapter 3

The sources of information for this chapter were largely Dominion Bureau of Statistics (and antecedent agencies) publications. The abbreviations for frequently cited words or phrases are given first. Titles of sources follow.

- **Abbreviations:**

DBS: Dominion Bureau of Statistics
CYB: *Canada Year Book*
GVP: Gross Value of Product

Statcan: Statistics Canada
HSC: *Historical Statistics of Canada (1965)*
GDP: Gross Domestic Product

- **Publications:**

Dominion Bureau of Statistics Publications

Canadian Forestry Statistics, Revised, 1959.
Operations in the Woods, Revised Estimates of Forest Production 1940-1953. Final Estimates 1954-1955.
The Lumber Industry, annual from 1917 onward.
Operations in the Woods published as part of *The Lumber Industry*, 1920 to 1924, then a separate publication.
The Pulp and Paper Industry, annual from 1917.
Railway Statistics, annual from 1876.
Trade of Canada, annual since 1867.
Handbook of Agricultural Statistics, Part II, Farm Income 1926-57.
Microfilm data of unpublished information on occupations and earnings (wage earner data) 1911 and 1921 censuses of Canada.
Decennial Census of Canada: all years.
Canada Year Book: Various issues.
The Fur Production of Canada, annual from 1919-20.
The Fur Farming Industry, annual from 1920.
Fisheries Statistics of Canada, annual from 1917.
Canadian Mineral Statistics, 1886-1956 (occasional 1957).
Annual Report on the Mineral Production of Canada, annual from 1921 to 1939.
Coal Statistics for Canada, annual from 1919.
Corporation Financial Statistics, (from 1965).
Historic Tables of the Mineral Production of Canada (1948).

Other Government Publications

Canada, Department of Marine and Fisheries, *Annual Report, Fisheries* for the years 1870 to 1917.

Other Publications

Historical Statistics of Canada: see bibliography, Chapter 2.

Non-Agricultural Primary Industries
Supplementary Tables

Forestry

Fur

Mining

Table 3.1. Farm and Nonfarm Production of Firewood, Census Years 1870–1930 (all production and consumption data in cords)

	1870	1880	1890	1900	1910	1920	1930
Number of farm houses (000)	328.0 *	398.8	436.9	450.3	600.9	666.1	703.9
Consumption per farm house (cords)	16.15	15.86	16.24	14.49	12.38	10.85	9.32
Total farm consumption (000 cords)	5,296	6,326	7,096	6,525	7,440	7,224	6,563
Number of nonfarm rural houses (000)	175.0 *	201.0	194.9	213.9	223.5	268.7	328.3
Consumption per nonfarm rural house (cords)	10.85	10.85	10.85	10.85	8.41	5.97	5.04
Total nonfarm rural consumption (000 cords)	1,899	2,181	2,115	2,321	1,880	1,605	1,655
Total consumption and production (000 cords)	7,195	8,507	9,211	8,846	9,320	8,829	8,219
Production per farm house (cords)	17.54	17.20	17.59	15.60	11.49	12.80	11.46
Total farm production (000 cords)	5,754	6,861	7,685	7,025	6,903	8,529	8,069
Total nonfarm production (000 cords)	1,441	1,646	1,526	1,821	2,417	300	150

* Both farm and rural nonfarm housing stock in 1870 were estimated from 1871, the first year for which Marion Steele's figures are available. This was done on the basis of Marion Steele's estimates of residential investment in 1870 and 1871.

Table 3.2. Production of Forest Products, Farm and Nonfarm, Canada, 1870–1920

Year	Logs and Bolts (millions fbm)	Pulpwood (cords)	Railway Ties (000)	Firewood (000 cords)	Exports of Squared Timber (000 tons)
1870	2,227	-	1,761	7,195	565
1871	2,358	-	2,390	7,294	569
1872	2,480	-	4,378	7,568	629
1873	2,751	-	3,357	7,642	567
1874	2,615	-	4,052	7,775	449
1875	2,135	8,141	3,559	7,926	568
1876	2,000	18,497	3,458	8,053	467
1877	2,030	28,853	4,080	8,185	651
1878	1,939	39,208	3,873	8,300	464
1879	2,008	49,564	4,604	8,394	211
1880	2,255	59,920	5,105	8,507	269
1881	2,392	70,276	5,448	8,635	524
1882	2,385	80,632	8,775	8,719	314
1883	2,414	90,987	6,856	8,768	351
1884	2,360	101,343	5,785	8,807	397
1885	2,226	111,699	5,277	8,864	281
1886	2,411	122,055	7,637	8,929	289
1887	2,623	132,411	6,450	8,993	171
1888	2,801	142,766	6,884	9,064	190
1889	3,044	153,122	7,059	9,144	228
1890	3,084	163,478	7,201	9,211	287
1891	3,144	230,943	7,391	9,159	222
1892	3,186	320,540	6,535	9,140	199
1893	3,223	395,565	6,918	9,126	178
1894	2,935	422,259	5,805	9,081	180
1895	3,065	523,972	5,622	9,014	126
1896	3,481	620,702	5,739	8,948	178
1897	3,587	682,171	5,869	8,888	164
1898	3,523	655,590	5,647	8,855	152
1899	3,674	593,152	5,909	8,849	175

Table 3.2. (continued)

Year	Logs and Bolts (millions fbm)	Pulpwood (cords)	Railway Ties (000)	Firewood (000 cords)	Exports of Squared Timber (000 tons)
1900	3,656	668,034	6,235	8,846	143
1901	3,900	750,431	6,403	8,777	125
1902	3,932	765,056	5,877	8,720	96
1903	3,869	753,199	6,580	8,724	126
1904	3,792	957,685	8,267	8,785	88
1905	4,107	1,063,063	7,746	8,906	70
1906	4,487	1,056,704	9,246	9,019	86
1907	4,385	1,414,702	7,983	9,081	64
1908	3,905	1,325,085	9,337	9,114	60
1909	4,448	1,557,753	9,635	9,170	63
1910	4,771	1,541,628	8,895	9,320	40
1911	5,176	1,520,227	9,630	9,449	42
1912	4,604	1,846,910	13,678	9,494	49
1913	4,028	2,144,064	13,885	9,484	53
1914	4,250	2,196,884	16,554	9,427	21
1915	4,327	2,355,550	16,797	9,321	23
1916	3,913	2,833,119	12,409	9,202	24
1917	4,578	3,122,179	10,123	9,106	17
1918	4,254	3,560,280	8,794	9,048	21
1919	4,262	3,498,981	10,201	8,933	68
1920	4,733	4,024,826	15,975	8,829	101

Table 3.3.   Forest Products on Farms, 1870–1920

Year	Logs and Bolts (Mfbm)	Price ($ per Mfbm)	Pulpwood (cords)	Price ($ per cord)	Railway Ties (thousands)	Price ($)	Firewood (thousand cords)	Price ($ per cord)	Adjusted Total Value* ($ 000)
1870	605,547	4.941	–	–	598	0.227	5,753	2.224	16,402
1871	641,010	4.913	–	–	812	0.225	5,824	2.365	17,621
1872	674,299	5.739	–	–	1,488	0.263	5,983	2.613	20,492
1873	747,881	5.935	–	–	1,141	0.272	6,018	2.743	21,896
1874	710,817	4.841	–	–	1,378	0.222	6,114	2.582	20,122
1875	580,485	4.202	3,582	1.787	1,210	0.200	6,233	2.197	16,773
1876	543,690	4.011	8,139	1.783	1,175	0.196	6,342	2.000	15,583
1877	551,766	4.181	12,695	1.859	1,387	0.237	6,477	1.964	15,873
1878	527,221	3.884	17,252	1.727	1,316	0.225	6,607	1.921	15,559
1879	545,816	3.870	21,808	1.721	1,565	0.186	6,725	1.931	15,941
1880	613,152	4.569	26,365	2.031	1,736	0.192	6,860	2.037	17,749
1881	650,311	5.625	30,921	2.501	1,852	0.192	7,014	2.149	19,840
1882	648,457	6.006	35,478	2.670	2,983	0.205	7,133	2.256	21,439
1883	656,360	5.483	40,034	2.438	2,331	0.234	7,218	2.294	21,553
1884	641,712	4.872	44,591	2.166	1,967	0.262	7,290	2.205	20,534
1885	605,138	4.738	49,148	2.107	1,794	0.262	7,372	2.100	19,627
1886	655,584	4.975	53,704	2.212	2,596	0.253	7,453	2.035	19,937
1887	713,160	5.315	58,261	2.363	2,193	0.223	7,517	1.8178	18,621
1888	761,332	5.793	62,817	2.576	2,340	0.188	7,574	1.8654	19,715
1889	827,403	6.384	67,374	2.838	2,400	0.175	7,634	1.8455	20,583
1890	838,472	6.773	71,930	3.011	2,448	0.183	7,684	1.8334	21,046
1891	854,631	7.199	101,615	2.781	2,513	0.168	7,604	1.8144	21,275
1892	866,072	7.557	141,038	3.011	2,222	0.144	7,523	1.7383	20,978
1893	876,113	8.037	174,049	2.921	2,354	0.141	7,465	1.6769	21,012
1894	797,941	8.053	185,794	2.991	1,973	0.141	7,396	1.6631	20,147
1895	833,166	8.170	230,548	2.816	1,911	0.158	7,313	1.6406	20,350
1896	946,210	8.296	273,109	2.836	1,951	0.164	7,230	1.5914	21,065
1897	974,983	8.341	300,155	3.706	1,995	0.137	7,148	1.5430	21,164
1898	957,635	8.528	288,460	3.066	1,920	0.151	7,085	1.5179	20,700
1899	998,641	8.555	260,987	3.056	2,009	0.163	7,051	1.5136	20,952

Table 3.3. (continued)

Year	Logs and Bolts (Mfbm)	Price ($ per Mfbm)	Pulpwood (cords)	Price ($ per cord)	Railway Ties (thousands)	Price ($)	Firewood (thousand cords)	Price ($ per cord)	Adjusted Total Value* ($ 000)
1900	993,970	8.147	293,935	3.246	2,120	0.173	7,025	1.645	1,604
1901	1,060,032	7.685	330,190	3.192	2,177	0.196	6,911	1.7939	22,868
1902	1,068,861	8.161	336,625	3.138	1,998	0.202	6,840	1.9357	24,128
1903	1,050,825	8.333	331,408	3.084	2,237	0.209	6,822	2.0564	25,014
1904	1,030,926	7.670	421,381	3.030	2,810	0.215	6,846	2.0930	24,848
1905	1,116,554	7.802	467,748	3.248	2,633	0.225	6,911	2.0318	25,612
1906	1,219,655	9.703	464,950	3.260	3,143	0.277	6,945	2.1843	30,275
1907	1,191,893	10.811	622,469	3,717	2,714	0.255	6,929	2.4810	34,076
1908	1,061,419	9.706	583,037	4.035	3,174	0.271	6,891	2.3770	30,792
1909	1,209,236	9.830	685,411	4.132	3,276	0.177	6,865	2.2636	31,765
1910	1,296,959	10.721	672,186	4.388	2,980	0.2643	6,902	2.1469	33,437
1911	1,325,709	10.074	641,065	4.506	3,042	0.216	7,201	2.7720	37,969
1912	1,107,104	10.620	752,350	4.675	4,060	0.248	7,371	2.8029	38,051
1913	905,482	11.143	842,666	4.936	3,855	0.267	7,501	2.8230	37,549
1914	888,769	11.411	831,936	5.083	4,280	0.262	7,624	3.2077	41,147
1915	836,996	11.390	858,259	5.108	4,022	0.254	7,741	3.1979	40,888
1916	695,613	11.575	991,654	5.564	2,734	0.263	7,871	2.9629	38,739
1917	742,076	14.180	1,048,081	6.895	2,036	0.307	8,031	3.7423	49,884
1918	622,801	16.944	1,144,114	8.745	1,601	0.369	8,213	4.9255	63,452
1919	557,184	18.307	1,074,261	10.050	1,662	0.440	8,380	4.5499	61,666
1920	544,563	21.323	1,178,019	13.007	2,297	0.592	8,529	4.3143	67,047

* Total adjusted value exceeds the sum of the quantities times prices by a factor 1.03: see the text for its basis.

Table 3.4. Volume of Nonfarm Production, Forest Products, and Unit Wage Costs, 1870–1920

Year	Wage Costs (per thousand cu.ft.)	Volume of Nonfarm Forest Products (millions cu.ft.)	Year	Wage Costs (per thousand cu.ft.)	Volume of Nonfarm Forest Products (millions cu.ft.)
1870	8.9894	573.9	1900	13.2890	880.9
1871	10.2808	603.3	1901	13.8376	929.8
1872	10.4075	656.7	1902	14.1283	930.2
1873	11.8508	689.9	1903	14.4772	930.0
1874	12.4079	664.8	1904	14.7097	944.7
1875	12.1800	598.7	1905	15.3493	1002.2
1876	11.1418	567.9	1906	15.9889	1084.9
1877	10.8126	597.0	1907	16.2214	1087.4
1878	10.4328	560.7	1908	15.7563	1020.7
1879	9.5718	550.3	1909	16.6284	1135.4
1880	8.7868	599.2	1910	17.2098	1190.6
1881	10.8886	648.4	1911	17.6168	1267.7
1882	12.2560	650.0	1912	18.1982	1240.3
1883	12.9397	640.2	1913	18.4889	1173.2
1884	12.3826	625.0	1914	17.2680	1240.9
1885	12.3826	585.5	1915	16.4540	1270.1
1886	13.1198	634.6	1916	19.6518	1188.4
1887	13.0022	648.2	1917	25.7566	1309.5
1888	13.2372	684.6	1918	29.6521	1270.7
1889	13.0236	731.9	1919	34.2452	1282.0
1890	13.0236	748.0	1920	38.3151	1482.4
1891	13.0236	759.8			
1892	13.2271	769.5			
1893	13.1254	785.8			
1894	13.0236	734.3			
1895	12.9219	756.7			
1896	12.9219	838.7			
1897	13.1254	862.0			
1898	12.9219	849.5			
1899	13.2271	877.1			

Note: The wage bill derived from the product of these two series was multiplied by the factor 1.01: see text.

Table 3.5. Fur Production, Gross Revenue and Sales of Fur Farms, Calendar Years, 1920–1929 (thousands of dollars)

Year	Gross Revenue	Sales of Fur Farms	Year	Gross Revenue	Sales of Fur Farms
1920	15,769	388	1925	15,256	783
1921	13,795	626	1926	16,968	1,226
1922	17,100	598	1927	18,811	2,163
1923	16,202	860	1928	18,752	2,389
1924	15,542	664	1929	15,452	2,305

Table 3.6. Value of Exports, Fur Trade, Calendar Years, 1870–1920 (thousands of dollars)

Year	Value of Exports	Year	Value of Exports
1870	312	1890	1,470
1871	453	1891	1,459
1872	763	1892	1,500
1873	1,284	1893	1,605
1874	1,478	1894	1,694
1875	1,551	1895	1,657
1876	1,550	1886	1,677
1877	1,324	1897	1,549
1878	1,258	1898	1,493
1879	1,113	1899	1,605
1880	1,509	1900	1,669
1881	1,630	1901	1,693
1882	1,182	1902	2,072
1883	1,103	1903	2,233
1884	1,368	1904	2,228
1885	1,630	1905	2,386
1886	1,673	1906	2,884
1887	1,845	1907	2,683
1888	1,896	1908	2,448
1889	1,680	1909	3,371

Table 3.6. (continued)

Year	Value of Exports	Year	Value of Exports
1910	4,110	1920	13,927
1911	3,912	1921	13,978
1912	4,812	1922	15,821
1913	5,456	1923	17,647
1914	3,434	1924	17,221
1915	4,182	1925	17,063
1916	5,430	1926	19,451
1917	7,439		
1918	12,130		
1919	18,837		

Table 3.7. Wages and Salaries, Mining, by Sector, 1870–1926 (thousands of dollars)

Year	Metallic Mines	Coal Mines	Asbestos Mines	Non-metallic Minerals and Fuels	Structural Materials	Total (unadjusted)	Total (adjusted)
1870	874	682	-	435	-	1,991	2,112
1871	1,102	745	-	525	-	2,372	2,528
1872	946	974	-	613	-	2,533	2,699
1873	779	1,082	-	696	-	2,557	2,725
1874	1,025	980	-	226	-	2,231	2,378
1875	1,365	979	-	406	-	2,750	2,931
1876	1,024	990	-	680	-	2,694	2,871
1877	988	1,024	-	429	-	2,442	2,602
1878	780	1,127	-	387	-	2,294	2,445
1879	802	1,206	10	570	-	2,587	2757
1880	661	1,549	12	470	-	2,692	2,869
1881	655	1,544	18	522	-	2,739	2,919
1882	632	1,871	26	477	-	3,006	3,204
1883	564	1,762	34	512	-	2,872	3,061
1884	536	2,106	38	558	-	3,238	3,451
1885	582	1,983	71	634	-	3,271	3,486
1886	742	2,164	103	521	520	4,050	4,316
1887	717	2,552	113	519	552	4,453	4,746
1888	898	2,737	128	593	622	4,977	5,304
1889	1,096	2,895	213	603	790	5,597	5,965
1890	1,203	3,369	630	682	834	6,719	7,160
1891	1,782	4,266	500	685	642	7,875	8,393
1892	1,199	3,832	295	720	663	6,709	7,150
1893	1,482	4,447	255	729	1,056	7,968	8,492
1894	1,479	4,473	210	664	1,056	7,882	8,400
1895	1,896	4,062	284	724	1,025	7,990	8,515
1896	2,466	4,323	215	685	893	8,582	9,146
1897	4,174	4,370	224	718	848	10,334	11,013
1898	6,492	4,981	246	739	1,065	13,523	14,412
1899	8,618	6,147	243	841	1,219	17,068	18,190

Table 3.7. (continued)

Year	Metallic Mines	Coal Mines	Asbestos Mines	Non-metallic Minerals and Fuels	Structural Materials	Total (unadjusted)	Total (adjusted)
1900	11,751	8,107	224	848	1,073	22,003	23,449
1901	11,672	7,646	624	869	1,399	22,209	23,668
1902	9,578	8,979	563	847	1,548	21,513	22,927
1903	8,469	9,338	451	903	1,553	20,714	22,075
1904	7,524	9,809	589	883	1,539	20,343	21,680
1905	8,557	10,385	714	992	1,425	22,073	23,523
1906	9,220	11,710	968	1,151	1,373	24,423	26,028
1907	8,833	14,547	1,165	1,360	1,129	27,034	28,810
1908	8,213	15,037	1,184	1,356	1,171	26,960	28,731
1909	8,165	15,009	1,047	1,258	1,694	27,173	28,958
1910	8,565	18,845	1,606	1,325	1,752	32,092	34,201
1911	8,179	15,819	1,324	1,549	2,303	2,9174	31,091
1912	11,109	21,635	1,412	1,961	2,436	38,553	41,086
1913	12,323	22,272	1,732	2,256	3,030	41,615	44,349
1914	11,278	11,918	1,309	2,197	3,112	37,814	40,298
1915	14,716	19,013	1,609	2,383	2,290	44,010	42,639
1916	21,083	23,180	2,353	2,904	2,177	51,697	55,009
1917	21,557	26,062	3,254	4,006	2,174	57,053	60,802
1918	23,666	35,943	4,037	4,172	2,109	69,927	74,521
1919	15,444	33,689	4,939	2,915	2,698	59,685	63,607
1920	16,757	49,978	4,765	3,329	4,645	79,474	84,697
1921	11,826	45,340	2,657	3,159	2,472	65,455	69,756
1922	13,319	39,501	2,582	3,094	3,358	61,853	65,917
1923	17,864	46,214	3,607	3,605	3,358	74,648	79,553
1924	21,557	35,121	2,977	3,833	3,617	67,105	71,514
1925	24,164	33,097	2,977	3,836	4,832	68,905	73,433
1926	26,449	35,841	3,544	4,994	5,321	76,149	81,153

Note: The wage and salary adjustment factor of 1.0657 was to adjust the level of the project series to the level of the official accounts.

Chapter 4. Manufacturing

M.C. URQUHART

Gross Domestic Product in Manufacturing, Canada, 1870-1926

A substantial statement on the general basis of the census of manufactures data is given in the published paper "New Estimates of Gross National Product, Canada, 1870-1926: Some Implications for Canadian Development" in Stanley L. Engerman and Robert E. Gallman, *Long-Term Factors in American Economic Growth* (published by the University of Chicago Press, 1986) which is volume 51 in the series of the Conference on Research in Income and Wealth sponsored by the National Bureau of Economic Research (NBER). That statement is repeated here and I carry on from it. The NBER text now follows.

Notes on the Estimates of Income Produced in Manufacturing, Canada, 1870-1926

The estimates for the manufacturing industry, like those of most other sectors, were prepared by the income-produced method.

The source data for manufactures estimates were of three main sorts. First, the most basic data were obtained from censuses of manufactures, which themselves were of three types: a census of manufactures was taken with each decennial census, from 1871 to 1911, the data applying to the calendar year preceding the census date — these censuses of manufactures were taken by enumerators; two postal censuses were taken for the years 1905 and 1915, both of which suffered from incomplete coverage; an annual census of manufactures was taken from 1917 onward. Second, a large quantity of data of many kinds and from many miscellaneous sources, nearly all of them official documents, were used to obtain estimates for the intercensal years. Third, quite extensive use was made of data on occupations and wages collected in the censuses of population. The 1911 census was the most valuable for this purpose. In that year the equivalent of an industrial classification of the labour force, very similar to the standard industrial classification of 1948, was used to classify the labour force. The part of the labour force classified to manufacturing matched very closely that of the numbers recorded in the census of manufactures. In addition, in 1911 the wages and salaries of every employed person collected in the census were useful for comparative purposes as well as for filling gaps for those industries employing fewer than five persons that were omitted from the 1911 census. Similar data from the 1901 and the 1921 censuses were likewise useful, though in a more limited fashion since there was not as satisfactory an industrial classification of the labour force for these years.

The information obtained in the censuses before 1917 was limited. The basic data obtained were gross value of products, costs of materials, payments of wages and salaries, cost of fuels beginning in 1900, and in one year, 1900, outlays on other miscellaneous expenses. In all of these early censuses there was a quite fine breakdown of industries, the number of individual industries varying from slightly less than 200 upward to 250, but there was no commodity detail.

For the years from 1917 onward the censuses contained considerably more information than hitherto. The largest change was the addition of the collection of commodity data. In addition, for the years 1917-23 data on "miscellaneous" expenses were obtained.

Three features of the set of data should be noted immediately. First, from 1870 to 1915 the census included what has variously been called custom and repair work or the hand trades, and, indeed, data were collected for these trades, although tabulated separately, in the annual census from 1917 to 1921. It was not feasible to separate the data for custom and repair from manufacturing proper before 1917, and consequently the estimates for 1870-1916 include these trades. In order to maintain comparability from 1917 onward, custom and repair, though tabulated separately, were also included with the various manufacturing industries to which they were related. This procedure is in contrast to the official estimates, which begin in 1926 and do not include custom and repair with manufactures.

Second, the censuses of 1900, 1905, 1910, and 1915 all fell somewhat short of complete coverage of the manufacturing industry. The census of 1900 did not cover businesses employing fewer than five persons, except in the cases of cheese factories and of brick and tile yards, which were covered completely. The census of 1910, in general, also did not include businesses employing fewer than five persons, but the exceptions for which full coverage was taken were extended to cover such industries as sawmills and flour and grist mills, with the result that the under-coverage was much less than in 1900. The censuses of 1905 and 1915, the first postal censuses, also had their shortcomings: the number of establishments covered in the census of 1905 appears small in comparison with the numbers in 1900 and 1910, and in any event, information on cost of materials was not obtained; the census of 1915 omitted collection of data from businesses producing products valued at less than $2,500, irrespective of the number of persons employed, except for flour and grist mills, butter and cheese factories, fish-preserving factories, sawmills, brick and tile yards, lime kilns, and electric light plants, which were covered whatever their size. The greatest shortfall in coverage in 1915 would be bakeries, tailoring, and black-smithing; sawmills were also considerably underreported. The short-falls in the coverage of 1900 and 1910 required the construction of special estimates to fill the gaps of the census data for those years.

Third, for the first volume of *Historical Statistics of Canada* (HSC), the manufacturing data for all censuses from 1870 to 1959 were classified, on as nearly a uniform basis as possible, into 17 industry groups in accordance with the Canadian standard industrial classification of 1948; this work was done in the DBS. This classification was most useful since the entire industrial distribution of GDP by industry in the official accounts for the years 1926-46 is based on the Standard Industrial Classification of 1948.

The Basic Estimates

The most basic estimates are those for the decennial census years of 1870, 1880, 1890, 1900, 1910, for 1915, and for each year from 1917 to 1926, all years in which a census of manufactures was taken. As has been noted, some supplemental estimation for the omitted establishments employing fewer than five persons in 1900, 1910, 1915, and 1917 was necessary, but a description of the method of calculating income generated in manufacturing in the decennial census benchmark years and in the later annual census of manufactures years is given.

The method is very simple. In the census of manufactures all business establishments reported the gross value of their products, the costs of materials, and wage and salary and piecework costs. In addition, in the 1900 census an estimate (provided by the establishments themselves) of the numbers engaged and of the value of labour services of owners and firm members was obtained. Also, in 1900 and in 1917-23 the costs of miscellaneous expenses, which included such items as rent of works and offices, insurance, travel, taxes, repairs, advertising, interest, royalties, and ostensibly all other expenses, were collected. If these expenses were complete, GDP at factor costs in manufacturing should be derivable by a process of subtracting the cost of materials, of fuel and power, and of such part of the miscellaneous expenses as contains items that are true costs and not themselves a part of factor returns from gross value of production. In fact, the method followed was actually to subtract relevant costs from gross value of production, the estimation process being done at the level of each of the 17 industry groups of the 1948 standard industrial classification.

The question then becomes one of trying to obtain estimates of gross value of product, of cost of materials, of cost of fuel and power, and of miscellaneous expenses that are as correct as possible. These items are dealt with in order.

Gross Value of Product

As for estimates of gross value of product (GVP), the amounts reported in the census returns themselves were accepted without amendment for the part of manufacturing that was covered in the censuses. It was accepted that the coverage was complete in 1870, 1880, 1890, and virtually complete in 1917-26; in 1900 and 1910, it was necessary to add estimates of output of those business employing fewer than five persons that were omitted in these censuses; in 1915 it was necessary to add estimates for those businesses producing less than $2,500 output; and for 1917-26 it was necessary to estimate custom and repair work. A rather extensive examination of some individual establishment returns for 1870, the only year for which individual establishment data are available, suggests that sometimes minor products and their values were not reported in that year. Hence the reported total of product values for that year is probably understated by an unknown amount. But there is no basis for making any revision of the reported figures. Further, it seems probable that in 1870 the cost of raw materials was also understated — the inspection noted above suggested that minor raw materials might have been omitted. If both GVP and costs of raw materials were understated, the biases would be offsetting for calculating GDP.

A scrutiny of the questionnaires used in the censuses shows the following. For 1870, 1890, and 1900, the questionnaires under the heading "Products" (1870 and 1890) or "Goods Manufactured" (1900) simply asked for "kind" or "classes" of products, "quantities", and "values" (1870 and 1890) or "value or price at work" (1900), with a single line being left for each of these stubs; in 1880 the request was limited to "aggregate value in $ of products"; in 1910 the headings were like those for 1890 but there were several blank lines to allow the listing of products. A request "Received for custom work and repairing" was added in 1900. It was not until 1915 that the instruction on the questionnaire specifically requested the inclusion of by-products and the value of containers sold with goods, and that a request for the item "all other products (value only)" was specifically printed on the questionnaire. The censuses from 1917 onward specified the commodity detail desired on forms that were specific to each industry and probably elicited full reporting.

Three other points are relevant. First, there is little or no information on instructions given to the enumerators about the taking of the censuses of manufactures. Second, there is no indication of whether or not construction work (of a capital account nature) done by establishments for their own use was included in value of product-it most likely was not. (Some information on establishments' construction with their own work force was sought in 1919, but there is no evidence that the resulting information was used.) Third, it is probably safe to say that goods were valued at the works from 1900 onward although the specific instruction to so value them was not contained in the 1910 schedule; the instructions for 1870, 1880, and 1890 do not specify the place of valuation.

Cost of Materials

The figures reported in the censuses for cost of materials were also accepted as reported (except for such adjustment as was necessary owing to the undercoverage of small businesses in 1900, 1910, and 1915 and custom work, 1919-26).

There are some uncertainties about the reliability of the recorded raw material costs on which some light is cast by the questions in the questionnaires. The exact wording of the relevant parts of the census questionnaire for censuses from 1870 to 1915 follows.

WORDING ON CENSUS OF MANUFACTURES

re. information on raw materials and entire exact wording on form

1870 Raw material
- 12. Kind
- 13. Quantities
- 14. Aggregate value, in dollars

1880 17. Aggregate value in $ of raw material

1890 Materials used
- 18. Kind
- 19. Quantities
- 20. Cost at the factory using them including freight charges

1900 Materials used
  In crude state
- 42. Kinds
- 43. Cost delivered, $
  In partly manufactured state
- 44. Kinds
- 45 Cost delivered, $

1905 No information on raw materials

1910 39. Kind or class of raw or partly finished materials used at the works in year.

    _____

    _____ (several lines left)

    _____

   40. Cost value of raw or partly finished materials used at works in year.

    _____

    _____ (several lines left)

    _____

1915 4. Materials used:
Give cost values including freight, duty, etc., of all materials actually used in the manufacture of goods, whether raw or partly manufactured or whether entering into the product, used as containers (boxes, barrels, cans, etc.), or consumed in the process or manufacturing. Do not consider stock used as identical with stock purchased. Materials produced by the establishment itself and used by it for further manufacture are not to be included.

Total cost value of all materials used — $_____.

Itemize principal materials used in the following schedule:

	Articles	Quantities	Cost Values

1.
2.
3.
4.
5.
6.
7.
8.   Fuel for power purposes
9.   All other   (value only)

1917 (onward)

From 1917 onward itemised forms for material costs specialised to industries were used. I have several of these. It would appear that in some industries in 1917 the listing of material inputs was not complete, since there was no heading for "all other materials" and containers were not included; in other industries the specifications were fairly complete even in 1917. In all industries the specifications were quite complete by 1920-22. From then on containers, etc., and other package materials were always included with costs where relevant. The consequence is that for some industries the 1917-19 figures for materials used are too low.

Cost of Fuel and Power

The data reported for cost of fuel and light and rent of power and heat are less well covered than those for GVP and for cost of material. Such data were not collected at all before 1900, although some part (probably small) of fuel costs may have been included in the cost of materials. In 1900, the money cost of "rent of power and heat" and expenses of "fuel and light" were collected explicitly; in 1910, the weight of coal used and the value of all fuels consumed were collected but not the cost of purchased power which, although requested on the form, was not tabulated; in 1915, although cost of fuel used for power purposes was collected, it was not tabulated separately and is most likely included in cost of materials for that year — fuel-for-power costs were collected in the same section as material costs; from 1917 onward, costs of fuel of all kinds and of rent of power were collected. It became necessary, then, to make estimates for the census years not covered. Only the simplest methods could be used. Purchased power for 1910 was estimated by first interpolating linearly the percentage of costs of purchased power to GVP for each of the 17 industry groups, between 1900 and 1917, and then applying the relevant percentage figure for each group in 1910 to the GVP in 1910. The purchased power costs were then added to fuel costs, which were collected in the census of 1910, to obtain fuel and power costs. Fuel and power costs for each industry in 1915 were estimated by linear interpolation between 1910 and 1917 of the ratio of such costs to GVP and then applying the 1915 ratios to GVP in 1915. For 1870, 1880, and 1890, the ratios of fuel and power costs to GVP for each of the 17 industries were taken as being the same as in 1900, and the estimates were made on that basis. The changes between 1900 an 1917 were sufficiently moderate that one has a reasonably comfortable feeling in following this procedure.

Miscellaneous Expenses

The most difficult problem to deal with was the estimation of "miscellaneous expenses". The purpose of obtaining these miscellaneous expenses presumably was to collect all expenses of manufacture other than material and fuel costs and salary and wage cost, excepting only capital consumption allowances.

The history of the collection of these costs is of some interest. "Miscellaneous expenses" under the headings given here were first requested on the questionnaire in the census of manufactures for 1900.

Headings of Miscellaneous Expenditure, 1900

Rent of works (if any), $
Rent of power and heat (if any), $
Fuel and light, $
Municipal taxes, $
Provincial taxes, $

Rent of offices, interest,
  insurance, internal revenue
  tax, etc. $
Amount paid for contract
  work (if any), $

The largest item reported is the second from the last in the list ("rent of offices", etc.): it was obviously a catchall item — it frequently amounted to one-half or more of the total — but just what was included is not clear. For example, it is not clear whether or not it includes costs of repairs and maintenance, office supplies, postage, travel, local transportation costs, and other such items.

It was not until 1917 that the same kind of information was collected again. From 1917 to 1921 "miscellaneous expenses" were collected under headings like those for 1919 enumerated here, which are typical of other years.

Miscellaneous Expenses during the Year 1919

Rent of offices, works, and machinery
Cost of purchased power
Insurance (premium for year only)
               Excise
Taxes: Excess Profits Tax
               Provincial and Municipal
Royalties, use of patents, etc.
Advertising expenses
Travelling expenses
Repairs to buildings and Machinery
All other sundry expenses (do not include fuel costs, materials used, salaries and wages).
                                  ·Total:

In 1922 and 1923 only the totals for all miscellaneous expenses (without any details) were collected; thereafter, this information was no longer obtained in the census of manufactures. In the enumerated data for 1917-21 the item "all other sundry expenses" was the largest one, often amounting to one-half or more of the total.

There was one other important body of data on miscellaneous expenses. At the time of preparation of the national income estimates for the Royal Commission on Dominion-Provincial Relations, in the late 1930s, a questionnaire requesting a great deal of information on value of products, cost of materials, wage and salary costs, depreciation, and a very wide range of miscellaneous expenses for the years 1929, 1933, and 1936 was sent to a very large number of manufacturing establishments, and a large response was obtained. The listing of expense items was quite exhaustive. By means of its use it was possible to ascertain that the "miscellaneous expenses" obtained by 1921 in the census of manufactures were quite complete, except for depreciation.

There are some items in the "miscellaneous expenses," as recorded in the census of manufactures data, that should not be treated as an expense for the purposes of estimating GDP. Thus, excess profits tax, royalties, use of patents, etc., and interest paid should not be deducted as expenses. A basis for calculating the interest payments (included in sundry expenses) was obtained from the royal Commission data alluded to above. These items were removed from the miscellaneous expense series used as a cost item in the calculation of GDP.

Basic data on miscellaneous expenses, then, were available by industrial groups for the years 1900 and 1917-23. Estimates for the years 1924-26 were made by interpolation of the ratios of miscellaneous expenses to GVP between 1923 and 1929, the data for the later year being the Royal Commission material. The data for 1900 yielded estimates that appeared to be much too low in comparison both with years 1917-26 in Canada and especially with estimates for the United States for 1889, 1899, 1904, and 1910. A considerable amount of supplementary material along with the material of the census was used to obtain individual industry benchmarks in 1900. Estimates for each year from 1901 to 1916 were made, for each of 17 industry groups, by linear interpolation of the ratio of miscellaneous expenses to GVP between 1900 and 1917. The expense ratios for the years 1870-99 were assumed to be the same as in 1900.

I have some reservations about these estimates of miscellaneous expenses for the earlier years. I believe that the supplementation of the data for 1900 with other information was justified: the figures that were used reflected my best judgement of reality. Yet it remains true that an element of estimation not based on complete information was involved. It is possible also that even if the 1900 figures are reasonably accurate, the ratios might have been somewhat lower in the 1870s and 1880s, but the absence of data precludes taking a different course than that followed.

(The NBER text ends here.)

AN ELABORATION OF THE ESTIMATES FOR MANUFACTURING

The published paper, noted above, contains a table of gross domestic product at factor cost in manufacturing classified into seventeen industrial groups and a total. These measures of gross domestic product in manufacturing were obtained by subtracting (i) cost of materials, (ii) cost of fuel and electricity and (iii) miscellaneous expenses, which include all other non-factor costs, from gross value of product within each category. We have separate estimates of wage and salary costs, by category, and by subtracting wages and salaries from gross domestic product at factor cost, we get what we call "gross property income" — this latter is a residual. It is useful at this point, to provide a setting for our further description of what was done, to present the following tables, which give data for each industrial category for each year for the above classes of manufacturing data.

4.1   Gross Value of Product (GVP)
4.2   Cost of Materials Used
4.3   Cost of Fuel and Electricity
4.4   Miscellaneous Expenses
4.5   Gross Domestic Product at Factor Cost
4.6   Cost of Wages and Salaries
4.7   Gross Property Income
4.8   Grand Summary

Table 4.1. Manufacturing: Annual Series of Gross Value of Product, by Industry, 1870-1926
(thousands of current dollars)

	1870	1871	1872	1873	1874	1875	1876	1877	1878	1879	1880	1881
Food and beverage	60847	68015	74806	81246	72818	67563	67162	83051	67649	72065	82409	91110
Tobacco and products	2435	2601	2793	3425	4155	4192	4132	3429	2560	2477	3060	3532
Rubber products	503	602	690	793	852	542	441	594	475	501	771	1262
Leather products	27911	33443	31098	26843	28367	22844	19300	24461	23068	26268	36456	40286
Textiles (ex. clothing)	9666	13214	12257	9196	9198	9971	9644	10265	10032	13181	15376	17846
Clothing	15019	20206	21461	19724	19833	18903	17707	19601	20196	24216	26698	29874
Wood products	40862	42206	42617	63986	60216	49819	39398	47165	38721	41546	54922	70218
Paper products	1725	2057	2046	2457	2647	2836	2767	2756	2771	2708	2976	3317
Printing and publishing	4128	4999	5372	6489	7171	7426	7112	7234	7342	7064	6785	9039
Iron and steel products	24675	32841	46797	69158	43799	43850	27965	30702	25197	23648	33937	39404
Transportation equipment	10128	10315	12519	23554	23512	17926	18880	18107	19339	15903	14513	19606
Non-ferrous metal products	1594	1835	2075	2316	2556	2797	3038	3278	3519	3759	4000	4017
Electrical apparatus and supplies												
Non-metallic minerals	3874	4105	4335	4566	4796	5027	5257	5488	5718	5949	6179	5861
Petroleum and coal	3095	3779	4642	5208	1738	3141	5388	3459	3192	4784	4050	4249
Chemical products	5022	5627	6068	6302	6685	6162	6277	6886	6638	6773	7058	7538
Miscellaneous industries	2408	2859	3203	3950	3581	3342	3050	3551	3229	3514	4301	5006
Total GVP	213892	248704	272779	329213	291924	266341	237518	270027	239646	254356	303491	352165

Table 4.1. (continued)

	1882	1883	1884	1885	1886	1887	1888	1889	1890	1891	1892	1893
Food and beverage	96406	93753	93566	84900	84174	90643	107648	112068	118911	126697	119992	109246
Tobacco and products	3796	4159	4975	4472	3596	4200	4601	4856	5743	6174	6109	6174
Rubber products	1306	1115	1225	1219	1267	1631	2101	2012	2060	2199	2226	2370
Leather products	39267	35840	35258	40141	41939	36169	31292	29254	35209	36284	35358	33038
Textiles (ex. clothing)	22906	20705	17902	18731	19812	20401	22032	24654	24705	25025	25793	23890
Clothing	3675	33681	30577	32229	35164	34943	36737	43699	45189	43937	44562	41664
Wood products	86320	95758	82888	73422	75334	76399	78197	79050	84544	85679	72079	73086
Paper products	3846	4525	4733	4821	4757	5174	5519	5856	6206	6641	7132	7644
Printing and publishing	10522	9786	8238	8303	8070	9705	12004	11562	10456	11010	13956	14226
Iron and steel products	48156	60752	45221	39554	40656	49778	49177	50870	55492	50832	49560	44401
Transportation equipment	22370	20686	18335	16664	17841	19711	20247	20518	23445	24550	25420	24690
Non-ferrous metal products	4221	3531	2542	2931	4265	4397	5422	6693	7400	9971	7582	7920
Electrical apparatus and supplies									866	903	954	1072
Non-metallic minerals	5544	5226	4908	4591	4273	4922	5159	6038	8199	6590	6327	8189
Petroleum and coal	3486	3739	3603	4086	4177	4470	3892	4063	4347	4296	4608	4733
Chemical products	8654	9355	9234	9274	9631	9834	9619	9743	10136	10067	9926	9317
Miscellaneous industries	5693	5842	5287	5042	5199	5471	5802	6076	6570	6653	6336	6012
Total GVP	399249	408453	368492	350380	360155	377848	399449	417012	449478	457508	437920	417672

Table 4.1. (continued)

	1894	1895	1896	1897	1898	1899	1900	1901	1902	1903	1904
Food and beverage	106169	112226	113856	142605	147160	140120	159402	165483	179130	192881	202974
Tobacco and products	6129	6077	6782	8674	8398	7549	8574	8668	9289	10495	11411
Rubber products	2136	2347	2818	3475	4153	4695	4728	4027	3869	4867	5923
Leather products	24666	30729	29185	44894	49417	45973	43059	46647	56454	56205	47186
Textiles (ex. clothing)	20914	20019	19116	23755	28537	31697	33010	34673	37536	38088	37055
Clothing	38438	38286	36858	39566	43597	48211	50264	53553	60745	65129	67154
Wood products	69393	59453	65750	68758	66751	77089	88238	84752	97078	107116	102668
Paper products	8260	8088	8054	8719	9340	10173	11413	11082	13243	14316	15366
Printing and publishing	11203	11087	11782	12006	12203	12899	14200	14244	14378	15224	16846
Iron and steel products	39043	30273	36643	30693	38507	41404	60014	48698	81317	80516	64532
Transportation equipment	24821	19027	14700	17177	20824	25404	25199	27622	35076	40184	37838
Non-ferrous metal products	7061	7144	7040	9364	11809	13033	14408	19365	20024	22625	26698
Electrical apparatus and supplies	1206	1297	1459	1611	2178	2562	3275	4421	4942	5303	6187
Non-metallic minerals	8197	10018	6795	6993	7960	8985	9460	10880	12207	12710	12618
Petroleum and coal	4902	4467	4098	3966	3990	3912	4417	4234	4426	5406	6653
Chemical products	8491	8656	8793	9323	10586	11487	12591	14275	15685	16230	17166
Miscellaneous industries	5536	5336	5374	6173	6624	6872	7642	7765	9043	9600	9446
Total GVP	386565	374530	379103	437752	472034	492065	549894	560389	654442	696895	687721

Table 4.1. (continued)

	1905	1906	1907	1908	1909	1910	1911	1912	1913	1914	1915
Food and beverage	225359	214510	230692	253963	274695	288881	295748	327937	327165	359869	434565
Tobacco and products	12212	11850	12665	16545	18082	18418	20598	21728	22064	23704	24328
Rubber products	6264	6924	7647	6282	9401	11063	13155	16474	14227	14448	20167
Leather products	57486	73795	54000	38980	71338	74543	84396	110132	77254	89543	76594
Textiles (ex. clothing)	40305	43708	40719	36061	42998	51673	43680	44901	47558	42622	56157
Clothing	75272	86353	90557	79478	102779	121123	109988	119815	125022	106402	118175
Wood products	114612	144148	162214	146438	166794	185093	197837	167430	152417	134733	133140
Paper products	17580	20862	24371	25075	28834	31644	29422	29861	34441	45183	52950
Printing and publishing	17826	19370	20066	23035	26092	26486	29030	31573	34535	35266	35274
Iron and steel products	103316	141985	181014	120381	144681	163027	170271	211251	232290	136574	166226
Transportation equipment	42894	54569	74586	62417	67266	71417	91082	107742	131504	109764	86783
Non-ferrous metal products	42503	51325	54933	45223	50112	60049	57244	72051	67806	52539	75117
Electrical apparatus and supplies	7760	10193	11973	13257	14130	15235	18443	17707	18075	18907	18637
Non-metallic minerals	14979	18289	20092	17973	17986	28154	32487	38646	41475	34126	26470
Petroleum and coal	7425	6774	8936	9213	8545	9553	11237	18129	22671	22160	16329
Chemical products	19380	21890	25239	24217	25605	30987	35921	44727	44879	41965	50122
Miscellaneous industries	11181	12828	14075	12640	14671	16242	16269	17382	16880	14791	15653
Total GVP	816354	939373	1033779	931178	1084009	1203588	1256808	1397496	1410263	1282596	1406687

Table 4.1. (continued)

	1916	1917	1918	1919	1920	1921	1922	1923	1924	1925	1926
Food and beverage	554180	790017	875389	991008	1036e3	755423	709069	717389	753262	829312	846885
Tobacco and products	26456	33759	35931	37413	44917	37608	36196	34346	34355	32547	35029
Rubber products	30889	43639	46280	56004	80717	39989	46487	56513	57412	78230	86508
Leather products	122204	115729	105787	142367	144931	96130	98283	98611	94462	93198	102574
Textiles (ex. clothing)	69428	106135	155195	173345	197191	131018	135016	151322	140948	147494	157126
Clothing	172358	201125	239866	285576	315656	237613	226644	233762	222234	234109	257905
Wood products	132979	202138	224335	262439	335592	208093	207894	244258	239341	233502	242425
Paper products	83907	120370	143880	169840	278728	179167	188074	216176	207790	222615	248831
Printing and publishing	45022	57513	60258	75633	104521	97393	93780	96355	98483	100428	105756
Iron and steel products	301826	474512	522776	380135	479408	293673	229463	306011	250732	264555	319065
Transportation equipment	95118	205896	251894	265370	301823	176556	165158	230638	196026	226188	278750
Non-ferrous metal products	114951	125702	114924	93503	97548	49371	53285	72093	78888	99611	113734
Electrical apparatus and supplies	26370	41165	31416	35552	55966	45093	41208	51360	56490	60159	69767
Non-metallic minerals	27823	33593	36417	38782	57430	47852	51230	57781	55269	57715	62028
Petroleum and coal	31765	48365	59070	66170	78913	68537	65166	63348	62487	64405	86458
Chemical products	110050	227512	334952	94095	130425	89755	96567	113840	111491	116290	129076
Miscellaneous industries	21452	30522	38296	44387	54788	41542	39590	41913	35608	38164	42661
Total GVP	1966778	2857692	3276666	3211619	3794431	2594813	2483110	2785716	2695278	2898522	3184578

248

Table 4.2. Manufacturing: Summary of the Cost of Materials Used, by Industry, 1870-1926
(thousands of current dollars)

	1870	1871	1872	1873	1874	1875	1876	1877	1878	1879	1880	1881
Food and beverage	46274	51793	57040	62039	55677	51726	51486	63750	52002	55468	63513	69799
Tobacco and products	1198	1285	1386	1707	2080	2108	2087	1739	1304	1267	1572	1787
Rubber products	358	423	478	543	575	361	290	385	303	315	478	791
Leather products	14846	18016	16964	14825	15860	12927	11053	14175	13525	15580	21870	23890
Textiles (ex. clothing)	6231	8446	7767	5778	5729	6157	5902	6227	6031	7852	9076	10451
Clothing	8619	11612	12349	11365	11442	10920	10242	11353	11712	14062	15522	17145
Wood products	21947	22631	22813	34194	32125	26539	20952	25040	20522	21982	29010	37019
Paper products	874	1050	1053	1274	1384	1494	1469	1474	1493	1470	1628	1802
Printing and publishing	1492	1818	1966	2389	2656	2768	2666	2729	2786	2696	2605	3445
Iron and steel products	9626	13018	18840	28279	18181	18478	11961	13322	11092	10556	15363	17716
Transportation equipment	3564	3730	4648	8976	9188	7179	7745	7603	8310	6988	6518	8778
Non-ferrous metal products	673	778	885	992	1100	1209	1320	1431	1543	1656	1770	1782
Electrical apparatus and supplies												
Non-metallic minerals	809	876	946	1019	1093	1170	1249	1330	1413	1499	1587	1468
Petroleum and coal	1739	2138	2644	2986	1003	1826	3152	2037	1892	2854	2432	2589
Chemical products	3049	3405	3660	3789	4006	3680	3736	4085	3925	3991	4145	4408
Miscellaneous industries	1088	1289	1442	1775	1606	1496	1363	1583	1437	1561	1907	2214
Total	122387	142308	154881	181930	163705	150038	136673	158263	139290	149797	178996	205084

Table 4.2. (continued)

	1882	1883	1884	1885	1886	1887	1888	1889	1890	1891	1892	1893
Food and beverage	73423	70971	70399	63497	62567	66958	79024	81765	86210	92020	87294	79618
Tobacco and products	1891	2039	2400	2123	1679	1928	2076	2154	2502	2693	2667	2699
Rubber products	828	715	794	799	839	1091	1421	1375	1422	1501	1503	1582
Leather products	23014	20762	20182	22700	23427	19954	17051	15739	18699	19459	19146	18065
Textiles (ex. clothing)	13306	11930	10231	10617	11136	11372	12177	13510	13422	13574	13967	12917
Clothing	20819	18824	16860	17533	18865	18485	19158	22461	22888	22232	22526	21040
Wood products	45430	50302	43458	38429	39354	39834	40694	41066	43836	44673	37791	38524
Paper products	2075	2424	2517	2546	2494	2693	2852	3004	3160	3361	3588	3822
Printing and publishing	3980	3675	3070	3071	2962	3536	4339	4147	3721	3836	4758	4743
Iron and steel products	21497	26931	19902	17285	17637	21439	21023	21589	23373	21426	20909	18746
Transportation equipment	9984	9203	8132	7367	7863	8659	8866	8956	10201	10868	11449	11308
Non-ferrous metal products	1877	1574	1136	1313	1916	1980	2447	3029	3357	4540	3465	3632
Electrical apparatus and supplies									338	351	369	413
Non-metallic minerals	1352	1241	1134	1031	932	1042	1059	1200	1577	1246	1175	1493
Petroleum and coal	2155	2344	2291	2634	2729	2960	2612	2762	2994	2955	3165	3247
Chemical products	5039	5425	5333	5333	5514	5606	5460	5507	5704	5661	5576	5231
Miscellaneous industries	2512	2572	2322	2209	2272	2385	2523	2636	2843	2871	2726	2580
Total	229182	230932	210161	198487	202186	209922	222782	230900	246247	253267	242074	229660

Table 4.2. (continued)

	1894	1895	1896	1897	1898	1899	1900	1901	1902	1903	1904
Food and beverage	77503	82071	83400	104644	108163	103170	117559	121762	131499	141247	148293
Tobacco and products	2681	2662	2973	3807	3689	3320	3774	3804	4066	4580	4966
Rubber products	1410	1532	1818	2215	2616	2922	2907	2376	2186	2629	3052
Leather products	13616	17122	16414	25482	28311	26577	25116	27139	32760	32531	27240
Textiles (ex. clothing)	11289	10788	10284	12759	15304	16971	17644	18963	20994	21779	21648
Clothing	19392	19296	18554	19898	21903	24197	25202	26803	30348	32480	33429
Wood products	36778	31683	35229	37040	36146	41967	48293	45385	50840	54822	51334
Paper products	4104	3995	3953	4252	4526	4899	5461	5305	6342	6857	7363
Printing and publishing	3651	3531	3664	3644	3612	3721	3990	3997	4027	4258	4703
Iron and steel products	16496	12802	15507	12998	16319	17564	25476	20565	34161	33640	26819
Transportation equipment	11559	9005	7069	8393	10333	12801	12889	14038	17713	20160	18862
Non-ferrous metal products	3250	3301	3264	4358	5515	6109	6778	9202	9612	10966	13069
Electrical apparatus and supplies	463	495	555	610	820	960	1222	1670	1889	2051	2422
Non-metallic minerals	1466	1759	1170	1180	1317	1456	1501	1733	1953	2041	2035
Petroleum and coal	3358	3057	2801	2707	2720	2663	3003	2849	2949	3565	4342
Chemical products	4763	4852	4925	5217	5920	6418	7030	7659	8073	8000	8087
Miscellaneous industries	2369	2277	2287	2620	2803	2900	3216	3250	3766	3977	3893
Total	214148	210228	213867	251824	270017	278615	311061	316500	363178	385583	381557

Table 4.2. (continued)

	1905	1906	1907	1908	1909	1910	1911	1912	1913	1914	1915
Food and beverage	164264	155884	167136	183463	197835	207417	214269	239755	241317	267815	326228
Tobacco and products	5299	5126	5464	7116	7755	7875	8940	9569	9858	10743	11182
Rubber products	3072	3425	3817	3162	4774	5665	6684	8305	7116	7169	9926
Leather products	33100	42639	31309	22682	41654	43675	49549	64791	45549	52902	45344
Textiles (ex. clothing)	24046	25845	23861	20937	24737	29454	25138	26087	27898	25236	33559
Clothing	37403	43107	45414	40041	52016	61579	56160	61441	64374	55020	61368
Wood products	55954	71267	81204	74215	85565	96100	100699	83514	74486	64470	62349
Paper products	8428	10041	11779	12166	14048	15477	14473	14769	17131	22596	26629
Printing and publishing	4970	5462	5725	6646	7614	7813	8488	9150	9915	10033	9944
Iron and steel products	42711	59435	76714	51655	62835	71650	75294	93986	103996	61513	75517
Transportation equipment	21241	26848	36450	30303	32436	34209	44539	53752	66922	56946	45891
Non-ferrous metal products	21009	25426	27280	22507	25001	30025	28685	36184	34134	26506	37979
Electrical apparatus and supplies	3073	4083	4851	5433	5855	6383	8052	8043	8528	9253	9449
Non-metallic minerals	2425	3047	3444	3165	3254	5225	6397	8050	9108	7883	6414
Petroleum and coal	4795	4412	5869	6101	5705	6431	7477	11922	14729	14225	10354
Chemical products	8707	9951	11610	11268	12052	14750	17246	21661	21919	20672	24896
Miscellaneous industries	4583	5230	5707	5099	5886	6481	6586	7139	7031	6248	6703
Total	445080	501228	547634	505959	589022	650209	678676	758118	764011	719230	803532

Table 4.2. (continued)

	1916	1917	1918	1919	1920	1921	1922	1923	1924	1925	1926
Food and beverage	417907	598517	665033	757377	775911	539327	503610	510393	536995	600908	603931
Tobacco and products	11455	13721	12000	18134	19413	15262	13253	11649	11779	17303	16286
Rubber products	15185	21418	22474	27535	41838	17104	19295	26336	24468	38389	49902
Leather products	72919	69599	62664	89623	89642	50460	49182	52170	49704	50221	55809
Textiles (ex. clothing)	40345	59913	93798	104187	120264	71272	69231	85525	88593	94668	94888
Clothing	89523	104484	128328	153365	176810	128743	114962	120658	116726	126025	139009
Wood products	62154	94277	104406	121876	167300	98910	104804	124369	131415	126920	128953
Paper products	39957	54094	59336	68412	106074	75382	78055	86795	86861	91815	102066
Printing and publishing	12908	16765	19454	22813	33415	29194	24560	26471	27868	28428	29302
Iron and steel products	142643	233518	254032	167505	212981	127975	98367	138390	105356	109421	135366
Transportation equipment	49128	103794	124118	134375	158812	97118	90332	141321	117376	125802	158082
Non-ferrous metal products	59683	66962	64084	47628	43766	20058	20487	31362	38279	48633	60417
Electrical apparatus and supplies	13330	20752	14686	16067	27221	19439	17547	26257	24371	25435	30196
Non-metallic minerals	6733	8116	9857	9210	8956	7086	7548	9353	9013	10650	12098
Petroleum and coal	20247	30987	39375	43449	50936	49348	44812	49636	45110	46792	60917
Chemical products	53880	109775	177760	44167	66618	44953	49388	57953	58025	59757	65488
Miscellaneous industries	9297	13384	15230	18539	23124	16411	14736	16205	14846	15776	17508
Total	1117294	1620076	1866635	1844262	2123081	1408042	1320169	1514843	1486785	1616943	1760218

Table 4.3. Manufacturing: Summary of the Cost of Fuel and Electricity, by Industry, 1870-1926 (thousands of current dollars)

	1870	1871	1872	1873	1874	1875	1876	1877	1878	1879	1880	1881
Food and beverage	773	864	950	1032	925	858	853	1055	859	915	1047	1157
Tobacco and products	15	16	18	22	26	26	26	22	16	16	19	22
Rubber products	10	11	13	15	16	10	8	11	9	10	15	24
Leather products	215	258	239	207	218	176	149	188	178	202	281	310
Textiles (ex. clothing)	229	313	290	218	218	236	229	243	238	312	364	423
Clothing	125	168	178	164	165	157	147	163	168	201	222	248
Wood products	278	287	290	435	409	339	268	321	263	283	373	477
Paper products	66	79	79	94	102	109	106	106	106	104	114	127
Printing and publishing	74	89	96	116	128	133	127	129	131	126	121	162
Iron and steel products	743	989	1409	2082	1318	1320	842	924	758	712	1022	1186
Transportation equipment	181	185	224	422	421	321	338	324	346	285	260	351
Non-ferrous metal products	71	82	93	104	115	125	136	147	158	168	179	180
Electrical apparatus and supplies												
Non-metallic minerals	528	560	591	622	654	685	717	748	779	811	842	799
Petroleum and coal	104	127	156	176	59	106	182	117	108	161	136	143
Chemical products	98	110	119	124	131	121	123	135	130	133	138	148
Miscellaneous industries	23	27	31	38	34	32	29	34	31	34	41	48
Total	3533	4165	4776	5871	4939	4754	4280	4667	4278	4473	5174	5805

Table 4.3. (continued)

	1882	1883	1884	1885	1886	1887	1888	1889	1890	1891	1892	1893
Food and beverage	1224	1191	1188	1078	1069	1151	1367	1423	1510	1609	1524	1387
Tobacco and products	24	26	31	28	23	26	29	31	36	39	38	39
Rubber products	25	21	23	23	24	31	40	38	39	42	42	45
Leather products	302	276	271	309	323	279	241	225	271	279	272	254
Textiles (ex. clothing)	543	491	424	444	470	484	522	584	586	593	611	566
Clothing	305	280	254	268	292	290	305	363	375	365	370	346
Wood products	587	651	564	499	512	520	532	538	575	583	490	497
Paper products	148	174	182	185	183	199	212	225	238	255	274	294
Printing and publishing	188	175	147	149	144	174	215	207	187	197	250	255
Iron and steel products	1449	1829	1361	1191	1224	1498	1480	1531	1670	1530	1492	1336
Transportation equipment	400	370	328	298	319	353	362	367	420	439	455	442
Non-ferrous metal products	189	158	114	131	191	197	243	300	332	447	340	355
Electrical apparatus and supplies									39	41	43	48
Non-metallic minerals	756	712	669	626	582	671	703	823	1118	898	862	1116
Petroleum and coal	117	126	121	138	141	151	131	137	146	145	155	160
Chemical products	170	183	181	182	189	193	189	191	199	197	195	183
Miscellaneous industries	55	56	51	48	50	53	56	58	63	64	61	58
Total	6482	6719	5909	5597	5736	6270	6627	7041	7804	7723	7474	7381

Table 4.3. (continued)

	1894	1895	1896	1897	1898	1899	1900	1901	1902	1903	1904
Food and beverage	1348	1425	1446	1811	1869	1780	2024	2085	2239	2392	2497
Tobacco and products	39	38	43	55	53	48	54	52	53	58	59
Rubber products	41	45	54	66	79	89	90	75	70	87	102
Leather products	190	237	225	346	381	354	332	364	440	444	373
Textiles (ex. clothing)	496	474	453	563	676	751	782	804	856	849	808
Clothing	319	318	306	328	362	400	417	423	456	469	457
Wood products	472	404	447	466	454	524	600	585	680	750	729
Paper products	317	311	309	335	359	391	438	432	523	574	625
Printing and publishing	201	198	211	215	218	231	254	246	242	247	263
Iron and steel products	1175	911	1103	924	1159	1246	1806	1476	2488	2480	2007
Transportation equipment	444	341	263	307	373	455	451	514	677	804	783
Non-ferrous metal products	316	320	315	420	529	584	645	840	843	923	1055
Electrical apparatus and supplies	54	58	66	73	98	116	148	183	188	182	191
Non-metallic minerals	1117	1365	926	953	1085	1225	1289	1479	1652	1715	1695
Petroleum and coal	165	151	138	134	134	132	149	138	139	165	196
Chemical products	166	170	172	183	207	225	247	281	312	323	345
Miscellaneous industries	53	51	52	59	64	66	73	76	89	94	92
Total	6913	6817	6529	7238	8100	8617	9799	10053	11947	12556	12277

Table 4.3. (continued)

	1905	1906	1907	1908	1909	1910	1911	1912	1913	1914	1915
Food and beverage	2727	2574	2745	2997	3214	3351	3401	3706	3632	3923	4693
Tobacco and products	61	56	56	68	71	66	78	87	93	104	114
Rubber products	106	114	122	99	143	164	197	252	222	230	327
Leather products	454	590	432	316	578	611	700	914	641	743	643
Textiles (ex. clothing)	863	913	831	718	838	982	817	822	856	754	977
Clothing	482	518	507	413	504	545	517	587	638	553	638
Wood products	825	1052	1200	1084	1251	1407	1563	1356	1280	1159	1185
Paper products	726	872	1033	1078	1254	1396	1415	1553	1929	2711	3389
Printing and publishing	271	283	281	309	337	326	354	382	418	420	416
Iron and steel products	3223	4473	5738	3840	4644	5282	5994	8049	9501	5968	7730
Transportation equipment	922	1206	1701	1473	1628	1785	2241	2607	3130	2558	1987
Non-ferrous metal products	1619	1889	1945	1547	1644	1892	1935	2601	2604	2112	3238
Electrical apparatus and supplies	212	242	242	220	184	143	173	165	168	176	173
Non-metallic minerals	2006	2440	2670	2380	2372	3699	4214	4943	5234	4249	3251
Petroleum and coal	211	185	235	232	207	220	321	622	905	1008	834
Chemical products	391	444	515	496	530	645	783	1029	1082	1062	1318
Miscellaneous industries	110	124	137	121	142	156	164	186	189	175	193
Total	15209	17975	20390	17391	19541	22670	24867	29861	32522	27905	31106

Table 4.3. (continued)

	1916	1917	1918	1919	1920	1921	1922	1923	1924	1925	1926
Food and beverage	5874	8254	10196	10174	13445	10972	10922	10983	11134	11882	12058
Tobacco and products	130	172	170	221	181	187	177	168	155	153	163
Rubber products	507	729	994	836	1379	1081	1112	1147	1083	1068	1198
Leather products	1027	972	1072	1038	1265	1203	1189	1174	1209	1065	1214
Textiles (ex. clothing)	1180	1772	2496	2588	3384	3313	3016	2876	2688	3144	3031
Clothing	965	1167	1775	1641	2051	1752	1830	1673	1554	1625	1718
Wood products	1210	1905	1980	2181	2666	2184	2192	2192	2303	2391	2339
Paper products	5697	8652	12386	12376	16814	15364	16173	18654	17776	18176	20792
Printing and publishing	527	662	804	792	1042	970	1024	1104	1166	1023	1095
Iron and steel products	14910	24770	37043	25936	19215	10747	9165	10254	11206	9857	10301
Transportation equipment	2140	4550	3343	3302	6505	4590	4528	6058	4883	6136	6968
Non-ferrous metal products	5219	6003	8727	5342	8696	4386	2472	6139	5686	6745	6830
Electrical apparatus and supplies	243	379	667	569	997	877	871	865	884	954	1065
Non-metallic minerals	3367	4006	4569	4606	8898	8394	7787	8575	8000	8077	8978
Petroleum and coal	1804	3016	3567	3266	5371	4557	4715	4459	4714	4670	4213
Chemical products	3026	6504	9149	3724	5064	3439	3349	3477	3384	3256	3811
Miscellaneous industries	277	409	435	365	833	672	690	629	586	594	614
Total	48103	73922	99373	78957	97806	74688	71212	80427	78411	80816	86388

Table 4.4. Manufacturing: Summary of Miscellaneous Expenses, by Industry, 1870-1926 (thousands of current dollars)

	1870	1871	1872	1873	1874	1875	1876	1877	1878	1879	1880	1881
Food and beverage	2537	2836	3119	3388	3037	2817	2801	3463	2821	3005	3436	3799
Tobacco and products	208	223	239	293	356	359	354	294	219	212	262	302
Rubber products	23	27	31	36	39	25	20	27	22	23	35	57
Leather products	1133	1358	1263	1090	1152	927	784	993	937	1066	1480	1636
Textiles (ex. clothing)	515	704	653	490	490	531	514	547	535	703	820	951
Clothing	889	1196	1270	1168	1174	1119	1048	1160	1196	1434	1581	1769
Wood products	2464	2545	2570	3858	3631	3004	2376	2844	2335	2505	3312	4234
Paper products	115	137	137	164	177	189	185	184	185	181	199	222
Printing and publishing	292	353	380	459	507	525	503	511	519	499	480	639
Iron and steel products	1503	2000	2850	4212	2667	2670	1703	1870	1534	1440	2067	2400
Transportation equipment	440	448	543	1022	1020	778	819	786	839	690	630	851
Non-ferrous metal products	80	93	105	117	129	141	153	166	178	190	202	203
Electrical apparatus and supplies												
Non-metallic minerals	139	148	156	164	173	181	189	198	206	214	222	211
Petroleum and coal	133	162	200	224	75	135	232	149	137	206	174	183
Chemical products	315	353	381	396	420	387	394	432	417	425	443	473
Miscellaneous industries	203	242	271	334	303	282	258	300	273	297	363	423
Total	10989	12825	14168	17415	15350	14070	12333	13924	12353	13090	15706	18353

Table 4.4. (continued)

	1882	1883	1884	1885	1886	1887	1888	1889	1890	1891	1892	1893
Food and beverage	4020	3910	3902	3540	3510	3780	4489	4673	4959	5283	5004	4556
Tobacco and products	325	356	426	383	308	360	394	416	492	528	523	528
Rubber products	59	51	56	55	58	74	95	91	94	100	101	108
Leather products	1594	1455	1431	1630	1703	1468	1270	1188	1429	1473	1436	1341
Textiles (ex. clothing)	1221	1104	954	998	1056	1087	1174	1314	1317	1334	1375	1273
Clothing	2176	1994	1810	1908	2082	2069	2175	2587	2675	2601	2638	2467
Wood products	5205	5774	4998	4427	4543	4607	4715	4767	5098	5166	4346	4407
Paper products	257	302	316	322	318	346	369	391	415	444	476	511
Printing and publishing	744	692	582	587	571	686	849	817	739	778	987	1006
Iron and steel products	2933	3700	2754	2409	2476	3031	2995	3098	3379	3096	3018	2704
Transportation equipment	971	898	796	723	774	855	879	890	1018	1065	1103	1072
Non-ferrous metal products	213	178	128	148	215	222	274	338	374	504	383	400
Electrical apparatus and supplies									73	76	81	91
Non-metallic minerals	200	188	177	165	154	177	186	217	295	237	228	295
Petroleum and coal	150	161	155	176	180	192	167	175	187	185	198	204
Chemical products	543	587	580	582	605	618	604	612	637	632	623	585
Miscellaneous industries	481	494	447	426	439	462	490	513	555	562	535	508
Total	21092	21844	19512	18479	18992	20034	21125	22087	23736	24064	23055	22056

Table 4.4. (continued)

	1894	1895	1896	1897	1898	1899	1900	1901	1902	1903	1904
Food and beverage	4427	4680	4748	5947	6137	5843	6647	6983	7631	8313	8829
Tobacco and products	525	520	581	742	719	646	734	757	827	952	1054
Rubber products	97	107	128	158	189	213	215	191	192	252	319
Leather products	1001	1248	1185	1823	2006	1867	1748	1927	2365	2394	2038
Textiles (ex. clothing)	1115	1067	1019	1266	1521	1689	1759	1886	2087	2160	2145
Clothing	2276	2267	2182	2342	2581	2854	2976	3224	3718	4051	4244
Wood products	4184	3585	3965	4146	4025	4648	5321	5305	6300	7198	7135
Paper products	552	540	538	582	624	680	762	749	907	992	1079
Printing and publishing	792	784	833	849	863	912	1004	1046	1094	1198	1371
Iron and steel products	2378	1844	2232	1869	2345	2522	3655	2975	4985	4960	3988
Transportation equipment	1077	826	638	745	904	1103	1094	1237	1624	1917	1858
Non-ferrous metal products	357	361	356	473	596	658	728	1007	1073	1247	1514
Electrical apparatus and supplies	102	110	124	136	184	217	277	378	427	463	546
Non-metallic minerals	295	361	245	252	287	323	341	435	538	611	659
Petroleum and coal	211	192	176	171	172	168	190	188	203	256	324
Chemical products	533	544	552	585	665	721	791	931	1062	1138	1246
Miscellaneous industries	468	451	454	522	560	581	646	676	809	883	893
Total	20390	19487	19956	22608	24378	25645	28888	29895	35842	38985	39242

Table 4.4. (continued)

	1905	1906	1907	1908	1909	1910	1911	1912	1913	1914	1915
Food and beverage	9916	9524	10358	11505	12581	13346	13811	15446	15573	17274	21076
Tobacco and products	1149	1135	1235	1641	1826	1892	2150	2305	2378	2596	2705
Rubber products	351	402	461	392	606	737	905	1168	1039	1085	1559
Leather products	2524	3284	2441	1785	3317	3511	4034	5330	3793	4450	3860
Textiles (ex. clothing)	2378	2627	2496	2250	2735	3343	2879	3008	3239	2954	3953
Clothing	4840	5639	6004	5349	7020	8394	7732	8543	9052	7810	8792
Wood products	8229	10681	12393	11525	13510	15418	16935	14717	13748	12463	12622
Paper products	1248	1500	1772	1846	2145	2383	2239	2299	2680	3556	4210
Printing and publishing	1499	1681	1794	2122	2474	2582	2906	3246	3643	3816	3908
Iron and steel products	6406	8831	11313	7548	9100	10287	10795	13436	14820	8741	10688
Transportation equipment	2166	2838	3983	3420	3787	4121	5383	6529	8153	6959	5624
Non-ferrous metal products	2474	3069	3367	2845	3227	3963	3864	4979	4787	3793	5536
Electrical apparatus and supplies	693	919	1091	1220	1313	1429	1747	1693	1746	1843	1834
Non-metallic minerals	842	1103	1292	1229	1302	2154	2615	3269	3675	3163	2560
Petroleum and coal	372	350	474	501	478	547	660	1091	1397	1396	1052
Chemical products	1454	1694	2017	1993	2171	2702	3222	4119	4241	4071	4982
Miscellaneous industries	1085	1276	1436	1321	1570	1778	1822	1990	1975	1768	1910
Total	47626	56553	63927	58492	69162	78587	83699	93168	95939	87738	96871

Table 4.4. (continued)

	1916	1917	1918	1919	1920	1921	1922	1923	1924	1925	1926
Food and beverage	27099	39027	43244	53614	59459	52653	53535	52298	54913	60457	61738
Tobacco and products	2987	3869	3701	5101	5766	5513	4408	5569	5542	5312	5662
Rubber products	2453	3557	3147	4704	6942	3707	3844	4600	4673	6368	7042
Leather products	6232	5978	5359	7769	8562	7751	7094	6606	6321	6212	6756
Textiles (ex. clothing)	4971	7716	11283	12429	14671	9708	8628	8822	8217	8599	9160
Clothing	12996	15366	18630	22766	27302	23869	21874	21801	20590	21649	23742
Wood products	12912	20093	24901	30994	28156	19811	16819	16304	17400	16976	17624
Paper products	6746	9774	11467	14810	21462	17218	15780	17834	17143	18366	20529
Printing and publishing	5110	6683	7496	9923	15741	15067	15961	15773	16122	16440	17312
Iron and steel products	19468	30701	33567	27818	39681	29499	23185	24512	20137	21184	25417
Transportation equipment	6306	20886	17453	16893	24972	13416	12255	14336	12576	14475	17709
Non-ferrous metal products	8656	7416	6447	7181	8116	7332	9122	7808	8543	10788	12317
Electrical apparatus and supplies	2619	4125	3955	4209	5535	4636	4187	4494	4943	5264	6105
Non-metallic minerals	2805	3521	4199	5302	6082	6891	7039	10793	10324	10781	11587
Petroleum and coal	2093	3831	2959	4725	5398	3690	4086	4542	4409	4618	6199
Chemical products	11203	17404	23246	11771	19055	13302	14126	14469	14171	14780	16518
Miscellaneous industries	2671	3875	5578	6143	5575	5043	4475	5061	4281	4596	5152
Total	137327	203622	226632	246152	302475	239106	226418	235622	230305	246865	270569

Table 4.5. Manufacturing: Summary of Gross Domestic Product, by Industry, 1870-1926 (thousands of current dollars)

	1870	1871	1872	1873	1874	1875	1876	1877	1878	1879	1880	1881
Food and beverage	11263	12522	13697	14787	13179	12162	12022	14783	11967	12677	14413	16355
Tobacco and products	1014	1077	1150	1403	1693	1699	1665	1374	1021	982	1207	1421
Rubber products	112	141	168	199	222	146	123	171	141	153	243	390
Leather products	11717	13811	12632	10721	11137	8814	7314	9105	8428	9420	12825	14450
Textiles (ex. clothing)	2691	3751	3547	2710	2761	3047	2999	3248	3228	4314	5116	6021
Clothing	5386	7230	7664	7027	7052	6707	6270	6925	7120	8519	9373	10712
Wood products	16173	16743	16944	25499	24051	19937	15802	18960	15601	16776	22227	28488
Paper products	670	791	777	925	984	1044	1007	992	987	953	1035	1166
Printing and publishing	2270	2739	2930	3525	3880	4000	3816	3865	3906	3743	3579	4793
Iron and steel products	12803	16834	23698	34585	21633	21382	13459	14586	11813	10940	15485	18102
Transportation equipment	5943	5952	7104	13134	12883	9648	9978	9394	9844	7940	7105	9626
Non-ferrous metal products	770	882	992	1103	1212	1322	1429	1534	1640	1745	1849	1852
Electrical apparatus and supplies												
Non-metallic minerals	2398	2521	2642	2761	2876	2991	3102	3212	3320	3425	3528	3383
Petroleum and coal	1119	1352	1642	1822	601	1074	1822	1156	1055	1563	1308	1334
Chemical products	1560	1759	1908	1993	2128	1974	2024	2234	2166	2224	2332	2509
Miscellaneous industries	1094	1301	1459	1803	1638	1532	1400	1634	1488	1622	1990	2321
Total GDP	76983	89406	98954	123997	107930	97479	84232	93173	83725	86996	103615	122923

Table 4.5. (continued)

	1882	1883	1884	1885	1886	1887	1888	1889	1890	1891	1892	1893
Food and beverage	17739	17681	18077	16785	17028	18754	22768	24207	26232	27785	26170	23685
Tobacco and products	1556	1738	2118	1938	1586	1886	2102	2255	2713	2914	2881	2908
Rubber products	394	328	352	342	346	435	545	508	505	556	580	635
Leather products	14357	13347	13374	15502	16486	14468	12730	12102	14810	15073	14504	13378
Textiles (ex. clothing)	7836	7180	6293	6672	7150	7458	8159	9246	9380	9524	9840	9134
Clothing	13456	12583	11653	12520	13925	14099	15099	18288	19251	18739	19028	17811
Wood products	35098	39031	33868	30067	30925	31438	32256	32679	35035	35257	29452	29658
Paper products	1366	1625	1718	1768	1762	1936	2086	2236	2393	2581	2794	3017
Printing and publishing	5610	5244	4439	4496	4393	5309	6601	6391	5809	6199	7961	8222
Iron and steel products	22277	28292	21204	18669	19319	23810	23679	24652	27070	24780	24141	21615
Transportation equipment	11015	10215	9079	8276	8885	9844	10140	10305	11806	12178	12413	11868
Non-ferrous metal products	1942	1621	1164	1339	1943	1998	2458	3026	3337	4480	3394	3533
Electrical apparatus and supplies									416	435	461	520
Non-metallic minerals	3236	3085	2928	2769	2605	3032	3211	3798	5209	4209	4062	5285
Petroleum and coal	1064	1108	1036	1138	1127	1167	982	989	1020	1011	1090	1122
Chemical products	2902	3160	3140	3177	3323	3417	3366	3433	3596	3577	3532	3318
Miscellaneous industries	2645	2720	2467	2359	2438	2571	2733	2869	3109	3156	3014	2866
Total GDP	142493	148958	132910	127817	133241	141622	148915	156984	171691	172454	165317	158575

Table 4.5. (continued)

	1894	1895	1896	1897	1898	1899	1900	1901	1902	1903	1904
Food and beverage	22891	24050	24262	30203	30991	29327	33172	34653	37761	40929	43355
Tobacco and products	2884	2857	3185	4070	3937	3535	4012	4055	4343	4905	5332
Rubber products	588	663	818	1036	1269	1471	1516	1385	1421	1899	2450
Leather products	9859	12122	11361	17243	18719	17175	15863	17217	20889	20836	17535
Textiles (ex. clothing)	8014	7690	7360	9167	11036	12286	12825	13020	13599	13300	12454
Clothing	16451	16405	15816	16998	18751	20760	21669	23103	26223	28129	29024
Wood products	27959	23781	26109	27106	26126	29950	34024	33477	39258	44346	43470
Paper products	3287	3242	3254	3550	3831	4203	4752	4596	5471	5893	6299
Printing and publishing	6559	6574	7074	7298	7510	8035	8952	8955	9015	9521	10509
Iron and steel products	18994	14716	17801	14902	18684	20072	29077	23682	39683	39436	31718
Transportation equipment	11741	8855	6730	7732	9214	11045	10765	11833	15062	17303	16335
Non-ferrous metal products	3138	3162	3105	4113	5169	5682	6257	8316	8496	9489	11060
Electrical apparatus and supplies	587	634	714	792	1076	1269	1628	2190	2438	2607	3028
Non-metallic minerals	5319	6533	4454	4608	5271	5981	6329	7233	8064	8343	8229
Petroleum and coal	1168	1067	983	954	964	949	1075	1059	1135	1420	1791
Chemical products	3029	3090	3144	3338	3794	4123	4523	5404	6238	6769	7488
Miscellaneous industries	2646	2557	2581	2972	3197	3325	3707	3763	4379	4646	4568
Total GDP	145114	137998	138751	156082	169539	179188	200146	203941	243475	259771	254645

266

Table 4.5. (continued)

	1905	1906	1907	1908	1909	1910	1911	1912	1913	1914	1915
Food and beverage	48452	46528	50453	55998	61065	64767	64267	69030	66643	70857	82568
Tobacco and products	5703	5533	5910	7720	8430	8585	9430	9767	9735	10261	10327
Rubber products	2735	2983	3247	2629	3878	4497	5369	6749	5850	5964	8355
Leather products	21408	27282	19818	14197	25789	26746	30113	39097	27271	31448	26747
Textiles (ex. clothing)	13018	14323	13531	12156	14688	17894	14846	14984	15565	13678	17668
Clothing	32547	37089	38632	33675	43239	50605	45579	49244	50958	43019	47377
Wood products	49604	61148	67417	59614	66468	72168	78640	67843	62903	56641	56984
Paper products	7178	8449	9787	9985	11387	12388	11295	11240	12701	16320	18722
Printing and publishing	11086	11944	12266	13958	15667	15765	17282	18795	20559	20997	21006
Iron and steel products	50976	69246	87249	57338	68102	75808	78188	95780	103973	60352	72491
Transportation equipment	18565	23677	32452	27221	29415	31302	38919	44854	53299	43301	33281
Non-ferrous metal products	17401	20941	22341	18324	20240	24169	22760	28287	26281	20128	28364
Electrical apparatus and supplies	3782	4949	5789	6384	6778	7280	8471	7806	7633	7635	7181
Non-metallic minerals	9706	11699	12686	11199	11058	17076	19261	22384	23458	18831	14245
Petroleum and coal	2047	1827	2358	2379	2155	2355	2779	4494	5640	5531	4089
Chemical products	8828	9801	11097	10460	10852	12890	14670	17918	17637	16160	18926
Miscellaneous industries	5403	6198	6795	6099	7073	7827	7697	8067	7685	6600	6847
Total GDP	308439	363617	401828	349336	406284	452122	469566	516339	517791	447723	475178

Table 4.5. (continued)

	1916	1917	1918	1919	1920	1921	1922	1923	1924	1925	1926
Food and beverage	103300	144219	156916	169843	187062	152471	141002	143715	150220	156065	169158
Tobacco and products	11884	15997	20060	13957	19557	16646	18358	16960	16879	9779	12918
Rubber products	12744	17935	19665	22929	30558	18097	22236	24430	27188	32405	28366
Leather products	42026	39180	36692	43937	45462	36716	40818	38661	37228	35700	38795
Textiles (ex. clothing)	22932	36734	47618	54141	58872	46725	54141	54099	41450	41083	50047
Clothing	68874	80108	91133	107804	109493	83249	87978	89630	83364	84810	93436
Wood products	56703	85863	93048	107388	137470	87188	84079	101393	88223	87215	93509
Paper products	31507	47850	60691	74242	134378	71203	78066	92893	86010	94258	105444
Printing and publishing	26477	33403	32504	42105	54323	52162	52235	53007	53327	54537	58047
Iron and steel products	124805	185523	198134	158876	207531	125452	98746	132855	114033	124093	147981
Transportation equipment	37544	76866	106980	110800	111534	61432	58043	68923	61191	79775	95991
Non-ferrous metal products	41393	45321	35666	33352	36970	17595	21204	26784	26380	33445	34170
Electrical apparatus and supplies	10178	15909	12108	14707	22213	20141	18603	19744	26292	28506	32401
Non-metallic minerals	14918	17950	17792	19664	33494	25481	28856	29060	27932	28207	29365
Petroleum and coal	7621	10531	13169	14730	17208	10942	11553	4711	8254	8325	15129
Chemical products	41941	93829	124797	34433	39688	28061	29704	37941	35911	38497	43259
Miscellaneous industries	9207	12854	17053	19340	25256	19416	19689	20018	15895	17198	19387
Total GDP	664054	960072	1084026	1042248	1271069	872977	865311	954824	899777	953898	1067403

Table 4.6. Manufacturing: Summary of the Cost of Wages and Salaries, by Industry, 1870-1926 (thousands of current dollars)

	1870	1871	1872	1873	1874	1875	1876	1877	1878	1879	1880	1881
Food and beverage	4783	5428	6059	6687	6080	5723	5769	7234	5980	6457	7483	8373
Tobacco and products	691	738	792	972	1179	1189	1172	973	726	703	868	1002
Rubber products	87	108	128	152	169	111	94	130	107	117	185	295
Leather products	6526	7769	7181	6158	6465	5174	4343	5467	5121	5795	7988	8879
Textiles (ex. clothing)	2073	2856	2670	2018	2034	2221	2163	2320	2283	3022	3550	4124
Clothing	3888	5243	5582	5142	5182	4953	4650	5159	5328	6403	7075	7914
Wood products	10522	10868	.10974	16476	15506	12828	10145	12145	9971	10698	14142	18081
Paper products	325	393	396	481	525	569	563	567	577	571	634	722
Printing and publishing	1702	2060	2212	2669	2947	3050	2919	2967	3008	2892	2776	3701
Iron and steel products	8429	11159	15817	23244	14642	14580	9248	10098	8239	7690	10975	12700
Transportation equipment	3598	3652	4414	8275	8227	6249	6557	6263	6664	5458	4962	6593
Non-ferrous metal products	500	574	648	721	794	868	941	1013	1085	1156	1228	1226
Electrical apparatus and supplies												
Non-metallic minerals	1576	1657	1736	1814	1890	1966	2039	2111	2181	2251	2318	2207
Petroleum and coal	222	271	333	373	125	225	386	248	229	343	290	305
Chemical products	691	783	855	899	965	900	928	1029	1004	1036	1092	1165
Miscellaneous industries	676	805	903	1115	1013	947	866	1010	920	1003	1230	1436
Total	46289	54364	60700	77196	67743	61553	52783	58734	53423	55595	66796	78723

Table 4.6. (continued)

	1882	1883	1884	1885	1886	1887	1888	1889	1890	1891	1892	1893
Food and beverage	8966	8822	8907	8176	8199	8928	10722	11285	12105	12860	12143	11023
Tobacco and products	1077	1180	1411	1269	1020	1192	1305	1378	1629	1768	1764	1799
Rubber products	298	248	265	257	259	325	406	377	374	406	418	452
Leather products	8705	7992	7908	9060	9520	8257	7185	6755	8176	8403	8168	7615
Textiles (ex. clothing)	5298	4793	4148	4346	4600	4741	5125	5739	5756	5848	6046	5617
Clothing	9737	8919	8097	8531	9304	9246	9717	11558	11948	11832	12219	11628
Wood products	22227	24658	21344	18906	19399	19673	20136	20355	21770	22122	18661	18973
Paper products	855	1026	1094	1137	1143	1267	1376	1486	1603	1686	1779	1873
Printing and publishing	4311	4011	3379	3408	3315	3990	4937	4759	4307	4566	5825	5978
Iron and steel products	15473	19453	14435	12582	12888	15730	15486	15968	17358	16048	15795	14279
Transportation equipment	7398	6725	5858	5231	5499	5965	6013	5979	6701	7213	7672	7649
Non-ferrous metal products	1279	1064	761	871	1259	1290	1580	1938	2128	2830	2124	2188
Electrical apparatus and supplies									277	288	303	339
Non-metallic minerals	2095	1982	1868	1753	1637	1893	1991	2339	3186	2562	2460	3184
Petroleum and coal	250	268	258	293	299	320	279	291	312	321	358	382
Chemical products	1335	1441	1420	1424	1477	1507	1471	1488	1546	1585	1611	1559
Miscellaneous industries	1638	1687	1531	1465	1515	1599	1702	1788	1939	2005	1950	1888
Total	90942	94269	82684	78709	81333	85923	89431	93483	101115	102343	99296	96426

Table 4.6. (continued)

	1894	1895	1896	1897	1898	1899	1900	1901	1902	1903	1904
Food and beverage	10681	11256	11374	14203	14613	13872	15733	16664	18397	20214	21678
Tobacco and products	1802	1802	2028	2617	2556	2316	2653	2593	2683	2923	3060
Rubber products	414	461	562	704	853	979	1000	851	816	1026	1247
Leather products	5671	7046	6675	10240	11247	10436	9749	10332	12228	11893	9753
Textiles (ex. clothing)	4932	4734	4532	5649	6806	7582	7919	8193	8735	8726	8356
Clothing	10916	11065	10833	11822	13240	14878	15758	16612	18637	19767	20153
Wood products	18063	15523	17213	18049	17569	20344	23348	22383	25590	28182	26961
Paper products	1987	1910	1866	1981	2081	2221	2441	2378	2850	3091	3328
Printing and publishing	4739	4721	5049	5178	5297	5634	6242	6377	6552	7061	7948
Iron and steel products	12673	9914	12107	10233	12950	14048	20537	16650	27770	27472	21993
Transportation equipment	7888	6199	4907	5871	7284	9090	9218	9908	12333	13847	12770
Non-ferrous metal products	1925	1921	1867	2449	3043	3310	3606	4857	5030	5695	6731
Electrical apparatus and supplies	380	408	457	502	676	792	1009	1344	1483	1570	1807
Non-metallic minerals	3188	3897	2644	2722	3098	3498	3684	4201	4673	4823	4747
Petroleum and coal	410	387	368	368	382	386	449	451	492	627	803
Chemical products	1462	1533	1600	1742	2031	2261	2540	2789	2966	2968	3032
Miscellaneous industries	1773	1743	1789	2094	2289	2418	2737	2798	3278	3502	3467
Total	88904	84520	85871	96424	106015	114065	128623	129381	154513	163387	157834

Table 4.6. (continued)

	1905	1906	1907	1908	1909	1910	1911	1912	1913	1914	1915
Food and beverage	24519	22995	24338	26387	28074	29061	29220	31843	31179	33684	39893
Tobacco and products	3149	3054	3263	4259	4652	4735	5075	5121	4964	5080	4953
Rubber products	1317	1356	1386	1048	1433	1526	1951	2614	2407	2595	3832
Leather products	11601	14958	10989	7968	14639	15363	17521	23029	16262	18983	16353
Textiles (ex. clothing)	8944	9467	8604	7429	8630	10097	8496	8693	9164	8175	10720
Clothing	22341	25509	26624	23247	29919	35089	31886	34758	36294	30910	34353
Wood products	30040	37709	42354	38162	43383	48050	51358	43465	39567	34977	34563
Paper products	3820	4546	5328	5499	6341	6981	6452	6510	7463	9728	11331
Printing and publishing	8555	9205	9441	10732	12034	12091	13458	14858	16497	17093	17348
Iron and steel products	35179	47139	58576	37932	44374	48615	51524	64833	72312	43103	53192
Transportation equipment	14172	17975	24487	20429	21942	23225	29082	33766	40424	33094	25653
Non-ferrous metal products	10736	11887	11569	8579	8454	8869	9440	13120	13521	11380	17562
Electrical apparatus and supplies	2236	2841	3224	3444	3538	3672	4603	4572	4822	5207	5293
Non-metallic minerals	5586	6760	7360	6524	6470	10034	11721	14117	15333	12770	10022
Petroleum and coal	932	851	1124	1161	1078	1207	1378	2156	2612	2471	1760
Chemical products	3300	3826	4525	4451	4821	5974	7234	9393	9806	9530	11814
Miscellaneous industries	4128	4598	4894	4258	4786	5123	5273	5785	5766	5181	5619
Total	190555	224676	248086	211509	244568	269712	285672	318633	328393	283961	304261

Table 4.6. (continued)

	1916	1917	1918	1919	1920	1921	1922	1923	1924	1925	1926
Food and beverage	43559	51663	58559	71648	83186	73544	73669	75830	81152	83257	86856
Tobacco and products	5043	5992	6500	7740	8619	7599	7415	7565	7338	7405	7623
Rubber products	5508	7270	8501	11546	16199	9868	10623	12329	11413	14144	14708
Leather products	23182	19183	19347	26898	29036	25250	27706	28111	27437	26292	28480
Textiles (ex. clothing)	11942	16249	18840	22212	29593	24282	26422	28191	25233	27240	29233
Clothing	46554	50170	50801	64270	76414	61566	61672	63973	60580	62660	67847
Wood products	32274	45637	47668	59041	78224	53514	55411	63476	64268	62734	65532
Paper products	17847	25450	32079	38841	53559	40746	39736	45825	44772	45431	51994
Printing and publishing	19080	20457	21922	28151	37337	35245	35610	37149	38177	39124	41501
Iron and steel products	80708	101939	116054	106646	130226	89818	75357	89454	80059	82816	96466
Transportation equipment	25653	50180	59659	69844	82665	41974	40514	54062	49166	64215	74771
Non-ferrous metal products	21323	17251	18627	18745	21962	13255	14332	17955	18165	19242	20575
Electrical apparatus and supplies	6360	8163	8599	9865	16587	13556	12162	14991	16090	16472	18627
Non-metallic minerals	9905	11199	10874	12900	19788	15230	15219	17143	16269	16326	18318
Petroleum and coal	3307	4855	5801	7722	8467	7531	6287	6826	6928	6936	6906
Chemical products	25289	50934	66120	15428	21520	15667	16257	18399	17027	17475	18592
Miscellaneous industries	7086	9203	9178	11964	17295	12982	12578	13344	11589	11505	12549
Total	384620	495795	559129	583461	730677	541627	530970	594623	575663	603274	660578

Table 4.7. Manufacturing: Summary of Gross Property Income, by Industry, 1870-1926 (thousands of current dollars)

	1870	1871	1872	1873	1874	1875	1876	1877	1878	1879	1880	1881
Food and beverage	6480	7094	7638	8100	7099	6439	6253	7549	5987	6220	6930	7982
Tobacco and products	323	339	358	431	514	510	493	401	295	279	339	419
Rubber products	25	33	40	47	53	35	29	41	34	36	58	95
Leather products	5191	6042	5451	4563	4672	3640	2971	3638	3307	3625	4837	5571
Textiles (ex. clothing)	618	895	877	692	727	826	836	928	945	1292	1566	1897
Clothing	1498	1987	2082	1885	1870	1754	1620	1766	1792	2116	2298	2798
Wood products	5651	5875	5970	9023	8545	7109	5657	6815	5630	6078	8085	10407
Paper products	345	398	381	444	459	475	444	425	410	382	401	444
Printing and publishing	568	679	718	856	933	950	897	898	898	851	803	1092
Iron and steel products	4374	5675	7881	11341	6991	6802	4211	4488	3574	3250	4510	5402
Transportation equipment	2345	2300	2690	4859	4656	3399	3421	3131	3180	2482	2143	3033
Non-ferrous metal products	270	308	344	382	418	454	488	521	555	589	621	626
Electrical apparatus and supplies												
Non-metallic minerals	822	864	906	947	986	1025	1063	1101	1139	1174	1210	1176
Petroleum and coal	897	1081	1309	1449	476	849	1436	908	826	1220	1018	1029
Chemical products	869	976	1053	1094	1163	1074	1096	1205	1162	1188	1240	1344
Miscellaneous industries	418	496	556	688	625	585	534	624	568	619	760	885
Total	30694	35042	38254	46801	40187	35926	31449	34439	30302	31401	36819	44200

Table 4.7. (continued)

	1882	1883	1884	1885	1886	1887	1888	1889	1890	1891	1892	1893
Food and beverage	8773	8859	9170	8609	8829	9826	12046	12922	14127	14925	14027	12662
Tobacco and products	479	558	707	669	566	694	797	877	1084	1146	1117	1109
Rubber products	96	80	87	85	87	110	139	131	131	150	162	183
Leather products	5652	5355	5466	6442	6966	6211	5545	5347	6634	6670	6336	5763
Textiles (ex. clothing)	2538	2387	2145	2326	2550	2717	3034	3507	3624	3676	3794	3517
Clothing	3719	3664	3556	3989	4621	4853	5382	6730	7303	6907	6809	6183
Wood products	12871	14373	12524	11161	11526	11765	12120	12324	13265	13135	10791	10685
Paper products	511	599	624	631	619	669	710	750	790	895	1015	1144
Printing and publishing	1299	1233	1060	1088	1078	1319	1664	1632	1502	1633	2136	2244
Iron and steel products	6804	8839	6769	6087	6431	8080	8193	8684	9712	8732	8346	7336
Transportation equipment	3617	3490	3221	3045	3386	3879	4127	4326	5105	4965	4741	4219
Non-ferrous metal products	663	557	403	468	684	708	878	1088	1209	1650	1270	1345
Electrical apparatus and supplies									139	147	158	181
Non-metallic minerals	1141	1103	1060	1016	968	1139	1220	1459	2023	1647	1602	2101
Petroleum and coal	814	840	778	845	828	847	703	698	708	690	732	740
Chemical products	1567	1719	1720	1753	1846	1910	1895	1945	2050	1992	1921	1759
Miscellaneous industries	1007	1033	936	894	923	972	1031	1081	1170	1151	1064	978
Total	51551	54689	50226	49108	51908	55699	59484	63501	70576	70111	66021	62149

Table 4.7. (continued)

	1894	1895	1896	1897	1898	1899	1900	1901	1902	1903	1904
Food and beverage	12210	12794	12888	16000	16378	15455	17439	17989	19364	20715	21677
Tobacco and products	1082	1055	1157	1453	1381	1219	1359	1462	1660	1982	2272
Rubber products	174	202	256	332	416	492	516	534	605	873	1203
Leather products	4188	5076	4686	7003	7472	6739	6114	6885	8661	8943	7782
Textiles (ex. clothing)	3082	2956	2828	3518	4230	4704	4906	4827	4864	4574	4098
Clothing	5535	5340	4983	5176	5511	5882	5911	6491	7586	8362	8871
Wood products	9896	8258	8896	9057	8557	9606	10676	11094	13668	16164	16509
Paper products	1300	1332	1388	1569	1750	1982	2311	2218	2621	2802	2971
Printing and publishing	1820	1853	2025	2120	2213	2401	2710	2578	2463	2460	2561
Iron and steel products	6321	4802	5694	4669	5734	6024	8540	7032	11913	11964	9725
Transportation equipment	3853	2656	1823	1861	1930	1955	1547	1925	2729	3456	3565
Non-ferrous metal products	1213	1241	1238	1664	2126	2372	2651	3459	3466	3794	4329
Electrical apparatus and supplies	207	226	257	290	400	477	619	846	955	1037	1221
Non-metallic minerals	2131	2636	1810	1886	2173	2483	2645	3032	3391	3520	3482
Petroleum and coal	758	680	615	586	582	563	626	608	643	793	988
Chemical products	1567	1557	1544	1596	1763	1862	1983	2615	3272	3801	4456
Miscellaneous industries	873	814	792	878	908	907	970	965	1101	1144	1101
Total	56210	53478	52880	59658	63524	65123	71523	74560	88962	96384	96811

Table 4.7. (continued)

	1905	1906	1907	1908	1909	1910	1911	1912	1913	1914	1915
Food and beverage	23933	23533	26115	29611	32991	35706	35047	37187	35464	37173	42675
Tobacco and products	2554	2479	2647	3461	3778	3850	4355	4646	4771	5181	5374
Rubber products	1418	1627	1861	1581	2445	2971	3418	4135	3443	3369	4523
Leather products	9807	12324	8829	6229	11150	11383	12592	16068	11009	12465	10394
Textiles (ex. clothing)	4074	4856	4927	4727	6058	7797	6350	6291	6401	5503	6948
Clothing	10206	11580	12008	10428	13320	15516	13693	14486	14664	12109	13024
Wood products	19564	23439	25063	21452	23085	24118	27282	24378	23336	21664	22421
Paper products	3358	3903	4459	4486	5046	5407	4843	4730	5238	6592	7391
Printing and publishing	2531	2739	2825	3226	3633	3674	3824	3937	4062	3904	3658
Iron and steel products	15797	22107	28673	19406	23728	27193	26664	30947	31661	17249	19299
Transportation equipment	4393	5702	7965	6792	7473	8077	9837	11088	12875	10207	7628
Non-ferrous metal products	6665	9054	10772	9745	11786	15300	13320	15167	12760	8748	10802
Electrical apparatus and supplies	1546	2108	2565	2940	3240	3608	3868	3234	2811	2428	1888
Non-metallic minerals	4120	4939	5326	4675	4588	7042	7540	8267	8125	6061	4223
Petroleum and coal	1115	976	1234	1218	1077	1148	1401	2338	3028	3060	2329
Chemical products	5528	5975	6572	6009	6031	6916	7436	8525	7831	6630	7112
Miscellaneous industries	1275	1600	1901	1841	2287	2704	2424	2282	1919	1419	1228
Total	117884	138941	153742	137827	161716	182410	183894	197706	189398	163762	170917

Table 4.7. (continued)

	1916	1917	1918	1919	1920	1921	1922	1923	1924	1925	1926
Food and beverage	59741	92556	98357	98195	103876	78927	67333	67885	69068	72808	83302
Tobacco and products	6841	10005	13560	6217	10938	9047	10943	9395	9541	2374	5295
Rubber products	7236	10665	11164	11383	14359	8229	11613	12101	15775	18261	13658
Leather products	18844	19997	17345	17039	16426	11466	13112	10550	9791	9408	10315
Textiles (ex. clothing)	10990	20485	28778	31929	29279	22443	27719	25908	16217	13843	20814
Clothing	22320	29938	40332	43534	33079	21683	26306	25657	22784	22150	25588
Wood products	24429	40226	45380	48347	59246	33674	28668	37917	23955	24481	27977
Paper products	13660	22400	28612	35401	80819	30457	38330	47068	41238	48827	53450
Printing and publishing	7397	12946	10582	13954	16986	16917	16625	15858	15150	15413	16546
Iron and steel products	44097	83584	82080	52230	77305	35634	23389	43401	33974	41277	51515
Transportation equipment	11891	26686	47321	40956	28869	19458	17529	14861	12025	15560	21220
Non-ferrous metal products	20070	28070	17039	14607	15008	4340	6872	8829	8215	14203	13595
Electrical apparatus and supplies	3818	7746	3509	4842	5626	6585	6441	4753	10202	12034	13774
Non-metallic minerals	5013	6751	6918	6764	13706	10251	13637	11917	11663	11881	11047
Petroleum and coal	4314	5676	7368	7008	8741	3411	5266	-2115	1326	1389	8223
Chemical products	16652	42895	58677	19005	18168	12394	13447	19542	18884	21022	24667
Miscellaneous industries	2121	3651	7875	7376	7961	6434	7111	6674	4306	5693	6838
Total	279434	464277	524897	458787	540392	331350	334341	360201	324114	350624	406825

277

Table 4.8.   Manufacturing: Grand Summary (thousands of current dollars)

Year	Gross Value of Product	Cost of Materials	Fuel and Electricity	Misc. Expenses	Gross Domestic Product	Wages and Salaries	Gross Property Income
1870	213892	122387	3533	10989	76983	46289	30694
1871	248704	142308	4165	12825	89406	54364	35042
1872	272779	154881	4776	14168	98954	60700	38254
1873	329213	181930	5871	17415	123997	77196	46801
1874	291924	163705	4939	15350	107930	67743	40187
1875	266341	150038	4754	14070	97479	61553	35926
1876	237518	136673	4280	12333	84232	52783	31449
1877	270027	158263	4667	13924	93173	58734	34439
1878	239646	139290	4278	12353	83725	53423	30302
1879	254356	149797	4473	13090	86996	55595	31401
1880	303491	178996	5174	15706	103615	66796	36819
1881	352165	205084	5805	18353	122923	78723	44200
1882	399249	229182	6482	21092	142493	90942	51551
1883	408453	230932	6719	21844	148958	94269	54689
1884	368492	210161	5909	19512	132910	82684	50226
1885	350380	198487	5597	18479	127817	78709	49108
1886	360155	202186	5736	18992	133241	81333	51908
1887	377848	209922	6270	20034	141622	85923	55699
1888	399449	222782	6627	21125	148915	89431	59484
1889	417012	230900	7041	22087	156984	93483	63501
1890	449478	246247	7804	23736	171691	101115	70576
1891	457508	253267	7723	24064	172454	102343	70111
1892	437920	242074	7474	23055	165317	99296	66021
1893	417672	229660	7381	22056	158575	96426	62149
1894	386565	214148	6913	20390	145114	88904	56210
1895	374530	210228	6817	19487	137998	84520	53478
1896	379103	213867	6529	19956	138751	85871	52880
1897	437752	251824	7238	22608	156082	96424	59658
1898	472034	270017	8100	24378	169539	106015	63524
1899	492065	278615	8617	25645	179188	114065	65123
1900	549894	311061	9799	28888	200146	128623	71526
1901	560389	316500	10053	29895	203941	129381	74560
1902	654442	363178	11947	35842	243475	154513	88962
1903	696895	385583	12556	38985	259771	163387	96384
1904	687721	381557	12277	39242	254645	157834	96811

Table 4.8. (continued)

Year	Gross Value of Product	Cost of Materials	Fuel and Electri-city	Misc. Expen-ses	Gross Domestic Product	Wages and Salaries	Gross Property Income
1905	816354	445080	15209	47626	308439	190555	117884
1906	939373	501228	17975	56553	363617	224676	138941
1907	1033779	547634	20390	63927	401828	248086	153742
1908	931178	505959	17391	58492	349336	211509	137827
1909	1084009	589022	19541	69162	406284	244568	161716
1910	1203588	650209	22670	78587	452122	269712	182410
1911	1256808	678676	24867	83699	469566	285672	183894
1912	1397486	758118	29861	93168	516339	318633	197706
1913	1410263	764011	32522	95939	517791	328393	189398
1914	1282596	719230	27905	87738	447723	286961	163762
1915	1406687	863552	31106	96871	475178	304261	170917
1916	1966778	1117294	48103	137327	664054	384620	279434
1917	2857692	1620076	73922	203622	960072	495795	464277
1918	3276666	1866635	99373	226632	1084026	559129	524897
1919	3211619	1844262	78957	246152	1042248	583461	458787
1920	3794431	2123081	97806	302475	1271069	730677	540392
1921	2594813	1408042	74688	239106	872977	541627	331350
1922	2483110	1320169	71212	226418	865311	530970	334341
1923	2785716	1514843	80427	235622	954824	594623	360201
1924	2695278	1486785	78411	230305	899777	575663	324114
1925	2898522	1616943	80816	246865	953898	603274	350624
1926	3184578	1760218	86388	270568	1067403	660578	406825

We will deal with how the estimates were made for each of these classes of economic phenomena, table by table.   Since the estimates for base years were made from census of manufactures data while the estimates for other years were obtained by interpolation among base years we will deal with the base years first, for each table, and then with the intervening years. The base years are 1870, 1880, 1890, 1900, 1910, 1917-1926, for most series 1915 and, for a very small number of series, 1905.

We should note, right at the outset, the set of most valuable material on manufacturing data that had been prepared at the Dominion Bureau of Statistics, under the direction of T.K. Rymes to whom we are indebted for so many sets of data.   The census of manufactures data of the base years were reclassified by T.K. Rymes at DBS into the 17 industry groups of the 1948 standard industrial classification: in the process estimates to provide full coverage of all manufacturing were made to correct for the omission of small businesses in 1900, 1905, 1910 and 1915.   These data were published in HSC, in Series Q1-137.   These data, especially for the gross value of product, were a starting point for our work.   The reader is referred to the extended note in the manufacturing industries statistics in HSC pages 455 to 457.   In addition, T.K. Rymes had prepared a special memo on the data of 1870 to 1915.   The contents of that memo follow almost immediately.

One other important acknowledgement is called for.   David Jones, who had played an important part in the development of official national accounts estimates in many years employment in Statistics Canada, assisted for several months with the work on manufacturing of this project.   His most valuable background along with the assiduous care and balanced judgement of his work meant that he made a most important contribution to the project's estimates on manufacturing.

T.K. Rymes Memorandum

"Some comments on the pre-Annual Census of Industry
data with respect to Manufacturing in Canada 1870-1915"

Introduction

One of the requirements of the Fixed Capital Stocks Project[1] of the Dominion Bureau of Statistics is estimates of gross capital formation in Manufacturing prior to the beginning of the official estimates in 1926.   To obtain such estimates it was found necessary to analyse the data with respect to Manufacturing which was collected and published prior to the commencement of the Annual Census of Industry in 1918.

Data with respect to Manufacturing were collected and published in the Decennial Censuses of Canada from the first Census in 1871 to the fifth Census in 1911.   In addition, data are available from the two Postal Censuses of Manufactures taken in 1906 and 1916.

These data, dealing with principal statistics and capital invested, have been re-tabulated on the basis of the DBS 1948 *Standard Industrial Classification*.   This re-tabulation involved certain problems, which, as well as their attempted solutions, are noted.   These comments are divided into three parts: Part 1 deals with the principal statistics of Manufacturing 1870-1915; Part 2 is a critique of the 'numbers employed' given in Part 1; and Part 3 deals with 'capital invested' in Manufacturing 1870-1915.

I should like to thank Professor M. Urquhart, Queen's University, T. Vout, formerly of the

---

[1]   See M. Tucker, "Recent development in the work of the Dominion Bureau of Statistics", *The Canadian Journal of Economics and Political Science*, XXV, 4, November 1959, 500.

Department of Trade and Commerce and, especially, Professor G.W. Bertram, Los Angeles State College, for their helpful advice and criticism.

General Problems:

  1. The industrial classification schemes followed in the various censuses are neither as precise nor as detailed as the *1948 SIC*. In the earlier censuses particularly, data for certain industries as reported should have been split into different major groups but it was only possible to classify them into one major group (i.e., data are given for an industry called 'Fittings and foundry workings in brass, iron, lead, etc.' This industry was arbitrarily included in the Non-Ferrous Metal Products major group in these re-tabulations). There were also some difficulties in this respect with the later sources, (e.g., from the *Census of Canada 1901* on, the industry reported as 'Oils', which is known to include linseed oil, fishoil and Neats-foot oil as well as refined oil, was included in the Products of Petroleum and Coal major group).

  This problem of reclassifying industries on the basis of the *1948 SIC* may lead, for a few major groups, to incorrect movements in the trends of the principal statistics.

  2. In all sources, industries such as 'House building', 'Plumbing, etc.' as well as others not now classified as Manufacturing were included in the data on Manufacturing. Wherever possible, these data were excluded from these re-tabulations.

  3. *The Census of Canada 1901 and 1911* give data relating only to those industrial establishments employing five hands and over. In addition the *Postal Census of Manufactures 1916* related only to those industrial establishments whose gross value of production was $2,500 and over. Adjustments to full coverage were attempted at a detailed level, but necessarily, some crudities were involved. These adjustments are noted in the discussions on each Census given below.

  4. Owing to the method of enumeration, the data dealing with the 'numbers employed' in the sources *Census of Canada 1870-71* to *Census of Canada 1911* contain considerable duplication. Discussion on this problem is reserved to Part 2 of these comments.

  5. In the *Censuses of Canada 1901 and 1911* and the two *Postal Censuses*, there was a group of industries denoted 'all other industries' with the principal statistics combined to meet the secrecy requirements of the *Statistics Act*. Since these re-tabulations are performed at the *1948 SIC* major group level, an attempt to distribute such data would not contravene the Act. In all of the sources, data for 'all other industries' are distributed over Census major groupings, while, in some of the sources, a list of the industries in 'all other industries', both at the aggregate level and within each census major group, is supplied.

Information available with respect to 'all other industries'

[1] Source	[2] List of 'all other industries'	[3] 'All other industries' data distributed over census major groups	List of 'all other industries' within each census group
Census of Canada 1901, III.	Yes	Yes	Yes
Postal Census of Manufactures 1906.	No	Yes	No
Census of Canada 1911, III.	Yes	Yes	No
Postal Census of Manufactures 1916.	Yes	Yes	No

It was decided that the least arbitrary distribution of these 'all other industries' data would be to assume that the census groups were roughly comparable to the *1948 SIC* major groups. For instance, the principal statistics for the 'all other industries' in the census group 'timber, lumber and their re-manufactures' were allocated to the *1948 SIC* major group Wood Products. This method of distributing the 'all other industries' data probably overweighted, to a slight extent, the *1948 SIC* major groups 5 and 8 and certainly overweights group 17. The distribution of the 'all other industries' data over the census groups and the assumed comparability between the census groups and the *1948 SIC* major groups are noted below.

Distribution of 'all other industries' data

Census groups	Census of Canada 1901	Postal Census of Manufactures 1906	Census of Canada 1911	Postal Census of Manufactures 1916
1. Food products	Yes	Yes	Yes	Yes
2. Textiles	Yes	Yes	Yes	Yes
3. Iron and steel products	Yes	Yes	Yes	Yes
4. Timber, lumber and their re-manufactures	Yes	Yes	Yes	Yes
5. Leather and its finished products			Yes	
6. Paper and printing	Yes	Yes	Yes	Yes
7. Liquors and beverages				
8. Chemicals and allied products	Yes	Yes	Yes	Yes
9. Clay, glass and stone products	Yes	Yes	Yes	Yes
10. Metals and metal products other than iron and steel	Yes	Yes	Yes	Yes
11. Tobacco and its manufactures				
12. Vehicles for land transportation		Yes		
13. Vessels for water transportation				
14. Miscellaneous industries	Yes	Yes	Yes	Yes
15. Hand trades				

Assumed comparability between Census and 1948 SIC groups

Census groups	*1948 SIC* major group
1. Food products	1. Food and beverages
2. Textiles	5. Textile products (excluding clothing)
3. Iron and steel products	10. Iron and steel products
4. Timber, lumber and their re-manufactures	7. Wood products
5. Leather and its finished products	4. Leather products
6. Paper and printing	8. Paper products
8. Chemicals and allied products	16. Chemical products
9. Clay, glass and stone products	14. Non-metallic mineral products
10. Metals and metal products other than iron and steel	12. Non-ferrous metal products
12. Vehicles for land transportation	11. Transportation equipment
14. Miscellaneous industries	17. Miscellaneous manufacturing industries

6. The conceptual basis for the valuation of capital invested is never, to my knowledge, clearly stated in the various Censuses. Thus, one is at a loss to know whether fixed reproducible capital is valued gross or net, at original cost or current market prices. A more complete examination of this problem is found in Part 3 of these comments.

7. In the *Census of Canada 1870-71*, it was noted that the gross value of production of 'Distilleries' included excise taxes. The data with respect to 'Distilleries' in the *Census of Canada 1880-81* would seem to indicate that gross value of production was recorded net of excise taxes. However, except for the reference in the *Census of Canada 1870-71*, there is no other mention of whether or not the gross value of production data for industries in the Foods and beverages and Tobacco and tobacco products major groups include or exclude excise taxes.

8. It is difficult to indicate quantitatively what errors are contained in the sources. One must consider the possibility of underenumeration, the unreliability of the respondents' answers and the errors, which are known to have occurred, in the tabulation of the results of the Censuses. In general, and with the exception of the 'numbers employed' data, I should expect some understatement to have occurred, particularly in the earlier Censuses owing to the practice of tabulating only those industries 'of importance'.

General procedure

A list of all industries reporting in each census was compiled. These industries were combined at the major group level on the basis of the *1948 SIC*. Non-manufacturing industries were, wherever possible, excluded from the re-tabulations. In Censuses requiring adjustment to full coverage the blow-up factors (obtained from Censuses where data were reported with both full and limited coverage) were applied at the individual (what would now be termed the three-digit) industry level. In Censuses where there existed data grouped under the heading 'all other industries,' these data were, as noted earlier, distributed over the *1948 SIC* major groups and added, with adjustment for limited coverage where necessary, to the re-tabulations.

Part 1 — Principal Statistics of Manufacturing 1870-1915

The following discussion outlines the enumerating concepts employed in each source of data, evaluates the data, and indicates, in some detail, the problems encountered and solutions used in these re-tabulations.

A.   Census Branch, Department of Agriculture, *Census of Canada 1870-71*, III (Ottawa: I.B. Taylor, 1875).

For the purposes of the *Census of Canada 1870-71* ...

An industrial establishment is a place where one or several persons are employed in manufacturing, altering, making up or changing from one shape to another, materials for sale, use, or consumption, quite irrespectively of the amount of capital employed or of the products turned out ...
All repairs, mending, or custom work, are understood to be industrial products; and are to be entered accordingly, by value, in the returns of industrial establishments.[2]

The Industrial data in the *Census of Canada 1870-71*

... apply to all industries *of any importance* conducted as separate establishments or work-

---

[2]   Census Branch, Department of Agriculture, *Manual Containing the Census Act and Instructions to Officers Employed in the Taking of the First Census of Canada (1871)* (Ottawa: Queen's Printer, 1871), 30.

shops, *ad hoc*. These (data) ... do not include the products of domestic industries such as building, furniture making, clothing, tools, boat and carriage building, etc., done by farmers and among the seaside population which in general cannot be separately classified. It is proper to remark that the importance of this unclassified industry is considerable ...[3]

The 'value of products' was reported on a gross value of production basis[4] and working proprietors, as well as salaried personnel, were included as employees.[5] It should be noted that the 'numbers employed', owing to the method of enumeration, contain considerable duplication (cf., Part 2 of these comments). The geographic coverage was for the four Confederated provinces only. Data for certain industries, which are not grouped within the Manufacturing Division in the *1948 SIC*, were excluded from these re-tabulations. These industries were: 'Carpenters and joiners'; 'Painters, glaziers, etc.'; 'Gas works'; and 'Photographic galleries'. There were two additional industries, whose inclusion in Manufacturing, because they might be for a large part in Retail Trade, seemed doubtful. They were: 'Bakeries of all sorts' and 'Tailors and clothiers'. However, the number of persons reported as being employed in these industries (allowing for over enumeration) matched closely to the number of people reported as being bakers and tailors in the occupation Census.[6] Therefore, the two industries were included in the Manufacturing data. Finally, in the report of the industry 'Distilleries' it was noted that the gross value of production included excise duties. The data from the *Census of Canada 1870-71* are to be found in Part 1, Appendix 1, Table A.

B.   Census Branch, Department of Agriculture, *Census of Canada 1880-81*, III (Ottawa: MacLean, Roger and Co., 1883).

The definition of an industrial establishment in the *Census of Canada 1880-81* was the same as that in the *Census of Canada 1870-71*. In addition, it was noted that

... in numerous cases where custom work is taken in and the raw material furnished by the consumer ... much difficulty was experienced in obtaining the value of raw material worked up.[7]

Again, the method of enumeration used to obtain the numbers employed resulted in considerable duplication (cf., Part 2 of these comments). The geographic coverage was extended to include the newly Confederated provinces of Manitoba, Prince Edward Island, and British Columbia. The Territories were covered as well. Certain industries, reported in the *Census of Canada 1880-81*, were excluded from these re-tabulations. They were: 'Carpenters and joiners', 'Painters and glaziers', 'Gas works', 'Dentistry', and 'Photographic galleries'. Two doubtful inclusions were 'Bakeries of all sorts' and 'Tailors and clothiers'. They were included after examination of the occupations Census.[8] The data from the *Census of Canada 1870-71* are to be found in Part 1, Appendix 1, Table B.

Replies to critics of the industrial data in the *Census of Canada 1880-81* are contained in J.C. Tache, "The third volume of the Census of 1881 and its critics". However, no additional data, useful for these purposes, are contained therein.

Special investigators were hired in 1884 to survey the state of Manufacturing, in particular to investigate the effects of the National Policy.[9] Some data are available, but on such a limited

---

[3]   *Census of Canada 1870-71*, III, pp. vii-ix (my italics).
[4]   *Op. cit.*, p. 19.
[5]   *Ibid.*, p. 31.
[6]   *Census of Canada 1870-71*, II, Table XIII.
[7]   *Census of Canada 1880-81*, III, p.x.
[8]   *Census of Canada 1880-81*, II, Table XIV.
[9]   *Report of the State of Manufactures.*

coverage as to be useless as far as these comments are concerned.

C.   Census Branch, Department of Agriculture, *Census of Canada 1890-91*, III (Ottawa: Queen's Printer, 1894).

The definition of an industrial establishment, as noted in previous Censuses, remained unchanged. However, as was noted earlier

> Many small industries were returned but were cut out of the tabulated statement ... because they were evidently adjuncts to the regular occupations by which livelihoods were obtained. In this respect, the lines of previous Censuses were closely followed, the object being to make the Census of 1891 strictly comparable, in its general results, with those of 1881 and 1871.[10]

The same definitions with respect to the value of output and employees as in previous censuses were maintained, and the geographical coverage was the same as for the *Census of Canada 1880-81*. Again, certain reported industries were excluded from the re-tabulations. They were: 'Carpenters and joiners', 'House decorator', 'Painters and glaziers', 'Plumbers and gas fitters', 'Gas works', 'Electric light works', 'Engravers' supplies', 'Dentistry', 'Photographic galleries', 'Marble and stone cutting' and 'Portrait painting'. Once again, after appealing to the occupations census,[11] 'Bakeries' and 'Tailors and clothiers' were included in these re-tabulations.

Owing to tabulation errors in the original data, some duplication in the 'number of employees', 'wages' and 'value of products' for six industries in the *Census of Canada 1890-91* occurred. These errors were noted in the *Census of Canada 1901*, III, p. lxv, n.1 and were eliminated in these re-tabulations which appear in Part 1, Appendix 1, Table E.[12]

D.   Census Office, *Census of Canada 1901*, III (Ottawa: Queen's Printer, 1905).

A major change occurred in the definition of an industrial establishment in the *Census of Canada 1901*. It was decided to limit the scope of the Census to statistics of the factory or workshop system as distinguished from those of the domestic or hand system of labour. Therefore

> ... no manufacturing establishment or factory will be so recognised for Census purposes which does not employ at least five persons, either in the establishment itself or as pieceworkers employed out of it.[13]

This limitation, however, did not apply in the enumeration and tabulation of data with respect to butter and cheese factories nor to brick and tile yards.

It was noted, for the first time, in the *Census of Canada 1901* that

> ... a reasonable allowance for salaries of owners and firm members should be entered ... whether they draw stated salaries or not[14]

This presumably implies that, in previous Censuses, working proprietors who drew salaries were

---

[10] *Census of Canada 1890-91*, III, p. iv. Thus, the view that the *Census of Canada 1890-91*, data on manufacturing were over stated, owing to over enumeration and irregularities in tabulations, would appear to be incorrect. See "The industrial census", *Facts for the People, 3, 1 March 1896*.

[11] *Census of Canada 1890-91*, II, Table XII.

[12] The correct data for the six industries are found in *Census of Canada 1901*, III, Table XXII.

[13] *Census of Canada 1901*, III, p. vi.

[14] *Fourth Census of Canada 1901. Instructions to Chief Officers, Commissioners and Enumerators.*

reported but 'unpaid' proprietors were not. Employees were divided into salary earners and wage earners. A good deal of further useful information was obtained in this Census. There are estimates, tabulated by industry, of fixed and working capital (cf. Part 3), aggregate working days, months in operation, rental of works, rental of power and heat, cost of fuel and light, municipal taxes, provincial taxes, rent of offices, interest paid, etc., amount paid for contract work, amount received for custom work and repairs, as well as statements of mechanical power in terms of type of power available (steam engines, electric motors, etc.), and horsepower thereof. This information, save with respect to capital invested, is not, however, reproduced in these re-tabulations.

The geographical coverage as well as the definition of value of production remained unchanged. Industries, which were reported, but not included in these re-tabulations were: 'Hay baled', 'Sea grass', 'Painting and glazing', 'Plumbing and tinsmithing', 'Electric light and power', 'Gas lighting and heating', 'Interior decorators', and 'Photography'. An error in the *Census of Canada 1901* was noted in the *Postal Census of Manufacturers 1906*[15] and the correction was introduced. Part 1, Appendix 1, Table D1 contains the re-tabulations *before adjustment for limited coverage*.

Part 1, Appendix 1, Table D2 contains the re-tabulations *after adjustment for limited coverage*. That adjustment was:

In the *Census of Canada 1901* III, the *Census of Canada 1890-91* data for industries was presented for all establishments and for establishments employing 'five hands and over' (cf., *Census of Canada 1901*, III, Table XXII). In addition, the data for establishments employing 'five hands and over' was presented by industry in a comparative table for 1891 and 1901 (cf., *Census of Canada 1901*, III, Table XXIII). These data permitted blow-up factors to be calculated by industry for employees, wages and salaries and value of products and these blow-up factors were applied to industries reporting in 1901 to adjust their data to full coverage. Unweighted mean blow-up factors were computed for each major group and these factors were applied to (i) industries reporting for the first time in 1901 and to (ii) the data, distributed by major group, contained in the category 'all other industries'.

E.   Census and Statistics Office, Department of Agriculture, *Postal Census of Manufactures 1906*. (Ottawa: King's Printer, 1907).

In this Census, industrial establishments were enumerated, regardless of the number of employees. However, the data was also presented on the basis of the industrial establishment used in the *Census of Canada 1901*. However, many of the smaller establishments which reported were apparently not tabulated[16]

In addition, it was noted that ...

In numerous industries, through misconceptions of mailed instructions, owners of establishments in receipt of stated salaries or allowances who in 1900 were counted as employees, have not been so returned in 1905; consequently, (some of) such returns have dropped into the category of establishments employing under five persons[17]

Employees were divided into salary earners and wage earners. No change in geographical coverage occurred but territories were now designated Alberta and Saskatchewan. The value of materials used was not reported. There is no discussion as to how the mailing list was compiled. Industries reporting in the *Postal Census 1906*, but not included in these re-tabulations, were: 'Painting and glazing', 'Plumbing and tinsmithing', 'Interior decorations', 'Photography', 'Electric light and power', and 'Gas, lighting and heating'.

---

[15] *Postal Census of Manufacturing* 1906, p. xv.

[16] *Ibid.*, p. vi.

[17] *Ibid.*, p. vii.

A problem was encountered in distributing the 116 establishments included in 'all other industries' in the full coverage data and the 115 establishments included in 'all other industries' in the data tabulated on the establishment basis of five employees and over. If one compares the data for 'all other industries' on the two bases, it is found that the data on the limited coverage basis are of greater magnitude than the data on the full coverage basis.

	Data with respect to 'all other industries' in the *Postal Census of Manufactures 1906*		
	Table 1 (full coverage)	Table 2 (limited coverage)	Table 4
Establishments	116	115	115
Value of land, buildings and plant	3,801,675		
Value working capital	4,028,375		
Total capital	7,830,050	9,025,275	9,025,275
Employees on salaries	460		
Salaries	419,202		
Employees on wages	3,516		4,215
Wages	1,206,403		1,537,165
Total employees	3,976	4,765	
Wages and salaries	1,685,605	2,047,234	
Value of products	7,225,103	8,536,193	8,536,193

The difference in the data greatly complicates the satisfactory distribution of the 'all other industries' data. The data with respect to 115 establishments in 'all other industries' are presented in Table 4 in the *Postal Census 1906* in groupings which are very roughly comparable to the *1948 SIC* major groups. They were distributed by means of this grouping and added to the re-tabulated limited coverage data, which are to be found in Part 1, Appendix 1, Table E1. The data with respect to the 116 establishments in 'all other industries' on the full coverage basis were distributed by means of the percentage distribution derived from the distribution of the 115 establishments in 'all other industries' on the limited coverage basis, and were added to the re-tabulated full coverage data, which are to be found in Part 1, Appendix 1, Table E2.

Anomalies with respect to Tables E1 and E2 must be mentioned. For a few principal statistics, the value recorded on the full coverage basis is less than that recorded on the limited coverage basis. This result occurs because (a) the 'all other industries' differ between bases and (b), in all likelihood the distribution technique is faulty.

In an attempt to obtain a better distribution of the 'all other industry' data, a search for the worksheets lying behind the *Postal Census 1906* was instigated. Unfortunately, only fragments were discovered and after examination, they were not deemed satisfactory to obtain a new 'all other industries' distribution.[18]

---

[18] For only a limited number of Census districts, compilation sheets for the *Postal Census of Manufactures 1906* are available in the Public Archives Record Centre at Tunney's Pasture in Ottawa. They are not catalogued but are stacked with the folios of the *Census of Canada 1870-71*. The compilation sheets, giving industry detail, which are available are:

Quebec Districts	137-154	
Quebec Districts	174-178	(City of Montreal)
Ontario Districts	43- 62	
Ontario Districts	114-125	

It should be pointed out that the *Postal Census of Manufactures 1906* is suspected of under-enumeration. The number of establishments employing 'five hands and over' was 14,285 in 1900, 12,057 in 1905, and 18,447 in 1910. However, the number of reporting establishments is not necessarily a good indication of underenumeration but the other principal statistics (cf., the discussion in Part 2 with respect to the 'numbers employed') would seem to indicate that under-enumeration occurred.

F.   Census Office, Department of Trade and Commerce, *Census of Canada 1911*, III (Ottawa: King's Printer, 1913)

This Census was of limited coverage, with the definition of an industrial establishment only applying to those establishments employing 'five hands and over'. However, the list of industries fully enumerated was extended to include, as well as butter and cheese factories and brick and tile works, flour and gristing mills, fish curing plants, lime kilns, and electric light and power plants. Industries reporting in the *Census of Canada 1911*, but not included in these re-tabulations, were: 'House-building', 'Plumbing and tinsmithing', 'Electric light and power', 'Gas lighting and heating', 'Interior decorations', and 'Sea-Grass'.

In the *Census of Canada 1911*, 121 establishments were grouped in 'all other industries'. The industries in the *Census of Canada 1911* were grouped by a classification system very roughly comparable to that of the *1948 SIC* and these groups reported 'all other industries'. This distribution, as noted earlier, was deemed acceptable for the purposes of these re-tabulations. The distribution of principal statistics by groups, however, only included wage-earners and wages and the percentage distribution of then was used to obtain the distribution of salary earners and salaries. The data for *Census of Canada 1911*, unadjusted for limited coverage are to be found in Part 1, Appendix 1, Table F1.

The data were adjusted to full coverage by applying individual industry blow-up factors from the *Postal Census of Manufactures 1906*. Where the blow-up factors obtained from that source could not be matched with the individual industries reported in the *Census of Canada 1911*, the data with respect to those industries were adjusted to full coverage by applying the unweighted mean *1948 SIC* major group blow-up factor obtained from the *Postal Census of Manufactures 1906*. This was also the procedure used in adjusting the distributed 'all other industry' data to full coverage. It should be noted that the blow-up factors may be too low, (cf., discussion on the *Postal Census of Manufactures 1916*). The data, adjusted to full coverage, will be found in Part 1, Appendix 1, Table F2.

G.   Census and Statistics Office, Department of Trade and Commerce, *Postal Census of Manufactures 1916* (Ottawa: King's Printer, 1917).

In this Census, industrial establishments were defined on a basis different from any used previously with only those industrial establishments where the gross value of production was $2,500 and greater being tabulated. This limitation did not apply to 'Flour and grist mills', 'Butter and cheese factories', 'Fish preserving stations', 'Sawmills', 'Brick and tile yards', 'Lime kilns', and 'Electric light plants'.

Industries reported in the *Postal Census of Manufactures 1916*, but not included in these re-tabulations, were: 'Hay baled', 'Electric light and power', 'Gas lighting and heating', 'Interior decorations', 'Painting and glazing', 'Plumbing and tinsmithing', 'Housebuilding', 'Photography'.

Also available are the industrial detail data with respect to manufactures in Ontario cities, towns and villages lying behind the published figures in Table III of the *Postal Census of Manufactures*.

In addition, it should be noted that the compilation sheets for Ontario Census districts 54-84 with respect (Footnote 18 continued) to manufacturing data for the *Census of Canada 1901* have been uncovered and are located in the Dead Storage Files in the DBS.

The data in 'all other industries' was distributed over the *1948 SIC* major groups on the basis of the grouping system used in the source. The data, on the basis of value of product of $2,500 or over, are presented in Part 1, Appendix 1, Table G1.

The *Postal Census of Manufactures 1916* also reported limited data with respect to industrial establishments employing 'five hands and over'. By means of blow-up factors obtained from the *Postal Census 1906* I originally felt I should be able to adjust the principal statistics to full coverage. When this was tried, however, the adjusted data for some industries were less than the data on the 'value of production of $2,500 and over' basis. Thus, the blow-up factors obtained from the *Postal Census 1906* are probably too low and, furthermore, the principal statistics of the *Census of Canada 1911*, adjusted to full coverage using the *Postal Census 1906*, are probably as well too low. In view of this problem, the data for 1915 on the basis of industrial establishments employing 'five hands and over', are not adjusted to full coverage and are presented in Part 1, Appendix 1, Table G2.

Part 2 — Numbers employed in Manufacturing 1870-1915

As noted in Part 1, the 'numbers employed' data in the Census from 1870 to 1910 can be suspected of overestimation.

In the *Census of Canada 1870-71*, it was noted that ...

> ... certain establishments do not employ workmen or labourers during the whole year, nor in any regular manner, and that men following certain occupations are successively engaged in the course of the year in various employments. The item of annual wages compared with the number of men employed, is consequently, not a fair indication, in many establishments, of the rate of pay for the day's work ...[19]

In the *Census of Canada 1880-81*, the same overestimation exists.

> It may be remarked that in many establishments the workmen are not regularly employed, nor during the whole year. Some saw mills, particularly in the lower provinces, are owned and run by farmers, and may work but a week or more in the year, and but a few anywhere, run more than six months, and so in other industries.[20]

In the *Census of Canada 1891*, no explicit mention is made of this problem either in the Third Volume or the Manual of Instructions to Enumerators. However, it can be assumed that the same overestimation exists in the number of employees.

In the *Census of Canada 1901*, again, there is no mention of the problem in either the Third Volume or the Manual of Instructions to Enumerators. However, in the Third Volume, Table IX, there are estimates of the aggregate number of working days for employees as well as estimates of the average hours of working time per week. From these data, some estimate of the full-time number of employees in Manufacturing could perhaps be made.

Again, in the *Postal Census of Manufactures 1906* and in the *Census of Canada 1911*, the problem is not mentioned. However, the *Census of Canada 1911* reported 'aggregate weeks of time employed in the year' defined to mean the whole amount of working time of all employees and 'average hours of working time per week' defined to mean the average hours of full time per week of all employees.[21] Again, some use could possibly be made of these data.

In the *Postal Census of Manufactures 1916*, the number of employees on salaries and wages (exclusive of piece workers) was asked on December 15, 1915 or the nearest pay day. In this

---

[19] *Census of Canada 1870-71*, III, p. x.
[20] *Census of Canada 1880-81*, III, p. x.
[21] *Census of Canada 1911: Instructions of Officers, Commissioners and Cumerators*, p. 58.

Census, it was noted that

> In previous censuses, the information asked for ... was less detailed, the manufactures being asked to state the total number of employees during the year, whereas in 1915, the number of the pay roll in each month was obtained. It is thought that the earlier method tended to increase somewhat the number of employees recorded, as manufacturers in industries like butter and cheese making, fruit canning, saw milling, fish preserving, brick and tile yards, etc., which vary considerably in activity with the season, tended to make their returns for the period of full activity.[22]

To make the 'numbers employed' data for Manufacturing in 1915 consistent with that for 1910, it was estimated that they would have to be increased by 12.3%.[23]

Some additional sources of information are available to check how much duplication is involved in the numbers of employees in Manufacturing reported in the earlier Censuses. The *Census of Canada 1870-71*, II, Table XIII, gives 'occupations of the people'. Some double counting may be involved in these figures (cf., *Manual of Instructions*, p. 23) and children under ten years of age are apparently included. The table provides a classification 'industrial class' which records 212,808 persons employed therein. This includes a number of occupations deemed not to be in Manufacturing, and the data was re-tabulated. Another possible source is that noted by O.J. Firestone.[24] Table 1, in the *Census of Canada 1921, IV*, gives occupations of the populations ten years of age and over for Canada 1881, 1891, 1901 and 1911. These data were re-tabulated to obtain the numbers reported in occupations which would most likely be found in Manufacturing.

The re-tabulations are shown in Part 2, Appendix 1, in which is found the number of people following occupations in 'Manufacturing' and 'Building Trades' in the various years with data from *Census of Canada 1870-71*, II, T. XIII and *Census of Canada 1921*, IV, T. 1, compared with number of people employed in 'Manufacturing' and 'Construction' with data from Part 1 of these comments and tabulations connected therewith.

The occupation data with respect to 'Building Trades' probably contain a number of persons who were engaged in Manufacturing industries. Nevertheless, the occupations data do indicate that, for the Censuses of Manufactures 1870, 1880, 1890 and 1900, the 'numbers employed' data in Manufacturing are overstated.

With respect to the 'numbers employed' data in the *Postal Census of Manufactures 1906*, I believe that the data are reasonably accurate. This is so because, while the method of enumeration would result in an overstatement, the *Postal Census* itself is suspected of undercoverage.

With respect to the 'numbers employed' data for the *Census of Canada 1911* (on a full coverage basis), I suspect that the inflation procedure used results in an under estimate and therefore data with respect to 'numbers employed' which are reasonably accurate. Again, the occupations data would seem to bear this out.

These comments are not meant to be exhaustive but are included merely to indicate the caution with which 'numbers employed' in Manufacturing data from the earlier Censuses must be used.

Part 3 - Capital Invested in Manufacturing 1870-1915

As mentioned earlier, in none of the sources am I able to locate a satisfactory discussion as to the principles of valuation used in reporting 'capital invested'. It must be pointed out that, in my opinion, the data with respect to 'capital invested' are of questionable reliability.

For the *Census of Canada 1870-71* and *1880-81* total 'capital invested' was reported. It is not known what components make up 'capital invested', but it is presumed, from the components

---

[22] *Postal Census of Manufactures 1916*, p. xi.
[23] *Loc. cit.*
[24] O.J. Firestone, *Canada's Economic Development 1867-1953, 318-19.*

noted in *Census of Canada 1891*, that they are land, buildings, machinery and working capital. For the *Census of Canada 1880-81*, it was noted that in 'capital invested' ...

> ... care must be taken to include the value of the buildings used, whether owned or rented, it matters not.[25]

For the *Census of Canada 1891*, the value of 'capital invested' was divided into four components: land, buildings, machinery and tools, and working capital. There is no discussion as to the content and evaluation principles to be attached to each component.

In the *Census of Canada 1901*, the value of 'capital invested', was divided into five components: land, buildings, machinery and motive power, tools and implements, and working capital. In the glossary of terms (cf. *Census of Canada 1901*, III, pp. viii-ix),

> Mechanical power was defined as ... the various kinds of power used to move the machinery and other accessory aids for promoting the interests of the establishment ... whether owned, leased or rented.

And 'working capital' was defined to include

> ... cash on hand, bills receivable, unsettled ledger accounts, raw materials, stock in process of manufacture and finished products on hand.

Also, it might be noted that the 'capital invested' in buildings, land, and machinery and tool and implements was designated 'visible' capital.

> Capital includes the values of lands, buildings, machinery and motive power, and of tools and implements necessary for a manufacturing industry, together with cash in hand, bills receivable, unsettled ledger accounts, raw materials, stock in process of manufacture and finished products on hand, on the basis of the last annual stock taking. These, however, are the usual terms of business rather than the scientific terms of political economy, which are exact and comprehensive.[26]

In the *Postal Census of Manufactures 1906*, the value of 'capital invested' (in the full coverage tabulations) was only divided between: value of land, buildings, and plant, and working capital. The terms employed have the same meaning as in the *Census of Canada 1901*[27]

> In this intercensal inquiry no separate statistics have been collected as to the value of land and buildings. Probably a considerable proportion of the increase in value under the heading of land, buildings and plant is due to appreciation in the value of previously existing property and not alone to the acquisition of additional land and the erection of new buildings.[28]

On the limited coverage basis, only the total 'capital invested' was reported.

In the *Census of Canada 1911*, the value of 'capital invested' was again only divided between: value of land, buildings, and plant; and working capital. Capital employed in a manufacturing establishment was defined as

> ... consisting of (1) value of land, buildings and plant occupied by the factory, and (2) the amount of the working capital employed, which may include money borrowed for carrying

---

[25] *Manual Instruction, Census of Canada 1880-81*, p. 40.
[26] *Census of Canada 1901*, III, p. lvi.
[27] *Postal Census of Manufactures 1906*, p. v.
[28] *Ibid.*, p. xi.

on the factory operations ... in many concerns where the business was simple the answer might be given off hand to the enumerator, while in others, which were extensive and complex, time might be gained by arranging with the owner or manager to make the entries carefully and in agreement with the book of entries or records of the factory[29]

In the glossary of terms (cf. *Census of Canada 1911*, III, pp. 414-417), the same definitions as for the *Census of Canada 1901* were noted.

In the *Postal Census of Manufactures 1916*, the value of 'capital invested' was defined to be: value of land, buildings and fixtures, machinery and tools, materials and stocks in hand, and cash, trading and operating accounts and bills receivable. In the glossary of terms (cf. *Postal Census of Manufactures 1916*, Appendix A, pp. 248-251) the same definitions as for the *Censuses of Canada 1901 and 1911* were noted.

For establishments enumerated on the basis of g.v.p. of $2,500 and greater, the value of capital is presented in the detail described above. For establishments enumerated on the basis of employing 'five hands and over', however, only total capital invested is reported.

As analysis of the 'capital invested' in the various sources indicates that it was capital used in an industry, not necessarily owned by that industry, which was reported. The information contained in the *Postal Census of Manufactures 1906* would seem to suggest that fixed reproducible capital invested was valued at current prices but, in view of the difficulties involved in revaluing capital, my suspicion is that it was valued in terms of original cost. Whether such valuation was gross or net of accumulated depreciation, I cannot say.

The data with respect to Capital invested is to be found in Part 3, Appendix 1, Tables A to C.

(signed)
T.K. Rymes
Central Research and Development Staff
DBS
21 September 1960

"Some comments on the pre-Annual Census of Industry data with respect to Manufacturing in Canada, 1870-1915"

T.K. Rymes
August 6, 1961
Addendum

For the purposes of the CPSA Historical Statistics volume, the data given in Part 1, Appendix 1 of the memorandum were tied into similar data for the period 1917-1958. Certain problems of reconciliation were encountered. For example, establishments engaged in the repair of transportation equipment were excluded from the latter data whereas, owing to the manner in which the basic data are found, they were included in the former. Another example with which this addendum is concerned is the treatment of establishments engaged in the manufacture of heating and lighting gas and those engaged in the distribution of such gas. In later Censuses of Manufactures, establishments of the former type were included while establishments of the latter were excluded. As one moves back in time, the available data are such as to reveal that in the earliest sources the distinction was not maintained and that later, when such distinction was indicated, it may have been less than satisfactory.

In Part 1, Appendix 1, industries classed as 'Gas works' and 'Gas, lighting and heating' were

---

[29] *Census of Canada 1911*, III, p. vi.

excluded from the re-tabulations. However, in preparing the data for the CPSA, they were added back into the Products of petroleum and coal major group. In accompanying Table 1, principal statistics data for 'Gas works' and 'Gas, lighting and heating' are presented on the same basis as for other Manufacturing industries in Part 1, Appendix 1 of the memorandum so that these data may be added to the major group and Manufacturing data if desired.

In Table 2, 'capital invested' data for 'Gas works' and 'Gas, lighting and heating' are presented on the same basis as for other manufacturing industries in Part 3, Appendix 1 of the memorandum so that these data may be added to the major group and Manufacturing data if desired.

[The following tables in Appendix to Parts 1, Parts 2 and Parts 3 and the two tables giving statistics of "Gas works" are all a part of the Rymes memorandum. M.C.U.]

Part 1, Appendix 1, Table A
Principal Statistics of Manufacturing – *Census of Canada 1870-71, III*

1948 SIC Major Group	Number of establishments (thousands)[1]	Number of employees (thousands)[2]	Wages and salaries (thousands of dollars)[2]	Value of materials used (thousands of dollars)[2]	Census value added (thousands of dollars)[2]	Gross value of production (thousands of dollars)[2]
1. Foods and beverages	4.1	12.4	2,978.2	48,215.1	15,177.4	63,382.6
2. Tobacco and tobacco products	0.1	2.2	407.1	1,197.7	1,237.6	2,435.3
3. Rubber products	–	0.5	83.3	357.7	144.9	502.6
4. Leather products	6.4	25.6	5,883.9	14,845.2	13,065.3	27,910.5
5. Textile products, ex. clothing	1.0	7.5	1,373.8	6,231.4	3,434.2	9,665.6
6. Clothing, textile and fur	2.6	17.1	2,753.7	8,619.7	6,399.5	15,019.2
7. Wood products	9.8	50.6	9,191.1	21,379.7	19,481.8	40,861.6
8. Paper products	–	1.5	295.0	873.7	851.2	1,724.9
9. Printing, publishing and allied industries	0.4	4.3	1,404.6	1,491.6	2,636.7	4,128.3
10. Iron and steel products	8.1	28.3	7,883.0	9,216.7	15,697.4	24,914.0
11. Transportation equipment	3.0	14.3	3,454.7	3,479.8	6,409.2	9,889.1
12. Non-ferrous metal products	0.3	1.6	476.1	673.3	920.8	1,594.1
13. Electrical apparatus and supplies	–	–	–	–	–	–
14. Non-metallic mineral products	1.8	8.5	1,506.0	857.8	3,015.9	3,813.7
15. Products of petroleum and coal	0.1	0.5	202.3	1,441.2	1,653.4	3,094.7
16. Chemical products	0.9	3.6	624.8	3,048.9	1,972.7	5,021.5
17. Miscellaneous manufacturing industries	0.4	2.9	628.8	1,087.9	1,320.2	2,408.1
Total manufacturing	38.9	181.4	39,146.3	123,007.5	93,418.3	216,425.8

1. Data for 2 April 1871
2. Data for the twelve months preceding 2 April 1871

Note: No breakdown of the numbers of employees or wages and salaries is available. No industries were reported in the *Census of Canada 1870-71* which could be classified in the Electrical apparatus and supplies major group. Totals may not add owing to rounding.

295

Part 1, Appendix 1, Table B
Principal Statistics of Manufacturing – *Census of Canada 1880-81, III*

1948 SIC Major Group	Number [1] of establishments (thousands)	Number [2] of employees (thousands)	Wages [2] and salaries (thousands of dollars)	Value of [2] materials used (thousands of dollars)	Census [2] value added (thousands of dollars)	Gross [2] value of production (thousands of dollars)
1. Foods and beverages	5.4	25.8	5,802.7	63,516.2	18,892.8	82,409.0
2. Tobacco and tobacco products	0.1	3.8	729.0	1,571.9	1,488.4	3,060.3
3. Rubber products	– –	0.5	177.4	478.1	292.9	771.0
4. Leather products	6.8	27.5	6,700.7	21,870.6	14,585.2	36,455.8
5. Textile products, ex. clothing	1.8	13.4	2,594.6	9,077.3	6,398.7	15,376.0
6. Clothing, textile and fur	4.5	32.2	5,347.1	15,521.0	11,176.5	26,697.5
7. Wood products	9.6	59.9	12,560.3	28,263.9	26,657.6	54,921.5
8. Paper products	0.1	2.2	576.1	1,627.5	1,348.2	2,975.7
9. Printing, publishing and allied industries	0.5	6.9	2,256.1	2,605.3	4,180.1	6,785.3
10. Iron and steel products	10.5	35.2	10,238.1	14,446.4	19,736.2	34,182.6
11. Transportation equipment	3.6	16.7	4,796.8	6,407.5	7,859.0	14,266.5
12. Non-ferrous metal products	0.5	3.3	1,770.4	1,770.2	2,230.0	4,000.3
13. Electrical apparatus and supplies	– –	– –	– –	– –	–	–
14. Non-metallic mineral products	2.4	11.0	2,215.6	1,912.8	4,266.5	6,179.3
15. Products of petroleum and coal	– –	0.5	194.0	2,241.3	1,808.4	4,049.7
16. Chemical products	0.6	3.8	989.2	4,144.9	2,912.9	7,057.8
17. Miscellaneous manufacturing industries	0.6	4.9	1,143.3	1,907.2	2,394.1	4,301.3
Total manufacturing	47.0	247.5	57,481.3	177,362.2	126,127.5	303,489.6

1. Data for 4 April 1881
2. Data for the twelve months preceding 4 April 1881

Note: No breakdown of the numbers of employees or wages and salaries is available. No industries were reported in the *Census of Canada 1880-81* which could be classified in the Electrical apparatus and supplies major group. Totals may not add owing to rounding.

Part 1, Appendix 1, Table C
Principal Statistics of Manufacturing – *Census of Canada 1890-91, III*

1948 SIC Major Group	Number [1] of establishments (thousands)	Number [2] of employees (thousands)	Wages [2] and salaries (thousands of dollars)	Value of [2] materials used (thousands of dollars)	Census [2] value added (thousands of dollars)	Gross [2] value of production (thousands of dollars)
1. Foods and beverages	12.6	57.0	10,580.7	85,045.6	33,865.6	118,911.2
2. Tobacco and tobacco products	0.1	5.3	1,461.5	2,502.1	3,240.4	5,742.5
3. Rubber products	- -	1.4	359.2	1,422.1	638.0	2,060.1
4. Leather products	7.8	25.7	7,552.6	18,699.6	16,509.1	35,208.7
5. Textile products, ex. clothing	4.0	25.5	5,848.4	13,536.9	12,506.4	26,043.3
6. Clothing, textile and fur	11.6	48.5	10,127.4	22,204.2	21,647.1	43,851.2
7. Wood products	11.6	80.0	21,405.0	42,661.5	41,882.7	84,544.1
8. Paper products	0.2	4.7	1,455.2	3,159.6	3,046.3	6,205.9
9. Printing, publishing and allied industries	0.7	9.8	3,852.5	3,721.4	6,735.1	10,456.5
10. Iron and steel products	12.7	45.6	16,186.4	23,542.9	32,328.2	55,871.1
11. Transportation equipment	4.0	18.5	6,561.1	10,156.6	13,186.3	23,344.9
12. Non-ferrous metal products	0.7	4.8	2,027.0	3,356.8	4,043.1	7,400.0
13. Electrical apparatus and supplies	- -	0.4	168.3	336.3	529.6	865.9
14. Non-metallic mineral products	2.2	12.7	3,040.8	2,011.1	6,187.4	8,198.5
15. Products of petroleum and coal	- -	0.3	159.1	1,482.1	673.0	2,155.1
16. Chemical products	0.8	4.6	1,400.1	5,703.4	4,432.0	10,135.5
17. Miscellaneous manufacturing industries	0.7	5.1	1,699.4	2,678.5	3,512.4	6,190.9
Total manufacturing	69.7	350.0	93,884.8	245,220.6	204,964.7	447,185.3

1. Data for 6 April 1891
2. Data for the twelve months preceding 6 April 1891

Note: No breakdown of the numbers of employees or wages and salaries is available. Totals may not add owing to rounding.

Part 1, Appendix 1, Table D1
Principal Statistics of Manufacturing – *Census of Canada 1901, III*
(Unadjusted for limited coverage)

1948 SIC Major Group	Number of establishments (thousands)	Number of salary earners (thousands)	Salaries (thousands of dollars)	Number of wage earners (thousands)	Wages (thousands of dollars)	Total number of employees (thousands)	Wages and salaries (thousands of dollars)	Value of materials used (thousands of dollars)	Census value added (thousands of dollars)	Gross value of production (thousands of dollars)
Foods and beverages	5.8	5.4	3,652.1	46.5	9,488.0	51.9	13,140.2	104,065.7	32,807.1	136,872.8
Tobacco & tobacco products	0.2	0.7	673.3	6.3	1,931.4	7.0	2,604.7	3,724.7	8,077.4	11,802.1
Rubber products	-	0.1	108.6	0.6	220.2	0.8	328.8	968.1	606.3	1,574.4
Leather products	0.4	1.6	1,389.7	19.2	6,040.9	20.8	7,430.6	21,725.6	12,944.9	34,720.5
Textile products, ex. clothing	0.3	1.1	921.9	23.5	6,403.8	24.6	7,325.7	15,749.8	13,716.3	29,466.1
Clothing, textile and fur	1.4	4.1	3,172.5	38.0	9,420.4	42.1	12,592.9	20,490.1	20,359.8	40,849.9
Wood products	3.0	6.7	4,346.6	72.1	17,820.5	78.7	22,167.1	37,601.4	38,264.7	75,866.1
Paper products	0.1	0.7	671.3	8.5	2,652.1	9.1	3,323.3	5,370.0	6,941.8	12,311.8
Printing, publishing and allied industries	0.5	2.1	1,706.2	10.2	4,144.0	12.4	5,850.2	3,698.1	9,459.5	13,157.6
Iron and steel products	0.7	3.5	3,064.0	31.7	12,378.9	35.1	15,442.9	19,743.6	26,520.5	46,264.1
Transportation equipment	0.5	1.2	919.7	17.9	7,210.8	19.1	8,130.5	11,565.4	11,042.7	22,608.1
Non-ferrous metal products	0.1	0.5	510.4	4.7	2,282.8	5.2	2,793.2	3,818.6	7,985.3	11,804.0
Electrical apparatus & supplies	-	0.1	103.9	1.9	846.6	2.0	950.6	1,131.0	1,901.2	3,032.3
Non-metallic mineral products	0.9	0.4	332.1	11.3	2,924.8	11.7	3,256.9	1,286.4	6,872.6	8,159.0
Products of petroleum & coal	-	0.1	80.3	0.6	251.0	0.7	331.2	2,392.6	1,126.9	3,519.6
Chemical products	0.2	0.8	749.0	3.5	1,092.0	4.3	1,841.0	5,658.3	4,474.9	10,133.2
Misc. manufacturing industries	0.2	0.7	534.5	5.6	1,981.5	6.3	2,516.0	2,991.6	4,116.9	7,108.5
Total manufacturing	14.3	29.7	22,935.9	302.1	87,089.7	331.8	110,025.6	261,981.3	207,268.7	469,249.9

Note: Data are for the year ending 31 March 1901, or 31 December 1900, or for the last business year of the establishment as was most convenient to enumerate. Data are for establishments employing 'five hands and over'. (See comments, Part 1, D). Totals may not add owing to rounding.

Part 1, Appendix 1, Table D2
Principal Statistics of Manufacturing – *Census of Canada 1901, III*
(Adjusted for limited coverage)

1948 SIC Major Group	Number of establishments (thousands)	Total number of employees (thousands)	Wages and salaries (thousands of dollars)	Value of materials used [1] (thousands of dollars)	Census value added (thousands of dollars)	Gross value of production (thousands of dollars)
1. Foods and beverages		59.2	15,810.9	116,975.1	36,878.8	153,853.9
2. Tobacco and tobacco products		7.1	2,652.8	3,774.3	8,184.8	11,959.0
3. Rubber products		0.8	335.7	976.7	611.9	1,588.6
4. Leather products		35.1	12,055.6	32,808.5	19,626.4	52,434.9
5. Textile products, ex. clothing		27.4	7,919.5	17,644.0	15,366.3	33,010.4
6. Clothing, textile and fur		68.3	16,987.2	27,176.7	27,014.1	54,190.8
7. Wood products		98.4	26,260.8	44,836.9	45,633.0	90,469.9
8. Paper products		9.2	3,347.1	5,416.3	7,003.6	12,419.9
9. Printing, publishing and allied industries		13.4	6,243.5	3,990.3	10,210.0	14,200.3
10. Iron and steel products		41.8	17,697.0	22,181.1	29,801.8	51,982.9
11. Transportation equipment		24.8	9,936.5	13,894.3	13,269.5	27,163.8
12. Non-ferrous metal products		6.2	3,199.7	4,135.9	8,648.9	12,784.7
13. Electrical apparatus and supplies		2.1	1,009.5	1,221.2	2,053.6	3,274.8
14. Non-metallic mineral products		14.0	3,684.2	1,490.9	7,969.2	9,460.1
15. Products of petroleum and coal		0.8	405.8	2,825.6	1,330.9	4,156.5
16. Chemical products		6.0	2,538.7	7,029.4	5,561.3	12,590.8
17. Miscellaneous manufacturing industries		7.2	2,829.7	3,325.3	4,577.0	7,902.2
Total manufacturing		421.8	132,914.1	309,702.4	243,741.2	553,443.6

1. Estimates of the value of materials used on a full coverage basis were obtained by applying the ratio (at the *1948 SIC* major group level) of the value of materials used to gross value of production on the limited coverage basis (cf. Part 1, Appendix 1, Table D1) to the gross value of production on the full coverage basis.

Note: Data are for the year ending 31 March 1901, or 31 December 1900, or for the last business year of the establishment as was most convenient to the enumeree. Data are adjusted to obtain estimates for all establishments, regardless of the number of employees. It should be noted that, in some cases, it is felt that the adjusted data are at too high a level. In the foods and beverages major group it was assumed that in 1901 'Flour and grist mills' and 'Fish curing plants' were fully enumerated (cf. *Census of Canada 1911, III*, p. vii).

Totals may not add owing to rounding.

Part 1, Appendix 1, Table E1
Principal Statistics of Manufacturing – *Postal Census of Manufacturing 1906*
(Unadjusted/ or limited coverage)

1948 SIC Major Group	Number of establishments (thousands)	Number of salary earners (thousands)	Salaries (thousands of dollars)	Number of wage earners (thousands)	Wages (thousands of dollars)	Total number of employees (thousands)	Wages and salaries (thousands of dollars)	Gross value of production (thousands of dollars)
Foods and beverages	5.0	5.4	4,229.4	49.3	13,726.9	54.7	17,956.3	189,170.1
Tobacco & tobacco products	0.1	0.5	489.0	7.1	2,326.3	7.6	2,815.3	15,189.7
Rubber products	--	0.2	212.6	1.0	403.2	1.2	615.8	3,047.0
Leather products	0.3	1.8	1,467.1	17.6	6,241.0	19.4	7,708.1	41,201.9
Textile products, ex. clothing	0.2	1.2	1,106.0	19.8	5,885.2	21.0	6,991.2	32,816.6
Clothing, textile and fur	1.3	3.9	2,987.8	39.0	12,241.3	42.9	15,229.1	58,309.6
Wood products	2.2	5.9	4,844.6	76.0	28,221.6	81.9	33,066.3	106,385.8
Paper products	0.1	1.0	964.0	10.1	3,718.7	11.1	4,682.6	18,742.7
Printing, publishing and allied industries	0.5	3.0	2,523.6	11.9	5,790.0	14.9	8,313.6	19,126.7
Iron and steel products	0.7	4.5	4,223.5	38.4	17,558.8	42.9	21,782.3	68,682.8
Transportation equipment	0.4	1.6	1,346.4	24.2	11,571.6	25.8	12,917.9	39,807.1
Non-ferrous metal products	0.1	1.3	1,359.6	13.7	7,794.1	14.9	9,153.8	36,440.2
Electrical apparatus & supplies	--	0.7	603.9	4.1	1,885.5	4.8	2,489.4	8,960.4
Non-metallic mineral products	0.7	1.1	912.1	15.4	5,605.9	16.6	6,518.0	15,766.8
Products of petroleum & coal	--	0.2	173.0	1.0	530.5	1.2	703.5	5,759.5
Chemical products	0.2	0.9	846.8	3.9	1,363.9	4.8	2,210.7	14,372.6
Misc. manufacturing industries	0.2	0.8	732.8	7.1	2,747.1	7.9	3,479.8	9,869.7
Total manufacturing	12.1	34.0	29,022.2	339.5	127,611.6	373.5	156,633.7	683,649.3

Note: The value of materials used and census value added were not reported in *Postal Census of Manufactures 1906*.

Note: Data are for the calendar year 1905 on the basis of establishments employing 'five hands and over'. Totals may not add owing to rounding.

Part 1, Appendix 1, Table E2
Principal Statistics of Manufacturing – *Postal Census of Manufacturing 1906*

1948 SIC Major Group	Number of establishments (thousands)	Number of salary earners (thousands)	Salaries (thousands of dollars)	Number of wage earners (thousands)	Wages (thousands of dollars)	Total number of employees (thousands)	Wages and salaries (thousands of dollars)	Gross value of production (thousands of dollars)
Foods and beverages	5.3	5.5	4,298.8	50.1	14,000.5	55.6	18,299.3	190,896.9
Tobacco & tobacco products	0.2	0.6	493.9	7.1	2,349.6	7.6	2,843.5	15,274.9
Rubber products	--	0.2	212.6	1.0	406.7	1.2	619.3	3,061.2
Leather products	0.5	1.8	1,492.4	18.0	6,399.3	19.8	7,891.7	42,132.0
Textile products, ex. clothing	0.3	1.3	1,114.7	20.0	5,930.4	21.2	7,045.1	33,061.5
Clothing, textile and fur	1.8	4.0	3,049.7	40.5	12,580.9	44.5	15,630.6	59,698.9
Wood products	3.1	6.1	4,924.2	78.5	28,800.1	84.6	33,724.3	109,721.0
Paper products	0.1	1.0	964.7	10.1	3,720.2	11.1	4,684.9	18,761.5
Printing, publishing and allied industries	0.8	3.2	2,611.9	12.6	6,047.7	15.7	8,659.6	20,040.6
Iron and steel products	1.0	4.6	4,249.8	28.9	17,768.2	43.5	22,018.0	69,513.6
Transportation equipment	0.5	1.6	1,364.0	24.6	11,743.7	26.2	13,107.7	40,305.3
Non-ferrous metal products	0.2	1.3	1,357.4*	13.6*	7,786.5*	14.9	9,143.9*	37,892.7
Electrical apparatus & supplies	- -	0.7	605.4	4.1	1,893.5	4.8	2,498.9	8,996.9
Non-metallic mineral products	0.8	1.2	934.0	15.7	5,733.8	16.9	6,667.8	16,272.2
Products of petroleum & coal	- -	0.2	177.3	1.0	546.6	1.2	723.8	5,829.9
Chemical products	0.2	1.0	883.1	4.0	1,420.1	5.0	2,303.3	14,854.6
Misc. manufacturing industries	0.2	0.8	727.3*	7.0*	2,751.0	7.8*	3,478.3*	10,086.6
Total manufacturing	15.2	34.9	29,461.3	346.9	129,878.7	381.7	159,340.0	696,400.3

* Data are less than for data for establishments employing 'five hands and over'. See Part 1, Appendix 1, Table E1 and comments.

Note: The value of materials used and census value added were not reported in *Postal Census of Manufactures 1906*

Note: Data are for the calendar year 1905 on a full coverage basis. Totals may not add owing to rounding.

Part 1, Appendix 1, Table F1
Principal Statistics of Manufacturing – *Census of Canada 1911, III*
(Unadjusted for limited coverage)

1948 SIC Major Group	Number of establishments (thousands)	Number of salary earners (thousands)	Salaries (thousands of dollars)	Number of wage earners (thousands)	Wages (thousands of dollars)	Total number of employees (thousands)	Wages and salaries (thousands of dollars)	Value of materials used (thousands of dollars)	Census value added (thousands of dollars)	Gross value of production (thousands of dollars)
Foods and beverages	7.3	5.9	5,607.1	58.4	17,387.9	64.3	22,995.0	185,440.0	92,394.9	277,835.0
Tobacco & tobacco products	0.2	0.7	932.0	8.8	3,325.0	9.5	4,257.0	12,129.8	13,199.5	25,329.3
Rubber products	-	0.2	167.5	1.7	767.0	1.9	934.5	3,602.4	3,436.8	7,039.2
Leather products	0.4	1.9	2,041.9	22.7	9,644.4	24.6	11,686.3	34,394.2	28,456.2	62,850.4
Textile products, ex. clothing	0.3	1.2	1,225.0	24.5	8,429.7	25.7	9,654.7	29,231.4	22,018.9	51,250.3
Clothing, textile and fur	1.2	4.8	4,585.3	51.6	19,382.7	56.4	23,968.0	47,058.1	45,767.7	92,825.8
Wood products	5.0	6.9	6,487.3	106.9	37,971.8	113.7	44,459.1	90,760.6	86,814.8	177,575.4
Paper products	0.2	1.3	1,520.6	14.2	6,094.7	15.5	7,615.4	15,448.1	17,479.6	32,927.7
Printing, publishing and allied industries	0.6	3.8	3,572.9	13.3	7,007.3	17.1	10,580.1	7,494.4	17,931.6	25,426.0
Iron and steel products	1.0	6.2	6,607.7	59.6	31,638.3	65.8	38,246.0	65,677.2	75,176.4	140,853.6
Transportation equipment	0.7	2.9	2,688.9	40.4	22,007.6	43.3	24,696.5	36,800.3	39,958.3	76,758.7
Non-ferrous metal products	0.2	1.4	1,475.0	11.3	6,934.9	12.7	8,409.9	26,644.6	32,812.4	59,457.0
Electrical apparatus & supplies	0.1	0.8	786.5	5.6	2,748.3	6.4	3,534.8	6,345.2	8,829.4	15,174.7
Non-metallic mineral products	0.8	1.4	1,332.7	19.1	8,155.5	20.5	9,488.2	4,299.7	23,153.3	27,453.0
Products of petroleum & coal	-	0.2	250.5	1.7	910.1	1.9	1,160.7	5,258.6	4,241.1	9,499.7
Chemical products	0.3	1.6	1,641.2	8.6	3,576.9	10.3	5,218.0	14,210.6	15,637.0	29,847.6
Misc. manufacturing industries	0.2	0.9	927.8	8.1	3,737.3	9.0	4,665.0	6,257.2	9,426.8	15,684.0
Total manufacturing	18.4	50.0	41,849.8	456.6	189,719.4	498.5	231,569.3	591,052.5	536,734.9	1,127,787.4

Note: Data are for the calendar year 1910. Totals may not add owing to rounding.

Part 1, Appendix 1, Table F2
Principal Statistics of Manufacturing – Census of Canada 1911, III
(Adjusted to full coverage)

1948 SIC Major Group	Number of establishments (thousands)	Number of salary earners (thousands)	Salaries (thousands of dollars)	Number of wage earners (thousands)	Wages (thousands of dollars)	Total number of employees (thousands)	Wages and salaries (thousands of dollars)	Value of materials used [1] (thousands of dollars)	Census value added (thousands of dollars)	Gross value of production (thousands of dollars)
Foods and beverages	6.1	5,703.6	59.4	17,799.9	65.5	23,503.5	187,259.8	93,489.5	280,749.3
Tobacco & tobacco products	0.7	941.3	8.8	3,360.1	9.6	4,301.5	12,206.9	13,277.2	25,484.0
Rubber products	0.2	167.5	1.7	769.7	1.9	937.2	3,607.7	3,438.6	7,046.3
Leather products	1.9	2,071.2	23.2	9,836.6	25.1	11,907.8	35,045.3	29,022.9	64,068.3
Textile products, ex. clothing	1.2	1,239.4	24.7	8,481.8	25.9	9,721.2	29,454.1	22,219.7	51,673.8
Clothing, textile and fur	5.0	4,680.3	53.2	19,821.2	58.2	24,501.4	48,241.5	46,909.4	95,150.9
Wood products	7.0	6,571.4	110.1	38,679.4	117.1	45,250.8	93,181.7	89,170.0	182,351.7
Paper products	1.0	1,523.9	14.2	6,102.4	15.2	7,626.2	15,476.7	17,522.7	32,999.5
Printing, publishing and allied industries	3.9	3,683.9	14.0	7,272.7	17.9	10,956.7	7,813.4	18,672.7	26,486.1
Iron and steel products	6.3	6,679.4	60.5	32,081.1	66.8	38,760.6	66,749.7	76,490.0	143,239.8
Transportation equipment	2.9	2,727.6	40.3	22,391.3	43.2	25,118.9	37,553.5	40,846.3	78,399.7
Non-ferrous metal products	1.4	1,483.8	11.4	6,981.5	12.8	8,471.3	26,810.7	33,034.6	59,845.8
Electrical apparatus & supplies	0.8	788.9	5.7	2,759.3	6.4	3,548.2	6,383.6	8,851.7	15,235.4
Non-metallic mineral products	1.4	1,355.2	19.4	8,287.6	20.8	9,642.8	4,420.3	23,734.3	28,154.6
Products of petroleum & coal	0.2	252.6	1.7	941.8	1.9	1,194.4	5,292.6	4,260.9	9,553.5
Chemical products	1.7	1,712.9	9.0	3,758.1	10.7	5,471.0	14,749.8	16,237.2	30,987.0
Misc. manufacturing industries	0.9	949.2	8.3	3,855.2	9.3	4,804.4	6,480.7	9,761.7	16,242.4
Total manufacturing	42.8	42,532.0	465.7	193,185.7	508.4	235,717.7	600,728.2	546,939.5	1,147,667.1

1. Estimates of the value of materials used on a full coverage basis were obtained by applying the ratio of the value of materials used to gross value of production on the limited coverage basis (cf. Part 1, Appendix 1, Table F1) to the gross value of production on the full coverage basis.

Note: Data are for the calendar year 1910. Meaningful number of establishments data not available. Totals may not add owing to rounding.

Part 1, Appendix 1, Table G1
Principal Statistics of Manufacturing – *Postal Census of Manufactures 1916*
(Unadjusted for limited coverage on the basis of establishments with g.v.p. of $2,500 and greater)

1948 SIC Major Group	Number of establishments (thousands)	Number of salary earners (thousands)	Salaries (thousands of dollars)	Number of wage earners (thousands)	Wages (thousands of dollars)	Total number of employees (thousands)	Wages and salaries (thousands of dollars)	Value of materials used (thousands of dollars)	Census value added (thousands of dollars)	Gross value of production (thousands of dollars)
Foods and beverages	6.8	8.4	9,221.9	60.2	25,289.8	68.6	34,511.7	315,761.3	113,167.8	428,928.1
Tobacco & tobacco products	0.2	1.1	1,445.5	8.5	3,083.0	9.6	4,528.5	16,017.7	12,969.5	28,987.3
Rubber products	-	0.8	920.1	3.5	1,830.8	4.4	2,750.9	7,370.5	7,604.7	14,975.2
Leather products	0.5	2.3	2,540.3	20.3	10,306.1	22.6	12,846.4	45,201.5	25,835.1	71,036.6
Textile products, ex. clothing	0.2	1.1	1,405.3	24.5	8,823.3	25.5	10,228.6	33,162.2	22,326.7	55,489.0
Clothing, textile and fur	2.5	5.3	5,497.2	46.4	18,869.8	51.7	24,367.0	50,546.1	43,017.2	93,563.3
Wood products	3.2	4.5	5,265.8	59.6	26,775.4	64.1	32,041.1	54,151.4	61,470.8	115,622.1
Paper products	0.3	2.3	3,018.2	19.9	10,904.2	22.1	13,922.4	26,628.2	26,321.6	52,949.8
Printing, publishing and allied industries	1.1	4.4	4,537.1	16.0	10,556.4	20.4	15,093.4	9,485.1	24,161.7	33,646.7
Iron and steel products	1.6	7.2	8,689.7	66.1	33,822.2	73.3	42,511.9	69,537.7	75,302.9	144,840.7
Transportation equipment	0.7	3.1	3,207.0	40.8	22,090.4	43.8	25,297.5	46,089.1	40,694.2	86,783.3
Non-ferrous metal products	0.2	1.8	2,399.9	21.1	14,281.4	22.9	16,681.3	37,533.6	36,704.5	74,238.2
Electrical apparatus & supplies	0.1	1.2	1,410.0	7.2	3,697.2	8.4	5,107.1	9,413.6	9,149.9	18,563.5
Non-metallic mineral products	0.8	1.4	1,938.7	17.1	9,321.7	18.5	11,260.4	12,212.7	18,650.8	30,863.6
Products of petroleum & coal	-	0.4	413.9	4.7	2,652.0	5.1	3,066.0	10,353.6	5,975.3	16,328.9
Chemical products	0.4	2.7	3,121.6	15.4	7,605.0	18.0	10,726.6	24,035.8	25,349.2	49,385.0
Misc. manufacturing industries	0.4	1.1	1,328.9	7.3	3,744.0	8.4	5,073.0	6,409.2	8,558.9	14,968.1
Total manufacturing	19.1	49.0	56,361.0	438.5	213,652.7	487.5	270,013.7	773,909.4	557,260.9	1,331,170.3

Note: Data are for the calendar year 1915. Totals may not add owing to rounding.

Part 1, Appendix 1, Table G2
Principal Statistics of Manufacturing – *Postal Census of Manufactures 1916*
(Unadjusted for limited coverage on the basis of establishments employing 'five hands and over')

1948 SIC Major Group	Number of establishments (thousands)	Wages and salaries (thousands of dollars)	Value of materials used (thousands of dollars)	Census value added (thousands of dollars)	Gross value of production (thousands of dollars)
Foods and beverages	5.8	32,695.2	311,073.4	108,763.0	419,836.4
Tobacco & tobacco products	0.1	4,483.2	15,937.8	12,902.8	28,840.6
Rubber products	- -	2,750.4	7,370.4	7,603.9	14,974.2
Leather products	0.3	12,661.3	44,856.7	25,198.6	70,055.3
Textile products, ex. clothing	0.2	10,177.1	32,830.8	20,800.2	53,631.0
Clothing, textile and fur	1.6	23,473.5	49,233.2	41,042.5	90,275.7
Wood products	3.0	31,875.9	54,070.4	61,208.6	115,279.0
Paper products	0.2	13,546.3	26,571.4	26,084.4	52,655.8
Printing, publishing and allied industries	0.6	14,567.3	9,163.3	22,760.9	31,924.2
Iron and steel products	0.8	41,384.7	69,459.7	73,426.3	142,886.0
Transportation equipment	0.3	24,849.3	45,698.8	39,920.5	85,619.3
Non-ferrous metal products	0.2	16,535.8	36,910.0	36,547.9	73,457.9
Electrical apparatus & supplies	- -	5,092.4	9,344.4	9,103.6	18,448.0
Non-metallic mineral products	0.6	12,068.4	12,244.8	18,671.7	30,916.5
Products of petroleum & coal	- -	2,961.0	9,334.5	6,965.8	16,300.4
Chemical products	0.3	10,371.3	23,850.3	24,429.6	48,279.9
Misc. manufacturing industries	0.2	4,906.7	6,741.0	8,519.8	15,260.8
Total manufacturing	14.4	264,399.5	764,691.0	543,950.2	1,308,641.1

Note: Data with respect to number of employees and breakdown of wages and salaries not available. Data for the calendar year 1915. Totals may not add owing to rounding.

Part 2, Appendix, Numbers Employed in Manufacturing 1870-1915
(thousands)

Censuses of Manufacture	1870	1880	1890	1900 [1]	1900	1905 [1]	1905	1910 [1]	1910	1915 [2]	1915 [1]
Number of people employed in Manufacturing as per Part 1, Appendix 1	181.4	247.5	350.0	331.8	421.8	373.5	381.7	498.5	508.4	487.5	n.a.
Number of people employed in Construction as per tabulations connected with Part 1, Appendix 1.	5.9	6.5	16.6	4.9		5.7	7.0	10.3		15,757	n.a.

Censuses of Occupations	1871	1881	1891	1901	1911
Number of people in Manufacturing occupations as per Census of Canada 1870-71, II, T.XIII and Census of Canada 1921, IV, T.1	120.7	173.4	237.3	283.3	485.9
Number of people in Building Trades occupations as per Census of Canada 1870-71, II, T.XIII and Census of Canada 1921, IV, T.1	47.4	230.9	185.6	213.3	246.2

1. Data on the basis of industrial establishments employing 'five hands and over'.
2. Data on the basis of industrial establishments having a gross value of production of $2,500 and greater.

Part 3, Appendix 1, Table A
Capital Invested in Manufacturing
(thousands of dollars)

1948 SIC Major Group	Census of Canada 1870-1871 [1] Total capital invested	Census of Canada 1880-1881 [2] Total capital invested	Census of Canada 1891 [3] Land	Buildings	Machinery and tools	Working capital	Total capital invested
Foods and beverages	15,184.7	29,762.8	4,985.3	13,747.9	14,170.2	34,228.9	67,132.3
Tobacco and tobacco products	573.1	1,829.4	201.1	668.9	433.0	2,528.3	3,831.3
Rubber products	454.6	851.5	181.0	365.0	439.6	1,345.1	2,330.7
Leather products	6,584.8	14,265.8	1,131.7	3,395.5	2,393.0	11,968.9	18,889.1
Textile products, ex. clothing	4,528.1	10,725.7	1,392.5	5,433.9	11,627.3	11,482.5	29,936.2
Clothing, textile and fur	3,441.1	10,503.7	996.5	2,299.1	1,672.9	11,126.7	16,095.2
Wood products	20,518.8	34,604.3	8,574.3	9,975.6	16,426.1	39,157.2	74,133.2
Paper products	933.7	2,738.0	1,226.7	1,706.0	2,269.9	4,000.9	9,203.5
Printing, publishing and allied industries	2,557.3	5,619.8	426.9	1,356.4	4,141.6	4,534.9	10,459.7
Iron and steel products	10,434.8	25,270.6	4,569.1	8,494.9	12,589.3	23,889.2	49,542.5
Transportation equipment	3,083.3	7,104.4	1,567.4	3,354.7	2,157.0	6,367.7	13,446.9
Non-ferrous metal products	788.0	2,610.5	438.9	1,326.9	1,549.8	5,251.9	8,567.5
Electrical apparatus and supplies	–	–	37.5	68.6	411.6	1,045.7	1,563.3
Non-metallic mineral products	2,119.0	3,578.6	1,717.0	1,365.7	1,435.2	4,665.3	9,183.1
Products of petroleum and coal	624.9	1,812.7	63.2	363.3	523.0	1,030.8	1,980.3
Chemical products	1,814.1	4,344.4	538.4	1,193.6	1,088.3	4,248.1	7,068.4
Miscellaneous manufacturing industries	794.8	2,382.5	177.2	470.7	477.3	2,515.3	3,640.5
Total manufacturing	74,435.3	158,004.8	28,224.6	55,586.7	73,805.3	169,387.2	327,003.8

1. Data for 2 April 1871
2. Data for 4 April 1881
3. Data for 6 April 1891

Note: Totals may not add owing to rounding.

Part 3, Appendix 1, Table B
Capital Invested in Manufacturing
(thousands of dollars)

1948 SIC Major Group	Census of Canada 1901 [1]					Postal Census of Manufactures 1906 [2]			Postal Census of Manufactures 1906 [3]
	Land	Buildings	Machinery and tools	Working capital	Total capital invested	Land, buildings and plants	Working capital	Total capital invested	Total capital invested
Foods and beverages	4,489.4	17,144.7	16,143.0	41,349.8	79,126.8	64,115.0	54,438.3	118,553.3	116,963.6
Tobacco and tobacco products	139.3	778.4	527.2	5,802.6	7,247.5	1,805.0	8,823.7	10,628.7	10,575.4
Rubber products	49.1	211.4	259.9	1,003.6	1,524.0	1,018.4	486.7	1,505.1	1,494.3
Leather products	888.4	2,596.2	2,739.7	15,212.3	21,436.6	8,847.8	19,819.4	28,667.1	27,681.9
Textile products, ex. clothing	2,156.5	7,692.4	12,766.3	14,592.4	37,207.6	25,713.9	13,743.9	39,457.8	38,984.1
Clothing, textile and fur	1,067.3	2,870.2	2,773.7	18,605.6	25,316.8	12,393.3	26,646.1	39,039.4	38,020.6
Wood products	5,223.0	9,461.4	17,539.6	45,767.0	77,990.9	70,191.2	70,452.1	140,643.3	137,167.2
Paper products	1,495.7	4,839.0	8,972.6	7,685.3	22,992.6	20,083.4	17,340.3	37,423.7	37,412.1
Printing, publishing & allied industries	1,043.1	2,306.5	6,014.9	7,280.9	16,645.4	13,185.2	10,344.2	23,529.4	22,288.6
Iron and steel products	3,204.7	7,117.3	14,866.7	35,550.3	60,739.0	40,073.9	52,742.0	92,815.9	91,749.1
Transportation equipment	2,782.9	4,039.9	4,604.7	8,461.9	19,889.5	22,645.4	13,374.5	36,019.9	35,165.3
Non-ferrous metal products	1,011.0	2,845.1	5,024.9	5,801.5	14,682.4	68,655.8	26,913.2	95,569.1	95,584.8
Electrical apparatus and supplies	198.1	432.7	1,908.6	2,727.9	5,267.4	7,389.0	7,010.6	14,399.7	14,367.4
Non-metallic mineral products	775.2	729.3	1,271.6	6,934.6	9,710.8	25,522.9	9,377.7	34,900.6	34,344.3
Products of petroleum and coal	88.0	328.3	395.6	1,119.3	1,931.3	3,726.4	1,907.7	5,634.1	5,470.5
Chemical products	546.2	1,822.5	1,800.2	6,049.7	10,218.6	6,643.2	9,145.1	15,788.3	15,367.4
Misc. manufacturing industries	340.7	1,457.2	2,482.7	6,655.4	10,936.1	4,550.4	7,594.1	12,144.4	12,136.3
Total manufacturing	25,410.6	66,344.4	99,696.3	229,480.8	420,932.1	396,560.4	350,159.4	746,719.8	734,773.0

1. Data for 31 March 1901, 31 December 1900, or date most convenient to enumerate, on the basis of industrial establishments employing 'five hands or over'.
2. Data for 31 December 1905.
3. Data for 31 December 1905 on the basis of industrial establishments employing 'five hands and over'.

Note: Totals may not add owing to rounding.

Part 3, Appendix 1, Table C
Capital Invested in Manufacturing
(thousands of dollars)

1948 SIC Major Group	Census of Canada 1911 [1]			Postal Census of Manufactures 1916 [2]					Postal Census of Manufactures 1916 [3]
	Land buildings and plants	Working capital	Total capital invested	Land buildings and fixtures	Machinery and tools	Material in stock fuel etc.	Cash accounts and bills receivable etc.	Total	Total capital invested
Foods and beverages	85,114.0	93,584.7	178,698.7	106,427.9	45,808.2	57,206.6	45,293.3	254,736.0	248,883.4
Tobacco and tobacco products	3,592.8	18,067.1	21,659.9	3,350.2	1,717.8	12,049.0	5,949.9	23,066.9	22,999.6
Rubber products	1,476.8	3,657.1	5,133.8	4,263.6	2,983.1	3,748.5	2,580.9	13,576.2	13,575.6
Leather products	16,695.3	32,093.5	48,788.8	12,510.4	9,013.3	23,980.4	14,765.4	60,269.5	59,483.0
Textile products, ex. clothing	32,106.7	26,775.1	58,881.8	19,301.3	13,979.4	18,223.7	10,065.7	61,570.1	61,230.4
Clothing, textile and fur	19,850.2	34,850.7	54,700.8	13,975.6	8,041.5	25,314.1	21,667.6	68,998.8	66,748.7
Wood products	120,841.2	108,383.0	229,224.2	79,959.4	47,734.9	56,385.3	32,824.7	216,904.4	216,501.2
Paper products	40,008.0	23,412.2	63,420.3	79,389.7	36,197.4	20,623.5	13,310.2	149,520.8	149,413.3
Printing, publishing & allied industries	17,494.6	14,680.6	32,175.2	10,610.7	16,995.4	3,760.7	7,505.9	38,872.6	36,854.8
Iron and steel products	79,783.9	96,201.0	175,984.8	70,130.0	59,746.8	55,586.6	88,682.9	274,146.3	271,176.1
Transportation equipment	27,045.6	33,441.0	60,486.7	53,299.0	24,575.1	23,847.2	40,424.3	142,145.5	139,512.9
Non-ferrous metal products	34,570.5	18,478.5	53,049.0	78,496.1	43,675.8	21,028.3	13,465.1	156,665.2	157,088.5
Electrical apparatus & supplies	8,886.1	8,498.5	17,384.6	11,527.1	7,723.7	9,180.8	10,542.4	38,973.9	25,576.6
Non-metallic mineral products	28,708.5	19,822.6	48,531.1	68,159.0	16,544.7	10,552.7	8,739.2	103,995.6	103,245.3
Products of petroleum & coal	5,989.9	3,652.9	9,642.9	6,493.6	1,574.1	3,324.1	1,677.7	13,069.4	13,036.9
Chemical products	15,606.3	16,554.9	32,161.3	24,984.0	10,538.4	15,126.1	9,241.9	59,890.3	58,481.0
Misc. manufacturing industries	6,480.0	9,438.6	15,918.6	6,230.2	4,111.7	6,160.1	5,441.7	21,943.7	21,784.6
Total manufacturing	544,250.5	561,592.0	1,105,842.5	649,107.7	350,961.1	366,097.6	332,178.8	1,698,345.3	1,665,592.0

1. Data are for 31 December 1910 on the basis of industrial establishments employing 'five hands and over'.
2. Data are for 31 December 1915 on the basis of industrial establishments having a gross value of production of $2500 and greater.
3. Data are for 31 December 1915 on the basis of industrial establishments employing 'five hands and over'.

Note: Totals may not add owing to rounding.

Table 1 – Principal Statistics of "Gas works" and "Gas, lighting and heating" Industries
Addition to "Products of Petroleum and Coal Major Group"

Year	Name of Industry in Basic Source Data	Number of Establishments	Total Number of Employers	Supervisory and Office Employees	Production Workers	Total Salaries and Wages ($'000's)	Supervisory and Office Employees ($'000's)	Production Workers ($'000's)	Gross Value of Production	Cost of Materials Used	Census Value Added
1870	Gas works	23	299			131			750	265	485
1880	Gas works	36	512			239			1,173	319	854
1890	Gas works	49	1,164			497			2,797	772	2,025
1900	Gas, lighting and heating (limited coverage of five employees and over)	27	961	105	856	504	98	406	2,327	752	1,575
	(adjusted for limited coverage)		1,014	111	903	538	105	433	2,432	786	1,646
1905	Gas,lighting and heating (limited coverage of five employees and over)	31	951	165	786	620	154	466	2,169	n.a.	n.a.
	(full coverage basis)	39	969	169	800	629	157	472	2,194	n.a.	n.a.
1910	Gas, lighting and heating (limited coverage of five employees and over)	31	1,519	172	1,347	949	163	786	4,006	908	3,098
	(adjusted for limited coverage)		1,547	176	1,371	962	166	796	4,054	919	3,135
1915	Gas, lighting and heating (limited coverage of five employees and over)	34				1,112			4,446	1,550	2,896
1915	Gas, lighting and heating (limited coverage of gmp of $2500 and more)	35	1,614	181	1,433	1,114	169	945	4,451	1,553	2,898

Fixed Capital Stock Project, Central Research and Development Staff, Dominion Bureau of Statistics, Ottawa, August, 1961.

Table 2 – Capital invested in "Gas works" and "Gas, lighting and heating"
(thousands of $'s)

Year	Name of Industry in Basic Source Data	Land	Buildings	Machinery and Tools	Working Capital	Total Capital Invested
1870	Gas works.............................					2,481
1880	Gas works.............................					5,358
1890	Gas works.............................	1,851	2,171	3,772	5,325	13,119
1900	Gas, lighting and heating (limited coverage of five employees and over).........	552	1,141	3,814	2,285	7,692
1905	Gas, lighting and heating (full coverage basis)............. (limited coverage of five employees and over)............		8,671		1,612	10,283
						10,142
1910	Gas, lighting and heating (limited coverage of five employees and over)............		12,308		1,875	14,183
1915	Gas, lighting and heating (limited coverage of gnp of $2500 and more)............... (limited coverage of five hands and over)	7,042		8,299	1,268*	16,609
						16,598

* Material in stock, fuel etc.: 841; Cash accounts and bills receivable, etc.: 427; Total: 1,268

Fixed Capital Stocks Project, Central Research and Development Staff, Dominion Bureau of Statistics, Ottawa, August, 1961.

The Rymes manuscript ends here and the regular text of the project carries on.

In the work of this project, the assignments of the 200 to 250 industry categories of the censuses of manufactures to the 17 major industry groups of the 1948 classification were replicated so that those of us in the project knew just what had been done in the DBS (Rymes) classification. Our data for base years for the seventeen industry groups differ moderately but not in a major way from the HSC data noted above. A comparison of our data, labelled "project" data and "DBS data" (HSC) on gross value of product from base years is given in Table 4.9. Data entries have been made only if the project and DBS entries differed; otherwise an asterisk is used if the entries are the same.

It will be noted that differences between the project estimates and DBS estimates are most common in 1900 and 1910; they are very few for the years 1870, 1880 and 1890; they apply to those industrial groups in which custom and repair work is significant for the years 1917 to 1926. The basis of the DBS tabulation of data for 1870, 1880, 1890, 1900 and 1910 are given in the DBS (Rymes) memo reproduced above. We note only the basis of the larger differences between the DBS and project estimates at this point.

These larger differences pertain to the data for 1900, 1910 and eight categories of the 1917-26 data. (Although called "larger" the differences are actually relatively small.) The differences for 1900 are accounted for by the fact that the census of manufactures in 1900 excluded businesses with fewer than 5 employees (with the exception of butter and cheese factories and brick and tile yards) and it was necessary to make estimates for the excluded businesses if our data were to be comprehensive. Fortunately, it was possible to separate the 1890-91 census returns of those businesses having 5 or more employees from those having less than 5 employees. In general, DBS adjusted upward, on an industry by industry basis, the 1900 data for the firms having 5 or more employees in the proportion that the 1890 data for firms with less than 5 bore to the data for firms with 5 or more employees.

The project used a different method of adjusting the 1900 census, based on the belief that the proportions of business and employees in concerns having less than 5 employees would be, in general, smaller than the same proportions in 1890, a belief supported by data for 1905 collected in the postal census of manufactures of 1905. The comparative data for 1890 and 1905 are given in the Table 4.10. Rymes believes that there was under-enumeration of business units with less than 5 employees in 1905. However, even if one allows generously for that circumstance, it looks as if the proportion of gross value of product produced by business units with less than 5 employees fell between 1890 and 1905.

Accordingly the project developed its own method of adjusting some of the data for 1900 and 1910 in order to have estimates that covered business units of all sizes. This work was done by David Jones formerly of DBS.

It should be noted that the undercoverage of industry in 1910 was much less than in 1900: in 1900 only butter and cheese factories and brick and tile yards were fully enumerated, i.e. exempted from the general practice of omitting businesses with less than 5 employees; in 1910, the fully enumerated industries, i.e., where businesses of all sizes were covered, included butter and cheese factories, brick and tile works, flour and grist mills, fish curing plants, log products, lime kilns and electric light and power plants — the last industry was removed from manufacturing. Hence much less adjustment for undercoverage was required in 1910 than in 1900.

Table 4.9. Checklist of Project and DBS Estimates of GVP, Base Years 1870, 1880, 1890, 1900, 1910, 1917–26 (thousands of dollars)

		1870	1880	1890	1900	1910	1917	1918	1919
Food & beverages	Project	60,847	*	*	159,402	288,881	*	*	*
	DBS	63,383	*	*	153,854	280,749	*	*	*
Tobacco & tobacco products	Project	*	*	*	8,574	18,418	*	*	37,413
	DBS	*	*	*	11,959	25,484	*	*	46,931
Rubber products	Project	*	*	*	4,728	11,063	*	*	*
	DBS	*	*	*	1,589	7,046	*	*	*
Leather products	Project	*	*	*	43,059	74,543	115,729	105,787	142,367
	DBS	*	*	*	52,435	64,068	103,952	93,118	126,738
Textiles, ex. clothing	Project	*	*	24,705	*	*	106,135	*	*
	DBS	*	*	26,043	*	*	105,650	*	*
Clothing, textile & fur	Project	*	*	45,189	50,264	121,123	201,125	239,866	285,576
	DBS	*	*	43,851	54,191	95,151	148,571	171,083	205,425
Wood products	Project	*	*	*	88,238	185,093	*	*	262,439
	DBS	*	*	*	90,470	182,352	*	*	322,211
Paper products	Project	*	*	*	11,413	31,644	57,513	*	*
	DBS	*	*	*	12,420	32,999	57,355	*	*
Printing, publishing & allied	Project	*	*	*	*	*	*	*	*
	DBS	*	*	*	*	*	*	*	*
Iron & steel products	Project	24,675	33,937	55,492	60,014	163,027	474,512	522,776	380,135
	DBS	24,914	34,183	55,871	51,983	143,240	448,576	496,305	351,103
Transportation equipment	Project	10,128	14,513	23,445	25,199	71,417	205,896	251,894	265,370
	DBS	9,889	14,267	23,345	27,164	78,400	197,795	240,871	251,739
Non-ferrous metal products	Project	*	*	*	14,408	60,049	*	*	*
	DBS	*	*	*	12,785	59,845	*	*	*
Electrical apparatus & supplies	Project	—	—	*	*	*	*	*	*
	DBS	—	—	*	*	*	*	*	*
Non-metallic & mineral products	Project	*	*	*	*	*	*	*	*
	DBS	*	*	*	*	*	*	*	*
Petroleum & coal products	Project	3,095	4,050	4,347	4,417	9,553	48,365	59,070	66,170
	DBS	3,845	5,223	4,952	6,589	13,608	59,057	67,483	77,514
Chemical products	Project	*	*	*	*	*	*	*	*
	DBS	*	*	*	*	*	*	*	*
Miscellaneous industries	Project	*	*	6,570	7,642	*	30,522	38,296	44,387
	DBS	*	*	6,191	7,902	*	29,195	37,302	43,334
Total manufacturing	Project	213,892	303,491	449,478	549,894	1,203,588	2,857,692	3,276,666	3,211,619
	DBS	217,176	304,663	449,982	555,876	1,151,722	2,768,046	3,165,139	3,152,237

Table 4.9. (continued)

		1920	1921	1922	1923	1924	1925	1926
Food & beverages	Project	*	*	*	*	*	*	*
	DBS	*	*	*	*	*	*	*
Tobacco & tobacco products	Project	44,917	37,608	36,196	34,346	34,355	32,547	35,029
	DBS	53,892	45,785	43,092	40,648	40,449	38,776	41,331
Rubber products	Project	*	*	*	*	*	*	*
	DBS	*	*	*	*	*	*	*
Leather products	Project	144,931	96,130	98,283	98,611	94,462	93,198	102,574
	DBS	129,788	82,751	84,034	84,942	81,515	80,776	90,191
Textiles, ex. clothing	Project	*	*	*	*	*	*	*
	DBS	*	*	*	*	*	*	*
Clothing, textile & fur	Project	315,656	237,613	226,644	233,762	222,234	234,109	257,905
	DBS	239,352	174,191	172,547	180,640	178,112	189,654	213,166
Wood products	Project	*	*	*	*	*	*	*
	DBS	*	*	*	*	*	*	*
Paper products	Project	*	*	*	*	*	*	*
	DBS	*	*	*	*	*	*	*
Printing, publishing & allied	Project	*	*	*	*	*	*	*
	DBS	*	*	*	*	*	*	*
Iron & steel products	Project	479,408	293,673	229,463	306,011	250,732	264,555	319,065
	DBS	449,221	267,405	206,519	283,207	230,133	245,176	300,546
Transportation equipment	Project	301,823	176,556	165,158	230,638	196,026	226,188	278,750
	DBS	285,230	158,050	144,706	207,310	169,672	196,366	244,185
Non-ferrous metal products	Project	*	*	*	*	*	*	*
	DBS	*	*	*	*	*	*	*
Electrical apparatus & supplies	Project	*	*	*	*	*	*	*
	DBS	*	*	*	*	*	*	*
Non-metallic & mineral products	Project	*	*	*	*	*	*	*
	DBS	*	*	*	*	*	*	*
Petroleum & coal products	Project	78,913	68,537	65,166	63,348	62,487	64,405	86,458
	DBS	94,623	87,309	84,255	82,953	79,589	82,279	104,723
Chemical products	Project	*	*	*	*	*	*	*
	DBS	*	*	*	*	*	*	*
Miscellaneous industries	Project	54,788	41,542	39,590	41,913	35,608	38,164	42,661
	DBS	43,296	32,635	31,453	33,557	27,806	30,102	33,901
Total manufacturing	Project	3,794,431	2,594,813	2,483,110	2,785,716	2,695,278	2,898,522	3,184,578
	DBS	3,667,579	2,491,280	2,389,216	2,690,344	2,606,650	2,808,485	3,090,179

Note: those entries that have a * are the same for both the Project and DBS

Table 4.10

Ratio of Total Gross Value of Product
for All Manufacturing Units to Gross Value of Product
of those Business Units with Less Than 5 Employees

Industry	1900 based on 1890	1905
Food and Beverages	1.124	1.004
Tobacco and Tobacco Products	1.013	1.006
Rubber Products	1.009	1.005
Leather Products	1.510	1.023
Textile excl. clothing	1.121	1.007
Clothing, textile and fur	1.327	1.024
Wood Products	1.192	1.031
Paper Products	1.009	1.001
Printing, Publishing and Allied	1.079	1.048
Iron and Steel Products	1.124	1.012
Transportation Equipment	1.202	1.013
Non-ferrous Metal Products	1.084	1.040
Electrical Apparatus and Supplies	1.080	1.004
Non-metallic Mineral Products	1.159	1.032
Products of Petroleum and Coal	1.181	1.012
Chemical Products	1.243	1.034
Miscellaneous Manufacturing Industries	1.112	1.017
Total Manufacturing	1.179	1.019

**Basis of Estimation of Aggregate GVP,
all Employed Persons, 1900 and 1910**
(David Jones Estimates)

1. Food and Beverages

The food and beverage industry group gross value of product figures were changed from the DBS (*Historical Statistics*) figures for 1900 at the level of 5 component (3-digit level) industries, *viz.*, (i) bread, biscuits and confectionary, (ii) flour and grist mills, (iii) slaughtering and meatpacking, (iv) canned and cured fish, (v) alcoholic beverages, and for 1910 at the level of 2 component industries (i) bread, biscuits and confectionary and (ii) alcoholic beverages. We deal with these in turn.

(i) Bread, biscuit and confectionery

The adjustment on undercoverage for this industry was done on the basis of the relationship between the numbers reported in the occupations of this industry from the occupational data of the individual censuses to the numbers of persons employed in the industry as reported in the census of manufactures. David Jones found that the numbers reported in the occupational data corresponded quite well with the numbers reported in the census of manufactures in the full enumerated years of 1890, 1920 and 1930. He then inferred the numbers employed in manufacturing in 1900 as follows.

The gainfully occupied in this industry were mainly "bakers" and "biscuit and confectionery" makers; the occupational data of the censuses from 1910 and especially 1920 onward recorded smaller numbers of ancillary workers such as labourers, managers, etc. The following data show how the calculations were made. The separate industrial and occupational recorded data for 1890, 1900 and 1910 (with minor inferred data for auxiliary workers in 1890 and 1900) are given in Table 4.11.

Table 4.11

Census of Manufactures Data

	1890			1900	1910
	Businesses With < 5 Employees	Businesses With 5 + Employees	All Busi- nesses	Businesses With 5 + Employees	Businesses With 5 + Employees
Employees, No.	2,747	4296	7,043	6,831	10,003
GVP per employee	$2,573	$1,947		$1,704	$2,556
No. of establishments	1,667	269	1,936	258	

Occupational Census Data (from each census as recorded)

	1890	1900	1910
No. of bakers	5161	6370	8731
No. of biscuit etc. makers	1499	2517	4920
No. of ancillary personnel	383*(inferred)	609**(inferred)	1569
Total employed	7043	9496	15220

Source: Census "occupations" 1911 Census, Table 1 to 4.

*The auxiliary persons among the gainfully occupied in 1890 are inferred from the difference between the number employed in the census of manufactures and the numbers of bakers and biscuit makers of the occupational census.
**The auxiliary persons in 1900 are inferred by assuming that the number of auxiliary employees increase from 1890 to 1900 in proportion to the numbers employed in businesses with 5 or more employees, i.e. by the amount (6831 ÷ 4296) x 383 = 609. The numbers employed in 1910 are taken as being equal to the total numbers reported employed.

From the data of Table 4.11, the numbers employed in establishments of less than 5 employees in 1900 and 1910 were calculated from the total numbers gainfully occupied less the numbers employed in establishments with 5 or more employed. This gave a number of gainfully occupied in establishments with less than 5 employees of 2,665 persons in 1900 and 5,217 persons in 1910. It was necessary also to calculate a GVP per worker in establishments with less than 5 employees in each of 1900 and 1910. The available data were GVP per worker for establishments with 5 employed persons or more in 1890, 1900 and 1910, and GVP per worker for establishments with less than 5 employees in 1890. To obtain an estimate of GVP per worker in establishments with less than 5 employees in each of 1900 and 1910 it was assumed that the ratio of GVP per worker for these small establishments (< 5 employees) bore the same relationship to GVP per worker in the establishments with more than 5 employees as in 1890.

The result of these procedures are illustrated in Table 4.12.

Table 4.12. Aggregate GVP, Establishments of All Sizes

	1890		
	< 5 employees	> 5 employees	All establishments
Number employed	2,747	4,296	7,043
GVP, $000	6,799	8,364	15,433
GVP per employee	2,573	1,947	-------

	1900		
	< 5 employees	> 5 employees	All establishments
Number employed	(2,665)	6,831	9,496
GVP, $000	(6,002)	11,640	(17,642)
GVP per employee	(2,252)	1,704	-------

	1910		
	< 5 employees	> 5 employees	All establishments
Number employed	(5,217)	10,003	15,220
GVP, $000	(17,623)	25,567	(43,190)
GVP per employee	(3,378)	2,556	-------

Note: figures in brackets for 1900 and 1910 are inferred figures derived in the manner described above.

(ii) Flour and grist mills

Flour and grist mills were fully covered in 1910; it was necessary to make an adjustment only for 1900. David Jones determined that DBS (Rymes) had assumed that these mills were fully covered in 1900 (see Rymes memo, Part 1, Appendix 1, Table D2 "Notes") and so had made no adjustment for mills employing less than 5 employees; he determined, in accordance with the census statements, that mills employing less than 5 persons had not been covered.

There were three parts to the estimation procedure for output of mills employing less than 5 employees in 1900. First, an estimate was made of the number of own account (i.e. self-employed) millers in each of 1890 and 1900: the number of own accounts in 1900 was estimated by subtracting the number of "millers" reported as being employed on wages, in the census of persons, from the number reported as being gainfully occupied in the same census; since data on those employed on wage or salary were not collected in the census of persons in 1890, an estimate of the number of self-employed millers was made by assuming that the proportion of "millers" that were self-employed (own accounts) within the occupational group "millers" in 1890 was the same as in 1900 — this procedure yielded a figure of 1,828 self-employed millers in 1890 which, reasonably, was less than the number of establishments employing less than 5 persons in 1890 reported at 2,320 since some of the latter would be incorporated. Second, the price of "strong bakers flour" in each of 1890 and 1900 was obtained from the Department of Labour *Wholesale Prices 1890-1909* (as reported in Michell). Third, the gross value of production of establishments employing less than 5 persons in 1890 was projected to 1900 on a combined (multiplied) index of the numbers of self-employed and the price of flour. The actual data follow.

	1890	1900
No. of self employed	1828	1592
Index of self employed	100	87.09
Index of flour price, strong bakers, 1890-99=100	119.2	90.0
Index flour price 1890=100	100	75.5
Combined index	100	65.753
GVP (establishments <5) $000	21,161	13,914

(iii) Slaughtering and meatpacking

It was only necessary to make an adjustment for 1900; the DBS (Rymes) adjustment for 1910 was accepted.

David Jones note is that the number of establishments (all size groups) was projected forward from 1890 on the trend of the number of self-employed. In the case of this particular industry it looks to me as if he obtained the number of establishments reported in each of the 1890 and 1917 censuses, both of which had full coverage, and then calculated the number of establishments of all sizes in 1900 and 1910 by linear interpolation between 1890 and 1917. (I give his numbers for the projection below). He then calculated the number of establishments employing less than 5 persons in 1900 by subtracting the number of establishments employing more than 5 employees as reported in the 1900 census. The gross value of product per establishment in establishments having less than 5 employees in 1890 was projected to 1900 on the basis of an index of meat prices (Department of Labour Canada, *Wholesale Prices, 1890-1909*, index animals and meats, and later annual publications *Wholesale Prices*). The gross value of product in 1900 was then the product of this projected GVP for small establishments (<5 employees) times the number of establishments. The results are summarized in the following figures, copied from Jones' worksheets.

	1890	1900	1910	1917
Full coverage number of establishments	528	(364)	(200)	86
Less establishments employing 5 or more persons	62	57	80	--
No. of establishments employing less than 5 persons	466	(307)	(120)	--
Price index animals and meats 1890-1899=100	111.2	103.4	163.6	--
Gross value of product				
establishments < 5 employees $000	1869	(1,145)	(708)	--

Note: bracketed figures are estimates.

The figure for adjustment for establishments with less than 5 employees in 1900 was then $1,145 thousand. This is much less than would be obtained by the DBS method which was to adjust the 1900 figure for GVP as follows.

$$\text{GVP all establishments } 1900 \quad = \quad \frac{\text{GVP all establishments } 1890}{\text{GVP establishments 5 or more employees } 1890}$$

$$x \quad \text{GVP establishments 5 or more employees } 1900$$

Yet the adjusted figure by our method seems to be amply high in comparison with the change in the numbers of gainfully occupied in the occupational census. Compare:

	1890	1900
GVP full coverage ($000)	7,133	23,363
Numbers gainfully occupied		
Butchers (occupational census)	7,288	9,889
Canners and curers, meat	205	677
Meat and fruit canners and preservers	294	--
Fruit and vegetable canners only	--	318

(iv) Canned and cured fish

This industry was fully covered in 1910; it remained only to make an estimate for 1900. Rymes had not adjusted it at all (see Rymes memo Part I, Appendix 1, Table D2, "Notes".)

The method used was almost identical with that for slaughtering and meatpacking with one exception. Since the census of manufactures of 1910 obtained a full count of all establishments, the estimate of the number of establishments of all sizes in 1900 was made by straight line interpolation between 1890 and 1910: otherwise the rest of the procedure is exactly similar in nature to that for slaughtering and meatpacking. The price index used was that for dried codfish.

(v) Alcoholic beverages

Alcoholic beverages were in two parts:

(a) Spirits. The coverage was complete in 1900 and census values were used: they were valued before the excise tax, which is treated as an indirect tax. In 1910, the census values included the excise tax which had to be subtracted. The excise taxes were obtained from internal revenue reports which were for fiscal year taxes. The fiscal year ended March 31 at that time: the excise tax for calendar 1910 was estimated by weighting the data for the fiscal year ended March 31, 1911 at 0.75 and that for fiscal 1910 at 0.25.

(b) Breweries. The GVP in the case of breweries should include the malt tax since it was added into the cost of materials because it was applied at a stage before the brewery production. The malt tax was included in the GVP reported in 1910 but was explicitly excluded in 1900 and had to be added in. It was obtained from internal revenue reports adjusted to a calendar year basis in the manner described for "spirits". (Incidentally, in the calculation of Gross Domestic Product at factor cost, the malt tax is included in the cost of materials and hence offsets its inclusion in GVP.) The malt tax for the calendar year 1900 was calculated at $950,805.

2. Tobacco and Tobacco Products

1900: The DBS census of manufactures figure included excise taxes on tobacco in Gross Value of Product from 1900 onward. These excise taxes were levied at different levels. For all years from 1871 onward, there were excise taxes collected at the finished manufactures level. From the 1900 census onward there was also a raw leaf tax levied on the raw materials of the manufactures. These excise taxes are reported in detail in internal revenue reports. After much investigation, it was decided that excise taxes were included in gross value of product as reported for 1900; it was further decided that excise taxes, including raw leaf tobacco tax were included in (and pretty well accounted for) in the category "general" or "other" which were reported in "miscellaneous" expenses for 1900 in the amount of $3,384,559. The 1900 GVP excluding taxes was estimated by subtracting this last figure from adjusted GVP (Rymes) for tobacco in 1900. This gives us in thousands of dollars, $11,959.0 - 3,384.6 \approx \$8,574$ thousand.

1910: It was judged that the 1910 GVP figure included all taxes: raw leaf tax plus all excise taxes on manufactures (possibly including a very small amount for licence fees). The tax data came from internal revenue records.

The 1910 GVP excluding excise taxes then is derived as follows (thousands of dollars):

Census GVP adjusted (Rymes)	25,484
Less all excise taxes (calendar year basis)	7,066
GVP excluding excise taxes	$18,418

3. Rubber Products

The rubber products in both 1900 and 1910 were changed from the adjusted census values by the addition of an estimate of that portion of boot and shoe production (assigned to the leather industry by the *1948 S.I.C.*) which comprised rubber footwear which was classified with rubber products; in Censuses before 1917 the census reported boots and shoes on a single industry assignment.

An estimate of the proportion of the category boots and shoes to be transferred to rubber products was made by assuming that the proportion would be the same as in the closest U.S. census of manufactures. In 1899, 12.5% of U.S. production of boots and shoes (and custom and repair) was made up of rubber footwear; it was assumed that the Canadian proportion was the same, giving

Rubber Products (Rymes adjusted in $000)   1,589 + (.125 x 25,109) = $4,728.

In 1909 the U.S. proportion was estimated at 9.3 percent (custom and repair was not reported in 1909 and it was assumed that it bore the same ratio to non-rubber factory production as in 1900).

This resulted in an estimate for 1910 of:

Rubber Products (Rymes adjusted in $000)   7,046 + (.093 x 43,195) = $11,063.

4. Leather Products

Adjustments to Rymes adjusted output included adjustments to the following components of leather products: (i) tanneries; (ii) harness and saddlery; and (iii) boots and shoes. Dave Jones calculations of adjustments for each of these items replaced the Rymes adjustments. The adjustments were as follows.

(i) Tanneries: The adjustment for the tanneries was made on the basis of the gainfully occupied (census of population) and numbers employed (census of manufactures) in the manner described for the category "bread biscuits and confectionery". The reader is referred to the text on the latter group for the method; only summary data are given here.

	1890	1900	1910
Estimate of number of self-employed	189	136	152
Price of leather (base 1890-99=100)	94.9	111.7	122.9
(From Department of Labour, *Wholesale Prices*)			
Gross value of product, establishments			
less than 5 employees, ($000)	2,644	2,126	2,612
(Replaces Rymes adjustment which was, $000)		(2,268)	(545)

(ii) "Harness and saddlery" was handled just like the tanneries. The relevant data for the adjustment of harness and saddlery are:

	1890	1900	1910
Number of own-accounts			
(Gainfully occupied less wage earners)	1,648	1,721	1,775
Price index, harness (1890-99=100)	96.0	110.0	130.7
Gross value of product, establishments			
less than 5 employees ($000)	2,644	3,162	3,878
(Replaces estimated Rymes adjustment			
which was, $000)		(6,745)	(545)

(iii) Boots and shoes: Jones identifies establishments with less than 5 employees with boot and shoe repair. The boot and shoe repair industry was not covered in the 1900 or 1910 census of manufactures, was only partly covered in the 1917-1921 census of manufactures (in the hand trades) and was not covered at all from 1923 onward.

The method used was the same, in principle with "Harness and saddlery" and tanneries but there was a twist. The number of self-employed for 1890 was estimated from the census of manufactures by assuming that there was one self-employed for each establishment having less than 5 employees and the total number of employees in the same establishments (including the self-employed themselves) was obtained from the same census. (It will be noted that most establishments were single person businesses.) The number of self-employed for each of 1900, 1910, 1920 and 1930 was estimated by subtracting the numbers of wage (and salary) earners from the numbers gainfully occupied as reported in the census of occupations, taken as part of the census of persons in these census years. The number of gainfully occupied in 1930 was taken as the number of gainfully occupied reported in the boot and shoe repair industry (industry classification) in the census of persons. This yielded a number of self-employed as follows for all census years and a number gainfully occupied for 1890 and 1930 as follows.

	1890	1900	1910	1920	1930
Self-employed (000's)	5,129	5,112	5,000	5,457	5,949
Gainfully occupied	6,410				7,536

For 1890 and 1930 the ratios of the gainfully occupied to the number of self-employed in this custom and repair industry (identified with establishments with less than 5 employees) were 1.25 for 1890 and 1.33 for 1930. Similar ratios were calculated from the census of industry data for 1917 to 1921 (boot and shoe repair) by dividing the numbers employed in the industry by the numbers of establishments which were taken as measures of the numbers of self-employed. These ratios were as follows (with interpolations as given in brackets for 1900 and 1910 and for 1922 to 1926).

Ratios Gainfully Occupied to Self-Employed

1890	1900	1910	1917	1918	1919	1920
1.25	(1.26)	(1.27)	1.29	1.24	1.31	1.23

1921	1922	1923	1924	1925	1926	1930
1.29	(1.29)	(1.30)	(1.30)	(1.31)	(1.31)	1.33

The numbers of gainfully occupied were then calculated by multiplying these ratios of gainfully occupied to numbers of self employed by the estimated number of self employed to obtain the following.

	1890	1900	1910	1920	1930
Numbers of gainfully occupied, custom and repair shoemaking	1,648	6,441	6,350	6,712	7,536

The next step was to obtain a gross value of product per employee for each of these years.

This was done in 2 steps. Gross value of product per employee was available in 1890 (establishments employing < 5) in 1920 and in 1930 from the census of industry (hand trades, boot and shoe, custom and repair). Next an index of average earnings per worker for 1890, 1900, 1910 and 1920 was prepared: for census years 1900, 1910 and 1920 the average earnings were obtained from wage earner data, boot and shoe activity, of the population census; since this datum was not collected in 1890, the earnings of the latter year were linked to 1900 by the formula noted next below.

$$\text{average earnings } 1890 = \frac{\text{Mfg census average earnings} \geq 5 \text{ employees group } 1890}{\text{Mfg census average earnings} \geq 5 \text{ employees group } 1900}$$

$$\text{x   average earnings } 1900 \text{ (population census)}.$$

These calculations yield the following result.

	1890	1900	1910	1920	1930
Gross value of product worker per ($)	980			2,256	1,371
Average earnings per worker	(296)	330	496	826	782
Index of average earnings per worker 1890=1.00	1.00	1.115	1.676	2.791	2.642
GVP per worker deflated by wage index	980	(923)	(865)	808	
GVP per worker in current $ (=(3)x(4))	980	1,029	1,450	2,256	
Number gainfully occupied	6,410	6,441	6,350	6,712	
Aggregate GVP ($000)	6,284	6,628	9,209	15,143	

The values of GVP measured in a sort of wage unit in line 4 for 1900 and 1910 are obtained by linear interpolation between 1890 and 1920.

Aggregate GVP for custom and repair is then obtained by multiplying the numbers of gainfully occupied by GVP per gainfully occupied person.

5. Textile Products (ex Clothing)

Rymes adjustment used.

6. Clothing, Textile and Fur

This group proved difficult because different methods of estimation yielded substantially different results. There were only two groups of manufacturing activities in 1890 in which there were substantial numbers employed in establishments with less than 5 employees: they were (i) tailors and clothiers; and (ii) dressmakers and milliners. For each of these Jones used two methods of estimation of the uncovered gross value of product for each of 1900 and 1910. He then averaged the two estimates for each year to obtain the first estimate.

Method 1. The first method involved projecting forward from the 1890 census of industry values in accordance with an estimate of the numbers of self employed and price indexes of textile goods. The numbers of self-employed in 1900 and 1910 were estimated from population census data on gainfully occupied persons (and earnings from wages) as the residuals of the numbers gainfully occupied less the numbers employed on wage or salary. In 1891, the numbers of gainfully occupied persons were also obtained in the census of persons, but wage earner data were not collected in that year in the census of persons. An estimate of the numbers of self-employed for each of tailors, seamstresses, dressmakers and milliners was obtained by assuming that the ratios of the number of self-employed to the numbers gainfully occupied was the same, in each case, as in 1900; the tailors were identified with the manufacturing industry "tailors and clothiers" and the three other groups with "dressmaking and millinery".

The data for the industry tailors and clothiers are:

	1890	1900	1910
Number of self-employed tailors	1,796	2,097	5,481
Index of number of self-employed	100	116.8	305.2
Price index, woollen yarn;			
1890-1899=100 (Dept. of Labour)	101.4	93.7	118.9
Price index, woollen yarn; 1890=100	100	92.41	117.26
Combined index, self-employed			
and prices	100	107.9	357.88
GVP tailoring establishments			
employing < 5 employees ($000)	3,979	4,293	14,240

(The 1890 GVP is from the 1890 census of manufactures)

The data for dressmaking and millinery are:

	1890	1900	1910
Number of self-employed female			
dressmakers and milliners	15,747	15,208	19,485
Index of number of self-employed	100	96.6	123.7
Price index, cottons; 1890-99=100	117.2	107.6	147.8
Price index, cottons; 1890=100	100	91.81	126.1
Combined index	100	88.68	156.0
GVP dressmaking & millinery			
small establishments < 5 ($000)	6,180	5,479	9,639

The 1890 GVP figures in each case is that for businesses employing less than 5 persons (from the census of manufacturing); the 1900 and 1910 GVP estimates are obtained by projecting the 1890 figures to those years on the bases of the combined indexes given above.

Method 2. The second method involved using 1931 data on gainfully employed in the custom, tailoring and dressmaking industry and, in a sense, casting backwards to 1900 and 1910 to get 1900, 1910 (and also 1920) values as follows.

The numbers gainfully occupied in the custom and repair industry in 1930 (according to the industrial distribution of the gainfully occupied in the 1931 population census) in custom tailoring, dressmaking and millinery were 7,795 males and 11,624 females (Census, 1931, Vol. VII, *Occupations and Industries,* p. 676-Table 56). The former figure was taken as representing the number employed in men's custom tailoring and repair, the latter figure as representing the numbers employed in dressmaking and millinery custom and repair in 1930; they would not be covered in census of manufactures in 1930.

In turn, while there would be a few women, in tailoring the vast majority would be men; in dressmaking, millinery, etc., while there would be a few men, the vast majority would be women. This last matter has a bearing on the techniques of projection back from 1931 that were followed.

The number of gainfully occupied in each of custom (and repair) tailoring and dressmaking, etc. were projected back to 1900, 1910 (and 1920) in three steps. First, the numbers of self employed male tailors and self-employed female dressmakers and milliners were calculated from the occupational classifications of gainfully occupied persons and corresponding classifications of wage earners for each census from 1901 to 1931 (self-employed equals gainfully occupied less wage-earners.) Second, the numbers of self-employed, calculated according to an industrial classification of the gainfully occupied persons and wage earners, which classification was available only in the 1931 census, were projected back from 1930 to 1900 for each of tailors and dressmakers and milliners, on the basis of numbers of self-employed calculated according to the occupational classification which was available in every census from 1901 to 1931. Third, the ratios of total employment of all employees (i.e., all gainfully occupied) to the numbers of self-employed, industrial basis, were calculated for 1930 from the data described above and similar estimates were made for establishments employing less than 5 employees in 1890 from the census of manufactures: the numbers employed for the latter establishments were as recorded in the census of 1901 in which the data for 1890 were separated between those establishments employing 5 or more employees and the numbers of self-employed were taken as being equal to the numbers of establishments. The ratios of all employed to self-employed were then calculated for 1930 and 1890 and linear interpolations of these ratios were made for in-between census years. The numbers employed in the in-between years were then calculated by multiplying these ratios by the numbers of self-employed as previously calculated (industrial classification basis). These numbers employed were multiplied by GVP per worker, calculated from the census of manufactures in each census year. Note that the 1890 data are used only to get ratios between the total numbers employed and the numbers of self-employed. The custom and repair tailoring in 1930 presumably includes output by establishments having more than 5 employees and hence the projections back from 1930 to 1900 and 1910 will include some output for establishments having more than 5 employees. Such output should be deducted from the totals in 1900 and 1910. Estimates for such output were obtained from the census of manufactures 1900, Table XXIII, "clothing men's" and "clothing women's" and census of manufactures 1910, "clothing, men's custom" and "clothing, women's custom".

The data of these steps are given in the Tables 4.13, 4.14, and 4.15.

Table 4.13. Custom and Repair Tailoring

	1890	1900	1910	1920	1930
Numbers of self-employed male tailors, occupational basis		2,594	4,801	5,914	5,268
Numbers of self-employed male tailors, industrial basis	2,609	(1,988)	(3,680)	(4,533)	4,038
Ratio of total employed to self-employed	1.95	(1.95)	(1.94)	(1.94)	1.93
Total number employed *	5,090	3,877	7,139	8,794	7,795
GVP per worker, $	782	894	1,541	3,555	2,666
Total GVP, custom and repair tailoring ($000)	3,979	3,466	11,001	31,263	20,731
Less output of establishments employing 5 or more persons ($000)	N.R.	8,775	8,724	N.R.	N.R.
Adjustment of net output for establishments employing fewer than 5 employees ($000)	N.R.	-5,309	2,277	N.R.	N.R.**

* from basic data for 1930 and 1890; line 2 x line 3 for intervening years

** N.R.: not relevant

Table 4.14. Dressmaking and Millinery

	1890	1900	1910	1920	1930
Numbers of self-employed female dress-makers, etc., occupational basis		15,117	20,165	10,911	8,459
Numbers of self-employed female dress-makers, etc., industrial basis	6,288	(13,846)	(18,470)	(9,994)	7,748
Ratio of total employed to self-employed	1.61	(1.58)	(1.55)	(1.52)	(1.50)
Total number employed *	10,152	21,877	28,629	15,191	11,624
GVP per worker, $	609	734	1,267	2,965	2,012
Total GVP, custom and repair tailoring ($000)	6,180	16,058	36,273	45,041	23,387
Less output of establishments employing 5 or more persons ($000)	N.R.	4,369	5,943	N.R.	N.R.
Adjustment of net output for establishments employing fewer than 5 employees ($000)	N.R.	11,689	30,330	N.R.	N.R.**

* from basic data for 1930 and 1890; line 2 x line 3 for intervening years

** N.R.: not relevant

Table 4.15. Sum of Adjustments for 1900 and 1910 for Establishments With < 5 Persons

	1900	1910
Method 2 adjustments:		
Tailors, custom and repairs	-5,309	+2,277
Dressmaking and millinery custom and repair	+11,689	+30,330
Sum	$6,380	$32,607
Method 1 adjustments:		
Tailors, custom and repairs	4,293	14,240
Dressmaking and millinery custom and repair	5,479	9,639
Sum	$9,772	$23,879
Average of 2 estimates	$8,076	$28,243

Subtract Rymes estimates for output of establishments employing less than 5 persons

		1900	1910
Rymes estimates:	Tailors	3,784	1,229
	Dressmakers and milliners	8,219	1,041
Sum		$12,003	$2,270
Net adjustment to Rymes adjusted figure		$-3,927	$25,973

(The estimate for Method 2 for tailors does not make sense – the subtraction for establishments employing more than 5 persons in the census of manufactures is too high. However, the net result of tailors and dressmakers, etc., together is close enough to the Method 1 result that we accepted the average of the estimates by the two methods.)

7. Wood Products

(i) Saw mills, sash and door factories, shingle mills

All saw mills were covered in 1910 and hence only an estimate for 1900 was necessary. The method of estimation was the same as that used for flour and grist mills and hence a description of it will not be repeated. The relevant data are the following:

	1890	1900
Number of self employed	4,508	3,537
Index 1890-100	100.0	.785
Price index, lumber (*Wholesale Trade of Canada*) 1890-99=100	103.5	114.0
Price index 1890=100	100	110.145
Combined index of self-employed and price index	100	.86464
GVP (establishments < 5 employees) $000	9,095	7,865

(ii) Furniture (cabinets and furniture)

It was necessary to make estimates for both 1900 and 1910. The method followed was the same as in saw mills (the method being actually described in flour and grist mills).

	1890	1900	1910
Number of self-employed	968	599	1,248
Index of number self-employed	100	61.88	128.93
Price index 1890-99=100	97.4	116.4	127.6
Price index 1890=100	100.0	119.5	131.0
Combined index 1890=100	100.0	73.9	168.9
GVP establishments employing < 5 persons ($000)	1,680	1,241	2,838

8. Paper Products

Rymes adjustments to paper products, for undercoverage, were accepted: they were very small.

There was another adjustment to be made however. My best judgement was that in 1900, 1905 and 1910 the paper products groups included some primary forestry for the production of the paper companies' own raw material and that some of this output was treated as a part of GVP in the paper companies returns. This matter of primary forestry in both the paper products and wood products industries is dealt with as a separate topic in connection with forestry. We only note here the amounts that were subtracted from GVP in the paper industry as reported in the census to remove that part which measured output of the forestry industry.

The amounts to be subtracted from GVP, Rymes basis, for double counting of forestry products were, in thousands of dollars

Deductions From GVP Paper Products
For Primary Forestry Products ($000)

1900	1,007
1905	1,181
1910	1,355

9. Printing, Publishing and Allied

Rymes adjusted figures were accepted.

10. Iron and Steel Products

Rymes adjustments were accepted except for two components of the iron and steel products group, *viz.* blacksmiths and foundries and machine shops. The estimates for each are as follows.

(i) Blacksmith shops operated by self-employed

All blacksmith shops were included in manufacturing in 1870, 1880, and 1890. Nearly all were omitted in 1900 and 1910 since most blacksmith shops had less than 5 employees. (From 1917 to 1921 substantial numbers of traditional blacksmith establishments were included in custom and repair.) We added blacksmith shops employing less than 5 persons for consistency.

Blacksmiths are employed in blacksmithing establishments predominantly of a size with less than 5 employees but also to a minor extent in establishments having more than 5 employees. In addition, many blacksmiths are engaged as employees in many other industries where metal working is of some significance: consequently, the number of blacksmiths in the blacksmithing industry is less than the number of blacksmiths classified on a strictly occupational basis.

The method is as follows. The year 1930 is included in the exposition to eliminate need for duplication later. First, estimates of the numbers of self-employed blacksmiths were made for 1890, 1900, 1910 (and 1917 to 1926). These members were determined for 1900, 1910, 1920 and 1930 from the occupational and wage earners data of the census of persons: the numbers of wage earners were subtracted from the numbers of gainfully employed to yield the self-employed. (For 1910 and 1920 microfilm of the unpublished wage earner data were used.) For 1890 the number of self-employed was taken as being equal to the number of establishments.

The total numbers gainfully occupied in the blacksmithing industry were then calculated. These figures were directly available only for 1890, 1920 and 1930. (As noted above the numbers of wage-earners in the occupational data of the personal census covered all blacksmiths and included those in industries other than blacksmithing itself.)

The total number of gainfully occupied persons in the blacksmithing industry in 1890 is that employment given in the 1890 census of manufactures for the blacksmithing (nearly all are in the under 5 employee group) industry. The comparable numbers of 1920 and 1930 are obtained from the industrial classifications of occupational groups, obtained from data calculated in the 1920 census of persons, the total in custom and repair only. (There were also over 3,000 blacksmiths reported in the main iron and steel manufacturing industry but by 1920 blacksmithing as an industry was treated as being confined to custom and repair.)

The rest of the procedure is best described by reference to Table 4.16. The estimated number of self-employed, described above, is given in line (1). The total numbers of gainfully occupied persons for 1890, 1920 and 1930, derived directly from data, are given in line 2. The ratio for each of these three years of gainfully employed to self employed is calculated in line (3). It is assumed that the 1920 ratio applied back to 1917 and ratios for 1900 and 1910 (in brackets) were obtained by straight line interpolation between 1890 and 1917. An estimate of the number of gainfully occupied persons in 1900 and 1910 is then made (line 4) by multiplying the ratios of line 3 by the number of self-employed persons (line 1). Gross value of product per employee is obtained directly from the census of manufactures in 1890 (all establishments) and 1920 (custom and repair blacksmithing). Estimates of gross value of product per employee were calculated by projecting the 1890 gross value of product per worker to 1900 and 1910 (in brackets in line 5) on the basis of the gross value per worker for blacksmithing establishments having 5 or more employees, which data are given in line 6. Gross value of product for the blacksmithing industry, line 7, is obtained directly from the census in 1890 and by multiplication of line (5) by line (6) for 1900 and 1910 (and 1920 and 1930).

Table 4.16. Gross Value of Product for Self-Employed Blacksmiths, 1900, 1910, 1920

Year	1890	1900	1910	1920	1930
Estimated number of self-employed	9,423	7,924	9,232	9,267	8,181
Total gainfully occupied in blacksmithing industry	12,070			15,386	11,949
Ratio, line 2 to line 1	1.28	(1.42)	(1.56)	1.66	1.54
Total gainfully occupied, all years, line 2 x line 3	12,070	11,252	14,402	15,386	11,949
Gross value of product per gainfully occupied person $	741	(695)	(1210)	1,962	1,092
Gross value of product per gainfully occupied person, establishments 5 + employees	(1107)	(1039)	(1807)		
Total GVP (line 2 x line 5) ($000)	8.942	7,820	17,246	30,187	13,048
Less output of establishments employing 5 or more persons in 1900 and 1910 ($000)		78	213	----	
Net adjustment of GVP for blacksmiths ($000)		7,742	17,033	30,187	

These estimates of GVP include output of business having more than 5 employees in 1900 and 1910 which are already covered in the census of manufactures (but are not covered in 1920). The net upward adjustment of GVP for blacksmiths in 1900 and 1910 is that given in the last line.

(ii) Foundries and machine shops

The estimate for the adjustment for this industry was done in exactly the same manner as for bread, biscuits and confectionary, for the tanneries and a number of other industries. The adjustment is summarized in the following tables.

The basic employment data are:

	1890	1900	1910
Estimate of number of self employed:			
Machinists	412	574	1,856
Foundry workers	---	61	330
Total	412	635	2,186

The calculations are as in the Table 4.17.

Table 4.17. Calculation of Foundry and Machine Shop Products Adjustment Coverage, 1900 and 1910

	1890	1900	1910
Numbers of self-employed	412	(574) 635	(1,856) 2,186
Price index, bar iron; 1890-99=100	129.5	114.9	106.6
Index of number employed	100	(139.3) 154.1	(450.5) 530.6
Index of price of bar iron; 1890=100	100	88.73	82.32
Combined index	100	(123.6) 136.7	(370.9) 436.8
GVP, establishments < 5 employees, $000	1,049	(1,296) 1,434	(3,891) 4,582

Data in brackets are figures for machinists only. The unbracketed figures include both foundries and machine shops and are the figures used.

Jones uses $1,286 ($000) for GVP 1900 which corresponds to counting machinists only and not foundries and checks with our data. Jones appears to have made both a mistake in calculation and a transposition of figures that make his figures wrong. He got a correction for 1910 of $3,459 thousand.

11. Transportation Equipment

The adjustments in this industry group were in the carriages and wagons industry for 1900 and 1910 and in the car repairs (railway) for 1910 only.

(i) Carriages and wagons

Jones' method of adjustment for 1900 and 1910 in this industry was the same as that used for flour and grist mills and many other industries: the gross value of product for establishment employing fewer than 5 employees in 1890 was projected to 1900 and 1910 on the basis of joint indexes of the numbers of self-employed persons and of a price index for these goods. (The most relevant available price index appeared to be that for "furniture".)

Jones' estimates were derived in the following way:

	1890	1900	1910
Number of self-employed	3,885	1,957	1,602
Index, 1890=100	100	50.4	41.2
Price index (furniture), 1890-99=100	97.4	116.4	127.6
Price index, 1890=100	100	119.5	131.0
Combined index	100	60.23	53.94
GVP (establishments < 5) ($000)	3,802	2,290	2,051

(ii) Car repairs plus car works (railways) appeared to be quite out of line with other data in 1910. These two quite large industries are a part of or sell almost entirely to the Canadian railway system. For comparison we get an amount spent by the railways on car repairs and new cars and equipment. (We actually use the railway data which are available annually as an interpolator.) The railway expenditure comes from Kenneth Buckley, *Capital Formation in Canada,* in which he gives total expenditure on equipment and repairs to equipment annually from 1896 onward from which we subtract imports of cars and locomotives and domestic production of locomotives to get an amount spent by the railways on railway cars and car repairs. The data follow.

Year	GVP Cars and Car Works Census ($000)	GVP Car Repairs, Census ($000)	Total Cars, etc., Census ($000) adjusted	Railway Expend. on Canadian Cars and Car Works ($000)	Ratio of Railway Data to Census Data
1900	3954.2	7,546.6	11,513.0	10,300	.8946
1905	14,430.2	12,290.3	26,720.5	22,500	.8421
1910	16.630.6	31,829.6	48,460.2	33,800	.6975
1915	24,951.9	14,842.5	39,794.4	35,200	.8845
1917	78,564.5	36,939.2	115,503.7	75,300	.6519

The 1917 data were undoubted influenced by the war, especially the census figures. Among the other years, the divergence between the railway expenditure data and the census production data in 1910 stands out. One set of data or the other (or even conceivably both sets) must vary in what is covered from the other years. My own best judgement, based on discussion with experts in the field (J.A. McDougall and A.G. Green) is that the railway data are probably the more invariable in content. It seems quite possible that the census covered some shop activities in the railways in 1910 that were not covered in other years and were perhaps more servicing than manufacturing in nature: this view is partly supported by the reporting of 34 car repair establishments in 1905, 114 such establishments in 1910 and 54 like establishments in 1915. We made the assumption then that the 1910 census figure for car works and car repairs included some non-manufacturing activity. We then made an estimate for manufacturing for 1910 based on making the ratio of railway expenditure to census production the same as in 1905 and assuming that the railway expenditure data are acceptable. We thus get:

GVP Cars and Car Repair ($000) 1910 = 33,800 ÷ .8421 = $40,138

This sum is $8,322 thousand less than the census figure (48,460 − 40,138).
The adjustments for the whole industry of transportation were:

	1900	1910
Rymes adjusted ($000)	27,164	78,399
Less Rymes adjustment, carriages and wagons	-4,255	-711
Add Jones adjustment, carriages and wagons	+2,290	2,051
Less correction of cars and car repairs	----	-8,322
Project total	25,199	71,417

12. Non-ferrous Metal Products

The adjustment for this group was for the component "Jewellery and Watches". The method of adjustment was the same as that for flour and grist mills which has been described.

Jewellery and repairs

Jones' estimates are derived as follows.

	1890	1900	1910
Number of self-employed	852	1,839	203
Index of self-employed (1890=100)	100	215.8	23.8
Price index (solder), 1890-99=100	134.1	134.8	127.9
Price index, 1890=100	100	100.5	95.4
Combined index	100	216.9	22.7
Gross Value of Product, establishments < 5 employees, $000	1,107	2,401	251

The finally adjusted figure for the whole of the non-ferrous metal products industry is

	1900	1910
Rymes adjusted, total ($000)	12,785	59,845
Less Rymes adjustment to Jewellery and watches ($000)	778	-47
Plus Jones' adjustment to Jewellery and watches	2,401	251
GVP Project total ($000)	14,408	60,049

13. Electrical Apparatus and Supplies

Rymes adjusted data were accepted as given.

14. Non-metallic Mineral Products

Rymes adjusted data were accepted as given.

15. Petroleum and Coal Products

There were only two coke plants reporting in 1900 and according to the newly adopted disclosure rules they could not be reported separately but instead were included in a group "All Other Industries" in the census publications. Rymes reallocated most of these "All Other Industry Components" to their two digit industry groups which could be done without making disclosure; however such was not possible in the case of the coke plants. Coke plants were included in 1890 and again in censuses from 1905 onward including the 1910 census of manufactures. It remained to make an estimate for 1900 to be added to the total for petroleum and coal: the procedure was the following.

The value of coke production was available for census dates, 1890, 1905 and 1910 in the censuses of manufactures for those years. In addition the Department of Mines collected data on the volume and value of coke production annually from 1886 onwards (see sessional paper 26b in sessional papers of 1907-88, p. 140 and *Annual Report on Mineral Production of Canada During the Calendar Year 1917,* a report of the Department of Mines of Canada.)

The Department of Mines annual series on the value of coke production was used as an interpolator between the census of manufactures production data for 1890 and 1905. Use of these census values and the interpolator yielded a figure of $260,000 for gross value of coke product in 1900. This was added to the Rymes adjusted figure for the whole industry group.

16. Chemical Products

Rymes adjustments were accepted for both 1900 and 1910.

17. Miscellaneous Industries

In 1900 the $260,000 GVP coke production that was transferred to Petroleum and coal products was subtracted from Miscellaneous products. Hence we have: subtract $260,000 from Rymes adjusted in 1900; Rymes adjusted is accepted for 1910.

Summary of Adjustments 1900 and 1910: Adjustments to Gross Value of Products
(All values in thousands of dollars)

1. Food and Beverages

	1900	1910
Rymes Adjusted ($000)	153,854	280,749
Project adjustments		
(i) Bread, biscuits and confectionary		
Subtract Rymes correction	-9,835	-1,662
Add Jones correction	+6,002	+17,623
(ii) Flour, grist mills		
Subtract Rymes	0	0
Add Jones	+13,914	0
(iii) Slaughtering and meatpacking		
Subtract Rymes	-7,889	-179
Add Jones	+1,145	+708
(iv) Canned and cured fish		
Subtract Rymes	0	0
Add Jones	+1,259	0
(v) Alcoholic beverages		
(a) Spirits		
Subtract Rymes	0	0
Add Jones	0	-7,727
(b) Breweries		
Subtract Rymes	0	0
Add Jones	+951	0
GVP Project ($000)	159,401	289,512

2. Tobacco and Tobacco Products

	1900	1910
Rymes adjusted ($000)	11,959	25,484
Subtract excise taxes	-3,385	-7,066
GVP excluding excise taxes ($000)	8,574	18,418

3. Rubber Products

Rubber boots were transferred from boots and shoes to rubber products yielding the following.

	1900	1910
Rymes adjusted ($000)	1,589	7,046
Rubber footwear ($000)	3,139	4,017
GVP Project ($000)	4,728	11,063

4. Leather Products

There were several adjustments to Leather Products.

		1900	1910
Rymes Adjusted ($000)		52,435	64,068
Adjustments for establishments employing < 5 persons			
Tanneries:	Project	2,126	2,612
	Less Rymes	-2,268	-545
Harness and saddlery:	Project	3,162	3,878
	Less Rymes	-6,745	-567
Boots and shoes:	Project	6,628	9,209
	Less Rymes	-9,140	-94
Less transfer of Rubber footwear		-3,139	-4,017
GVP Project ($000)		43,059	74,544

5. Textile Products (ex. Clothing)

There were no changes here. The figures used were:

	1900	1910
Project: Rymes adjusted ($000)	33,010	51,673

6.   Clothing, Textile and Fur

There were several adjustments.

		1900	1910
Rymes adjusted ($000)		54,191	95,151
Adjustments for establishments employing < 5 persons			
Tailors and clothiers:	Project	-508	8,259
	Less Rymes	-3,784	-1,229
Dressmaking and millinery:	Project	8,584	19,984
	Less Rymes	-8,219	-1,041
GVP Project ($000)		50,264	121,124

7.   Wood Products

Several adjustments.

		1900	1910
Rymes adjusted ($000)		90,470	182,352
Adjustments for establishments employing < 5 employees			
Saw and shingle mills:	Project	7,865	0
	Less Rymes	-9,401	0
Furniture and cabinets:	Project	1,241	2,838
	Less Rymes	-1,937	-96
GVP Project ($000)		88,238	185,094

8.   Paper Products

Rymes adjustments accepted. But some primary wood operatives transferred.

	1900	1910
Rymes adjusted ($000)	12,420	33,000
Transfer to Forestry	-1,007	-1,355
GVP ($000)	11,413	31,645

9.   Printing Publishing and Allied Industries

No changes to Rymes adjusted.

	1900	1910
GVP Project ($000)	14,200	20,041

10. Iron and Steel Products

There were two adjustments by the project as follows:

	1900	1910
Rymes adjusted ($000)	51,983	143,240
Adjustment for establishments employing < 5 persons		
Blacksmiths: Project	7,742	17,033
Less Rymes	0	0
Foundry and machine shop products:		
Project (Jones' figures)	1,286	3,459
Less Rymes	-996	-702
GVP Project ($000)	60,015	163,030

11. Transportation Equipment

There were two project adjustments.

		1900	1910
Rymes adjusted ($000)		27,164	78,400
Carriages and wagons:	Project	2,290	2,051
	Less Rymes	-4,255	-711
Car repairs and car works:			
	Project	0	-8,322
	Less Rymes	0	0
GVP Project ($000)		25,199	71,418

12. Non-ferrous Metal Products

Project adjustment for jewellery and repairs.

		1900	1910
Rymes adjusted ($000)		12,785	59,845
Jewellery and repairs:	Project	2,401	251
	Less Rymes	-778	-47
GVP Project ($000)		14,408	60,049

13. Electrical Apparatus and Supplies

No adjustment of Rymes data by the Project.

	1900	1910
GVP Project ($000)	3,275	15,235

14. Non-metallic Mineral Products

No adjustment of Rymes data by the project.

	1900	1910
GVP Project ($000)	9,460	28,155

15. Petroleum and Coal Products

There was only one adjustment in 1900.

		1900	1910
Rymes adjusted ($000)		4,157	9,554
Coke:	Project	+260	0
	Less Rymes	0	0
GVP Project ($000)		4,417	9,554

16. Chemical Products

No adjustment to Rymes figures by the project.

	1900	1910
GVP Project ($000)	12,591	30,987

17. Miscellaneous Industries

Only one adjustment to Rymes (in 1900).

		1900	1910
Rymes adjusted ($000)		7,902	16,242
Coke:	Project	-260	0
	Rymes	0	0
GVP Project ($000)		7,642	16,242

		1900	1910
Grand Total GVP:	Project($000)	549,894	1,203,588
	Rymes($000)	553,444	1,147,667

Adjustments to Rymes Data for Other Years Than 1900 and 1910

Year 1870

Two adjustments were made.

(i) Food and Beverages was reduced in the project by the amount of the excise tax on spirits which was included in GVP in 1870 in the census but not in most later years and not in our data. Rymes had not removed this excise tax in 1870.

The excise tax on spirits amounted to $2,536 thousand (calendar year estimate) and it was subtracted from Rymes total for food and beverages. So we have:

	1870
Food and Beverages, Rymes adjusted ($000)	63,383
Adjustment for excise tax, Project	-2,536
Final GVP, Food and Beverages ($000)	60,847

(ii) One item was transferred from the "iron and steel" industry to the "transportation" industry, *viz.*, spring, axle factories in the amount of $238.8 thousand. The changes then were:

	1870
Iron and Steel, Rymes Adjusted ($000)	24,914.0
Subtract spring, axle factories ($000)	-238.8
Final GVP, Project ($000)	24,675.2
Transportation Industry: Rymes ($000)	9,889.1
Add spring, axle factories ($000)	238.8
Final GVP, Project ($000)	10,127.9

Year 1880

There was only one project adjustment. Axle, spring factories in the amount of $246.4 thousand were transferred from the "iron and steel" industry and added to the "transportation" industry. So we have

	1880
Iron and Steel industry, Rymes adjusted ($000)	34,182.6
Less: Spring, axle factories ($000)	246.6
Final GVP; Iron and Steel, Project ($000)	33,936.0
Transportation Industry, Rymes ($000)	14,266.5
Add: Spring, axle factories ($000)	246.6
Final GVP, Transportation Industry ($000)	14,513.1

Year 1890

The changes were:

(i) Knit goods was transferred from the industry "textiles (excluding clothing)" to the industry "clothing, textile and fur". Accordingly for these two industries we have

	1890
Textiles (excluding Clothing), Rymes adjusted ($000)	26,043.3
Subtract knit goods ($000)	1,338
Final GVP, textiles excluding clothing ($000)	24,705.3
Clothing, Textile and Fur: Rymes Adjusted ($000)	43,851.2
Add knit goods ($000)	1,338
Final GVP: Clothing, Textile and Fur ($000)	45,189.2

(ii) Iron and Steel: Springs and axles were mistakenly subtracted from iron and steel to be transferred to transportation as was correct in 1870 and 1880. We therefore have with regard to iron and steel

	1890
Rymes adjusted ($000)	55,871
Less springs and axles ($000)	379
Final GVP, Project ($000)	55,492

(iii) Transportation: It appeared that there had been a mistake in addition of $100 thousand in Rymes calculations. Therefore we have

	1890
Transportation: Rymes adjusted ($000)	23,345
Add correction for addition ($000)	100
Final GVP, transportation	23,445

(iv) Petroleum and Coal Products: Estimates for petroleum: It seems almost certain that at least one large refinery was missed in the 1891 census of manufactures. A large refinery in Middlesex county was reported in 1880 but not 1890 (and 1900 cannot be used as a check since by then disclosure rules prevented publication of data relating to less than 3 companies). The 1890 census figure of GVP refined petroleum products was about one half the 1880 figure and about 60 percent of the 1900 figures. The annual series of government inspections of Canadian oil products from Canadian refineries shows no such big drop (actually a substantial increase in gallonage between 1880 and 1890).

Accordingly an estimate was made for 1890 as follows:

The gallonage of refined Canadian oil inspected by the Canadian government was valued by the price of coal oil for every year from 1880 to 1900. Since the reports of inspected oil began only in 1881, it was assumed that the 1880 gallonage figure was the same as the 1881 figure: the credibility of this assumption can be gauged by noting that Canadian production of crude oil was 369 thousand barrels in 1881 and 350 thousand barrels in 1880 (HSC, p. 437-348, Series N174.)

The ratio of the resultant values of oil inspected for 1880 and 1900 to the corresponding GVP of the petroleum refining industry were calculated. The respective values were (1890 GVP is an estimate):

	1880	1890	1900
1. Estimated value of oil refined ($000)	1,866	2,035	2,014
2. GVP, products of petroleum ($000)	4,050	(4,302)	4,157
3. Ratio, (1) to (2)	.461	(.473)	.484

The ratios of line (3) were linearly interpolated to get a ratio for 1890. This ratio for 1890 along with the value of oil inspected (line 1) was used to infer a GVP for petroleum products in 1890 at $4,302 thousand. The actually reported figure in the census of 1890 was $2,064 thousand; the difference is $2,238 thousand. The project adjustment is shown then as follows.

	1890
Products of Petroleum and Coal, Rymes ($000)	2,155
Add adjustment for oil refining ($000)	2,238
Sub-total	4,393
Subtract lubricating oil factories	-6
Paraffin and wax factories	-40
Final GVP ($000)	4,347

(v) Miscellaneous Industries. Since the interpolations had been done already in the iron and steel industry when it was found that "springs and axles" should not have been subtracted and since the relative amount was small, the iron and steel industry was not changed. However, an amount equal to the springs and axles entry was added to the "miscellaneous" industries so that the overall total was maintained. Thus we have

	1890
Miscellaneous Industries, Rymes ($000)	6,191
Add axles and springs ($000)	379
Final GVP, Project ($000)	6,570

Adjustments In 1905

The 1905 census suffered from undercoverage. Therefore it was used in only limited measure to make 1905 a base year. The limited number of cases in which 1905 data were used as base year data are described below.

1. Alcoholic Beverages

(a) Breweries — were interpolated between 1900 and 1910.
(b) Distilleries — It seemed that the census of manufactures coverage of distilleries was good. (There were as many establishments as in 1900.) Therefore the census of manufactures figure was accepted for 1905: it reported GVP excluding excise duty. The latter was added. The relevant quantities are:

GVP distilleries 1905 — census GVP $000	2,343.7
Excise taxes, calendar year	6,373.3
GVP including excise tax used for interpolation	8,717.0

2. Butter and Cheese

The interpolator for 1882 to 1917 comprised two parts (i) the annual Ontario Bureau of Industries production for Ontario. (ii) The ratios of Ontario production to Canadian Production. The postal census of manufactures in 1905 seemed deficient on a country wide basis for this industry (only 2,958 establishments vs. 3,625 in 1910 and 3,576 in 1900). However, there was no reason to believe that the proportion covered (or the proportion not covered) varied among provinces. Hence the 1905 census data could be used to estimate the ratio of Ontario production to total Canadian production for that year and so it became a base year for carrying out the second step noted immediately above. (Incidentally, 1907 became a third year since an estimate for cheese and butter production for all Canada and Ontario was obtained from the *Canada Year Book* 1921, p. 252 ff.) These ratios of Ontario production to all Canada production were interpolated linearly between base years.
These ratios will be given in the section on interpolation.

3. Tobacco Products

The GVP for 1905 was obtained by accepting the 1905 census returns, as given in Rymes, and then by subtracting the cost of excise taxes, and raw leaf taxes. The figure thus attained for 1905 for GVP less excise and raw leaf taxes was $12,212 thousand.
The use of the 1905 as a base year applied to the entire tobacco products industry.

4. Paper Products

Data on production of paper and wood pulp separately appeared to be reasonably complete in 1905. The census GVP's of each were

Census GVP	
Pulp and Paper products (Rymes) $000	18,762
Less transferred to woods operations	1,181
Final GVP Project $000	17,580
Divided as follows	
Paper production	12,075
Pulp production	5,505

The item "transferred to woods operations" is involved because the pulp and paper companies have their own woods operations and some of the production of pulpwood logs gets into the GVP of the pulp and paper industry. (See paper products, 1900 and 1910 surplus.) The amount to be subtracted in 1905 was taken as being half way between the values for 1900 and 1910.

The division of the industry between paper and pulp was obtained by estimating pulp output and taking paper as a residual. The GVP of the pulp part of the industry was obtained by assuming that it had the same ratio to exports of pulp in 1905, which are available in the trade data, as the like GVP figure for 1910 had to exports of pulp in 1910.

5. Non-ferrous Metals

The non-ferrous metals group was interpolated between 1900 and 1910 in two parts *viz.* (i) smelting (ii) all others. The coverage of the smelting appeared to be high (probably about complete) in 1905 and so the 1905 figure for smelting was taken from the postal census of 1905. The GVP smelting was $28,462 thousand.

The non-smelting part was not properly covered. The 1905 figure for it was obtained by interpolation between 1900 and 1910.

6. Petroleum and Coal Products

This group was interpolated between base years according to (i) coke production and (ii) petroleum products production.

The coke appeared to be well covered in the census of manufactures for 1905 and the census figure for it in 1905 was used.

The GVP, coke production, 1905, was $1,279.3 thousand.

Petroleum products were not well enough covered in 1905 for the data to be used. The GVP petroleum products, 1905, was obtained by interpolation between 1900 and 1910.

7. Transportation Equipment

"Railway equipment and repairs" was one component of the transportation industry. It was regarded as being fully reported in the census of manufactures of 1905 (two items "car repairs" and "cars and car works".)

The total GVP for railway equipment and repairs for 1905 was $26,721 thousand.

Other items of transportation equipment were not sufficiently comprehensively reported in the 1905 census to be usable and the figure for 1905 were obtained by interpolation between 1900 and 1910.

Adjustments to Rymes 1915 Figures

In general, the postal census of manufactures of 1915 did not have tabulated complete coverage. Apparently, returns were obtained from companies of all sizes but the two alternative tabulations included (i) all establishments having a gross value of production of $2,500 or more or (ii) all establishments having 5 or more employees. Therefore some small establishments are not covered in the published census data and it seems possible that even some of the larger companies may have been missed. However, the 1915 postal census of manufactures was much more complete than the 1905 postal census. Accordingly the 1915 data are frequently but not always used as base year data.

In this section of the notes the sources of all components of the 1915 data on manufactures that are used in base year fashion are given. Unless otherwise indicated the references to 1915 tabulations are to the tabulations of establishments with $2,500 or more GVP. It should be noted that in other base years before 1915 the Rymes totals for whole industry groups were adjusted by the sum of our adjustments for the individual components. This procedure then gave us a total for each of the seventeen industry groups. We did not obtain industry totals in this way in 1915 for all groups.

1. Food and Beverages

(i) Alcoholic beverages

The GVP's for both malt and distilled liquors were taken directly from the census.

(ii) Bread, biscuits and confectionery

The 1915 figure as derived from the interpolation between 1910 and 1917 was used. Checks against other data (for 1915 and other years) supported the use of this figure. Therefore, 1915 was not a base year for this component.

(iii) Butter and cheese

We used the 1915 figure as given in the census of manufactures. There were 3,307 establishments in 1915 vs. 3,625 in 1910. There was full coverage in 1910.

(iv) Flour and grist mill products

The year 1915 was not a base year for this component (only 644 establishments recorded for 1915 vs. 1,141 in 1910).

(v) Sugar refining

We use the GVP as reported in the postal census for 1915. It is a base year.

(vi) Slaughtering and meatpacking

The census of manufactures 1915 reported 17 fewer establishments in 1915 than in 1910, which latter did not cover any establishments having less than 5 employees. The adjustment of the census figure for 1915 to full coverage was done in two steps.

First, in the tabulations for 1915, 59 establishments with a GVP of $2,500 or more reported total GVP of $78,431 thousand while, in a separate tabulation of establishments with 5 or more employees reported 54 establishments with a GVP of $78,334 thousand so that 5 establishments with a GVP larger than $2,500 but employing less than 5 persons had an average GVP per establishment of $19,400. On the assumption that there would have been as many establishments with 5 or more employees in 1915, as in 1910, a value was imputed for the shortfall of 17 establishments, noted above, at the rate of $19,400 per establishment, adding $330 thousand to the 1915 total. In addition, there was an adjustment to be made for plants with less than 5 employees that were not covered. Jones had estimated that these accounted for 1.459 per cent of plants with 5 or more employees in 1910 and we made the same assumption for 1915. The figure for 1915 then became: the 1915 census of GVP of reported plants at $96,790 thousand plus $330 thousand for the 17 uncovered plants with 5 or more employees, the sum of these two then being multiplied by the Jones adjustment factor of 1910 of 1.01459 to yield an estimated total in 1915 of $98,537 thousand. It will be noted that these adjustments are not large. They are probably an underestimate but were the best that could be done.

(vii) The sum of the above six components accounted for more than 85 per cent of the total for all food and beverages in 1915. There was not a direct estimate for the remaining less-than-15 per cent; it was derived in the interpolation process which is described later.

2. Tobacco and Tobacco Products

Rymes GVP for establishments with $2,500 or more product was accepted as covering the total industry but it seemed apparent (after an enormous amount of checking) that it included raw leaf tobacco tax and small taxes on other materials. The project estimate was derived as follows.

	1915
GVP Rymes $2,500+ ($000)	28,987.3
Less excise taxes on materials	
Raw leaf ($000)	4,454.3
Other materials ($000)	204.9
Final GVP project ($000)	24,328.1

Source of tax data: Canada Sessional Papers 1917 #12, pp. 24-25.

(The excise taxes noted above appear to be for fiscal 1915; fiscal 1916 has almost the same figure as the one here for the raw leaf tax only, *viz.* 4,676.8. We note that these cost-of-material excise taxes are subtracted from both GVP and cost of materials. Therefore GDP at factor cost is unaffected by small apparent variations from the correct raw material excise taxes.)

3. Rubber Products

For 1915, the 1916 census figure of GVP for plants employing 5 + persons was adjusted in two ways. First, the Rymes very small (one-tenth of 1 percent) proportional adjustment for plants employing less than 5 persons of 1910 was applied to the census GVP (5 + plants) in 1915. Second, an estimate for rubber boots, transferred from general boots and shoes in the leather goods group, was added. This latter estimate was made by making a linear interpolation of the ratio of rubber boots and shoes to total boots and shoes between 1910 and 1917 to obtain a ratio for 1915 and then multiplying census GVP for 1915 for boots and shoes by this ratio. These adjustments are summarized:

	1915
Census figure, GVP rubber products for plants 5 + employees ($000)	14,974
Census figure adjusted in proportion to Rymes adjustment for 1910 ($000)	14,989

Proportion of rubber shoes to total shoes

For 1910 —	.118
For 1917 —	.165
interpolated 1915 —	.152

Total production of boots and shoes, 1915, from census ($000)	34,065
Estimate of rubber boots and shoes (.152 x 34,065) ($000)	5,178
Final GVP, rubber products, 1915 ($000)	20,167

This gives a base year figure.

4. Leather Products

Leather products were interpolated in two components (i) tanneries (ii) all other leather goods. Each is dealt with in turn.

(i) Tanneries: The GVP reported in the census for 1915 was adjusted in the same ratio as for 1910. Its calculation follows.

GVP 1910, Census (5 or more employees)	$19,972,178
GVP 1915, Census (5 or more employees)	$23,472,017
Adjusted GVP, 1910	$22,584,000
Adjusted GVP, 1915 = 22,584 ÷ 19,972 x 23,472 =	$26,542,000

Even this adjusted figure seems low. We will deal with this matter when we deal with interpolation. (We just note here that cost of material behaves well between 1910 and 1915 relative to the interpolator). To make an estimate of GVP based on our interpolator would have meant a GVP value in 1915 enormously above the census GVP.

(ii) All other leather goods

This component was calculated as the residual of total GVP for the whole industry group in 1915, which was estimated independently, less the tanneries and rubber boots and shoes. The question then is how the total was estimated.

The total was estimated as follows. Jones estimated the GVP of plants with less than 5 employees in the boot and shoe and the harness and saddlery industries (as well as the tanneries already noted above). He also estimated cost of boot and shoe repairs in 1917 which he associated with plants of less than 5 employees and there was a figure for total harness and saddlery GVP in 1917 which seemed complete.

For this project an estimate for 1915 was made by taking a linear interpolation for each of boot and shoe repair and harness and saddlery between the 1910 and 1917 figure to yield the following.

Jones added $9,208,000 for boot and shoe employees in plants employing less than 5 persons in 1910 and estimated $11,777,000 for boot and shoe repairs in 1917. The interpolation between these 2 figures gave GVP shoe repairs 1915 (in $000) = 9,208 (2 ÷ 7) + 11,777 (5 ÷ 7) = 11,043. The 1915 census already included $328,000 for business. The net to be added for boots and shoes then was, (in $000) 11,043 - 328 = 10,715.

The harness and saddlery industry needed little adjustment. Jones' adjustments for under 5 yielded an output (in $000) of all harness and saddlery of $9,083 in 1910 and in 1917 GVP was $8,769. A linear interpolation between these two figures gave:

For 1915 GVP entire harness and saddlery industry (in $000) was estimated at 9,083 (2 ÷ 7) + 8,769 (5 ÷ 7) = $8,859. The 1915 census already reported a GVP (in $000) at $8,839. Therefore only $20 (8,859 − 8,839) was added for small concerns.

The total for all leather goods in 1915 then was estimated at (in $000) 71,037 (unadjusted +2500) + 10,715 (boots and shoes) + 20 (harness) = $81,772. Of this $5,178 was transferred to rubber for rubber boots and shoes and if the figure for tanneries of $26,542 is subtracted, we have a figure of $50,052 for all leather other than tanneries. (Note: although the figure for tanneries was adjusted we did not add anything to the total for this adjustment. In the case of the tanneries the cost of materials as recorded in the census of 1915 had risen from 1910 almost exactly in proportion to the value of domestic disappearance of hides, separately calculated. The ratio of cost of materials to GVP had become very high in the 1915 data.)

5. Textiles (ex. Clothing)

The GVP's for woollens, cottons and cordage rope and twine were taken directly from the 1915 census. "All Other" was calculated as a ratio to the sum of the woollens, cottons and cordage rope and twine. The ratio was obtained by interpolation between similar ratios for 1910 and 1917. The relevant ratios are

	1910	1915	1917
Ratio of sum of woollens, cottons and cordage to total for the group	.841	(.843)	.844

The 1915 figure was inferred.

Owing to peculiarities that we will note when we come to the interpolators, the 1915 figures were not much used as a base year to facilitate interpolation.

6. Clothing: Textile and Fur

The year 1915 was not used as a base year in any form for this group: it was determined by regular interpolation between 1910 and 1917. The resultant total figure for 1915 at $118,175 thousand compares with a figure of $112,129 thousand actually recorded in the 1915 census: the latter had some unmeasured undercount.

7. Wood Products

The saw mills ("log products" in the census) component of this industry group was clearly under reported (the number of plants reported was 1,000 less than 1910 and even further short of the number reported in 1917). An estimate was made for uncovered saw mills by interpolating the ratio of the value of lumber production (HSC Series K130) to gross value of production of saw mill products in 1910 and 1917 linearly to get a value of this ratio in 1915. The value of lumber production in 1915 (HSC Series K130) was divided by the interpolated ratio for 1915 to give an estimate of the gross value of product of saw mills (log products) in 1915. The relevant data follow.

	1910	1915	1917
1. GVP log products, census, (saw mills) $000	105,506	68,815	115,885
2. Value of lumber production (HSC) $000	70,609	61,020	83,655
3. Ratio, line 2 to line 1	.6692	.8867	.7219
4. Interpolated ratio for 1915	.6692	.7068	.7219
5. GVP log products (line 2 ÷ line 4) $000	105,506	86,333	115,885

The upward adjustment for 1915 in $000 is 86,333 - 68,815 = +17,518.

The final total GVP for all wood products then became

Rymes ($2500+) 1915 ($000)	115,622
Add for unreported saw mills ($000)	17,518
Final GVP Wood Products 1915 ($000)	133,140

8. Paper Products

The Rymes total for plants with $2500+ GVP was accepted. There are no small firms in this group (or not many).

9. Printing, Publishing and Allied

There are a substantial number of quite small plants in this industry group and the 1915 census of manufactures fell short of covering all of them. The method of making an estimate for the omitted group is:

First, in three of the four components of this group an average GVP was calculated for those plants in the $2500+ category but not in the 5 employee category; in the fourth category the number of establishments with $2500+ GVP and the number employing 5+ persons was exactly the same as were their joint attributes. The second step involved calculating the differences between the numbers of plants reported in each category in 1917 and in 1915, which was taken as the shortfall of reported plants in 1915. The third step involved attributing a GVP for these numbers measuring the shortfalls by attributing average GVP's of step one to the shortfalls measured in step 2. Accordingly we have the following adjustment.

Industry Component	Average GVP For Plants Having $2500+ GVP But Less Than 5 Employees (dollars)	Shortfall of Numbers Reported in 1915	Attributed GVP For These Shortfall Numbers
Printing and bookbinding	2,811	212	595,932
Printing and publishing	3,712	270	1,002,240
Lithographing and engraving	2,228	13	28,964
Stereotyping and electrotyping	N.A.	-2	Nil

Aggregate GVP to be added	1,627,136	
Rymes (plants $2500+)	33,646,736	
Final aggregate GVP for industry group	$35,273,872	

This became a base year for the entire industry group.

10. Iron and Steel Products

Jones made two adjustments to the 1910 census of manufactures data. First, he added an estimate for the blacksmiths who were scarcely covered at all since most blacksmith shops had less than 5 employees. Second, he made an adjustment for the foundries. The same adjustments are made to the iron and steel group data in the census of manufactures for 1915. They are considered in order.

(i) Blacksmiths

In 1915, a total of 963 blacksmithing establishments produced a total GVP of $1,431,172 (census). (Note in the summary for Canada the number of establishments is given as 611. However, the sum of the numbers reported for the provinces is 963.) The average product per establishment is $1,492.16

The total number of blacksmithing establishments was assumed equal to the number in 1917. The latter figure was obtained by dividing D. Jones estimate of total GVP blacksmiths 1917 (the origins described with the data on 1917) by the output per establishment as reported in the 1917 census of manufactures, which was $1,891.58. This gave a number of establishments as 13,711.

The total GVP blacksmiths 1915 was 13,711 x 1,492.16 =	20,460,000
Subtract GVP reported in census 1915	1,437,000
Adjustment to Rymes figures for $2500+ for blacksmiths	19,023,000

(ii) Foundries

The adjusted GVP foundries in 1915 was estimated in the fashion

$$\frac{\text{Jones adjusted GVP 1910}}{\text{Census GVP 1910 for plants employing 5 + persons}} \times \left(\begin{array}{c}\text{Census GVP 1915 for plants}\\ \text{employing 5 + persons}\end{array}\right)$$

This gave a value of $39,098,000 in 1915 from which was subtracted the output reported in 1915 census ($2500 plants) 36,736,000. Net adjustment to foundries +$2,362,000.

Final GVP for 1915

Rymes ($2500+) ($000)		144,841
Plus:	addition for blacksmiths	19,023
	addition for foundries	2,362
Final GVP ($000)		$166,226

This was a base value.

11. Transportation Equipment

Used Rymes figure for GVP establishments having output of $2,500 or more as a base year quantity.

12. Non-ferrous Metal Products

A small adjustment to Rymes figure was made for jewelry and repairs as follows:

There were 34 more establishments reported in the classification with GVP ≥ $2,500 than in the classification with 5 or more employees, and these 34 accounted for $91,674 or $2,696 each.

The number of establishments reporting in the 1917 census was 438 and in the 1915 census for the classification ≥ $2,500 was 86. It was assumed that there were the same number of establishments in 1915 as in 1917 and hence that the number of unreported establishments in 1915 was 352. These 352 establishments were attributed an average GVP of $2,500 (of the figure of $2,696 noted above). We therefore had adjustment for uncovered jewelry plants = 352 x 2,500 = $880,000.

The final aggregate GVP for non-ferrous metal products was

Rymes (plants ≥ $2,500) ($000)	74,238
Adjustment for jewelry plants	880
Final total GVP ($000) (a base year value)	$75,118

13. Electrical Apparatus and Supplies

The project GVP was obtained by multiplying Rymes reported GVP figure for establishments producing a product of $2,500 or more by the adjustment factor Rymes used in 1910 to take account of those establishments with less than 5 employees. (Rymes 1910 adjustment factor was 1.0040.)

Note: For strict comparability the 1910 correction factor should have been applied to the 1915 GVP for establishment with less than 5 employees. An adjusted GVP obtained in this way would have been less than the figure actually published for 1915 for establishments with $2,500 GVP. Perhaps the 1915 figure should just have been left at this 1915 published figure but it was deemed that coverage would not be entirely complete and the adjustment only amounts to four-tenths of 1 per cent, a very small figure.

1915 is a base year.

14. Non-metallic Mineral Products

The entry for this year is obtained by ordinary interpolation between 1910 and 1917; the year 1915 was not a base year for this industry.

15. Petroleum and Coal Products

Rymes figure for establishments producing $2,500 product or more was accepted: it was broken into two parts as recorded in the 1915 census of manufactures. The two GVP's were:

Coke production ($000)	4,416.5
Petroleum products ($000)	11,912.0
Total ($000)	16,328.5

These values were used as base year values for each of the two components.

16. Chemical Products

The Rymes 1910 adjustment factor was used to adjust the Rymes 1915 figure for establishments with 5 or more employees.

Rymes adjustment ratio was 1.038.

17. Miscellaneous Industries

For 1915 Rymes GVP for establishments with $2,500 or more product was actually less than Rymes GVP for establishments of 5 or more employees, which is quite the reverse of the usual.

In these unusual circumstances the average of the Rymes GVP's for 1915 (i.e. GVP $2,500 and GVP employees 5+) was adjusted on the basis of Rymes adjustment for 1910 which was to add an estimate for establishments with less than 5 employees.

$$\text{Rymes adjustment ratio } 1910 = \frac{\text{Rymes adjusted}}{\text{Rymes unadjusted}} = 1.035578$$

1915 GVP for establishments $2,500 + ($000)	14,968
1915 GVP for establishments 5+ employees ($000)	15,261
Average of establishments $2,500 and 5+ employees ($000)	15,115
Final adjusted project figure ($000) 15,115 x 1.035578 =	$15,263

Basis of Data on Gross Value of Product, 1917 to 1926

The basic data for 1917 to 1926 came from HSC, Section Q, Manufactures. Series Q 30 to 137. These which essentially continued the Rymes data (and, I believe, were prepared under Rymes direction) provided a classification of the data of the census of manufactures on the basis of the

1948 Standard Industrial Classification.

The census of manufactures was taken annually at this time and the coverage was full, in the sense that small plants were not omitted on the basis of their size only.

For seven industry groups the data were taken without adjustment from HSC: these industries are the following:

> Bread, Biscuits and Confectionery
> Rubber Products
> Paper Products
> Non-ferrous Metal Products
> Electrical Apparatus and Supplies
> Non-metallic Mineral Products
> Chemicals and Allied Products

For three industry groups the HSC data were used with only minor adjustments for single years: these industries (years of adjustment in brackets) were

> Textile Products, excluding Clothing   (1917)
> Wood Products   (1919)
> Printing, Publishing and Allied   (1917)

For two industry groups subtractions from HSC were made, *viz.* Tobacco and Tobacco Products, 1919-1926, excise taxes subtracted; Products of Petroleum and Coal 1917-1926, manufactured gas removed.

For five industries, there were additions to all years to take account of the so-called hand trades: these industry groups included

> Leather Products
> Clothing, Textile and Fur
> Iron and Steel Products
> Transportation Equipment
> Miscellaneous Industries

The nature of the adjustments follows.

(i) The three industry groups with single year adjustments

(a) For textiles excluding clothing, the 1917 figure was adjusted upward by the small amount of $485 thousand to include the category "flax dressed", which had been included in earlier years but not in the tabulation for 1917.

(b) For wood products in 1919, the HSC 1919 figure for GVP was adjusted downward by $59,772 thousand. This adjustment was made using data of the *The Lumber Industry* 1919 in which a GVP of $222,322,975 is given on p. vii, which figure includes log products produced in the forest (forestry); the correct figure for us appears to be $162,759 found on p. ix of the same report.

(c) For printing, publishing and allied in 1917, the project added blue printing to the HSC figure in the amount of $158,536 to yield a total of $57,513 thousand.

(ii) The two industry groups for which simple subtractions were made

(a) Tobacco and Tobacco Products. Deductions from the HSC data for excise taxes were made in the following amounts, obtained from Government of Canada, Department of Internal Revenue.

Year	Amount ($000)	Year	Amount ($000)
1919	9,518	1923	6,302
1920	8,975	1924	6,094
1921	8,177	1925	6,229
1922	6,896	1926	6,302

(b) Petroleum and Coal Products. Manufactured gas was removed from petroleum and coal. (It had not been included in the data for this industry for prior years.)

The GVP for manufactured gas is given separately in the section of these notes on manufactured gas.

(iii) The five industry groups to which the hand trades were added

The size of these additions can be readily calculated by taking the difference between the GVP for the relevant industry group in the tables in this document and the GVP given for the same industry group in HSC: they are summmarized in Table 4.18, which follows on page 354.

(a) Leather Products

The additions to the leather products group for 1917 to 1926 were entirely for the boot and shoe custom and repair industry. The method of adjustment has been described in the previous part that dealt with the adjustments to 1900 and 1910 and will not be repeated in detail here. The method essentially was to estimate the numbers employed in this sub-group and the gross value of product per worker and then to obtain the adjustment for shoe making as the product of the number employed and the GVP per worker.

The number of self-employed boot and shoe workers has been given already (in the discussion for 1900 and 1910) for 1910, 1920 and 1930. The numbers of self-employed for 1917 to 1919 were obtained by linear interpolation between 1910 and 1920; likewise the numbers of self-employed for 1921 to 1926 were obtained by linear interpolation between 1920 and 1930.

The numbers gainfully occupied (employed) in each year were then obtained by multiplying the numbers of self-employed by the ratios of gainfully occupied to self-employed given in the 1900 and 1910 exposition. The gross value of product per worker was then calculated for 1917 to 1921 from the average product per worker derived from the report on shoemakers in the part on hand trades in censuses of manufactures 1917 to 1921; since these data were no longer collected after 1921, the GVP per worker for 1922 to 1926 was extrapolated from 1921 on the basis of estimates derived from the average earnings per worker in the boot and shoe industry of the census of manufactures and the ratio of these earnings to GVP per worker. The relevant data follow.

Table 4.18. Adjustments for Handtrades 1917-1926 (thousands of dollars)

	1917	1918	1919	1920	1921
Iron and Steel Products: blacksmithing	25,936	26,471	29,032	30,187	26,268
Leather Products: boot and shoe repair	11,777	12,669	15,629	15,143	13,379
Clothing: custom tailoring	18,646	25,375	30,400	31,263	25,447
Clothing: dressmaking and millinery	33,908	43,408	49,751	45,041	37,975
Transportation Equipment: garages and auto repair	8,101	11,023	13,631	16,593	18,506
Miscellaneous Custom and Repair	1,327	994	1,033	11,278	8,723
Total Custom and Repair	99,695	119,940	139,476	149,505	130,298

	1922	1923	1924	1925	1926
Iron and Steel Products: blacksmithing	22,944	22,804	20,599	19,379	18,519
Leather Products: boot and shoe repair	14,249	13,669	12,947	12,422	12,383
Clothing: custom tailoring	22,998	23,087	18,769	19,342	20,321
Clothing: dressmaking and millinery	31,099	30,035	25,353	25,113	24,418
Transportation Equipment: garages and auto repair	20,452	23,328	26,354	29,822	34,565
Miscellaneous Custom and Repair	8,137	8,356	7,802	8,062	8,486
Total Custom and Repair	119,879	121,279	111,824	114,140	118,692

	1921	1922	1923	1924	1925	1926	1930
GVP per worker (dollars)	1,894	(2,010)	(1,907)	(1,800)	(1,708)	(1,697)	1,371
Earnings per worker $	923	1,010	993	968	949	981	924
Ratio, GVP to earnings	2.05	(1.99)	(1.92)	(1.86)	(1.80)	(1.73)	1.48

The GVP per worker in 1921 and 1930 are for the hand trades part of the industry. The average earnings in line 2 are from the boot and shoe manufacturing industry. It will be noted that the ratio of the hand trades GVP to industry earnings fell from 2.05 in 1921 to 1.48 in 1930. It was assumed that the decline in this ratio occurred in linear fashion as shown in the bracketed figures of line 3. The GVP's per worker for 1922 to 1926 (in brackets) were then obtained as the product of the entries in lines 2 and 3.

(b) Clothing, Textile and Fur

The category "knitting mills" of HSC was included with the category "clothing, textile and fur". There were adjustments to the HSC to add estimates for two categories known by names such as "clothing, men's custom" and "clothing, women's custom" — sometimes designated as "custom and repair". There were such categories in the censuses of manufactures for 1917 to 1921 but they were left out in the HSC tabulations; the categories were not included in the census of manufactures from 1922 onward.

The method of making the estimates has been described, in large part, in the prior description of method 2 for making estimates for these two categories in 1900 and 1910.

The method for each category separately for each year was to make an estimate of, first, the numbers employed in each category and second, the gross value of product per worker and finally to produce the product of these two measures which gave the amounts to be added to the HSC data for each category.

An explanation of how an estimate of the numbers employed in 1910, 1920 and 1930 were determined has been given already in the discussions of the 1900 and 1910 estimates. Estimates of the numbers employed in each category in the years 1917 to 1919 were obtained by linear interpolation between the figures for 1910 and 1920 and in the years 1921 to 1926 by linear interpolation between 1920 and 1930.

Data for gross value of product per employee for years 1917 to 1921 were obtained from the census of manufactures from the categories "clothing, men's custom" and "clothing, women's custom". The GVP per employee for each category, respectively, was extrapolated from 1921 through 1922 to 1926 on the basis of average earnings per employee for "men's factory clothing" and "women's factory clothing".

The aggregate gross value of product in each year was obtained as the product of the number of gainfully occupied persons and the gross value of product per worker. The additions giving the aggregate gross value of product for the industry group appear in the following table.

Gross Value of Product, Clothing, etc. 1917-1926
(all values in $000)

Year	HSC	Custom and Repair Tailors	Custom and Repair Dressmaking	Grand Total, Project
1917	148,571	18,646	33,908	201,125
1918	171,083	25,375	43,408	239,866
1919	205,425	30,400	49,751	285,576
1920	239,352	31,263	45,041	315,656
1921	174,191	25,447	37,975	237,613
1922	172,547	22,998	31,099	226,644
1923	180,640	23,087	30,035	233,762
1924	178,112	18,769	25,353	222,234
1925	189,654	19,342	25,113	234,109
1926	213,166	20,321	24,418	257,905

(c) Iron and Steel Products

The HSC estimates were adjusted upwards to take account of independent blacksmith shops. The general method used is the same as that described in the explanation of the preparation of the data for 1900 and 1910. It is necessary to add only some additional information relevant to this period. The general method was to obtain an estimate of the number of gainfully occupied in each year, and an estimate of gross value of product per worker. The aggregate gross value of product then followed as the product of these two quantities.

It has been explained already, in the description of the 1900 and 1910 estimates how the figures for the numbers of self-employed blacksmiths and of gainfully occupied persons in these shops were obtained. The numbers of gainfully occupied for all years 1917 to 1926 were obtained as follows:

	1910	1920	1930
Number of self-employed	9,232	9,267	8,181
Number of gainfully occupied	14,402	15,386	11,949
Ratio of gainfully occupied to self-employed	1.56	1.66	1.46

The numbers of, first, self-employed and, second, all gainfully occupied (including the self-employed) in blacksmith shops were obtained from the censuses for census years as described before. The numbers of self-employed for 1917 to 1919 were then estimated by linear interpolation between the census figures for 1910 and 1920; likewise the self-employed for 1921 to 1926 were estimated by linear interpolation between 1920 and 1930. Ratios of the numbers gainfully occupied to numbers of self-employed were then calculated from the census data for each census year 1910, 1920 and 1930 and for 1917 to 1919 were obtained by linear interpolation between 1910 and 1920 and for 1921 to 1926 by linear interpolation between 1920 and 1930. The numbers of gainfully occupied for 1917 to 1919 and 1921 to 1926 were then obtained by multiplying the number of self-employed by the relevant ratio of gainfully occupied to self-employed.

Gross value of product per worker was available for 1917 to 1921 but had to be estimated for 1922 to 1926. For 1917 to 1921, the gross value of product per worker was obtained from the reports on blacksmith shops in the section on hand trades in the census of manufactures; these data were not collected after 1921. For 1922-26 the gross value of product per worker was projected from 1921 on the basis of average earnings in the iron and steel industry calculated from data in HSC and the ratio of these average earnings to GVP in each year. This latter ratio was obtained for 1921 and 1930 from actual values as obtained directly in these years; it was interpolated linearly for 1922 to 1926. For the years 1922 to 1926 the product of this ratio and the average earnings provided the estimate of gross value of product per worker.

The totals for the iron and steel industry was then obtained as shown in the following table.

Gross Value of Product, Iron and Steel Industries
Adjusted for Blacksmith Shops ($000)

Year	Gross Value of Product, HSC	Gross Value of Product, Blacksmith Shops	Grand Total, Gross Value of Product, Project
1917	448,576	25,936	474,512
1918	496,305	26,471	522,776
1919	351,103	29,032	380,135
1920	449,221	30,187	479,408
1921	267,405	26,268	293,673
1922	206,519	22,944	229,463
1923	283,207	22,804	306,011
1924	230,133	20,599	250,732
1925	245,176	19,379	264,555
1926	300,546	18,519	319,065

(d) Transportation Equipment

The HSC estimates were adjusted upward to take account of automobile repairs. (Railway car repairs had been included in 1911 and earlier and are specifically designated also in the 1917, 1918 and 1919 census of manufactures.)

Automobile repair work was covered in the hand trades of the census of manufactures from 1917 to 1921. The gross values of product of this segment as reported in the census of manufactures for 1920 and 1921 were accepted as reported; it appeared that this industry segment suffered from under coverage in 1917 to 1919 and it was not reported in the census of manufactures at all after 1921. It was necessary then to make estimates for 1917 to 1919 and 1922 to 1926.

The years that served as base years for these estimates were 1921 and 1930. The gross value of product for 1921 was plucked out of the census of manufactures for 1921. The gross value of product for 1930 came from the Merchandising (Retail) and Services (Retail) Census 1930, 1931 Census, Volume 10, pp. 70 and 1046, Volume 11, pp. 68. It includes the service and parts components only from each of garage operatives of motor vehicle dealers, the services garages and merchandising garages.

The interpolator-extrapolator series was the total number of motor vehicle registrations reported in HSC, Series S222. The use of the interpolator and the derivation of the series for 1917 to 1926 is shown in the following table.

Basis of Estimation of Gross Value of Product
and Entire Automobile Repair, 1917-1926

Year	Number of Motor Vehicle Registrations	Ratio of Gross Value of Product to Vehicles Registered	Gross Value of Product Automobile Repair ($000)	HSC, Transport Equipment ($000)	Grand Total, Gross Value of Product, Project
1917	203.5	(39.81)	(8,101)	197,795	205,896
1918	276.9	(39.81)	(11,023)	240,871	251,894
1919	342.4	(39.81)	(13,631)	251,739	265,370
1920	408.8	-------	16,593	285,230	301,823
1921	464.8	39.81	18,506	158,050	176,556
1922	509.4	(40.15)	(20,452)	144,706	165,158
1923	576.0	(40.50)	(23,328)	207,310	230,638
1924	645.3	(40.84)	(26,354)	169,672	196,026
1925	724.0	(41.19)	(29,822)	196,366	226,188
1926	832.3	(41.53)	(34,565)	244,185	278,750
1930	1,232.5	42.91	52,889		

The number of motor vehicles registered (Column 1) was available from the source for every year. The gross value of product, automobile repair was available for 1920, 1921 and 1930. The ratio of gross value of product to the number of motor vehicles registered was calculated for 1921 and 1930 from the base data. This ratio was interpolated linearly between 1930 and 1921, for years 1922 to 1926; it was assumed that the 1921 ratio applied also to 1917 to 1919. The gross value of product for 1917 to 1919 and 1922 to 1926 for each year was calculated by multiplying the number of vehicles registered by the corresponding ratio. (Estimated figures are in brackets.) ,

The addition of this gross value of product for automobile repair, column 3, to the HSC figure for the transport equipment industry (Column 4) yields the project figure for transportation equipment.

(e) Miscellaneous

The HSC gross value of product for the miscellaneous group was adjusted upward by allowances for custom and repair items that had been included in earlier censuses of manufactures but were not included in the later censuses. The items to be added include: for 1917 to 1919 the single item "lock and gunsmithing" as reported in the hand trades of the census of manufactures for those years; for 1920 to 1926 the added items were electrical repairs, elevator repairs, harness and saddlery repairs, jewellery repairs and lock and gunsmithing repairs.

The values for 1920 and 1921 were obtained from the appropriate items in the "hand trades" category of the census of manufactures for those years. These items for 1920 and 1921 were:

Gross Value of Product, Miscellaneous Items
of Miscellaneous Industries Group ($000)

	1920	1921
Electrical contracts and repairs (1/2 of reported item)	2,460	2,527
Elevator repairs	1,719	1,914
Harness and saddlery repairs	2,432	940
Jewellery repairs	4,506	3,246
Lock and gunsmithing repairs	161	96
Total	11,278	8,723
Unaccounted for	214	184
	11,492	8,907

The values for 1922 to 1926 were obtained by interpolation between 1921 and 1930 as follows:

From the Services Census (for 1930) in the 1931 decennial census an estimate of gross value of product of equivalent items as those to be estimated for 1922 to 1926 was calculated. This estimate basically depended on obtaining from the census of occupations and industries, the numbers engaged in these items of activity and multiplying the numbers engaged by a gross value of product per worker determined from such activities in the services industries census. The activities covered were carriage repairs, harness repairs, locksmith, radio and electrical repairs, watch and jewellery repairs, furniture repairs and a small group of miscellaneous. The result of these steps was to yield:

6,360 employees at a GVP of $1,516.77 per employee, yielding a total of gross value of product of $9,647,000 for 1930.

The interpolator used was the gross value of product of other "hand trades" industries, with which we have already dealt, *viz.* the hand trades in leather products, in clothing (textile and fur), in iron and steel products and in transportation equipment. The ratios of the gross value of product in the hand trades of the miscellaneous industry group to the interpolator were calculated for 1921 and 1930. By linear interpolation, like ratios were calculated for 1922 to 1926. These latter ratios were multiplied by the relevant value of the interpolator to yield the gross values of product year by year.

The material follows.

Year	Gross Value of Product, Miscellaneous Hand Trades ($000)	Ratio of GVP to Interpolator	Interpolator ($000)
1921	8,723	.072	121,575
1922	(8,137)	(.073)	111,742
1923	(8,356)	(.074)	112,923
1924	(7,802)	(.075)	104,022
1925	(8,062)	(.076)	106,078
1926	(8,486)	(.077)	110,206
1930	9,647	.080	120,430

The items in brackets are estimated.

The Interpolations Between Base Years

Primary data were available only for base years until the annual census of manufactures was begun with the year 1917. This circumstance meant that to obtain estimates of production for all years it would be necessary to interpolate between base years for the period for 1870 to 1917. This section provides a description of the way in which the interpolation was done.

The interpolations were done at various levels of disaggregation for industry groups. At one extreme, in practice, the food and beverage industry group interpolations were done at the level of seven component industries plus a residual of all other components; at the other extreme the electrical apparatus and supplies industry group interpolations were done at the single aggregate level for the whole group.

There was no one method of interpolation that was used in all cases. However, there was one method that was used much the most commonly and a description of that method at this time will have wide relevance as the individual industry groups are examined.

This widely used method involved first finding some series of annual data of an economic quantity that would be expected to bear a regular relationship to the component industry values that were to be interpolated: for example, the importation of raw cotton (and to a lesser extent cotton yarn) in providing input materials for the Canadian cotton textile industry might be expected to move closely in sympathy with the output of cotton textiles: the data for the component industries to be interpolated were always gross value of product; the interpolators also were usually in value form. These annual series when found became the interpolator series. In their use, a ratio of the interpolator to the gross value of product of the component industry in each base year was calculated. These interpolator ratios were then linearly interpolated between each pair of juxtaposed base years to provide ratios for the in-between years. The interpolator series in the in-between years were then divided by the interpolator ratios to give gross value of product for the in-between years. This method will be called the regular or standard method.

Other interpolation methods were used in a small number of instances. They will be described when particular instances of their use are involved.

The years 1870, 1880, 1890, 1900, 1910 and 1917 were almost always base years; 1905 was seldom a base year and in what follows it has been made a base year only when that fact is explicitly mentioned; 1915 was usually a base year and in its case, special mention will be made only when it is not a base year. The interpolations are now described, industry group by industry group.

1. The Food and Beverages Industry

This industry group was interpolated by seven component groups, *viz.* (i) malt liquors, (ii) spirits, (iii) bread, biscuits and confectionary, (iv) butter and cheese, (v) flour and grist mill products, (vi) sugar refining, and (vii) slaughterhouses, and a residual group in the following manner.

(i) Malt liquors

The interpolator for malt beverages is constructed from two series. The first series is the amount (in gallons) of malt liquor released from bond for consumption: these data are given in individual annual reports of the Internal Revenue Department of the federal government and the information is also given in the *Canada Year Book*. Since these data were reported on a fiscal year basis they were converted to calendar year basis, after having been valued, by weighting the value of the interpolator of each fiscal year by the proportion of that fiscal year which lay within the calendar year concerned. The second series is a series of wholesale prices of malt liquor: for 1890 to 1917 the price of malt liquor per barrel was obtained from Department of Labour *Wholesale Prices, 1890 to 1909* and subsequent annual reports on *Wholesale Prices* of the Department of Labour; for 1870 to 1890 the Coats wholesale price for 1890 was projected backward on the basis of the price of barley obtained from Taylor and Michell, *Statistical Contributions to Canadian Economic History*. It was assumed that there were forty gallons per barrel.

The interpolator was the product of the above series, quantity times price. (Note from what follows that the level of the price would not matter — just the proportionate movement from year to year is important.)

The next steps were to (a) calculate the ratio of the value of the interpolator to the gross value of product in base years (b) to interpolate this ratios linearly between base years and (c) for non-basis years to divide the interpolator by the ratio obtained in step (b) in order to get a gross value of product for interpolated years.

The interpolation ratios were as follows:

Base Year	Ratio of Interpolator to Gross Value of Product of Malt Liquors
1870	0.6828
1880	0.4968
1890	0.5128
1900	0.5625
1910	0.5352
1915	0.5448
1917	0.4016

At this point it should be noted that both the interpolator prices and gross values of product have included excise taxes. They were removed later.

(ii) Spirits

The principle of interpolation was the same as that used for the malt liquors.

The selection of the appropriate annual interpolator of quantity of spirits produced raised a problem. Internal Revenue, Canada, reported both spirits manufactured and spirits released for consumption. The two did not correspond well which is not surprising in view of the large stocks held in this industry. When a value was put on each of these sets of data, the changes in the value of spirits released for consumption (plus the value of exports which was very small) corresponded much more closely to changes in gross value of product from the census of manufactures in the base years than did changes in the value of manufactures reported by Internal Revenue. In the light of this testing the interpolator series used was the value of spirits released for consumption plus the value of exports of spirits.

The value of spirits released for consumption was obtained by valuing the gallonage of spirits released, as reported by the Internal Revenue Service, and converted from a fiscal year to a calendar year basis, by a price for spirits. The prices series were obtained as follows: 1870 to 1889 from Michell (32 U.P. whisky per gallon); 1890 to 1909 *Wholesale Prices*; 1910 to 1917

Dept. of Labour, *Wholesale Prices* (20.8 U.P. whiskey per gallon). The Michell and the Department of Labour series were linked at 1890. Although there was not a year of overlap of prices at 1890 it was assumed that the 1889 and 1890 prices were the same since prices did not change between 1886 and 1889 and again between 1891 and 1906. The spirits released for consumption were then valued at the prices that have been described. To this value of spirits released for consumption the value of exports of spirits (including very small amounts of beer and ale) was added. The resultant series then become the interpolator.

The method of use of the interpolator was exactly the same as the method used in the case of beer. Since the prices included excise taxes the gross values of product interpolated were gross values including excise taxes. Once the interpolation was done the excise taxes were subtracted to yield gross value of product excluding excise taxes.

As well as the usual base year, 1905 was also used as a base year. The interpolation ratios were as follows.

Base Year	Ratio of Interpolator to Gross Value of Product of Spirits
1870	0.8907
1880	0.7863
1890	0.8483
1900	0.8123
1905	0.8270
1910	0.8715
1915	0.6753
1917	0.6668

(iii) Bread, biscuits and confectionery

The two annual basic component series of the interpolator were the value of domestic disappearance of flour and the value of domestic disappearance of refined sugar. The value of the domestic disappearance of flour comes from the section on the interpolator for flour and grist mills products below; the value of the domestic disappearance of sugar comes from the section on the interpolation for the products of sugar refineries from below. The way in which the two series were calculated is explained in those sections.

The process of using these series involved some additional steps. First, each series of values was put into index form with base 1900=100. These indexes were then combined as a single weighted interpolator index, the weights being 0.8 for flour and 0.2 for sugar. This index of the combined value of the component series values then yielded the interpolator between the base years. (Note: this index just had one base year, 1900: it is distinct from what have been called the base years of the data set.) The adjustment was made by first calculating the ratio of the composite index value of the interpolator to an interpolator that had the same values for base years but for non-base years had linearly interpolated values between the base year values: this adjusting series showed how much each non-base year stood, in relative terms, above or below a simple linear trend between base year figures. Second, a dollar value for gross value of product interpolated linearly between basis year values was multiplied by this ratio that had just been calculated, to take account of year to year variations from straight lines interpolations from one base year to the next. The interpolation ratios were as follows.

Base Year	Ratio of Interpolator to Gross Value of Product of Bread, Biscuits & Confectionery
1870	0.848
1880	1.018
1890	1.128
1900	1.000
1910	1.696
1917	4.536

(iv) Butter and cheese, factory product

The basic interpolator was Ontario production of cheese and butter which was recorded annually from 1883 onward; before 1883 resort was had to straight line interpolation between 1870 and 1880 and between 1880 and 1883. Each of these interpolation periods is considered in turn: the last will be dealt with first.

Value of cheese production was recorded in the census of manufactures for both 1870 and 1880; values for intervening years were estimated by linear interpolation. The large growth of gross value of production from 1.5 million dollars in 1870 to 5.5 million dollars in 1880 may mean that a linear interpolation is not very accurate but it was the best that could be done. There was no record of factory production of butter in Canada in 1870; the relatively small amount of 0.3 million dollars worth was recorded in the 1880 census. It was assumed that factory production of butter began in Canada in 1875 and grew by equal annual increments to 1880.

Since there was no record of cheese and butter production in any part of Canada for 1881 and 1882, resort to linear interpolation between the census of 1880 values and the project estimate for 1883, described below, was used for the Province of Ontario. These Ontario values were then used in the same way as described for the years 1883 onward.

For 1883 onward until 1916 the Ontario Bureau of Industries collected data on butter and cheese production annually and reported them in its annual report. These data were used from 1883 onward as follows. For census of Canada years, production of cheese and butter in Ontario as reported by the federal census and by the Ontario Bureau of Industries were compared with the following results.

Gross Value of Product, Butter and Cheese
($000)

Year	Ontario, Census of Canada	Ontario Bureau of Industries	Ratio: Census of Canada to Ontario Bureau of Industries
1890	7,569.3	7,410.8	1.0214
1900	14,968.9	14,842.3	1.0085
1910	18,148.6	17,507.5	1.0366
1915	28,518.5	26,233.0	1.0871

(It will be noted that the data from each source correspond quite well.)

The Canadian Census data for Ontario were used for each census year; for intervening years it was assumed that the ratio of the census-based estimate for Ontario to the Ontario Bureau of Industries estimates followed a linear interpolation between each adjacent pair of census years; since the Ontario Bureau of Industries data only went back to 1883, it was assumed that the ratio of production, had it been obtained by the census to Ontario Bureau of Industries data, was 1.0214, the 1890 ratio. The estimates of production in Ontario were then obtained by multiplying the annual Ontario Bureau of Industries data on production by the relevant ratio from the foregoing calculations. As already noted, estimates of production for Ontario for 1881 and 1882 were obtained by linear interpolation between the Canadian census figure for 1880 and the figure obtained in the immediately preceding estimate for 1883. In addition, the Ontario Bureau of Industries did not publish data for 1907: the data for this year were obtained from the *Canada Year Book* 1921, pp. 252 ff. for both Ontario and Canada.

The next steps were to go from Ontario to Canada. The steps involved were: first, a ratio of the value of production in Ontario to that in all Canada was calculated for census years (including 1905, in which the ratio seemed appropriate but not absolute levels of output, and 1907 from the *Canada Year Book* data noted immediately above); second, linear interpolations of these ratios of between the base years, noted above, were made; third, the annual data on gross value of production for Canada, from 1880 to 1915 were calculated for each year by dividing the value of Ontario production by the estimated ratio of Ontario production to all-Canada production. The following were the ratios of Ontario to all-Canada.

1870	1880	1890	1900	1905	1907	1910	1915
.9070	.8406	.7076	.5081	.5047	.4986	.4874	.5068

A special note for 1916 is necessary. The figure actually used for 1916 was based on the assumption that the *Canada Year Book* figure for 1916 was understated in the same proportion as for 1915. The 1916 estimate was obtained from the process:

$$\frac{\text{Census figure for Canada 1915}}{\text{Canada Year Book for 1915}} \times \text{Canada Year Book for 1916}$$

An alternative method of estimation based on using the 1916 Ontario Bureau of Industries figure multiplied by the 1915 value 1.0871 (see the ratio of Canadian census to OBI above) and divided by the 1915 value .5068 (ratio of Ontario to Canada) yields almost the same result.

(v) Flour and grist mill products

The interpolator is the value of flour produced in Canada. This value was comprised of the sum of two parts, value of exports of flour and value of domestic consumption. (Imports were not significant.) The values of exports of flour were obtained from the foreign trade data of the sessional papers of Canada: nearly the whole series came from Sessional Papers of Canada 1916, sessional paper 10; the remaining trade data came from Sessional Papers, 1919, no. 10. The trade data which were for fiscal years, were converted to calendar years.

The process of estimation of domestic consumption of flour was a little more elaborate. The physical domestic consumption of flour was obtained by assuming consumption of wheat per capita in Canada at 5.5 bushels per capita — this latter figure was a very widely given estimate throughout the period of these estimates. Multiplication of population by 5.5 bushels per capita yielded wheat consumption in bushels. At 44.2 pounds of flour per bushel of wheat and 196 pounds of flour per barrel measure, the estimated consumption of wheat was converted to barrels of flour. These were then valued at the price of "flour, strong baker's" obtained for 1890 onwards from *Wholesale Prices 1890-1909* and annual publications of the Department of Labour from 1910 onward. (I have not found the exact source of the price before 1890. I would guess it is related to export unit values.)

The year 1915 was not used as a base year. The interpolation ratios were as follows:

Base Year	Ratio of Interpolator to Gross Value of Product of Flour & Gristmill Products
1870	0.6508
1880	0.7245
1890	0.6080
1900	0.6334
1910	0.7047
1917	0.8727

(vi) Sugar refineries

The basic interpolation data were the value of raw sugar imported for the refineries including the customs duties levied on the raw sugar. The source was Canadian Trade data obtained from the basic Canadian government publications. Since the original data were for fiscal years they were converted to a calendar year basis.

The procedures in making the interpolations were: first, the ratio of the interpolator to the gross value of product was calculated for each of the base years; these base years ratios were interpolated linearly between adjacent base years; the estimates of gross value of product for non-base years were then obtained by dividing the value of the interpolator by the interpolated ratio. The ratios of the interpolator to base year values of gross value of product were:

Year	Ratio	Year	Ratio
1870	0.4128	1900	0.6664
1880	0.5705	1910	0.7717
1890	0.6670	1915	0.7022
		1917	0.6087

(vii) Meat-packing and slaughterhouses

The interpolator between base years was the value of cattle and calves disposed of from Canadian farms for consumption in Canada. This was obtained from estimates of the number of Canadian produced cattle consumed in Canada valued at a price per head. The number of Canadian-produced cattle consumed in Canada was estimated by subtracting the numbers of live cattle exported from the total production of cattle for off-farm sales or slaughter. (Importation of live cattle into Canada were almost certainly mainly for breeding stock and not for slaughter.) The description of the source data is given in the section on the agricultural production in Canada.

Ratios of the interpolator to gross value of product in the base years were calculated. These ratios were then interpolated linearly between each adjacent pair of base years and the interpolator was then divided by the interpolation ratios in non-base years to yield estimates of gross values of product in non-base years. The base year ratios follow.

Ratio of Value of Cattle and Calves Slaughtered in Canada to Gross
Value of Production of Slaughterhouses and Meatpacking Plants

Year	Ratio
1870	6.4478
1880	4.8511
1890	3.4366
1900	1.1908
1910	1.0409
1915	0.7312
1917	0.4566

It might well be argued that the value of hogs slaughtered in Canada should have been included in the interpolator. The production of hogs relative to cattle increased substantially during this period. Yet the relative increases between pairs of base years took place relatively smoothly so that the addition of hogs to the interpolator would not have made much change to the interpolator estimates. It must be remembered that the interpolators are used only for interpolation between successive pairs of base years. Inclusion of hogs in the interpolator would have raised the interpolation ratios as well as the interpolators themselves in all years but more in the later years than in the earlier years.

The actual fall in the interpolation ratios based only on cattle probably takes place initially with the removal of much slaughtering from farms to slaughterhouses; they are also based on the relative increase in the value of pork production; in the 1915 to 1917 period they are affected by wartime effects on prices.

(viii) The residual and total food and beverage production

The above seven components accounted for by far the larger part of food and beverage production but there was a small residual production of other products. These were accounted for by direct estimate of total production of non-alcoholic food and beverage production as follows.

The ratios to the total gross value of product for the whole non-alcoholic food and beverage group of the sum of the gross values of production for the five individually interpolated non-alcoholic categories were calculated for base years. These new ratios were interpolated, in turn, between adjacent pairs of base years by linear interpolation. The gross values of production for the whole industry exclusive of alcoholic categories for non-base years were obtained by dividing the sums for the five components by the new ratios of gross values of products of the sums of the five components to the entire non-alcoholic beverage group.

The ratios that permitted the latter projection are the following.

Base Years	Ratio of Sum of Gross Value of Product of Five Non-Alcoholic Industries to Entire Non-Alcoholic Food and Beverage Group
1870	0.97312
1880	0.93297
1890	0.87189
1900	0.85518
1910	0.85790
1917	0.87037

The year 1915 was not a base year in the last calculation.

The total for the entire industry group of food and all alcoholic beverages was obtained simply by adding the alcoholic beverage values to the non-alcoholic group.

2. The Tobacco Products Industry

The interpolator was the value of tobacco, snuff and cigarettes taken out of bond. This value was obtained as the product of the physical quantities in pounds of tobacco, snuff and cigarettes taken out of bond and the price per pound excluding excise duties on tobacco products.

The weight of tobacco products taken for consumption (out of bond) in Canada is obtained from the Internal Revenue Reports of the Canadian Government. They were reported in the *Canada Year Book* and actually taken therefrom. The prices per pound exclusive of excise duty were obtained in two steps. Wholesale prices per pound of cut tobacco products were obtained from Michell for 1870 to 1889 and from the Department of Labour *Wholesale Prices* from 1890 onward. These wholesale prices appeared to include excise duties; they often continued without change for several years. Excise duties per pound were calculated from data on pounds of tobacco consumption per head in Canada and tobacco duty paid per head. A price per pound excluding excise duties was then obtained for each year by subtracting the excise duty per pound from the wholesale price per pound. The resulting price (excluding excise duty) was multiplied by the quantity of tobacco released for consumption to yield an annual figure of value excluding excise duty of tobacco products consumed on a fiscal year basis. This series was then converted to a calendar year basis to yield the interpolator.

The next steps were: a ratio of the interpolator to gross value of product was calculated for each base year; in this case both 1905 and 1915 were base years; the ratios were then interpolated linearly between adjacent pairs of base years to obtain ratios for non-base years; the interpolator values for non-base years were then divided by the corresponding ratios to yield a gross value of product estimate for non-base years. The interpolation ratios follow.

Ratio of Interpolator to Gross Value of Product of Tobacco Products

Base Year	Ratio	Base Year	Ratio
1870	0.4883	1905	0.4048
1880	0.4186	1910	0.4021
1890	0.4369	1915	0.3561
1900	0.3934	1917	0.2821

3. Rubber Products Industry

The interpolator was the value of imports of raw rubber obtained from the annual reports of *Trade of Canada*. The data, which were reported on a fiscal year basis were converted to a calendar year basis.

The procedure for making the interpolation of gross value of product was: first the ratio of the interpolator to gross value of product in each base year was calculated; second, these ratios were then linearly interpolated between adjacent base years; third the gross value of product for non-base years was derived by dividing the interpolator by the relevant ratio of interpolator to gross value of product. The ratios of the interpolator to gross value of product in base years follow.

Base Years	Ratio of Value of Imported Raw Rubber to Gross Value of Product
1870	0.322
1880	0.341
1890	0.334
1900	0.455
1910	0.423
1915	0.277
1917	0.192

4. Leather Products Industry

The leather products group was interpolated in two parts: (i) the product of leather tanneries; (ii) all other leather products. The interpolator for the tanneries was the value of the domestic disappearance of hides of cattle and calves; the interpolator for "all other leather products" was the value of the domestic disappearance of leather. These two components are dealt with in turn.

(i) The leather tanneries

The value of the domestic disappearance of hides was obtained from values of domestic production plus value of imports minus value of exports of hides.

The calculation of the domestic production of hides involved several steps. The number of such hides was taken as being equal to the number of cattle and calves slaughtered in Canada, the derivation of which has been described already in the section on slaughterhouses in the food and beverage group. It was assumed that two thirds of the animals slaughtered were adults and one third was calves. An adult green hide weighs 60 pounds and a green calfskin 20 pounds yielding an average of 47 pounds per hide for the whole group; the total number of pounds of hides is then the number of cattle and calves multiplied by 47. The prices of hides and of calfskins per pound were obtained from Michell, p. 73 for 1870 to 1889 and from Department of Labour *Wholesale Prices 1890-1909*, pp. 152, 153 and successor annual volumes for 1910 to 1917. Since there were 6 pounds of cattle hides for every one pound of calfskin the weighted average price of the total of the adult hides and the calfskins was obtained by weighting the adult prices by six and prices of calfskins by unity. The values of domestically produced hides and skins were then obtained from the product of quantity and price. The value of the domestic disappearance of hides and skins was then obtained by subtracting the value of exports from the value of domestic production and adding the value of imports. The external trade data were obtained from *Trade of Canada* and were converted to a calendar year basis. The resulting value of domestic disappearance of hides in Canada was the interpolator.

The gross value of product of the tanneries was then calculated as follows: first, the ratio of the interpolator to gross value of product in base years was determined; second, these ratios are linearly interpolated between adjacent base years; third, the gross value of product for non-base years is derived by dividing the interpolator by the interpolated ratio. The ratios of the gross value of domestic disappearance of hides to gross value of product of the tanneries in base years follow.

Year	Ratio of Gross Value of Domestic Disappearance of Hides to Gross Value of Product of Tanneries
1870	0.314
1880	0.286
1890	0.311
1900	0.493
1910	0.502
1915	0.671
1917	0.492

(ii) All other leather products

The interpolator was the value of the domestic disappearance of leather. This interpolator was obtained from the gross value of the tanneries of Canada (from immediately above) less the value of exports of leather plus the value of imports of leather (from Canadian Trade data adjusted to a calendar year basis).

The gross value of product of all other leather products is then interpolated in the usual way: the ratios of the interpolator to the gross values of product for base years are calculated; these ratios are then linearly interpolated between adjacent base years; finally, the gross value of product for non-base years is obtained by dividing the interpolator by the interpolation ratio.

The interpolation ratios for base years were as follows:

Year	Ratio of Value of Domestic Disappearance of Leather to Gross Value of Product "All Other Leather"
1870	0.546
1880	0.727
1890	0.475
1900	0.463
1910	0.441
1915	0.443
1917	0.497

The total gross value of product for the entire industry group is simply the sum of the two components.

5. Textile Products (Excluding Clothing) Industry

This industry group was interpolated in four components, *viz*., (i) woollen textiles, (ii) cotton textiles, (iii) cordage, rope and twine, and (iv) all other textiles. The interpolators of the first three components, in order, were: (i) the domestic disappearance of wool; (ii) the domestic disappearance (importation) of raw cotton; (iii) the domestic disappearance (imports) of hemp, manilla grass and Mexican grass. "All other textiles" was treated as a residual and handled in the same manner as "all other" in the food and beverage group.

(i) Woollen textiles. Woollen textiles included the categories: carding and fulling; woollen goods; woollen yarns, wool pulling.

The interpolator, the value of the domestic disappearance of raw wool, was obtained by adding the value of imports to the value of domestic production and then subtracting the value of exports. The value of domestic production of raw wool was estimated in the work on the income of agriculture and the method of estimation is described in the section on agriculture. The values of imports and exports both came from the official trade data: import values were taken from Taylor in *Statistical Contributions* for 1870 to 1915; all other trade values were from the trade data of the Sessional Papers or of the Dominion Bureau of Statistics. Trade data were converted from a fiscal year to a calendar year basis.

The usual method of interpolation was followed. Ratios of domestic disappearance of raw wool to gross value of production of the woollen textiles were calculated for the base years, these ratios were interpolated linearly for non-base years from 1870 to 1910 and by special treatment described below for 1910 to 1917, the interpolator was then divided by the interpolation ratio to yield an estimate of gross value of product for non-base years.

There was a special problem of estimation for 1910 to 1917. Beginning moderately in 1914 but burgeoning in 1915 there were very large imports of wool related to the war, which initially must have led to large accumulations of inventory. For example, the ratio of apparent domestic disappearance of raw wool to gross value of product which could be estimated by the census of manufacturers for 1915 became inordinately high and then that for 1917 became inordinately low. In these circumstances the interpolation ratios for 1911 to 1914 were made the same as for 1910; the ratios for 1915 and 1917 were obtained from the raw material values as calculated in the ordinary way and the gross value of product figures of the censuses of manufactures and the ratio for 1916 was half way between the 1915 and 1917 values.

The relevant ratios for base years follow.

Base Year	Ratio of Domestic Disappearance of Wool to Gross Value of Product of Woollen Textiles
1870	0.301
1880	0.333
1890	0.338
1900	0.361
1910	0.396
1915	0.727
1917	0.197

(ii) Cotton textiles. The items included in cotton textiles are: awnings, tents and sails; bags (cotton); threads; yarn and duck (1890 only); cottons.

The interpolator was the value of imports of raw cotton, which came originally from official trade statistics but were taken from Taylor for 1870 to 1915 and from the trade reports for fiscal 1916, 1917, 1918. The data were converted from a fiscal to a calendar year basis.

The usual ratio method was used. Ratios of value of raw cotton imports to gross value of product of cotton textiles were calculated for base years; these ratios were linearly interpolated between adjacent base years; gross value of product for non-base years were estimated by dividing the interpolator by the interpolation ratios. Interpolation ratios for 1911 to 1914 and 1916 were obtained by linear interpolation between the 1910 and 1917 ratios; the gross value of product for 1915 was obtained from the census of manufactures for 1915 but 1915 was not made a base year.

The interpolation ratios follow.

Year	Ratio of Value of Imports of Raw Cotton to Gross Value of Production of Cotton Textiles
1870	0.435
1880	0.419
1890	0.387
1900	0.327
1910	0.341
1917	0.326

(iii) Cordage, rope and twine. This category was usually reported as one item under the above name.

The interpolator was the value of imports of dressed hemp from 1870 to 1900 and value of imports of hemp, manilla grass and Mexican grass for 1900 to 1917. These data came from official trade data.

The usual ratio method was used. The ratio of the interpolator to gross value of product was calculated for base years; the ratio was linearly interpolated between adjacent base years; the interpolator was then divided by the interpolation ratio to yield gross value of product in non-base years.

The base year interpolation ratios follow.

Base Year	Ratio of Value of Interpolator to Gross Value of Product of Cordage, Rope and Twine
1870	0.377
1880	0.443
1890	0.476
1900 (hemp only)	0.366
1900 (all products)	0.376
1910	0.550
1915	0.675
1917	0.854

(iv) Total for all textiles (excluding clothing).   All other textiles (excluding clothing) were essentially estimated in the process of estimating the total gross value of product for the whole industry group. This was done by: first, total gross value of product for woollen textiles, cotton textiles and cordage rope and twine was obtained, by summation, for base years; second the ratio of this summed gross value of product for the above three categories to the gross value of product for the whole industry group was calculated for each base year; third, these ratios were linearly interpolated between adjacent base years; finally non-base year estimates of gross value of product for the total group were obtained by dividing the summed values for the three categories by the interpolation ratios.

The interpolation ratios follow — 1915 was not used as a base year in this step.

Base Year	Ratio of Summed Gross Values of Product For Three Component Categories, to Gross Value of Product of Entire Textile Group (Excluding Clothing)
1870	0.964
1880	0.924
1890	0.840
1900	0.714
1910	0.841
1917	0.844

6. Clothing: Textile and Fur Industry

The interpolation was done in one step for the group as a whole. The interpolator was a series made up of the sum of cloth imports, predominantly cotton and woollen but including also silk and linen, values of yarn imports, and the values of domestic production of woollen and of cotton textiles.

The sources of the data for the interpolator are pretty straight forward excepting the case of imports for 1869-70 to 1873-74. Imports of cloth of all kinds were available in the official Canadian trade data from 1874-75 onward and were taken therefrom: the values included duty. The trade data on textiles were given in more aggregated form prior to 1874-75 than from 1874-75 onward. Cloth imports for fiscal years 1869-70 to 1873-74 were estimated by applying average ratios for 1874-75 to 1878-79 of the value of cloth including duty to total values imports of textile manufactures to years 1869-70 to 1873-74. Values of imports of yarn, including duty, were also obtained from the official trade data: they were relatively small. These trade data were converted to a calendar year basis. The values of production of woollen textiles and of cotton textiles separately were obtained from the material of the data on textiles (excluding clothing) of the industry group of that name.

Once the interpolator was constructed the common procedure of using it to interpolate the gross value of products between base years was followed. A single interpolation was done for the industry as a whole. The steps were: first, the ratios of the interpolator to gross value of product for the industry group for base years were calculated; second, these ratios were interpolated in linear fashion between adjacent base years to get non-base year interpolation ratios; finally, the interpolator was divided by the base year ratio year by year to obtain non-base year values. The year 1915 was not used as a base year in this industry group.

The ratios of the interpolator to gross value of product follow.

Base Year	Ratio of Interpolator to Gross Value of Product of Industry Group
1870	1.160
1880	0.821
1890	0.706
1900	0.773
1910	0.652
1917	0.729

7. Wood Products Industry

There was a single interpolator for the whole wood products group but the interpolator itself is a product of interpolation and was derived in different ways for different time periods. The interpolator was the gross value of product of sawmills and planing mills which, of course, was a component of the wood products group.

It should be noted at the outset that it was not easy to obtain the inter census gross value of product of the saw and planing mills only. Such estimates required derivations of interpolators for the sawmills and log product mills themselves. David Jones tested several different methods and those that he adopted appeared to be the best for the particular time period concerned. His procedure for each time period follows. Basic to the whole series, of course, were the census of manufactures values obtained for the years 1870, 1880, 1890, 1900, 1910, 1915 and 1917.

(i) The decade 1870 to 1880

For the years from 1870 to 1880 Jones used the tonnage of lumber passing through the Ottawa canals, obtained from the Inland Revenue reports in the Canadian Sessional Papers, adjusted by movements in the prices of wood products, obtained from HSC, Series J39, in such a way as to make the interpolator reflect the value of the lumber shipments on the Ottawa canals.

(ii) The decades 1880 to 1890 and 1890 to 1900

The construction of the interpolator itself involved a number of steps. First, value of exports of lumber and squared timber were obtained from *Trade of Canada* figures for every year. Second, for each of the census years 1880, 1890, 1900, internal use of Canadian lumber products was obtained by subtracting export values from gross value of production of the saw and planing mill sector. Third, the value of importation of a wide range of building materials was obtained for each year. This last series was then used to interpolate the values of internal usage of Canadian lumber products between the census years 1880 and 1890 and, again, 1890 and 1900. Fourth, the exports of lumber and like products were added to the domestic usage of the product of the saw and planing mill group for all years to yield the interpolator for the period from 1880 to 1900.

(iii) The period 1900 to 1910

For 1900 to 1908, Ken Buckley's estimates of production of construction materials, available in *Capital Formation in Canada,* p. 198 and for 1908 to 1910 (overlapping at 1908), total value of lumber production from HSC, Series K130, were used to fill in values between the census of 1900, that of 1905 and that of 1910.

(iv) The periods 1910 to 1915 and 1915 to 1917

I have not found the final explanation in my notes.
The ratios of the interpolator to gross value of product for base years follow.

Base Year	Ratio of Interpolator to Gross Value of Production in Wood Industry
1870	0.835
1880	0.827
1890	0.820
1900	0.787
1910	0.786
1915	0.786
1917	0.718

The usual method of interpolation for the whole industry group was followed. For intercensal years the above ratios were interpolated linearly. The interpolator was then divided by the corresponding ratio to yield the estimate of gross value of product.

8. Paper Products Industry

The estimates for the paper products group was done in two parts, *viz.* "paper" and "wood pulp". Each part is dealt with in turn.

(i) Paper

The steps in the estimate of the paper component were: first, the gross value of product of paper products were obtained from the censuses of 1870, 1880, 1890, 1900, 1905, 1910, 1915 and 1917 (note 1905 and 1915 are base years). (The paper component was obtained by subtracting the wood pulp component from the total for the paper products group; the derivation of the wood pulp component is explained in the next section of this note.) For each of these base years, the value of paper imports was added to gross value of product and value of paper exports was subtracted. (Trade data were converted to a calendar year basis.) This process yielded the value of domestic disappearance of paper in current dollars. Division of these annual totals by population gave a per capita figure for domestic disappearance in current dollars.

Second, the per capita values of domestic disappearance for base years were converted to a constant dollar base by deflation by a price index (base year 1900). The price index for 1870 to 1900 was the wholesale price index for wood, wood products and paper, obtained from HSC Series J39; the price series from 1900 to 1917 was the unit values of imports of paper n.e.s. obtained from trade data. The per capita constant dollar domestic disappearance values were then linearly interpolated between adjacent pairs of base years. The whole annual per capita series was then reinflated to current dollar values by use of the above-noted price indices and then multiplied by population to give value of domestic disappearance of paper for the country.

Third, for each year, value of imports was then subtracted from the value of domestic disappearance and value of exports was added to give gross value of product for the paper component of this group.

The interpolation ratios were as follows:

Base Year	Ratio of Interpolator to Gross Value of Product of Paper
1870	1.133
1880	1.387
1890	1.485
1900	1.734
1905	1.994
1910	3.158
1915	2.830
1917	3.847

(ii) Wood pulp

Wood pulp production for sale begins in these data with 1890, the first census year for which a wood pulp item was reported. The gross values of production for base years 1890 and 1900 were obtained directly from the census. After 1900 a different method was followed since much wood pulp was used directly in production of paper and was not consistently reported separately from the latter. Accordingly, the relevant wood pulp component of the industry gross value of product for years 1905 to 1917 was obtained by assuming that the ratio of the value of exports to this relevant wood pulp production remained constant at the ratio of the value of exports in 1910 to the value of wood pulp production as reported in the census of 1910. It should be noted that this assumption for the base years 1905, 1910, 1915 and 1917 affected not only the size of the wood pulp component of the total but also the paper component as noted in the part of the note dealing with paper.

The gross value of product for interbase years for the wood pulp component was obtained by using value of exports as the interpolator. The actual process was that export values were taken as a percentage of gross value of wood pulp product in base years. These ratios were linearly interpolated between adjacent base years and the export values were divided by these ratios to give gross value of product. (Note that the export ratio was constant from 1905 onward.) The interpolation ratios were as follows:

Base Year	Ratio of Interpolator to Gross Value of Product of Wood Pulp
1890	0.2117
1900	0.4420
1905	0.6247
1910	0.6247
1915	0.6247
1917	0.6247

(iii) The total for the group

The total is the sum of the two components.

9. Printing, Publishing and Allied Industries

The interpolations between base years were done for the entire industry as a whole.

Since a part of the procedure involves the use of a price index for the product of the industry group, the derivation of that index is described first.

For 1886 to 1917 the price index is an index of the unit values of imported pamphlets and periodicals, base 1900=100. The source material came from Canadian trade data. The items included were: advertising pamphlets, pictorial showcards, illustrated advertising periodicals, illustrated price books, catalogues and price lists; advertising calendars and almanacs; patent medicine or other advertising circulars, fly sheets or pamphlets. The items were given in pounds weight and dollar value and the unit price is price per pound.

For 1880 to 1886 the unit values were for the same items from Canadian trade data but the quantities were in number of pamphlets and the unit price was per pamphlet. Fortunately, there were data in 1886 given in numbers and data in pounds of weight. The series for 1880 to 1886 and 1886 to 1917 were linked at 1886. All of these price data were adjusted from a fiscal year to a calendar year basis.

For 1870 to 1880 the unit values of imports were not available and it was necessary to use the wholesale price index of wood, wood products and paper obtained from HSC, Series J39. This series was linked at 1880 to the series from 1880 onward.

Procedure: The current gross value of product data for base years were deflated by the price index. The resulting constant dollar per capita figures were then interpolated in linear manner between base years. The resulting per capita data were then converted to current dollars for all years by means of the price index. The annual current dollars per capita data were then multiplied by the population to yield a series of gross value of product in current dollars for all years.

The interpolation ratios were as follows:

Base Year	Ratio of Interpolator to Gross Value of Product of Industry Group
1870	0.844
1880	1.208
1890	1.563
1900	2.679
1910	3.509
1915	3.946
1917	5.755

10. Iron and Steel Products Industry

The interpolator for iron and steel products was made up of the sum of values of domestic pig iron production and of domestic production of ingots, castings and rails together with values of imports of iron and steel including import duties. The ratios of the interpolator to gross value of production for base years were then calculated. These ratios were linearly interpolated between base years. The division of the interpolator values by these ratios, year by year, then yielded the annual values of gross value of product. The 1880 data were used in two versions owing to a change in classification of imports. Hoop, bands and bridges were included in the 1870 data but were not given in the 1890 data; for comparison of 1870 and 1880, this import item was included in the interpolator in 1880; for comparison of 1880 with later years this import item was omitted from the interpolator.

Sources of data

Data for base years are, of course, from the census of manufactures for those years. Imports are from the annual *Trade of Canada* returns.

Domestic production of pig iron from 1875 onward and domestic production of steel ingots, castings and rails from 1894 onward are from the *Canada Year Book* and the *Statistical Year Book,* various issues.

The ratios of the interpolators to gross values of production in base years follow.

Base Year	Ratio of Interpolator to Gross Value of Product, Entire Group
1870	0.137
1880	0.143/0.138
1890	0.121
1900	0.223
1910	0.417
1915	0.433
1917	0.394

11. Transportation Equipment Industry

The transportation equipment group was interpolated by four fairly narrow specific categories and "all other" as follows: carriages and wagons; railway equipment; shipbuilding; autos, auto parts and repairs; all other. The interpolation process for each is dealt with in turn.

(i) Carriages and wagons

The interpolator for carriages and wagons was the dollar value of imports of carriage parts including duty. The carriage parts included hubs, spokes and fellows of wood as well as categories called carriage parts. This import series which accounted for a very small fraction of the cost of Canadian built carriages and wagons may appear to be a slender reed on which to interpolate. The circumstance that contributes to some reduction of uneasiness about its use is that the ratio of the value of these imports to gross value of production of the Canadian carriage and wagon industry had a quite steady trend from one census year to the next when the actual census data were available.

The interpolation ratios were as follows:

Base Year	Ratio of Interpolator to Gross Value of Product of Carriages and Wagons
1870	0.005
1880	0.010
1890	0.013
1900	0.019
1910	0.029
1917	0.028

(ii) Railway equipment

An enormous amount of work was done on estimating this component which in turn comprised three parts, *viz.*: locomotives; freight and passenger cars; cars and locomotive repairs. Two or three features of these data require attention. First, there are substantial quantities of annual data, available in the annual reports *Railway Statistics* which go back to 1876. Second, the census of manufactures for 1905 is sufficiently good for it to be a base year. Third, much manufacturing activity was carried on in the railway companies' own shops, which shops reported to the census of manufactures. Fourth, and related to the third point, it appears that in 1910 the railways or subsidiaries must have reported to the census of manufactures much more of the shop activity than in other years, with the result that there appeared to be a great bulge in car and locomotive repairs in 1910. There is an abundance of evidence that points toward this abnormality as being an artifact of the reporting to the census of manufacturers in 1910: much more of the ordinary shop activity must have been reported as manufacturing than in other census years. Fifth, it seemed apparent that locomotives were not included in the reports for railway rolling stock manufacturing plants: they appear to have been included in boilers and engines which were in the iron and steel category. Hence they are not included here. It was decided not to try to transfer them since they were lumped together with other boilers and engines and it would have been guesswork to try to break down cost of materials and other expenses between locomotives and other engines and boilers. Sixth, that great workman, Kenneth Buckley, had made estimates of annual outlay on gross capital formations of railways as well as repair expenditure for the period from 1896 to 1926 (and beyond) as well as some estimates for the earlier periods.

The processes of estimation for this category then were somewhat different before 1896 than from 1896 to 1926.

For the period 1896 to 1917 the procedure was the following:

The data for base years came from the census of manufactures for 1900, 1905, 1915 and 1917; the year 1910 was treated specially as noted below. These data were usually reported in two separate items "cars and car works" and "car repairs".

The railway equipment interpolator was derived from Buckley's estimate of new and replacement expenditure on equipment and repair expenditure on equipment (from *Capital Formation in Canada 1896-1930* p. 215). From it were subtracted the value of imports of rolling stock and the value of domestically produced locomotives. The ratio of the interpolator to the gross value of product in the car works and car repair industries were then calculated for base years and were linearly interpolated between adjacent base years subject to the following exceptions: the ratios for the years 1896 to 1899 were made the same as that for 1900; the 1905 ratio was applied to all years from 1905 to 1910 since as was noted earlier the 1910 census figure appeared to suffer from substantial over reporting. The gross values of product for inter-base years were then obtained by dividing the interpolator by the interpolation ratio. The ratios used for this period were as follows:

Base Year	Ratio of Interpolator to Gross Value of Product of Railway Equipment
1896	0.8946
1900	0.8946
1905	0.8421
1910	0.8421
1915	0.8845
1917	0.6519

For the years 1875 to 1896 a series for repairs to railway cars and locomotives and a series on new railway cars produced were used as a base for the interpolators for the whole. Repair expenditure on cars and locomotives was estimated from the annual data in statistics of railways on "working and repair of engines" and "working and repair of cars" (HSC, Series S60-61). Buckley's estimates of repair expenditures proper was equal to 41 per cent of these items for the years 1896 to 1900. The car and engine repair expenditures proper for 1876 to 1896 were estimated at 41 per cent of the two series on working and repair. Buckley's estimates of repair expenditure were, on average, 1.14 times the repair gross value of product reported in the censuses of 1900 and 1905. To bring it in line with the census estimates, the foregoing series was divided by 1.14 to yield the final estimate for repair.

Estimates of annual production of new passenger and freight cars in Canada were made by adding together the change in stock from year to year plus an estimate of replacement of old stock minus the number of cars imported. These cars were then valued at import unit values to get a value series of new cars.

The next and final step was to add together the repair series and the value of domestically produced new cars for each year to give an interpolator series to interpolate the census gross values of production between base years: the ratios of the interpolator to the base values of gross value of product were taken for 1880, 1890 and 1896 (the last year base figure was that calculated in the derivation of estimates for the 1896 to 1917 period).

The ratios were as follows:

Year	Ratio of Interpolator to Gross Value of Product
1880	0.9858
1890	0.8350
1896	0.9825

These interpolation ratios were linearly interpolated between base years. The 1880 ratio was extrapolated unchanged to 1876. The interpolator was then divided by these ratios to yield the annual gross value of product estimates.

Rates of Replacement of Equipment of Canadian Railways
(percentages of stock)

Year	Locomotives	Passenger Train Cars	Freight Train Cars
1876	1.0	3.52	1.21
1880	1.0	3.52	1.21
1883		3.52	1.21
1885	1.21		
1890	1.87	2.48	2.56
1895	2.53	1.73	3.53
1900	3.26	2.58	3.83
1903	3.70		
1910	3.00		
1917	3.00		
1920	3.00		

Unit Values of Equipment
(dollars)

Year	Locomotives	Passenger Cars	Freight Cars
1880	8,000	6,291	529
1890	8,893	7,162	602
1900	10,593	6,426	540

For the years 1870 to 1876, in the pre-statistics-of-Railway period, still another procedure was followed. In two memoranda, of 1960 and 1962, Kenneth Buckley had estimated, for these years, among others, first, annual investment spending of a sample of railways for construction and machinery and equipment separately and, second, subsequently an estimate of total investment spending for all railways in which construction and equipment outlays are not given separately. For this project it was assumed that equipment outlays were the same proportion of Buckley's later more comprehensive outlays on investment expenditure that they were in the earlier estimates in which equipment was given separately. From the resultant estimate of expenditure on equipment there was subtracted the value of imports of railway rolling stock. This procedure provided the interpolator series for interpolating between the 1870 figures for expenditure on railway cars from the census of manufactures and the estimates of the like figure for 1876 that had been obtained in making the 1876 to 1896 estimates. The usual methods of interpolation between 1870 and 1876 were followed. The interpolation ratios were as follows:

Base Year	Ratio of Interpolator to Gross Value of Product of Railway Equipment
1870	1.4063
1876	0.6305

It should be kept in mind that all of these estimates of annual data of railway equipment were directed to getting interpolators between census of manufactures base year data; the basic data were, of course, the base year data which came from the various censuses of manufactures.

(iii) Shipbuilding

The values for the base years, 1870, 1880, 1890, 1900, 1905, 1910 and 1917 were taken from the census of manufactures. Note that 1905 was a base year, in this case, and 1915 was not a base year.

The interpolator between base years was an index of the values of ships built obtained as follows.

The tonnages of sailing and steam ships built were available annually in the reports of the Department of Trade and Navigation and successor departments. A combined tonnage and from it an index of tonnage volume built was obtained by giving a weight of 0.7 to steamship tons and 0.3 to sailing tons; these weights reflected relative unit values per ton of exports of ships. A price index per ton of shipping was constructed from an index of wage rates weighted 0.5, an index of wood and wood products prices, weighted 0.25 and an index of iron and its products weighted 0.25. The index of construction wage rates was that used by Marion Steele in her estimates of expenditure on residential housing and described in connection with it; the indices of wood and wood products and of iron and its products were obtained from HSC, Series J39 and J40. The product of the index of volume and index of construction costs yielded an index of value of ships built. This index was then used as the interpolator between base years. The interpolation ratios were as follows:

Base Year	Ratio of Interpolator to Gross Value of Product of Shipbuilding
1870	244.9
1880	183.4
1890	145.9
1900	100.0
1905	96.8
1910	130.5
1917	437.0

(iv) Autos and auto parts

The basic estimates were from the census of manufactures for base years 1910, 1915 and 1917. The interpolator was obtained by subtracting from Buckley's estimates of expenditure on automobiles (Buckley, *Capital Formation in Canada*) the value of imports and adding the value of exports to obtain a measure of the value of sales of domestically produced automobiles. This series was then used as the interpolator between the base year values; it was assumed that the ratio of the interpolator to gross value of products for the years 1903 to 1909 were the same as that for 1910.

The interpolation ratios were as follows:

Base Year	Ratio of Interpolator to Gross Value of Product of Autos and Auto Parts
1910	0.881
1915	0.978
1917	0.807

(v) There was a very small remainder of "other transportation equipment", usually less than 5 per cent of the total. This component was in effect obtained by using the sum of the four components described above, which had been interpolated individually, as the interpolator for the whole industry. The interpolation ratios of this last step were:

Year	Ratio of Sum of Four Components to Total Gross Value of Product of Industry Group
1870	0.9905
1880	0.9879
1890	0.9755
1900	0.9375
1910	0.9594
1915	1.0000
1917	1.0939

12. Non-ferrous Metal Products Industry

The non-ferrous metal products group was interpolated between base years by two components: (i) smelting; and (ii) non-smelting activity.

(i) Smelting

The interpolator for 1886 to 1917 was the sum of the value of domestic production of copper, lead, nickel and zinc, obtained from HSC, Series N4, N10, N14 and N26, plus the imports of aluminum, bauxite, crylate, HSC, Series N28, minus exports, lead ore and scrap, HSC, Series N65. (The so-called "production" figures include some quantities of metals in ores or other primary form that were exported.) The ratio of the interpolator to the value of the product of smelters, obtained from the censuses of manufactures were then calculated for base years. (1905 was a base year for non-ferrous smelters.) From 1900 on these ratios were interpolated linearly between base years; for 1886 to 1895 the 1890 base year ratio was used for each year and for 1896 to 1899 the ratio was obtained by linear interpolation between 1895 and 1900. The rationale for using the 1890 ratio for 1890 to 1895 was that there was small change in the interpolator in these years but from 1895 onward the interpolator itself increased quite rapidly from year to year. Once the interpolated ratios were obtained, the interpolated estimates for smelters were obtained by dividing the interpolator itself by the interpolation ratio for each year.

Since the amount of production was small in 1886 and there was no basis for going further back, no estimates were made for years before 1886. The ratios of the interpolator to the base years values were as follows:

Year	Ratio of Interpolator to Base Year Gross Values of Product
1890	0.619
1900	1.024
1905	0.596
1910	0.536
1915	0.794
1917	1.020

(ii) Non-ferrous metal products excluding smelting

For 1890 to 1917: the interpolator was the value of imports of aluminum, copper, lead, zinc, (HSC, Series N30, N34, N38, N42, and N49) plus value of domestic production of aluminum (HSC, Series Q293 valued at export unit prices) less value of exports of aluminum in primary forms and scrap. (HSC, Series N51).

For 1880 to 1890: the interpolator was the value of imports of lead.

For 1870 to 1880: there was not an annual interpolator: the data were obtained by straight line interpolation between 1870 and 1880.

The usual procedures were followed in interpolation: the interpolation ratios were interpolated linearly between adjacent base years. As usual, the actual interpolation values of gross value of product were obtained by dividing the interpolator by the interpolation ratio for each year. The interpolation ratios were:

	Base Year	Ratio of Interpolator to Gross Value of Product
	1870	no ratio
lead only interpolator:	1880	0.0315
	1890	0.0728
full interpolator:	1890	0.110
	1900	0.150
	1910	0.243
	1915	0.346
	1917	0.248

An alternative interpolator, using product of the smelter, derived in the interpolation of the first sector, plus imports of metals was tried but did not do as well as the actual import series that was used.

The total for the whole industry group is the simple sum of the two components.

13. Electrical Apparatus and Supplies Industry

The interpolator of this group, which is interpolated only at the single aggregate level, is the horsepower of hydraulic industrial and central electrical power installations. It is the only annual series that goes back beyond 1917. Thermal stations accounted for less than 15 per cent of total power production from 1917 on until after 1926.

The ratios were the following:

Ratio of Installed Hydroelectric Turbines Horsepower (in thousands of H.P.)
to Gross Value of Production (thousands of dollars)

Base Year	Ratio	Base Year	Ratio
1890	0.08257	1915	0.11297
1900	0.5292	1917	0.05557
1910	0.06414		

Although the interpolator is measured in physical units and gross value of product in current dollars, the interpolation ratios are reasonably steady except for 1915. There could be concern about the 1915 census figure being too low but a check on details of number of establishments etc. does not suggest that there were great omissions. An alternative explanation of the surge of the interpolation ratio in 1915 (and immediately preceding years) is that a large part of the Niagara based power was exported in the period from 1910 to 1915 (and later) and a good part of the installation of turbines at that time would be for that purpose.

14. Non-Metallic Mineral Products Industry

A single interpolator for the group as an aggregate was used.

There was no reasonable interpolator between 1870 and 1880 and between 1880 and 1886. Therefore, straight line interpolation was used for each of these pairs of years. The 1870 and 1880 figures came from the censuses of manufactures; the 1886 figure came from the annual data for 1886 to 1917 obtained as follows.

For 1886 to 1917 the interpolator was the sum of the values of production of asbestos, gypsum, quartz, salt, cement, lime, limestone, sandstone, granite, and clay products all of which data were obtained from HSC, pp. 426-429. The usual method of using the interpolator was followed: ratios of the interpolator to the census of manufactures gross value of product for the years 1890, 1900, 1910 and 1917 were calculated; the 1890 ratio was used for the years 1886 to 1889; the other ratios were interpolated linearly between adjacent base years. (The year 1915 was not used as a base year since the census figures for Portland cement, which is a huge part of the total group, were anomalous: the ratio of cost of materials to gross value of product was over 50 per cent in 1915 compared with less than 25 per cent in other census years; a guess is that the 1915 figures included some finished products, such as, for example, cement pipe.) The gross value of product were then interpolated by dividing the interpolator by the interpolation ratios for each year.

The ratios of the interpolator to gross value of product for base years follow.

Base Year	Ratio of Interpolator to Gross Value of Product
1890	0.640
1900	0.802
1910	0.806
1917	0.801

15. Petroleum and Coal Products Industry

The petroleum and coal products group was interpolated by two components *viz.* (i) coke production and (ii) petroleum products. The total for the whole group was merely the sum of these components.

(Rymes had not included manufactured gas in this group and hence it is not included here.)

(i) Coal products: coke

The interpolator for the gross value of product of coke production was the annual value of coke produced. This series goes back only to 1886 — the value of coke produced in that year was only 28 thousand dollars and since it was on the uptrend at that time, the value of coke production was undoubtedly less before 1886. There was not any record of coke production in the census of manufactures for 1880.

The interpolator, the value of coke produced, was obtained from the *Annual Report on the Mineral Production of Canada* of the Department of Mines. The whole series could be obtained from two reports, that for 1906 (sessional papers 1907-08) and that for 1917 (not in sessional papers).

The year 1900 could not be used as a base year since there were only 2 companies reporting in that year and to maintain confidentiality the data of the coke industry were not published separately.

The coverage in both the 1905 and 1915 postal censuses was good enough for them to be used as base years.

The ratios the interpolator to gross value of product in base years follow.

Base Year	Ratio of Value of Interpolator to Census Gross Value of Product of Coke
1890	3.696
1905	1.904
1910	2.372
1915	0.964
1917	0.626

(The 1890 figure should have been 1.848. In some manner a figure of $45 thousand was used as census value of production in 1890 rather than $90 thousand which I had indicated. Fortunately the amounts are so small until 1900 as to not matter much and by 1900 our ratio was approaching the 1905 ratio.)

(ii) Petroleum products

This component includes variously such industries as oil refineries, lubricating oils, paraffin and wax, asphalt.

After much consideration of and experimentation with different types of interpolator series a choice of three different series for different time periods was made.

For the period 1870 to 1880 the interpolator was the value of production of crude petroleum: the quantity of crude oil produced was obtained from HSC, Series N180; the quantity data were converted to a valuation basis (essentially yielding an index of the value of crude oil production) by use of annual data for the price of coal oil from Michell, p. 83.

For the period 1880 to 1900 the interpolator was the value of oil inspected: the number of gallons of Canadian refined oil imported were obtained from Department of Mines, *Annual Report on the Mineral Production of Canada during the Calendar Year 1912*, p. 255; this quantity series was then valued at the price of coal oil per gallon obtained from Michell, p. 83, for 1880 to 1889 and from Department of Labour, *Wholesale Prices*, p. 198, for 1890 to 1900. The Department of Labour and Michell series were linked at 1889 to 1890 by assuming that prices had not changed between 1889 and 1890 (unit values of imports show a decline between 1889 and 1890; unit values of domestic production rise between 1890 and 1900). The data on refined oil inspections go back only to 1881; it was assumed that the volume in 1880 was the same as in 1881; (the Canadian production series shows only a rise from 350 thousand barrels of crude in 1880 to 369 thousand barrels in 1881).

The year 1890 was not used as a base year. From inspection of the census data it appeared that a large refinery was omitted in 1890 (in Middlesex County, Ontario). Hence the interpolation was made directly from 1880 to 1900.

It was not possible to use a series on domestic disappearance of crude petroleum as interpolator in this period since until 1898 imports of refined and crude oils are not separated.

For the period 1900 to 1917, the interpolator was the value of the domestic disappearance of crude petroleum. The domestic disappearance is derived from values of production plus imports minus exports obtained respectively from HSC, Series N175, N181, N187.

The interpolator ratios for the various periods were as follows:

Base Year	Ratio of Interpolator to Gross Value of Product of Petroleum Products
1870	0.0304
1880 (1870 comparison)	0.0249
1880 (1880 to 1900 comparison)	0.461
1900 (1880 to 1900 comparison)	0.484
1900 (1900 to 1917 comparison)	0.283
1910	0.251
1915	0.334
1917	0.397

16. Chemical Products

A single interpolator was used for the entire chemical group. It was comprised of the value of imports, including duty, of drugs, dyes, chemicals, explosives, gunpowder, paints, colours and linseed oil, all taken from *Trade of Canada* reports and converted from a fiscal to a calendar year basis.

The ratios of the interpolator to gross value of product for base years follow.

Base Year	Ratio of Interpolator to Gross Value of Product in Base Year
1870	0.351
1880	0.427
1890	0.471
1900	0.550
1910	0.512
1915	0.413
1917	0.144

In 1917, of 227,512 thousand dollars worth gross value of product $112,867 thousand was ammunition and $26,163 thousand was explosives.

17. Miscellaneous Manufactures Industry

The interpolator for this industry group was the sum of gross value of production of the other 16 groups. The usual method of using the interpolator was followed.

The interpolation ratios are:

Base Year	Ratio of Interpolator to Gross Value of Production, Miscellaneous Manufacturing
1870	87.826
1880	69.563
1890	67.414
1900	70.858
1910	73.103
1915	88.741
1917	92.627

Gross Value of Product by Components of Major Industry Group Series

Table 4.19 contains the gross value of product data for the component elements of those industries for which interpolation was done at a level of detail that involved component parts of the industry concerned. (By "industry" we mean one of the 17 industry groups of the *1948 S.I.C.*)

Table 4.19. Gross Value of Product for Manufacturing, Industry Components, 1870-1917 (thousands of dollars)

	1870	1871	1872	1873	1874	1875	1876	1877
Malt liquors (breweries)	2,141	2,638	3,584	4,971	5,398	4,473	3,620	3,558
Spirits (distilleries)	1,557	1,183	910	894	1,494	1,480	1,506	1,580
Bread, biscuits and confectionery	6,942	8,103	8,954	9,767	8,720	8,218	8,429	11,018
Butter and cheese	1,602	1,988	2,374	2,761	3,147	3,590	4,033	4,476
Flour and grist mill products	39,136	45,453	50,295	53,188	44,813	40,145	40,488	52,815
Sugar refining	4,133	2,853	2,147	2,545	2,908	3,461	2,609	1,583
Slaughterhouses	3,800	3,815	4,087	4,186	3,507	3,303	3,315	3,737
Other non-alcoholic food and beverages	1,536	1,983	2,455	2,934	2,831	2,893	3,162	4,284
Tanneries	9,185	11,246	10,889	9,599	10,401	8,800	7,714	9,818
Other leather products	18,726	22,197	20,210	17,244	17,966	14,044	11,586	14,642
Woollen textiles	7,762	10,845	9,795	6,865	6,634	7,274	6,856	7,198
Cotton textiles	784	848	854	877	1,121	1,424	1,480	1,618
Cordage, rope and twine	770	992	1,069	1,013	965	715	729	792
Other textiles, ex. clothing	350	529	539	441	478	558	579	657
Paper	1,725	2,057	2,046	2,457	2,647	2,8836	2,767	2,756
Wood pulp	-	-	-	-	-	-	-	-
Carriages and wagons	5,088	4,500	5,167	8,000	10,143	7,375	8,375	9,333
Railway equipment	512	587	160	6,346	3,284	1,249	3,145	3,145
Shipbuilding	4,432	5,127	7,067	8,965	9,838	9,108	7,150	5,424
Auto and auto parts	-	-	-	-	-	-	-	-
Other transportation equipment	96	101	115	243	247	194	210	205
Smelting	-	-	-	-	-	-	-	-
Non-ferrous metals, excluding smelting	1,594	1,835	2,075	2,316	2,556	2,797	3,038	3,278
Coke production	-	-	-	-	-	-	-	-
Petroleum products	3,095	3,779	4,642	5,208	1,738	3,141	5,388	3,459

Table 4.19. (continued)

	1878	1879	1880	1881	1882	1883	1884	1885
Malt liquors (breweries)	3,729	3,997	4,768	5,594	5,708	5,483	5,366	5,414
Spirits (distilleries)	1,919	1,703	1,791	2,415	4,069	3,468	3,035	2,133
Bread, biscuits and confectionery	8,369	8,532	9,477	10,597	11,041	10,870	10,946	9,976
Butter and cheese	4,920	5,363	5,806	6,254	6,717	7,196	9,120	7,720
Flour and grist mill products	39,234	39,163	41,772	44,384	44,999	41,056	38,765	35,086
Sugar refining	2,199	5,448	9,627	11,229	11,818	12,500	12,372	11,357
Slaughterhouses	3,621	3,677	4,084	4,559	5,189	5,943	6,173	5,667
Other non-alcoholic food and beverages	3,658	4,182	5,084	6,078	6,865	7,238	7,789	7,547
Tanneries	9,333	10,723	15,145	16,317	15,466	13,779	13,303	14,685
Other leather products	13,735	15,545	21,311	23,969	23,802	22,060	21,954	25,456
Woollen textiles	6,709	8,688	9,611	10,497	13,039	10,970	8,976	8,545
Cotton textiles	2,085	2,945	3,822	4,899	6,499	6,399	5,823	6,826
Cordage, rope and twine	556	599	775	951	1,238	1,245	1,134	1,150
Other textiles, ex. clothing	682	949	1,168	1,499	2,130	2,091	1,969	2,210
Paper	2,771	2,708	2,913	3,154	3,584	4,163	4,272	2,260
Wood pulp	–	–	63	163	262	362	461	561
Carriages and wagons	10,889	8,800	6,825	10,200	12,545	11,000	8,636	8,083
Railway equipment	3,449	2,942	3,956	5,563	5,651	5,528	5,943	5,712
Shipbuilding	4,777	3,973	3,557	3,582	3,847	3,831	3,442	2,564
Auto and auto parts	–	–	–	–	–	–	–	–
Other transportation equipment	224	188	175	261	327	327	314	305
Smelting	–	–	–	–	–	–	–	–
Non-ferrous metals, excluding smelting	3,519	3,759	4,000	4,017	4,221	3,531	2,542	2,931
Coke production	–	–	–	–	–	–	–	–
Petroleum products	3,192	4,784	4,050	4,249	3,486	3,739	3,603	4,086

Table 4.19. (continued)

	1886	1887	1888	1889	1890	1891	1892	1893
Malt liquors (breweries)	5,541	6,000	5,899	5,454	5,718	5,622	5,426	5,588
Spirits (distilleries)	1,988	1,918	1,911	2,330	2,200	2,283	2,122	2,297
Bread, biscuits and confectionery	9,579	10,398	13,900	14,644	15,433	16,515	14,986	13,231
Butter and cheese	8,128	9,769	8,582	9,878	10,698	11,784	14,258	13,549
Flour and grist mill products	34,002	35,516	46,613	48,461	51,883	54,742	48,221	40,945
Sugar refining	11,426	12,078	12,821	12,429	11,627	12,807	11,771	11,260
Slaughterhouses	5,563	5,882	6,352	6,149	7,133	7,527	8,427	8,883
Other non-alcoholic food and beverages	7,947	9,082	11,570	12,723	14,219	15,417	14,781	13,493
Tanneries	14,886	12,438	10,469	9,636	11,407	11,861	11,457	10,897
Other leather products	27,053	23,731	20,823	19,618	23,802	24,423	23,902	22,141
Woollen textiles	8,560	8,012	7,490	9,065	9,168	8,912	9,175	8,594
Cotton textiles	7,613	7,940	8,982	9,741	9,859	9,911	9,613	8,724
Cordage, rope and twine	1,143	1,695	2,409	2,101	1,724	1,873	2,233	1,842
Other textiles, ex. clothing	2,496	2,754	3,151	3,747	3,954	4,329	4,772	4,730
Paper	4,097	4,414	4,660	4,897	5,148	5,286	5,557	5,856
Wood pulp	660	760	859	959	1,058	1,355	1,575	1,788
Carriages and wagons	9,833	10,167	9,833	9,462	10,308	10,285	12,357	13,000
Railway equipment	5,920	7,612	8,437	8,470	9,461	10,470	9,500	8,693
Shipbuilding	1,740	1,522	1,532	2,108	3,101	3,100	2,747	2,111
Auto and auto parts	–	–	–	–	–	–	–	–
Other transportation equipment	348	410	445	478	575	695	816	886
Smelting	624	606	1,546	2,326	3,046	5,892	3,633	4,879
Non-ferrous metals, excluding smelting	3,641	3,791	3,876	4,367	4,354	4,079	3,949	3,041
Coke production	28	37	36	42	45	49	46	49
Petroleum products	4,150	4,433	3,855	4,021	4,302	4,247	4,562	4,685

Table 4.19. (continued)

	1894	1895	1896	1897	1898	1899	1900	1901
Malt liquors (breweries)	5,551	5,455	5,501	5,732	6,164	6,622	7,155	7,831
Spirits (distilleries)	2,295	2,022	1,995	1,631	1,236	1,486	1,621	1,671
Bread, biscuits and confectionery	12,548	14,487	14,479	17,692	18,610	15,923	17,642	19,288
Butter and cheese	16,354	15,822	16,809	23,391	21,927	26,516	29,462	28,037
Flour and grist mill products	36,121	41,630	39,881	52,467	55,930	42,753	45,750	46,798
Sugar refining	11,935	10,228	11,413	10,878	8,935	10,854	12,595	12,782
Slaughterhouses	8,112	8,288	9,085	11,905	14,586	17,068	23,363	26,528
Other non-alcoholic food and beverages	13,253	14,294	14,693	18,908	19,773	18,897	21,814	22,547
Tanneries	8,334	10,306	9,803	14,530	15,940	14,887	14,195	15,503
Other leather products	16,332	20,423	19,382	30,364	33,477	31,087	28,864	31,145
Woollen textiles	6,415	4,583	3,847	5,791	8,244	9,237	7,565	6,759
Cotton textiles	8,829	9,347	9,199	10,690	10,894	11,306	13,775	15,814
Cordage, rope and twine	1,278	1,625	1,559	1,383	1,951	2,501	2,213	2,634
Other textiles, ex. clothing	4,392	4,464	4,511	5,891	7,448	8,653	9,457	9,466
Paper	6,384	6,149	6,028	6,102	6,203	6,486	7,166	6,919
Wood pulp	1,876	1,939	2,026	2,617	3,137	3,687	4,247	4,163
Carriages and wagons	13,933	10,313	6,353	7,118	8,222	10,389	10,210	10,400
Railway equipment	8,357	6,786	6,819	7,825	9,725	11,625	11,513	13,799
Shipbuilding	1,546	1,100	833	1,356	1,734	1,899	1,900	1,757
Auto and auto parts					–	–	–	–
Other transportation equipment	985	828	695	878	1,143	1,491	1,576	1,666
Smelting	4,283	3,706	3,533	4,321	5,006	5,601	7,082	11,874
Non-ferrous metals, excluding smelting	2,778	3,438	3,507	5,043	6,803	7,432	7,326	7,491
Coke production	46	46	37	62	104	134	260	516
Petroleum products	4,855	4,421	4,061	3,904	3,886	3,778	4,157	3,718

Table 4.19. (continued)

	1902	1903	1904	1905	1906	1907	1908	1909
Malt liquors (breweries)	8,286	8,622	9,411	10,426	11,304	12,030	11,850	12,088
Spirits (distilleries)	1,547	1,774	2,105	2,344	2,784	4,804	4,272	4,201
Bread, biscuits and confectionery	20,045	22,219	28,167	31,176	26,739	32,151	40,365	42,667
Butter and cheese	33,973	38,779	29,648	39,610	43,091	34,547	32,211	34,459
Flour and grist mill products	46,668	50,657	62,024	64,303	52,668	63,414	75,417	83,280
Sugar refining	12,316	12,446	13,102	14,721	14,483	15,290	18,136	19,811
Slaughterhouses	31,870	32,106	30,999	32,281	34,743	37,891	37,787	41,400
Other non-alcoholic food and beverages	24,426	26,278	27,518	30,498	28,698	30,565	33,926	36,789
Tanneries	18,643	18,591	15,641	18,695	23,326	17,049	12,720	21,882
Other leather products	37,811	37,615	31,546	38,790	50,469	36,951	26,260	49,456
Woollen textiles	6,791	6,903	7,456	8,140	7,175	6,915	5,838	6,336
Cotton textiles	17,527	18,012	17,375	19,826	23,104	20,694	19,186	25,568
Cordage, rope and twine	3,421	3,727	3,516	3,391	4,250	5,088	4,402	3,698
Other textiles, ex. clothing	9,797	9,446	8,708	8,948	9,179	8,022	6,635	7,396
Paper	8,197	9,276	10,429	12,075	14,893	17,930	18,558	20,992
Wood pulp	5,046	5,040	4,937	5,505	5,969	6,441	6,517	7,842
Carriages and wagons	12,714	14,364	13,913	11,875	13,440	16,577	10,630	13,964
Railway equipment	18,201	20,739	19,353	26,721	33,963	45,719	41,919	41,444
Shipbuilding	2,123	2,483	2,276	1,648	3,941	8,065	5,649	4,838
Auto and auto parts	–	352	264	441	529	705	1,410	4,141
Other transportation equipment	2,038	2,246	2,032	2,209	2,696	3,520	2,809	2,879
Smelting	11,758	14,456	15,735	28,462	38,354	40,082	32,750	33,420
Non-ferrous metals, excluding smelting	8,266	8,169	10,963	14,041	12,971	14,851	12,473	16,692
Coke production	672	809	1,004	1,279	1,433	1,714	1,579	1,530
Petroleum products	3,755	4,597	5,648	6,146	5,341	7,222	7,634	7,016

Table 4.19. (continued)

	1910	1911	1912	1913	1914	1915	1916	1917
Malt liquors (breweries)	12,469	13,493	14,818	17,320	18,164	15,796	15,704	15,426
Spirits (distilleries)	4,337	5,195	6,536	7,314	6,367	5,991	7,564	8,025
Bread, biscuits and confectionery	43,190	37,625	38,204	34,897	38,397	46,508	53,331	77,224
Butter and cheese	37,233	41,014	45,949	41,982	43,090	56,275	68,295	85,731
Flour and grist mill products	82,495	78,053	85,253	83,338	93,918	118,728	136,913	224,192
Sugar refining	21,260	23,672	26,932	25,940	29,380	37,753	56,525	73,329
Slaughterhouses	49,235	57,819	67,771	75,001	85,293	98,537	146,081	206,721
Other non-alcoholic food and beverages	38,662	38,877	42,474	41,374	45,261	54,978	69,767	99,369
Tanneries	22,584	25,504	32,384	23,450	29,601	26,542	39,847	41,117
Other leather products	51,959	58,893	77,748	53,803	59,942	50,052	82,357	74,612
Woollen textiles	7,072	7,154	8,336	8,394	10,556	11,583	16,686	23,365
Cotton textiles	32,745	26,218	25,323	28,352	22,105	31,518	37,765	57,863
Cordage, rope and twine	3,624	3,363	4,148	3,298	3,269	4,239	4,146	8,323
Other textiles, ex. clothing	8,232	6,945	7,094	7,514	6,692	8,817	10,831	16,584
Paper	22,527	21,573	20,333	24,974	30,992	38,096	56,143	78,441
Wood pulp	9,117	7,849	9,528	9,467	14,191	14,854	27,764	41,929
Carriages and wagons	16,991	18,690	21,448	18,552	12,786	11,964	10,643	13,464
Railway equipment	40,138	50,553	61,343	75,735	55,251	39,794	51,289	115,504
Shipbuilding	5,136	9,159	9,350	19,500	23,480	10,667	13,010	35,281
Auto and auto parts	6,252	9,720	12,972	15,587	17,358	24,358	24,647	60,986
Other transportation equipment	2,900	2,960	2,629	2,130	889	0	-4,471	-19,339
Smelting	37,352	31,320	44,477	42,265	35,601	52,782	74,954	69,263
Non-ferrous metals, excluding smelting	22,697	25,924	27,574	25,541	16,938	22,335	39,997	56,439
Coke production	1,460	1,737	2,855	3,877	2,936	4,417	7,609	10,635
Petroleum products	8,093	9,500	15,275	18,794	19,224	11,912	24,156	37,730

Note: Other non-alcoholic food and beverages, Other textiles, excluding clothing, and Other transportation equipment categories were not specifically interpolated, but rather done implicitly when the total was done for the relevant industry group as a whole. Therefore, the figure quoted here was obtained by subtraction.

The Various Input Series and Related Series

Cost of Materials

Cost of materials was the single most important item of the set of items to be subtracted from gross value of product in order to calculate gross domestic product at factor cost; the other two items to be subtracted for this purpose were cost of fuel and electricity and miscellaneous expenses.

Cost of materials was obtained in each census of manufactures except that for 1905. These values, as collected in the census, were accepted for the census years.   In cases where the coverage of the census was incomplete, as in 1900, 1910 and, to some extent, in 1915, the cost of materials as reported was supplemented at a detailed level of industry breakdown in accordance with the additions made to gross value of product to obtain full coverage.   The base years, so to put it, were the years 1870, 1880, 1890, 1900, 1910, 1915 and each year from 1917 to 1926.

The calculation of cost of materials for years between the base years was obtained by use of ratios of such material costs to gross value of product in base years for each of the 17 main industry groups.   These ratios were interpolated in straight line fashion between each adjacent pair of base years.

The actual ratios for base years are given in Table 4.20; the data for the years after 1917 are available in the census for each year but only the figure for 1926 is given for comparative purposes.

Cost of Fuel and Electricity

The data reported for cost of fuel and light and rent of power and heat are less well covered than those for GVP and for cost of material.   Such data were not collected at all before 1900, although some part (probably small) of fuel costs may have been included in the cost of materials.   In 1900, the money cost of "rent of power and heat" and expenses of "fuel and light" were collected explicitly; in 1910, the weight of coal used and the value of all fuels consumed were collected but not the cost of purchased power which, although requested on the form, was not tabulated; in 1915, although cost of fuel used for power purposes was collected, it was not tabulated separately and is most likely included in cost of materials for that year — fuel-for-power costs were collected in the same section as material costs; from 1917 onward, costs of fuel of all kinds and of rent of power were collected.   It became necessary, then, to make estimates for the census years not covered.   Only the simplest methods could be used.   Purchased power for 1910 was estimated by first interpolating linearly the percentage of costs of purchased power to GVP for each of the 17 industry groups, between 1900 and 1917, and then applying the relevant percentage figure for each group in 1910 to the GVP in 1910.   The purchased power costs were then added to fuel costs, which were collected in the census of 1910, to obtain fuel and power costs.   Fuel and power costs for each industry in 1915 were estimated by linear interpolation between 1910 and 1917 of the ratio of such costs to GVP and then applying the 1915 ratios to GVP in 1915.   For 1870, 1880, and 1890, the ratios of fuel and power costs to GVP for each of the 17 industries were taken as being the same as in 1900, and the estimates were made on that basis.   The changes between 1900 and 1917 were sufficiently moderate that one has a reasonably comfortable feeling in following this procedure.

The ratios for 1900, 1910, 1917, and for comparative purposes for 1920, 1923 and 1926 are given in Table 4.21.

Table 4.20

Ratio of Cost of Materials to Gross Value of Products
for Census Years by Main Industry Groups

Industry	1870	1880	1890	1900	1910	1915	1917	1926
Food and beverages	.7605	.7707	.7250	.7375	.7180	.7507	.7576	.7131
Tobacco products	.4920	.5137	.4357	.4402	.4276	.4596	.4064	.4649
Rubber products	.7117	.6200	.6903	.6149	.5121	.4916	.4908	.5768
Leather products	.5319	.5999	.5311	.5833	.5859	.5920	.6014	.5441
Textiles (ex. clothing)	.6446	.5903	.5433	.5345	.5700	.5976	.5645	.6039
Clothing: textile and fur	.5739	.5814	.5065	.5014	.5084	.5193	.5195	.5390
Wood products	.5371	.5282	.5185	.5473	.5192	.4683	.4664	.5319
Paper products	.5066	.5470	.5092	.4785	.4891	.5029	.4494	.4102
Printing and publishing	.3614	.3839	.3559	.2810	.2950	.2819	.2915	.2771
Iron and steel products	.3901	.4527	.4212	.4245	.4395	.4531	.4921	.4243
Transportation equipment	.3519	.4491	.4351	.5115	.4790	.5288	.5041	.5671
Non-ferrous metal products	.4222	.4425	.4536	.4704	.5000	.5056	.5327	.5312
Electrical apparatus and supplies	--	--	.3907	.3731	.4190	.5070	.5041	.4328
Non-metallic mineral products	.2087	.2568	.1924	.1587	.1856	.2423	.2416	.1951
Petroleum and coal products	.5618	.6005	.6887	.6798	.6732	.6341	.6407	.7046
Chemical and allied industries	.6071	.5873	.5627	.5583	.4760	.4967	.4825	.5074
Miscellaneous industries	.4518	.4434	.4327	.4208	.3990	.4282	.4385	.4104

Miscellaneous Expenses

Miscellaneous expenses include a wide range of non-factor costs that are not included in cost of materials or fuels. They include items such as repair of machinery and buildings, cost of rental plant (the factor returns of which go to the real estate industry), insurance, advertising, travel, stationery and telephone, office supplies, and like items; they do not include depreciation.

There were three sources of information that helped in the making of our estimate of these "miscellaneous" expenses.

(i) From 1917 to 1923 the census of manufactures collected such expenses in total and in a considerable amount of detail for 1917 to 1921. There were some shortcomings for 1917 and even 1918 but from then on these expenses seemed fairly complete. Since they were collected in the same questionnaire as "cost of materials" and "fuel" there should not be duplication with them: in particular they should not include cost of containers or mill supplies which would be included in cost of materials. In addition to the foregoing, the manufactures questionnaire in 1900 also requested data of miscellaneous expenditure and while the acquired information was

Table 4.21

Ratios of Cost of Fuel and Electricity
to Gross Value of Product

Industry	1900	1910	1917	1920	1923	1926
Food and beverages	.0127	.0116	.0104	.0130	.0153	.0142
Tobacco products	.0063	.0036	.0051	.0040	.0049	.0047
Rubber products	.0190	.0148	.0167	.0171	.0203	.0138
Leather products	.0077	.0082	.0084	.0087	.0119	.0118
Textiles (ex. clothing)	.0237	.0190	.0167	.0172	.0190	.0193
Clothing: textile and fur	.0083	.0045	.0058	.0065	.0072	.0067
Wood products	.0068	.0076	.0094	.0079	.0098	.0096
Paper products	.0384	.0441	.0719	.0603	.0863	.0836
Printing and publishing	.0179	.0123	.0115	.0100	.0115	.0104
Iron and steel products	.0301	.0324	.0522	.0401	.0335	.0323
Transportation equipment	.0179	.0250	.0221	.0216	.0263	.0250
Non-ferrous metal products	.0448	.0315	.0478	.0891	.0852	.0601
Electrical apparatus and supplies	.0451	.0094	.0092	.0178	.0168	.0153
Non-metallic mineral products	.1363	.1314	.1193	.1549	.1484	.1447
Petroleum and coal products	.0337	.0230	.0624	.0681	.0704	.0487
Chemical and allied products	.0196	.0208	.0286	.0388	.0305	.0295
Miscellaneous industries	.0096	.0096	.0134	.0152	.0150	.0144
Total production	.0178	.0188	.0259	.0258	.0289	.0271

undoubtedly incomplete in its coverage it contained some useful material.

(ii) The group who prepared the national income estimates for the Rowell-Sirois Royal Commission in the 1930s circulated a very elaborate and carefully specified questionnaire about costs to 1000 of the largest manufacturing enterprises — 358 fully usable returns, which appeared to be quite representative of manufacturing as a whole, were used for tabulations. The cost estimates were obtained for each year of 1929, 1933 and 1937. This material contained most valuable statements of all costs that were comprehensive and at the same time mutually exclusive.

(iii) The United States census of manufactures had obtained information on "miscellaneous" expenses in its censuses for 1889, 1899, 1904 and 1909. The material was classified and tabulated in such a way that it was very useful to this project in the preparation of estimates of miscellaneous expenses in 1900.

The Canadian Census of Manufactures data for miscellaneous expenses for 1917 to 1923 provided the basis of estimation of such items for 1917 to 1926. Certain items such as purchased power were removed since they appeared in other cost categories; in addition, factor cost items such as interest payments and royalties were also removed. (Fortunately the original unpublished tabulations of these data were available in Statistics Canada; they were tabulated in accordance with the 1948 standard industrial classification specifically for this project. Some limited adjustment of the 1917 data, the first such yearly data, was made by use of information on later years.)

The "miscellaneous expenses" estimates for 1900 from the census were only a starting point for that year. On the one hand, they included certain factor costs, such as interest, and fuel costs, both of which had to be removed. On the other hand, the instructions in the questionnaire gave such limited detail that many expense items were omitted — for example, repair and maintenance expenditures seemed absent. In these circumstances, the following method of estimation for 1900 was followed separately for each of the seventeen 1948 S.I.C. classifications. Rent of works, provincial and municipal taxes and outlays for work contracted out were obtained directly from the 1900 census of manufactures. Repair and maintenance expenditure and insurance cost were assumed to bear the same relationship to depreciation of plant and equipment in 1900 as they did in 1921. Each of advertising and travel was assumed to bear the same relationship to gross value of product in 1900 as they did in 1921. Finally each of "stationery", etc. and "miscellaneous administrative" costs were assumed to bear the same ratio to GVP as in 1929 at 0.3 per cent and 0.6 per cent respectively. (These last two items could not be differentiated among the seventeen industry groups since the 1929 data were just tabulated for the group as a whole.)

The use of the depreciation figures, noted above, requires some elaboration. First, it seemed appropriate to relate repair expenditure to depreciation since the latter reflects machinery and equipment components in greater measure than does the capital stock itself. Second, the estimates of depreciation were made by assuming depreciation rates of 2 per cent per year for plant and 10 per cent per year for machinery. In 1900 these rates could be directly applied to each component since plant (buildings, etc.) exclusive of land and machinery were given separately. In 1921, machinery was given separately but since buildings and structures and land were all given in one category, the land component had to be separated. The separation was made by a method which approximately estimated the land ratios to buildings and structures including land at about the same values in 1921 as in 1900.

The resulting estimates of "miscellaneous expenses" in 1900 checked out very well with the estimates of the U.S. census of manufactures of the time. This check was reassuring since the project estimates for 1900 are substantially above those in the Canadian census of manufactures.

Estimates for all other years were by interpolation or extrapolation. For years before 1900, the ratios of miscellaneous expenses to gross value of product were assumed to be the same, industry group by industry group, as in 1900. For years between 1900 and 1917 a linear interpolation between these two years of the miscellaneous expenses to gross value of product ratios was done for each industry group. For 1924 to 1926 the ratios were interpolated between 1923 and 1929. The product of the resultant ratios and the relevant gross values of product in each year then gave the estimates of "miscellaneous expenses".

A sample of the procedures for estimating 1900 ratios is given for the food and beverage industry.

Miscellaneous Expense Ratios, 1900: Food and Beverage Group
Gross Value of Product = $159,401,000

Type of Miscellaneous Expenditure	Dollar Amounts ($000's)	Percentage of GVP
Rent of works plus provincial and municipal taxes plus contract work (from 1900 census adjusted to full coverage)	1,729	1.08
Repair expenditure (related to depreciation in 1900)	1,203	0.75
Insurance (related to depreciation in 1900)	564	0.35
Sub total		2.18
Advertising (from 1921 ratio to GVP)		0.50
Travel (from 1921 ratio to GVP)		0.59
Stationery (from 1929 ratio to GVP)		0.30
Miscellaneous administrative (from 1929 ratio to GVP)		0.60
Total		4.17

Table 4.22 gives the ratios of miscellaneous expense to GVP for key years for each of the 17 industry groups of the *1948 S.I.C.*

Table 4.22

Proportions of Miscellaneous Expenses to Gross Value
of Product by Industry Group (per cent of GVP)

Industry	1900	1920	1921	1922
Food and beverages	4.17	5.74	6.97	7.55
Tobacco and products	8.56	12.84	14.66	12.18
Rubber products	4.54	8.56	9.27	8.27
Leather products	4.06	5.91	8.06	7.22
Textile products	5.33	7.44	7.41	6.39
Clothing	5.92	8.65	10.05	9.65
Wood products	6.03	8.39	9.52	8.09
Paper products	6.68	7.70	9.61	8.39
Printing and publishing	7.07	15.06	15.47	17.02

Table 4.22 (continued)

Industry	1900	1920	1921	1922
Iron and steel products	6.09	8.28	10.04	10.10
Transportation equipment	4.34	8.27	7.60	7.42
Non-ferrous metal products	5.05	8.91	8.88	4.64
Electrical apparatus and supplies	8.47	9.89	10.28	10.16
Non-metallic mineral products	3.60	10.59	14.40	13.74
Petroleum and coal products	4.30	6.84	5.38	6.27
Chemical products	6.28	14.61	14.82	14.63
Miscellaneous manufacturing	8.45	10.18	12.14	11.30

Table 4.23

Ratios of Miscellaneous Expenses to Gross Values of Product,
United States, Industry Group
(miscellaneous expenses as percent of GVP)

Industry Group	1889	1899*	1899	1904
Food and kindred products	3.24	(3.42)	3.45	4.63
Textiles	6.21	(7.85)	7.87	9.27
Iron and steel and their products	5.04	(5.10)	5.09	7.67
Lumber and its remanufactures	5.18	(3.90)	6.35	10.69
Leather and its finished products	3.81	(3.93)	3.82	5.77
Paper and printing	13.36	(12.55)	12.56	16.13
Liquors and beverages	34.31	(28.72)	48.58	44.58
Chemicals and allied products	7.76	(9.01)	10.01	12.49
Clay, glass and stone products	6.13	(6.54)	6.70	9.67
Metals and metal products other than iron and steel	4.65	(2.84)	2.75	4.51
Tobacco	17.74	(28.08)	29.93	24.20
Vehicles for land transportation	2.75	(3.90)	3.89	4.52
Shipbuilding	3.45	(4.94)	4.94	6.35
Miscellaneous industries	7.59	(8.16)	7.41	10.75
Hand trades	4.53	(10.53)	n.a.	n.a.

* comparable with 1889

Source: Calculated from U.S. *Census of Manufactures*, 1900, Vol. I, p. CXLV and U.S. *Census of Manufactures*, 1905, Vol. I. p. CXXIV.

Data on United States miscellaneous expenses as a percentage of Gross Value of Products provide useful comparative information. The United States began collecting miscellaneous expenses for its manufacturing industries in its census of manufactures for 1889 and continued collecting such data for the censuses for 1899, 1904 and 1909.

The relevant ratios for quite comprehensive industry groups are given in Table 4.23 for comparison with project estimates of the Canadian figures for 1900.

These U.S. miscellaneous expenses, up to 1904, included some items that should be omitted as expenses: the largest of these items was internal revenue taxes which were very large

Table 4.24

Ratios of Miscellaneous Expenses to Gross Values of Product,
United States, Selected Industries 1904 and 1909
(miscellaneous expenses as percent of GVP)

Industry	1904	1909
Automobiles	14.20	8.38
Boots and shoes (leather)	5.79	5.46
Bread and other bakery products	7.60	7.39
Cars and general shop construction and repairs by steam railway cos.	3.19	1.81
Clothing, men's	16.22	14.61
Clothing, women's	9.83	8.76
Cotton goods	6.77	5.72
Electrical machinery, apparatus and supplies	12.75	10.68
Flour mill and grist mill products	2.77	2.94
Foundry and machine shop products	8.81	9.97
Furniture and refrigerators	9.88	9.70
Hosiery and knit goods	7.56	6.52
Iron and steel, steel works, rolling mills	5.21	4.32
Leather, tanned, curried and finished	4.95	5.66
Lumber and timber products	11.70	10.50
Paper and wood pulp	8.71	8.05
Petroleum refining	3.03	3.99
Printing and publishing	20.65	20.23
Slaughtering and meat packing	3.35	3.13
Smelting and refining copper	1.97	1.05
Sugar refining	3.10	3.59
Tobacco manufactures	22.69	24.64
Woollen, worsted, and felt goods and wool hats	5.46	5.18

Source: U.S. Census of Manufactures, 1905 (1904) Vol. I, Table 1.
              U.S. Census of Manufactures, 1910 (1909) Vol. I, Table II.

in spiritous beverages and tobacco but quite small in nearly all other industries; the other main item that should be omitted is interest on borrowed money. There is evidence regarding these two matters in the census of manufactures for 1909. In that census the taxes, including internal revenue taxes, were tabulated as a separate item and it is clear that the incidence of the internal revenue taxes is predominantly in the tobacco products and alcoholic beverages industries. Also for 1909, the instructions were to not include interest payments in the miscellaneous expenses as they are really a factor cost. Unfortunately, the miscellaneous expenses data were not tabulated by industry groups as had been done in prior censuses but the data were published by industry at a quite detailed level. They could have been tabulated by the larger industry grouping as a part of this project but such a tabulation would have required substantial work. Instead, relevant comparisons were made at the finer industry classification level for every industry that had a product of $200 million dollars in 1909. The relevant ratios of miscellaneous expenses to gross value of product for them are given in Table 4.24. In viewing it, it should be kept in mind that the one clear item of difference between the two years was that interest expenses were included in miscellaneous expenses in 1904 but not in 1909.

It seems probable that it was not until the census of manufactures for 1904 that the coverage of the miscellaneous expenses became reasonably complete (and even then there may have been omissions, such as, for example, bad debts). The differences between the 1904 and 1909 ratios may well be explained mainly by the presence of the interest component in 1905 and its absence in 1910 — the Canadian interest on all borrowed money of the Rowell-Sirois large sample of companies covered was 1.2 per cent of gross value of product in 1929, 1.5 per cent in 1933 and 0.9 per cent in 1936. In any event, it seems doubtful that the differences in the percentages between 1899 and 1904 in the United States reflect real changes in practice. Consequently, it would appear that the best basis of comparison of the ratio used for Canada in 1900 would be with the 1905 ratios in the United States. On that basis the ratios for Canada do not appear to be too high.

Gross Domestic Product at Factor Cost

Gross domestic product at factor cost is obtained simply, on a year to year basis, by subtraction of non-factor costs from gross value of product. It is obtained then by subtraction of cost of materials, costs of fuel and electricity, and miscellaneous expenses from gross value of product. In this method of estimation of gross domestic product at factor cost it has not been necessary to estimate wages and salaries. However, it is desirable to try to see what proportion of factor costs is accounted for by labour costs. It is for this reason that the wage and salary estimates were made.

Wages and Salaries

The basic source of the wage and salary data was the census of manufactures: these data were obtained in every census of manufactures. The base years in this case included 1905. The data were handled in much the same way that cost of materials was handled. There were four main types of adjustment.

1. In cases where there was undercoverage owing to businesses with less than 5 employees (or with GVP less than $2500 – 1915) both gross value of product and wages and salaries in-

volved upward adjustment to take account of the omitted businesses. This adjustment, of both gross value of product and wages and salaries, was done at a considerably finer level of detail than the industry group of the 1948 standard industrial classification. The result was that for each industry group as an entity wages and salaries, at the aggregate level for the group, were not necessarily adjusted in the same proportion as GVP. This feature of the data is desirable since if an industry component of the group that had, let us say, an atypically high ratio of wages and salaries to GVP was adjusted relatively more than an industry component with a low ratio of wages and salaries to GVP, the ratio of wages and salaries to the whole industry group would be increased by the adjustments.

2. In a very few industries non-manufacturing activities were sometimes included with manufacturing activities. For example, some woodsmen, engaged in the felling of trees, were included with the wood products manufacturing activities. These employees and their wage and salary incomes were removed from the manufacturing sector.

3. The 1870 and 1880 ratios of wages and salaries to GVP when compared with the 1890 ratios were so much out of line that it seemed apparent that the wages and salaries had not been fully reported in the censuses of 1870 and 1880. Accordingly at the individual industry component level, before aggregation to groups, the ratios of wages and salaries to GVP in 1870 and 1880 were assumed to be the same as the ratios in 1890 unless the ratios using the actually recorded wages and salaries for 1870 or 1880 were higher, a very, rare occurrence, in which event they were used.

4. It seemed evident, from the instructions to enumerators, from tabulations and from texts in census volumes, that the wages and salaries reported in the census did not ordinarily include remuneration for many of the self-employed except in 1900; however, in years other than 1900, self-employed who had specifically put themselves on salary may have been included.

In 1900 the instructions were that remuneration was to be recorded for the self-employed that fairly reflected the work that owners or firm members did themselves whether on salary specifically or not. Further, in the tabulation of the returns, the numbers and remuneration, actual or imputed, of the self-employed (owners and firm members) were recorded separately from salaries of hired persons and wages of hired persons. From these data it was possible to tabulate the ratio of remuneration for the self-employed to the wage and salary remuneration of employees for each of the seventeen industry groups of the 1948 standard industrial classification. The average ratio of remuneration of the self-employed, as reported, to wages and salaries of employed workers for all manufacturing in 1900 was 0.09625; the ratios for the individual groups departed widely from this average.

For later years Sydney Smith of the Dominion Bureau of Statistics in his DBS paper *National Income of Canada, 1919-1928*, p. 72, estimated income of the self employed (entrepreneurial withdrawals) at an amount that worked out at a ratio of 0.06831 to the wage and salary bill on the average for the years 1919-1928: for project purposes this was taken as representative of the year 1924. For the project purposes it was assumed that the ratio of remuneration of self-employed to total salaries and wages of hired workers for each individual group was scaled down linearly from 1900 to 1915 according to a straight line interpolation between the actually observed ratios of 1900 and 1924.

Thus the 1900 ratios were scaled down for later years as follows: for 1905 by .0943 ÷ .09625; for 1910 by .08461 ÷ .09625; for 1915 by .07879 ÷ .09625.

The actual 1900 ratios of remuneration of the self-employed to wages and salaries of all hired workers were as follows for industry groups.

Food and beverages	0.11403
Tobacco and tobacco products	0.11442
Rubber products	0.04216
Leather products	0.08235
Textiles (excluding clothing)	0.04399
Clothing: textile and fur	0.14209
Wood products	0.12430
Paper products	0.10166
Printing publishing and allied	0.11769
Iron and steel products	0.07978
Transportation equipment	0.01704
Non-ferrous metal products	0.04971
Electrical apparatus and supplies	0.03954
Non-metallic mineral products	0.04623
Petroleum and coal products	0.01087
Chemical products	0.10412
Miscellaneous industries	0.07547
All industries	0.09625

For the years 1917 to 1926, the data on manufactures appearing in HSC had been reclassified according to the 1948 standard industrial classification and the wage and salary data had been amended to include estimates of labour income for the self-employed. For several of the industry groups, the wage and salary item was taken directly from HSC. However, HSC data on manufactures for these years did not include the hand trades which have been included with manufactures in this project. The way in which estimates of gross value of product for the hand trades for these years were made has been described in the section of these notes on gross value of product. The wage and salary ratios to gross value of product for the hand trades came from data on the hand trades obtained in the census of manufactures from 1917 to 1926. The industry groups for which additions for the hand trades in the 1917 to 1926 years were:

Industry Group	Hand Trade
Iron and steel products	Blacksmiths
Transportation equipment	Auto repair and garage
Clothing	Custom tailoring and repair
	Dressmaking and millinery (women's custom)
Leather and leather products	Boot and shoe repair
Miscellaneous	Locksmiths, gunsmiths

In addition, the census of manufactures had included some woodsmen with the wood products group for 1917 to 1919. The wages for these workers were removed from the woods product group for these years. Also, the retabulated data by Rymes for 1870 to 1915 had excluded manufactured gas and accordingly, for consistency, manufactured gas was removed from the petroleum and coal products group data of HSC. The original data in the census of manufactures publications for 1917 to 1926 was in the detail to make its removal just a mechanical matter.

Gross Property Income

Gross property income is, in every case, just the difference between gross domestic product at factor cost and the wage and salary item.

Gas: Illuminating and Fuel

This item, mainly involving the production of coal gas in the period of this project, but with some supplementation by gas derived from petroleum refining, is based on data collected in the censuses of manufactures. It is given separately in our estimates because Rymes did not include it with his estimates for manufacturing. The justification of separating it from manufacturing arises from characteristics that makes it very much like a public utility. (In the interest of brevity this industry will just be called the illuminating gas industry hereafter.)

The basic data came from the censuses of manufactures taken by the census office from 1870 to 1915 and the annual census of manufactures taken by DBS from 1917 onward, although as will be explained, the 1917 data themselves were not used. The other data of significance were the interpolator data for years before 1918.

The basic method of calculating gross domestic product was to subtract cost of materials, cost of fuel and electricity and miscellaneous expenses from gross value of product.

Gross value of product for base years was obtained directly from the relevant censuses of manufactures. Interpolation between base years was done by use of the annual series on gross value of product in the coal and petroleum sector of the manufacturing industries (already described in the section on manufacturing). Ratios of gross value of product in the illuminating gas industry to gross value of product in the "coal and petroleum" manufacturing industry for base years were calculated; these ratios were linearly interpolated for years between base years; the product of the resulting ratios and the gross value of product in the coal and petroleum yielded gross value of product for the illuminating gas industry between base years.

The relevant gross value of product for base years and the ratios for the base years of gross value of product in the illuminating gas industry to the gross value of product in the coal and petroleum industry are given in the next following table.

There was a census of industry for this industry taken in 1917, the first of the annual censuses. However, the data, especially "miscellaneous" cost data, appeared to be inconsistent with the conformation of data in following years. Accordingly, the reported data for 1917 were not used: estimates for 1917 were derived in the same manner as for other intercensal years.

The gross value of product being thus estimated for all years, it followed to subtract the relevant expenses to acquire an estimate of gross domestic product. The relevant expenses were: (i) cost of materials of which coal was by far the largest item, (ii) cost of fuel and electricity necessary for ordinary plant operations such as boiler fuel but not including basic material for making coal gas or petroleum by-product gas, (iii) miscellaneous expenses. The available data varied a good deal among census years both in terms of total coverage and in the nature of assignment of costs among the three categories noted above. Given that the data for 1917 as recorded were not used, the only census years for which all three categories of expenditure were reported were the years 1918 to 1923. Cost of materials, and cost of boiler fuel and electricity but not miscellaneous costs were available for 1900, 1910 and 1924 to 1926. Costs of materials alone were available for 1870, 1880 and 1890. Allusion has been made to the fact that the assignment of expenses among the three categories of expenditure was not always the same in

Year	Gross Value of Product of of Illuminating Gas Industry	Ratio of Gross Value of Production of Illuminating Gas to Gross Value of Production in the Petro- leum and Coal Industry
1870	750	0.2423
1880	1,173	0.2896
1890	2,797	0.6434
1900	2,327	0.5268
1910	4,006	0.4193
1915	4,451	0.2726
1918	8,413	0.1424
1919	11,967	(0.1809)
1920	17,758	(0.2250)
1921	18,772	(0.2739)
1922	19,089	(0.2922)
1923	19,605	(0.3095)
1924	18,102	(0.2897)
1925	17,874	(0.2775)
1926	18,265	(0.2113)

Source: Column (1) from Census of Manufactures for all years given.

Ratios in column (2) are obtained as the quotient of column (1) divided by gross value of product of the petroleum and coal sector of the manufacturing industries. The ratios in brackets are inserted for information purposes only.

different censuses years. In particular, owing to coal (and coke) being both a raw material for the generation of gas and a boiler fuel, the assignment of costs to "cost of materials" or "cost of fuel and electricity" was not done uniformly in all years. For this reason, the behaviour of the sum of these two categories together in relation to gross value of products is perhaps more meaningful than the ratios of the two categories considered separately.

The ratio of each of the three categories of cost to gross value of product in the base years (including the first year, 1918, and the last year, 1923, for which the information is complete) are given in the next table.

Cost of Materials

For all years the ratio of cost of materials was derived from data reported in the relevant census. In 1910, the materials costs and fuel costs were not clearly separable, though together fully covered: separation was done by making the ratio of fuel costs to GVP the same in 1910 as in 1918; the remainder was then material costs.

Ratios of Costs to Gross Values of Product,
Gas Manufacturing

	1870	1880	1890	1900	1910	1915
Cost of materials	0.3533	0.2720	0.2760	0.3232	0.2844	0.2726
Cost of fuel and electricity	0.0133	0.0133	0.0133	0.0133	0.0958	0.0958
Miscellaneous expenses	0.1011	0.1011	0.1011	0.1011	0.1011	0.1011

	1918	1923	1924	1925	1926
Cost of materials	0.4126	0.3822	0.3742	0.3457	0.3409
Cost of fuel and electricity	0.0958	0.0722	0.1495	0.0632	0.0557
Miscellaneous expenses	0.1197	0.0902	0.1011	0.1011	0.1011

Sources: The sources for 1870, 1880, 1890, 1900, 1910, 1915 are the Census of Canada *Manufactures*. The sources for 1918 onward are DBS *Manufactures of Non-Metallic Minerals in Canada*, annual.

Cost of Fuel and Electricity

These costs were reported separately in 1901 and from 1919 onward; David Jones made estimates for 1918 when separating "manufactured gas" from the "coal and petroleum" industry of manufacturing sector. The ratio for 1910 was made the same as the ratio for 1918 (see the note on cost of materials above). The ratio for 1900, calculated from reported data, was used also for 1870, 1880 and 1890, for which years no cost of fuel and electricity was reported.

Miscellaneous Costs

These costs were reported only for years 1918 to 1923. The average ratio of these costs to GVP for these years was 0.1011; there was narrow dispersion around this average. This ratio was used for all years, 1870 to 1917, and for 1924 to 1926.

A check of the realism of these ratios was made by comparison with the industry in the United States. The comparisons follow.

Ratios of Materials Plus Fuel
Costs to Gross Value of Product,
Canada and United States

	1870	1880	1890	1900	1910	1919	1920
Canada	0.3666	0.2853	0.2893	0.3365	0.3802	0.5107	0.4943
United States	0.3392	N.A.	0.2463	0.2721	0.3143	0.4785	0.4919

Note: Until 1910 the U.S. census data refer to the year preceding the census, that is to 1909, 1899, 1889, etc.

Sources: Canadian data — already given; U.S. data — U.S. Census of Manufactures, e.g. for 1889 to 1914: U.S. Census of Manufactures 1914, Vol. 2, p.535; for 1919 onward, biennial Census of Manufactures, e.g. 1921, p.799.

     The total costs in the base years were obtained from the sum of the three categories of costs — some of these costs had to be calculated as the product of gross value of product and the ratio of cost to this gross product value. Gross domestic product then was calculated as the remainder when the sum of these costs was subtracted from gross value of product.

     For calculations for other than the base years, for example, 1871-79, 1881-89, 1891-99, 1901-09, 1911 to 1915 and 1916-17, the estimates of the categories of expenses were calculated by interpolating the ratios of the category of expense to gross value of product, linearly, between base years and then multiplying the interpolated gross value of product by the relevant ratio. The resultant costs of materials, costs of fuel and electricity and miscellaneous costs were then added together to get total costs. Subtraction of these total costs from gross value of product then yielded the estimates of gross domestic product.

Bibliography of Sources Cited in Chapter 4

The census of manufacturing was by far the most important source of data for this section. This census was taken with the decennial census from 1871 to 1911, and the data which applied to the preceding year were published in the census reports; postal censuses of manufactures were taken by the Census and Statistics Office (CSO) of Canada in 1906 and 1916 for the immediately preceding years and the data were published; the Dominion Bureau of Statistics took an annual census of manufactures for 1917 and later years and published the data of these censuses both as a whole and for component industry parts. For abbreviations of bibliographic references see the bibliography of Chapter 2.

Major References:

CSO; *Census of Manufactures*, 1871, 1881, 1891, 1901, 1906 (postal), 1911 and 1916 (postal).

DBS; *Census of Manufactures*, annual since 1917.

CSO and DBS; Decennial Census of Canada, 1871 to 1931, data on occupations and earnings of persons covered in the census of persons.

DBS; censuses of 1911 and 1921, unpublished data on individual earnings of persons, available on microfilm from DBS.

DBS and antecedents; *Trade of Canada*, annual from 1867.

DBS and antecedents; *Railway and Statistics*, annual since 1876.

HSC, *Historical Statistics of Canada*: see bibliography to Chapter 2.

Engerman, Stanley L. and Robert E. Gallman, *Long Term Factors in American Economic Growth* (University of Chicago Press, 1986).

Department of Labour, Canada; *Wholesale Prices 1890 to 1909* and succeeding annual volumes, *Wholesale Prices*, to 1917.

Department of Mines, Canada; *Annual Report on Mineral Production of Canada during the Calendar Year*, annual since 1886, published in sessional papers of Canada.

Buckley, Kenneth, *Capital Formation in Canada 1860-1930* (University of Toronto Press, 1955).

Taylor K.W., "Statistics of Foreign Trade", in K.W. Taylor and H. Michell, *Statistical Contributions to Canadian Economic History*, Volume II (Macmillan of Canada, 1931).

U.S. Bureau of the Census; *Census of Manufactures*, 1870 to 1900 every tenth year; 1904-1919, every fifth year; and biennially for 1921-1939.

Chapter 5. Construction

M.C. URQUHART

Gross Domestic Product in the Construction Industry, Canada, 1870-1926

Income produced in the construction industry was obtained in two steps. First, an estimate was prepared of total capital formation in building and engineering construction. Second, gross domestic product was obtained by use of estimates of the ratio of gross domestic product in construction to total gross capital formation in construction. These steps are described in turn.

Capital Formation in the Form of Construction

The basic sources for these data, exclusive of residential construction, were Statcan, *Fixed Capital Flows and Stocks 1926-1978*; DBS, *Fixed Capital Flows and Stocks in Manufacturing 1926-1960*; and, more importantly, detail of the Statcan estimates, not published in the original, that were obtained from a printout of material on a tape borrowed from Statcan — this source is designated as Maclist in the project files and is identified by that description in references to it herein. In fact, all the actual data used in this project were obtained from this last source.

The capital formation estimates of Statcan were prepared as part of a project to estimate the capital stock in Canada, beginning with 1926, by the perpetual inventory method. The use of this method meant that it was necessary to prepare estimates of capital formation for years before 1926 at least as far back as a period equal to the length of life of the fixed asset. The assumed lengths of life of various structures are given in the original sources. The larger part of the estimates of capital formation in the form of construction go as far back as 1871; a smaller part, comprised of data for agriculture, forestry, mines and the construction industry itself did not go quite so far back.

The origins of the estimates of capital formation in construction are now given in as much industrial detail as was required from the nature of the original estimates; a description of Statcan's general methodology is deferred until consideration is given to the accuracy of the estimates. In the source, building and engineering construction were given separately. In what follows, they are treated separately except in the case of manufacturing.

Manufacturing, Building and Engineering Construction

Whilst the lengths of life of both building and engineering structures varied considerably among various categories of manufacturing, the estimates of capital formation in these structures were carried right back to 1871, in the sources, for all categories of manufacturers. Hence, these data were obtained for all years from Maclist.

Agriculture, Building Construction

The comprehensive Statcan estimates for building construction in agriculture go as far back as 1876 even though building structures in agriculture were assumed to have a life of 40 years; there was not any engineering construction. Hence, the data for 1876 to 1926 were obtained from the Maclist printout.

The estimates for 1871 to 1875 remained to be made. The value of other non-manufacturing building construction, excluding forestry, mines, and the construction industry, (and, of course, agriculture) was available in the source for the years 1871 to 1875 (see below). The average ratio of building capital formation in agriculture to total non-manufacturing building construction, excluding forestry, mines, and the construction industry, in the years 1876 to 1880 was 0.44162. The estimates for agriculture for 1871-75 were made by using this ratio to extrapolate building construction in agriculture for 1876 to 1871 on the basis of the building construction in non-manufacturing industries excluding agriculture, forestry, mines and the construction industry itself.

Forestry, Mining and the Construction Industry Building Construction

Forestry, mining and the construction industry were treated as a group. The Statcan estimates for them, available from Maclist, ran back as far as 1896; it was necessary to make estimates for 1871 to 1895. A technique similar, in principle, to that used in agriculture for 1871 to 1875 was used to extrapolate building construction estimates for these industries as a group from 1896 back to 1871. The average ratio of building construction in forestry, the mines and the construction industry to building construction in all non-manufacturing industry for the years 1896 to 1900 was 0.04585 or, equivalently, the average ratio of building construction in this group of the industries to building construction in all other non-manufacturing industry was 0.04805.

The estimates for forestry, mines, and the construction industry were extrapolated back to 1871 by multiplying the latter ratio by the figures for building construction in all other non-manufacturing industry which comes from Maclist back to 1876 but which includes the project estimate for agriculture for 1871 to 1875.

Residual Non-Manufacturing Non-Residential Building Construction

It has been pointed out already that all other non-manufacturing building construction, i.e. non-manufacturing building construction excluding agriculture, forestry, mines and the construction industry, was available right back to 1871 from the Maclist. It is also to be pointed out that Statcan has no building construction entered for the fisheries at any time.

Residential Building Construction

Building construction in housing was estimated (re-estimated) for this project by Professor Marion Steele. Her methods are described in her own manuscript which is given in her description of housing, contained in Chapter 8 of this volume.

Fisheries Engineering Construction

The Statcan estimates for engineering construction in the fisheries go back to 1901 and are available in Maclist: they were uniformly at $0.40 million for each year from 1901 to 1906. This industry was arbitrarily given a value for this project of $0.4 million for 1890 to 1899 and a value of $0.30 million for 1871 to 1889.

Water Transport Engineering Construction

The Statcan estimates, available from Maclist, go back to 1874. Since each of the entries for 1874 to 1916 was either $0.10 million or $0.20, the entry for each year from 1871 to 1873 was made $0.10 million in the light of the values for the following years.

Forestry, Mining, and Urban and Suburban Transport Engineering Construction

The Statcan estimates, taken from Maclist, run back to 1896 for forestry and mines and to 1895 for the urban and suburban transport component. For the years before 1896, except the years 1882 to 1884, the project estimates were extrapolated for all three industries as a single group, from the Statcan data by the same method as used for the extrapolation of the forestry, mines, and construction industry building construction estimates: the average ratio of the sum of forestry, mines and urban etc. transport engineering construction to all non-manufacturing engineering construction was calculated from the Statcan data for 1896 to 1900, at a value of 0.08446; data for all other non-manufacturing engineering construction were already available in Maclist or in our estimates for fisheries prior to 1901 and for water transport prior to 1874; on the assumption that the ratio of the sum of forestry, mines and urban etc. transport to all other non-manufacturing engineering construction would be constant at 0.08446 the estimates for this group of three industries was extrapolated back to 1871.

This method could not properly be used for the years 1882 to 1884 owing to the very large such expenditures of the Canadian Pacific Railway for those years. For these years, the procedure simply was to interpolate, almost linearly, between our calculated values for 1881 and 1885 which were, in dollars: for 1881, 1.7 million; for 1885, 2.7 million. The derived figures were, in dollars: for 1882, 2.0 million; for 1883, 2.2 million; for 1884, 2.5 million.

Residual Non-Manufacturing Engineering Construction

The data for this category which includes all those industries not dealt with so far, were available right back to 1871 from Maclist. The industries for which there were entries are broadcasting (from 1923), telephones (from 1891), water systems (rounded to zero before 1896), railway transport, electric light and power and gas distribution, trade, and, federal, provincial and municipal governments.

The Ratio of Gross Domestic Product in Construction to Capital Formation in New Building and Engineering Construction

An estimate of the ratio of gross domestic product in the construction industry to gross capital formation in building and engineering construction may be derived from the official national accounts. Just such a ratio was obtained by averaging the ratios of gross domestic product in the construction industry to gross building and engineering construction for all years from 1926 to 1974, except the wartime years of 1940 to 1945, which were excluded because they were so much out of line with the peacetime activities. There was variation among the ratios for indi-

Ratio of Gross Domestic Product in the Construction Industry to Gross
Capital Formation in Building and Engineering Construction, 1926-1974

Year	Ratio	Year	Ratio	Year	Ratio
1926	.3785	*1942	.5722	1958	.3347
1927	.3236	*1943	.5574	1959	.3402
1928	.3025	*1944	.4256	1960	.3517
1929	.3266	*1945	.4167	1961	.3550
1930	.3286	1946	.4142	1962	.3602
1931	.3492	1947	.4674	1963	.3583
1932	.3681	1948	.4141	1964	.3454
1933	.3561	1949	.4143	1965	.3620
1934	.3227	1950	.3959	1966	.3821
1935	.3300	1951	.3744	1967	.3972
1936	.3503	1952	.4032	1968	.3899
1937	.3392	1953	.3988	1969	.3989
1938	.3684	1954	.3661	1970	.4050
1939	.3780	1955	.3370	1971	.4080
1940*	.4528	1956	.3412	1972	.4180
1941*	.4934	1957	.3500	1973	.4104
				1974	.4018

* Wartime years

Source of original data: *National Accounts, 1926-74, Volume 1*, Table 2 and Table 28.

vidual years but there was not a trend. The source document was Statistics Canada, *National Income and Expenditure Accounts, Volume 1, 1926-1974* (National Accounts 1926-1974). Capital formation in the form of building and engineering construction was obtained from Table 2 and gross domestic product in the construction industry from Table 28. The ratio as calculated was 0.37.

The estimates of gross domestic product in the construction industry were obtained by taking it as the proportion of 0.37 of gross capital formation in construction for years 1900 to 1926, as the proportion 0.40 from 1871 to 1895 and for the years 1896 to 1899 as a proportion linearly interpolated between 0.37 in 1900 and 0.40 in 1895. The reason for using a higher ratio for the years before 1900 was that it seemed probable that the hand trades in construction were relatively more important before 1900 than in the boom period that followed 1900.

Some Checks for Reliability

A number of things bearing on the reliability of these estimates are now considered.

A matter of general methodology is noted first. Probably the best method of obtaining capital outlays is by explicit survey of those buying the capital goods if such survey can be reasonably complete. Such has been the method used by Statistics Canada since the fairly early post-war years. Alternatively, data for some industry groups may be derivable from industry reports prepared for other purposes or from income tax returns. A third method, developed originally by Simon Kuznets, has involved preparation of estimates of flows of construction materials from production and trade data and then adding allowances for transportation costs, labour costs and various overhead costs to obtain a figure for the total value of construction put in place. If a reasonably good estimate of the flows of construction materials can be made and if, as seems to be the case, the ratio of labour and overhead costs to construction materials costs is fairly stable, this method has the advantage of providing consistent year to year estimates of overall construction expenditure. The absolute level of such an estimate may be too high or too low but such bias as there is tends to be consistent from year to year. If a good base year estimate can be made, such a series can provide a good extrapolator to obtain estimates for many years. This method was used in the first capital formation estimates for Canada for 1926 to 1941 (Dominion-Provincial Conference on Reconstruction, *Public Investment and Capital Formation*, Ottawa, 1945) and while estimates prepared later from much more comprehensive data showed that the general level of the first estimates was too low, the year to year movements were quite good. The disadvantage of this method, by itself, is that it does not give much detail on the distribution of construction among sectors; the advantage of the method is that it gives a control total to which individually and separately estimated sector components should add up. All this presupposes, of course, a reasonably good estimate of the construction material flows.

The method used by Statcan in making its estimates for 1871 to 1926 was to make estimates for individual sectors of the economy. For manufacturing, the railways, and presumably government and education, there are basic data throughout the period, such as, for example, in manufacturing the capital stock estimates of the censuses of manufacturing. Most of the rest of the estimates for non-residential construction were prepared, sector by sector if my suppositions of Statcan's methodology are right, by using some kinds of extrapolators to project the official figures back from 1926 to the earlier years. And the extrapolators sometimes had a rather loose connection with construction expenditure. Further, the residential construction did not come from Maclist but was separately estimated within this project itself, albeit with a good deal of direct information, such as housing stocks at census dates and estimates of number of units constructed on an annual basis. There was no overall controlling total in the Statcan methodology although it should be added that use of Buckley's data, noted below, for making some of the individual projections, provided some part of this function.

For comparison, there are Buckley's estimates (Buckley, Kenneth, *Capital Formation in Canada, 1896-1930*, University of Toronto Press, 1955) of construction for 1896 to 1925, of which the total was prepared first, by estimating the flow of construction materials and then adding the wage costs, transportation costs and overhead costs to get a series for the total and then, second, using this series to extrapolate a base-period construction expenditure for 1921 which, in turn, was based upon a fairly good construction census for that year. Buckley made separate estimates for certain sectional components of construction expenditure but his total was not derived from addition of separately and independently estimated components.

The Buckley data for 1896 to 1925 may, of course, have problems of their own. The measures of the flows of construction materials are based on partial data and they probably became less reliable the further back one goes. In addition, over long periods the ratios of labour costs, or overhead, to construction materials may have changed in ways that are not known. Again, the proportion of construction materials used for repair purposes rather than for construction of new facilities may have changed. Nevertheless, it is worthwhile to compare Buckley's results with the project data and various comparisons are now made.

First, in Table 5.1, a comparison is made between the project figures and Buckley's figures for all construction, for residential construction and for non-residential construction. With the exception of the wartime years, the project figures are above Buckley's figures in every temporal category — there is a difference in level — a not-surprising state of affairs since the official estimates for 1926-30 are above the P.I.C.F. estimates, which are almost the same as Buckley's.

Table 5.1
Comparison of Buckley's Estimates and Project Estimates:
Total Construction, Residential Construction and Non-Residential Construction
(All values in million of current dollars)

Period	Total Construction			Residential Construction			Non-Residential Construction		
	Project	Buckley	P/B	Project	Buckley	P/B	Project	Buckley	P/B
1896-1900	357	269	1.33	125	104	1.20	232	165	1.41
1901-1905	792	681	1.16	230	222	1.04	562	459	1.22
1906-1910	1623	1439	1.13	481	468	1.03	1142	971	1.18
1911-1915	2467	2007	1.23	645	568	1.14	1822	1439	1.27
1916-1920	1841	2122	0.87	401	641	0.63	1440	1481	0.97
1921-1925	2611	2271	1.15	922	742	1.24	1689	1529	1.10
1926-1930	*3655	3109	1.18	*1114	1060	1.05	*2541	2049	1.24

* From official national accounts. The Maclist figure is slightly higher.

Source: Buckley, Tables B and IV; Project, from Maclist; residential, Marion Steele.

Table 5.1 — Continued

Total Construction, Railways
(All values in millions of current dollars)

Period	Project	Buckley	Ratio, P/B
1896-1900	55	55	1.00
1901-1905	124	124	1.00
1906-1910	381	381	1.00
1911-1916	537	537	1.00
1916-1920	252	253	1.00
1921-1925	253	253	1.00
1926-1930	447	389	1.15

Source: Buckley, p.45, Table XII; project, Maclist.

All Government Investment
(All values in millions of current dollars)

Period	Project Estimates Gross Investment	Buckley Gross Investment[1]	Ratio P/B	Project Construction	Buckley Construction only[2]	Ratio P/B
1896-1900	49.7	--	--	41	--	--
1901-1905	94.6	94.0	1.01	79	79	1.00
1905-1910	174.7	247.9	0.70	146	149	0.98
1911-1915	399.9	439.7	0.91	335	342	0.98
1916-1920	237.5	292.1	0.81	250	256	0.98
1921-1925	504.3	438.8	1.15	427	436	0.98
1926-1930	--	602.0	--	566	578	0.98

Sources: (1) Buckley C.F.I.C. p.82
(2) *ibid.* p.57

Non-Residential Construction in Agriculture
(All values in $ mm)

Period	Project	Buckley (Prairies only)
1896-1900	33.0	--
1901-1905	87.9	37.6
1906-1910	134.6	57.9
1911-1915	93.0	23.8
1916-1920	--	60.2
1921-1925	--	15.2
1926-1930	--	64.8

Given this fact there remain two anomalies: the ratio of the project's estimates to Buckley's are relatively low in the wartime period; the same ratio is relatively high in the 1896-1900 period. The general difference in level is not a matter of concern; the project estimates may be regarded, in a sense, as an extrapolation of the official national income estimates of 1926-30. Nor is the divergence in the wartime years of the pattern of the relationship of project estimates to those of Buckley of great concern. I believe that the more recent figures for that disturbed period must be accepted. In this period of great escalation of prices and of real problems in separating the repair and maintenance expenditure from the new capital expenditure in the construction industry, there may be merit in the component by component estimation of construction outlay. For that time, independently made estimates for outlay on construction in railways, manufacturing, housing, agriculture and governments should be reasonably accurate and, by the project estimates, they comprise nearly 80 percent of all construction expenditure at that time. At the same time, it is in just such a period that estimates derived from flows of construction materials are least reliable.

The divergence of the ratio of project estimates to Buckley's estimates in the period 1896-1900 is of more concern, connecting as it does to the entirely new overall estimates for 1870 to 1895. It raises the possibility that the new estimates for the period 1870 to 1900 may be too high. It should be noted at once, for whatever it is worth, that Buckley's estimates for this period were based on less complete data than for the later period. In particular, the data on domestic disappearance of lumber, a most important component of the building material series, is not viewed as being very reliable before 1908. In addition, Buckley extrapolated his construction series from 1900 back to 1896 on trend rather than by working out domestic disappearance year by year from production plus imports less exports as he did for the years from 1900 onward. (See the introductory note to the Appendix in Buckley.) Therefore his series for 1896-1900 is probably considerably more subject to diversion from a consistent value than in any other peacetime quinquennium of the period with which he dealt. However, despite the possibility of the Buckley series being out of line for 1896-1900, we should check our own estimates further.

Second, the project (Statcan) estimates for construction in railroads and those of Buckley are identical for each five year period from 1896 to 1926. (Rather strangely, the project estimates exceed those of Buckley for 1926-30 despite the facts that both Buckley and Statcan state that they took their estimates from the same source.)

Third, the project estimates for residential construction were prepared anew by Professor Marion Steele for this project and without question are the authoritative estimates. It should be pointed out that Buckley's inclusion of separate estimates for housing was not an item that affected his estimates of total construction. The Steele estimates for 1896-1900 are of the same quality as her estimates of the entire period from 1870 to 1926 and hence cannot be regarded as a special cause of the divergence of the project and the Buckley estimates in 1896-1900 period.

Fourth, since the project (Statcan) estimates for manufacturing were prepared by use of capital stock data of the census of manufacturers as part of the basic data, the capital stock data provide anchor years in 1870, 1880, 1890, 1900, 1905, 1910, 1915 and annually from 1917 onward. Hence, while the capital stock data may become somewhat less good the further back in time one goes, there is no reason to expect a discrete break at 1900.

Fifth, project estimates and Buckley's for direct government expenditure are almost identical for 1901-05 to 1926-30. Project estimates are 98 percent of Buckley's for each quinquennial period from 1905-10 to 1926-30 and exactly equal to Buckley's 1901-05; Buckley did not publish a separate figure for 1896-1900. It appears that methods of estimation have been about the same. Buckley's estimates were prepared from government accounts and presumably Statcan's estimates were constructed likewise. One would expect that estimates of investment expenditure on schools would likewise have been prepared from government publications.

Finally, one would not expect that the estimates for non-residential agricultural construction, described earlier, would be biased upward in the earlier years since the series for extrapolation backward from 1926-30 was based half on purchases of farm machinery and half on construction of farm houses (each of which incidentally increased slightly over five times between 1896 and 1930) and there is no apparent reason that agricultural non-residential construction should have moved much differently.

The estimates for railways, residential construction, manufacturing, government and agri-

Table 5.2
Industrial Division of Construction Expenditure
Amount of Gross Capital Expenditure
(millions of current dollars)

Period	Manufac-turing	Railway and Telegraph	Agricul-ture	Other Business (Residual)	Housing Construc-tion	Public Schools	Govern-ment	Total
1871-75	12.3	89.7	61.4		154.1	6.8	18.5	342.8
1876-80	12.7	40.4	20.7	26.7	98.8	5.4	38.7	243.4
1881-85	31.1	171.8	24.0	40.5	75.5	4.0	28.6	375.5
1886-90	26.7	79.5	19.0	43.8	174.1	6.7	29.2	379.0
1891-95	21.9	41.4	24.4	37.9	153.4	5.8	36.1	320.9
1896-1900	39.4	54.6	33.0	58.6	125.1	5.2	41.1	357.0
1901-05	107.7	124.2	87.9	154.4	229.5	9.3	78.5	791.5
1906-10	169.4	380.7	134.6	281.3	480.5	30.7	145.7	1622.9
1911-15	309.2	537.2	93.0	473.3	644.9	74.5	334.6	2466.7
1916-20	274.5	252.7	162.8	438.6	401.3	62.3	249.5	1841.0
1921-25	237.7	252.7	84.9	568.7	921.9	117.9	426.7	2610.5

Percentage distribution of above

Period	Manufac-turing	Railway and Telegraph	Agricul-ture	Other Business (Residual)	Housing Construc-tion	Public Schools	Govern-ment
1871-75	3.6	26.2	17.9		44.6	2.0	5.4
1876-80	5.2	16.6	8.5	11.0	40.6	2.2	15.9
1881-85	8.3	45.8	6.4	10.8	20.1	1.1	7.6
1886-90	7.0	21.0	5.0	11.6	45.9	1.8	7.7
1891-95	6.8	12.9	7.6	11.8	47.8	1.8	11.2
1896-1900	11.0	15.3	9.2	16.4	35.0	1.5	11.5
1901-05	13.6	15.7	11.1	19.5	29.0	1.2	9.9
1906-10	10.4	23.5	8.3	17.3	29.6	1.9	9.0
1911-15	12.5	21.8	3.8	19.2	26.1	3.0	13.6
1916-20	14.9	13.7	8.8	23.8	21.8	3.4	13.6
1921-25	9.1	9.7	3.3	21.8	35.3	4.5	16.3

culture account for 83.6 percent of total construction expenditure in 1896-1900. There does not appear to be any reason for a significant deterioration in the quality of these individual estimates between 1901-05 and 1896-1900. The remaining part of the estimate for residual construction for all other businesses was made on a shakier basis. Nevertheless, it is worth noting that this latter component made up a smaller proportion of total construction expenditure in 1896-1900 than in 1900-1905 or any subsequent period.

Given the foregoing information, then, there does not appear reason to expect that the 1896-1900 overall estimate of construction expenditure will be significantly biased upward relative to those after 1900. One is led to wonder whether the divergence relative to the Buckley data in 1896-1900 is not caused by the Buckley data for this quinquennium being less reliable than that after 1900. The extension by Buckley of his construction total at least partly on trend for 1896-1900 may have led to his estimates for those years being too low. In any event, the relative similar movements of the totals after 1900 are gratifying.

The project estimates of the construction expenditure for the entire period 1870 to 1925 according to the industrial categories noted above are given in Table 5.2.

There remains to be made such evaluations as can be done for the 1870 to 1895 data. The first thing to be noted is that the project estimates for manufactures, residential and government construction were prepared in the same manner as for the period from 1896 onward. The method of estimation for agriculture back as far as 1876 described earlier appears to be not unreasonable.

The estimates for railways require comment. Statcan estimated the railway construction expenditure for 1871 to 1895 by projecting the average 1896 to 1900 construction expenditure backward on the basis of an index of imported railway construction materials. However, Buckley had estimated railway investment expenditure in total including rolling stock and machinery (but excluding capital expenditure charged to current account) for the same period

Table 5.3
Buckley's C.F.I.C. Fixed Capital Formation
in Railroads Compared with his 1962 Estimates
(All values in millions of dollars)

Period	C.F.I.C. Estimates (1)	1962 Estimates (excludes capital outlay charged to current acct.) (2)	Ratio (1)/(2)
1896-1900	71	67	1.06
1901-1905	165	149	1.11
1906-1910	473	453	1.04
1911-1915	682	669	1.02
1916-1920	423	321	1.31
1921-1925	386	264	1.46
1926-1930	583	433	1.35

Source: Buckley, C.F.I.C., page 44; Buckley, *Capital Formation in Railway Transport and Telegraphs in Canada, 1850-1930*, Table 1, C.P.S.A. Conference on Statistics, McMaster University.

and earlier by use of very considerable detail for individual lines and his estimates should be regarded as authoritative. Buckley's estimates appear in HSC, Series R156. Buckley's estimates for 1850 to 1895 do not include capital outlay charged to current account. Some rough estimate of the shortfall caused by this omission can be made. When Buckley made his estimates for 1850-1895 he carried them through again to 1930 using the same methodology throughout; that is, his estimates for the whole period exclude capital items charged to current account. He had

Table 5.4
Buckley's Replacement Capital Expenditure as a
Proportion of "Net" Capital Expenditure
(values in millions of dollars)

Period	Net Capital Expenditure	Replacement Capital Expenditure	Total	Ratio of Total to "Net"
1896-1900	54	17	71	1.31
1900-1905	136	29	165	1.21
1906-1910	430	43	473	1.10
1911-1915	622	60	682	1.10
1916-1920	299	124	423	1.41
1921-1925	234	152	386	1.65
1926-1930	404	180	584	1.45

Source: Buckley, C.F.I.C., Table XIII.

Table 5.5
Investment in Railways, Structures and Equipment
($ mm)

Period	Buckley (excludes capital items charged to current acct.)	Statcan		Ratio
		Construction only	Total (Project)	Statcan to Buckley
1871-1875	88.1	83.7	118.1	1.34
1876-1880	70.7	40.4	53.2	0.75
1881-1885	151.6	171.8	226.1	1.49
1886-1890	112.4	79.9	105.2	0.94
1891-1895	41.4	41.4	54.5	1.31
1896-1900	66.7	54.8	71.2	1.07
Total	530.9		628.3	1.18

Average ratio (1871 - 1900) = 1.15

previously in C.F.I.C. made estimates for 1896 to 1930 that did include capital outlays charged to current account. A comparison of his two series for 1896 to 1930, given in Table 5.3, shows the size of capital outlay charged to current account in that period. It will be seen that the item is relatively small when much new track and equipment are being acquired as in the years 1906 to 1915. In other years, it is relatively much larger.

An alternative check may be made. The fact that the railways charged considerable amounts of their capital expenditure to current account was a consequence of the railways not using depreciation accounting; rather they charged replacement of retired equipment and the like to current account. However, not all replacements were charged to current account. For example, the replacement of iron rails by steel rails was charged to capital account. Buckley had separated his estimates of capital formation in railways in Canada for 1896 to 1930 in C.F.I.C. into "net" and "replacement", terms used by the railways to designate investment outlay charged to capital account and to operating account respectively. The ratio of total investment to "net" investment in the Buckley estimates is given in Table 5.4. The pattern of this table is much the same as the preceding table.

From these two tables one can only make a guess of what should be added to the Buckley estimates for 1870 to 1895 to adjust for the capital outlay charged to current expense. The most that one can do is to see whether the project estimates compare with the Buckley "net" estimates for 1870 to 1895 in a way that seems reasonable. The project estimates used the Statcan estimates for construction outlay from 1870 to 1895. However, since the Statcan estimates for equipment only went back to 1896, the project estimates for this item for 1870 to 1895 were made by assuming that annual equipment expenditures bore the same relation to construction as they did on the average in the Statcan estimates for 1896 to 1905.

A comparison of the project and Buckley net estimates for 1870 to 1895 is given in Table 5.5. From it one might conclude that on the average for each quinquennium over the period the project estimates may be reasonably satisfactory. One could argue from the data of Tables 5.2 and 5.3 that the average excess of the project estimates over Buckley's of 15 percent or the excess of the project's aggregate for the period over Buckley's of 18 percent could be taken as a reasonable measure of the capital items charged to current not covered by Buckley's data. My own view is that the project's excess, whether of the average or the aggregate, is possibly a bit high but not uncomfortably so. At the same time the distribution of the differences by periods is not satisfactory. The project estimates are especially too high in 1871-75 and 1881-85, the active periods of building of the intercolonial railways and the Canadian Pacific Railway respectively; they are considerably too low in 1876-80 and 1886-90: However, the averages for each decade, 1871-80, 1881-90 and 1891-1900 are possibly acceptable

The remaining construction expenditure, the residual non-residential construction, is relatively small — it may be a little too small — so that even a 50 percent error in it would not greatly affect the overall totals.

Bibliography of Sources Cited in Chapter 5

Buckley, K.A.H., *Capital Formation in Canada*, University of Toronto Press, 1955.

Buckley, K.A.H., *Capital Formation in Railway Transport and Telegraphs in Canada 1850-1930*, mimeograph from Conference on Statistics, McMaster University, 1962.

Dominion Bureau of Statistics, *Fixed Capital Flows and Stocks in Manufacturing, 1926-1960* (Catalogue No. 13-522).

Statistics Canada, *Fixed Capital Flows and Stocks 1926-1978* (Catalogue 3-568 Occasional).

Statistics Canada, *Maclist*, not a publication of Statistics Canada but a set of data obtained from a Statcan tape giving much detail that lies behind *Fixed Capital Flows and Stocks 1926-1978*.

Urquhart, M.C. and Buckley, K.A.H., *Historical Statistics of Canada*, The Macmillan Company of Canada Ltd. and Cambridge University Press, 1965.

Chapter 6. Transportation and Public Utilities

ALAN GREEN

Gross Domestic Product At Factor Cost In Transportation And Public Utilities, 1870–1926

This section outlines, in detail, the estimation procedures used to measure gross domestic product (GDP) and its components for the following industries: steam railways and railway express; electric railways; water transport; telephone and telegraph. The final series (gross domestic product) is the sum of wages and salaries paid; interest paid; dividends disbursed and gross savings. Only the last series needs some explanation. Gross savings (which in this case is gross of depreciation allowance) is the residual amount remaining after taxes, interest and dividend payments have been deducted from net operating revenue.

Two factors dictated the allocation of GDP into the industrial divisions outlined above. First, statistical limitations forced certain series amalgamations. In the case of railway express, as is shown in the appropriate section which follows, it was intricately bound up with steam railroads. The former often was owned by the latter and in all cases used the railways facilities for the movement of goods. Separate estimation, although possible for years towards the end of the period, was not possible for the early decades. A very similar argument dictated the amalgamation of the telegraph and steam railway industries for the years before 1907. Second, for analytical purposes, certain divisions seemed more useful. For example, it is important to separate land from water transport since in a number of instances they were direct competitors in the movement of goods (and people) and they represent, as well, two different forms of transportation technology. A separate record of the growth of electric railways is also useful since, to a large extent, they were used for intra and inter-urban transportation and as such reveal something about the growth of Canadian cities.

There is a frequent reference to Dominion Bureau of Statistics, *National Income 1910-1940*. This was a document along with supporting papers obtained from the archives of DBS. It was prepared by Sydney Smith, who, in addition to using the sources cited herein, had correspondence with many of the individual bodies who had provided data on which the cited sources were based. This is not a published document.

The discussion of the methods and sources used to derive these estimates is organized around the various forms of factor payments; that is, by wages and salaries, interest payments, divided payments and savings This was done not only to provide an easy comparison of the variety of approaches adapted among industries in deriving specific factor payments but also because the factor payments, by category, represent the basic building blocks upon which the GDP figures are derived. Besides factor payment estimates, two additional series have been developed — gross revenue (except for water transport), and employment, by industry. The table numbers and headings are set out below.

6.1 Gross Revenue by Industrial Division
6.2 Gross Domestic Product by Industrial Division
6.3 Wages and Salaries by Industrial Division
6.4 Interest Payments by Industrial Division
6.5 Dividend Payments by Industrial Division
6.6 Total Payments to Individuals by Industrial Division
6.7 Gross Savings by Industrial Division
6.8 Employees by Industrial Division
6.9 Total Payments by Type

Gross Revenue by Industrial Division

The annual gross revenues of the various components of this industry group are given in Table 6.1. The derivation of the data for each industry is described, item by item.

The Derivation of the Data of Table 6.1: Gross Revenue by Industrial Division

Column 1, **Electric Light and Power:** For 1918 to 1926 from Dominion Bureau of Statistics (DBS) *Central Electric Stations* and for 1911, 1901 and 1891 respectively the *Census of Canada 1911* Vol. III (pp.114-15); *Census of Canada 1901*, Vol. III (pp.142-3) and *Census of Canada 1891*, Vol. III (p.142); and cover the calendar years 1910, 1900 and the census year 1891 — see Table A. The estimates for 1918 to 1926 are "net" of inter-utility company purchases [for a discussion see *Historical Statistics of Canada* (hereafter HSC), p.445, "Revenue from the Sale of Electricity". It was not possible to remove this element of inter-utility company purchases for the earlier census estimates (i.e., for 1890, 1900 and 1910) since no information on the extent of such purchases was available for the late 19th and early 20th Centuries. Simple extrapolation from the later years yield unsatisfactory results. Annual estimates for 1911 to 1917, inclusive, are interpolations based on a weighted average of gross revenues of a sample of firms reporting in *Moody's* and *Standard and Poor's* annual financial statements of corporations. The sample covers three provinces — Nova Scotia, Quebec and Ontario with one reporting unit located in each province. The interpolation procedure used here (and elsewhere unless explicitly stated), is that shown in S. Kuznets, *National Income and Its Composition: 1919-1938*, Vol. II, pp.479-80, "which apportions any change in the relative disparity between the partial or indirect data and the two terminal years [with complete data] along a straight line". A partial check on this interpolation procedure was made by comparing the estimated figure for 1915 with the adjusted gross output figure for the same year, as reported in the *Postal Census of Manufacturers 1916*, pp.8-9. The latter differed from the formula by approximately 5%.

Table 6.1. Gross Revenue by Industrial Division (thousands of dollars)

Year	Electric Light & Power (1)	Steam R.R. and R.R. Express (2)	Electric R.R. (3)	Water Transport (4)	Telephone (5)	Telegraph (6)
1871	-	15,187	-	-	-	-
1872	-	17,913	-	-	-	-
1873	-	19,860	-	-	-	-
1874	-	19,471	-	-	-	-
1875	-	19,471	-	-	-	-
1876	-	19,358	-	-	-	-
1877	-	18,742	-	-	-	-
1878	-	20,520	-	-	-	-
1879	-	19,925	-	-	-	-
1880	-	23,561	-	-	-	-
1881	-	27,988	-	-	-	-
1882	-	29,028	-	-	-	-
1883	-	33,245	-	-	-	-
1884	-	33,422	-	-	-	-
1885	-	32,227	-	-	-	-
1886	-	33,389	-	-	-	-
1887	-	38,842	-	-	701	-
1888	-	42,159	-	-	730	-
1889	-	42,142	-	-	847	-
1890	1,154	46,828	-	-	993	-
1891	1,239	48,173	-	-	1,139	-
1892	1,325	51,530	-	-	1,226	-
1893	1,410	51,822	-	-	1,548	-
1894	1,496	49,137	1,941	-	1,548	-
1895	1,581	46,248	1,824	-	1,548	-
1896	1,666	49,906	1,928	-	1,548	-
1897	1,752	51,562	2,109	-	1,548	-
1898	1,837	58,670	2,385	-	2,015	-
1899	1,923	61,065	2,718	-	2,132	-
1900	2.008	69,370	3,389	-	2,424	-
1901	2,572	72,687	5,768	-	2,920	-
1902	3,326	83,458	6,486	-	3,222	-
1903	3,934	95,836	7,234	-	3,927	-
1904	5,862	100,000	8,454	-	4,531	-
1905	6,730	106,250	9,357	-	5,437	-
1906	7,869	125,017	10,967	-	6,343	- [3]
1907	9,012	146,738	12,630	-	7,450	3,012
1908	10,466	146,918	14,007	-	7,048	3,323
1909	11,832	144,779	14,611	-	7,652	3,569

Table 6.1. (continued)

Year	Electric Light & Power (1)	Steam R.R. and R.R.Express (2)	Electric R.R. (3)	Water Transport (4)	Telephone (5)	Telegraph (6)
1910	12,917	173,669	17,101	-	8,558	4,571
1911	16,992	198,623	20,357	-	10,068	4,721
1912	19,376	230,427	23,499	-	12,273	5,359
1913	20,826	269,575	28,216	-	14,897	6,095
1914	22,230	255,755	29,691	-	17,297	5,983
1915	23,825	210,848	26,923	-	17,601	5,536
1916	28,280	274,764	27,416	-	18,594	6,256
1917	35,117	327,607	30,238	-	20,122	7,273
1918	43,908	348,900	32,486 [2]	-	22,753	7,771
1919	47,933	433,531 [1]	40,699 [1]	-	29,401 [1]	9,499 [1]
1920	53,436	522,614	47,047	-	33,474	11,337
1921	58,272	490,514	44,537	-	36,987	11,311
1922	62,173	469,384	49,660	-	39,559	11,019
1923	67,497	492,151	50,191	-	42,133	11,417
1924	74,617	459,022	49,440	-	44,323	10,930
1925	79,342	468,322	49,626	-	47,234	11,520
1926	88,934	506,823	51,723	-	50,523	12,143

R.R.: abbreviation for railroads

1   From 1919 onward, the data for the steam railways, electric railways, telephone and telegraph industries are given, as reported, on a calendar year basis; prior to 1919, the data for these industries are on a fiscal year basis ending June 30 of the year given. For comparative purposes, the data for the fiscal year ending June 30, 1919 are also given as follows, in thousands of dollars: steam r.r. and r.r. express, 404,135; electric r.r, 35,697; telephone system, 24,601; telegraph, 8,812.
2   In 1918 Montreal Tramways did not report earnings or expenses. Earnings for this year were estimated by interpolating between the 1917 and 1919 estimates for this company and adding this figure ($8,185,524) to the total.
3   Prior to 1907 telegraph is included with steam railroad statistics.

For 1900, the benchmark estimate was derived from the *Census of Canada 1901*, Vol. III. The interpolation procedure between 1910 and 1900 is identical to that used for the later years except here the corporate sample was for one company only — Montreal Light Heat and Power. This was the only company with annual estimates back to 1902. It was one, if not the largest, of its type operating in Canada and since the majority of electric power generation and distribution during this period was carried on in Ontario and Quebec, is likely to be representative of the general trends during this decade. The estimates for 1901 and 1900 were derived by extrapolating the Montreal firm's estimates by the annual change in total lamps (arch and incandescent) in operation during these two years.

For the decade 1890 to 1900 interpolation between the census estimates used a simple straight-line method since no suitable index could be found. This obviously imparts an error into the annual estimates, although given the smallness of the industry at this time it is doubtful whether this straight-line approach creates a significant bias in the sector and/or the national results. There was no census information available on this industry prior to 1890.

Column 2, **Steam Railroads and Railway Express:** For the years 1917 to 1926 the figures were obtained from the summary tables on gross earnings as shown in the DBS publication, *Statistics of Steam Railways in Canada* and for the period 1875 to 1916 they are from the *Sessional Papers of Canada* which published the annual reports of the Department of Railways and Canals (the latter began reporting in 1875). In 1919 the reporting year was switched from a fiscal year basis (July 1 to June 30) to a calendar year basis. The year 1919 was recorded on a calendar year basis, as well as fiscal year basis. The gross revenue for the twelve months ending June 30, 1919 was $383.0 million.

In order to make the figures internally consistent over the period, revenue derived from the St. Clair Tunnel, the International Bridge and the Detroit Tunnel were excluded. For a more complete discussion of inclusion, exclusions, etc., in this series over time see HSC, p.517 and 519, in particular the discussion relating to Series S53-63 and S129-144. With only minor exceptions the series shown here and those recorded in HSC were identical.

Two other adjustments were made to the series shown in HSC. First, gross earnings from express company operations were added. For the years 1923 to 1926 inclusive, Canadian National Express revenue was deducted from the total since the latter had been brought into the railway accounts beginning in that year. The source of express revenue for the period 1911 to 1926 (inclusive), is the *Canada Year Book* (CYB). No separate record of express company activity is shown prior to 1911. Second, for the years 1894 to 1900, inclusive, gross revenue for electric railways was removed from the total and shown separately (i.e., in Column 3 of Table 6.1).

The years 1875 to 1910 are taken directly from the *Annual Report* of the Department of Railway and Canals as shown in the *Sessional Papers of Canada*. The figures for the years 1871 to 1874 are extrapolations based on the trend values of gross earnings for the Grand Trunk Railway for these years.

Column 3, **Electric Railways:** From 1919 to 1926, DBS, *Electric Railways of Canada*, in "Railway Statistics", from the section on "Electric Railways". For the years 1894 to 1901 the figures are the sum of gross revenue shown in the *Sessional Papers, ibid.*, plus operating revenue for the Montreal, Toronto and British Columbia electric railway systems. These three large systems did not report their financial statements to the government during these years. However, since they needed capital, they gave this information to *Poor's* which recorded it beginning in the early 1890s.

Column 4, **Water Transport:** The water transport industry (inland water transport, movement on the Great Lakes and the St. Lawrence and other river systems; ocean shipping, including coastal shipping; stevedoring, and the like) was not regulated in the sense that the railroad industry was from the latter's inception. Beginning in the mid 19th Century each steam railway company was required to submit annual report to the Commissioner of Railways and Canals outlining the basic operations of the company during the previous twelve months. This report included such information as operating revenue and expenses (by type), the stock of equipment (number of engines, freight or passenger cars, etc.), new capital investment, sources of financing, freight and passenger tariffs, and so on. No such reports were requested of vessel operators either those operating on the Great Lakes or on the High Seas.

The water transport sector operated at two different levels. At the government level full reports were kept on the capital and current expenditure of canals, wharves, navigational aids, etc., plus a count of the number, type, size and cargo tonnage and type of vessels passing through the inland canals. In addition a count of these vessels arriving and departing from Canadian ports was made. The actual owners and operators of the vessels, however, were not required to report information on earnings, expenses, capital investments, etc., and since, in the main the firms were small, extant company records are virtually non-existent or at best scattered too widely for easy retrieval. The main exceptions are the Canada Steamship Lines and the Canadian Pacific Steamship Lines. The former is an amalgamation, in 1913, of several companies — the Canada Inter-Lake Line, Quebec Steamship Co., Lake Ontario and Bay of Quinte Steamboat Co., and the Ontario and Quebec Navigation Company. This last has a long history stretching back to 1845 when it was formed as La Societe de Navigation du Riviere Richelieu to transport produce from farms located along the Richelieu River to Montreal. This firm subsequently (in 1856) became the central unit around which the Canada Steamship Lines were built (see Desmond Allard, "Canadian Carriers of the Great Lakes" in *Canadian Shipping and Marine Engineering*, November 1971, a Maclean-Hunter Publication available from the Canada Steamship Lines, Ltd., Montreal).

The main result of these two factors — no government regulations requiring firms to report operating revenues, expenses, and other data, and the small scale nature of the industry (one or two large firms plus a large number of businesses operating only one or two vessels) is that information on gross revenue, interest charges, and other such information, is not available over long periods of time (the industry, in addition to being comprised of privately owned firms, unlike large railway companies, did not submit information — except for the Ontario and Quebec Navigation Company to *Moody's*). Indeed, even with the information gathering resources of DBS, the National Accounts group working on the estimates for the period 1919 to 1940 were only able to collect scattered years' estimates on net dividends and interest payments for two firms — Canadian Pacific Steamship and Canada Steamship Lines. Most of the annual estimates shown are interpolations between these points of observation, with the interpolators drawn from U.S. water transport data (Kuznets, *National Income, 1919-1938*).

In order, therefore, to give as consistent a series as possible over time, no estimates on total revenue, interest payments, dividends paid or net savings are included. Although subject to variation, labour income (wages and salaries paid plus subsistence allowance) appears to represent between 85 and 90% of total factor payments in this industry — a share which approaches more closely the 90% level as one goes back in time when the vessels were smaller in size, and being sailing vessels required more manpower per ton of cargo carried.

Column 5, **Telephones:** For the period 1911 to 1926 inclusive, various issues of CYB under the section "Telephone Statistics". There were no statistics reported to the Department of Railways and Canals prior to 1911 (the latter issued its first report on telephone statistics in the fiscal year 1913). The estimates for the years 1901 to 1910, inclusive, are based on extrapolations using an annual index of total operating revenue of the Bell Telephone Company. In 1913, the latter accounted for approximately 56% of total telephone revenue generated in Canada. Indeed in the earlier years Bell Canada controlled the development of telephones in all provinces, except British Columbia. In 1888 the lines of Bell in the Maritime Provinces were sold to the Maritime Telegraph and Telephone Company and in 1908 the lines in Manitoba and Alberta were sold to their respective governments. Bell lines were sold to the Saskatchewan government in 1909. Since 1908/09 the telephone systems in the Prairie Provinces have been government operated (see CYB, 1922-23, p.686). It was assumed, therefore, that trends in Bell Canada activity reflected annual and long run changes in the system as a whole. There may, however, be some underestimate of the systems growth between 1908 and 1910 when the Bell Co. statistics no longer contain activity for the Prairie Provinces — a rapidly growing region. For example, although a very small system in terms of gross revenues, the Alberta Telephone system grew by 30% between 1909 and 1910, while the Bell Company's revenues grew only by 12% over the same period. The Bell Telephone data were derived from *Moody's*, *Poor's* and the *Annual Financial Review*

The estimates for the years 1887 to 1900 were obtained by extrapolating backward on the basis of number of sets of instruments (number of telephones in operation) recorded, annually, in the *Statistical Yearbook of Canada* (section on "Telephones"). This is far from an optimal match since it is in real terms when what is needed are trends in financial variables. A forward projection from 1901 to 1903 of both gross income and the number of instruments, though, provide almost equal growth rates in the system — approximately 30% in each case. The index is also flawed in that it covers only Ontario and Quebec. Estimates of the growth of the Maritime telephone system and the system being formed in Manitoba are omitted. The latter two systems (especially Manitoba's), however, were small and their omission, it is believed, does not significantly alter the basic patterns shown here.

The assumptions involved in this procedure are as follows: (1) that financial variables move with real variables — "number of instruments". There is some support for this assumption in that changes in the number of instruments gives an indication of investment in the system as well as the potential customer use, and so revenue and the attendant operating costs; (2) that all components of the system — revenue, wages, interest, and so forth — move along the same path. This assumption seems the weakest to justify especially when one reviews the movement in these separate series for later years. Given the declining absolute size of the system, and therefore its components, these fixed relationships should not create significant distortions in the overall sector estimates. However, it should be noted that trends in average income per week cannot be discerned. Again this is not a great problem for the 1890s since it appears that during these years, nominal wage levels (in a period of fairly stable prices), changed very little (see HSC, p.111, Series D471-484).

One other feature to note about this extrapolated series is the absence of change in the absolute values over the years 1893 to 1897, inclusive. The *Statistical Year Books* for these years state that the companies reporting stated no change in the number of instruments, miles of wire, and similar items, occurred during this period. Absence of growth can be found for steam railways also in this period — in 1893 gross income for the latter was $51,822 million while in 1897 it was $51,562.

Column 6, **Telegraph:** For the years 1912 to 1926 inclusive the source is HSC, p.561 (Series 350). Operating revenue includes both transmission and non-transmission revenue. Since 1912 was the first year that statistics on the telegraph industry were collected, the estimates for 1907 to 1911 were obtained by running back the 1912 estimate on the basis of an index constructed from the revenue figures of telegraph reported by the Canadian Pacific Railroad in its *Annual Reports*. Prior to 1907 it is assumed, since Canadian telegraphs were, in the main, operated by the railways, to be included with the estimates for the latter.

Gross Domestic Product at Factor Cost by Industrial Division

The gross domestic product at factor cost by industrial division is given in Table 6.2, followed, as usual, by a description of the derivation.

Table 6.2. Gross Domestic Product at Factor Cost by Industrial Division (thousands of dollars)

Year	Electric Light & Power (1)	Steam R.R. and R.R. Express (2)	Electric Railway (3)	Water Transport (Wages only) (4)	Tele-phone (5)	Tele-graph (6)	Total GDP at Factor Cost (1)+(2)+(3)+ (4)+(5)+(6) (7)
1871	-	9,413	-	13,196	-	-	22,609
1872	-	10,483	-	11,531	-	-	22,014
1873	-	11,322	-	12,050	-	-	23,273
1874	-	14,148	-	9,629	-	-	23,777
1875	-	11,606	-	8,084	-	-	19,690
1876	-	11,528	-	8,321	-	-	19,849
1877	-	11,030	-	8,293	-	-	19,323
1878	-	12,513	-	8,941	-	-	21,454
1879	-	12,008	-	9,241	-	-	21,249
1880	-	15,191	-	9,810	-	-	25,001
1881	-	17,992	-	9,937	-	-	27,929
1882	-	18,482	-	10,569	-	-	29,051
1883	-	21,848	-	9,453	-	-	31,301
1884	-	21,642	-	9,373	-	-	31,015
1885	-	20,997	-	7,675	-	-	28,672
1886	-	24,739	-	7,429	-	-	32,168
1887	-	26,222	-	7,382	526	-	34,130
1888	-	28,280	-	7,897	548	-	36,725
1889	-	28,318	-	8,002	636	-	36,956
1890	936	32,099	-	8,361	745	-	42,141
1891	1,012	32,119	-	7,721	855	-	41,707
1892	1,089	34,951	-	7,478	921	-	44,439
1893	1,166	35,006	-	7,228	1,162	-	44,562
1894	1,241	32,457	1,852	7,735	1,162	-	44,447
1895	1,320	32,540	2,357	3,761	1,162	-	41,140
1896	1,395	34,986	2,406	6,096	1,162	-	46,045
1897	1,471	36,220	2,893	5,994	1,162	-	47,740
1898	1,546	42,207	3,243	6,627	1,512	-	55,135
1899	1,625	44,453	3,592	7,544	1,600	-	58,814
1900	1,700	49,986	4,136	7,961	1,818	-	65,601

Table 6.2. (continued)

Year	Electric Light & Power (1)	Steam R.R. and R.R. Express (2)	Electric Railway (3)	Water Transport (Wages only) (4)	Tele- phone (5)	Tele- graph (6)	Total GDP at Factor Cost (1)+(2)+(3)+ (4)+(5)+(6) (7)
1901	2,124	51,185	5,026	7,583	2,192	-	68,110
1902	2,652	58,898	5,580	9,096	2,548	-	78,774
1903	3,234	67,167	6,084	11,283	2,981	-	90,749
1904	4,985	68,056	7,033	11,256	3,429	-	94,759
1905	6,023	72,029	7,721	13,010	4,164	-	102,947
1906	6,790	84,764	9,106	14,791	4,860	-	120,311
1907	7,660	102,766	10,747	19,286	5,532	2,691	148,682
1908	8,533	101,132	10,969	19,384	5,987	2,820	148,845
1909	9,512	105,225	12,795	14,849	6,310	2,996	151,668
1910	9,503	122,946	13,306	17,339	6,796	3,605	173,495
1911	13,786	138,797	16,931	19,127	7,487	3,900	200,028
1912	16,103	166,636	16,962	24,345	8,909	4,558	237,513
1913	17,995	196,932	20,607	29,131	10,762	5,033	280,460
1914	20,611	174,153	23,641	24,214	12,665	4,842	260,126
1915	22,080	155,306	19,819	14,900	13,122	4,427	229,654
1916	23,861	194,024	18,473	17,120	15,300	4,827	273,605
1917	27,551	222,984	19,207	18,316	16,908	5,595	310,561
1918	30,858	216,510	22,463	17,427	19,519	5,825	312,602
1919	32,963	279,644 [1]	28,896 [1]	26,015	25,094 [1]	6,937	399,549
1920	37,353	315,284	33,275	32,957	22,723	8,312	449,904
1921	39,495	287,821	32,129	28,037	25,907	8,249	421,638
1922	43,718	290,013	39,659	25,655	26,899	7,481	433,425
1923	46,733	295,723	39,265	29,005	27,924	7,494	446,144
1924	51,635	275,951	39,115	30,005	29,000	8,216	433,922
1925	59,354	296,740	40,125	32,117	30,773	9,042	468,151
1926	69,877	330,480	42,015	32,684	37,600	9,088	521,744

[1]　See footnote 1 to Table 6.1. The gross domestic products for the fiscal year ending June 30, 1919, in thousands of dollars, were as follows: steam r.r. and r.r. express, 289,276; electric railway, 21,481; telephone, 21,482.

The Derivation of the Data of Table 6.2: Gross Domestic Product at Factor Cost by Industrial Division

This table, being derived from later tables, needs little explanation. The table shows the sum for each industrial division of total payments to individuals (Table 6.6) and gross savings (Table

6.7) respectively, except for water transport where only wages and salary payments are included (See the "notes" on gross revenue). National Income for Water Transport as reported by DBS for 1919 to 1926 is as follows (figures are in thousands of dollars):

Year	Income	Year	Income
1919	39,122	1923	38,052
1920	48,930	1924	37,693
1921	35,904	1925	38,469
1922	40,161	1926	41,406

Column 7 shows the sum of all industrial divisions in this sector and as such represents the gross domestic product at factor cost for transportation and other public utilities. However as one moves from later to earlier periods certain industry series either become amalgamated with other series (for example, telegraph is included with steam railways beginning in 1906) or disappear due to lack of statistical evidence or non-existence (e.g., electric power or telephones). The respective changes create breaking points in the total series and to aid users Table A has been constructed. The periods for which there are entries are marked with an 'X'.

Table A

Industrial Divisions Included in Total Gross
Domestic Product, By Period, 1926-1871

Period	Electric Light & Power (1)	Steam R.R. and R.R. Express (2)	Electric R.R. (3)	Water Transport (4)	Telephone (5)	Telegraph (6)
1886-1871		X		X		
1889-1887		X		X	X	
1893-1890	X	X		X	X	
1906-1894	X	X	X	X	X	
1926-1907	X	X	X	X	X	X

Wages and Salaries by Industrial Division

There now follows Table 6.3 which gives wages and salaries by industrial component, and a description of the derivation of the data.

The Derivation of the Data of Table 6.3:   Wages And Salaries By Industrial Division

Since these data are limited to wages and salaries, that fact will not be repeated in the following explanations of derivations.

Column 1, **Electric Light and Power:** For 1917 to 1926 from HSC, p.452 (Series 51) and for

Table 6.3. Wages And Salaries By Industrial Division (thousands of dollars)

Year	Electric Light & Power (1)	Steam R.R. and R.R. Express (2)	Electric R.R. (3)	Water Transport (4)	Telephone (5)	Telegraph (6)
1871	-	7,190	-	13,196	-	-
1872	-	7,819	-	11,531	-	-
1873	-	8,538	-	12,050	-	-
1874	-	10,964	-	9,629	-	-
1875	-	8,987	-	8,084	-	-
1876	-	9,054	-	8,321	-	-
1877	-	8,669	-	8,293	-	-
1878	-	9,164	-	8,941	-	-
1879	-	9,259	-	9,241	-	-
1880	-	9,573	-	9,810	-	-
1881	-	11,382	-	9,937	-	-
1882	-	12,673	-	10,569	-	-
1883	-	13,951	-	9,453	-	-
1884	-	14,471	-	9,373	-	-
1885	-	13,615	-	7,675	-	-
1886	-	13,725	-	7,429	-	-
1887	-	15,776	-	7,382	306	-
1888	-	17,443	-	7,897	319	-
1889	-	17,684	-	8,002	370	-
1890	298	18,700	-	8,361	434	-
1891	327	19,834	-	7,721	497	-
1892	357	20,639	-	7,478	536	-
1893	386	20,668	-	7,228	676	-
1894	415	19,851	897	7,735	676	-
1895	445	18,479	928	3,761	676	-
1896	474	19,718	1,023	6,096	676	-
1897	503	19,779	1,107	5,994	676	-
1898	532	22,058	1,173	6,627	880	-
1899	562	22,956	1,338	7,544	931	-
1900	591	26,849	1,696	7,961	1,058	-
1901	718	28,617	2,504	7,583	1,275	-
1902	864	32,626	2,772	9,096	1,407	-
1903	974	38,436	3,261	11,283	1,714	-
1904	1,181	42,169	3,883	11,256	1,979	-
1905	1,263	45,450	4,314	13,010	2,374	-
1906	1,402	49,394	4,866	14,791	2,769	- [3]
1907	1,544	58,719	5,922	19,286	3,254	1,677
1908	1,535	60,377	5,758	19,384	3,078	1,685
1909	1,919	63,217	6,761	14,849	3,342	1,773

Table 6.3.   (continued)

Year	Electric Light & Power (1)	Steam R.R. and R.R. Express (2)	Electric R.R. (3)	Water Transport (4)	Telephone (5)	Telegraph (6)
1910	2,367	67,168	6,317	17,339	3,737	2,010
1911	2,722	77,520	8,559	19,127	4,397	2,274
1912	2,960	97,654	9,261	24,345	5,730	2,727
1913	3,390	119,771	11,048	29,131	7,041	3,104
1914	4,163	116,136	11,845	24,214	8,250	3,345
1915	4,047	94,159	10,782	14,900	8,357	3,061
1916	4,763	108,358	8,768	17,120	7,853	3,025
1917	7,778	135,009	9,452	18,316	8,882	3,518
1918	10,354	158,824	15,775 [2]	17,427	10,410	4,075
1919	11,487	240,377 [1]	20,212 [1]	26,015	15,775 [1]	5,251 [1]
1920	14,627	299,875	24,236	32,957	17,294	6,565
1921	15,235	256,631	23,977	28,037	19,000	6,672
1922	14,495	240,428	24,988	25,655	17,306	6,308
1923	14,784	256,368	25,039	20,005	18,182	6,092
1924	17,947	241,359	24,964	30,005	18,293	7,016
1925	18,756	238,641	24,544	32,117	19,106	7,692
1926	19,943	254,689	24,687	32,684	25,219	7,640

1   See footnote 1 to Table 6.1. The wage estimate for the year ending June 30, 1919 for those industries for which the data were changed from a fiscal year to a calendar year in 1919 are, in thousands of dollars: steam r.r. and r.r. express, 208,990; electric railways, 17,211; telephone, 13,048; telegraph, 4,485.

2   To the total of wages and salaries shown for electric railways in 1918 was added an additional amount of $3,934,338 to cover the omission of statistics for the Montreal Tramway Co. The latter did not report operating information for 1918. The estimating procedure was same as that set out in the notes to Table 6.4 for steam railroads.

3   Prior to 1907 telegraph statistics are included with those for steam railroads.

1911, 1901 and 1891 from the respective *Census of Canada* for 1911, Vol. III, pp.4-5; for 1901, Vol. III, p.142-143; and for 1891, Vol. III, p.142. Annual estimates for 1910 to 1916, inclusive, are interpolations — see Note 3 of Table 6.1 for sources and methods. The corporate sample series used here, however, is "General Expenses".

In this case the check with the *Postal Census of Manufactures, 1916* revealed a wide difference between the interpolated estimates for 1915 and those presented in the Census. One possible explanation is that the *Postal Census* captured construction as well as operations workers. The census estimates (for 1915) are greater than the official estimate of wages and salaries for 1917, while the time pattern of "Operating Expenses" shown in a wider sample of corporate reports than is used here reveals no such discrepancy between 1915 and later years.

The benchmark estimates for 1900 are derived from the *Census of Canada 1901* Vol. I, p.xxxvi. Interpolation between 1900 and 1910 follows the procedures and sources outlined in the notes to Table 6.1.

For the decade 1890 to 1900 see the notes to Table 6.1 and for the benchmark estimates see Table 6.1.

Column 2, **Steam Railroads and Railway Express:** For the years 1919 to 1926 the estimates are derived from the wages and salaries series of steam railways and railways express as recorded in the work sheets of the DBS estimates of *National Income 1919-1940*. The steam railway series is net of wages paid to Canadian National express employees (1923 to 1926 inclusive). These were brought into the railway accounts in 1928 (net of C.P.R. telegraph wages), and are included in outside operations. The series shown here, then, is simply the sum of these latter estimates for steam railways and the series for railway express workers.

For the years 1911 to 1918, which are on a fiscal basis, the series, again, is the sum of the salary and wage bill for steam railways and railway express. Now, however, no adjustments have been made to steam railway salary and wages since there are no data on the extent of C.P.R. telegraph salary and wages incorporated in the former. This potential double counting would seem to amount to about 1% of the total steam railway wage and salary bill. In the case of railway express, no official estimate of the wage bill was constructed prior to 1926, although DBS did make an estimate based on the trend of operating expenses for earlier years. A similar practice was followed for this period (i.e., 1911 to 1918), using a fixed ratio 0.70 of operating expenses. The latter was approximately the average of wages and salaries to total operating expenses over the period 1919 to 1922. This ratio is relatively high since, with the exception of some buildings and equipment, the express industry used the railways for transporting goods, hence the wage bill tends to be higher here than its normal share of total expenses in related industries. For the years prior to 1911 wages of express workers outside those directly employed by the railroads are included.

Since express firms were generally subsidiaries of the railway companies (see the discussion of the historical development of express companies in the CYB, 1926, p.611 ff.), they had little need to go to capital markets for funding; consequently individual company reports do not appear in the earlier issues of *Poor's Manual*. Thus no additional information could be obtained on the trend or size of revenue or expenditures. The absence of an express wage bill, in the total of wages and salaries, would not seem too serious as the share, even in 1911, was fairly small. Some idea of the relationship between total wages and salaries for steam railways and express companies, can been seen by examining the figures for the former between 1914 and 1911. These are, in order from 1914 to 1911, in thousands of dollars, $111,763, $115,750, $94,238, and $74,614. Wage and salary estimates for the period 1907 to 1910, inclusive, are from the *Sessional Papers of Canada* for 1916, No. 20b, "Summary Table", p.LX.

The annual reports of *Railways and Canals* did not record wages and salaries prior to 1907. Consequently, it was necessary to estimate the latter by indirect means. This was accomplished by multiplying the ratio of wages to operating expenses by annual total operating expenses for the years 1875 to 1906. The estimating procedure may be formulated as follows: $W = b \times E$ where W is the total wage bill, b is a constant based on the ratio between wages and operating expenses for selected years beginning in 1907, and E is the total current operating expenses.

The coefficient of E was obtained by a two stage method. First, total operating expenses were partitioned into two parts — one covered the expenditures associated with the maintenance of ways, buildings, etc., while the other covered the remaining expenses. Second, total compensation, as a percentage of operating expenses, for each category was calculated for the years 1907 and 1908, and from this an average ratio of compensation to expenses in each of the two groups was obtained. In the case of the former (maintenance of ways, buildings, etc.), the average ratio was 0.7227 while for "all other" it was 0.5253.   Thus for any year $b = 0.7227 \times E_1 + 0.5263 \times E_2$ where E_1 is expenditures on maintenance, ways, etc., and E_2 covers "all other" expenditures.   The annual wage bill from 1875 to 1906 then, was found by multiplying these two components of annual expenditures by these coefficients.

The productivity assumptions implicit in this type of estimation procedure are set out in the discussion on employment — Table 6.8.   It is worth noting, however, that this approach may dampen the true variation in wages paid over the business cycle.   For example in later periods, when information on wages by occupational category are available, it appears that a reduction in demand for railway services was met partly by layoffs (generally among the unskilled workers), and partly by reassignment of duties; i.e., foremen demoted to ordinary workmen, with the reverse occurring in periods of growing demand.   This type of change is not adequately covered by the procedure outlined above.

Total compensation for the years 1871 to 1875, was obtained by extrapolating backwards from 1875 on the basis of annual total expenditures recorded by the Grand Trunk Railway. The latter are available in *Poor's Manual*.

Column 3, **Electric Railways:** For the source of estimates of salaries and wages over the period 1919 to 1926, and 1907 to 1918 see notes to Table 6.1.   The figures for 1901 to 1906, inclusive, were derived in a manner similar to that outlined for steam railways for the years prior to 1907. The same qualifications apply in this case.   Here the coefficient of operating expenses was the average of wages and salaries over the years 1907 to 1909, inclusive.   The average used was 0.729 (i.e., $W = 0.729 \times E$ where W = the wage bill and E = operating expenses).

For the years 1894 to 1900, total operating expenses shown in the *Sessional Papers* were augmented by the expenses recorded for the Montreal Street Railroad, the Toronto Railway and the British Columbia Electric Railway.   These three estimates were reported in *Poor's Manual* for 1901 and 1902.   The wage and salary estimation procedure is identical to that described in the preceding paragraph.

Column 4, **Water Transport:** As outlined in the discussion of this industry in the "Notes" to Table 6.1 the absence of operating reports by shipping companies means that only income which can be measured is wages and salaries.   The latter, itself, can be obtained by multiplying annual employment figures by a derived average earnings series.   Construction of the employment series is set out in the "Notes" to Table 6.8.

The annual earnings series was derived using two different methods.   For the period 1901 to 1931 the respective Censuses provide an estimate of average earnings for Water Transport. However, the latter refer to the earnings of only that segment of wage earners who report wages. To correct for the omission of wage earners not reporting earnings, Table B was constructed. The procedure used was taken from the DBS *National Income 1910-1940* working papers for 1921 and 1931, and extended to include the census of 1901 and 1911.   The assumptions for full-time equivalence (lines (4) and (5)) are that the number of wage earners not reporting were placed on a full time basis by allowing them 50.0 percent average wage rate and 75.0 percent time.   The main affect of adjusting total employment on this basis was, in all cases, to raise average earnings; e.g., in 1901 from $393 a year to $496 (the latter estimate is more in line with average wages in other industries, at this time).   Annual movements in wages and salaries for steam railway workers were used as interpolators between these respective census estimates of average earnings (see Table 6.3, Column 2).   The interpolation procedure is identical to that described in Table 6.1 for Electric Power.

Since the Census prior to 1901 did not report earnings, it was necessary to construct an

436

Table B. Estimation Procedure, For Water Transport, Of Full Time Equivalent Employment and Full Time Average Earnings For 1901, 1911, 1921 & 1931 (Males Only)

	1901 (1)	1911 (2)	1921 (3)	1931 (4)
1) Total wage earners (reporting and not reporting)	13,474	23,067	20,238	36,159
2) Total wage earners (reporting earnings)	12,010	20,661	19,385	30,688
3) (1) – (2)	1,464	2,406	853	5,481
4) (2) + 50% of (3)	12,741	21,864	19,811	33,428
5) (2) + 75% of (3)	13,108	22,466	20,024	34,798
6) Total earnings (w/e reporting) ($)	4,715,328	11,340,100	18,583,400	28,375,200
7) (6) ÷ (2) ($)	393	549	964	925
8) (7) x (4) ($)	5,002,331	12,003,336	19,097,804	30,920,900
9) Number of weeks worked	N.A.	788,141	821,018	1,191,162
10) Average number of weeks worked	40 *	38.1	42.4	38.8
11) (10) x (5)	524,320	855,955	849,018	1,350,162
12) (11) ÷ 52 (Number on full time basis)	10,083	16,461	16,327	25,964
13) (8) ÷ (12) ($)	496	729	1,169	1,190

* Assumed on the basis of average weeks worked for period 1911-1931.

Sources:

Column 1. Census of Canada 1901, Census and Statistics Bulletin XI

Column 2. Census of Canada 1911, Tabulated but unpublished census data on file at Queen's University

Column 3. Census of Canada 1921, Tabulated but unpublished census data on file at Queen's University

Column 4. Census of Canada 1931, Vol. V, pp.124-126.

Chart I

Water Transport – Average Earnings
Per Employee (in current dollars)

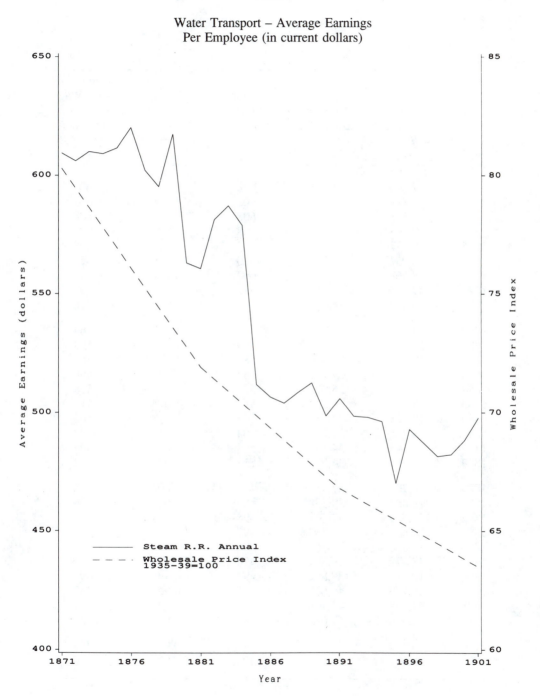

Table C. Water Transport

Index of Average Earnings Per Worker
in Steam Railways, 1871-1901

Year	Total Earnings ($000) (1)	Number Employed (2)	Average Earnings (2) ÷ (1) ($) (3)	Index of Column (3) 1901=1.000 (4)	Estimated Avg. Wage For Water Transport 1901=496 (5)
1871	7,190	11,816	608	1.226	609
1872	7,819	12,850	608	1.226	608
1873	8,538	14,032	608	1.226	608
1874	10,964	18,019	608	1.226	608
1875	8,987	14,770	608	1.226	608
1876	9,054	14,590	620	1.250	620
1877	8,669	14,382	602	1.214	602
1878	9,164	15,358	596	1.202	596
1879	9,259	15,030	616	1.242	616
1880	9,573	16,952	564	1.137	564
1881	11,382	20,347	559	1.127	559
1882	12,673	21,765	582	1.173	582
1883	13,951	24,569	567	1.143	566
1884	14,471	25,020	578	1.165	578
1885	13,615	26,573	513	1.034	513
1886	13,725	27,135	505	1.018	505
1887	15,776	31,286	504	1.016	504
1888	17,443	34,332	508	1.024	508
1889	17,684	34,537	512	1.032	512
1890	18,700	37,486	498	1.004	498
1891	19,834	39,182	506	1.020	506
1892	20,639	41,368	498	1.004	498
1893	20,668	41,533	497	1.002	497
1894	19,851	39,666	500	1.007	500
1895	18,479	39,304	470	0.948	470
1896	19,718	39,882	494	0.996	494
1897	19,779	40,607	487	0.982	487
1898	22,058	45,756	482	0.972	482
1899	22,956	47,635	481	0.970	481
1900	26,849	54,953	489	0.986	489
1901	28,617	57,741	496	1.000	496

earnings series by extrapolating backwards from the 1901 estimate ($496). The procedure adopted was to construct an index of earnings based on average wages and salaries paid to steam railway workers over the period 1871 to 1901 (See Table C). This series was derived by dividing Column 2 of Table 6.3 by Column 2 of Table 6.8. The resulting series is shown in Chart I, along with the wholesale price index, the latter at decadal points (see O.J. Firestone, *Canada's Economic Development 1867-1952*, Table 63). The two series imply an increase in real wages in the 1870s and then a constancy afterwards; that is, both series falling at about the same rate. An index was made of the average earnings series, and estimates of wage levels (annually) were derived for Water Transport. The latter were then multiplied by the employment series (Column 4, Table 6.8) to derive the basic wage and salary series.

Water transport employees, like farm labourers, received part of their income in the form of room and board. In the 1931 Census (Vol. V, Table 28) the level of subsistence allowance was shown. The DBS, in its National Income estimates for 1910-1940, obtained an annual series for subsistence allowance by extrapolating the 1931 estimate backward, and forward, on the basis of an index of the cost of living for food. The subsistence allowance over this period amounted to approximately 20% of total earnings (i.e., including the allowance). Thus, for the years 1871 to 1918, the estimated wage and salary bill was multiplied by 1.20 to give the series shown in Column 4 of Table 6.3.

Column 5, Telephone: For the period 1911 to 1926 inclusive the source was the CYB section on "Telephone Statistics" (HSC also gives a wage and salaries series for telephone companies over this period see p.560). However, for the first three reporting years — 1911, 1912 and 1913 — there is apparently an undercount of the total wage bill. In fact the CYB, 1914, states that for these years, a number of companies, although reporting accurate employment levels, did not inform the Department of Railways and Canals on wages and salaries paid. In order to adjust for this deficiency an average ratio of wage and salaries to operating expenses (0.60) was multiplied by operating expenses for these three years to obtain more reasonable estimates.

For the decade 1901 to 1910, annual wage and salary estimates were obtained by extrapolating the 1911 figure to earlier years on the basis of annual changes in gross revenue for Bell Canada (see notes to Table 6.1). In 1901 this yielded an average wage of $422. The 1901 Census's average for Telephone and Telegraph workers was $463. Given that the telephone industry employed proportionately more women than the telegraph industry, this close agreement between the two independently derived averages suggested that the extrapolation procedure (and its counterpart for employment), gives a reasonably good representation of trends in wages and employment over this period.

For the years 1887 to 1900 see the notes to Table 6.1.

Column 6, Telegraph: For the years 1919 to 1926 the figures are drawn for the annual reports of "Telegraph and Cable Statistics". The latter was published separately by DBS beginning in 1919. The years 1912 to 1918 were drawn from the annual reports entitled, "Telegraph Statistics" (fiscal year end 30 June). This publication appeared as a supplement to the *Annual Report of the Department of Railways and Canals*.

The estimates shown here includes commission payments to telegraphers. However, even with this inclusion they are less than those recorded by the DBS reports for "wages and salaries" in the *National Income 1919-1940* estimates, although figures for 1919 to 1926 are drawn from the same source. At this time there is no explanation for this discrepancy unless DBS included an estimate for "other income"; i.e., pension payments, workmen's compensation payments, etc. If the latter are included no mention is made of the fact.

Interest by Industrial Division

The presentation of interest by industrial division and the explanation of its derivation is the next task. The relevant information follows in Table 6.4.

Table 6.4. Interest by Industrial Division (thousands of dollars)

Year	Electric Light and Power (1)	Steam R.R. and R.R. Express (2)	Electric R.R. (3)	Water Transport (4)	Telephone (5)	Telegraph (6)
1871	-	3,123	-	-	-	-
1872	-	3,546	-	-	-	-
1873	-	3,684	-	-	-	-
1874	-	4,084	-	-	-	-
1875	-	4,004	-	-	-	-
1876	-	4,039	-	-	-	-
1877	-	4,129	-	-	-	-
1878	-	4,531	-	-	-	-
1879	-	4,254	-	-	-	-
1880	-	4,364	-	-	-	-
1881	-	4,490	-	-	-	-
1882	-	6,083	-	-	-	-
1883	-	4,644	-	-	-	-
1884	-	5,005	-	-	-	-
1885	-	8,766	-	-	-	-
1886	-	8,838	-	-	-	-
1887	-	9,405	-	-	60	-
1888	-	9,715	-	-	62	-
1889	-	10,296	-	-	72	-
1890	64	11,139	-	-	84	-
1891	82	11,819	-	-	97	-
1892	99	12,724	-	-	104	-
1893	117	13,408	-	-	131	-
1894	134	14,620	233	-	131	-
1895	152	15,369	380	-	131	-
1896	169	15,603	383	-	131	-
1897	187	16,017	466	-	131	-
1898	204	15,968	519	-	171	-
1899	222	16,055	552	-	181	-
1900	239	16,326	615	-	205	-
1901	290	16,661	668	-	248	-
1902	360	16,910	702	-	324	-
1903	748	16,917	749	-	333	-

Table 6.4. (continued)

Year	Electric Light and Power (1)	Steam R.R. and R.R. Express (2)	Electric R.R. (3)	Water Transport (4)	Telephone (5)	Telegraph (6)
1904	1,815	17,933	823	-	333	-
1905	2,068	19,161	905	-	343	-
1906	2,161	19,672	1,147	-	486	-
1907	2,265	20,007	1,237	-	600	-
1908	2,381	20,969	1,180	-	610	-
1909	2,430	22,012	1,318	-	610	-
1910	2,462	23,095	1,606	-	619	-
1911	2,917	21,581	1,781	-	791	-
1912	3,395	23,213	1,763	-	953	-
1913	4,080	25,073	3,124	-	1,327	-
1914	5,018	26,960	2,466	-	1,684	-
1915	6,021	27,765	3,589	-	1,878	-
1916	5,799	24,020	4,818	-	1,984	-
1917	7,125	43,795	4,876	-	2,112	-
1918	7,900	46,900	3,764	-	2,462	-
1919	8,450	54,697 [1]	4,980 [1]	-	2,863 [1]	-
1920	9,484	59,270	5,949	-	3,185	-
1921	11,636	74,750	6,021	-	3,818	-
1922	13,643	78,378	7,362	-	3,913	-
1923	14,475	54,666	7,860	-	3,970	-
1924	16,731	59,448	8,220	-	4,194	-
1925	18,596	60,498	8,857	-	4,427	-
1926	21,660	59,241	8,926	-	4,831	-

1   See footnote 1 to Table 6.1. The values for years ending June 30, 1919 were as follows (in thousands of dollars): steam r.r. and r.r. express, 43,097; electric r.r., 3,833; telephone, 2,643.

The Derivation of the Data of Table 6.4: Interest by Industrial Division

Column 1, **Electric Light and Power:** For 1919 to 1926, from estimates prepared by the DBS study on *National Income 1919-1940*. This interest rate series is taken from the "Sources and Methods" sheets for the "Electric Power Industry". It was derived from "Corporate Securities Annual Financial Review". The series represents the net bond interest paid by public utility companies and the Hydro Electric Commission of Ontario.

A two stage procedure was adopted to obtain the earlier estimates. First, the ratio of net interest to capital invested in the fixed assets in this industry [fixed capital was defined as the sum of the value of lands, buildings, sites, and transmission and distribution equipment, see *National Income, 1919-1940*], was calculated annually for the period 1919 to 1926, inclusive.

Table D. Electric Light and Power

Estimates of Net Dividends and Net Savings at
Census Dates 1915, 1910, 1900 and 1891
(thousands of dollars)

Item	1915 (1)	1910 (2)	1900 (3)	1891 (4)
1) "Net" revenue	22,914	10,050	1,562	898
2) Less expenses (incl. taxes)	6,645	2,914	453	260
3) GNP (1)-(2)	16,269	7,136	1,109	638
4) Less interest paid	6,021	2,462	239	64
5) Amount available for dividends	10,248	4,674	870	574
6) Dividends paid (5) x 0.21	2,152	982	183	120
7) Surplus (savings inc. dep.)	8,096	3,692	687	454

Notes and Sources

Line 1: Gross revenue reduced by 0.22 for inter-industry purchases.
Line 2: This is a derived figure and is comprised of the sum of "fuel used" in the production of electric power, basically coal and gas, and other expenses, rent, taxes, installation in homes, etc. The former ratio (cost of materials) was in "Electric Power Industries" sector of *National Income 1919-1940* for the years 1919 to 1926. Since there was a distinct trend in this ratio (falling sharply for later years — a function of the increasing shift towards water as the chief source of power), an average for only the years 1919 to 1921 was used. This gave a figure of approximately 5.5%. The figure for general or other expenses was derived similarly; i.e., finding the ratio of "general expenses" to revenue for the period 1919 to 1926 as shown in *National Income, 1919-1940*. This ratio proved to be much more stable to the average figure (24%) than it was for the years 1919 to 1926. The sum of these two figures (24+5 = 29%) was the ratio used to derive the "Expenses" figure. The 1910 Census (Vol. III, p.134), provided a rough check on the "General Expenses" ratio since it gave direct estimates of what was termed "Misc. Expenses". The ratio of the latter figure to gross output was approximately 23% which, if the 5% figure for fuel used is added, gives a total of 28% — roughly the same as derived using the later data from DBS.
Line 4: See note to Table 6.4.
Line 5: See notes to Table 6.5.
Line 7: This figure represents the difference between income payments to individuals and the gross domestic product originating in the industry. In this case the savings estimate is gross of depreciation since the cost of equipment consumed in the process has not been deducted from the gross value of production.

The mean (and median) value was approximately 2.75%. This rate was then multiplied by the values of capital invested in fixed assets. Fixed assets, for Census purposes, are defined as the sum of lands, buildings, plant and machine tools. The estimates used here are recorded in the *1916 Postal Census of Canada*, p.62 (for the calendar year 1915); *1911 Census of Canada*, Vol. III, p.28 (for the calendar year 1910); *1901 Census of Canada*, Vol. IV, p.108 (for the calendar year 1900) and *1891 Census of Canada*, Vol. III, p.142 (for the Census year ending April 1, 1891). The product (fixed assets x 2.75%), yielded estimates of net interest paid for the calendar years 1915, 1910 and 1900 and for the census year 1891.

The second stage involved the determination of annual estimates for net interest paid. The interpretation procedure used is that set out in Table 6.1 except the "index" here was for fixed charges reported by the sampled corporations. For the period 1915 to 1919, the corporate sample was identical to that used in Table 6.1, but for the period 1915 to 1910 figures for the Ontario Power Company were substituted for the Ottawa Light and Power Company since data on fixed charges were not available for the latter. For the decade 1900 to 1910 the interpolation procedure is set out in the notes to Table 6.1 (fixed charges were used for the "index").

For the decade 1890 to 1900 see the procedures outlined in the notes to Table 6.1. The decadal benchmark estimates are shown in Table D.

Column 2, **Steam Railway and Railway Express:** Throughout the series only gross interest payments are shown; i.e., no deduction has been made for interest receipts, although the latter probably appear in "Other Income" and so are included in the net income figure. For 1919 to 1926, the source is "Steam Railway Estimates" of the DBS report on *National Income 1919-1940*. The DBS figures adjust the interest on funded and unfunded debt for the C.N.R. The latter is shown in "Statistics of Steam Railways of Canada" on an accrued basis. The interest payment figures shown here have been reduced as a result of changes effected by the Canadian National Railways Capital Revision Act of 1937. There are no recorded interests payments for railway express since they were for the most part, wholly owned by the railway companies. Any debt charges, then, would appear under the general total for the latter.

For the years 1911 to 1918 the source is the *Sessional Papers of Canada*, section on "Steam Railway Statistics". To the interest payments shown in this report have been added Canadian Pacific Railway's 4% debenture stock costs. These were included with interest payments beginning in 1919 when their omission was discovered. However, the correction was not carried back to 1911 by the Bureau. This error has now been corrected.

For the years prior to 1911, the government reports did not record total interest payments. However, the railway companies in the *Sessional Papers*, did report the size of the "bonded" and "floating" debt of each railroad reporting to the Commission, plus the coupon interest payment for many of these outstanding issues. This debt information was available annually over the period 1875 to 1911. The overlap (in 1911) allowed us to check whether an estimate of total interest payments could be made by multiplying the amount of debt outstanding by the recorded interest rate. An experiment was tried (in the case where no interest rate was recorded a rate based on an average of all rates shown was used the interest rates were for 1905), for 1911 when both sets of information, for each railroad (150 were available). A large discrepancy was observed, but this was virtually eliminated when the extension lines for the Canadian Northern, the Canadian Pacific and the Grand Trunk were subtracted from the total. This left, in essence, the "small" railroads. Since interest payments' information — plus other fixed costs and dividend payments — were available for these three railroads in *Poor's Manual*, it was decided to obtain these payments from this source — for the Canadian Pacific the Annual Statements were used — and estimate, via the extension procedure, interest payments for the balance of the railway system. This exercise involved multiplying the outstanding fixed and floating debt of between 80 and 150 railroads for each year from 1875 to 1910. To the latter total the interest payments of the three large railways, as well as the interest costs for the Canadian Northern Quebec and the Canadian Northern Ontario were added. Where small lines become merged with one of the larger companies their interest rate payments were dropped from the extensions series in order to avoid any double counting. The results of these calculations and additions are shown in Table 6.4.

For the years 1871 to 1875, prior to the publication of the *Railways and Canals* annual reports, the interest payments series was extrapolated on the trend series of total operating revenue for the Grand Trunk Railway.

Column 3, **Electric Railway:** For the years 1919 to 1926, inclusive, data are taken from DBS *Electric Railways in Canada* 1926 and 1924 volumes and for 1918 to 1909, from the *Sessional Papers of Canada* No. 20B, "Electric Railway Statistics". The estimates are taken in all cases from the statement on "Income Account". The figures shown here do not coincide precisely with those shown in the Bureau's figures in *National Income 1919-1940* for electric railways. In the sources and methodological section the source for interest payments is the same as that noted above, with the following additional statement:

> "Includes interest of all divisions of certain companies engaged in power production on distribution and motor transportation. However, the duplication with the Electric Power Industry would be very small."

Since there is no further direction on what "divisions of certain companies engaged in power production..." means and since the Bureau's figures apparently cover only funded but not floating debt it was decided to use the original sources exclusively.

The period from 1894 to 1908 was estimated in two parts. For the years 1894 to 1900, inclusive, total interest payments (funded and floating) are the *Railway and Canals* reports in the *Sessional Papers*. The total funded and floating debt for each railway line is recorded plus, in most cases, the interest charge for this outstanding debt. The interest payments were obtained by extending these two figures (where interest rates were not shown those developed for steam railways were used). Although the railway reports covered up to 13 separate accounts, nevertheless the large street railway systems — Toronto and Montreal — were omitted. Interest payments for these last two systems were obtained from *Poor's Manual* and were then added to the above totals. Linear apportionment was used to cover the period 1901 to 1908. The annual trends were taken from a small sample of street railway companies operating during this period. These "indices" were recorded in *Poor's Manual*.

Column 4, **Water Transport:** See the notes on gross income for this industry. The net interest payments reported by the DBS, *National Income, 1919-1940* are as follows.

Interest on Bonds and Debentures
(thousands of dollars)

Year	Interest	Year	Interest
1919	350	1923	743
1920	622	1924	713
1921	644	1925	684
1922	720	1926	1,202

However, the earlier data were not good enough to yield reliable estimates of interest payments. Hence there is not an estimate of interest payments for this group.

Column 5, **Telephone:** For the years 1919 to 1926 inclusive, the estimates are taken from the

DBS study, *National Income 1919-1940*. The figures here are gross interest payments. Since no interest payment data were presented before 1919, the estimates for 1912 to 1918 were derived by multiplying the funded debt in 1912 by an average bond yield figure. The latter was obtained by averaging yields over period 1901 to 1912 (3.85%). For each year thereafter the interest payment was found by multiplying the incremental increasing funded debt by the yield on provincial bonds for that year (see HSC, p.275; Series 606), and adding this extension to the 1912 estimate. Three assumptions are implied in this approach:

(1) No funded debt is retired over the period: this is not unreasonable given the late start of this industry (1890s).
(2) No funded debt was "rolled-over" during this period: this seems unlikely since interest rates were generally climbing during the period.
(3) Telephone companies could obtain rates equivalent to those paid by the provinces: this seems reasonable since, for the main growth period, the majority of telephone companies issuing debt instruments were provincially owned or very large (i.e., Bell Canada).

It is difficult to say whether the resulting estimate have an upward or downward bias. The possibility of the latter is stronger if telephone companies tended to use a great deal of floating debt — no statistics have been reproduced on such debt. However for 1919, this procedure yielded an interest payment of $2,643 million while the DBS figure for the same year was $2,863 million.

To obtain annual estimates for 1901 to 1911 inclusive, an extrapolation procedure was adopted. The index used was "fixed charges" as recorded by the Bell Company over the years.

For the years 1887 to 1900 see the notes to Table 6.1.

Column 6, **Telegraph:** As the Canadian Telegraph System is largely operated by railways they own few physical assets except for some telegraph offices. Thus their funded debt can be assumed to be negligible. In fact for the DBS estimates on National Income for the period 1919 to 1940 no attempt was made to estimate interest payments.

Dividends by Industrial Division

The next set of data, dividends by industrial division, are given in Table 6.5. As usual, it is followed by a description of the derivation of the estimates.

The Derivation of the Data of Table 6.5: Dividends by Industrial Division

Column 1, **Electric Light and Power:** For the period 1919 to 1926 estimates are taken from DBS, *National Income 1919-1940*. This series is derived from the *Financial Post Securities* list and the *Annual Financial Review*. Estimates found in these two sources were increased by 10 percent to allow for undercoverage. For the calendar years 1900 and 1910 and the census year 1891 estimates of gross output and for 1900 expenses incurred, were derived from the respective Censuses of 1911 (Vol. III), 1901 (Vol. III) and 1891 (Vol. III). From these figures dividends paid were obtained by multiplying, at each census date, the estimated value of the amount available for the payment of dividends (see Table D in the "General Notes") by the average of this amount divided into net dividends paid between 1919 and 1926 (the latter estimates were

Table 6.5. Dividends by Industrial Division (thousands of dollars)

Year	Electric Light and Power (1)	Steam R.R. and R.R. Express (2)	Electric R.R. (3)	Water Transport (4)	Telephone (5)	Telegraph (6)
1871	-	100	-	-	-	-
1872	-	100	-	-	-	-
1873	-	100	-	-	-	-
1874	-	100	-	-	-	-
1875	-	100	-	-	-	-
1876	-	100	-	-	-	-
1877	-	100	-	-	-	-
1878	-	100	-	-	-	-
1879	-	100	-	-	-	-
1880	-	100	-	-	-	-
1881	-	100	-	-	-	-
1882	-	100	-	-	-	-
1883	-	2,985	-	-	-	-
1884	-	1,533	-	-	-	-
1885	-	100	-	-	-	-
1886	-	1,036	-	-	-	-
1887	-	1,872	-	-	94	-
1888	-	906	-	-	98	-
1889	-	2,101	-	-	114	-
1890	120	2,612	-	-	133	-
1891	126	2,168	-	-	153	-
1892	132	2,200	-	-	165	-
1893	139	3,001	-	-	208	-
1894	145	1,920	400 [2]	-	208	-
1895	152	1,257	539	-	208	-
1896	158	2,321	633	-	208	-
1897	164	5,006	643	-	208	-
1898	170	4,944	781	-	270	-
1899	177	6,941	798	-	286	-
1900	183	6,954	909	-	325	-
1901	235	7,088	985	-	392	-
1902	300	7,516	1,075	-	482	-
1903	319	9,378	1,183	-	542	-
1904	419	9,318	1,252	-	648	-
1905	566	10,841	1,352	-	844	-
1906	678	12,198	1,792	-	935	-
1907	809	15,434	2,024	-	980	-
1908	976	14,443	2,455	-	1,342	-
1909	1,086	16,649	2,635	-	1,372	-

Table 6.5. (continued)

Year	Electric Light and Power (1)	Steam R.R. and R.R. Express (2)	Electric R.R. (3)	Water Transport (4)	Telephone (5)	Telegraph (6)
1910	982	18,563	2,587	-	1,402	-
1911	1,844	24,989	2,732	-	1,342	-
1912	2,382	25,140	3,229	-	1,507	-
1913	2,765	27,333	2,626	-	1,861	-
1914	3,243	30,434	4,174	-	2,005	-
1915	3,680	32,341	4,338	-	2,026	-
1916	4,403	36,452	2,835	-	2,059	-
1917	4,526	30,145	2,469	-	2,063	-
1918	5,124	30,156	1,671	-	2,086	-
1919	5,462	30,157 [1]	2,685 [1]	-	2,607 [1]	-
1920	5,552	29,943	3,376	-	2,992	-
1921	4,455	30,157	2,280	-	3,130	-
1922	5,771	30,155	2,555	-	3,737	-
1923	6,610	30,356	2,323	-	4,391	-
1924	8,103	30,512	2,396	-	4,470	-
1925	9,834	30,410	2,535	-	4,929	-
1926	12,965	30,449	2,647	-	4,935	-

1   See footnote 1 of Table 6.1. For the fiscal year ending June 30, 1919, the estimates for dividends are (in thousands of dollars): steam r.r. and r.r. express, 37,230; electric railways, 1,509; telephone, 2,274.
2   Estimated on basis of trend in dividend payments for previous years.

reported in *National Income 1919-1940*). The mean (and median) value of this ratio was approximately 21%. The interpolation procedure, for the period 1910 to 1919, is identical to that outlined in the notes to Table 6.1 except the particular corporate series employed here is "Surplus Above Charges". For the period 1900 to 1910, see the methods outlined in Table 6.1.

For the decade 1890 to 1900 see the notes to Table 6.1. The decadal benchmark estimates are shown in Table D.

Column 2, **Steam Railways and Railway Express:** For the period 1926 to 1919 (calendar year basis), data are from the DBS *National Income 1919-1940*, section on Transportation. In the latter study dividend payments are recorded net of dividend receipts. Since, for earlier years, dividend receipts are not available only gross payments are used. For the period 1919 to 1926, the average level of dividend receipts was approximately $1.7 million. For the same reasons as outlined in the "Notes" to Table 6.4 no dividend payment information is available for railway express companies. For the period 1911 to 1918, inclusive (fiscal year ending June 30th), see "Railway Statistics", in the *Sessional Papers of Canada*. The consolidated debenture payments of the C.P.R. which are included in the interest rate series have been deducted from dividend payments.

Dividend payments were not reported prior to 1911. The estimates shown here are the sum of dividends paid by the Canadian Pacific Railway and the Grand Trunk Railway (the latter's payments converted to Canadian dollars at the fixed rate of $4.867). In 1911 this sum accounted for approximately 98% of all dividends paid by Canadian railroads. Accordingly this sum was divided by 0.98 to give the figures shown. For 1885 and the period 1871 to 1882 no dividend payments were recorded by the Grand Trunk. On the assumption that the small railroads may indeed have been paying some dividends $100,000 was inserted. This was derived by taking 10% of the roughly 1 million dollars paid in dividends by the Grand Trunk. At this stage there is no way of knowing precisely what, if any, dividends were paid by these smaller lines. The actual number is probably small. Data on dividends for the C.P.R. were obtained from the companies "Annual Reports" while for the Grand Trunk, the source is *Poor's Manual*

Column 3, Electric Railways: The sources are the same as outlined in the notes to Table 6.4 back to 1910. The 1909 estimate from the "Electric Railway" report seems underestimated *vis-à-vis* the 1910 figure. Thus for the period 1895 to 1909 the estimates were derived by dividing the sum of dividend payments reported by five electric railway companies (Halifax R.R., Montreal Street R.R., Ottawa Electric, Toronto R.R. and the Winnipeg Electric) by 0.90. The divisor was based on the relationship of this sample total to the official estimate for dividends paid in 1910.

Column 4, Water Transport: See the "Notes" on gross income for this industry.

The net dividend payments on stocks reported by the DBS, *National Income, 1919-1940* are as follows (in thousands of dollars).

Year	Dividends	Year	Dividends
1919	2,373	1923	419
1920	2,350	1924	302
1921	1,280	1925	407
1922	407	1926	461

Column 5, Telephones: For the years 1926 to 1919 inclusive, DBS *National Income 1919-1940*. The figures are for gross dividend payments. No dividend estimates were collected before 1919. The estimates shown for the period 1918 to 1921 (fiscal year 30th June) were obtained by multiplying the value of outstanding stock for the given year by 0.070. The latter was the average ratio of gross dividends paid to capital stock for the years 1919 to 1921. Although this was a period of slightly below average stock prices for utilities (see HSC, p.277, Series 640), the average yield was taken as a constant since we do not know the earlier trends in utility stock prices; i.e., the presumption is they were lower and this probably raised the yield rates. The basic assumption is that the stocks are shown at market value rather than at cost.

For the years 1887 to 1900 see the notes to Table 6.1.

Column 6, Telegraph: See the comments for interest payments. Again any dividends collected would be absorbed in the accounts of the steam railway companies.

Table 6.6. Total Payments to Individuals by Industrial Divisions (thousands of dollars)

Year	Electric Light and Power (1)	Steam R.R. and R.R. Express (2)	Electric R.R. (3)	Water Transport [2] (4)	Tele-phone (5)	Tele-graph (6)
1871	-	10,413	-	13,196	-	-
1872	-	11,483	-	11,531	-	-
1873	-	12,322	-	12,050	-	-
1874	-	15,148	-	9,629	-	-
1875	-	13,091	-	8,084	-	-
1876	-	13,193	-	8,321	-	-
1877	-	12,898	-	8,293	-	-
1878	-	13,795	-	8,941	-	-
1879	-	13,613	-	9,241	-	-
1880	-	14,037	-	9,810	-	-
1881	-	15,972	-	9,937	-	-
1882	-	18,856	-	10,569	-	-
1883	-	21,580	-	9,453	-	-
1884	-	21,009	-	9,373	-	-
1885	-	22,481	-	7,675	-	-
1886	-	23,599	-	7,429	-	-
1887	-	27,053	-	7,382	460	-
1888	-	28,064	-	7,897	479	-
1889	-	30,081	-	8,002	556	-
1890	482	32,451	-	8,361	651	-
1891	535	33,821	-	7,721	747	-
1892	588	35,563	-	7,478	805	-
1893	642	37,077	-	7,228	1,015	-
1894	694	36,391	1,530	7,735	1,015	-
1895	749	35,105	1,847	3,761	1,015	-
1896	801	37,642	2,039	6,096	1,015	-
1897	854	40,802	2,216	5,994	1,015	-
1898	906	42,970	2,473	6,627	1,321	-
1899	961	45,952	2,688	7,544	1,398	-
1900	1,013	50,129	3,220	7,961	1,588	-
1901	1,243	52,366	4,157	7,583	1,915	-
1902	1,524	57,052	4,549	9,096	2,213	-
1903	2,041	64,731	5,193	11,283	2,589	-
1904	3,415	69,420	5,958	11,256	2,960	-
1905	3,897	75,452	6,571	13,010	3,561	-
1906	4,241	81,264	7,805	14,791	4,190	-
1907	4,618	94,160	9,183	19,286	4,834	1,677
1908	4,892	95,789	9,393	19,384	5,030	1,685
1909	5,435	101,878	10,714	14,489	5,324	1,773

Table 6.6.   (continued)

Year	Electric Light and Power (1)	Steam R.R. and R.R. Express (2)	Electric R.R. (3)	Water Transport [2] (4)	Tele-phone (5)	Tele-graph (6)
1910	5,811	108,826	10,510	17,339	5,758	2,010
1911	7,483	124,090	13,072	19,127	6,530	2,274
1912	8,737	146,007	14,253	24,345	8,190	2,727
1913	10,235	172,177	16,798	29,131	10,229	3,104
1914	12,424	173,530	18,485	24,214	11,939	3,345
1915	13,748	154,265	18,709	14,900	12,261	3,061
1916	14,965	168,830	16,421	17,120	11,896	3,025
1917	19,429	208,949	16,797	18,316	13,057	3,518
1918	23,378	235,880	21,210	17,427	14,958	4,075
1919	25,399	325,321 [1]	27,877 [1]	26,015	21,245 [1]	5,251
1920	29,663	389,088	33,561	32,957	23,471	6,565
1921	31,326	361,538	32,278	28,037	25,948	6,672
1922	33,909	348,961	34,905	25,655	24,956	6,308
1923	35,869	341,390	35,222	29,005	26,543	6,092
1924	42,781	331,319	35,580	30,005	26,957	7,016
1925	47,186	329,549	35,936	32,117	28,462	7,692
1926	54,568	344,379	36,260	32,684	34,985	7,640

1   See footnote 1 of Table 6.1. For the fiscal year ending June 30, 1919, the estimates of total payments to individuals are, in thousands of dollars: steam r.r. and r.r. express, 289,318; electric railways, 21,045; telephones, 17,965.

2   Includes only wage and salary payments. See the "notes" on interest and dividend payments for explanations on their exclusion from this total.

Total Payments to Individuals by Industrial Division

There now follows estimates of total payments to individuals by industrial division and the explanation of their derivation.   Table 6.6 gives total payments to individuals by industrial division.

The Derivation of the Data of Table 6.6: Total Payments to Individuals By Industrial Division

The total payments to individuals by industrial division comprise the sum for each industrial division of wages and salaries (Table 6.3); net interest payments (Table 6.4) and net dividend payments (Table 6.5).

Column 4, **Water Transport:** For a general discussion of this industry see the "Notes" on gross revenue following Table 6.1. Total factor payments (in thousands of dollars) as reported by the DBS, *National Income 1919-1940* are as follows:

Year	Payment	Year	Payment
1919	35,618	1923	35,382
1920	47,500	1924	36,023
1921	36,196	1925	36,980
1922	38,417	1926	40,315

These include (in thousands of dollars), entrepreneurial withdrawals as follows:

Year	Withdrawl	Year	Withdrawl
1919	2,194	1923	1,923
1920	2,164	1924	1,915
1921	2,085	1925	1,875
1922	2,066	1926	1,883

Savings by Industrial Division

The next set of data, savings by industrial division, is given in Table 6.7, followed by an explanation of their derivation.

The Derivation of the Data of Table 6.7: Gross Business Savings By Industrial Division

Although there are some minor variations in the methods of calculating savings between industrial divisions, essentially they are calculated as the difference between net income and dividends paid out. The savings estimates are in the main gross of depreciation allowances.

Column 1, **Electric Light and Power:** For the period 1919 to 1926 the source was the same as shown in Table 6.5. For the procedures used on years prior to 1919, see the discussion for Table 6.4. Here net savings includes depreciation charges and is calculated according to the method shown in Table D.

For decennial benchmark estimates see Table D. The interpolation procedures used are set out in the discussion to the notes for Table 6.1. The "index" used for the period 1900 to 1919 was the "surplus above charges" described in the notes to Table 6.5.

For the decade 1890 to 1900 see the notes to Table 6.1. The decadal benchmark estimates (and procedures) are shown in Table D.

Column 2, **Steam Railway and Railway Express:** For the period 1919 to 1926 inclusive (calendar year basis) the figures represent the total of net saving (gross of depreciation) in the two industries. Thereafter the total is for steam railways only. Net savings here is the difference between net earnings for the railway system as a whole and gross dividend payments.

Net earnings for the railway system as a whole for 1911 to 1926 is that reported in *Railway Statistics* in the table "Income Account". For the earlier years it was calculated by adding to net operating revenue, "Other" income (this gives gross corporate earnings), and deducting from the latter all fixed charges plus interest payments on C.P.R. 4% debenture stock; C.P.R. steamship replacement fund; and C.P.R. contributions to its pension fund. All taxes paid before

Table 6.7. Gross Savings by Industrial Division (thousands of dollars)

Year	Electric Light and Power (1)	Steam R.R. and R.R. Express (2)	Electric R.R. (3)	Water Transport [2] (4)	Tele-phone (5)	Tele-graph (6)
1871	-	(1,000) [3]	-	-	-	-
1872	-	(1,000)	-	-	-	-
1873	-	(1,000)	-	-	-	-
1874	-	(1,000)	-	-	-	-
1875	-	(1,485)	-	-	-	-
1876	-	(1,665)	-	-	-	-
1877	-	(1,868)	-	-	-	-
1878	-	(1,282)	-	-	-	-
1879	-	(1,605)	-	-	-	-
1880	-	1,154	-	-	-	-
1881	-	2,020	-	-	-	-
1882	-	(374)	-	-	-	-
1883	-	268	-	-	-	-
1884	-	633	-	-	-	-
1885	-	(1,484)	-	-	-	-
1886	-	1,140	-	-	-	-
1887	-	(831)	-	-	66	-
1888	-	216	-	-	69	-
1889	-	(1,763)	-	-	80	-
1890	454	(352)	-	-	94	-
1891	477	(1,702)	-	-	108	-
1892	501	(612)	-	-	116	-
1893	542	(2,071)	-	-	147	-
1894	547	(3,934)	322	-	147	-
1895	571	(2,565)	510	-	147	-
1896	594	(2,656)	367	-	147	-
1897	617	(4,582)	677	-	147	-
1898	640	(763)	770	-	191	-
1899	664	(1,499)	904	-	202	-
1900	687	(143)	916	-	230	-
1901	881	(1,181)	869	-	277	-
1902	1,128	1,846	1,031	-	335	-
1903	1,193	2,436	891	-	392	-
1904	1,570	(1,364)	1,075	-	469	-
1905	2,126	(3,423)	1,150	-	603	-
1906	2,549	3,500	1,301	-	670	-
1907	3,042	8,606	1,564	-	698	1,014
1908	3,661	5,343	1,576	-	957	1,135
1909	4,077	3,347	2,082	-	986	1,223

Table 6.7. (continued)

Year	Electric Light and Power (1)	Steam R.R. and R.R. Express (2)	Electric R.R. (3)	Water Transport [2] (4)	Tele- phone (5)	Tele- graph (6)
1910	3,692	14,120	2,796	-	1,038	1,595
1911	6,303	14,707	3,859	-	957	1,626
1912	7,366	20,620	2,709	-	719	1,831
1913	7,760	24,755	3,809	-	533	1,929
1914	8,187	623	5,156	-	726	1,497
1915	8,332	1,041	1,110	-	861	1,366
1916	8,896	25,194	2,052	-	3,404	1,802
1917	8,122	14,035	2,410	-	3,851	2,077
1918	7,480	(19,370)	1,253	-	4,561	1,750
1919	7,564	(45,587) [1]	1,019 [1]	-	3,849 [1]	1,686
1920	7,690	(73,804)	(286)	-	(748)	1,747
1921	8,169	(73,717)	(149)	-	(41)	1,577
1922	9,809	(58,948)	4,754	-	1,943	1,173
1923	10,864	(45,667)	4,043	-	1,381	1,402
1924	8,854	(55,368)	3,535	-	2,043	1,200
1925	12,168	(32,809)	4,189	-	2,311	1,350
1926	15,309	(13,899)	5,755	-	2,615	1,448

1   See footnote 1 of Table 6.1. The estimates of gross savings for the fiscal year ending June 30, 1919, are, in thousands of dollars: stream r.r. and r.r. express, (42,171); electric railways, 436; telephones, 3,516.
2   Not available — see "Notes".
3   Brackets indicate negative savings (dissavings).

were deducted. The latter are very small before 1907.

For the years 1871 to 1874, inclusive it was assumed, in the absence of other hard data, that the railroad system exhibited a steady net savings deficiency of one million dollars. The latter appears reasonable in light of the performance of the system in the last half of the decade of the seventies.

Column 3, **Electric Railroads:** For the years 1926 to 1919 see the sources set out in the text on Table 6.4. In order to be consistent with gross savings estimates for electric power and steam railway it was necessary to include depreciation charges in the net savings figures. It was assumed that the category "Reserves, etc.", shown in the income statements, was a measure of the annual amount set aside for this purpose and so this was added to the net savings figure shown in these statements.

For the years 1909 to 1918, inclusive, gross savings were obtained from the "Income Account" for "Electric Railway Statistics" as recorded in various issues of the *Sessional Papers of Canada*. As in the comments above, since gross savings in the other industry groups was defined as including depreciation charges the "Reserves" shown in these accounts were added to the surplus to yield the estimates shown. The figures for the period 1901 to 1908 were obtained by filling out the missing components to the "Income Account" for these years. In the case of miscellaneous income it was assumed, based on the ratio of this figure to gross earnings for the previous five years, that the latter be multiplied by 55 to yield an estimate for this source of income. For the most part this income was earned by the sale of excess power to commercial and non-commercial users. From total corporate income taxes were deducted (assumed to decline from the 1909 figure at the rate of $100,000 a year) interest payments (see Table 6.4) and dividend payments (see Table 6.5).

For the years 1894 to 1900, net savings were extrapolated back from 1901 on the basis of an index constructed from the annual movements in "Surplus" recorded by the Montreal and Toronto Street railway systems — these two systems dominated electric railroad revenue earned during this period.

Column 4, **Water Transport:** See the "Notes" on gross revenue, for this industry.

The gross savings estimates — really undistributed corporate profits — as recorded by the DBS, *National Income 1919-1940* are as follows (in thousands of dollars):

Year	Savings	Year	Savings
1919	3,504	1923	2,670
1920	1,430	1924	1,670
1921	708	1925	1,489
1922	1,744	1926	1,091

Column 5, **Telephones:** For the years 1911 to 1926, inclusive, net savings (including depreciation reserves) were calculated by subtracting from net revenue (CYB, 1922-1923 and 1914 issues) gross interest payments (see Table 6.4). This operation yielded a figure for net corporate income and from this figure gross dividend payments (see Table 6.5) were subtracted. The final result is a close approximation to gross savings. For the years 1919 to 1926 the net savings figures shown differ slightly from those recorded in the DBS estimates. This difference is due to the omission from these figures of the category "Other Income". The latter figure is available only for large telephone systems and beginning only in 1920. To give consistency to the full range of estimates this category of income was eliminated throughout. The DBS study records "Other Income" as follows (in millions of dollars):

Year	Other Income	Year	Other Income
1920	653	1924	965
1921	284	1925	996
1922	367	1926	903
1923	866		

The DBS report fails to mention that these figures apply only to "Large Telephone Systems", not to the telephone system as a whole.

For the years 1901 to 1911, inclusive, the net savings estimates were derived by extrapolating backward from the 1911 estimate using an annual index based on the trend in "Net Surplus" as recorded by the Bell Company.

For the years 1887 to 1900 inclusive see the notes to Table 6.1.

Column 6, **Telegraph:** The estimates for 1919 to 1926, inclusive, were taken from the telegraph industry section of the DBS study on *National Income, 1919-1940*. Undistributed profits or savings in this case are represented by "net revenue" for the years 1919 to 1922 and "net corporate income" for 1923 to 1926. For the years 1912 to 1918 the estimates are for net corporate income as recorded in the supplement to the *Annual Report of the Department of Railways and Canals* entitled, *Telegraph Statistics*.

   Net corporate income; i.e., net revenue less taxes and other incidental payments is a good proxy for savings since, as discussed in the notes to interest and dividend payments, no deductions are made, in this case, from net corporate income for these two expenditures. The estimates for 1907 to 1911 were made on the basis of an index constructed from annual changes in net revenue earned by the Canadian Pacific Railway on their telegraph operations. The revenue and expenditures figures used to derive net revenue appear in the companies' *Annual Report*. As in the other components of the telegraph industry earlier figures are included with the estimates for steam railways.

Employees by Industrial Division

The data on employees by industrial division are given in Table 6.8. As before, the table is followed by an explanation of the derivation of the data.

The Derivation of the Data of Table 6.8: Employees by Industrial Division

Column 1, **Electric Light and Power:** For the period 1919 to 1926, see HSC, p.452. Benchmark estimates for the calendar years 1900 and 1910 and the "census year" 1891 were taken from the *1911 Census of Canada*, Vol. III, p.376; *1901 Census of Canada*, Vol. III, p.356; and *1891 Census of Canada*, Vol. III, p.142; respectively. The interpolation procedure for the years 1910 to 1917 was identical to that described in Table 6.1 except here the index used was a weighted average of "current expenditures" as recorded in the corporate annual statements. For the period 1900 to 1910 the sample "index" is similar to that set out in Table 6.1.

   The interpolation procedure for the decade 1890 to 1900 is set out in the notes to Table 6.1. The decadal benchmark estimates can be found in the respective census as set out above.

Column 2, **Steam Railway and Railway Express:** For the years 1919 to 1926, inclusive, the figures are the sum of employees in these two industries as shown by DBS in a table entitled "Numbers of Employees in Canada 1919-1944". This table was derived as part of the larger project on *National Income in Canada 1919-1940*. For the years 1911 to 1918 (fiscal year basis), steam railway figures were derived from the various issued of the *Sessional Papers of Canada* which record "Railroad Statistics". Employment in railway express is a derived figure — see the "notes" to Table D for the method of computation (qualifications on the accuracy of these estimates are similar to those for estimates of the number of steam railway employees set out below). In order to minimize double counting telegraph workers have been eliminated from this total back to 1907.

   For the years prior to 1911 (i.e., 1871 to 1910), only steam railway employees are recorded in the series shown. "Statistics on Steam Railways" did not record employment in the industry prior to 1907. It was necessary therefore, to estimate the level of annual employment using ra-

Table 6.8. Employees by Industrial Division (number of employees)

Year	Electric Light and Power (1)	Steam R.R. and R.R. Express (2)	Electric R.R. (3)	Water Transport (4)	Tele- phone (5)	Tele- graph (6)
1871	-	11,816	-	18,087	-	-
1872	-	12,850	-	15,805	-	-
1873	-	14,032	-	16,516	-	-
1874	-	18,019	-	13,198	-	-
1875	-	14,770	-	11,080	-	-
1876	-	14,590	-	11,184	-	-
1877	-	14,382	-	11,480	-	-
1878	-	15,358	-	12,502	-	-
1879	-	15,030	-	12,502	-	-
1880	-	16,952	-	14,494	-	-
1881	-	20,347	-	14,813	-	-
1882	-	21,765	-	15,133	-	-
1883	-	24,569	-	13,918	-	-
1884	-	25,020	-	13,514	-	-
1885	-	26,573	-	12,467	-	-
1886	-	27,135	-	12,259	-	-
1887	-	31,286	-	12,206	726	-
1888	-	34,322	-	12,955	756	-
1889	-	34,537	-	13,024	876	-
1890	763	37,486	-	13,991	1,027	-
1891	795	39,182	-	12,715	1,179	-
1892	827	41,368	-	12,513	1,270	-
1893	859	41,533	-	12,119	1,602	-
1894	891	39,666	1,390	12,891	1,602	-
1895	923	39,304	1,373	6,667	1,602	-
1896	954	39,882	1,485	12,097	1,602	-
1897	986	40,607	1,614	10,257	1,602	-
1898	1,018	45,756	1,765	11,458	2,086	-
1899	1,050	47,635	2,011	13,070	2,207	-
1900	1,082	54,953	2,529	13,567	2,509	-
1901	1,270	57,741	4,006	12,741	3,023	-
1902	1,502	66,028	4,470	14,089	3,336	-
1903	1,637	76,731	5,118	15,677	4,066	-
1904	1,952	82,403	6,037	14,936	4,691	-
1905	2,044	87,974	6,696	16,809	5,630	-
1906	2,232	99,598	7,698	18,675	6,568	-
1907	2,370	121,025	9,031	21,836	7,714	2,969
1908	2,526	103,718	9,954	22,687	7,298	2,984
1909	2,804	122,296	10,557	18,144	7,923	3,138

Table 6.8. (continued)

Year	Electric Light and Power (1)	Steam R.R. and R.R. Express (2)	Electric R.R. (3)	Water Transport (4)	Tele- phone (5)	Tele- graph (6)
1910	3,406	117,243	11,390	21,032	8,861	3,558
1911	3,774	140,834	13,671	21,864	10,425	4,027
1912	3,960	155,629	14,760	23,186	12,783	4,828
1913	4,378	178,401	16,351	24,059	12,867	6,006
1914	5,206	159,630	16,195	21,767	16,799	6,150
1915	4,896	126,110	14,795	17,815	15,072	6,243
1916	5,576	146,506	10,622	18,822	15,247	6,581
1917	8,847	149,215	11,696	17,504	16,490	7,100
1918	9,696	157,498	14,567 [2]	15,191	17,336	7,212
1919	9,656	180,608 [1]	16,940 [1]	16,461	20,491 [1]	7,696 [1]
1920	10,693	191,713	17,341	18,164	21,187	7,508
1921	10,714	174,103	17,015	20,107	19,943	7,818
1922	10,684	171,362	18,099	21,105	19,321	8,500
1923	11,094	180,837	17,779	22,422	21,002	8,565
1924	13,263	170,949	17,379	23,347	21,685	8,909
1925	13,406	165,995	16,933	24,759	21,831	8,965
1926	14,708	174,012	16,961	25,057	23,083	8,914 [3]

1   See footnote 1 of Table 6.1. For the fiscal year ending June 30, 1919, total employment was: steam r.r. and r.r. express, 158,777; electric r.r., 17,542; telephones, 19,057; telegraph, 7,705.
2   Due to the failure of Montreal Tramways to report operating statistics for the fiscal year 1918 it was necessary to estimate employment for this firm and add this number (2,921) to that recorded in statistics on electric railways. The estimation procedure is identical to that used for steam railways and set out in the notes to Table 6.8.
3   As the 1926 figures omitted commission operators, the figure shown was derived as an average of those employed in 1925 and 1927.

tios based on the relationship between the wage bill and operating revenue and expenses for years since 1907. Details of this procedure, plus qualifications, are set out in the "Notes" to Table D. The first aspect revealed by the latter is the apparent downward bias in the census estimates of steam railway employment. Apparently census takers assigned to this group only those workers who were directly connected with operating the railroad; i.e., engineers, firemen, conductors, trackmen, etc. Those engaged in maintenance of road and repair of equipment were assigned in all likelihood to the manufacturing sector or as unclassified labour. The second point to note is the magnitude of the difference. For example in 1911, when we have both census and railway statistics estimates, the difference shows approximately 51,000 more workers reported themselves as working for steam railway companies than were assigned to this category in the census. Fishlow (*op.cit.*, pp.402 and 408) found that in the U.S. census of 1849 and 1959 the number of "railroad men" were 4,831 and 35,567 respectively. Using estimation techniques identical to those employed here he found railway employment to be 18,000 in 1849 and 85,000 in 1859. The estimates shown in Column 5 of Table E, then, would seem to be not unreasonable in light of Fishlow's work. Although at this time it is difficult to state firmly whether the Canadian employment estimates have an upward or downward bias; there is a presumption towards the latter. Finally, Fishlow shows that for 1849 U.S. railroads output was approximately 29.3 million dollars (p.326) and he estimated employment (as shown above) at 18,000. Although railroad technology may have been slightly different between the two countries, and over these two time periods, nevertheless the latter figure seems to be a reasonable approximation for employment in steam railways.

The estimates for the years 1871 to 1874 were found by extrapolating the 1875 figure backward on the basis of the trend in total operating expenses recorded by the Grand Trunk Railway.

Column 3, **Electric Railroad:** The sources were: for the years 1926 to 1919, DBS Electric Railways in Canada and for 1918 to 1907, *Sessional Papers in Canada* No. 20b section on "Electric Railway Statistics". In the case of estimates for the period 1894 to 1906 the procedure is identical to that outlined for steam railways for the years before 1907. Here the coefficients for operating expenses and revenue are 0.00114 and 0.00071 respectively. The figures shown, as for steam railways are simply averages of the two estimates derived by using operating expenses and output. Again, as for steam railways, the biases are likely to appear due to the underlying productivity assumptions inherent in this approach.

For the period 1894 to 1900, inclusive, the revenue and expense data were augmented by the figures for Montreal Street Railway, Toronto Railway and British Columbia Electric Railway as recorded in *Poor's Manual* 1901 and 1902. These three street railway systems did not report to the Department of Railways and Canals.

Column 4, **Water Transport:** Since the individual shipping companies were not required to report operating revenue or expenses (see the "Notes" to this sector for gross income), employment estimates could only be derived from the decennial census reports. The basic procedure was to use the figures for wage earners in the censuses of 1901, 1911, 1921 and 1931 while for the censuses of 1881 and 1891 only estimates of gainfully occupied were available. The annual estimates, over the whole period, were derived by linear interpolation between successive census dates.

For the census covering the period 1901 to 1931 two estimates of wage earners were available. The number of wage earners who reported their earnings and those who did not provide such information. The assumption used was that half of the difference between the total wage earners (reporting earnings as well as though not reporting earnings), provides a rough estimate of full time equivalent workers and this number was added to those reporting earnings. The full time equivalent estimates are shown in Table 6.8 at the respective census dates; i.e., 1901, 1911, etc.

The procedure to obtain annual intercensal estimates of employment is identical to that outlined in Table 6.1 for Electric Power. In this case the interpolators used were the number of Canadian vessels passing through Canadian canals. These series appeared to be an appropriate interpolator for the following reasons.

(1)   Since water transport is such a labour intensive industry, the number employed at any one time must be closely related to the number of vessels actually in operation. Note that the underlying assumption here is that the ratio of employees per vessel is approximately constant. This assumption needs to be checked, especially since the shares of sailing

vessels in the total declined sharply towards the end of the 19th Century.

(2)   Annual variations in the number of vessels passing through Canadian canals apparently
follows fairly closely a direct estimate of employment variation (see Chart II). The
number of vessels index, however is not without its biases. In particular it apparently
overstates the increase in employment at cyclical peaks and understates employment in
troughs. The actual conditions might be such that in times of heavy demand vessels make
more trips then normal and fewer than normal during slow seasons. However, the actual
size of the crews might not vary quite as widely.

(3)   Finally the number of vessels using the canals seems to represent fairly well the observed
trend changes between census dates in the levels of employment in this industry.

For the period 1881 to 1901, only the number of gainfully occupied workers was available.
The census of Canada for 1911 (Vol. VI) sets out (Table 1, pp. 8-9), a comparative study of
workers 19 years of age and over for this industry. The presumption here is that the figures
represent a consistent definition of workers to be included in this industry. The estimates for
1881 and 1891 were taken from this table adjusted to an approximate wage earner basis by
multiplying each census estimate by 0.75. This latter ratio was the one which held between wage
earners and the gainfully occupied for the early decades of the 20th Century. The net result
was to lower the level of employment in 1881 and 1891 but to leave the trend line unaffected.

Annual intercensal estimates were obtained by the same procedure as for the later estimates
(i.e., by linear apportionment). However the interpolation index was changed to the number of
Canadian and British vessels (seagoing and inland) arriving and departing from Canadian ports
(HSC, p.542). The inclusion of British vessels did not distort the overall trend since their
number remained small until the opening of the new St. Lawrence locks in the 1950s.

A comparison of the annual movements in this series with a similarly constructed series
(i.e., sum of Canadian and British vessels), for passage through Canadian canals is shown in
Chart III [parts (A) and (B)]. Although the dates of the main peak and trough are similar for
both series, there is a difference in trends. The Canadian canal series shows a positive trend after
1886 whereas the arrival and departures series is much flatter (i.e., less positive trend). Since
the number of gainfully occupied workers remains relatively constant over the period, it was felt
that the latter index was not inappropriate, especially since the peaks and troughs roughly match
the known periods of high and low economic activity in Canada (e.g., the troughs of 1873-75
and 1895 match closely periods of known economic recession).

The census of 1871 does not show a consistent set of estimates for employment in Water
Transport. Thus annual employment estimates were derived by simply running the 1881 figure
back on an index based on the number of Canadian and British vessels arriving and departing
from Canadian ports — HSC, *ibid.*, i.e., the same series used for interpolation over the period
1881 to 1901.

Column 5, **Telephone:** For 1911 to 1926, see notes to Table 6.3. The extrapolation procedure
back to 1901 was identical to that described in the "notes" to this table. Bell Canada gross revenue was used as the extrapolator in both cases instead of operating expenses since the latter
series moved erratically over this period due to changing definitions of current expenses.

For the years 1887 to 1900 inclusive, see the notes to Table 6.1.

Column 6, **Telegraph:** For the years 1919 to 1926, inclusive the estimates are from the DBS publication *Telegraph and Cable Statistics* while for the years 1912 to 1918, they are from a supplement to the *Annual Report of the Department of Railways and Canals* entitled, *Telegraph Statistics* which appears in the *Sessional Papers of Canada*.

The estimates for the years 1907 to 1911 were derived from an index based on annual changes in total operating expenses of the telegraph department of the Canadian Pacific Railway. These data appear in the companies' *Annual Reports*.

Appendix to Table 6.8

Table E. Comparison of Census with Derived Estimates of Employment in the Operation of Steam Railways, 1871-1931

	Actual		Estimated Employment		
Year	Census Estimates [1] (1)	Steam Railway Reports [2] (2)	Employment, from Operating Revenue (3)	Employment, from Operating Expenses (4)	Final Estimate = Midpoint Between Col. 3 and Col. 4 (5)
1871	2,739	-	-	-	-
1881	8,520	-	22,670	18,023	20,347
1891	23,446	-	39,020	39,344	39,182
1901	30,259	-	58,576	56,605	57,741
1911	92,716	143,922	-	-	-
1921	30,560	174,103	-	-	-
1931	83,748	148,790	-	-	-

Notes: 1. Excludes telegraph and telephone workers.
            2. Includes railway express workers.

Sources and Methods:

Column 1:   1871, *Census of Canada, 1871*, Vol. II, p.334 ff.
             1881, *Census of Canada, 1881*, Vol. II, p.316 ff.
             1891, *Census of Canada, 1891*, Vol. II, p.191.
             1901, *Census of Canada, 1901*, Bulletin 1, p.87.
             1911, *Census of Canada, 1911*, Vol. VI, p.8.
             1921, *Census of Canada, 1921*, Vol. IV, p.26.
             1931, *Census of Canada, 1931*, Vol. 7, p.68.

Column 2:   The figure for 1921 and 1931 is the sum of employees in steam railways and express recorded by the DBS, *National Income 1919-1940*. For 1911 the figure is the sum of railway workers shown in the "Report of Railways and Canals", in the 1916 *Sessional Papers of Canada*, No.20b, table entitled "Railway Employees". To this figure was added the estimated employment of express workers. The latter was derived by multiplying operating expenses in express by 0.650 (an average of E ÷ O for the years 1920 to 1922 inclusive, where E = employment and O = total operating expenses).

Columns 3&4: The estimates for the census years 1901, 1891, 1881 and 1871, as for the annual estimates beginning in 1907 and going back to 1875 were obtained by finding the ratio of employment to gross operating revenue, and to gross operating expenses for the period 1907 to 1914. Examination of these ratios indicated that, in terms of the latter ratio E ÷ O, where E = railway employment and O = total operating expenses, a sharp break in productivity occurred beginning in 1920. The value of the ratio for 1920 was only one third its value in 1910. It was decided, therefore, to use an average of the two ratios (i.e., employment to revenue and to expenses) for the years 1907 to 1909 inclusive. These are E ÷ R = 0.000810 and E ÷ O = 0.001126 respectively. Operating employment levels annually for the period 1906 to 1875 inclusive were found by multiplying annual revenue and expenses by these ratios; i.e., E= b x R (1) and E= c x O (2) where b=0.000810 and c=0.001126.

The basic assumption of the above exercise is that productivity is constant, and equal to that observed in the period 1907 to 1909. This may be seen by rewriting equations (1) and (2) as follows: E = R x (O/R) x (W/O) x (1/w) where E = total employment; R = operating revenue; O = operating expenses; W = the wage bill and w = the wage rate. The estimation exercise then requires that the coefficient of revenue [in equation (1)], i.e., the product of the ratio of expenses to revenue; the share of wages in operating expenses; and the reciprocal of the wage rate, be the same for each year. Similarly equation (1) can be rewritten as E = O * (W/O) * (1/w) where the coefficient of O (i.e. c), is the product of the share of wages in operating expenses, and the reciprocal of the wage rate. These expanded coefficients are the average ratio outlined above, and cover the years 1907 to 1909. For an earlier attempt at estimating employment using this approach for the United States, see A. Fishlow, *American Railroads and the Transformation of the Ante-Bellum Economy* (Harvard University Press, 1965), pp.403-08.

Column 5:   The final estimates of operating employment are the midpoint levels between the two estimating ratios (output and expenses). Using a midpoint estimate, then allows the incorporation in the final figure of changes in the relationship between output and expenses as they occur over time. This "averaging" approach was adapted for the annual as well as for the decennial estimates.

Employment Estimates, Steam Railways, From Total Revenue

Year	Employment	Operating Revenue (thousands of dollars)	Ratio (1) : (2)
	(1)	(2)	(3)
1907	124,012	146,738	0.000845
1908	106,404	146,918	0.000721
1909	125,195	144,779	0.000863
1910	123,768	173,669	0.000714
1911	141,224	188,440	0.000748
1912	155,882	219,107	0.000712
1913	178,614	256,355	0.000698
1914	159,242	242,736	0.000655
			0.005956

Average for years 1907-1912 inclusive = 0.0007671 $\overline{X}$ = 0.0007445

Employment Estimates, Steam Railways, From Total Revenue

Year	Employment	Operating Revenue (thousands of dollars)	Ratio (1) : (2)
	(1)	(2)	(3)
1915	124,142	199,509	0.000622
1916	144,770	261,889	0.000554
1917	146,359	310,717	0.000470
1918	153,559	330,220	0.000466
1919	170,320	408,598	0.000416
1920	185,745	492,101	0.000378

For the reasons set out for expenses, it was decided to use the average for estimation purposes of the years 1907-1909 inclusive = 0.000810.

Employment Estimates, Steam Railways, From Total Operating Expenses

Year	Employment	Operating Expenses (thousands of dollars)	Ratio (1) : (2)
	(1)	(2)	(3)
1907	124,012	103,749	0.001195
1908	106,404	107,304	0.000988
1909	125,195	104,600	0.001195
1910	123,768	120,405	0.001030
1911	141,224	131,035	0.001076
1912	155,882	150,726	0.001035
1913	178,614	182,012	0.000983
1914	159,242	178,925	0.000389
			0.008391

Average for period 1907-1909 inclusive = 0.001126 $\overline{X}$ = 0.001049

Average for period 1907-1912 inclusive = 0.1088 ≈   0.11

Year	Employment	Operating Expenses (thousands of dollars)	Ratio (1) : (2)
1915	124,142	147,604	0.000840
1916	144,770	180,542	0.000803
1917	146,359	222,955	0.000655
1918	153,559	273,955	0.000562
1919	170,320	376,789	0.000451
1920	185,745	478,248	0.000389

Given the sharp increase in productivity beginning in the second decade (i.e., in 1920 the ratio E ÷ O was only one third of this 1910 value), it was decided to use the ratio average for years 1907-09 inclusive = 0.001126.

Chart II

Water Transport – Employment

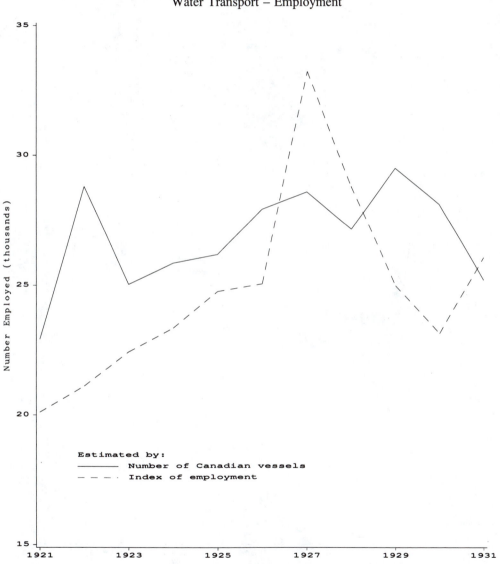

Chart IIIa

Numbers of Canadian and British Vessels Arriving and Departing
Canadian Ports, and Passing Through Canadian Canals

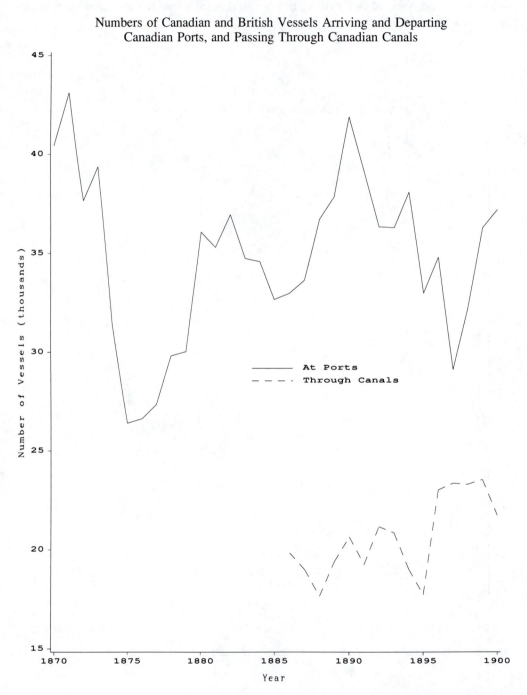

Chart IIIb

Numbers of Canadian and British Vessels Arriving and Departing
Canadian Ports, and Passing Through Canadian Canals

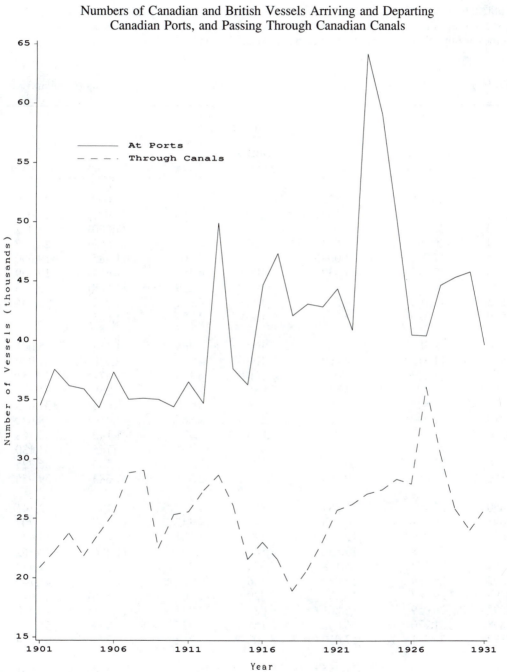

Gross Domestic Product at Factor Cost by Factor Income

Table 6.9 presents the summary factor income components for all parts of this industry (Transportation and Public Utilities). There is no need for descriptive notes because these factor incomes are merely the sums of the incomes measured in Tables 6.3 to 6.7.

Table 6.9.   Factor Income Components of Gross Domestic Product (thousands of dollars)

		Property Income				
Year	Wages or Salaries	Interest Payments	Dividend Payments	Total	Net Savings	GDP at Factor Cost
1871	20,386	3,123	100	3,223	(1,000)	22,609
1872	19,350	3,564	100	3,664	(1,000)	22,014
1873	20,588	3,684	100	3,784	(1,000)	23,372
1874	20,593	4,084	100	4,184	(1,000)	23,777
1875	17,071	4,004	100	4,104	(1,485)	19,690
1876	17,375	4,039	100	4,139	(1,665)	19,849
1877	19,962	4,129	100	4,229	(1,868)	19,323
1878	18,105	4,531	100	4,631	(1,282)	21,454
1879	18,500	4,254	100	4,354	(1,605)	21,249
1880	19,383	4,364	100	4,464	1,154	25,001
1881	21,319	4,490	100	4,590	2,020	27,929
1882	23,242	6,083	100	6,183	(374)	29,051
1883	23,404	4,644	2,985	7,629	268	31,301
1884	23,844	5,005	1,533	6,538	633	31,015
1885	21,290	8,766	100	8,866	(1,484)	28,672
1886	21,154	8,838	1,036	9,874	1,140	32,168
1887	23,464	9,465	1,966	11,431	(765)	34,130
1888	25,659	9,777	1,004	10,781	285	36,725
1889	26,056	10,368	2,215	12,583	(1,683)	39,956
1890	27,793	11,287	2,865	14,152	196	42,141
1891	28,379	11,998	2,447	14,445	(1,117)	41,707
1892	29,010	12,927	2,497	15,424	5	44,439
1893	28,958	13,656	3,348	17,004	(1,400)	44,562
1894	29,574	15,118	2,673	17,791	(2,918)	44,447
1895	24,289	16,032	2,156	18,188	(1,337)	41,140
1896	29,987	16,286	3,320	19,606	(1,548)	46,045
1897	28,059	16,801	6,021	22,822	(3,141)	47,740
1898	31,270	16,862	6,165	23,027	838	55,135
1899	33,331	17,010	8,202	25,212	271	58,814
1900	38,155	17,385	8,371	25,756	1,690	65,601

Table 6.9.   (continued)

| Year | Wages or Salaries | Property Income | | | Net Savings | GDP at Factor Cost |
		Interest Payments	Dividend Payments	Total		
1901	40,697	17,867	8,700	26,567	846	68,110
1902	46,765	18,296	9,373	27,669	4,340	78,774
1903	55,668	18,747	11,422	30,169	4,912	90,749
1904	60,468	20,904	11,637	32,541	1,750	94,759
1905	66,411	22,477	13,603	36,080	456	102,947
1906	73,222	23,466	15,603	39,069	8,020	120,311
1907	90,402	24,109	19,247	43,256	14,924	148,682
1908	91,817	25,140	19,216	44,356	12,672	148,845
1909	91,861	26,370	21,742	48,112	11,715	151,688
1910	98,938	27,782	23,534	51,316	23,241	173,495
1911	114,599	27,070	30,907	57,977	27,452	200,028
1912	142,677	29,324	32,258	61,582	33,254	237,513
1913	173,485	33,604	34,585	68,189	38,786	280,460
1914	167,953	36,128	39,856	75,984	16,189	260,126
1915	135,306	39,253	42,385	81,538	12,710	229,654
1916	149,887	36,621	45,749	82,370	41,348	273,605
1917	182,955	57,908	39,203	97,111	30,495	310,561
1918	216,865	61,026	39,037	100,063	(4,326)	312,602
1919	319,117	70,990	40,911	111,901	(31,469)	399,549
1920	395,554	77,888	41,863	119,751	(65,401)	449,904
1921	349,552	96,225	40,022	136,247	(64,161)	421,638
1922	329,180	103,296	42,218	145,514	(41,269)	433,425
1923	349,470	80,971	43,680	124,651	(27,977)	446,144
1924	339,584	88,593	45,481	134,074	(39,736)	433,922
1925	340,856	92,378	47,708	140,086	(12,791)	468,151
1926	364,862	94,658	50,996	145,654	11,228	521,744

Bibliography of Sources Cited in Chapter 6

Allard, Desmond, "Canadian Carriers of the Great Lakes: The CSL Story", *Canadian Shipping and Marine Engineering* (Toronto, November, 1971), A Maclean-Hunter Publication.

Standard and Poor's Industry Surveys, New York: Standard and Poor's Corporation.

Moody's Manual of Railroads and Corporation Securities, New York: Poor's Publishing Corporation.

Fishlow, Albert, *American Railroads and the Transformation of the Ante Bellum Economic* (Cambridge, Mass: Harvard University Press, 1965).

Pomeroy, L.A., Jr., "The Bulk Freight Vessel", *Quarterly Journal of the Great Lakes Historical Society*, "Inland Seas", Volume 23, Summer, 1967, No. 2, pp. 191-200.

Chapter 7. Finance, Insurance, and Real Estate

THOMAS K. RYMES

Gross Domestic Product in the Finance, Insurance, and Real Estate Industry, 1870-1926

The GDP_f for this industry becomes very small before 1890 and the data scarce. Therefore the estimates are made in detail only for 1891 to 1926. The estimates are extrapolated from 1891 to 1870 on the basis of a few financial series as will be explained later.

Published official Statistics Canada estimates of gross domestic product at factor cost for the Finance, Insurance and Real Estate Industry appear in Statistics Canada, *National Income and Expenditure Accounts, 1926-1974, Volume I* (hereafter called the Orange Book). For the years 1926-1930, the estimates are those given in the entry (a) of each category in Table 7.1.

Since these estimates for gross domestic product at factor cost in finance, insurance, and real estate (GDP_f) are those into which those produced by this project must tie, it is useful to examine their content and historical background more closely. Accordingly, in Table 7.1, I set out the Orange Book, the Brown Book (DBS, *National Accounts Income and Expenditure 1926-1956*), and such worksheet level estimates (WSS) as I was able to find from Statistics Canada.

This part of the Queen's University Project deals only with the Finance, Insurance and Real Estate Industry and does not include the estimates of gross market and imputed rents on residential capital prepared by Dr. Marion Steele of the University of Guelph.

I would like to thank two research assistants who worked one after another on the project, Messrs D. Whillans and R. Pant, and the following, who provided me with invaluable assistance and archival information I would not have otherwise obtained: Mr. D.M. Macpherson, Assistant to the Inspector General Banks; M. Claude Doucet, Archives Assistant, Bank of Nova Scotia, Toronto; Mr. G.M. Rostrup, Corporate Reporting Manager and Mr. Freeman Clowery, Archivist, Bank of Montreal, Montreal; and Mr. Dave Jones, formerly of Statistics Canada.

Table 7.1. Gross Domestic Product at Factor Cost by Factor Component, 1926-1930
(millions of dollars)

		1926	1927	1928	1929	1930
(1)	Labour income					
	(a) Orange Book	103	112	128	142	139
	(b) Brown Book	103	112	128	142	139
	(c) WSS	103	112	128	142	139
(2)	Net income of non-farm unincorporated business					
	(a)	167	176	186	181	170
	(b)	16	19	27	31	24
	(c)	16	19	27	31	24
(3)	Corporate profits before taxes					
	(a)	58	67	72	82	55
	(b)	58	67	72	83	55
	(c)	58	66	67	77	49
(4)	Profits and other investment income					
	(a)	84	98	106	119	99
	(b)	235	255	209	268	245
	(c)	179	189	197	191	196
(5)	Inventory valuation adjustment					
(6)	Capital consumption allowances and miscellaneous valuation adjustments					
	(a)					
	(b)					
	(c)	138	142	149	160	160
(7)	GDP_f					
	(a)	497	532	575	607	578
	(b)	492	528	513	601	568
	(c)	492	528	568	601	568

Sources and comments: The rows (a), (b), and (c) are designated respectively the Orange Book,
the Brown Book, and such worksheet level estimates as I was able to find (with the assistance

of Dave Jones). With respect to: "labour income", row (a) has as its source the Orange Book, Table 29, (b) the Brown Book, T.22 and (c) worksheets (WSS); "net income of non-farm unincorporated business" (a) the Orange Book figures (Table 31) include the net rents on residential real estate (paid and imputed) in tenant- and owner- occupied residential real estate, (b) the Brown Book, T.24 and (c) WSS; "corporate profits before taxes" (a) the Orange Book, Table 34, (b) Brown Book, T.27, (c) WSS; "investment income" (a) Orange Book, Table 30, designated as profits and interest, and miscellaneous investment income, (b) Brown Book, T.23 designated as profits, *rent*, interest, dividend and miscellaneous investment income, (c) WSS, designated as rent, interest, dividend and miscellaneous investment income (not including corporate profits); no estimate is made for the inventory valuation adjustment (IVA) for this industry; "capital consumption allowances and miscellaneous valuation adjustments": not published in (a) or (b) but available at the worksheet level of detail (largely the estimated capital consumption allowances on residential real estate).

With respect to the Brown Book figure for GDP_f for 1928, 7(b) the number 513 should have been 568 as given by the WSS (this error being noted on the WSS). The error as published occurred also in Brown Book, Investment income for 1928 which, as 209, should be 264. By means of comparing these sources, it is possible to obtain estimates in greater detail. For example, an estimate of the net rents can be obtained by subtracting either lines 2(b) or 2(c) from 2(a).

	1926	1927	1928	1929	1930
2(a)	167	176	186	181	170
subtract 2(b) or 2(c)	16	19	27	31	24
Estimate net rents	151	157	159	150	146

Furthermore, the investment income data can be roughly reconciled. The additions of rows 3(c) and 4(c) corporate profits and rents, interest, dividend and miscellaneous investment income ought to give the investment income as published in the Brown Book

	1926	1927	1928	1929	1930
3(c)	58	66	67	77	49
add 4(c)	179	189	197	191	196
	237	255	264	268	245
4(b) for comparison	235	255	209	268	245

and the figure for 4(b) 1928 ought to be 264 as previously indicated. If from 4(c) one deducts our estimate for net rents, one obtains an estimate of the interest, dividend and other miscellaneous investment income arising in this industry and then if one adds to this the information on corporate profits first as published (rows 3(a) or 3(b)) or on the WSS (rows 3(c)), one has:

	1926	1927	1928	1929	1930
4(c)	179	189	197	191	196
less estimate of net rents	151	157	159	150	146
Interest, dividends, and					
other investment income	28	32	38	41	50
add 3(a)	58	67	72	82	55
	86	99	110	123	105
cf., 4(a) Investment income	84	98	106	119	99

or

	1926	1927	1928	1929	1930
Interest, dividends, etc. – estimate	28	32	38	41	50
add 3(c)	58	66	67	77	49
	86	98	105	118	99
cf., 4(a) Investment income	84	98	106	119	99

If the published corporate profits are correct, then our estimates of interest, dividends, etc., are, in general, somewhat too high.

Taking into account that the labour income figures appear firm — at least from WSS to published figures — I reconstruct below GDP_f and its components for the industry (based on the procedures outlined above).

Table 7.2. Estimated GDP_f by Factor Components (millions of dollars)

	1926	1927	1928	1929	1930
Labour income	103	112	128	142	139
Net income of non-farm					
unincorporated business	16	19	27	31	24
Interest, dividends, etc. (estimate)	28	32	38	41	50
Corporate profits	58	67	72	82	55
Net rents (estimate)	151	157	159	150	146
Capital consumption allowances	138	142	149	160	160
Total GDP_f	494	529	573	606	574
GDP_f (a)	497	532	575	607	578
(b) as corrected	492	528	568	601	568

Table 7.2 is used to shed light on the basic problems confronting this project for this industry. First, I assume that the WSS capital consumption allowances (CCA) may be used to

derive estimates of net domestic product at factor cost in this industry (NDP_f).

	1926	1927	1928	1929	1930
GDP_f (a)	497	532	575	607	578
subtract CCA	138	142	149	160	160
NDP_f (est.)	359*	390	426	447	418
CCA ÷ GDP_f (a), %	27.8	26.7	25.9	26.3	27.7

* In D. Jones, "Canada: Estimates of Net Domestic Income at Factor Cost and Labour Income by Industry, 1919-26" mimeo April 1961, the figure of $381 is reported for 1926 (Jones reports the same figure for labour incomes $103 as it is in this report) and allows as how his figure includes the net imputed rent of government buildings.

If I assume that the net rents pertain largely to residential real estate (and similarly for the capital consumption allowances) and bearing in mind that there is *assumed* to be no labour income for residential real estate, I have:

	1926	1927	1928	1929	1930
NDP_f (estimate)	359	390	426	447	418
less Net rents	151	157	159	150	146
NDP_f (ex-residential real estate) (estimate)	208	233	267	297	272
less Labour income	103	112	128	142	139
Net non-labour income (ex-residential real estate)	105	121	139	155	133
Labour income ÷ GDP_f (a), %	20.7	21.0	22.2	23.4	24.0
Labour income ÷ NDP_f , %	28.6	28.7	30.0	31.8	33.3
Labour income ÷ NDP_f (ex-residential real estate), %	49.5	48.1	47.9	47.8	51.1

These rough calculations indicate (if the argument that net rents and capital consumption allowances pertain largely to residential real estate is correct) that historical estimates of GDP_f in the Finance, Insurance and Real Estate industries are required to focus on three main areas

(i)   Labour income arising in the Finance and Insurance industries
(ii) Non-labour income arising in the Finance and Insurance industries
(iii) Non-labour income arising in the Real Estate Industry

In this report, I focus only on areas (i) and (ii) but I provide some estimate of labour income in the Real Estate Industry.

(i) Labour Income

As is well known, the early (1926-1930) estimates of National Income which concern us were prepared by Sydney B. Smith and, in particular, for the Finance, Insurance and Real Estate Industry, by R.G. Bangs.[1] Bangs' estimates of income originating in this Industry are based on post-distribution concepts, not the pre-distribution concept of GDP_f by industry which lies behind the official estimates outlined in Tables 7.1 and 7.2. With respect to Labour income for the Finance, Insurance and Real Estate Industry, I provide in Table 7.3, estimates by Bangs for the period 1919-1930, based on an examination of his worksheets and final compilation sheets in Statistics Canada files (again, I express my thanks to Dave Jones for his help in locating these materials). It is clear from Table 7.3 that, for this Industry, the estimates of Labour income for the Insurance and Banking industries are all important.[2]

Labour Income: Insurance. SIC 806 and 808

With respect to Labour income for Insurance, Bangs obtained, for the period 1919-36, data on salaries, wages and commissions directly from the Canadian Life Insurance Officers' Association. For 1937-39, the data for Life Insurance was obtained from the Reports of the Superintendent of Insurance and Insurance Branches of the provinces of Ontario, Quebec and Manitoba. An adjustment was made for the fact that the reported salaries and wages and commissions in the Superintendent reports were for the total operations of the companies both inside and outside Canada.

For Fraternal and Mutual Benefit Societies, data for the period of concern in this study were obtained from the Reports of the Superintendent of Insurance and Insurance Branches of the provinces of Ontario, Quebec and Manitoba.

For Fire and Casualty Insurance, again the same sources as for Fraternal and Mutual Benefit Societies were used and again an adjustment was made for the fact that the reported figures were for the total operations of the reporting companies.

For this Project, a procedure, similar to that of Bangs was pursued. Company by company reports to the Superintendent of Insurance for Dominion registered Life, Fire and Casualty and Fraternal and Mutual Benefit Societies were tabulated and examined for the years 1890-1931 (provincial data for Ontario and B.C. were tabulated by company only for selected years). For purpose of comparison with Bangs' estimates, the Dominion registered company data tabulated by this Project, together with Bangs' estimates, are reported in Table 7.4 for Life Insurance.

---

[1]   See DBS, *National Income of Canada 1919-1938, Part I* (Ottawa: Department of Trade and Commerce, 1941, unpublished).

[2]   The percentage contributions of Insurance and Banking for 1926-1930 to estimated Labour income is as follows:

	1926	1927	1928	1929	1930
Insurance	60.1	60.1	59.9	60.5	59.8
Banking	35.6	35.5	35.4	34.5	34.9
Total	95.7	95.6	95.3	95.0	94.7

though not on Bangs' worksheets (see below).

Table 7.3. Labour Income: R.G. Bangs' Estimates; Finance, Insurance and Real Estate Industry, 1919-1930
(thousands of dollars)

	1919	1920	1921	1922	1923	1924	1925	1926	1927	1928	1929	1930
(a) Insurance	36,960	45,052	45,845	45,444	48,756	51,658	56,693	60,546	64,292	69,660	74,488	75,610
(b) Contributions to pension funds	15	20	26	68	80	127	173	185	219	240	269	290
(c) (a)+(b)	36,975	45,072	45,871	45,512	48,836	51,785	56,866	60,731	64,511	69,900	74,757	75,900
(d) Banking	34,567	38,524	35,790	33,488	33,304	33,668	35,071	35,970	38,123	41,287	42,602	44,252
(e) Loan + mortgage cos.	1,110	1,133	1,192	1,171	1,358	1,306	1,255	1,321	1,340	1,338	1,387	1,385
(f) Trust companies	1,900	2,091	2,395	2,338	2,427	2,696	2,838	3,096	3,440	4,190	4,802	5,289
(g) Total: (c)+(d)+(e)+(f)	74,552	86,820	85,248	82,509	85,925	89,455	96,030	101,118	107,414	116,715	123,548	126,826
(h) Labour income: Table 7.1								103	112	128	142	139

Sources:

(a) Bang's compilation sheet "National Income, 1919-1939 — Insurance". Bangs, given his post-distribution concept, deducted contributions to pension funds which I have added back.

(d) Bang's compilation sheet "National Income (1919-1939) — Banking"

(e) Bang's compilation sheet "National Income (1919-1939) — Loan and Mortgage Companies"

(f) Bang's compilation sheet "National Income (1919-1939) — Trust Companies"

(g) My totals.

(h) The labour income for this Industry as reported in Table 7.1. The discrepancy between Bangs' totals and the published figure is due to labour income in miscellaneous finance industries (primarily stock brokers, real estate), estimates of which for this early period must be regarded as most tenuous. See the Brown Book, paragraphs 217, 231. See text below.

Labour Income: Life Insurance SIC 806

The Project's tabulations of salaries and fees and commissions and brokerage fees are reported first in Table 7.4. Officers of the Superintendent of Insurance were not able to provide us with copies of the schedules used by the reporting companies but recent schedules were examined together with instructions to the reporting companies to ascertain the following:

For example, from Form Ins.54 Canadian Life, Exhibit 9 dealing with General and Investment Expense: Salaries, wages and allowances include head and branch office employee salaries and wages, managers and agents salaries and directors fees. The contributions to pension plans, etc., were not tabulated since they were a small, vanishingly small, component of Labour Income for the period covered by this Project (See Table 7.3 line (b)). No special instructions worth noting are provided in the instructions to the reporting companies, 1959: Exhibit 2 consists of commissions on Insurance Premiums and Annuity Considerations and again the instructions provide no information worthy of special consideration.

For this project, it was assumed that part of Commissions, etc., paid to agents, etc., not resident in Canada would be captured by adjusting the reported Commissions by the ratio of Canadian premiums to total premiums paid as in the reports of the Superintendent. The adjusted Commissions, etc., are shown in the third section of Table 7.4. Bangs' estimates are shown in the second section of the Table.[3]

Some comments on Table 7.4 follow. The Projects' estimates (tabulations) of salaries and wages are for the early years below those reported to, and used by, Bangs by the Canadian Life Insurance Officers Association while for later years the Project's tabulations are somewhat higher. Conceptually, the Project's tabulation should always be above those provided by the CLIO Association. When the Project's tabulations of commissions and brokerage fees are adjusted in the manner outlined, the two series showed remarkable similarity in level and behaviour (except for the year 1927, but a check of the original tabulations, particularly for Canadian Life companies, revealed no error in the Project's tabulations). When Bangs' estimates and those of the Project for labour income are compared, again there is exhibited similarity with respect to level and movement (again excluding the recalcitrant 1927 observation). This is exhibited on the Chart for Table 7.4.

Accordingly, the Project's estimates of labour income in the Life Insurance industry are accepted and are carried back to 1891. See Table 7.9.

Labour Income: Fire and Casualty Insurance SIC 808

In Table 7.5 labour income for the Fire and Casualty Insurance industry, as estimated by this Project and Bangs are reported. With respect to that Table, for Bangs' work, lines (a), (b), (d) and (e) are obtained from final summaries (initialled by Bangs) whereas line (h) is from his final compilations sheet for income originating. The adjustment for Bangs' estimates for provincially registered companies is made to compare with the Project's tabulations which are for Dominion registered companies reporting to the Superintendent of Insurance.

The salaries and wages figures from Bangs and the Project exhibit the same level and movement (as Chart to Table 7.5 shows) with Bangs' estimates being slightly lower throughout. (This is to be expected because of the adjustment Bangs made to the reported Salaries and wages of Fire and Casualty Insurance Companies). The close similarity of the two series, however, is

---

3   The source of Bangs' estimates is *National Income of Canada*, Disbursements made in Canada by Life Insurance Companies, compiled by the Canadian Life Insurance Officers Association, 1938.

Table 7.4. Labour Income: Life Insurance Industry, 1919 to 1931
R.G. Bangs' Estimates and Project Estimates
(thousands of dollars)

	1919	1920	1921	1922	1923	1924	1925	1926	1927	1928	1929	1930	1931
Project													
(a) Salaries + fees	5,926	6,996	7,523	9,253	10,111	12,000	13,650	14,669	16,743	18,363	21,546	24,636	25,497
(b) Commissions + brokerage	13,977	15,516	16,697	14,256	16,554	19,666	22,824	24,783	39,937	34,565	39,850	39,081	33,572
Bangs													
(a) Salaries + wages	6,847	7,991	8,999	10,260	11,244	13,150	15,088	16,561	17,609	19,139	21,367	23,081	23,351
(b) Commissions	10,464	12,480	11,793	10,592	11,576	13,023	14,221	15,618	16,984	18,209	19,503	18,588	16,573
(c) Total: Bangs	17,311	20,471	20,792	20,852	22,820	26,173	29,309	32,179	34,593	37,348	40,870	41,669	39,924
Project													
(c) Commissions + brokerage (adjusted)	10,217	11,280	11,872	10,264	11,704	13,137	15,475	15,316	23,603	19,587	21,160	20,283	16,920
Total:													
Project (a)+(c)	16,143	18,276	19,395	19,517	21,815	25,137	29,125	29,985	40,346	37,950	42,706	44,919	42,417

Chart for Table 7.4

Labour Income: Life Insurance
1919-1931

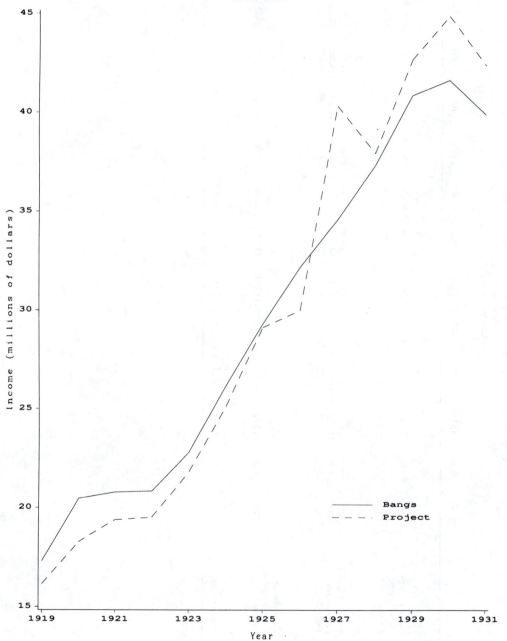

Table 7.5. Labour Income: Fire and Casualty Insurance Industry, 1919 to 1931
R.G. Bangs' Estimates and Project Estimates
(values in thousands of dollars)

	1919	1920	1921	1922	1923	1924	1925	1926	1927	1928	1929	1930	1931
Project													
(a) Salaries + fees	4,588	5,527	6,517	6,650	6,644	6,353	7,612	7,087	7,481	8,040	8,953	9,386	9,293
(b) Commissions	10,062	12,766	11,899	12,246	13,386	13,075	15,194	15,765	15,861	17,146	17,261	16,601	15,882
(c) Commissions (adjusted)	5,606	8,048	8,036	7,736	7,888	7,382	9,316	9,812	9,938	11,115	11,009	10,565	10,101
(d) Labour income: (a)+(c)	10,194	13,575	14,553	14,386	14,532	13,735	16,928	16,899	17,419	19,155	19,962	19,951	19,394
Bangs													
(a) Salaries + Wages	5,012	6,177	6,973	7,019	7,096	7,217	7,481	7,671	7,642	8,358	8,846	9,722	9,756
(b) Provincial companies	755	794	986	814	690	623	735	786	631	662	583	935	999
(c) (a)-(b)	4,257	5,383	5,987	6,205	6,406	6,594	6,746	6,885	7,011	7,696	8,263	8,787	8,757
(d) Commissions	13,882	17,112	16,847	16,541	17,424	17,009	18,476	19,274	20,628	22,505	23,375	22,921	21,450
(e) Provincial companies	1,323	1,252	1,512	1,121	921	895	1,081	1,271	1,203	1,261	1,145	1,588	1,614
(f) (d)-(e)	12,559	15,860	15,335	15,420	16,503	16,114	17,395	18,003	19,425	21,244	22,230	21,333	19,836
(g) Labour Income (a)+(d)	18,894	23,289	23,820	23,560	24,520	24,226	25,957	26,945	28,270	30,863	32,191	32,643	31,206
(h) Labour Income Bangs' final	18,538	23,146	23,608	23,372	24,560	24,123	25,937	26,958	28,254	30,862	32,144	32,626	30,903
Project: Provincial adjustment													
(i) Bangs (b) + (c), %	17.7	14.8	16.5	13.1	10.8	9.4	10.9	11.4	9.0	8.6	7.1	10.6	11.4
(j) Bangs (e) + (f), %	10.5	7.9	9.9	7.3	5.6	5.6	6.2	7.1	6.2	5.9	5.2	7.4	8.1
Labour Income: Final (Dom. + prov.)													
(k) Salaries + wages: P(a)+B(b)	5,343	6,321	7,503	7,464	7,334	6,976	8,347	7,873	8,112	8,702	9,536	10,321	10,292
(l) Commissions: P(c)+B(e)	6,929	9,300	9,548	8,857	8,809	8,277	10,397	11,083	11,141	12,376	12,154	12,153	11,715
(m) Total: (k)+(l)	12,272	15,621	17,051	16,321	16,143	15,253	18,744	18,956	19,253	21,078	21,690	22,474	22,007

Chart for Table 7.5

Labour Income: Fire and Casualty
Insurance Industry, 1919-1931

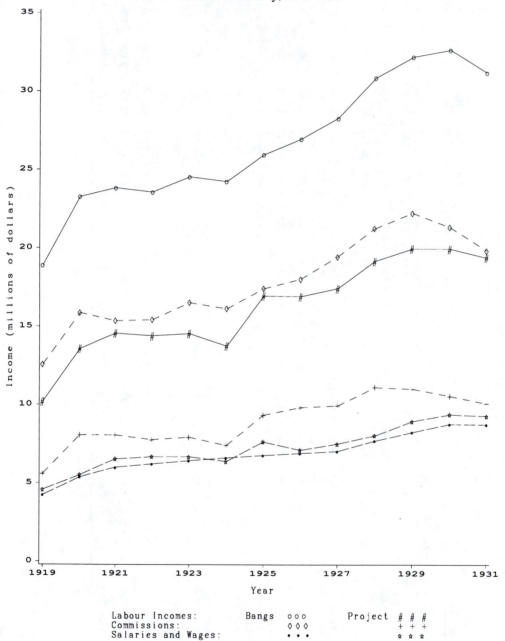

Labour Incomes:	Bangs	o o o	Project	# # #
Commissions:		◊ ◊ ◊		+ + +
Salaries and Wages:		• • •		☆ ☆ ☆

evidence that the source data behind them is the same — that is, the tabulations from the Reports of the Superintendent of Insurance.

The Commissions data from Bangs and the Project, while exhibiting similar movement (cf. Chart to Table 7.5), have a serious discrepancy with respect to the level — a discrepancy I have been unable to resolve. With respect to Table 7.5, one observes first for the Project a level of commissions, etc., [line (b) for Project] *as tabulated* (i.e., unadjusted for the non-Canadian business of the companies) which always lie below those of Bangs as adjusted by Bangs [line (f) for Bangs]. As a consequence when the Project's tabulations are adjusted [line (c) for Project] the estimate of Commissions, etc., component of Labour Income for the Project lies *substantially* below that of Bangs. Indeed, for the period 1926-1931, the discrepancy as an annual average is in the order of $10 million.

It is possible to examine the discrepancy more closely. In Table 7.6A, for the years 1919-1921, the Project's and Bangs' estimates for salaries and wages and commissions are set out by company of ownership nationality. Again, the similarity for the salaries and wages data (with Bangs' adjustment) offers evidence confirming that the original tabulations are drawn from the same sources. The difference, however, for commissions — and the differences appear substantial regardless of the nationality of ownership — remains and implies that Bangs adjustment still fails to pull the estimates below the tabulated figures (which is what one would expect).

I have found it impossible to account for this discrepancy. In my opinion, Bangs' estimates for commissions are simply too high and I have used therefore the Project's estimates. As a consequence, it must be remembered that the official published estimates of labour income for the Finance, Insurance and Real Estate Industry are also too high to the extent Bangs' estimates are used therein.

The final section of Table 7.5 shows the adjustment made to the Projects' estimates to account for provincially registered Fire and Casualty Insurance Companies. A check was provided, as mentioned, by the Project's tabulations of insurance companies provincially registered for Ontario and British Columbia, and it was decided to accept Bangs' estimates for this (small) component of Labour income for Fire and Casualty Insurance. Bangs' estimates were then extrapolated historically on the Project's tabulations. The resultant estimates of salaries and wages component stands slightly above Bangs but the "Commissions, etc.", component substantially below. The Project's estimates of Labour income in the Fire and Casualty Insurance industry are reported in Table 7.9.

Labour Income: Fraternal, Benefit Societies SIC 808

This is a very small component of the labour income arising in the Insurance industry. Again, the Project's tabulations from the Reports of the Superintendent of Insurance for fraternal, mutual and pension benefit societies are compared in Table 7.6B (and accompanying Chart) with Bangs estimates. (No adjustment was made by Bangs to his tabulations from the reports for income (labour) paid to nonresidents.)

With the exception of 1931 (when the Project's tabulations of commissions appear suspect), the two series again show the same movement but again Bangs' series is much higher. In this case, it would appear that the important additions are the estimates for provincially registered fraternal, benefit societies. The evidence for this conjecture is provided in Table 7.7A. In that table, estimates of salaries and wages and commissions for all insurance companies reporting to the Insurance Branch of the Province of Ontario are noted for selected years around which the Project's tabulations for Dominion registered companies and Bangs' estimates can be made.

Table 7.6A

Examination of Commissions Discrepancy for Fire and Casualty Insurance
Companies (Dominion registered), Bangs vs. Project Estimates, 1919-1921.
(thousands of dollars)

		1919	1920	1921
Project:	Salaries and wages:			
	Fire insurance:			
	Canadian companies	1,693	2,066	2,284
	American companies	603	820	1,081
	British companies	1,635	1,980	2,492
	Casualty insurance:			
	Canadian companies	353	382	278
	Foreign companies	303	279	381
	Totals:			
	Canadian companies	2,046	2,448	2,562
	British companies	1,635	1,980	2,492
	Foreign companies (incl. Amer.)	906	1,099	1,462
	(cf. Table 7.5)	4,588	5,527	6,516
Bangs:	Salaries and wages:			
	Fire and casualty insurance:			
	Canadian companies	1,871	2,201	2,326
	British companies	1,583	2,114	2,309
	Foreign companies	803	1,068	1,352
	(cf. Table 7.5)	4,257	5,383	5,987
Project:	Commissions (Tabulated):			
	Fire insurance:			
	Canadian companies	1,985	2,368	2,134
	American companies	2,744	3,609	3,477
	British companies	4,182	5,392	4,943
	Casualty insurance:			
	Canadian companies	385	466	351
	Foreign companies	765	932	993
	Totals:			
	Canadian companies	2,370	2,834	2,485
	British companies	4,182	5,392	4,943
	Foreign companies (incl. Amer.)	3,509	4,541	4,470
	(cf. Table 7.5)	10,061	12,767	11,898
Bangs:	Commissions (adjusted):			
	Fire and Casualty insurance:			
	Canadian companies	3,025	3,203	3,266
	British companies	5,350	7,240	6,828
	Foreign companies	4,184	5,417	5,241
	(cf. Table 7.5)	12,559	15,860	15,335

Sources: Project – Tabulations.
          Bangs   – Summary WSS initialled by Bangs.

483

Table 7.6B. Labour Income: Fraternal, Mutual and Pension Benefit Societies, 1919 to 1931
R.G. Bangs' Estimates and Project Estimates
(thousands of dollars)

	1919	1920	1921	1922	1923	1924	1925	1926	1927	1928	1929	1930	1931
Project													
(a) Salaries + fees	470	460	492	519	561	596	634	578	639	670	661	612	617
(b) Commissions	95	290	274	218	207	226	339	348	325	333	329	272	509
(c) (a)+(b)	565	750	766	737	768	822	973	926	964	1,003	990	884	1,126
Bangs													
Salaries + Commissions	1,126	1,455	1,471	1,388	1,456	1,489	1,620	1,594	1,664	1,690	1,743	1,605	1,586

Chart for Table 7.6B

Labour Income: Fraternal, Benefit Societies,
Salaries and Commissions, 1919-1931

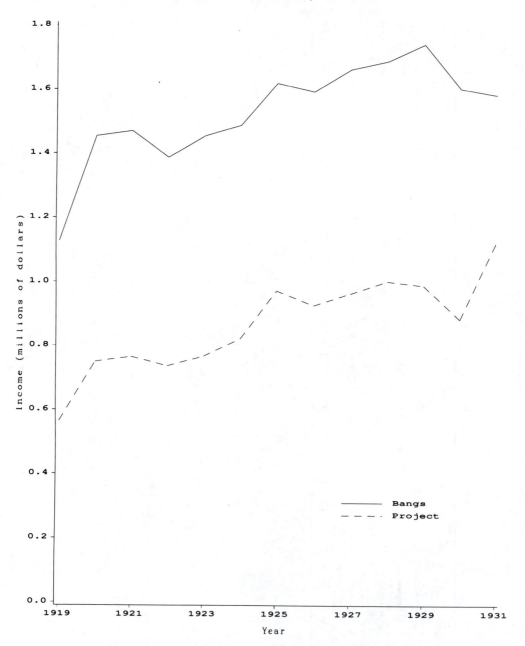

Table 7.7A

Selected Data for the Ontario Insurance Industry
(thousands of dollars)

	1911	1912	1913	1914	1915	1916	1917	1918	1919
Salaries and wages									
(a) All companies	320	364	324	687	486	440	410	270	386
(b) Friendly societies	150	159	166	470	173	195	183	201	301
(c) (b) ÷ (a), %	46.9	43.7	51.2	68.4	35.6	44.3	44.6	74.4	78.0
Commissions									
(a) All companies	766	864	689	815	842	786	806	779	850
(b) Friendly societies	284	389	156	293	253	220	325	258	298
(c) (b) ÷ (a), %	37.1	45.0	22.6	36.0	30.0	28.0	40.3	33.1	35.1

In addition to the importance of the Friendly societies, provincially registered fire insurance companies are the other predominant sector of the Ontario insurance industry for this period (and the importance of the provincial estimates has already been noted for the Fire and Casualty Insurance Industry). Some data for selected years for B.C. confirm the impression exhibited in Table 7.7A but it must be pointed out that the Project's provincial tabulations (because of the frequency of reclassification in both the Ontario and B.C. data) present no more than an impressionistic view of the relative importance of fraternal, benefit societies at the provincial *vis-à-vis* the Dominion level.

Based on these impressions, however, it was decided to accept Bangs' estimates as firm and to extrapolate them backwards beyond 1919 on the basis of the Project's tabulations for Dominion registered companies. These estimates are provided in Table 7.9.

Labour Income: Banking SIC 802

The official estimates for this Industry are again based on Bangs' data, which are provided in Table 7.7B. The sources of Bangs' data are as follows: first, with respect to the Ontario and Alberta Provincial Postal Banks, the Montreal City and District Savings Banks and the co-operative Peoples Bank, the estimates — to the best of my knowledge — are arbitrary and, given their vanishingly small importance and the manner in which the chartered bank estimates were prepared, can be ignored for the early period 1919-1925. The estimates of wages, salaries and allowances for the chartered banks for the period 1926 and following years were apparently obtained from the Canadian Bankers Association (CBA) (though I could find no file in Bangs' records containing these estimates nor any descriptions by the CBA as to how they were prepared). The CBA estimates were run back to 1919 on the basis of Canadian dollar deposit liabilities of the chartered banks.

In this section of the report, I concentrate on the estimates for the chartered banks. As is well known, the principal difficulty is that, though the reported assets and liabilities of the banks are available through the monthly reports of the Inspector General of Banks and earlier historical records of agencies to whom the banks were required to report,[4] with the exception of annual reports to shareholders which contain virtually no revenue and expense data for the early period and a net profit to shareholders figure which is worthless (for our purposes), the data available for chartered banks with respect to wages and salaries are not available. Through the Inspector General's office and the archives of the Bank of Nova Scotia and the Bank of Montreal, data are available which permitted this Project to attempt an estimate of Labour income for its chartered banks back to 1890.

First, from the Inspector General's Office, I received the following information (with respect to the financial years of the reporting banks) — data in millions of dollars:

		1929	1930	1931
Remuneration to employees		47.0	48.0	45.0
Contributions to pension fund		1.1	1.3	1.3
	Total	48.1	49.3	46.3
Bangs (Table 7.7B line (g) includes pension fund contributions)		42.6	44.3	41.5

I was advised by the Inspector General's Office that ten banks reported in 1930 and 1931 and nine in 1929 (the data not being available for all ten banks). This limited information is based on the fact that the banks did not begin reporting income and expense data to the Inspector General until 1929.

From these data it would appear that the estimates Bangs used (from the CBA) underestimated the labour income in banking, at least for the years 1929-1931, assuming that the difference is not entirely accounted for by foreign operations. Second, there are some useful data in the archives of the Bank of Nova Scotia (Head Office, Toronto).[5] In these archives, we obtained profit and loss data, 1893-1927,[6] net profit data (which, though this is not clear, may not be that reported to the shareholders) for the years 1876-1914,[7] a summary of current charges, including salaries, taxes, rents and number of staff, 1893-1927,[8] and salaries and number of staff, 1882-1914.[9] (In these last two sources, for the overlap period 1893-1914, the data are the same.) Thus, there is available from the Bank of Nova Scotia, a series on labour income for the whole

---

[4] See C.A. Curtis, "Banking Statistics in Canada," *Statistical Contributions to Canadian Economic History*, Vol. 1 (Toronto: Macmillan, 1931).

[5] We examined evidence provided by the Home Bank to the Supreme Court, Public Archives, File No-MG 23 II-11 and though there are some revenue and expense data for half-years 1913-23 they were not too useful for our purposes.

[6] BNS Statistics Ledger 8, (Archives, BNS, Toronto)

[7] BNS Statistics, Ledger 3, 123 (Archives, BNS, Toronto).

[8] BNS Statistics, Ledger 3, Table 1 (Archives, BNS, Toronto).

[9] BNS Statistics, Ledger 3, 123 (Archives, BNS, Toronto).

Table 7.7B. Labour Income: Banking, 1919 to 1930
R.G. Bangs' Estimates and Project Estimates
(thousands of dollars)

	1919	1920	1921	1922	1923	1924	1925	1926	1927	1928	1929	1930
R.G. Bangs												
Banking:												
(a) Chartered banks	33,900	37,700	35,100	32,800	32,600	33,000	34,350	35,269	37,400	40,500	41,760	43,423
(b) Ontario Provincial				23	53	80	87	102	105	111	126	135
(c) Alberta Provincial	2	5	6	4	4	5	5	6	6	6	6	6
(d) Montreal City and District	150	170	160	160	160	165	170	180	200	220	260	255
(e) Cooperative Peoples Bank	10	11	11	11	11	12	13	15	16	17	18	18
(f) Total: (a) to (e)	34,062	37,886	35,277	32,998	32,828	33,262	34,625	35,572	37,727	40,854	42,170	43,837
(g) Total: final compilations	34,597	38,524	35,790	33,488	33,304	33,668	35,071	35,970	38,123	41,287	42,602	44,252
Project												
Chartered banks	25,373	32,046	31,652	28,626	30,656	32,271	32,245	34,082	35,891	39,654	39,973	42,051
Total Assets: BNS + BM All Banks	.265	.254	.268	.336	.330	.330	.347	.345	.341	.331	.333	.340
Ratio: Labour income to assets	.00900	.01069	.01100	.01120	.01195	.01210	.01172	.01216	.01203			
Project												
Miscellaneous banks (b)+(c)+(d)+(e)	162	186	177	198	228	262	275	303	327	354	410	414

Chart for Table 7.7B

Labour Income: Banking
1919-1930

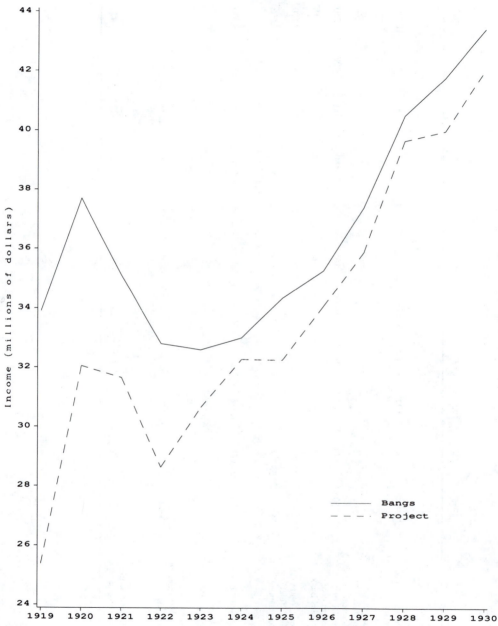

bank (including foreign operations) from 1882-1927.[10]

From the archives of the Bank of Montreal (the vaults in the old Molsons Bank and the archives of the Chief Accountant's Office, including the Bank of Montreal in Montreal), I was able to obtain (with some interpolation), salaries and wages[11] for 1892-1931 and, with some estimation on my part, total expenses 1892-1931, net profits after expenses but including depreciation and transfers to Rest Fund (or additionals to inner reserves), 1892-1931 and other expense items permitting one to tie into net profits as reported to the shareholders of the Bank of Montreal 1896-1931.

Based on these data, I constructed an estimate of Labour income by assuming that

$$W_T = A_T \times \left[\frac{W_{BNS} + W_{BM}}{A_{BNS} + A_{BM}} \right]$$

total Labour income for the chartered banks would be equal to *total* assets multiplied by the ratio of Labour income for the Bank of Nova Scotia and the Bank of Montreal divided by the sum of the total assets for the two banks. A small allowance, based on the data in footnotes 10 and 11 of this report, was made for labour income in foreign branches. The resulting estimates are compared with those of Bangs in Table 7.7B and on the Chart accompanying Table 7.7B.

With respect to Table 7.7B, the Project's estimates are very similar to those of Bangs for the years 1926-1930 (particularly when the adjustment for salaries and wages paid in foreign branches is added back into the Project's estimates), but earlier the Project's estimates fall below those of Bangs. Trials with a number of deposit liabilities data, which it must be remembered were used as an extrapolator for the period prior to 1926, failed to reproduce Bangs' figures. Moreover, the total Canadian dollar liabilities series moved very closely with the total assets figure employed in this study. As reported on Table 7.7B, the ratio of total assets for the two banks to total assets (all banks) fell in 1921 — the only year in which the ratio changed substantially in all years 1890-1930 — but since the ratio of Labour income to total assets for the two banks remained fairly stable, they should not adversely affect the Project's estimates.

It was concluded that the Project's estimates of labour income, based as they are on reliable information for at least two banks, would be accepted and they are provided for the years 1891 to 1931 on Table 7.9. While it should be borne in mind that, compared with the figures supplied by the Inspector General of the Banks, Bangs' estimates may entail an underestimate of the labour income originating amongst the chartered banks, for Bangs' earlier estimates to be accepted as valid would imply, in my opinion, far too high a ratio of labour income to total assets for all

---

10 In only one year (1924) could I find salaries for Canadian Operations and foreign operations [Newfoundland, Jamaica, Cuba and U.S.A. (New York and Chicago)]. The ratio of Canadian to total salaries was .840. For the years 1923-1927, I could find "profits" broken down the same way. The ratios reported were

1923	1924	1925	1926	1927
.507	.543	.450	.513	.610

11 These include director fees, gratuities to officers and are available for foreign branches as well (1892-1913). The ratio of Canadian salaries and wages to total salaries and wages for the Bank of Montreal was

1895	1896	1897	1898	1899	1900	1901	1902	1903	1904	1905	1906	1907	1908	1909
.821	.828	.817	.832	.862	.873	.944	.960	.955	.969	.885	.916	.838	.853	.847

banks when compared to the data obtained from the archives of the Bank of Nova Scotia and the Bank of Montreal.[12]

Labour Income: Miscellaneous Banks SIC 802

As previously indicated, Bangs' estimate include a very small allowance for labour income originating amongst Quebec Savings Banks and provincial government Postal Savings branches. As shown in Table 7.7A these amounted to no more than 0.86% of the estimated labour income of the chartered banks in 1926 and 0.48% in 1919. Bangs' estimates for these miscellaneous banks were accepted and were carried back into the earlier period on the basis of annual Canadian asset data found in the Statistical appendix in E.P. Neufeld, *The Financial System of Canada* (the series for the Quebec Savings Banks). These additional estimates are shown in Table 7.9.

Labour Income: Investment and Loan Industries SIC 804

Compared with insurance and banking, the labour income estimates of these industries are relatively unimportant (cf. Table 7.3) and, for this Project are weak and arbitrary. First, Bangs' estimates for Loan and Mortgage Companies and Trust Companies are accepted as valid. Second, the treatment of the labour income of stock brokers and bond dealers leaves a great deal to be desired.

Bangs' estimates of labour income for Loan and Mortgage companies were based on data in the annual reports of the Ontario Registrar of Loan Corporations and the reports of the Dominion Superintendent of Insurance dealing with "Loan and Trust Companies" and "Small Loan Companies" and for, Trust Companies were based on data from the Ontario Registrar, a summary of financial statements of trust companies in Quebec and again the reports of the Superintendent of Insurance dealing with "Loan and Trust Companies". A rough check on Bangs' data was performed by a comparison of our own data for the Provinces of Ontario and B.C. but the extent of the tabulations which would be necessary to extrapolate Bangs' estimates historically by his procedures was deemed unwarranted. Instead, Bangs' estimates were accepted as valid and extended back on the assets series found in E.P. Neufeld, *op. cit.,* respectively for Building Societies and Mortgage Loan Companies and Trust Companies. As Neufeld points out (pp.583-4) these series cannot be regarded as entirely satisfactory.

The relationship between Bangs' estimates of labour income and Neufeld's asset data are exhibited in Table 7.8.

The labour income for loan and mortgage companies and trust companies is reported in Table 7.9.

An estimate for the labour income originating amongst stock brokers and bond dealers (as part of the Investment and loan industries) was also made by Bangs. The estimates (along with those for Real Estate SIC 809) were very crude and were based on decennial census data and annual interpolators. But the difficulty which arises is that when Bangs' total labour income for the Finance, Insurance and Real Estate Industry is struck, his estimates exceed the published

---

12 There is, on the other hand, some evidence that the tabulated "Labour income" for the Bank of Montreal might be an underestimate since, though for only two years, there are allowances for lunches and dinners appearing in the current expense ledgers of the Bank which, if incorporated into the tabulated "Labour income" of the Bank would raise it respectively 2.3% and 2.59% for the two years. Given the greater relative importance of the salaries and wages paid in foreign branches and the adjustment for them in the Project's estimates, concern over this potential understatement was deemed unwarranted.

official labour income for the Industry. This is illustrated in the following table (units are thousands of dollars except where noted).

	1926	1927	1928	1929	1930
Table 7.3, line (g)	101,118	107,414	116,715	123,548	126,826
Stock and bond dealers	13,300	13,900	15,200	16,600	15,370
Real estate	4,753	5,452	5,891	6,957	4,811
Total (rounded, millions of dollars):					
Bangs	119	127	139	147	147
Orange Book	103	112	128	142	139

Before indicating the Project's procedure with respect to stock and bond dealers and Labour income in real estate, I examine various pieces of information available from the Decennial Censuses.

1931 Census

In the 1931 Census, Vol. V., Table 27 there are reported wage earners for the Finance, Insurance Industry broken down as follows:

	Total Wage Earners	Persons Reporting	Earnings ($ 000's)	Weeks Employed (000's)
Total	82,963	78,278	114,590	3,839
Banking	28,800	28,278	38,401	1,426
Insurance	36,132	32,877	50,510	1,617
Investment and loan	14,225	13,508	21,109	631
Real estate	3,806	3,615	4,569	159

The estimates of earnings of wage earners as reported are blown up (by sex) by the ratio of persons reporting to total wage earners. It yields the following earnings (in thousands of dollars).

Banking	39,117
Insurance	56,534
Investment and loan	22,371
Real estate	4,836
Total	122,858

When contrasted with the figures shown on Table 7.9 the estimates derived by the Project for Banking are remarkably close:

Table 7.8. Labour Income: Loan and Mortgage Companies, and Trust Companies, 1919 to 1930

	1919	1920	1921	1922	1923	1924	1925	1926	1927	1928	1929	1930
Loan and Mortgage Companies												
Bangs * Labour income ($000)	1,110	1,133	1,192	1,171	1,358	1,306	1,255	1,321	1,340	1,338	1,387	1,385
Neufeld-Canadian dollar assets ($mm)	259	277	263	275	274	273	277	289	295	296	287	291
Ratio: Labour income to assets	.00429	.00402	.00453	.00426	.00496	.00478	.00453	.00457	.00464	.00452	.00483	.00476
Trust Companies												
Bangs * Labour income ($000)	1,900	2,091	2,395	2,338	2,427	2,696	2,838	3,096	3,440	4,190	4,802	5,289
Neufeld-Canadian dollar assets ($mm)	67	67	67	83	94	98	104	117	135	154	224	250
Ratio: Labour income to assets	.02836	.03121	.03575	.02817	.02582	.02751	.02729	.02646	.02548	.02721	.02144	.02116

* Initialled sheets and final compilations.

Project	39,846
Census	39,117

for Insurance they are,

Project	66,477
Census	56,534

indicating that the Projects' estimates include some allowances for gainfully occupied labour income not recorded as wage earnings in the Census. For investment and loan activity, however, the divergence is sharp

Project	6,611
Census	22,371

and it is believed that the major missing component here is the labour income for stock brokers and bond dealers.

In the 1931 Census, Vol. VII, Table 40, there are reported the gainfully occupied by 'industry' — but the major difficulty is that clerks, stenographers, messenger boys, etc., *were not* included in the occupational industry classifications as can be seen from the following:

Gainfully Occupied	Males	Females	Total
Finance, insurance	36,262	571	36,833
Officers, finance	35,512	12	35,524
Insurance, officials	3,045	26	3,071
Insurance, agents	17,049	350	17,399
Pawn and money brokers	60	-	60
Real estate agents & dealers	5,518	146	5,664
Stock and bond brokers	4,873	36	4,909

In the 1931 Census, Vol. V, Table 31 wage earners are given by occupation by province. When tabulated, one has

	Persons			Earnings (thousands of $'s)		
	M	F	T	M	F	T
Officials – finance	5,117	0	5,117	17,476	0	17,476
Insurance officials	2,814	20	2,834	11,409	44	11,453
Insurance agents	11,153	224	11,377	19,368	250	19,618
Real estate agents and dealers	1,721	21	1,742	2,845	25	2,870
Stock and bond brokers	2,430	19	2,449	5,771	28	5,799
Others	81	0	81	189	0	189
Totals	23,316	284	23,600	57,058	347	57,405

1921 Census

For other purposes, we examined Vol. III of the 1921 Census, Table 40, dealing with wage earners, 10 years of age and over living in cities of 30,000 and more in population. The data are as follows:

	Persons			Earnings (thousands of $'s)		
	M	F	T	M	F	T
Managers & Superintendents						
Banks	1,983	1	1,984	5,856	2	5,858
Insurance companies	1,105	0	1,105	3,324	0	3,324
Loan + trust companies	379	0	379	1,356	0	1,356
Clerks						
Banks	4,804	3,142	8,546	5,181	3,331	8,512
Insurance, loan, etc.,	3,878	4,906	8,785	3,948	4,361	8,309
Managers and office boys						
Finance	1,034	0	1,034	968	0	968
						28,327

If from such data we combine the information for the banks, we get a figure for 1921 of $14.4 million whereas our own estimate of Labour income for the banking in 1921 is $31.8. Of course, since the data are restricted to cities of 30,000 and more in population,[13] the Census misses all of the labour income in branches of banks in smaller centres.

Finally, we consider the tabulations by the Queen's Project for the 1911 Census. The data as tabulated by us are given in the next Table.

Queen's Project – 1911 Census

	Wage Earnings Reported	Wage Earnings (inflated)	Earnings of the Gainfully Employed
01 Banking	10,793	12,780	12,878
02 Brokers, stock	312	362	516
Brokers, ns	771	907	2,367
04 Fire Insurance	2,463	3,154	3,461
05 Life and accident insurance	2,935	5,130	5,596
06 Loan and trust	815	1,011	1,284
07 Real estate	2,741	3,449	11,603
Totals	20,880	26,793	37,189

---

[13] The cities were Calgary, Edmonton, Halifax, Hamilton, London, Montreal, Ottawa, Quebec, Regina, St. John, Toronto, Vancouver, Victoria, Windsor and Winnipeg.

Compared with the Project, we estimate the total labour income for Banking in 1911 at $10.6 million whereas the Queen's study shows it between $10.8 and $12.9 million. We estimate the labour income for Loan, Mortgage and Trust Companies at $2.2 million whereas the Queen's study shows it between $0.8 and $1.3 million. We estimate labour income for the Insurance industry to $14.5 million whereas the Queen's study (combining 04 and 05) shows it between $5.4 and $9.1. From the Project's worksheets, we have salaries and wages reported to the Dominion Superintendent of Insurance. They are as follows, in thousands of dollars.

		Wages + Salaries	Commissions
1.	Life insurance	3,216	4,765
2.	Fire	1,593	4,875
3.	Accident, etc.	535	1,271
4.	Fraternal	299	64
	Totals	5,643	10,975

Combining just life and accident insurance, one has compared with Queen's study

		Wage Earnings (thousands of dollars)	
		Above	Queen's Study
1.	Life and accident insurance	3,751	5,130
2.	Fire insurance	1,593	3,154

When account is taken of our inclusion of estimates of the labour income component of commissions, etc., we do not believe the Project's estimates are too far off the Queen's study figures which, as the previous pages dealing with the Census data in this Industry indicate, cannot themselves be regarded as firm. Let us recapitulate the information available to use. In the Census information on p. 491, stock and bond dealers are included in Investment and loan 'industries'. From p. 493, among the gainfully occupied it would appear that the number of gainfully occupied classified as real estate agents and dealers and as stock and bond brokers was about equal, roughly confirmed by the provincial data on p. 493 [the 1921 Census data reported on p. 494 is, in my opinion, of little use]. The estimated total earnings are, however, for 1931

Real estate agents and dealers	2,870
Stock and bond brokers	5,799

For 1911 from the Queen's study we have

		Gainfully Occupied (adj.)
Real estate	3,449	11,603
Brokers (combined)	1,269	2,883

From Bangs' worksheets, we obtained the following estimates for Labour income for 1921[14]

Real estate	5,491
Stock and bond dealers	12,000

(Bangs, it must be pointed out, relied partially on the 1921 Census data commented on above).

The basic problems are: the estimated labour income in this part of the Industry is (at least much of it is) indistinguishable from the income of unincorporated enterprises, salesmen commissions, etc., and there is no way a non-arbitrary estimate of the labour income for stock and bond dealers and in the real estate industry can be constructed to my knowledge. As a consequence, it was decided

(i) to accept Bangs' estimates of labour income for these two subcomponents and to extrapolate them back to the Queen's study on the basis of the movement of the estimated Labour income constructed for this Project for Loan and Mortgage and Trust companies — with one alteration: the Queen's study figure for Brokers (1,269) was raised to bring into line with the relationship observed in the 1931 Census and in Bangs' study between labour income for real estate agents and dealers and stock and bond dealers, pointed out above, and (ii) for years prior to 1911, the estimates are combined and run back on the extrapolator mentioned which, of course, implies they move with Neufeld's assets series.

It is to be clearly pointed out that the estimates of labour income for these two subcomponents of the Finance, Insurance and Real Estate Industry must be regarded as highly unsatisfactory. They are provided in Table 7.9.

The GRAND TOTAL of Labour income for the Finance, Insurance and Real Estate Industry also is provided on Table 7.9. The bottom section of Table 7.9 represents, then, our estimates of Labour income for this sector. We may again compare them to other estimates and official figures.

	1919	1920	1921	1922	1923	1924	1925	1926	1927	1928	1929	1930
Project	73	87	91	86	91	96	106	107	122	127	136	138
Official								103	112	128	142	139
D. Jones	77	91	90	84	88	92	97	103				

Sources: Project – Table 7.9
            Official – Table 7.1
            D.H. Jones

Comments: with respect to the official estimates, the only serious discrepancy arises in 1927 when the Project's estimates lie $10 million above the official estimates. The problem arises in the Project's estimates of Commissions for life companies in that year and as stated, a check of the Project's worksheets indicated no error. With respect to Jones' estimates the only serious discrepancy arises in the timing of the peak (1920 – Jones; 1921 – Project). I believe this can be explained by the fact that Jones relied on Bangs' estimates and they pick up peaks in Bangs' series for the Chartered banks and Stock and bond dealers. It must be remembered that (a)

---

[14] Bangs' estimates were accepted back only to 1921 as inspections indicated that the movement for the period 1920 for Stock and bond dealers (even given the inflation of that year) and for real estate in 1919 appeared without foundation.

Bangs' stock and bond dealers series (which was used only back to 1921 for this Project) are arbitrary — the stock and bond series of Bangs moves with an index of stock prices on the TSE (among others) and he received Wages and Salaries data from the Canadian Bankers Association only back to 1926.

(ii) Non-Labour Income

It is well-known that there are interesting conceptual problems connected with the estimation of gross domestic product originating in the Finance, Insurance and Real Estate Industry. Though this is not the place to provide an exhaustive account, a brief mention of them is necessary to shed light on the estimation of non-labour income originating in this Industry constructed by this Project.

First, consider a pure bank (i.e., a financial intermediary engaged in pure financial inter-mediation and thus making up no payrolls other than its own and charging for such services, renting no safety deposit boxes, etc.). Suppose it uses no intermediate inputs of any kind but that the service it provides is produced solely by means of labour and capital. It makes loans on which it receives interest receipts and incurs in so doing deposit liabilities on which it makes interest payments. Its profit (or loss) picture will then be (in simplest possible terms)

Expenditures	Revenues
Interest on deposits	Interest on loans
Wages and salaries	
Depreciation	
Net profits	

Some (or all) of the net profits will be distributed to shareholders, some paid in taxes and the remainder (if any) will be retained by the bank.

Consider figures roughly representative of the chartered banks in Canada.

Current Operating Expenses		Current Operating Earnings	
Interest on deposits	50	Interest on loans	100
Wages and salaries	45		
Depreciation	1		
Net profits before taxes	4		

At first blush, it appears that the gdp_f for this 'bank' would be

Wages and salaries	45
+ Depreciation	1
+ Net profits before taxes	4
	50

Table 7.9. Labour Income: Finance, Insurance and Real Estate Industry, 1891 to 1931

	1891	1892	1893	1894	1895	1896	1897	1898	1899	1900
	(thousands of dollars)									
1) Labour income: Insurance										
(a) Life insurance 806	1,242	1,291	1,440	1,635	1,678	1,677	1,850	2,141	2,302	2,808
(b) Fire and casualty 808	1,674	1,986	2,099	2,109	2,147	2,218	2,214	2,357	2,423	2,840
(c) Fraternal, benefit 808	70	78	88	123	129	343	367	397	433	468
(d) Total: (a)+(b)+(c)	2,986	3,355	3,627	3,867	3,954	4,262	4,431	4,895	5,158	6,116
2) Labour income: Banking										
(e) Chartered banks 802	2,933	2,896	2,822	2,959	2,769	2,815	2,895	3,091	3,177	3,492
(f) Miscellaneous banks 802	39	42	42	42	45	47	47	50	53	59
(g) Total: (e)+(f)	2,972	2,938	2,864	3,001	2,814	2,862	2,942	3,141	3,230	3,551
3) Labour income: Investment and Loan 804										
(h) Loan and mortgage cos.	540	566	579	583	587	591	583	587	579	579
(i) Trust companies	-	-	25	50	75	100	113	170	199	284
(j) Stock brokers and bond dealers										
(j)+(l)	(200)	(300)	(400)	(500)	(600)	741	837	889	1,474	2,103
4) Labour Income: Real Estate 809										
(l) Real estate operators (j+l)										
Total: 1+2+3+4	6,698	7,159	7,495	8,001	8,030	8,556	8,906	9,682	10,640	12,633
SUMMARY (millions of dollars)										
Insurance (d)	3	3	4	4	4	4	4	5	5	6
Banking (g)	3	3	3	3	3	3	3	3	3	4
Investment and loan (k)										
Real estate (l)	1	1	1	1	1	1	2	2	2	3
GRAND TOTAL	7	7	7	8	8	9	9	10	11	13

Totals do not necessarily add owing to rounding

Table 7.9. (continued)

	1901	1902	1903	1904	1905	1906	1907	1908	1909	1910
	(thousands of dollars)									
1) Labour income: Insurance										
(a) Life insurance	3,005	3,400	3,877	4,422	4,849	4,595	4,535	4,753	4,970	5,626
(b) Fire and casualty	2,949	2,783	3,315	4,401	3,985	4,597	4,530	4,579	4,410	6,550
(c) Fraternal, benefit	491	480	508	540	561	583	612	646	690	696
(d) Total: (a)+(b)+(c)	6,445	6,663	7,700	9,363	9,395	9,775	9,677	9,978	10,070	12,872
2) Labour income: Banking										
(e) Chartered banks	3,751	4,145	4,876	5,335	5,424	6,644	7,289	7,618	7,952	8,707
(f) Miscellaneous	61	64	70	75	81	87	87	89	95	103
(g) Total: (e)+(f)	3,812	4,209	4,946	5,410	5,505	6,731	7,376	7,707	8,047	8,810
3) Labour income: Investment and loan 804										
(h) L+M companies	591	587	600	617	639	651	664	703	763	827
(i) Trust companies	312	340	425	482	567	709	794	822	908	964
(j) Stock brokers + bond dealers										
(j)+(l)	2,310	2,518	3,147	3,569	4,199	5,250	5,880	6,087	6,724	7,138
4) Labour Income: Real Estate										
(l) Real Estate operators										
Total: 1+2+3+4	13,470	14,317	16,818	19,441	20,305	23,116	24,391	25,297	26,512	30,611
SUMMARY (millions of dollars)										
Insurance (d)	6	7	8	9	9	10	10	10	10	13
Banking (g)	4	4	5	5	6	7	7	8	8	9
Investment and loan (k)	3	3	4	5	5	7	7	8	8	9
Real estate (l)										
GRAND TOTAL	13	14	17	19	20	23	24	25	27	31

Totals do not necessarily add owing to rounding

Table 7.9. (continued)

(thousands of dollars)

	1911	1912	1913	1914	1915	1916	1917	1918	1919	1920
1) Labour income: Insurance										
(a) Life insurance	6,441	6,549	7,258	6,163	8,408	9,211	11,093	11,757	16,143	18,276
(b) Fire and casualty	7,401	8,248	8,675	9,969	9,420	8,195	8,743	9,823	12,272	15,621
(c) Fraternal, benefit	701	713	783	644	498	488	564	909	1,126	1,455
(d) Total: (a)+(b)+(c)	14,543	15,510	16,716	16,776	18,326	17,894	20,400	22,489	29,541	35,352
2) Labour Income: Banking										
(e) Chartered banks	10,478	12,095	13,427	14,611	12,662	12,843	15,184	18,511	25,373	32,046
(f) Miscellaneous banks	117	128	123	117	123	134	137	148	162	186
(g) Total (e)+(f)	10,595	12,223	13,550	14,728	12,785	12,977	15,321	18,659	25,535	32,232
3) Labour Income: Investment and loan 804										
(h) L+M companies	900	977	1,041	1,093	1,114	1,106	1,119	1,089	1,110	1,133
(i) Trust companies	1,276	1,503	1,730	1,758	1,787	1,786	1,957	1,815	1,900	2,091
(j) Stock brokers + bond dealers	6,000	7,572	8,887	9,955	10,387	10,233	10,500	9,884	10,315	10,788
(k) Total: (h)+(i)+(j)	8,176	10,052	11,658	12,806	13,288	13,125	13,576	12,788	13,325	14,012
4) Labour Income: Real Estate 809										
(l) Real estate operators	3,449	3,978	4,428	4,780	4,936	4,880	4,981	4,772	4,919	5,079
Total: 1+2+3+4	36,763	41,763	46,352	46,090	49,335	48,876	54,278	58,708	73,320	86,675

SUMMARY
(millions of dollars)

	1911	1912	1913	1914	1915	1916	1917	1918	1919	1920
Insurance (d)	15	16	17	17	18	18	20	22	30	35
Banking (g)	11	12	14	15	13	13	15	19	26	32
Investment + loan (k)	8	10	12	13	13	13	14	13	13	14
Real estate (l)	3	4	4	5	5	5	5	5	5	5
GRAND TOTAL	37	42	46	49	49	49	54	59	73	87

Totals do not necessarily add owning to rounding.

Table 7.9. (continued)

	1921	1922	1923	1924	1925	1926	1927	1928	1929	1930	1931
	(thousands of dollars)										
1) Labour Income: Insurance											
(a) Life insurance	19,395	19,517	21,815	25,137	29,125	29,985	40,346	37,950	42,706	44,919	42,417
(b) Fire and casualty	17,051	16,321	16,143	15,253	18,744	18,956	19,253	21,078	21,690	22,474	22,474
(c) Fraternal, benefit	1,471	1,388	1,456	1,489	1,620	1,594	1,664	1,690	1,743	1,605	1,586
(d) Total: (a)+(b)+(c)	37,917	37,226	39,414	42,879	49,489	50,535	61,263	60,718	66,139	68,998	66,477
2) Labour Income: Banking											
(e) Chartered banks	31,652	28,626	30,656	32,271	32,245	34,082	35,891	39,654	39,973	42,051	39,426
(f) Miscellaneous banks	177	198	228	262	275	303	327	354	410	414	420
(g) Total (e)+(f)	31,829	28,824	30,884	32,533	32,520	34,385	36,218	40,008	40,383	42,465	39,846
3) Labour Income: Investment and loan 804											
(h) L+M companies	1,192	1,171	1,358	1,306	1,255	1,321	1,340	1,338	1,387	1,385	1,381
(i) Trust companies	2,395	2,338	2,427	2,696	2,838	3,096	3,440	4,190	4,802	5,289	5,230
(j) Stock brokers and bond dealers	12,000	11,400	12,400	12,200	12,200	13,300	13,900	15,200	16,600	15,370	13,600
(k) Total: (h)+(i)+(j)	15,587	14,909	16,185	16,202	16,293	17,717	18,680	20,728	22,789	22,044	20,211
4) Labour Income: Real Estate 809											
(l) Real estate operators	5,491	5,171	4,784	5,101	4,727	4,753	5,452	5,891	6,957	4,811	4,682
Total: 1+2+3+4	90,824	86,130	91,267	95,715	106,029	107,390	121,613	127,345	136,268	138,318	131,216
SUMMARY (millions of dollars)											
Insurance (d)	38	37	39	42	49	51	61	61	66	69	66
Banking (g)	32	29	31	33	33	34	36	40	40	42	40
Investment and loan (k)	16	15	16	16	16	18	19	21	23	22	20
Real estate (l)	5	5	5	5	5	5	5	6	7	5	5
GRAND TOTAL	91	86	91	96	106	107	122	127	136	138	131

Totals do not necessarily add owning to rounding.

but if the argument is made that the 'bank's' net profits were increased by interest receipts (which reflect the distribution of returns to capital earned elsewhere in the economy) and were decreased by interest payments (which reflect the distribution elsewhere of returns to capital earned by the bank) and if the net profits are 'corrected' by the implied reversals of the interest receipts and payments, then

Wages and salaries	45
+ Depreciation	1
+ Net profit before taxes	4
− Interest receipts	−100
+ Interest payments	+ 50
	0

the result would appear that no gdp_f would be generated by a pure bank and that pure financial intermediates make no contribution to overall GDP_f.[15] (This result is, of course, absurd and, while it has led some observers to argue that it is the reversal of the interest flows which is incorrect,[16] it is generally maintained that this anomaly, with respect to financial intermediaries, arises because they do not charge a full market price for their services by charging a higher interest rate on the monies they lend compared to the lower interest rate they pay on the monies they borrow). If, so the argument goes, the banks fully charged for their services, then the interest rates on monies lent and borrowed would be the same and no problems would arise with the interest reversals or in estimating the gdp_f for the bank. The exemplary figures, suitably amended, illustrate

---

[15] If the simple example were recast to include intermediate inputs to read

Interest on deposits	50	Interest on loans	100
Wages and salaries	45		
Intermediate inputs	1		
Depreciation	1		
Net profits before taxes	3		

Then with the interest adjustment, one has

Wages and salaries	45
+ Depreciation	1
+ Net profits before taxes	3
	49
− Interest receipts	100
+ Interest payments	50
	− 1

or, a negative gdp_f is recorded — that is, the use of intermediate inputs by the pure financial intermediary would be recorded as entailing a net loss to overall economic system.

[16] Such an argument would imply a substantial revision in the current "industrial" distribution of GDP_f found in most countries' National Accounts.

Current Operating Expenses		Current Operating Earnings	
Interest on deposits	75	Interest on loans	75
Wages and salaries	45	Service charges	50
Depreciation	1		
Net profits before taxes	4		

So that, after adjustment

Wages and salaries	45
+ Depreciation	+ 1
+ Net profits before taxes	+ 4
− Interest receipts	−75
+ Interest payments	+75
gdp_f	50

or

Gross output	50
− Intermediate inputs	ϕ
gdp_f	50

The so-called "banking imputation" in the national accounts then is merely an attempt to impute a measure of the value of the services provided by banks and other financial intermediaries for which the banks do not charge and then, when the interest reversal is performed, to impute an offsetting interest payment. The following example again illustrates

Current Operating "Expenses"		Current Operating "Earnings"	
Interest on deposits	50	Interest on loans	100
Imputed interest payments	50	Imputed service rendered	
Wages and salaries	45	by bank	50
Depreciation	1		
Net profits before taxes	4		

So that, after adjustment

Wages and salaries		45
+ Depreciation		1
+ Net profits before taxes		4
− Interest receipts		−100
+ Interest payments:	paid	50
	imputed	50
	gdp_f	50

or	Gross input (Imputed services rendered by the banks)	50
	− Intermediate input	ϕ
	gdp$_f$	50

The banking imputation in the national accounts then

(i)   essentially takes the sum of the reported wages and salaries, depreciation and net profits as constituting a 'correct' measure of the banks' gdp$_f$,

(ii) to the extent that part of the imputed gross outputs of the banks are deemed to flow to final consumers (more precisely, deemed to be part of the overall final demand of the economy), total GDP$_f$ will be correspondingly higher (and, on the income side of the Accounts, an addition to returns to capital is made in the form of the imputed interest payments),

(iii) that the remainder of the imputed gross output of the bank is deemed to be imputed intermediate inputs flowing into other 'industries' thereby leaving total GDP$_f$ unchanged (so that the additional returns to capital arising in financial intermediation are offset by the corresponding reductions in gdp$_f$ originating in all other industries).

In practical terms, the allocation of the imputed gross output of financial intermediaries (e.g., banks, trust companies, instalment finance companies) as between final and intermediate output (and, with respect to the latter, its allocation amongst "using industries") has always been extremely arbitrary.[17] Indeed, when attention is turned to the problem of estimating the "real" output of banks (and other financial intermediaries) — i.e., the imputed gross output of the banks in constant price terms — the arbitrary and unsatisfactory nature of the banking imputation in the National Accounts becomes manifest.

For this project, of course, no attempt at a resolution of the problem of the "banking imputation" will be attempted.[18] For our immediate purposes, however, it is clear that the recorded labour income and profits of the banks (by profits, one means here before deductions for depreciation and appropriations to inner reserves) can be taken as a proxy to the gdp$_f$ originating amongst the banks. This then is the procedure followed by the Project in estimating the gdp$_f$ originating in the Finance Industry.

Second, consider a pure insurance company. Suppose that it insures against loss of some kind (damage to crops by hail, accident, or loss of life or limb) and in no way operates to provide any other service such as provision of pension funds or any other form of savings. The insurance company will incur a variety of costs such as those connected with the mere administration of the receipt of premiums and the payment of benefits to its policy holders, the investigation of claims and all other expenses connected with the problem of enforcing against the phenomenon

---

[17] The practice amongst financial intermediaries of calling part of their charges levied on loans they make (or customers' paper discounted) service charges has, of course, focused upon the practical problem of distinguishing between the service charges levied by financial intermediaries and the "true" interest being charged on such loans or involved in discounting the liabilities of the customers of the financial intermediaries. Furthermore, many "firms" in non-financial intermediation "industries" are partially engaged in the *activity* of financial intermediation and the treatment of the "banking imputation" should really be extended to the *activity* regardless of the "industry" in which it arises.

[18] The basic problem is, of course, that of conceptualising in a manner amenable to the measurement the services of money and more immediately for modern monetary economies the output of a central bank and the output of the activity of pure financial intermediation, produced in public or private institutions.

of "moral hazard" which arises in the insurance business, and so forth. For an insurance company which has built up no reserves for its contingent liabilities (say, a state-owned insurance company operating on the basis that the difference between premiums and benefits must be such as to cover costs of operations) then the accounts (ignoring intermediate inputs would be)

Expenditures	Revenues
Benefits paid	Premiums received
Wages and salaries	
Depreciation	
Profits (or net returns to capital) before taxes	

For such an insurance company the gdp_f originating would be merely the difference between premiums received and benefits paid (less any intermediate inputs which, in this simple exposition, we are ignoring). In the National Accounts at present, if such insurance was purchased solely by individuals, then consumer expenditures on goods and services would be written up by the difference between premiums received and benefits paid — the argument being that the premiums and benefits are merely inter-person transfers and consumer outlays are only for the value of the services rendered by the insurance companies. If such insurance is purchased by "firms", however, the current treatment is that the premiums are treated as intermediate inputs into all other activities with the benefits being treated as a positive component of the capital consumption allowances and miscellaneous valuation adjustments. Here, the rationale would appear to be that the premiums represent the value of the service purchased by Industry from the insurance companies — the argument being, of course, that a premium (for insurance against a specific risk) equals the probability of the value of the loss for that risk plus the cost of the primary inputs (again, ignoring intermediate inputs) used by the insurance company in providing the administration services involved in covering that risk. The following illustrates why the miscellaneous valuation adjustment is necessary. Assume that the non-insurance Industry is wholly integrated (save *vis-à-vis* the Insurance company) and we have

Non-Insurance Industry

Intermediate input		Final output	1000
Insurance premiums	100		
Primary input			
Wages and salaries	500		
Depreciation	100		
Net profit (before taxes)	300		

Insurance Company

Benefits	50	Premiums	100
Wages and salaries	45		
Net profits (before taxes)	5		

Total GDP_f is

Wages and salaries	545	1000
Net profits (before taxes)	305	
Depreciation	100	
+ MVA (benefits)	50	
	1000	1000

The adjustment is necessary since the cost of final goods sold includes the value of primary inputs involved in the insurance activity (measured by Premiums-Benefits) so that the elimination of the premiums paid for the GDP_f of the Non-Insurance Industry eliminates not just the gdp_f for the Insurance Company but the losses being experienced as well, a legitimate charge perhaps[19] against NDP_f but not against GDP_f.

For an insurance company which is growing or for one in which the contingent liabilities involved in its promise to pay benefits in certain eventualities must be matched by income — earning assets[20] premiums would exceed benefits by a greater amount than for a stationary non-funded insurance company, but again premiums minus benefits would be the correct measure of gdp_f for the company. This is illustrated below (in utmost simplicity)

Benefits paid	Premiums received
Wages and salaries	Net interest
Depreciation	
Net profits before taxes	

so that immediately

$$\text{Premiums} - \text{Benefits} \equiv \text{Wages and salaries} + \text{Depreciation}$$
$$+ \text{ Net profits before taxes} - \text{Net interest received}$$
$$\equiv gdp_f$$

The previous distinction, where the insurance was purchased by individuals or "firms", and the resulting different treatment followed in the National Accounts applies again.

Thus, with respect to this project, the method so far of estimating gdp_f for the Insurance Industry will be

Premiums received − Benefits paid − Intermediate input expenses

---

19 There has always been some dispute in National Accounting as to whether losses of property due to fire or other insurable accidents should be charged against NDP_f (and hence against net capital formation) or treated as a capital loss in the revaluation accounts linking stock accounts (e.g., national balance sheets). Losses not insurable through a market (e.g., losses owing to war, revolution, etc.) are, of course, not included in the miscellaneous valuation adjustments of the National Accounts (though they could be treated as part of capital consumption).

20 A collective insurance scheme requires no fund since the premiums are really taxes and the benefits transfers (with the difference between them being the resource costs of so collectively pooling risk). A private insurance company itself, of course, confronts the risk that its premiums will dry up and, to remain solvent, it must have a source of revenue (interest receipts and amortization of bonds) to cover both the benefits it is obliged to pay and costs in administrating the benefits so that its shareholders, in winding up the business, do not see their capital dissipated in benefits and costs.

and given the estimates of labour income derived in part (i) of this report, the estimates of the non-labour income component of gdp$_f$ should follow residually.

There is another further complication with respect to the Insurance Industry which pertains almost exclusively to the Life Insurance Industry. The life companies offer not only insurance to their policy holders (and being private companies hold interest-earning assets to support their contingent liabilities) but also a variety of savings programmes. In the National Accounts, the activities of life insurance companies are treated as if they were conducted by "associations of individuals" — that is, the premiums received and benefits paid are treated as transfers amongst individuals and the expenses of the companies in carrying out the insurance and portfolio management activities are deemed to be part of Personal Expenditures on Goods and Services with the net investment income of the companies being treated as accruing to that of individuals as policyholders, bond and stock holders of the companies. Thus, the investment income of the life companies is deemed to originate elsewhere and to flow through them as intermediaries to households and once again the current price contribution of the life insurance companies to GDP$_f$ will be equal to the costs of the administration, management, etc., of the insurance and portfolio programmes the companies are deemed to be running on behalf of the policyholders.

Third, there is some confusion at present in the National Accounts as to what constitutes the Real Estate Industry. There are some matters on which there is little dispute. Paid and imputed gross rents[21] (including that is, capital consumption allowances on residential real estate) on owner-occupied and tenant-occupied (of all kinds, e.g., apartments, condominiums, etc.) residential real estate is deemed to originate in the Real Estate Industry. There are relatively tiny problems such as houses owned by mining companies and rented to employees in which the question is: should the gross rents be shown as originating in the Mining or the Real Estate Industry. This problem illustrates, of course, the well-known difficulties of trying unambiguously to classify gdp$_f$ originating along activity versus industry lines where the basic reporting unit for industry statistics is engaged in a variety of activities. There are pure intermediaries which we may call real estate brokers whose prime source of income are the commissions they earn from acting as agents in transactions in real estate.

The problems emerge when one considers (say) a major real estate developer which runs large office buildings and retail trade complexes such as shopping centres. The various offices and stores can be treated as fixed capital the services of which are being used in Mining, Manufacturing, etc., Industries (e.g., a manufacturing company may rent its head offices from the developer) and in the Retail Trade Industry — in which case one would want the gross rents arising in connection with the rented offices and stores to be shown as originating, respectively, in the Manufacturing and Retail Trade Industry. On the other hand, the allocation of gross rents originating could be followed on an ownership basis in which case the gross rents would be treated as part of the gdp$_f$ on the Real Estate Industry.

The same problem arises, of course, with respect to rented equipment — should the gross rents originating be deemed to originate in the industry using the equipment or the industry

---

[21] Gross rents, it is understood, are the following:

Gross market rents − Intermediate inputs − Wages and salaries = Gross rents
Gross rents − Depreciation = Net rents
Net rents − Interest payments = Net profits before taxes

Thus, gross rents are not the rents a tenant pays but are the gross market rents less any payments for intermediate and labour inputs involved in the provision of the service and so represent the gross returns to the rented capital good.

owning the equipment. This problem is further complicated by the existence of rent-option-to-buy and lease-back arrangements with respect to a large amount of fixed capital and land. Though I personally believe that the ownership approach is the one which makes economic sense it must be confessed that puzzles result. For example, today a major real estate developer (or owner of large commercial aircraft) may be a Life insurance company. A portion, therefore, of gdp$_f$ which would otherwise be shown as originating in the Retail Trade and Transportation industries will, under the ownership approach, be shown as originating in the Life Insurance Industry which would seem to conflict with our earlier treatment of Life Insurance Companies which dealt with their interest receipts as if they were returns to capital generated elsewhere and distributed to individuals through the Life Insurance companies acting as intermediaries or portfolio managers on behalf of the individuals.

My support of the ownership approach rests on the contention that interest and dividend payments are phenomena sufficiently conceptually dissimilar to that of rent payments so that one need not be concerned with the seeming paradoxes just discussed. Once again though, (just as in the case of the "banking imputation") it must be admitted that, as yet, both in economic theory and in National Accounting no satisfactory theoretical framework exists which would both explain the ownership-rental distinction with respect to fixed assets and which would permit the National Accountant to arrive at a wholly satisfactory treatment with respect to gdp$_f$ originating in the Real Estate Industry.

For the period prior to 1930 with which this project is concerned, it is the case, however, that a very large component of the gdp$_f$ originating in the Real Estate Industry will be the paid and imputed gross rents connected with tenant- and owner- occupied residential real estate and the gross income of (largely unincorporated) real estate dealers and brokers. Any imputed gross rents on fixed assets owned by the three levels of governments (not government business enterprises) should, in my view, be allocated as part of gdp$_f$ of the Public Administration and Defence Industry.

This completes the conceptual sketch of the problems of estimating Non-labour income component of gdp$_f$ in the Finance, Insurance and Real Estate Industry, estimates which I now outline and provide.

Non-Labour Income: Banking SIC 802

Bangs' estimates of Non-labour income for Banking for the period 1919-1931 are provided in Table 7.10.

Bangs' estimates are for the chartered banks, Quebec Savings Banks and the Alberta and Ontario Provincial Banks. (It is not possible to get a breakdown, as was the case for his estimates of Labour income but it is safe to say that these estimates of Non-labour income pertain largely if not entirely to the Chartered banks.) Bangs' estimates are prepared in a manner similar to that outlined in the text above dealing with conceptual problems. Briefly, Bangs' estimates interested paid out by the Banks on debentures and bonds by multiplying securities (apparently, largely Dominion and provincial short and long term securities, including Treasury bills and municipal and corporation bonds) by an annual estimate of average yields. Interest on Savings deposits were similarly estimated. Dividends paid out were obtained from the chartered banks and the reported net profits of the banks were adjusted for "transfers to rest and reserve funds". Thus, the net profits adjusted by Bangs are net of depreciation allowances, Dominion and provincial government taxes but are gross of the "transfers to rest and reserve funds".

In his "interest reversal" approach to the estimation of Non-labour income originating in Banking, the major error which Bangs made (so far as I can tell) is that no allowance was made

Table 7.10. Non-Labour Income: 802, Banking, 1919 to 1931
(thousands of dollars)

	1919	1920	1921	1922	1923	1924	1925	1926	1927	1928	1929	1930	1931
Bangs' estimates:													
(a) Interest (net) on bonds and debentures	-31,959	-25,894	-25,032	-20,710	-23,534	-28,048	-30,501	-28,977	-26,978	-26,479	-27,837	-25,960	-36,957
(b) Interest on savings deposits	22,220	24,506	25,364	25,346	25,625	26,381	25,708	26,996	28,103	29,869	29,514	28,536	28,759
(c) Dividends (net) on stocks	14,348	16,557	16,887	16,299	16,125	15,943	16,018	15,957	16,615	16,960	18,563	19,786	18,006
(d) 'Savings' – net profits, adjusted	4,601	4,332	3,351	1,537	879	275	874	1,457	1,988	2,638	4,151	1,408	1,235
(e) Total: a+b+c+d	9,210	19,501	20,570	22,472	19,095	14,551	12,099	15,433	19,728	22,988	24,391	23,770	11,043
(f) Labour income: Bangs (see Table 7.7 line (g))	34,597	38,524	35,790	33,488	33,304	33,668	35,071	35,970	38,123	41,287	42,602	44,252	41,490
(g) Ratio (e) + (f)	.266	.506	.575	.671	.573	.432	.345	.429	.517	.557	.573	.537	.266

Sources: See Table 7.3

for interest received by the banks on loans. (His notes seem to suggest that no loan categories of any kind are included in bonds and debentures — a surprising omission which I am unable to explain.) In addition, of course, from the viewpoint of this project, the estimation of gross domestic product at factor cost would necessitate the inclusion of depreciation allowances and Dominion and provincial government (income) taxes.

Even with these difficulties taken into account, it is clear that Bangs' estimates cannot be considered too reliable. Again, the central problem is that no "revenue and expense" data are available for the chartered banks. From incomplete information on revenues and expenses provided by the office of the Inspector-General for the years 1929-1931, one has the data of Table 7.11.

Table 7.11

Estimates of Gross Domestic Product, Chartered Banks, 1929-1931, Inspector-General
(millions of dollars)

	1929	1930	1931
Remuneration to employees	47.0	48.0	45.0
Contributions to pension fund	1.1	1.3	1.3
Provision for taxes	8.3	8.1	8.4
Provision for depreciation of bank premises	3.1	2.9	1.6
Balance of current operating earnings	51.7	34.7	30.2
" GDP_f "	111.2	95.0	86.5
Less: Interest and discounts on loans	150.5	131.5	108.4
Interest, dividends and trading profits on securities	22.8	22.0	28.8
Plus: Interest on deposits	65.0	58.7	55.1
GDP_f	2.9	0.2	4.4

Note: In Table 7.11, only 9 banks reported for 1929 and 10 reported for 1930 and 1931 even though 11 banks reported assets and liabilities to the Inspector-General. The 'Balance of Current Operating Earnings' includes Exchange Commissions and other services and is not net of "transfers to net and reserve funds".

Thus, it is clear that if Bangs had made an estimate of interest received by the banks on loans, his estimates of national income originating in Banking would have been sharply reduced. Moreover, from the data supplied by the Inspector-General (IG), we can recapitulate an estimate, trying to match Bangs', of the components of Non-labour income in Banking (net of depreciation and net of government (income) taxes). That is provided in Table 7.12A.

While Bangs' estimates of Interest (net) on bonds and debentures appear somewhat too high (and his estimates of dividends paid by the banks to their shareholders are, of course,

Table 7.12A
(millions of dollars)

	1929	1930	1931
Bangs: Interest (net) on bonds & debentures	27.8	26.0	37.0
IG: Interest, dividends and trading profit on securities	22.8	22.0	28.8
Bangs: Interest on savings deposits	29.5	28.5	28.8
IG: Interest on deposits	65.0	58.7	55.1
Bangs: Dividends (net) on stocks	18.6	19.8	18.0
IG: Dividends to shareholders	18.1	19.3	17.5

accurate), his estimates of interest on deposits appear far too low.

Taking what information is available from the Inspector-General and the conceptual basis of Bangs' estimates into account, it is clear that they cannot be considered satisfactory.

Based on data obtained from the previously mentioned archives of the Head Office of the Bank of Montreal, it was possible to build up, for that Bank, a statement from 1897-1931 of the gross operating profits of that bank, which includes depreciation of bank premises, taxes and, most importantly, transfers to rest fund and inner reserves. Thus, for that Bank, it was possible to develop a series indicating the ratio of gross Non-labour income to Labour income originating. Following the conceptual discussion previously outlined, we, accordingly, on the assumption that the Bank of Montreal was representative, applied that ratio to the Labour income estimates previously reported for the chartered banks.

This arbitrary procedure was fleshed out, to some extent, by a checking of related data. From the archives of the Bank of Nova Scotia, some components of the reported net profits of the BNS were compared with those available from the Bank of Montreal. While it was not possible on the basis of the BNS data to construct the required figures as was the case for the Bank of Montreal, the assumption that the profitability of the Bank of Montreal was similar to that of the Bank of Nova Scotia (though there is some evidence, based on respective ratios of reported net profits to subscribed capital, to suggest some difference between them) was not entirely unwarranted. In addition, the ratio of the Bank of Montreal's reported net profits was compared with the ratio of the Bank of Montreal's gross profits (as obtained from the archives) to the Project's estimates of total gross profits. That comparison is provided below in Table 7.12B.

The chartered banks included in this comparison were: Bank of Nova Scotia, Sterling Bank of Canada, United Empire Bank of Canada, Bank of Vancouver, Security Bank, Bank of Ottawa, Traders Bank of Canada, Imperial Bank of Canada, Metropolitan Bank, Home Bank of Canada, Northern Crown Bank, Bank of Montreal, Bank of New Brunswick, Quebec Bank, Bank of British North America, Bank of Toronto, Molson Bank, Eastern Township Bank, Banque Nationale, Merchants Bank, Provincial Bank of Canada, Union Bank of Canada, Canadian Bank of Commerce, Dominion Bank (dropped from tabulations because data not available), Royal Bank of Canada, Bank of Hamilton, Standard Bank and Banque de Hochalaga.[22] (This list

---

22   These data were obtained from the BNS archives (and were checked for the Home Bank with data from the National Archives, for the Bank of Nova Scotia with other data from the BNS archives, and for the Bank of Montreal with the data obtained from the archives of the Bank of Montreal).

Table 7.12B

	Ratios	
	Reported Net Profits, Bank of Montreal, to Total Profits (see notes p. 511)	Gross Profits, Bank of Montreal, to Total Gross Profits Estimated
1908	0.168	0.192
1909	0.156	0.190
1910	0.135	0.185
1911	0.147	0.169
1912	0.151	0.158
1913	0.159	0.155
1914	0.158	0.175
1915	0.148	0.177
1916	0.152	0.177
1917	0.154	0.171
1918	0.147	0.160
1919	0.168	0.180

corresponds almost entirely with the list of the banks reporting to the Inspector-General over the period concerned.)

Another rough check — though certainly not independent — was to compare the ratio of gross profits to reported net profits from the Bank of Montreal to that of the estimated gross profits for all the chartered banks to their reported net profits. This is provided in Table 7.13.

Finally, the Project's estimates of labour and non-labour income for the Chartered Banks were compared with data from the Inspector-General's office for the years 1929-1931. This is illustrated in Table 7.14.

From Table 7.14, it would appear that the Project's estimates of gross profits for the chartered banks are too low but it should be remembered that the Inspector-General's data include all the operations of the chartered banks while the Project's estimates, as reflected in the labour income data, pertain to their domestic operations only.

Finally, for the years 1891-1896, the Non-labour income for the chartered banks was quite arbitrarily estimated.

The project's estimates of the Non-labour income component of the gdp$_f$ originating for the Chartered Banks is reported in Table 7.17.

Non-Labour Income: Miscellaneous Banks

In the section of this report dealing with Labour income, it was reported that the Labour income for Miscellaneous banks was vanishingly small, being less than 1% of that of the Chartered Banks over the period 1919-1926. Accordingly, a token allowance for Non-labour income originating amongst the miscellaneous banks is made in this Report and that allowance is constructed by assuming that the ratio Non-labour income to Labour income observed for the

Table 7.13

Ratios of Gross Profits to Net Profits

	Bank of Montreal	Estimates for All Chartered Banks
1908	2.111	2.408
1909	1.702	2.073
1910	1.419	1.945
1911	1.359	1.568
1912	1.422	1.490
1913	1.713	1.672
1914	1.225	1.359
1915	1.075	1.287
1916	1.301	1.518
1917	1.730	1.921
1918	1.886	2.052
1919	2.168	2.321

Table 7.14

	1929	1930	1931
Labour income: Project, Table 7.9	40.000	42.100	39.400
Remuneration for employees, including pension contributions: Inspector-General	48.100	49.300	46.300
Ratio: Project to Inspector-General	.832	.854	.851
Gross non-labour income: Table 7.17	55.600	36.000	21.700
Balance of current operating expenses, depreciation and taxes: Inspector-General	63.100	45.700	40.200
Ratio: Project to Inspector-General	.881	.788	.540

Chartered Banks (i.e., observed for the Bank of Montreal, to all intents and purposes) is valid for these miscellaneous banks. It is to be reiterated that this estimate is a mere token and is recorded in Table 7.17.

Non-Labour Income: Investment and Loan Industries SIC 804

Bangs' estimates of Non-labour income for Loan and mortgage companies and for Trust companies are reproduced on Table 7.15. His estimates, derived in a manner similar to that of the chartered banks were judged to be equally unsatisfactory. Unfortunately, for this Project, no satisfactory method of estimating Non-labour income for these industries was possible. There are no satisfactory operating statistics for these companies, particularly in view of the importance of provincially incorporated companies. One attempt was to distribute Non-labour income (with the Project's estimates for the chartered banks taken as a benchmark) amongst the Loan and mortgage and Trust companies on the basis of Bangs' estimates, using the proportions amongst those estimates. The attempt resulted in quite unsatisfactory estimates for Non-labour income for these industries. It was finally decided to take the ratio of Non-labour to Labour income as established for the chartered banks and to apply these ratios annually to the Project's estimates of Labour income for these industries. This procedure, with its heavy reliance on the basic data from the archives of the Bank of Montreal, is admittedly unsatisfactory but no better procedure was deemed available. The estimates are given in Table 7.17.

Non-Labour Income: Insurance SIC 806 and 808

Bangs' estimates of Non-labour income for Insurance for the period 1919-1931 are provided in Table 7.16.

It is clear from Table 7.16 that, contrary to the conceptual discussion of the measurement of gdp_f in the Insurance industry, Bangs attempted, in this case, a procedure similar to that he followed for the banking industry. There are two major differences: i) there is an allowance for interest arising on insurance and annuity contracts and ii) there is an allowance for the capital gain earned by policyholders in insurance and pension reserves. All the components of Table 7.16 were derived by Bangs by a variety of estimating procedures, among which for the last component, the year-to-year change in the adjusted net liabilities of the insurance companies and societies was taken as representing the net equity of the policyholders arising from the yearly operations of the companies and societies. Not only is Bangs' procedure unsatisfactory from a conceptual viewpoint, but as Table 7.16 would reveal, it results in measures of the Non-labour income originating among the non-life-insurance industries (fire and casually) which are extremely difficult to interpret. In the thirteen years reported in Table 7.16, the non-life-insurance industry reported negative Non-labour income originating in six years of which perhaps only 1930 and 1931 may be understandable.

An attempt was made in this Project to obtain what could only be an approximation to the desired total Non-labour income. The basic data consist essentially of net cash premiums and total expenditures (including losses) as reported to the Superintendent of Insurance by federally incorporated life insurance, fire insurance, accident, burglary insurance companies and fraternal benefit societies. An allowance was made for taxes and the ratio of the estimate so derived to the reported commissions and salaries (previously discussed) was computed. This ratio, computed for life, fire and casualty insurance companies and fraternal benefit societies was then applied to the estimated Labour income estimates for this Industry as reported earlier in this Project. The procedures appeared to give valid results for the life insurance companies and the ratios for that sector were also applied to derive the data for the fraternal benefit societies. For the fire and casualty insurance companies, the procedure resulted in unwarranted low estimates (indeed, for many years, the calculation yielded negative figures). Accordingly, for the fire and casualty insurance companies, the total income was used in place of net cash premiums.

The results, shown in Table 7.17 must be regarded as less satisfactory than the corresponding Labour income estimates. The volatility of the series, particularly its behaviour around 1920 and 1930, can, I believe, be defended but questions can be raised regarding the level throughout.

Table 7.15. Non-Labour Income: 804, Investment and Loan Industries, 1919 to 1931
(thousands of dollars)

	1919	1920	1921	1922	1923	1924	1925	1926	1927	1928	1929	1930	1931
Bangs' estimates:													
Loan and Mortgage Companies													
(a) Interest (net) on bonds and debentures	1,441	769	1,007	1,258	1,538	1,725	1,836	2,175	2,708	3,433	3,511	3,870	4,173
(b) Interest on savings deposits	941	1,020	1,101	1,056	906	967	1,060	1,106	1,226	1,332	1,364	1,366	1,444
(c) Dividends (net) on stocks	3,056	2,852	3,139	3,147	2,763	2,985	4,571	4,855	3,524	4,026	3,971	4,036	3,971
(d) Net profits, adjusted	2,216	2,153	1,823	1,535	1,789	2,300	824	498	1,776	1,546	2,367	1,181	1,122
(e) Total: a+b+c+d	7,654	6,794	7,070	6,996	6,996	7,977	8,291	8,634	9,234	10,337	11,213	10,453	10,710
Trust Companies													
(a) Interest (net) on bonds and debentures	-879	-951	-953	-934	-1,039	-1,139	-1,167	-1,319	-1,531	-1,746	-2,046	-2,095	-1,961
(b) Interest in savings deposits	2,107	2,067	1,961	1,963	2,375	2,740	3,002	3,317	3,812	4,429	5,979	6,974	7,604
(c) Dividends (net) on stocks	1,697	1,962	2,159	2,120	2,118	1,798	1,807	1,909	2,086	2,406	2,708	2,914	2,834
(d) Net profits, adjusted	685	627	343	450	528	1,347	1,552	1,567	2,007	2,512	2,255	1,609	1,189
(e) Total: a+b+c+d	3,610	3,705	3,510	3,599	3,982	4,746	5,194	5,474	6,374	7,601	8,896	9,402	9,666

Sources: See Table 7.3

516

Table 7.16. Non-Labour Income: Insurance 806-808, 1919-1931 — Bangs' estimates: (thousands of dollars)

	1919	1920	1921	1922	1923	1924	1925	1926	1927	1928	1929	1930	1931
Interest (net) from bonds and debentures													
806 Life insurance	-15,796	-18,216	-20,696	-23,567	-26,899	-30,688	-33,109	34,925	-38,141	-39,828	-42,142	-44,396	-46,408
808 Non-life insurance	-3,417	-4,024	-4,760	-5,114	-5,422	-5,943	-6,236	-6,416	-6,994	-7,280	-7,809	-8,330	-8,120
Sub-total	-19,213	-22,240	-25,456	-28,681	-32,321	-36,631	-39,345	-41,341	-45,135	-47,108	-49,951	-52,726	-54,528
Interest from insurance and annuity contracts													
806	14,979	14,469	14,117	16,990	18,889	20,746	23,240	23,900	26,766	29,896	36,024	41,710	46,972
808	1,506	1,956	2,582	2,228	2,725	2,346	2,299	2,679	3,204	3,734	3,471	3,662	3,457
Sub-total	16,485	16,425	16,699	19,218	21,614	23,092	25,539	26,579	29,970	33,630	39,495	45,372	50,429
Dividends (net) from stocks													
806	-785	-702	-946	-918	1,306	-1,356	-3,622	-5,096	-8,624	-13,585	-17,984	-18,994	-16,073
808	816	1,026	773	775	562	664	728	651	937	902	906	943	2,891
Sub-total	31	324	-173	-143	-744	-692	-2,894	-4,445	-7,687	-12,683	-17,878	-18,051	-13,182
Savings: net equity of policyholders in insurance and pension reserves													
Total													
806	42,463	48,895	59,552	72,567	74,387	111,563	94,691	122,195	120,601	179,626	141,714	125,074	111,658
808	7,599	7,807	-188	2,394	710	-41	1,381	3,515	4,301	6,776	7,872	44	-396
Sub-total	50,062	56,702	59,364	74,961	75,097	111,522	96,072	125,710	124,902	186,402	149,586	125,118	111,262
Total													
806	40,861	44,446	52,027	65,072	65,071	100,265	81,200	106,074	100,602	156,109	117,612	103,394	96,149
808	6,504	6,765	-1,593	283	-1,425	-2,974	-1,828	429	1,448	4,132	4,440	-3,681	-2,168
GRAND TOTAL	47,365	51,211	50,434	65,355	63,646	97,291	79,372	106,503	102,050	160,241	121,252	99,713	93,981
Labour Income:													
Bangs (Table 7.3)	36,975	45,072	45,871	45,512	48,836	51,785	56,866	60,731	64,511	69,900	74,757	75,900	
Ratio: Grand Total to Labour Income	1.281	1.136	1.099	1.436	1.303	1.879	1.396	1.754	1.582	2.292	1.622	1.314	

Sources: See Table 7.3

Table 7.17. Non-Labour Income: Finance, Insurance and Real Estate Industry, 1891 to 1900 (thousands of dollars)

	1891	1892	1893	1894	1895	1896	1897	1898	1899	1900
1) Non-labour income: Insurance										
(a) Life insurance 806	1,490	2,582	2,118	1,980	2,014	1,929	1,767	2,569	2,472	2,381
(b) Fire and casualty 808	753	661	420	675	661	1,151	983	813	751	-1,003
(c) Fraternal, benefit 808	84	156	129	149	155	394	350	476	465	397
(d) Total: (a)+(b)+(c)	2,327	3,399	2,667	2,804	2,830	3,474	3,100	3,858	3,688	1,775
2) Non-labour income: Banking										
(e) Chartered banks 802	8,799	8,688	8,466	8,877	8,307	8,445	9,189	10,188	11,612	16,458
(f) Miscellaneous banks 802	117	126	126	126	135	141	149	165	194	278
(g) Total: (e)+(f)	8,916	8,814	8,592	9,003	8,442	8,586	9,338	10,353	11,806	16,736
3) Non-labour income: Investment and Loan 804										
(h) Loan and mortgage cos.	1,620	1,698	1,737	1,749	1,761	1,773	1,850	1,935	2,116	2,729
(i) Trust companies			75	150	225	300	359	560	727	1,338
(j) Stock brokers and bond dealers										
(j)+(l)	(366)	(600)	(686)	(857)	(943)	1,270	1,435	1,556	2,948	3,996
4) Non-labour income: Real Estate 809										
(l) Real estate operators										
Total: 1+2+3+4	13,229	14,511	13,757	14,175	14,201	15,403	16,082	18,262	21,285	26,574

SUMMARY
(millions of dollars)

	1891	1892	1893	1894	1895	1896	1897	1898	1899	1900
Insurance (d)	2	3	3	3	3	3	3	4	4	2
Banking (g)	9	9	9	9	8	9	9	10	12	17
Investment and loan (k)										
Real estate (l)	2	2	2	3	3	3	4	4	6	8
GRAND TOTAL	13	15	14	14	14	15	16	18	21	27

Totals do not necessarily add owing to rounding

Table 7.17. (continued)

	1901	1902	1903	1904	1905	1906	1907	1908	1909	1910
1) Non-labour income: Insurance										
(a) Life insurance	2,837	3,740	3,877	3,913	4,170	5,431	5,038	5,262	6,148	5,114
(b) Fire and casualty	1,012	4,347	3,505	-2,718	5,511	4,238	3,512	3,016	5,061	4,586
(c) Fraternal, benefit	463	528	508	478	482	689	680	715	854	633
(d) Total: (a)+(b)+(c)	4,312	8,615	7,890	1,673	10,163	10,358	9,230	8,993	12,063	10,333
2) Non-labour income: Banking										
(e) Chartered banks	14,606	15,867	20,328	15,754	14,742	22,623	26,138	24,538	19,960	18,903
(f) Miscellaneous banks	238	245	292	222	211	296	312	286	238	224
(g) Total: (e)+(f)	14,844	16,112	20,620	15,976	14,953	22,919	26,450	24,824	20,198	19,127
3) Non-labour income: Investment and loan 804										
(h) L+M companies	2,301	2,247	2,501	1,822	1,737	2,217	2,381	2,264	1,915	1,795
(i) Trust companies	1,215	1,302	1,772	1,432	1,541	2,414	2,847	2,648	2,279	2,093
(j) Stock brokers and bond dealers										
(j)+(l)	4,389	5,723	7,021	4,590	7,000	10,190	12,107	11,498	11,955	9,408
4) Non-labour income: Real Estate 809										
(l) Real estate operators										
Total: 1+2+3+4	27,061	33,999	39,804	25,493	35,394	48,098	53,015	50,227	48,410	42,756

SUMMARY
(millions of dollars)

	1901	1902	1903	1904	1905	1906	1907	1908	1909	1910
Insurance (d)	4	9	8	2	10	10	9	9	12	10
Banking (g)	15	16	21	16	15	23	26	25	20	19
Investment and loan (k)	8	9	11	8	10	15	17	16	16	13
Real Estate (l)										
GRAND TOTAL	27	34	40	25	35	48	53	50	48	43

Totals do not necessarily add owing to rounding

Table 7.17. (continued)

	1911	1912	1913	1914	1915	1916	1917	1918	1919	1920
1) Non-labour income: Insurance										
(a) Life insurance	6,518	6,005	6,140	6,083	2,228	6,567	7,454	4,632	8,443	18,843
(b) Fire and casualty	6,578	7,526	12,654	12,860	7,326	8,039	13,048	11,678	14,650	18,092
(c) Fraternal, benefit	709	654	662	636	132	348	379	358	589	1,900
(d) Total (a)+(b)+(c)	13,805	14,185	19,456	19,579	9,686	14,954	20,881	16,668	23,682	38,435
2) Non-labour income: Banking										
(e) Chartered banks	21,092	23,706	28,559	19,403	15,308	18,892	27,847	32,876	42,652	64,765
(f) Miscellaneous banks	236	251	262	156	149	200	252	262	272	376
(g) Total (e)+(f)	21,328	23,957	28,821	19,559	15,457	19,092	28,099	33,138	42,924	65,141
3) Non-labour income: Investment and Loan 804										
(h) L+M companies	1,812	1,915	2,214	1,452	1,347	1,627	2,052	1,934	1,866	2,290
(i) Trust companies	2,569	2,956	3,680	2,335	2,160	2,627	3,589	3,223	3,194	4,226
(j) Stock brokers and bond dealers	11,005	13,641	18,047	16,007	10,710	11,226	14,700	12,058	12,337	16,581
(k) Total: (h)+(i)+(j)	15,386	18,512	23,941	19,794	14,217	15,480	20,341	17,215	17,397	23,097
4) Non-labour income: Real Estate 809										
(l) Real estate operators	4,642	5,410	6,855	5,975	3,978	5,353	6,973	5,822	5,883	7,806
Total: 1+2+3+4	55,161	62,064	79,073	64,907	43,338	54,879	76,294	72,843	89,886	134,479
SUMMARY (millions of dollars)										
Insurance (d)	14	14	19	20	10	15	21	17	24	38
Banking (g)	21	24	29	20	15	19	28	33	43	65
Investment + loan (k)	15	19	24	20	14	15	20	17	17	23
Real estate (l)	5	5	7	6	4	5	7	6	6	8
GRAND TOTAL	55	62	79	65	43	55	76	73	90	134

Totals do not necessarily add owing to rounding

Table 7.17. (continued)

	1921	1922	1923	1924	1925	1926	1927	1928	1929	1930	1931
1) Non-labour income: Insurance											
(a) Life insurance	25,892	27,538	20,353	19,657	25,368	33,253	41,677	40,303	31,432	18,911	5,599
(b) Fire and casualty	8,416	3,893	5,408	9,656	12,498	14,671	17,623	19,192	18,822	4,496	-2,593
(c) Fraternal, benefit	1,964	1,958	1,358	1,164	1,411	1,768	1,719	1,795	1,282	676	209
(d) Total (a)+(b)+(c)	36,272	33,389	27,119	30,477	39,277	49,692	61,019	61,290	51,536	24,083	3,215
2) Non-labour income: Banking											
(e) Chartered banks	41,496	30,057	23,360	25,849	22,152	30,469	26,380	40,090	55,602	36,038	21,684
(f) Miscellaneous banks	232	208	174	210	189	271	240	358	571	355	231
(g) Total: (e)+(f)	41,728	30,265	23,534	26,059	22,341	30,730	26,620	40,448	56,173	36,393	21,915
3) Non-labour income: Investment and loan											
(h) L+M companies	1,563	1,230	1,035	1,046	862	1,181	984	1,353	1,929	1,187	760
(i) Trust companies	3,140	2,455	1,849	2,159	1,950	2,768	2,528	4,236	6,680	4,533	2,877
(j) Stock brokers and bond dealers	13,368	10,887	9,040	9,113	9,077	12,675	12,607	15,200	16,915	8,300	3,210
(k) Total: (h)+(i)+(j)	18,071	14,572	11,924	12,318	11,889	16,624	16,119	20,789	25,524	14,020	6,847
4) Non-labour income: Real Estate 809											
(l) Real estate operators	6,117	4,938	3,488	3,810	3,517	4,530	4,945	5,891	7,089	2,596	1,105
Total: 1+2+3+4	102,188	83,164	66,065	72,664	77,024	101,576	108,703	128,418	140,322	77,092	33,082
SUMMARY (millions of dollars)											
Insurance (d)	36	33	27	30	39	50	61	61	52	24	3
Banking (g)	42	30	24	26	22	31	27	40	56	36	22
Investment and loan (k)	18	15	12	12	12	17	16	21	26	14	7
Real estate (l)	6	5	3	4	4	5	5	6	7	3	1
GRAND TOTAL	102	83	66	73	77	102	109	128	140	77	33

Totals do not necessarily add owing to rounding

Non-Labour Income: Stock Brokers and Bond Dealers and Real Estate Operators

Here an estimate is provided which must be interpreted as pure conjecture. For the sectors already covered, a ratio of Non-labour income to Labour income originating was computed and applied to the Labour income estimates for the brokers, dealers and operators already described above. This must be regarded as unsatisfactory but the estimates are found in Table 7.17.

Finally, the estimates of gdp$_f$ originating by major groups within this industrial division are provided in Table 7.18. It must be remembered that herein there is no estimate of the market and imputed gross rent on owner-occupied and tenant-occupied dwellings in the Real Estate Industry — an estimate provided by the overall Queen's Project.

Here then are estimates of GDP$_f$ originating in the Finance, Insurance and Real Estate Industry, Canada, 1891-1930.

Finance, Insurance and Real Estate, 1870-1890

The contribution of the finance, insurance and real estate sector to total GDP becomes quite small as one goes backward in time. In 1891, GDP in this sector at 20 million dollars, made up of 12 million dollars for banking, 5 million dollars for insurance and 3 million dollars for all other, was 2.9 per cent of overall gross domestic product at factor cost. In light of this fact and also owing to the lower quality of data for earlier years, the gross domestic product was extrapolated backward from 1891 to 1870 for each of banking, insurance and the "all other" category by use of available related time series as now will be explained.

The GDP at factor cost for banking was extrapolated backward from 1891 on the basis of a series comprised of the sum of the values of the chartered bank note issue (HSC, Series H19), chartered bank Canadian deposits (HSC, Series H20) and the Dominion of Canada note issue held outside-banks (HSC, Series H15). This sum in 1891 was comprised of the chartered bank Canadian deposits at 161.5 million dollars, chartered bank note issue of 35.6 million dollars, and Dominion note issue held by the general public of 6.1 million dollars: thus the extrapolating series was predominantly the value of chartered bank notes and deposits.

The GDP at factor cost for insurance was extrapolated from 1891 by an index giving equal weights to the value of net new life insurance policies written each year (HSC, Series H347) and the value of fire insurance policies taken during the year (HSC, Series 437)

The GDP at factor cost for the "all other" component was extrapolated from 1891 by the single series of the value of new insurance policies written (HSC, Series H347).

Thomas K. Rymes
Department of Economics
Carleton University
March 1981

522

GDP in the Finance, Insurance and Real Estate Industry (GDP$_f$), Canada, 1890-1930
(millions of dollars)

	1891	1892	1893	1894	1895	1896	1897	1898	1899	1900	1901	1902	1903	1904
Insurance 806/808														
Labour	3	3	4	4	4	4	4	5	5	6	6	7	8	9
Non-labour	2	3	3	3	3	3	3	4	4	2	4	9	8	2
GDP$_f$	5	7	6	7	7	8	8	9	9	8	11	15	16	11
Banking 802														
Labour	3	3	3	3	3	3	3	3	3	4	4	4	5	5
Non-labour	9	9	9	9	8	9	9	10	12	17	15	16	21	16
GDP$_f$	12	12	11	12	11	11	12	13	15	20	19	20	26	21
Investment & loan 804														
Labour	1	1	1	1	1	1	2	2	2	3	3	3	4	5
Non-labour	2	2	2	3	3	3	4	4	6	8	8	9	11	8
GDP$_f$	3	3	4	4	4	5	5	6	8	11	11	13	15	13
Real Estate 809														
Labour														
Non-labour														
GDP$_f$														
Total *														
Labour	7	7	7	8	8	9	9	10	11	13	13	14	17	19
Non-labour	13	15	14	14	14	15	16	18	21	27	27	34	40	25
GDP$_f$	20	22	21	22	22	24	25	28	32	39	41	48	57	45

GDP in the Finance, Insurance and Real Estate Industry (GDPf), Canada, 1890-1930
(millions of dollars)

	1905	1906	1907	1908	1909	1910	1911	1912	1913	1914	1915	1916	1917	1918
Insurance 806/808														
Labour	9	10	10	10	10	13	15	16	17	17	18	18	20	22
Non-labour	10	10	9	9	12	10	14	14	19	20	10	15	21	17
GDPf	20	20	19	19	22	23	28	30	36	37	28	33	41	39
Banking 802														
Labour	6	7	7	8	8	9	11	12	14	15	13	13	15	19
Non-labour	15	23	26	25	20	19	21	24	29	20	15	19	28	33
GDPf	20	30	34	33	28	28	32	36	42	34	28	32	43	52
Investment & loan 804														
Labour	5	7	7	8	8	9	8	10	12	13	13	13	14	13
Non-labour	10	15	17	16	16	13	15	19	24	20	14	15	20	17
GDPf	16	21	25	25	24	22	24	29	36	33	28	29	34	30
Real Estate 809														
Labour							3	4	4	5	5	5	5	5
Non-labour							5	5	7	6	4	5	7	6
GDPf							8	9	11	11	9	10	12	11
Total *														
Labour	20	23	24	25	27	31	37	42	46	49	49	49	54	59
Non-labour	35	48	53	50	48	43	55	62	79	65	43	55	76	73
GDPf	56	71	77	76	75	73	92	104	125	114	93	104	131	132

524

GDP in the Finance, Insurance and Real Estate Industry (GDP), Canada, 1890-1930
(millions of dollars)

	1919	1920	1921	1922	1923	1924	1925	1926	1927	1928	1929	1930	1931
Insurance 806/808													
Labour	30	35	38	37	39	42	49	51	61	61	66	69	66
Non-labour	24	38	36	33	27	30	39	50	61	61	52	24	3
GDP_r	53	74	74	71	67	72	89	100	122	122	118	93	70
Banking 802													
Labour	26	32	32	29	31	33	33	34	36	40	40	42	40
Non-labour	43	65	42	30	24	26	22	31	27	40	56	36	22
GDP_r	68	97	74	59	54	59	55	65	63	80	97	79	62
Investment and loan 804													
Labour	13	14	16	15	16	16	16	18	19	21	23	22	20
Non-labour	17	23	18	15	12	12	12	17	16	21	26	14	7
GDP_r	31	37	34	29	28	29	28	34	35	42	48	36	27
Real Estate 809													
Labour	5	5	5	5	5	5	5	5	5	6	7	5	5
Non-labour	6	8	6	5	3	4	4	5	5	6	7	3	1
GDP_r	11	13	12	10	8	9	8	9	10	12	14	7	6
Total *													
Labour	73	87	91	86	91	96	106	107	122	127	136	138	131
Non-labour	90	134	102	83	66	73	77	102	109	128	140	77	33
GDP_r	163	221	193	169	157	168	183	209	230	256	277	215	164

* Totals do not necessarily add owing to rounding

Bibliography of Sources Cited in Chapter 7

Statistics Canada, *National Income and Expenditure Accounts, 1926-1974*, Volume 1.

Dominion Bureau of Statistics, *National Income and Expenditure 1926-1956*.

Canada Superintendent of Insurance, *Report*, annual.

Curtis, C.A., "Banking Statistics in Canada" in Statistical Contributions to Canadian Economic History, Volume 1 (Toronto: Macmillan, 1931).

Neufeld, E.P., *The Financial System of Canada* (Macmillan, Canada, 1972).

Ontario Registrar of Loan Corporations, *Report*, annual.

Dominion Bureau of Statistics (and predecessor) *Census of Canada*.

In addition to the previous cited sources, a great deal of information came from unpublished sources, including unpublished material of Statistics Canada and of two chartered banks.

Chapter 8. Residential Rents and Residential Construction

MARION STEELE

This chapter has two distinct parts, related to one another by both dealing with residential housing. Residential rents measure the contribution of residential structures to gross domestic product. Residential construction is a component of gross national expenditure. Residential rents are presented first, followed by residential construction. In what follows all references by name are elaborated in the bibliography.

Part A

Gross Domestic Product at Factor Cost in Residential Rents

1. Introduction

Estimates of residential rent in Canada 1871-1925 currently do not exist, except for those of Firestone (*Canada's Economic Development 1867-1953*, (1958)) for decade-ending years. In this note we present and describe new annual estimates for 1871-1930. The fundamentals of our estimation procedure are simple. First we estimate mean paid and imputed rent in 1931, using the Census data of that year. Next we estimate an index of mean rents back to 1870; this index is a patchwork of separate indexes which we estimate from sources as diverse as surveys carried out by Ontario Bureau of Industries (OBI) in the 1880s and James Mavor's Toronto survey (Mavor) in the 1900s. Third we estimate the stock of dwelling units by urbanization level — urban, rural nonfarm, farm — and so derive gross rents by urbanization level. Finally we estimate deductions from gross rents: expenditure on repairs and maintenance, for sevices and facilities included in rent, and on fire insurance premiums.

2. The Estimate of 1931 Paid and Imputed Rent by Area

Our estimates of 1931 rent are based on data collected in the 1931 Census. Our first step is the estimation of average urban rents and average urban values from the Census frequency distributions. The simplest estimating procedure is based on the assumption that the mean of each class is the class mid-point. Some exhaustive research by Wickens (*Residential Real Estate*, 1941, pp.32, 33), however, suggests that this procedure yields an upward-biased estimate. In particular, in Wickens' sample of U.S. Census data, class means consistently fell below class mid-points. Wickens does not offer any explanation for this striking phenomenon but it seems plausible that it arises because of the way value and rent classes were specified. Classes used in the U.S. Census, like those used in the 1931 Canadian Census, typically opened with a number ending in zero or five but closed with a number ending in nine. For instance, in the Canadian Census one rent class was $10 to $15.99 and one value class was $1,000 to $1,999. It seems likely that a respondent who thought his house was worth $1,800 to $2,200 would focus on the even number $2,000 and so would choose the class $2,000 to $2,999 rather than the $1,000 to $1,999.[1] In view of the substantial similarity of the Canadian and American specifications, we have assumed values for class means (Table 8.1) using Wickens' findings as a guide.[2]

Because the 1931 Census collected rent and selling value data for urban dwellings only, we use ratios from the 1941 Census to estimate rents and values for rural dwellings. The 1941 ratio of rural nonfarm to urban is 0.62 for rents and 0.52 for values; and the 1941 ratio of farm values to rural nonfarm values is 0.66. These low values of rural housing are not surprising in view of the substandard nature of the rural housing, as indicated in Table 8.2. In particular, in 1941 only 13 percent of urban dwellings had no flush toilet while 81 percent of rural dwellings did not have one. (Lower land values, of course, would also help account for the lower values and rents in less urban areas.)

We note that we considered deriving rural values and rents by using the 1941 ratio for rural nonfarm to urban areas of *1,000 or less* population, rather than the 1941 ratio of rural nonfarm to *all* urban. The former ratio is appealing because it relates rural rents to rents in rural-like urban places. Unfortunately, however, there are only a small number of dwellings in these places and the Prairie Provinces are substantially over-represented. In 1941, 48 percent of all dwellings and 53 percent of rental dwellings in these tiny places were on the Prairies, as compared with only 44 percent of all in 1931 (*1941 Census*, Volume IX, Table 20; *1931 Census*, Volume V, Table 54). Under these circumstances there are no grounds for confidence that rent ratios will be stable between Censuses. In fact, the ratio of rents in such places to rents in all urban places fell substantially between 1931 and 1941 (*1941 Census*, Volume IX, Table 21; Royal Commission on Dominion-Provincial Relations, *National Income*, p.34 and Table 8.1, above). We conclude that a ratio based on **all** urban is more robust.[3]

For owner-occupied dwellings a further step is required, in order to get gross rent. We need to impute rent and to do this it is necessary to decide on the appropriate rent-to-value ratio. In equilibrium the net rent or return to the capital asset, housing, should be equal to the rate of interest plus an appropriate risk factor. Thus one way of arriving at an appropriate rent-to-value ratio would be to start with an appropriate rate of return on the above principles and then add on various items such as depreciation to yield a gross ratio. In this method the most difficult problem is determining the appropriate risk premium. It will be greater the greater is the probability that the house will decline in value — or even be abandoned, as many were during this period. It is also true that there will be a deduction required to the extent that owner-occupiers gain utility from ownership *per se*.

We avoid these difficulties by using United States empirical evidence on rent-to-value ra-

Table 8.1
Average Rent by Area, 1931

	Number of Households	Average Annual Gross Rent Per Household	Average Gross Rent Per Dwelling Unit
Urban owners	565,084	$ 405.8	$ 358.7
Urban renters	675,631	297.6	
Rural non-farm owners	181,302	191.8	189.0
Rural non-farm renters	145,830	183.1	
Farm owners	616,510	126.6	127.3
Farm renters	68,372		

Sources by column:

(1) *1931 Census*, Volume V, Table 61; *1931 Census*, Volume VIII, Table VIII. Farms include only farms of 10 acres or more.

(2) *1931 Census*, Volume V, Tables 71, 77, 79, 81, 83.

Urban Rents: Gross imputed average rent of owners computed assuming a mean value of $350 for the class "less than $500", and for other classes, $650 ($500-$999), $1,300 ($1,000-$1,999), $2,300 ($2,000-$2,999), $3,400 ($3,000-$3,999), $4,400 ($4,000-$4,999), $6,600 ($5,000-$9,999), $13,000 ($10,000 and over). Rent-to-value ratio assumed 0.10.

Gross paid rents of renters computed assuming rents for non-husband-wife households equal to 0.8 of husband-wife households and assuming a mean value of $7 for the class "less than $10" and assuming for other classes respectively, $12.50 ($10-$15.99), $19 ($16-$24.99), $30 ($25-$39.99), $46 ($40-$59.99), $70 ($60 and over).

Rural Nonfarm Rents: Average gross imputed rent of owners estimated as urban average for owners times (rural nonfarm average, 1941 divided by urban average value, 1941) times 10/11. The 10/11 ratio is required by the assumption that the rent-to-value ratio for rural nonfarm is only 0.0909 while for urban areas it is 0.10.

Gross paid average rent estimated as urban average, 1931, times (rural nonfarm average, 1941 divided by urban average, 1941) (*1941 Census*, Volume IX, Tables 21, 27).

Farm Rent: Estimated as 0.66 of average imputed rent for rural nonfarm owned dwellings.

(3) Weighted average from columns 1 and 2 times ratio of dwelling units to households. This ratio is 1.0342 for urban and 1.0054 for rural. (*1931 Census*, Volume V, Table 61)

tios. For single-family housing in the United States, evidence assembled by Grebler, Blank and Winnick (*Capital Formation in Residential Rents*, 1956), suggests a ratio of more than 0.10 in 1919, but 0.12 in the 1930s (1956, pp.408-414). Wickens, however, on the basis of a large, careful study of 1930 data, found ratios for areas with weather like Canada's of only 0.076 to 0.093 (1941, pp.35-37 and Table B20).

In view of this discussion, we assume a ratio of 0.10 for urban dwellings. This is equivalent to assuming a ratio of 0.091 for single-family, a ratio of 0.14 for multiple-family, and as-

Table 8.2
Quality Indicators, Rural and Urban Dwellings 1931 and 1941
(percentage)

		Wood Con-struction	Located in the Prairie Provinces	No Flush Toilet
Urban	1931	56	16	n.a.
	1941	43	16	13
Rural	1931	87	31	n.a.
	1941	81	30	81

Source: *1931 Census*, Volume V, Table 51 (refers to buildings containing dwellings),
and Table 54.
1941 Census, Volume IX, Tables 2, 16.

suming that 75 percent of owner-occupiers in 1931 occupied a single-family dwelling.[4] We note that in his housing study of 1931 Census data Greenway (*Housing in Canada*, 1941) used a ratio of 0.10 (1941, p.120).[5]

For rural nonfarm dwellings we assume a ratio of 0.0909. Rural nonfarm dwellings are almost all singles. It might be argued that the ratio for rural nonfarm singles should be less than the ratio for urban singles, because of the very low property taxes in rural areas. Offsetting this, however, is the poor fire protection in these areas which increases fire insurance premiums, and the higher risk of abandonment. The latter partially explains the higher interest rate charged on farm mortgages (*Historical Statistics of Canada* (HSC), Series H414, H417).

3. The Average Rent Index

For estimation of average rents prior to 1931 we are fortunate to have available the Statistics Canada series, average rents of six-room workmen's houses with sanitary conveniences, based on data collected by local correspondents of the *Labour Gazette* in 60 cities (HSC, pp.287-8). These data do not start until 1900 and omit 1901-1904 and 1906-08, so that the use of other data is also required.[6]

For the year 1871-1885 we use the construction cost index shown in Table 8.8, because we have no rent data prior to 1885. In the medium run one would expect rents to be substantially affected by construction costs, but of course other costs such as land costs and interest rates also have an effect; and in the short run demand fluctuations might cause substantial deviations from the longer-term trend. In view of these possibilities and in view of the crudeness of our construction cost index, sketchy evidence suggests the index does a surprisingly good job in capturing rent movements. Testimony before the Royal Commission on the Relations of Labour and Capital (Canada) in 1888 (RCRLC) is consistent with rents falling after 1878 but then rising again in the mid 1880s to a level in 1888 above the 1878 level,[7] and this is the pattern shown by our construction cost index.

For 1885-1889, we use an index based on rent data collected by Archibald Blue (later of the Dominion Bureau of Statistics) and published in the *Annual Reports* of the Ontario Bureau of Industries (OBI). These data are average rents by city, based on returns from about 3,000 workers; from these data we have computed a weighted average (see Table 8.3), using 1891 city populations as weights. Bits of rent information in the testimony before the RCRLC support the use of these data. In 1888, the average OBI monthly rent for Toronto was $10.14 (*Report*, 1889, p.54), while a working man testified to the Royal Commission that he paid $12 for a "comfortable" six-room house (*Report*, RCRLC, p.155). For Chatham the average OBI rent was $5.34 while a witness to the Royal Commission claimed a mechanic's comfortable house could be obtained for $4, while a five-room house in a "respectable locality" rented for $5-$6.

For 1889-1910 our index is computed in two stages, because of evidence that the indexes we use in the first stage very substantially understates the rise in average rent over this period. In the first stage, for 1889-1900 we use the construction cost index, linked at 1900 to the Statistics Canada rent index. As noted earlier, the Statistics Canada rent index is missing 1901-1904. So, for these years we interpolate using James Mavor's index of Toronto rents. Mavor's index is a pure price index — unlike the Statistics Canada (Statcan) rent index of this era — based on a sample of 68 Toronto houses, all with no improvements during the period of the index. As is apparent in Table 8.3 Mavor's index increased 1901-1905 by 20.1 percent or nearly twice the (Canada) average rent index increase,[8] but we presume it captured year-to-year movements well. Certainly the surge in Mavor's index 1904-1905 is consistent with the rapid increase in nonfarm housing starts in 1904 and 1905. If we used the alternative possible interpolator, the construction cost index, we would show a fall in rents in 1905. Mavor's index is not available for 1905-1910 and so we use the construction costs index for those years.

In the second stage of the estimation for 1889-1910 we correct for understatement of the change in average rent over this period. The extent of understatement is revealed by the following. For 1888, using mean rents computed from data in the RCRLC[9] for each of Nova Scotia, New Brunswick, Quebec and Ontario we derive weighted mean rent for Canada, using the number of permanent occupied dwelling units in 1891 (Pickett, *Residential Capital Formation in Canada 1871-1921*, 1961) as weights. The result is $6.87. For 1910 we use provincial mean rents (*Wholesale Prices Canada, 1916*) and Pickett's data to compute an analogous weighted mean. It is $13.55. This shows an increase of 97.2 percent in average rents between 1888 and 1910, as compared with an increase of only 37.5 percent shown by our first stage index.

Part of this difference is attributable to the fact that the Statistics Canada index is based on rents which are unweighted averages of rents in 60 cities. Thus, between 1900 and 1910 the Statistics Canada index does not reflect the increasing importance of Prairie dwelling units which commanded very high rents in this period.[10] The required adjustment is estimated as follows. The appropriate ratio, 1910 average rent to 1900 average rent, is

$$\frac{\sum r_{1i} d_{1i} \div \sum d_{1i}}{\sum r_{0i} d_{0i} \div \sum d_{0i}}$$

where r_{0i} and r_{1i} is average rent in province i in 1900 and in 1910 respectively, and d_{0i} and d_{1i} is number of permanent occupied dwelling units in 1900 and 1910 respectively. This ratio may be expressed by

Table 8.3
Components of Average Rent Index

Year	Construction Cost Index 1913=100	Ontario Bureau of Industries Index 1889=100	Toronto Index (James Mavor) 1900=61.7	Six-Room Work-Men's Houses (Statcan Index) 1913=100	Average Rent Index 1931=100
1870	63.33				24.89
1871	65.10				25.58
1872	74.00				29.08
1873	76.29				29.98
1874	75.30				29.59
1875	70.22				27.60
1876	66.80				26.25
1877	64.42				25.32
1878	62.54				24.59
1879	61.41				24.13
1880	61.21				24.45
1881	64.28				25.26
1882	68.64				26.98
1883	66.93				26.30
1884	64.82				25.47
1885	62.90	96.45			24.72
1886	62.83	86.17			23.67
1887	66.16	98.35			27.02
1888	69.13	100.10			27.50
1889	68.90	100.00			27.47
1890	66.86				27.32
1891	65.04				27.39
1892	65.89				28.29
1893	64.39				28.34
1894	63.89				28.82
1895	62.09				28.71
1896	62.27				29.51
1897	59.11		46.74		28.71
1898	60.22		51.42		29.98
1899	62.09		58.90		31.69
1900	67.25		61.70	61.7	35.18
1901	67.28		65.44		37.34
1902	70.34		67.78		38.41
1903	75.54		69.65		39.33
1904	76.90		73.39		40.92
1905	78.40		81.80	73.5	44.17
1906	82.40		91.15		46.75
1907	85.64				48.93
1908	90.36				51.47
1909	90.02			83.6	51.66
1910	89.96			86.9	54.08

Table 8.3 (continued)

Year	Construction Cost Index 1913=100	Ontario Bureau of Industries Index 1889=100	Toronto Index (James Mavor) 1900=61.7	Six-Room Work-Men's Houses (Statcan Index) 1913=100	Average Rent Index 1931=100
1911	94.84			88.4	55.01
1912	96.82			94.9	59.05
1913	100.00			100.0	62.23
1914	96.36			97.0	60.36
1915	93.65			94.1	58.56
1916	102.46			95.0	59.12
1917	122.66			102.0	63.47
1918	142.17			108.0	67.21
1919	166.69			117.9	73.37
1920	201.66			134.9	83.95
1921	177.50			147.0	91.47
1922				153.0	95.21
1923				156.9	97.64
1924				158.0	98.32
1925				158.0	98.32
1926				156.0	97.08
1927				154.1	95.89
1928				157.9	98.26
1929				161.1	100.24
1930				165.2	102.80
1931				160.7	100.00

Sources:

Column (1): Table 8.8, Column 3.
Column (2): Computed from data given in *Annual Report* of OBI, various issues. For each year a weighted average rent is computed with 1891 population as weight. For the computation of the proportional change between adjacent years, the sample of cities is kept the same. These proportional changes are then chained to produce the index. Thirteen places are present in all five years, with as many as 8 additional places in other years.
Column (3): James Mavor Papers (Robarts Library), File ARel, table headed "Rents in Toronto 1896-1906 in Dollars per Month". This is an index using a sample of 68 houses, with 1896=100.
Column (4): Greenway (1941, p.106). This index is apparently the same as HSC Series J142.
Column (5): 1871-1885: Column (1) converted to 1885=24.72
1885-1889: Column (2) converted to 1885=24.72 and with the value for 1885 in column (2) assumed at 90. Food and clothing per capita were higher in 1885 than in other years and there were fewer dependents than in 1886 and 1887; therefore we presume the 1885 sample yields upward-biased rents.
1889-1900: Column (1) times an index showing a 2.5 percent annual cumulated increase; converted to 1889=27.47
1900-1910: Column (4) with interpolation 1901-04 using column (3) and 1906-08 using column (1) x (index showing a 2.5 percent increase), converted to 1900=35.18. The 1901-04 interpolation is computed by taking 0.5871 times the proportional year-to-year change shown by (3); this ratio, 0.5871, is the ratio of the proportional change 1900-1905 of the average rent index to the proportional change of the Mavor index.
1910-1931: Column (4)

$$\frac{(\sum r_{1i}\, d_{1i} \ \div \ \sum d_{1i})}{(\sum r_{1i}\, d_{0i} \ \div \ \sum d_{0i})} \qquad \frac{\sum r_{1i}\, d_{0i}}{\sum r_{0i}\, d_{0i}}$$

and we note that

$$\frac{\sum r_{1i}\, d_{0i}}{\sum r_{0i}\, d_{0i}}$$

is approximately the same as the ratio of the Statistics Canada index in 1910 to the Statistics Canada index in 1900. Plugging the data[11] into this expression yields

$$(\ \frac{13.550}{12.643} \ ) \ 1.4083 \ = \ 1.07178 \times 1.4083$$

In other words, the very great increase in the number of Prairie and B.C. dwelling units between 1900 and 1910 accounted for seven percentage points of the increase in average rents during that period.

The remaining differential is, we assume, the result of quality improvements. There were three kinds of quality improvements taking place in this era. First, there was an increase in the size of dwellings. We see this in Table 8.4; the average number of rooms per dwelling increased by six percent between 1891 and 1901, decreased very slightly in the following decade and then fell quite substantially in succeeding decades.[12] Examination of the detailed room distributions between 1891 and 1901 shows that this drop may be attributed partly to the "disappearance" of large numbers of very small houses, either through abandonment or because rooms were added, turning them into large houses.

The second kind of improvement was in the use of higher quality materials of construction. As is the case for number of rooms, of course, the improvement in the stock may have come about largely via the abandonment of poorer quality houses, rather than via a change between the 1880s and the 1890s in the materials used to build new housing. The percentage of dwellings built of wood fell from 80 percent in 1891 to 73 percent in 1901 and then stayed about the same in 1911 and 1921 (*1921 Census*, Volume III, Table 5).[13]

Another important improvement which occurred during these years was the installation of indoor plumbing. We know that by 1941, all but 13 percent of urban dwellings had an inside flush toilet (Table 8.2, above). Unfortunately there is nothing like comprehensive data for earlier years, but impressionistic evidence suggest that few dwellings had such facilities in 1891 and a substantial number had them in 1901. For instance, testimony before the RCRLC indicates that in 1888 dwellings with plumbing rented at well above the average rent.[14] Then, in the 1890s and 1900s municipal sewage systems were installed and building regulations relating to plumbing and to fire residence were tightened.[15] In fact, R.H. Coats (Canada, Board of Inquiry into the Cost of Living, 1915, *Report*, Vol. 1, P. 1) gives the following reasons for the increase in rents 1900-1914.

(1)   The increased cost of building material
(2)   The increased cost of labour

Table 8.4
Average Number of Rooms at Census Dates 1891-1931

	1891	1901	1911	1921	1931
Adjusted for definition changes: average number of rooms per occupied permanent dwelling unit					
Canada	5.80	6.14	6.08	5.90	5.76
Unadjusted for definition changes:					
Canada	5.80	5.86	6.09	6.00	5.64
Prince Edward Island	6.24	6.76	7.43	7.26	7.48
Nova Scotia	6.24	6.41	7.15	6.94	6.55
New Brunswick	6.23	6.40	7.46	7.17	6.71
Quebec	5.21	5.46	6.28	6.36	5.90
Ontario	6.25	6.44	6.93	6.67	6.24
Manitoba	4.00	4.16	5.09	5.07	4.82
Saskatchewan	3.44	3.24	3.22	4.23	4.29
Alberta			3.51	4.27	4.15
British Columbia	4.31	4.16	5.13	4.88	4.56

Notes:

1. Figures for Canada exclude Yukon and Northwest Territories.

2. "Unadjusted" figures were estimated as follows. From the 1931 Census were available, by province, households by number of rooms occupied. From this we derived by province the average number of rooms in the classes 6-10 rooms, 11-15 rooms, 16+ rooms, and 11+ rooms. The results were applied, by province, to the room distributions in earlier Census years, to yield the average number of rooms. This procedure by itself probably overstates rooms per dwelling in 1891 and to a lesser extent in 1901 and 1911.

3. The adjusted figures were derived as follows: for 1891 no adjustment was required because the rooms distribution was for "houses", i.e. occupied dwellings excluding temporary dwellings (vessels and shanties) (*1891 Census*, Volume I, Table II). For 1901 the rooms distribution was for "families occupying" (*1901 Census*, Volume IV, Table XVII). The number of families per dwelling unit is 1.0397 (*1941 Census*, Volume V, Table 1) yielding 6.09 rooms per dwelling unit. To get rooms per *permanent* dwelling unit we subtract total temporary units (Steele, 1976 Table 1) minus those in unorganized territories (Pickett, 1961, Table 1A) from total units and assumed temporary units were one room units. For 1911 and 1921 the room distribution was for dwellings but dwellings were undercounted (Steele, 1976, Table 1). Adjustment for this yields average number of room 5.99 in 1911 and 5.87 in 1921. Further adjustment for temporary units (see explanation for 1901) yields the numbers given in line one. For 1931 the room distribution was for *households* excluding rooming houses, tents, etc. The number of households per dwelling unit, 1.022, yields 5.76 rooms per dwelling.

(3)   Higher standards of construction fixed by more stringent building by-laws.
(4)   General demand for conveniences which a few years ago were luxuries.

It remains to decide how to allocate this quality improvements over the 1889-1910 period.

We allocate it all to the years 1889-1901. The major reason for doing this is the evidence of the average room data from the Censuses. They show that while dwellings improved in all provinces over the 1901-1911 decade as well as over the previous decade, the greatly increased importance of provinces with a lower, although improving, quality of stock kept the 1911 Canada average at about the same level as the 1901 Canada average.

The final average rent index for 1889-1910 is the first index times the adjustment index just described. The adjustment index shows a 2.5 percent increase (cumulated) per year until 1901 and then a 0.7 percent increase until 1910; thus the adjustment index has a value of 1.025 in 1890, 1.345 in 1901 and 1.43 in 1910.

We conclude this section by presenting evidence on the validity of using the Statcan rent index to represent the movement in average rent by urbanization level between 1910 and 1931. Without confronting this index with any alternative data there is a *prima facie* case for accepting it, because it is in concept a cross between a unit value index and a price index, unlike the current rent component of the CPI. In particular it is based on rents of a six-room workmen's house with sanitary conveniences, and after 1926 "includes apartments and flats for both workmen's and middle class dwellings" (Greenway, 1941, p.106 and *Wholesale Prices, 1916,* Appendix A). If the typical workmen's house increased in the quality of materials used, the index would reflect this. In fact, from Table 8.1 we have from Census data that average urban paid rent was $24.80 per month in 1931. Using the Statcan Canada index to project this back we get a rent for 1910 of $12.90. Above, we computed average rent for 1910 from the *Labour Gazette* returns as $13.55. The correspondence is remarkable.

4. Occupied Dwelling Unit Stock, Farm, Rural Nonfarm and Urban

We compute gross rent separately for farm, rural nonfarm and urban dwelling units. This requires estimation of dwelling stocks for these three components. We use the data in Steele (1976) for the years up to 1921, estimating stock as 1871 stock plus cumulated net change, where net change is starts minus (loss minus conversions). The tedious details of this estimation, plus details of the estimation for 1921-1931 are given in the source notes to Table 8.5. It is worthwhile to note here that we obtained urban stock from total nonfarm stock by assuming that the proportion of urban dwellings to all nonfarm changed linearly between adjacent Census years.

The question might be raised as to the suitability of assuming that the ratio of urban average rent to rural average rent existing in the 1931 persisted back into earlier years. As Table 8.1 shows, rural rents were very much lower than urban rents in 1931. It would of course be naive to imagine that the ratio remained precisely the same in earlier years. The alternative assumption (used by Firestone, 1958) that in early years average global rent was unaffected by the much higher ratio of rural to urban seems much more untenable, however, than our assumption. For instance, in 1913, average rent reported by *Labour Gazette* correspondents was $25 for Toronto, as against $16 for urban Ontario as a whole (*Wholesale Prices, Canada, 1916*, pp.231, 237) and in 1888, Toronto rent was $10 as compared with $6.50 for urban Ontario (OBI, *Report*, 1889, Part V, p.154).

This great differential between the rent of a large urban place and smaller urban places is like the pattern in 1931 and 1941 and suggests that the 1931 and 1941 pattern of much lower rents in rural than in urban areas also existed in the later nineteenth century. There are good economic reasons to expect this pattern to persist over time. First, land costs are higher in more densely settled places. Perhaps more important, quality is generally substantially higher in more densely settled places because of the concern for negative externalities caused by characteristics such as nonfire-resistance construction, and because of the higher average income of those in more densely settled places.

Gross rent is estimated as available private permanent dwelling unit stock times the occupancy rate times average rent. The occupancy rate between Census years is estimated by linear interpolation between adjacent Census years.

We note that we do not attempt to estimate the stock separately by tenure. One reason for not doing so is the absence of Census information on tenure prior to 1921. Some reassurance for the validity of our estimates despite this omission comes from the 1921 and 1931 Censuses. In 1931, 45.9 percent of urban households were owners, as compared to 46.1 percent of urban families in 1921; for rural areas, the numbers are 79.4 percent and 78.5 percent (*1931 Census*, Volume V, Table 61; *1921 Census*, Volume III, Table 15).[16] The stability of the ownership ratio 1921-1931, in view of the apartment-building boom in the late twenties suggests that there was a substantial change occurring in the type of structure used as a rental unit, from the typical single-detached unit of earlier years.

Prior to 1921 the only data on ownership we have is from the OBI survey of wage-earners. In 1886 the ratio of owners to owners plus tenants was 28.4 percent (*Report*, 1886, p.20). The ratio for larger places was much lower than for the smaller places; for instance the ratio for Toronto was 11.2 while that for Guelph was 38.2. The ratio for all urban Ontario wage *and* salary earners in 1931 was 45.4 percent. Because salary earners would have a higher incidence of ownership than wage earners, it appears plausible that the urban ratio of owners was not lower by more than 10 percentage points in the nineteenth century as compared with the 1920s.

5. Deductions from Gross Rent

To obtain gross domestic product originating from the residential rental, it is necessary to deduct allowances for services and facilities included in rent, for repair and maintenance expenditure and/or fire insurance premiums. There is virtually no contemporary Canadian evidence on these first two items. For the United States, in 1933, Wickens found that the cost of facilities *and* services provided to the tenant was 9 to 10 percent of gross rent for single-family dwellings, 11 percent for two-family and 25 percent for apartments (Wickens, 1941, p.141). These ratios are undoubtedly substantially too high as estimates of the situation in 1931 and most earlier years because of the greater drop in rents than in utility prices over 1931-1933. At the same time, the proportion of dwellings with facilities included in rent in the United States cities sampled by Wickens was not much different from the proportion in Canada in 1941; the proportion of rental dwellings furnished was 10.8 percent in the United States, as compared with 4.9 percent for urban Canada while the proportion with heat included was 15.2 percent in the U.S. as compared with 22.8 percent (Wickens, 1941, p.134 and *1941 Census*, Volume IX, Table 22). In view of this we assume that facilities accounted for six percent of gross rent for urban units and three percent for rural non-farm units.[17] We use the same percentage for all years. Grebler, Blank and Winnick (1956, pp.414-416, esp. Table I-4) present evidence that although this ratio likely rose sharply after 1930, prior to that it was remarkably stable.

For repair and maintenance expenditure estimation we have data from a survey of 473 civil service families for the year ended October 31, 1931. These families spent an average of 15.9 percent of imputed gross rent (where imputed gross rent is taken as 10 percent of selling value) on repairs and replacements (Greenway, 1941, p.172). The ratio is remarkably consistent from income class to income class, never differing from the mean overall ratio by more than a percentage point. We note that these families lived mostly in the City of Ottawa where building

Table 8.5
Stock of Dwelling Units, by Area

| | Number of Units (thousands) | | | | Vacancy Rate (per cent) | |
	Farm	Nonfarm Total	Urban		Farm	Nonfarm
1871	332.7	298.3	120.3		4.5	4.3
1872	342.4	323.3	133.5		4.6	4.5
1873	345.1	335.1	141.6		4.8	4.6
1874	351.3	347.8	150.3		4.9	4.8
1875	358.8	360.5	159.2		5.1	4.9
1876	365.8	371.1	167.5		5.2	5.0
1877	374.3	378.9	174.7		5.4	5.2
1878	382.6	384.5	180.9		5.5	5.3
1879	390.2	389.0	186.8		5.6	5.5
1880	398.8	394.0	193.0		5.8	5.6
1881	406.8	398.8	199.1		5.9	5.7
1882	412.8	402.4	205.2		5.9	5.7
1883	416.8	405.3	210.9		5.9	5.7
1884	420.0	408.8	217.0		5.9	5.7
1885	423.8	414.0	224.0		5.9	5.6
1886	427.5	421.5	232.5		5.8	5.6
1887	430.2	432.5	243.1		5.8	5.6
1888	432.5	446.8	255.8		5.8	5.6
1889	435.0	463.1	270.0		5.8	5.5
1890	436.9	479.3	284.4		5.8	5.5
1891	437.3	496.4	299.8		5.7	5.5
1892	437.6	514.2	312.7		5.4	5.2
1893	439.3	528.3	323.5		5.1	4.9
1894	440.4	537.8	331.6		4.8	4.6
1895	440.7	545.1	338.4		4.5	4.3
1896	441.0	552.8	345.5		4.2	4.0
1897	441.3	562.5	354.0		3.9	3.8
1898	442.9	574.2	363.8		3.6	3.5
1899	446.3	586.5	374.1		3.3	3.2
1900	450.3	597.3	383.4		3.0	2.9
1901	455.0	607.5	392.5		2.7	2.6
1902	462.9	619.1	406.0		2.8	2.7
1903	474.9	633.3	421.5		2.9	2.8
1904	490.6	651.6	439.9		3.0	2.9
1905	510.3	675.1	462.3		3.1	3.0
1906	528.9	704.8	489.4		3.2	3.1
1907	544.7	736.5	518.6		3.3	3.2
1908	559.8	764.5	545.7		3.4	3.3
1909	577.0	795.3	575.3		3.5	3.4
1910	600.9	837.6	614.1		3.6	3.4

Table 8.5 (continued)

	Number of Units (thousands)			Vacancy Rate (per cent)	
	Farm	Nonfarm Total	Urban	Farm	Nonfarm
1911	619.8	890.3	661.3	3.7	3.5
1912	627.3	953.2	710.9	3.6	3.4
1913	631.3	1016.0	761.0	3.4	3.3
1914	634.6	1063.5	799.9	3.3	3.1
1915	637.4	1090.1	823.3	3.1	3.0
1916	641.1	1105.2	838.2	3.0	2.9
1917	647.2	1119.0	852.1	2.8	2.7
1918	654.9	1131.6	865.2	2.7	2.6
1919	661.3	1149.3	882.3	2.6	2.5
1920	661.1	1172.7	904.0	2.4	2.4
1921	670.4	1193.2	923.5	2.3	2.2
1922	674.1	1213.6	939.8	2.5	2.4
1923	677.8	1237.2	958.5	2.7	2.6
1924	681.6	1261.7	978.0	3.0	2.8
1925	685.3	1287.8	998.8	3.2	3.0
1926	689.0	1319.6	1024.0	3.4	3.1
1927	692.7	1360.3	1056.1	3.7	3.3
1928	696.5	1405.4	1901.7	3.9	3.5
1929	700.2	1445.3	1123.2	4.1	3.7
1930	703.9	1476.0	1147.7	4.3	3.9

Sources:

Columns (1) & (2):

Stock year t is 0.5 (Stock, end year t plus stock, end year t-1).

1871-1920: Stock end year t is 1871 stock of permanent occupied dwellings (Steele, 1976, Table 1 and Table 4, "favoured farm starts" footnote) plus starts (Steele, 1976, Table A1) minus (loss minus conversions). Our (loss minus conversions) per *decade* is in Steele (1976, Table 1, note). We assume 0.1 of decade loss occurred in each year of the decade.

1921-1931: For stock end 1921 to end 1931 a different procedure is required because of the different basis of starts (Steele, 1972). The change in farm stock 1921-1931 is computed as 1931 farm stock (occupied plus vacant minus all temporary units) minus farm stock end 1920 as cumulated from the 1871-1920 calculation. Farm occupied is defined as occupied farms of 10 acres or more. Sources of farm: *1941 Census*, Volume VIII, Pt. 1, Table 2; *1931 Census*, Volume VIII, Table 32. All temporary units (Steele, 1976, Table 1 for 1921 and Steele, 1972, Table 6.8 for 1931) are taken as farm. The change in farm stock per year is taken as 0.1 times decade change.

The net change in nonfarm stock 1921-1931 is computed as nonfarm starts minus (loss minus conversions). Nonfarm starts are total starts (Steele, 1972) minus 0.1 decade farm starts, where farm starts are estimated in a fashion consistent with estimation of total starts (Steele, 1972, Table 6.8). Decade nonfarm loss is urban demolitions plus rural nonfarm abandonments plus nonfarm fire loss minus conversions (Steele, 1972). Each annual figure is 0.1 of this figure.

(sources continued at the bottom of page 539.)

standards would be higher than in the typical urban place; and we note that civil service families probably included many fewer manual workers, able to do their own repairs, than the typical Canadian family of the time. Grebler, Blank and Winnick's data for the U.S., however, suggest a ratio about the same as this for rental units in New York City over the 1900-1924 period.[18] In view of this, we assume a ratio of 13 percent for urban and rural nonfarm, and a ratio of 8 percent for farm.

In the era we are concerned with fires caused relatively much more damage than they do now. The civil service owners in the 1931 survey paid only 2.4 percent of gross rent in fire insurance premiums but they lived in a city well protected by a fire department and they probably also lived in housing much more fire resistant than the typical house. We assume that fire insurance premiums were 6 percent of gross rent in the case of rural and urban nonfarm and 10 percent in the case of farm. This results in an estimate of residential fire insurance premiums paid in 1925 or $24 million, or not much more than half the $57 million total fire insurance premiums paid (HSC, Series H448).[19] In 1871 the amount is $1.4 million as compared with (for reporting companies) $2.3 million (HSC, Series H436); in 1891, $2.4 million ($6.2); in 1911 $9.3 million ($21).

The cost items described above were calculated by applying the percentages to potential gross rent, i.e. gross rent before allowance for vacancies. For example, if the vacancy rate were 5 percent, the gross rent in column 1 of Table 8.6 would be 95 percent of the potential gross rent and fire insurance premiums would be 10 percent of potential gross rent.

Table 8.5 Sources (continued)

Column (3):
    Census years: Urban stock is occupied urban units excluding Yukon and Northwest Territories (*1931 Census*, Volume V, Table 48 and *1921 Census*, Volume III, Table 6). To the 1921 Census figure is added 41,200 to adjust for the multiple-unit problem (Steele, 1976). Urban stock in Census years 1871-1911 is estimated as total occupied private permanent dwellings (Steele, 1976 times proportion of population urban times 1.03624. The proportion of population urban is from Stone (1967, Table 2.2, p.29). The ratio 1.03624 is urban dwelling units as a percentage of all dwelling units divided by the percentage of population urban, for 1931.

    For other than Census years: The ratio of urban to nonfarm is 0.403, computed at Census years (the results are, starting with 1871, 0.499, 0.604, 0.646, 0.743, 0.774, 0.778) and for other years is obtained by linear interpolation.

Columns (4) & (5):
    For Census years 1871-1921: The vacancy rate is vacancies (Steele, 1976, Table 1) divided by private permanent units. Vacancies are divided between farm and nonfarm in proportion to the number of occupied units. For 1931, nonfarm vacancies are urban vacancies (Steele, 1972, Table 6.8) divided by the ratio (0.778) of urban to non-farm occupied units. For 1931, farm vacancies are farm vacant and abandoned.

    For non-Census years: The vacancy rate is obtained by linear interpolation between adjacent Census years.

Table 8.6
Gross Rental Revenue and Deductions, Farm
(thousands of dollars)

	Gross Rental Revenue	Repair and Maintenance Services and Facilities	Fire Insurance Premium	Gross Domestic Product 1−(2+3)	Depreciation
	(1)	(2)	(3)	(4)	(5)
1871	10348.1	1191.7	1083.4	8073.1	1787
1872	12090.6	1394.5	1267.8	9428.3	2092
1873	12542.1	1448.8	1317.1	9776.2	2173
1874	12583.0	1455.8	1323.4	9803.9	2183
1875	11964.8	1386.3	1260.3	9318.1	2079
1876	11586.3	1344.6	1222.3	9019.5	2017
1877	11414.0	1326.6	1206.3	8881.4	1990
1878	11316.7	1317.3	1197.6	8801.9	1976
1879	11240.3	1310.5	1191.4	8738.6	1965
1880	11691.5	1365.2	1241.0	9085.2	2047
1881	12304.2	1439.0	1308.1	9557.2	2159
1882	13335.3	1559.1	1417.4	10358.6	2339
1883	13131.7	1535.0	1395.5	10201.2	2303
1884	12418.9	1498.2	1361.9	9958.8	2247
1885	12554.0	1466.9	1333.5	9753.6	2200
1886	12128.0	1416.8	1288.0	9423.2	2125
1887	13932.2	1627.2	1479.3	10825.7	2441
1888	14259.8	1665.1	1513.7	11081.0	2498
1889	14329.9	1672.9	1520.8	11136.2	2509
1890	14318.4	1671.2	1519.3	11127.9	2507
1891	14369.4	1676.8	1524.4	11168.3	2515
1892	14899.3	1733.1	1575.5	11590.6	2600
1893	15030.4	1742.8	1584.4	11703.2	2614
1894	15371.1	1776.7	1615.2	11979.3	2665
1895	15372.7	1771.3	1610.2	11991.3	2657
1896	15862.2	1821.9	1656.3	12384.0	2733
1897	15494.3	1774.1	1612.8	12107.4	2661
1898	16289.4	1859.3	1690.3	12739.9	2789
1899	17400.0	1979.9	1799.9	13620.3	2970
1900	19550.5	2217.7	2016.1	15316.8	3327
1901	21033.1	2378.5	2162.2	16492.4	3568
1902	21988.8	2489.0	2262.7	17237.1	3733
1903	23076.9	2614.8	2377.1	18085.1	3922
1904	24778.0	2810.3	2554.8	19412.9	4215
1905	27796.2	3155.5	2868.9	21771.5	4734

Table 8.6 (continued)

	Gross Rental Revenue	Repair and Maintenance Services and Facilities	Fire Insurance Premium	Gross Domestic Product 1−(2+3)	Depre- ciation
	(1)	(2)	(3)	(4)	(5)
1906	30461.1	3461.8	3147.1	23852.2	5193
1907	32799.0	3731.2	3392.0	25675.8	5597
1908	35422.8	4033.7	3667.0	27722.1	6051
1909	36609.2	4173.0	3793.6	28642.6	6259
1910	39868.5	4549.1	4135.5	31183.9	6824
1911	41793.9	4773.5	4339.6	32680.7	7160
1912	45473.5	5186.2	4714.7	35572.6	7779
1913	48292.9	5499.7	4999.7	37793.5	8250
1914	47157.6	5362.5	4875.0	36920.0	8044
1915	46017.6	5225.3	4750.2	36042.0	7838
1916	46794.4	5305.7	4823.4	36665.2	7959
1917	50793.3	5750.8	5228.0	39814.6	8626
1918	54504.7	6162.0	5601.8	42740.9	9243
1919	60171.5	6792.8	6175.3	47203.5	10189
1920	69443.9	7828.2	7116.5	54499.1	11742
1921	76270.5	8585.3	7804.8	59880.4	12878
1922	79637.6	8985.4	8168.5	62483.7	13478
1923	81925.9	9265.4	8423.1	64237.5	13898
1924	82758.3	9381.6	8528.7	64848.0	14072
1925	83014.2	9432.9	8575.4	65005.9	14149
1926	82213.9	9364.1	8512.9	64336.9	14046
1927	81458.0	9300.1	8454.7	63703.2	13950
1928	83716.0	9580.7	8709.7	65425.5	14371
1929	85664.8	9827.2	8933.8	66903.8	14741
1930	88101.3	10130.9	9209.9	68760.5	15196

Sources:

Column (1): Gross rent is stock (Table 8.5) times 0.01 times average rent index (Table 8.3) times 1931 farm rent (Table 8.1) times (one minus vacancy rate) (Table 8.5).

Column (2): Gross rent gross of vacancy allowance times 0.11

Column (3): Gross rent gross of vacancy allowance times 0.10

Column (5): Gross rent gross of vacancy allowance times 0.165

"Gross Domestic Product" is gross of depreciation.

Table 8.7
Gross Rental Revenue and Deductions, Nonfarm
(thousands of dollars)

	Gross Rental Revenue	Repair and Maintenance Services and Facilities	Fire Insurance Premium	Gross Domestic Product 1−(2+3)	Depreciation
	(1)	(2)	(3)	(4)	(5)
1871	18797.4	3733.4	1179.0	13885.1	2948
1872	23271.7	4628.9	1461.8	17181.1	3654
1873	24980.5	4976.1	1571.4	18432.9	3929
1874	25715.0	5130.1	1620.0	18964.9	4050
1875	24973.4	4989.5	1575.6	18408.2	3939
1876	24571.8	4916.6	1552.6	18102.5	3881
1877	24305.0	4870.4	1538.0	17896.5	3845
1878	24067.8	4830.1	1525.3	17712.4	3813
1879	23861.3	4795.8	1514.5	17551.0	3786
1880	24743.8	4980.6	1572.8	18190.3	3932
1881	25991.3	5239.5	1654.6	19097.1	4137
1882	28197.9	5682.8	1794.6	20720.7	4486
1883	27877.7	5616.6	1773.7	20487.4	4434
1884	27419.4	5522.6	1744.0	20152.8	4360
1885	27121.2	5461.0	1724.5	19935.6	4311
1886	26611.7	5356.9	1691.6	19563.2	4229
1887	31374.2	6313.7	1993.8	23066.7	4985
1888	33204.6	6680.1	2109.5	24414.9	5274
1889	34600.3	6958.9	2197.5	25443.8	5494
1890	35849.0	7208.0	2276.2	26364.9	5690
1891	37463.7	7530.4	2378.0	27555.2	5945
1892	40303.7	8076.9	2550.6	29676.2	6376
1893	41702.1	8332.0	2631.2	30738.9	6578
1894	43411.6	8647.6	2730.8	32033.1	6827
1895	44068.5	8752.3	2763.9	32552.5	6910
1896	46187.0	9145.7	2888.1	34153.1	7220
1897	45973.5	9076.4	2866.2	34030.8	7166
1898	49274.1	9699.3	3062.9	36511.9	7657
1899	53477.3	10495.6	3314.4	39667.2	8286
1900	60787.5	11895.3	3756.4	45135.8	9391
1901	65974.4	12872.4	4065.0	49037.0	10162
1902	69472.2	13567.7	4284.5	51620.0	10711
1903	73095.8	14288.9	4512.3	54294.7	11281
1904	78588.9	15377.2	4856.0	58355.7	12140
1905	88293.5	17292.4	5460.8	65540.3	13652

Table 8.7   (continued)

	Gross Rental Revenue	Repair and Maintenance Services and Facilities	Fire Insurance Premium	Gross Domestic Product 1−(2+3)	Depre- ciation
	(1)	(2)	(3)	(4)	(5)
1906	97986.7	19209.1	6066.0	72711.6	15165
1907	107650.9	21123.6	6670.6	79856.7	16677
1908	118050.5	23186.3	7322.0	87542.2	18305
1909	123798.9	24338.5	7685.8	91774.7	19215
1910	137071.0	26973.4	8517.9	101579.8	21295
1911	148843.5	29317.9	9258.3	110267.3	23146
1912	171591.2	33752.5	10658.7	127180.0	26647
1913	193314.1	37973.8	11991.7	143348.6	29979
1914	196876.6	38621.0	12196.1	146059.5	30490
1915	196370.9	38469.6	12148.3	145753.0	30371
1916	201601.2	39440.7	12455.0	149705.5	31137
1917	219819.3	42946.7	13562.1	163310.5	33905
1918	236071.2	46059.6	14545.1	175466.5	36363
1919	262528.9	51152.6	16153.5	195222.8	40384
1920	307428.1	59820.3	18890.6	228717.2	47227
1921	341885.7	66435.7	20979.7	254470.3	52449
1922	361319.2	70344.1	22213.9	268761.2	55535
1923	377110.9	73557.0	23228.5	280325.4	58071
1924	386612.8	75552.8	23858.8	287201.2	59647
1925	393974.7	77137.1	24359.1	292478.5	60898
1926	397920.9	78057.5	24649.7	295213.7	61624
1927	404507.3	79500.2	25105.3	299901.8	62763
1928	427498.8	84178.7	26582.8	316737.3	66457
1929	447779.5	88340.3	27896.9	331542.2	69742
1930	468149.6	92535.5	29221.7	346392.4	73054

Sources:

Column (1): Gross rent is gross urban rent plus gross rural nonfarm rent. Gross urban rent is urban stock (Table 8.5) times 0.01 times average rent index (Table 8.3) times 1931 average urban rent (Table 8.1) times (one minus vacancy rate) (Table 8.5). Rural nonfarm gross rent is estimated analogously using rural nonfarm stock (by subtraction, Table 8.1).

Column (2): Gross rent gross of vacancy allowance times 0.19

Column (3): Gross rent gross of vacancy allowance times 0.06

Column (5): Gross rent gross of vacancy allowance times 0.15

Table 8.8
Construction Cost Index
1913=100

Year	Construction Materials Index	Construction Wage Index	Construction Cost Index
1870	73.60	(48.18)	63.33
1871	76.86	48.18	65.10
1872	89.41	52.43	74.00
1873	93.60	52.43	76.29
1874	91.19	53.12	75.30
1875	83.72	51.04	70.22
1876	77.44	51.04	66.80
1877	73.08	51.04	64.42
1878	69.73	51.04	62.58
1879	67.58	51.04	61.41
1880	69.05	51.04	62.21
1881	72.83	51.04	64.28
1882	77.61	54.70	68.64
1883	72.79	51.44	66.93
1884	82.79	52.23	64.82
1885	70.57	50.75	62.90
1886	69.21	52.72	62.83
1887	72.21	56.57	66.16
1888	76.97	57.16	69.13
1889	76.43	56.97	68.90
1890	73.29	56.67	66.86
1891	69.89	57.36	65.04
1892	70.84	58.05	65.89
1893	69.89	55.68	64.39
1894	69.75	54.60	63.89
1895	66.75	54.70	62.09
1896	66.48	55.58	62.27
1897	61.72	54.99	59.11
1898	63.07	55.68	60.22
1899	66.76	54.70	62.09
1900	74.93	55.09	67.25
1901	72.48	59.04	67.28
1902	74.93	63.06	70.34
1903	80.79	67.23	75.54
1904	83.11	67.08	76.90
1905	82.43	72.02	78.40
1906	86.51	75.89	82.40

Table 8.8 (continued)

Year	Construction Materials Index	Construction Wage Index	Construction Cost Index
1907	89.65	79.29	85.64
1908	96.86	80.06	90.36
1909	94.55	82.84	90.02
1910	92.51	85.94	89.96
1911	97.14	91.19	94.84
1912	96.87	96.75	96.82
1913	100.00	100.00	100.00
1914	93.87	100.31	96.36
1915	90.33	98.92	93.65
1916	103.81	100.31	102.46
1917	130.52	110.20	122.66
1918	150.54	128.90	142.17
1919	174.93	153.63	166.69
1920	214.71	180.99	201.66
1921	183.11	168.62	177.50

Sources by Column:

Column (1): Building materials index for 1885 to 1921 is Rymes *Fixed Capital Flows and Stocks, Manufacturing, Canada, 1926-1960* (1967, Table 17, P.77) converted to base 1913=100.00; building materials index for 1870 to 1884 gives equal weight to Rymes and index of wood and wood products (HSC Series J39).

Column (2): 1871-1901: Construction wage index constructed using a weighted average of backward percentage changes (i.e. $((t-1) - t)/t)100$) of various series yielding an index reflecting these series as follows:

1900 back to 1894: 0.25(a) + 0.75(b)
1893 back to 1891: 0.50(a) + 0.50(b)
1890 back to 1889: 0.75(a) + 0.25(b)
1887 back to 1884: 0.50(a) + 0.50(c)
1883 back to 1871:   (a)

Series (a) was constructed back to 1881 using wages reported by immigration agents for carpenters and labourers (HSC, Series D198, D199, D204, D205). Within occupations, percentage changes by cities were averaged, and then the simple average of the percentage changes in the two occupations was obtained. The percentage change for Winnipeg between 1882 and 1883 was omitted because of its enormous size. The series before 1881 is a rougher and more arbitrary one, constructed also from immigration agents' data (HSC, Series D189, D192).

Series (b) was constructed using the unweighted average of percentage changes in construction wage rates in the Ottawa area and in the Toronto area (HSC, Series D487 and D488).

Series (c) was constructed using the unweighted average of percentage changes of wage per hour of Ontario carpenters and Ontario labourers (HSC, Series D168, D169, D177).

1901-1921: Labour index is Rymes (1967, Table 17, p.177) converted to base 1913=100.00.

Column (3): (0.613 x Column (1)) + (0.387 x Column (2)).

Notes to Part A

* I am very much indebted to Professor D.C. MacGregor for making me aware of the Mavor Toronto survey, to Professor T.K. Rymes for discovering and sending me Bangs' paper, and to Professor M.C. Urquhart for making me aware of various other sources and for commenting on the estimation procedure. I am also indebted to Mrs. Karen Dares and Mrs. Jenny Arnott for help with the computations, and to Mrs. Sue Patterson for typing the manuscript.

1.   The phenomenon revealed by Wickens' sample is probably allied to the humping of reported *ages* at numbers ending in zero or five, an artifact caused by respondent error.

2.   In *National Income* (App. 4, Royal Commission on Dominion-Provincial Relations, p.32) are assumed means for rent suggested by H.F. Greenway. These are $9, $14, $20, $28, $45, $65 respectively, as compared with our assumed means of $7, $12.50, $19, $30, $46, $70 (see Table 8.1).

3.   We note that the ratio of *values* for owner-occupied units in tiny places to values in all urban areas was almost precisely the same in 1931 and in 1941 (Steele, 1972, Table 7.3). We also note that Bangs (1945) in his estimation of rents 1919-1941 for Statistics Canada used the ratio of urban less than 1,000 to rural. Consequently his rural rents are considerably above ours.

4.   Wickens found ratios for 3-family buildings of 0.096 to 0.156 in regions where ratios for 1-family buildings were 0.76 to 0.093. We note that in the 1931 Census values for units in multi-family buildings sometimes referred to the whole building. This would support use of a relatively low rent-to-value ratio; however, the quantitative importance of this phenomenon is slight (Bangs, 1945).

5.   Bangs (1945) assumed a ratio of 0.12.

6.   In fact we use Greenway (1941, p.106) as our source of this series because the HSC Series excluded 1909.

7.   The evidence is that the individuals appearing before the Royal Commission in the spring of 1888. In St. John, N.B. a witness testified that rents were lower than in 1877 (*Report*, Vol. 2, p.6); in Halifax, a witness testified that rents had risen 10 percent in 15 years (*Report*, Vol. 3, p.33). In Toronto, a witness reported rents higher than 16 years ago (*Report,* Vol. 5, p.3). In Hamilton, "rents slightly higher but there is better accommodation for the money" (p.1111). In Kingston, rents increased 20 percent in "last five years" (p.956). In Montreal, the "rent is rather higher" than formerly (*Report,* Vol. 4, p.582); according to a landlord, rents the same prior to 1878 as in 1888 but "when the hard times came they were put down at a much lower rate" (p.660). In Quebec City, "rents have increased 25-30 percent of late years" (p.924).

8.   Rents for Toronto reported by *Labour Gazette* correspondents show an increase for Toronto slightly less than that shown by Mavor's index, but still much greater than the increase in the Canada index (*Wholesale Prices, Canada, 1916*, p.231).

9.   We extracted values for rent given in testimony. There were 21 observations for N.B.

(average $5.40); 16 for N.S. (average $5.54), 30 for Quebec (average $6.57) and 11 for Ontario (average $7.50).

10.   In Regina average monthly rent (with sanitary conveniences) in 1910 was $18 in 1900 and $31 in 1910, as compared with $13 and $17 respectively for Toronto (Department of Labour *Wholesale Prices, Canada, 1916*, pp.231, 239).

11.   For the d's we use Pickett's permanent occupied units, *except* that in the case of Saskatchewan we use only 1/3 of the number of units, in order to take account of the fact that an especially large proportion of Saskatchewan units were rural, and the average rent index is an urban index.

12.   It can be seen from the table that Buckley's statements, "The trend was slightly downward in all provinces except the prairie provinces where the pioneer influence was very apparent ..." (1974, p.191) is somewhat misleading. As the table shows, in all provinces but Alberta and Saskatchewan, the trend was quite strongly upward at first, only turning down at 1911.

13.   This overstates the improvement between 1891 to 1901 and understates it 1901-11 because it appears that a substantial number of houses of "other" material of construction in 1901 were regarded as wood in 1911.

14.   In St. Stephen, N.B. a house without all "modern conveniences" rented at $6.67 to $8.33 (*Report*, Vol. 2, p.468); a house with modern conveniences in Chatham, N.B. rented at $8 to $10 (p.366). The mean rent for New Brunswick is estimated at $5.40 (see above, note 9). In Montreal, the rent is given at $6 or $7 for a flat with "outside closet, no drainage" (*Report*, Evidence-Quebec, p.548) while a cottage designed to be rented to a mechanic or bookkeeper with a bath, water closet and stove heating rented for $10 to $15 (p.660). The mean rent for Quebec was $6.57.

15.   One may infer from reports on local conditions in 1913 that sewage systems and tougher bylaws were established before 1900 in the larger cities, especially in central Canada. We make this inference because no reference is made to the recent installation of such facilities in the case of larger places, while there are frequent such references in the case of smaller places. For St. John, N.B., "About two years ago the Board of Health compelled the installation of sanitary conveniences ... " (Board of Inquiry into the Cost of Living, 1915, *Report*, Vol. II, p.384). For Brantford, " ... sanitary conveniences are now more general". For Guelph, because of a "new" building bylaw, "there has been a tendency for the labouring classes to move to outlying portions of the city and to build cheap houses without sanitary conveniences" (p.385). For Lethbridge, Alberta, "The progress of the Town was slow up to five years ago when a sewage system was installed." (p.379).

16.   Bangs, in his estimation for Statistics Canada, states that the urban percentage owners in 1921 was 55.9 (1945, p.2). He derived this by taking as the number of owned dwellings the number of owner private *families*, while taking as the number of dwellings, the actual number of dwellings given in the 1921 Census. This is only appropriate if the number of owner families per owned dwelling is one. Yet "owned home" was defined as "... if it is owned wholly or in part by the head of the family, or by ... a son, or a daughter, or

other relative living in the same house with the family. It is not necessary that ... the family should be sole owner." This clearly allows two related families eating separately in the same house each to be called owner. In 1931 there were 1.076 owning families for every owning household, in urban areas (*1931 Census*, Volume V, Table 61).

17.   Bangs assumed a ratio of 6.6 percent of urban units, i.e. $23 of a gross rent of $348 (1945, p.6).

18.   They show net to gross rent at about 51 percent, taxes about 12 percent. Assuming *roughly* on the basis of Wicken's data, a ratio of 15 percent for facilities and services, we get a ratio for maintenance and repairs plus insurance of 22 percent.

19.   The question of doublecounting arises here. Did fire insurance claims account for some of the cash outlay on repair and maintenance? Undoubtedly it did account for some small amount; however, a large part of the total dollar value of claims probably went to dwellings completely destroyed by fire and so not in the dwelling stock. In addition, our repairs and maintenance assumption is a quite conservative one.

Part B

Residential Construction in Canada, 1867-1920

1. Introduction

Virtually no analysis exists of the causes of fluctuations in Canadian residential construction before 1920, except for the essentially incidental analysis of this sector in Buckley's important path-breaking work on capital formation (1955), and on population as an engine of growth (1963). The historian J.T. Saywell (*Housing Canadians: Essays on the History of Residential Construction in Canada*, 1975) has written a history of housing[1] which is a delight to read, daring in its analysis and rich in quotations of contemporary comments; however, it is essentially a work of institutional and social analysis. An economic study in depth of residential construction before 1920 has still to be written.

We propose to help fill this lacuna with new estimates of residential construction. The estimates of residential construction in existence by James Pickett (*Residential Capital Formation in Canada, 1871-1921*, 1963) are estimated in a scholarly and ingenious way, which is, however, unsatisfactory both in terms of its technique and its results. On the latter point, as Buckley (HSC, p.501) and recently, Saywell, have commented, Pickett's estimates for the period around World War I are too out of line with other indicators to be acceptable. Of more fundamental concern, our work on a later period (Steele, 1972) has made it clear that estimation, such as Pickett's which is substantially based on the use of domestic disappearance of building materials will in general yield poor estimates.[2]

In this paper, we estimate a new dwelling starts series, 1867-1920. Unlike Pickett, we estimate farm and nonfarm starts separately; global estimation like that of Pickett will just not do, for reasons affecting the validity of the estimation technique and for the purposes of later analysis. During this period, unlike the period after 1920, farm starts were of substantial importance — obviously so during the wheat boom, but also in the years after Confederation. And farm starts were a quite different phenomenon from nonfarm because of the extent to which their construction was a nonmarket activity; they were strongly affected by population changes but only relatively weakly influenced by income levels and thus were probably relatively untouched by the vagaries of financial markets.

A novel, distinguishing, feature of this study is its emphasis on error indicators. These are computed using series generated by running the estimating procedure many times plugging in a variety of alternative assumptions. Examination of these error indicators as well as the series from which they were computed makes it possible to comment much more fully than is usual about the quality of the estimates.[3]

The basic estimating procedure is essentially the following. First, we derive estimates of decade farm and nonfarm starts using Census stock data and various other information (Section 1). This involves putting data on a consistent basis, to get net decade changes, and estimating decade flows other than starts. Secondly, we derive annual distributor series (Section 2). Thus far our basic procedure is essentially the same as Pickett's, except for our farm/nonfarm split and our use of several distributors to yield alternative series. Our integration of the Census-derived decade estimates and the annual distributors (Section 3 and 4) however, differs rather substantially from Pickett's; we develop a fairly elaborate integration procedure in an attempt to ensure that year-over-year percentage changes are not just statistical artifacts of the estimating procedure.

Table 8.9
Estimates of Dwelling Starts by Decade, 1871–1920
(thousands of units)

Census Year	Decade	Total Occupied (1)	Vacant (2)	Temporary (3)	Institutions and Hotels (4)	Decade Change in Stocks (5)	Loss Conversions (6)	Timing Adjustment (7)	Starts (5)+(6)+(7) (8)
1871		606.3	27.4	12.4	1.1				
	70s					162.5	24.2	-0.1	186.5
1881		753.0	45.8	14.7	1.4				
	80s					121.8	29.6	0.6	152.0
1891		877.6	50.6	22.1	1.7				
	90s					131.6	46.3	-1.1	176.9
1901		1029.9	27.6	19.4	2.0				
	00s					412.7	32.7	9.1	454.4
1911		1428.3	52.2	28.6	3.2				
	10s					375.4	34.6	-9.0	401.0
1921		1805.3	40.9	18.3	3.8				
	20s								

Notes by Column:

(1) 1871: *1871 Census*, Volume I, Table I, except Pickett's figures for P.E.I. and the West (1961, App. Table 1).
1881-1901: *1881 Census*, Volume I, Table I; *1891 Census*, Volume I, Table II; *1901 Census*, Volume V, Table XIV.
1911, 1921: Number of households (*1941 Census*, Volume V, Table 1) times 1.029 (for 1911) and 1.034 (for 1921).

(2) 1871-1911: Vacancies excluding prairies. 1871-1901, sources as for (1); 1911, Pickett (1961, App. Table I).
1921: 2.24 percent of stock.

(3) 1871-1891: Vessels and shanties.
1901, 1921: 1891 vessels and shanties (excluding prairies) plus contemporary prairie occupied dwellings of other materials of construction.
1911: As for 1901, 1921 *plus* 1/2 (1911-1921 change in prairie one and two-room occupied dwellings.)

(4) Institutions from Pickett (1961, Table 1). Hotels assumed in 1871 and succeeding Censuses as 600, 700, 800, 1000, 2000, 2500 (in 1931 there were 5,000 hotels (*1931 Census*, Administrative Report p.61).

(5) Change in ((1) + (2) − (3) − (4)).

(6) Rates, as a percentage of decade-beginning stock, for farm assumed as 6, 6, 8, 6, 5 and for nonfarm, at 1.5, 1.5, 1.5, 1.0, 0.5.

(7) Calculated assuming that change between Census dates includes 30 percent of dwellings actually started the year preceding the Census for the 1871-1901 Censuses (which took place about April 1); ratio was assumed 18 percent for the 1911 and 1921 Censuses (which took place about June 1).

For 1871-1901 Censuses, starts in the year prior to Census were estimated from dwellings reported under construction, assuming a 15 percent under count and assuming dwellings under construction around April 1 represented 60 percent of the previous year's starts. Dwellings under construction are from *1871 Census*, Volume I, Table 1, *1881 Census*, Volume I, Table II, *1891 Census*, Volume I, Table XIV and Pickett (1961, App. Table 1). For 1910 and 1920 dwellings started were assumed as 80 and 30 thousand units, based on estimates from an earlier run of the estimation.

The assumptions about the relation of dwelling under construction to earlier starts are based on the construction pattern of the early 1950s and revealed in *Housing in Canada* (various issues, e.g. April, 1950, Table 4, p.28 and Table 54, p.88).

For the reader who is only interested in substantive results, the most important sections of the paper are 7, in which we comment on the behaviour of starts, especially with respect to the revisionist view of 1873-96, and 6 where we evaluate the results of our estimation. In addition, in other sections (except 4) incidental comment on aspects of housing and urban development is fairly frequent.

2. The Census-Derived Decade Starts Estimates

The anchor to our annual starts estimates is our series of Census-derived decade estimates. The Census, of course, provides only stock data and the starts are not the same as the simple increment in the stock. The simple increment will tend to understate starts to the extent that demolition, fire or abandonment causes houses to be lost from the stock; the simple increment will tend to overstate starts to the extent that buildings are converted so as to add dwelling units to the stock, as for instance, when a single-family house is duplexed. And in some cases Census stock data are missing or defective. The following identity gives the required components of decade starts estimates more precisely:

Starts =   [Occupied (n) + Vacant (n) − Temporary (n) − Institutions (n)] − [Occupied (n−1) + Vacant (n−1) − Temporary (n−1) − Institutions (n−1)] + Losses − Conversions + Timing adjustment

where the items in brackets are stocks some months after the end of decade n, and losses, conversions and starts are flows during decade n. The timing adjustment is required because stock data refer to completed dwellings existing at a Census date some months after the end of the decade. Estimates of the components, discussed below, are given in Table 8.9.

The Occupied Dwelling Counts

Occupied dwelling counts are taken directly from the Census except in 1911 and 1921. In those two Censuses muddy instruction led enumerators to report some buildings containing several dwelling units as only one dwelling. It is easy to exaggerate the importance of this; Table 8.10A suggests that the problem was manifested as much in the diversion of apartment units into the wrong category as in the omission of dwelling units.[4]

To arrive at new estimates we first examined households per unit, province by province. The pattern of households per dwelling unit for those provinces like B.C. with very few multiple dwelling units (see Table 8.10B) makes it clear that the building boom which was well underway some years before the 1911 Census allowed the massive immigration after the turn of the century to occur without much overcrowding in 1911; on the other hand, it confirms that the wartime and early postwar slump in housing did in fact result in overcrowding.[5] Our estimation reflects this. For all provinces except Alberta and Saskatchewan, and the Yukon and Northwest Territories, we added to the dwelling count an amount equal to about one-third the reported apartment plus row dwellings in 1921; for 1911 the percentage adjustment was somewhat less than for 1921. The resultant households per dwelling for Canada are 1.029 (1911) and 1.034 (1921) as compared with the 1901 and 1931 ratios of 1.04 and 1.02 respectively.[6]

Vacancies

Except for 1921, we estimate vacancies as the global Census count, excluding Prairie Province vacancies. The basis for ignoring Prairie vacancies is the especially strong likelihood that virtually all these "vacancies" were not dwellings still part of the market stock, but instead were abandoned dwellings which we take care of in our loss and temporary dwelling adjustments. For 1921, when no Census count is available, we estimate vacancies using Firestone's rate for four cities (Firestone, 1951, p.380); this rate, 2.24 percent, reflects the tight housing market following several years of depressed building activity.

Temporary Dwellings

Census dwellings encompass all types of human shelter, including tents and shacks. Makeshift, temporary dwellings are a phenomenon of the rural frontier and so vary considerably in importance from Census to Census; thus, it is important to remove them from the stock count to ensure our estimates of starts exclude "buildings" representing only a trivial amount of capital. Our estimates for 1901, 1911 and 1921 (when no Census counts are available) assume that changes in these temporary dwellings were only of consequence on the Prairies. Consequently our temporary dwellings are Prairie dwellings of "other" materials of construction. For 1911 we add to that one-half the decline in Prairie one and two room dwellings between 1911 and 1921. Our adjustments are thus less than those of Pickett (1963, Table I, p.43) and more than those of Buckley (1955, p.120). Like Buckley and unlike Pickett, we are convinced that the number of dwellings of "other" material of construction category is a much better guide to the importance of temporary dwellings than the number of one-room dwellings. Our cautious use of one-room dwellings as an indicator of temporary units is warranted by the shifts in size of the Prairie stock between Census dates. The substantial increase in three-room units in 1921 accompanying the large decrease in one-room units suggests that while many of the latter fell apart or were turned into granaries, many others were turned into three-room units by an addition, or perhaps merely by partitioning off a kitchen and bedroom.

Occupied Farm Dwelling

Our occupied farm dwelling units estimator is the number of occupied farms of 11 acres or more. A worrying problem here is the appropriate definition of a farm. Until the 1921 Census, there was no minimum agricultural production criterion to distinguish a farm from other "occupied land". The detailed returns of the 1891 Census show that a very large number of properties of 1-10 acres included in the agricultural census were located in towns, village and even cities; the 1901 Census report acknowledged this and suggested five acres as the division between farms and "lots". This is the convention followed by Pickett. If this convention were followed, the data would show an increment in occupied farms in the 1880s almost twice that shown by our figures, with virtually no increment in the 1890s. That this rise and great fall in the farm increment is a mirage is supported by the data in Table 8.11. We presume that the disappearance of many Ontario and Quebec "farms" in 1901 reflects, instead, the subdivision of some of the larger lots in the 1890s, as urban areas became more densely settled — and perhaps also the merger of some other lots as speculators defaulted when the expected strong urban growth in the 1890s did not materialize.

Loss

One important reason for disaggregation into farm and nonfarm is the very different loss experience in these two sectors. Direct loss evidence simply does not exist, and data on loss

Table 8.10

A. Dwelling By Type, 1921 and 1931, for Toronto and Montreal
(thousands of dwellings)

	Apartments	Row	Single Detached	Semi Detached	Total[a]
Montreal					
1921	12.8	37.5	24.1	19.6	94.9
1931	149.2	2.7	10.7	6.9	170.0
Toronto					
1921	2.2	14.0	35.1	46.0	98.6
1931	23.5	10.5	46.9	55.7	136.0

a Included in the total are unspecified and other.

Sources: *1921 Census*, Volume III, Table II; *1931 Census*, Volume V, Table 56.

B. Households Per Dwelling Unit, 1921 and 1931 and Multiple Units

	Percentage By Which Households Exceed Dwelling Units				Percentages of All Dwelling Units in 1921	
	1901	1911	1921	1931	Apartments	Apartments and Row
Canada	4.0	5.3	7.5	2.2	2.0	6.3
P.E.I.	1.2	1.0	0.9	0.6	0.2	1.3
N.S.	4.8	5.0	5.8	2.3	2.3	3.5
N.B.	7.7	10.1	9.3	1.2	2.7	3.1
Que.	5.4	9.2	11.0	1.0	4.4	16.2
Ont.	2.2	3.0	6.9	3.0	1.3	5.1
Man.	2.6	6.4	9.7	3.1	1.0	2.1
Sask.	8.2	2.1	3.0	1.7	0.6	0.7
Alta.	10.5	3.1	3.7	2.0	0.6	0.9
B.C.	4.1	6.9	9.3	2.4	1.8	3.2

Notes by Column:

(1), (2), (3), (4)	*1941 Census*, Volume V, Table 1.
(5), (6)	*1921 Census*, Volume III, Table 9.

Table 8.11
Farm and Lots by Size, Ontario and Quebec, 1881-1901
(thousands of units)

		1881	1891	1901
Ontario	< 10 acres	36	109	46
	11 – 50 acres	42	38	35
	51+ acres	129	138	143
Quebec	< 10 acres	19	51	24
	11 – 50 acres	25	22	20
	51+ acres	94	102	106

Source: *1901 Census*, Volume II, Table XXXVII.

Table 8.12
Alternative Estimates, Census-Derived Decade Dwelling Starts, 1871-1920
(thousands of units)

	Farm Starts			Nonfarm Starts		
	Favoured	Quasi-Pickett	High Loss	Favoured	Quasi-Pickett	High Loss
1871-80	87.7	87.3	100.9	98.9	99.5	106.1
1881-90	57.8	59.1	73.7	94.2	95.8	103.8
1891-1900	48.9	23.0	57.5	123.3	118.4	135.1
1901-10	192.2	181.2	210.1	262.3	290.8	274.0
1911-20	84.6	99.3	102.6	316.4	367.2	329.3

Notes:

Quasi-Pickett: As for "favoured" except occupied, vacant, and temporary dwellings are from Pickett, 1963, Table 8.9, p.43.

High Loss: As for "favoured" except loss-conversion percentage rate for farm assumed for decades 1870s to 1910s respectively at 10, 10, 10, 10, 8 and for nonfarm, respectively 4, 4, 4, 3, 2.

Favoured:

Farm Starts – Estimated using identity for total starts given in Table 8.9. Farm occupied units taken as number of farms more than ten acres. These are for census years 1871-1921, respectively, 327.6, 388.7, 428.9, 453.5, 613.9, 667.0 (in thousands) (*1871 Census*, Volume III, Table XXI, p.100; *1901 Census*, Volume II, Table XXXVII, p.275; *1921 Census*, Volume V, Table 2, p.3). Farm vacancy and "timing adjustment" rates taken as same as global rates. All temporary units are taken as farm units and all institutions as nonfarm.

Nonfarm Starts – Total starts (Table 8.9) minus farm starts.

are very scanty even for other periods, so that our loss estimates must be based to large extent on hypotheses about the urban and farm housing markets. In the urban housing market, when a house decays or becomes obsolescent it is seldom destroyed; rather it trickles down to the poor. Alternatively, its location may be desirable for denser residential development and so it may be demolished. Demolitions may also occur to accommodate other buildings, roads and other public works. Apartment building and road building to accommodate the automobile did not assume importance until the twenties; this, and the relatively young age of dwellings in urban areas in our period suggest that the loss rate then must have been substantially less than in the twenties. On the other hand, fire loss was probably more than negligible. Firestone's large city rate for the 1920s is 2.9 and for the 1930s, 1.8 (1951, pp.382-383). We assume a nonfarm rate of two percent[7] (of beginning decade stock) for each decade.

Losses of dwelling stock on farms were doubtless much greater than in urban areas. First, throughout this period, farms and the houses on them were abandoned. More important is the fact that when a farm house becomes obsolete because of growth in the wealth of the farmer, there is generally no other family for the house to trickle down to; consequently, it is apt to trickle down to the pigs — and so be lost from the housing stock.

Our removal of "temporary" dwellings, which were especially important as the Prairies became settled, partly accommodates for this problem. And of course, in many cases, farmers would improve their housing accommodation simply by putting an addition onto their current house.

Keeping all this in mind we use rates of 6, 6, 8, 6, 5 percent for our five decades. We use the eight percent rate for the 1890s because it is clear that in decade abandonments were unusually great; the tiny increment in farms over 10 acres during the 90s, in Ontario and Quebec suggests that many of the great number of rural vacant units there in 1891 had deteriorated or collapsed by 1901 and that this is more important than the reoccupation of vacant units as an explanation of the big drop in vacancies between the two Censuses.[8] We use the five percent rate for the 1910-20s because we have already made a substantial adjustment for that decade, in our treatment of temporary units. These rates we regard as conservative,[9] although they are greater than Pickett's (three percent for farm and nonfarm except for six percent for farm in the 90s (1963, p.45)) and Buckley's (3.9 (90s), 4.5 (00s and 10s) (File 69, Saskatchewan Archives)).

Conversions (in nonfarm stock)

As in the case for loss, direct information about the number of dwelling units added to the stock because of the conversion of existing buildings, is virtually nonexistent. What we know about the income and life style of this era, however, suggests that there would have been few apartments in converted houses. Some of the people who would now live in apartments would have been roomers or boarders, because single people did not commonly set up separate households. And families would be inclined to reject an apartment in favour of a house, in that era when cheap houses could be built untrammelled by building codes or zoning laws.

In its housing preferences as in so many other matters, however, Quebec was not a province like the others. Building reports in the Montreal archives indicate that the characteristic duplex with its outside staircase was predominant in residential building right back to the 1870s. With the Quebec fact in mind we set the ratio at 0.5 percent for each of the three 19th century decades.

In recognition of the great urbanization occurring in the 1900s we set the ratio at 1 percent, assuming that some trivial amount of the great demand pressure reflected in the building boom got deflected into conversions. For the 1910s we set the ratio at 1.5 percent because of the collapse of residential building during World War I and the resultant very tight market by 1921, a market somewhat like that after World War II, when we know the conversion rate was high.[10]

3. The Annual Distributors

The Census-derived decade estimates are merely the anchor for our annual series. They must be used in conjunction with annual distributors. The distributors used in all existing series, except Buckley's prairie farm series, are building-materials based. But the problems associated with using the pattern of consumption of building materials are legion. First, there is leakage out of new dwelling construction: building materials have other uses — lumber is used for furniture, fences, and wagons, and brick for paving, for instance; and building materials are used for non-residential building and for alterations and repair. An important technical problem is the correction for inventory changes.[11] Rather less important for our purposes are two trend-affecting factors: the changing proportion of building materials manufactured outside the market, and the changing amount of materials used per dwelling. The extraordinarily odd results of Firestone, derived using such a series, for 1921-1944 (1951, pp. 385, 386) and 1900-20 (1958, p.299) serve as horrible examples to warn the unwary. In our view[12] building-material based distributors are the least attractive of available alternatives.

While building-material distributors are objectionable, the alternatives are ridden with problems as well, although less serious ones. For this reason, we have combined several distributors, where feasible, on the grounds of offsetting biases. The distributor series we label Buckley urban, urban mortgage, residential, Pickett glass and farm.

The Buckley Urban Index

"Buckley urban" is the Buckley urban building index, constructed from permit numbers in Montreal until 1886, and thereafter with deflated permit values; the index reflects Toronto as well as Montreal in 1887, in 1892 also reflects Hamilton and in 1901, St. John, Brantford, Winnipeg and Victoria.[13] Permit series like this have the outstanding advantage of being almost totally uncontaminated indicators of *new* building. Even where permits are legally required for repairs and alterations, much work of this sort would not be done under permit.

This type of series is, however, not without defects. Urban building is likely to move differently from rural non-farm buildings, especially on the fringe of urban areas. The problem of the fringe is especially evident in the 1911-21 decade when increased use of the car and the decline in vacant land in cities led to a swing to the fringe (Stone, 1967, Chart 6.2, p.135). The fringe problem has as almost its mirror image the annexation problem: if a city without much vacant land does not enlarge its legal borders by annexation the trend of its building will be a downward-biased indicator of the trend for all nonfarm building, but if a city annexes an area which is rapidly developing at the time of annexation, its permits series will show an upward shift in building which is merely a statistical artifact. It is to be expected that these biases will tend to offset each other.[14] In fact, annexations were fairly important 1870-1911 but faded[15] after that, while fringe population grew dramatically relative to city growth after 1911 (Stone, 1967, Chart 6.2, p.135); 1911 could be said to mark the zenith of the central city — not surprisingly, in view of the history of the car. For our purposes the annexation-fringe problem is probably not very important; it is clearly less important for the period after 1900 when the size of Buckley sample would smooth the effects of annexation.

Another defect in the Buckley index, for our purposes, is its inclusion of non-residential building. This is not as serious as a look at individual city non-residential and residential detail might suggest: jogs in the proportion of commercial and industrial building should be smoothed with the inclusion of several cities in a series. The Riggleman-Isard index for the U.S. during this period in fact does rather well; its most serious failing is a pronounced upward trend relative to housing after 1900 (see Gottlieb, *Estimates of Residential Building, United States, 1840-1939*, 1964, Chart 21, p.83), and this failing does not matter for our purposes.

The Residential Distributor

Nonetheless, we have constructed a pure residential index primarily in an attempt to eliminate this defect of the Buckley index. Especially for the early period, the inclusion of offices, stores and factories is worrisome, because of the Buckley's use of only Toronto, Montreal and Hamilton. In Toronto in the 80s and 90s residential building was generally somewhat less than half the total but it jumped to 70 percent in 1891 and dropped as low as 17 percent in 1895; it was consistently well over half the total in the 1900s but in 1920 it was just 29 percent.[16]

The residential index is essentially the same as the Buckley's urban index until 1883 when the former starts to reflect Toronto residential activity; also, beginning in 1885 the Montreal portion refers to dwelling units, unlike the Buckley's which refers to *all* buildings. From 1915 the index reflects all residential building in Quebec, as well as Toronto residential building.[17] The global coverage of Quebec is particularly important for this period because the data show that rural building dropped much less than urban during World War I (a pattern repeated during the World War II), as rural areas on the fringe of cities became built up.

The Urban Mortgage Distributor

We have constructed a third distributor index which as a very different foundation from the two permit-based indexes — the mortgage assets of insurance companies. Mortgage financing is not, of course, confined to dwellings built within the legal boundaries of cities, and so a mortgage series will not be affected by annexations and the changing importance of fringe building. Too, a mortgage series will not be affected by the possible unrepresentativeness of building in a few cities, so that there is not the sampling problem here that there is with permit series, although there may be some bias caused by the preference of insurance companies for lending in central, well-established areas.

These are strengths of a mortgage based series. But there are a host of weaknesses. First, mortgages are used for farms as well as non-farm dwellings. We have accommodated for this by using the mortgage assets only of insurance companies. There is abundant evidence that the building societies and loan and trust companies were heavily involved in farm mortgages in the late nineteenth century (see Easterbrook, 1937, pp.25 and Neufeld, 1972, pp. 205, 208) and one may infer that the insurance companies left this field more or less alone. The *Canada Year Book* (1927, p.197) makes the distinction explicit:

While every company lends on urban property to some extent, the proportion of urban loans to farm loans is not considerable. This refers, of course, to loan companies.

The other objections may be easily seen by examining the following identities which make clear the rather loose formal connection between net increments in mortgage assets and starts:

Change in insurance mortgage assets = SL + EL + CL − repayments

$$SL = (\frac{L}{V} \times V \times \frac{ISM}{M} \times \frac{M}{S})S$$

where: SL = loans for dwelling starts; EL = loans for existing dwellings; CL = loans for commercial buildings; $\frac{L}{V}$ = the loan-to-value ratio; V = the value per dwelling; ISM = insurance company mortgage lending on new dwellings; M = total mortgage lending on new buildings; S = starts

For our purposes the question of concern is: which of the variables in these identities did not move in a relatively smooth secular fashion? In the second identity, V, the value per dwelling is the greatest question mark. Until 1914 we have no yearly data on this other than an input price index, but there is some presumption from the rooms per dwelling unit data that the real value per nonfarm dwelling unit rose in the nineties but fell in the nineteen-tens.[18] We may take some comfort in the fact that in the U.S. in the period 1891-1920 the real value per dwelling did not change by as much as 10 percent in any year until 1918, when it fell, and the only important cyclical movement was a rise in the 1890s peaking in 1896 (Blank, 1954, Table 19, p.70). Nonetheless the lack of correction for changing real value must be regarded as a serious defect in this index.

With respect to the first identity we dismiss loans for commercial building as being of negligible importance for this period — contemporary accounts do not mention this use of funds. Turning to the second item, loans on existing dwellings, we presume that increased activity in new residential construction was accompanied by increased trading in — and lending on — existing dwellings; thus, the presence of loans on them likely does little damage to the change in mortgage assets as an indicator of starts, except perhaps to dampen it.

Perhaps more doubt should be entertained about the fourth item in the identity, repayments. These would rise with a rise in outstanding mortgages (although in this period of unamortized mortgages, cash flow from principle repayments might be relatively less than now). We would also expect repayments to rise with a rise in the change in real money. We test for the importance of repayments by running regression (see Table 8.13) incorporating these repayment-determining variables. More generally, the results of these regressions indicate the worth of the change in mortgage assets as an indicator of starts and provide a guide for construction of a mortgage index.

In Part A of Table 8.13 are equations "explaining" the real change in insurance mortgage companies' mortgage assets.[19] We see that urban starts powerfully affect the mortgage asset increment: its t statistics is 15.2 even when the constant term is removed. Its coefficients imply that around $700 or $800 (1913 dollars) were added to insurance company mortgage assets for every urban start; to put this in perspective, we note that urban single-detached and duplex units were valued at about $3,200 (in 1913 dollars) during the twenties (Steele, 1972, Table A3.4, p.221, plus $500 allowance for lot value) and the usual loan was about 60 percent of value.

The mortgage asset increment is also strongly related to the two repayment-determining variables, the level of mortgage assets and the change in the real money. At first sight the estimated coefficients of mortgage assets may appear implausibly low: one would expect repayment of the principle of existing mortgages to be much more like 10 or 15 percent per year

Table 8.13
Mortgage Increment Regression Results, 1921-1932

A: Dependent Variable: real change in insurance company mortgage assets

Constant	US	RM$_{-1}$	CRMY	R^2	SEE	Average Absolute Percentage Error
-6.61	0.824	-0.38	0.012	0.99	8.3	4.2
(-6.2)	(36.0)	(-10.8)	(-5.7)			
	0.693	-0.055		0.93	26.4	22.6
	(15.2)	(-6.5)				

B: Dependent Variable: urban starts

RCMT	RM$_{-1}$	R^2	SEE	Average Absolute Percentage Error
1.38	0.083	0.90	3.7	10.1
(15.2)	(10.6)			

Notes: Numbers in brackets are t statistics. Estimation is OLS.

Sources: US: urban starts in thousands: Steele, 1972, Table A3.2, p.219.
RCMT: real change in insurance company mortgage assets in millions of 1913 dollars. See notes to Table A3.
RM$_{-1}$: real insurance company mortgage assets in millions of 1913 dollars. See notes to Table A3.
CRMY: change in real money: change in ((H13 + H16 + H19 + H20) divided by wholesale price index) where the wholesale price index is J34 put on basis 1913=1.00 and series references are to HSC.

than the 3.8 or 5.5 percent indicated by the regressions. However, fragmentary evidence suggests repayment of well under 10 percent in 1930-31.[20] More important, much of the repayment flow would go to finance sales of existing houses; the amount of this financing would be directly related to the size of the housing stock and accordingly, to the amount of mortgage assets, thus reducing in a systematic way the proportion of gross repayments available for financing new dwellings.

With the evidence of our regressions in mind we construct our mortgage index (see Table A3) as the real increment in insurance company mortgage assets, adjusted to a starts basis, plus 5.5 percent of real mortgage assets at the beginning of the year. The 5.5 percent ratio is perhaps too high, but a lower ratio yielded a negative number during the World War I depression in house-building. We did not feel sufficiently confident in the stability of the change in money supply coefficient to build it into our index. A direct indication of the value of our index is shown in Table 8.13, Part B. We note that the coefficient of the level of assets is 6.0 percent of the coefficient of the change in assets. The average absolute percentage error, 10.1 percent, is reduced to 7.3 if we ignore 1921, a year of extreme turnaround in construction prices, unparalleled in the earlier period.

Pickett's Glass Series

We have already listed problems in residential building materials distributors. Pickett's series of real imports of window glass adjusted to a work-put-in-place basis (1963, pp.46-48) over-comes two of these objections: first, window glass, unlike lumber and some other construction materials, does not have an obvious non-construction use; secondly, there is little evidence of any domestic production, so that the problem of changing coverage of domestic disappearance is reduced. Still problems remain. The chief of these is probably the use of window glass for non-residential building and for repair. For instance, the peculiar rise in starts shown in Pickett's completion series in 1917, remarked upon by Buckley (HSC, p.501) is almost certainly the outcome of a case of extreme repair requirements, the Halifax Explosion:

> On December 6, 1917, the city was rocked by a giant explosion, which broke windows at Truro, 60 miles distant, and damaged every building in Halifax.[21]

The Farm Distributor

For our farm dwelling starts estimates we have constructed just one distributor series, for two reasons: there is very little annual information for this sector, and it is less important than the nonfarm sector. Our series depends on Buckley's farm estimates after 1891, and on a mortgage series prior to that.

As we have noted above, during this period most of the mortgage lending of building societies and loan companies was on farm property and there is reason to believe that expenditure on farm dwellings is a fairly constant ratio of total expenditure on farm buildings (Buckley, 1955, p.121). On these grounds, our farm distributor index for the period up to and including 1891 is the real increment in building society and loan company mortgage assets, adjusted to a starts basis, plus 5.5 percent of real mortgage assets at the beginning of the year.

Our farm distributor index starting in 1892 reflects Buckley's annual farm series. Using Census prairie farm data — including data from the special prairie census taken midway between national censuses — Buckley estimated five-year changes and then distributed these using the value of the wheat crop as distributor (Buckley, 1955, p.121). He distributed the (small) 10-year change in non-prairie farms using the domestic disappearance of building materials.

4. Integration of the Decade Estimates and the Annual Distributor Estimates

The third step in our estimation is the integration of the Census-derived decade starts estimates and the annual distributor estimates. There is no integration problem, of course, if both estimates are precise, i.e. if the decade estimates are without error and if the annual distributor's value is always in the same ratio to starts. In that case, there would obviously be no point in estimating decade starts for more than one decade, since this one estimate would yield the appropriate blow-up ratio for the annual distributor.

For further discussion of this problem it is useful to state the simple general estimator of overall starts more formally, i.e.

$$\hat{S}(n,t) = AD(n,t) \times r(n,t)$$

where $\hat{S}(n,t)$ is the estimate of starts in year t of decade n, AD (n,t) is the value of the distributor series and r (n,t) is the estimated blow-up ratio. The integration problem is to determine the best estimate of r (n,t). We have already noted the error-free case where $\hat{r}(n,t)$ is a constant given by

$$\hat{r} = \frac{\sum_{t=1}^{10} AD(n,t)}{DS(n)}$$

where DS (n) is the Census-derived decade starts estimate for any decade n.

In general, we cannot assume the decade estimates are error free. In the face of this, one way of proceeding is to assume that the decade estimates are error free and the distributors are not, but that the relation of the distributor to starts does not change within any decade. The distributor series is then used to distribute the decade total. Put more formally, this estimator assumes r (n,t) is a constant only over any decade, i.e. $\hat{r}(n,t)$ is given by

$$\hat{r}(n) = \frac{\sum_{t=1}^{10} AD(n,t)}{DS(n)} \qquad [1]$$

where $\hat{r}(n)$ will in general be different for different n's.

If there are in fact errors in the decade estimates this estimator will yield a series showing breaks at decade-linking years. Unwarranted sharp breaks will also occur if the decade estimates are error-free but the average relation of the distributor to starts changes between decades: in general there will be no reason to believe that all the change in r (n,t) indicated by $\hat{r}(n+1) - \hat{r}(n)$ occurs between the last year of the decade n and the first year of (n+1). The existence of change is also prima facie evidence for the case that this estimator will also yield distorted patterns within decades. For instance, building in sample cities may be relatively more important at the beginning of a decade than at the end, making $\hat{r}(n)$ relatively upward biased at the beginning and downward biased at the end.

The defects of this estimator are evident in the implausible movements at decade endings shown in some NBER series. Thus Gottlieb's estimates for the U.S. show virtually no fall in 1900, surely a statistical artifact in view of the substantial drop manifest in residential series which are constructed without any break between 1899 and 1900 (see Gottlieb, 1964, Chart 21, p.83). If western building grew relative to building in the rest of the U.S. in the later nineties, the estimating technique used would produce this artifact (see Gottlieb, 1964, pp. 59-61 and Blank, 1954, pp. 35-38, 45-48, 73, 74). The 1900 problem is the most obvious in Gottlieb's results, but movements at other decade-beginning years look suspect as well. This is true despite Gottlieb's clever integration of a lot of information and his concern in choosing decade indexes "to keep in mind decade fittings at decade endings" (Gottlieb, 1964, p.59). Blank did not show explicitly even an awareness of the problem, sticking rigidly to a sophisticated, but blinkered and mechanical estimating procedure.[22]

The crudeness of Pickett's glass series did not allow him the luxury of assuming the ratio of this distributor to starts was constant over any decade. As the ratios in Table 8.14, column 1 show, this would have resulted in extreme distortion at decade endings. So Pickett essentially assumed that r (n,t) changed linearly over the years between mid-decade, i.e.:

$$\hat{r}(n,t) = \hat{r}(n) + 0.1(t-5)(\hat{r}(n+1) - \hat{r}(n)) \qquad \text{if } 10 \geq t > 5$$
$$\hat{r}(n,t) = \hat{r}(n-1) + 0.1(t+5)(\hat{r}(n) - \hat{r}(n-1)) \qquad \text{if } 5 \geq t \geq 1$$

where $\hat{r}(n)$ is defined in [1] above.

We find this estimator unappealing because it assumes that the ratio of the value of the distributor to starts changes in a smooth absolute fashion rather that in a smooth percentage fashion. Our estimator assumes that this ratio changes in a smooth percentage fashion — and that the percentage changes themselves change smoothly. More precisely, our estimator is given by

$$\hat{r}(n,t) = \hat{r}(n, t-1)(1 + \hat{g}(n,t-1))$$

where the rate of change, $\hat{g}$, is derived by first computing the average annual rate of change between decades, as given by $\hat{g}(n)$ in the following,

$$\hat{r}(n+1) = \hat{r}(n)(1 + \hat{g}(n))^{10}$$

and then by smoothing these rates of change as follows[23]

$$\hat{g}(n,t) = \hat{g}(n-1) + (0.05 + 0.1(t-1))(\hat{g}(n))$$

The base $\hat{r}$ to which these rates of change are applied is the $\hat{r}$ for 1876[24] given by

$$\hat{r}(1876) = \hat{r}(7,6) = \hat{r}(7)(1 + 0.5\hat{g}(7))$$

We iterated on $\hat{r}(n)$ until the decade sums of our annual estimates were within five percent of our Census-derived decade starts.[25]

Displayed in Table 8.14 are the values for $\hat{r}(n)$ using our various indexes. This shows, not too surprisingly, that the ratios from the urban mortgage and glass indexes, which have a broad, if not precise coverage are much more stable than ratios from the Buckley urban index or our residential index.[26] The ratios for the latter two indexes climb tremendously in the twentieth century, after a drop in the 1890s. At first glance the drop suggests that the Census-derived decade estimates are too high in the 1890s, but this is contradicted by the evidence form the other two indexes. Looking further, we see from Table 8.15 that the rate of population in-crease in Montreal and Toronto, the base of our residential index, fell by much more there in the 1890s than it did elsewhere; in fact the rate of growth of the urban fringe actually rose in the 1890s. These population relationships, however, do not explain the steep rise in the ratios

Table 8.14

Ratios, Distributor Decade Sums to Census-Derived Decade Starts, 1871-80 to 1911-20

	Pickett Glass Index to Pickett Total Completions	Farm Distributor to Farm Starts	Distributor Ratios to Nonfarm Starts			
			Buckley Urban	Resid-ential	Urban Mortgage	Pickett Glass
	(1)	(2)	(3)	(4)	(5)	(6)
1871-80	6	23.2	5.8	5.6	0.07	10.2
1881-90	22	61.9	7.4	5.9	0.24	35.8
1891-1900	27	70.8	7.1	4.6	0.42	30.6
1901-10	18	62.2	12.2	11.3	0.37	26.3
1911-20	14	72.0	13.7	15.1	0.37	26.6

Sources by Column

(1):   Pickett, 1963, p.48. His 1871-80 figure is affected by an arithmetic error and should be 7.2.
(2) – (6):   Farm and nonfarm starts are from Table 4. Distributors are from Table A3.

in the 1900s; this rise is likely a manifestation of the tendency for fluctuations in building to be accentuated in large cities, with residential building, even when deflated by the change in population, booming more there than elsewhere.

5. The Favoured Nonfarm Starts Estimates

In the Appendix (Table A2) are displayed nonfarm starts estimates based on the use of each of our four annual distributors. After assessing each of these series we may construct our favoured estimates. Because the distributors each have quite different biases, one important criterion for a series is the extent to which its movements are like the movements of the other three. As an additional aid we have important information from the Censuses: dwelling units under construction (Table 8.16). The relation of this figure to starts clearly depends crucially on the date the Census was taken. From 1871 to 1901 this was about the beginning of April. Because for several months before this the ground in most of Canada is frozen, dwellings under construction then would virtually all be dwellings started the previous year. Thus, starts counts for 1870, 1880, 1890, 1900 should have roughly the same pattern as under construction counts in the corresponding year-later Census.[27]

Turning to Table A2, it is immediately clear that the glass-based series should be discarded. Its movements bear little relationships to those of any of the other series. In particular, it shows starts implausibly low in the late 1880s and implausibly high in the early 1880s, the early 1900s and during World War I.

The two largely urban permit-based series, not surprisingly, generally are characterized by fluctuations of too-great amplitude. This aside, these series are quite well supported by the under

Table 8.15
Estimated Decade Rates of Population Growth, 1870s to 1910s

| Decade | Toronto | Montreal | Incorporated Urban Areas | | | Subdivisions Adjacent to Cities 30,000 and Over |
| | | | Canada | Quebec | Ontario | |
	(1)	(2)	(3)	(4)	(5)	(6)
1870s	54	18	32	27	40	20
1880s	87	44	33	29	36	12
1890s	20	23	18	23	13	15
1900s	75	47	52	39	41	36
1910s	37	27	28	26	31	56

Sources by Column

(1), (2):	Read off Chart 6.3, Stone 1967, p.137.
(3), (4), (5):	Stone, 1967, Table 5.3, p.89.
(6):	Read off Chart 6.2, Stone, 1967, p.135.

construction data. Confidence in our narrowly-based residential distributor in the nineteenth century is strengthened by the remarkable closeness of starts based on this series and starts based on the Buckley urban series for 1901-11, when the latter series is broadly based.

The construction of our "favoured" estimates reflects our favourable view of these last two series. Our favoured estimates for 1867 and 1868 are essentially the only one available — the residential-based estimate. For 1869-1900 our favoured estimate weights the residential distributor-based estimate 0.75 and the mortgage distributor-based estimate 0.25. This weighting for the mortgage-based estimate is a saw-off between our fairly substantial faith in the amplitude it shows for cycles in this period, and, on the other hand, our queasiness about using a relatively untried kind of starts indicator. In addition, until the late 1870s, the basic insurance company mortgage asset data are shaky; we did not junk the series in the early years, however, because during these years the residential index is just a Montreal index.

For 1901 to 1914 our favoured estimate weights the two series used above at 0.25 each and the urban index-based series at 0.50. During these years the urban index incorporates the activity of a very large number of cities and towns.

For 1915 to 1920, we drop the mortgage index-based series; it rises much too much in 1920 and generally behaves erratically during this period, possibly because of price and asset distortions caused by the war. Instead, our favoured estimate is a simple mean of the residential and urban-based series. We put increased importance on the former for these years, partly because starting in 1915 it incorporates information covering all dwellings built in Quebec, rural as well as urban. In addition, we suspect that during this period the inclusion of nonresidential building in the urban series would distort it unduly; in fact our residential series shows a much greater recovery in 1919-21 than the urban series.

6. Evaluation of the New Estimates

For the nineteenth century, our estimates, despite their rather flimsy basis, fit the under construction counts taken at Census dates very nicely (Table 8.16), (although our "high loss" results suggest that there is a case for using them as our favoured decade estimates). At the end of our estimation period, our extrapolation to 1921 yields almost precisely the existing estimate for 1921 (33.5 thousand against 33.9 thousand (Steele, 1972, Table A3.2)). We do not pretend that the extreme precision of this fit is anything other than coincidence but this fit, like any fit within 10 or 15 percent, is substantial support for our new series.

Our estimates of starts, however, are strikingly different from Pickett's (Tables A1 and A2). The greatest differences are in the early 1870s and in 1915-20; in each of these periods our estimates are at only about half the level of Pickett's. The high level of activity shown by Pickett's estimates in the 1870s is, however, essentially merely the result of an arithmetic error magnified by his annual distribution procedure.[28] The major source of the high level of activity shown by Pickett's series during World War I is probably the bias caused by the use of a building materials index in a period when there was stepped up use of building materials in nonresidential construction related to the war.[29] In addition, Pickett's Census-derived change for 1911-21 is very high, mostly because of his very large upward adjustment to occupied dwelling units in 1921 and his assumption of high vacancy rates in 1921. These two adjustments yield a ratio of dwelling units to households indicating a loose housing market, contrary to other evidence for this year.[30] Under these circumstances it is not surprising that the annual estimates generated by Pickett's estimator for 1915-20 are greatly out of line not only with our favoured estimates but also with every one of our alternative series as well as with residential contracts awarded (HSC, Series R170, p.514).

All comment about possible error in our series so far has used essentially external indicators. We also have internal indicators of error for our nonfarm series, yielded by comparison of our favoured series with six alternative nonfarm starts series. Four of these are merely the nonfarm series yielded by using each of the four annual distributors for the whole period (see Table A2). The other two series were derived by plugging into the favoured annual estimator procedure alternative Census-derived decade starts estimates; one of these alternatives assumes relatively large losses (the "high loss" estimates) and one assumes Pickett's values for occupied, vacant and temporary units. Table 8.17 makes it immediately clear that the annual estimates are much more sensitive to differences in the annual distributor than to changes in the assumptions underlying the raw decade estimator. Thus, when we use the Pickett assumptions for various stock values at Census dates we get a maximum absolute percentage derivation from our favoured series of only 18 percent (column 6) compared with 43 percent using the residential distributor. Yet we regard the stock values of Pickett as exceedingly implausible.

The most noteworthy fact Table 8.17 points out is the remarkable agreement in the estimates for the 1901-10 decade. Even the Pickett glass distributor does not do too badly for that decade. Looking at the whole period after 1880, on the basis of these results, we would find it surprising if our favoured nonfarm series were ever more than 20 percent in error and we expect the average error is less than ten percent. Further, Table A2 suggests that within most periods errors are apt to be strongly serially correlated (e.g. 1895-99 and 1915-21) so that appropriate autocorrelation correction should undo a lot of the damage to regression results arising from this source.

Looking at particular periods in a more qualitative way we can say the following. First, the weight of available evidence supports our picture of a peak in total starts in 1874. The mortgage series, which does not show such a peak, is based on quite questionable asset data

Table 8.16

Dwellings Under Construction and Total Dwelling Starts, Selected Years

(thousands of units)

	Dwellings Under Construction* (1)	Pickett (2)	Using Favoured Decade Estimates: Nonfarm Distributors				Using Favoured Annual Estimators: Decade Estimates		
			Buckley Urban (3)	Resid-ential (4)	Urban Mortgage (5)	Pickett Glass (6)	Favoured (7)	Quasi-Pickett (8)	High Loss (9)
1870			17.8	18.0	16.2	n.a.	17.6	17.2	18.7
71	10.1		27.3	27.6	13.3	17.7	24.0	23.6	25.7
72		30.0	17.0	17.2	9.0	14.7	15.2	15.0	16.3
1880		15.2	14.5	14.6	24.3	21.3	17.0	17.4	19.8
81	9.9	17.4	12.7	12.8	17.4	20.8	14.0	14.3	16.4
1890	10.9	13.8	20.7	21.8	15.4	14.0	20.2	20.1	23.4
91		13.5	18.7	24.5	14.5	12.0	22.0	21.4	25.0
1900		17.8	18.4	16.2	19.9	23.3	17.1	14.3	18.7
01	9.1	19.6	21.2	20.6	17.3	23.8	20.1	17.5	21.8
1910		60.7	76.5	78.7	83.8	66.9	78.9	87.2	84.9
11	20.2	73.4	73.6	67.3	70.2	57.0	71.2	80.4	75.6

* As of about April 1, except about June 1 for 1911.

Sources by Column

(1) Census figures plus in 1871, Pickett's estimates for areas other than Ontario, Quebec, Nova Scotia and New Brunswick (1871 Census, Volume I, Table I; 1881 Census, Volume I, Table I; 1891 Census, Volume II, Table II; 1901 Census, Volume IV, Table IV: Pickett, 1961, Appendix, Table I).

(2) Pickett, 1963, Table IV, p.47 adjusted to a starts basis using the following estimator: $0.786\,C(t) + 0.214\,C(t+1)$ where $C(t)$ is Pickett completions in year t.

(3)-(7) Tables A1 and A2 below.

(8), (9) Estimated as described in text, using Census-derived decade starts estimates given in Table 8.12.

Table 8.17
Robustness Indicators, Nonfarm Starts Estimates:
Measures of Deviation from the Favoured Series

	Series Using Favoured Raw Decade Estimates and Using As Distributor				Series Using Favoured Annual Estimator and Using As Raw Decade Estimates	
	Buckley Urban	Resi-dential	Urban Mortgage	Pickett Glass	High Loss	Quasi-Pickett
1871-1920						
Avg. abs. % dev.	13.0	12.1	30.7	7.4	7.2	
Max. abs. % dev.	44.0	43.0	129.0	189.0	11.0	18.0
Avg. abs. dev.	1.8	2.1	3.8	4.7	1.1	1.8
Dev. sum of sq's	296.0	621.0	1375.0	1835.0	81.0	467.0
1871-1880						
Avg. abs. % dev.	19.4	17.5	52.5	31.1	7.4	2.0
Max. abs. % dev.	44.0	43.0	129.0	84.0	8.0	4.0
Avg. abs. dev.	1.7	1.5	4.5	2.3	0.7	0.2
Dev. sum of sq.'s	33.5	32.2	289.7	92.6	5.6	0.3
1881-1890						
Avg. abs. % dev.	9.9	8.1	24.2	73.2	10.0	3.9
Max. abs. % dev.	26.0	23.0	70.0	189.0	11.0	6.0
Avg. abs. dev.	0.8	0.7	2.0	4.9	1.0	0.3
Dev. sum of sq's.	14.6	6.8	61.1	284.0	13.7	0.9
1891-1900						
Avg. abs. % dev.	16.0	10.6	31.7	25.1	10.3	4.5
Max. abs. % dev.	28.0	21.0	64.0	62.0	11.0	6.0
Avg. abs. dev.	1.9	1.3	3.8	3.1	1.3	0.5
Dev. sum of sq's.	42.8	21.6	194.7	180.8	17.7	3.3
1901-1910						
Avg. abs. % dev.	5.7	6.4	9.3	20.3	5.1	9.1
Max. abs. % dev.	10.0	15.0	24.0	60.0	7.0	14.0
Avg. abs. dev.	1.3	1.3	2.1	4.4	1.3	2.8
Dev. sum of sq's.	20.2	28.7	66.3	334.4	17.4	115.1
1911-1920						
Avg. abs. % dev.	14.2	17.7	35.9	36.6	4.2	16.5
Max. abs. % dev.	27.0	27.0	90.0	104.0	4.0	18.0
Avg. abs. dev.	3.6	5.6	6.8	8.5	1.4	5.2
Dev. sum of sq's.	185.2	532.0	763.9	944.0	26.7	347.8

Sources: Tables 4, A1 and A2.

before about 1876; as well, the change in Ottawa assessment,[31] and the number of instruments registered in Toronto, York and Winnipeg (Buckley, 1955, Tables O, P, pp. 140-143) all show a peak in 1874.

For the period from about 1875 to 1893, doubt is cast on the picture shown by our favoured estimates, by the cycle of much less amplitude shown by the mortgage series (Table A2); the series based on the Pickett glass distributor tells an exaggerated version of this same story. The major source of this apparent anomaly looks to be the behaviour of the farm starts (Table A1). The mortgage distributor to some minor extent, and the Pickett glass distributor to a much greater extent, reflect farm starts as well as the nonfarm starts we are taking them to represent. Over the period 1875 to 1893, this resulted in important bias because of the opposite directions in the movements of starts in these two sectors. So, we see no need to reject our estimates for this period.

The discrepancy between our favoured series and the mortgage series over 1894 to 1900 cannot be explained so easily. The mortgage series — and the glass series — show nonfarm starts substantially greater than our favoured estimates despite the relatively depressed state of farm starts in this period. The Census under construction data for 1901, however, especially for individual cities, strongly support our favoured estimates. Other Census data for this period suggest an explanation for the behaviour of mortgage series. This series assumes a constant real value during the nineties, but there is evidence that starts were of better materials and larger than the existing stock: over 75 percent of the net change in occupied dwellings were as large as six rooms or more, while only 49 percent of the stock in 1891 were of this size.[32] So we presume the relatively high level of starts indicated by the mortgage and glass series is a statistical artifact produced by an increase in the quality and size of dwellings as builders withdrew from the speculative building of small houses for immigrants in the larger cities but continued the construction of larger houses.

The most important questionable aspect of our picture for the early 1890s is the peak we show in nonfarm starts in 1891. The number for 1891 is, in fact, a rather artificial one. In constructing the residential series we, following Buckley (1955, p.123), reduced the reported number for 1891 in Toronto. We are less convinced, however, than Buckley that lapsed permits in 1891 in Toronto were very important; after all, lapsing of permits is usually the sign of the end of a speculative fever and yet in 1892 residential permits taken out remained higher than in 1889.[33] Our major reason for reducing the spectacularly high number for Toronto is its unrepresentativeness; we reduced it to show a substantially smaller percentage drop between 1891 and 1892 than the Hamilton total value series.[34]

It appears that in 1891 and possible 1892 there were wide regional variations, with residential construction strong in Toronto and the west and declining elsewhere. Thus, Montreal declined substantially, and there are signs that happened also in Ottawa. In contrast, Winnipeg apparently improved substantially (with property transfers not reaching a peak until 1892 (Buckley, 1955, Table O, p.140)) and Vancouver also grew (Nicolls, 1954, p.10). We presume that eastern bias plays some part in the relatively low figure our mortgage series shows for 1891; the glass series in fact shows a peak in 1892.

As we have noted earlier, the alternative series are remarkably unanimous in their picture of the years from 1901 to 1911. The downturn in the residential series in 1912 casts some doubt, however, on the stratospheric heights our series show for the nonfarm peak reached in that year. Increased commercial and industrial building may have pushed the urban distributor up and increased loans per dwelling unit may have pushed the mortgage distributor up, together producing an unwarrantedly high peak in our favoured estimates. On the other hand, property transfer data for York and for Greater Toronto show a very pronounced peak in 1912 (Buckley, 1955, Table

P, p.144). Greater Toronto includes suburban areas which grew much faster after 1910 than the City of Toronto; the downturn of the residential distributor in 1912 likely merely reflects this shift to the suburbs in Toronto, and to a lesser extent, in Montreal.

7. The Behaviour of Dwelling Starts

The new estimates show total starts hitting a high in 1874 of 24,000 units, a level not equalled until after the turn of the twentieth century. Following this, starts drifted down for several years, as strong farm starts prevents a sharp fall. Perhaps propelled by easier credit, there was a weak recovery in 1879 and 1880 but starts fell back again in 1881, and this time farm starts as well as nonfarm starts fell, until a trough was reached in 1883. Farm starts did not really pick up steam again until the last year of the century, but nonfarm starts revived in 1884 following the big rise in immigration the year earlier. This expansion lasted until 1892; starts fell off sharply in 1893, a year after the precipitous drop in immigration, and hit bottom in 1895, with total starts at 12,000 units, 46 percent above the previous low. By 1899 total starts were getting an important boost from farm starts and were close to the previous peak level.

The twentieth century did not open auspiciously, with a decline in immigrants and total starts in 1900. Starts rose the following year, however, and in 1903 took off. In residential construction, from then until 1912, the twentieth century certainly belong to Canada. Although the credit crunch in 1906 and 1907 and the sharp fall in immigrants in 1908 took their toll, especially in 1908, the recovery in 1909 was very great. By 1912 the level of starts was over four time as great as in 1900.

The earlier high expectations looked like a mirage as residential construction crashed in the following three years, especially in western Canada. At the trough in 1915, starts, at 22 thousand units, were almost down to the level of the late nineteenth century. Indeed the percentage decline was even greater — albeit only slightly — than that suffered later in the depression of the thirties. Starts did not really improve until after World War I with a surge in 1919 followed by insubstantial increases in the next two years.

Residential Construction and the Revisionist View of 1873-1896

Essentially, our estimates show that residential construction depressed per capita income over the years from 1873 to 1896 but this negative effect was not great except in comparison with United States experience over the same years (Table 8.18). Starts per capita fell by only 38 percent from the seventies to the eighties and then remained in the nineties at a level substantially higher than that achieved in the 1930s. In fact, evidence adduced above on the increased quality and size of starts in the nineties suggests that the nineties may have seen a substantial rise in real residential capital formation per capita.

Decade aggregates, however, hide cyclical movements, and in particular, what should perhaps be termed the agonizing depression in housebuilding which began in 1875 — agonizing because of its length, because of the unfulfilled promise of the slight 1879 and 80 upturn and because of its contrast with the United States. As Table 8.19 shows, the decline in this depression was almost as great as in the 1930s in percentage terms and the depression lasted much longer, not really ending until 1885. It was after the 1879 and 80 upturn that Canadian housebuilding parted company with that in the United States; while U.S. building continued to boom (Gottlieb, 1964, Table 15, p.61), Canadian building flopped as Canadians emigrated to the United States and immigrants to Canada came, looked and left. This contrast with the United

States was especially severe for nonfarm building and apparently, for the west.[35]

This disappointing decade from the mid-seventies to the mid-eighties was not repeated. The depression of the mid-nineties was relatively short-lived and the decline relatively moderate. So, as far as house-building goes, the revisionists' view of the 1873-1896 period is half right. Furthermore, much of the investment in railways and telegraphs came at just the right time (HSC, Series R156) surging ahead in the early 1880s when house-building was in the doldrums and helping to keep the depression in house-building from spreading beyond that sector.

8. Residential Construction Expenditure

The estimates of residential construction expenditure given in Table 8.20 were approached in seven steps.

(i) The number of new dwelling units constructed, distributed between farm and nonfarm were estimated for each year: the derivation of these estimates has just been described.

(ii) An average value for the cost of construction for nonfarm residences in 1926 was

Table 8.18

Average Annual Dwelling Starts Per Thousand Population,
Canada and the United States, by Decades

	Canada		United States	
Decade	Total Starts	Nonfarm Starts	Total Starts	Nonfarm Starts
1870s (1871-1880)	4.7	2.5	5.5	2.9
1880s	3.4	2.7	6.0	4.8
1890s	3.4	2.5	5.2	3.5
1900s	7.6	4.4	6.2	5.3
1910s	6.0	4.0		4.0
1920s	4.9			6.8
1930s	2.7			
1960s	8.3			

Sources:

Columns (1) and (2):   Data obtained by dividing total starts by total population: Starts from Table A1 and *Canadian Housing Statistics* (CHS), 1972, Table 1, p.1; Population from HSC, Series A1 (mid-decade, e.g. 1875).

Columns (3) and (4):   Nonfarm Starts from dwellings "produced" in Gottlieb, 1964, Table 15, p.61; Total Starts from Nonfarm Starts, plus farm starts estimated at six percent of beginning decade stock plus Gottlieb's estimated increment (1964, Table 9, p.36); Population from *Historical Statistics of the United States*, A1-3.

Table 8.19

Characteristics of Residential Building Cycles,
1871-1941 and 1965-1973

Cycles	Mean Starts	Mean Starts Per Thousand Population	Length of Cycle (Peak to Peak)	Fall, Trough from Initial Peak	Rise, Final Peak from Trough
	(000s)		(years)	(percent)	(percent)
1874-92	17.2	3.9	18	66	176
1892-1905	22.9	4.4	13	48	344
1905-10	55.8	8.7	5	19	87
1910-22	43.6	5.5	12	73	102
1922-27	45.8	5.0	5	6	36
1927-41	36.9	3.4	14	71	265
1965-69	174.5	8.6	4	19	56
1969-73	230.6	10.7	4	9	41

Sources: computed using total starts from Table A1; from Steele, 1972, Table A3.2, p.219; from Steele, 1969, Table 8, p.19; and from *Canadian Housing Statistics*, 1973, Table 1; from *Canadian Statistical Review* (CSR) June 1969, Table 1, p.1; from CSR, August, 1973, Table 1, p.18).

estimated.

(iii) An index for the cost of construction per unit of nonfarm dwellings was prepared for all years from 1926 back to 1870: this index was used to extrapolate the 1926 average cost of construction of nonfarm residences back year by year to 1870.

(iv) The average cost of construction of farm dwelling units was calculated as a proportion of the construction cost for nonfarm dwelling units: the proportion of farm to nonfarm dwelling unit construction costs varied over the period 1870 to 1926.

(v) For each year, for 1870 to 1925, the estimate of construction cost of a nonfarm dwelling unit was multiplied by the number of nonfarm dwelling units started to obtain the estimated aggregate value of nonfarm starts; similarly, for each year the estimated average construction cost of a farm dwelling unit was multiplied by the number of farm dwelling units started to obtain the estimated aggregate value of farm starts. The value of non-farm and farm starts were added together to give the aggregate value of housing starts.

(vi) The value of starts was put on a work-put-in-place basis by calculating a weighted sum of the current year value of starts and the previous year value of starts. Specifically, aggregate construction expenditure on new housing in any year was estimated as 0.85 times the value of starts in the current year plus 0.15 times the value of starts in the previous year.

Table 8.20. Total Residential Construction in Current and Constant Dollars, 1870 to 1920

	New Residential Construction	Alterations and Additions	Total Residential Construction	New Residential Construction	Alterations and Additions	Total Residential Construction
	(thousands of current dollars)			(thousands of 1913 dollars)		
1870	20176	3051	23227	32629	4931	37560
1871	27567	3623	31190	42476	5548	48024
1872	24033	3488	27522	34479	4931	39410
1873	26014	3599	29613	35797	4931	40728
1874	31288	4010	35298	43237	5548	48784
1875	26824	3655	30478	38214	5239	43454
1876	20515	3263	23778	30700	4931	35631
1877	16631	2960	19591	25822	4623	30445
1878	14758	2647	17405	23891	4315	28206
1879	14806	2550	17356	24918	4315	29233
1880	17974	2608	20581	29824	4315	34139
1881	15460	2761	18221	24412	4315	28727
1882	11471	2805	14276	17702	4315	22017
1883	9025	2934	11959	13383	4315	17698
1884	11352	3005	14357	17377	4623	21999
1885	13506	3057	16564	21653	4931	26584
1886	19068	3615	22683	27974	5239	33213
1887	27173	4509	31682	35742	5856	41597
1888	33589	4626	38215	42658	5856	48513
1889	36627	5178	41805	45866	6472	52338
1890	34277	5424	39701	42846	6780	49627
1891	36714	5529	42243	46907	7088	53996
1892	33788	5387	39175	44270	7088	51358
1893	25223	5221	30444	32843	6780	39623
1894	17329	4854	22183	22982	6472	29454

Table 8.20. (continued)

Year	New Residential Construction	Alterations and Additions	Total Residential Construction	New Residential Construction	Alterations and Additions	Total Residential Construction
	(thousands of current dollars)			(thousands of 1913 dollars)		
1895	14748	4660	19408	20348	6472	26820
1896	15725	4466	20191	22659	6472	29131
1897	19076	4407	23483	29134	6780	35914
1898	22217	4678	26896	33731	7088	40820
1899	23832	5030	28862	35199	7397	42595
1900	20405	5178	25582	29301	7397	36698
1901	22709	5609	28318	32442	8013	40455
1902	27000	5825	32825	38572	8321	46893
1903	36102	6749	42852	49699	9246	58945
1904	46974	7495	54469	62113	9862	71975
1905	62691	8269	70961	79794	10479	90272
1906	74743	9203	83946	90710	11095	101806
1907	76675	9564	86239	89470	11095	100565
1908	68105	10128	78233	75349	11095	86444
1909	90586	10593	101179	100049	11711	111760
1910	119589	11426	131015	132250	12636	144886
1911	135687	12540	148227	144313	13252	157566
1912	157598	13385	170983	163717	13869	177586
1913	142446	13252	155698	143319	13252	156571
1914	97307	11288	108594	100176	11711	111888
1915	50262	11107	61369	48689	10479	59168
1916	47630	12534	60165	40515	10479	50994
1917	45372	12737	58109	38345	10787	49132
1918	45383	13686	59070	37034	11095	48129
1919	79273	17306	96579	55850	12020	67869
1920	104164	23091	127254	60105	12944	73049

(vii) Estimates of aggregate outlay on alterations and additions to existing dwelling units were made, year by year, and added to the outlay on new dwelling units to yield the overall estimate of construction expenditure on capital formation in residential dwelling units.

Value of Nonfarm Housing, 1926

Nonfarming housing was divided into two components, first, urban housing equated with housing in centers of 5,000 population and over and, second, other nonfarm housing. A value equal to the average construction cost of urban dwelling units in one-to-three unit buildings multiplied by 1.03 to allow for supplementary costs was assigned as the average construction cost of urban units in 1926. This average value was estimated from "contracts awarded" which information was derived largely from building permits for residential building from MacLean Building Review, Hugh C. MacLean Publications Ltd. The ratio of the value of "other" nonfarm housing to urban (5,000 and over population) was calculated from 1941 Census data (*1941 Census*, Volume IX, Tables 20, 21, 23). In this computation it was assumed that the value of rented units is 100 times monthly rent and that the value of land per dwelling unit is $300 for urban units of 5,000 and over and is zero for other nonfarm. These calculations led, in 1941, to a construction cost of $2,792 per urban unit and $1,744 construction cost per unit for "other" nonfarm dwellings. The resultant ratio of nonfarm per unit construction costs to urban per unit construction costs is 0.6246. In 1926 then the ratio of the construction value per unit of all nonfarm starts (both urban and other) to urban starts only is

$$\frac{22.1 + 0.6246\,(10.1)}{32.2} = 0.882250$$

where 22.1 is thousands of urban starts in 1926 and 10.1 is thousands of other non-farm starts in 1926. The average construction cost of urban dwelling starts in one-to three unit buildings in 1926 was $4,205.

We note that value ratios for different areas appear to be rather stable; the 1931 Census yields a ratio of 0.481 for owner-occupied dwellings in urban centers of less than 1,000 relative to those in urban centers of 1,000 or more, as compared with a ratio of 0.472 from the 1941 Census (Steele, 1972, Table 7.3, p.155). This stability suggests that there is a problem in our estimates to the extent that (the less valuable) nonfarm rural starts were a more important component of total nonfarm starts in earlier years than in 1926; i.e. our estimate for earlier years may be upward biased. If it is any comfort, the official estimation for the 1950s and 1960s takes no account of this problem.

The Value Index: The Index of Construction Costs for Non-Farm Dwelling Unit Starts.

Back to 1914, this value index is based on the average value of rural units in Quebec as reported in Quebec Municipal Statistics. The value index was linked at 1914 to the residential construction price index. This was linked in 1905 to what will be called the "Toronto adjusted" index. This index was constructed by weighting a Toronto index and the residential construction prices index equally and then arbitrarily smoothing the resultant index. The Toronto index is an index of mean values per dwelling, derived from building permit data. The Toronto adjusted index was linked in 1881 to the residential construction price index. An index of construction input costs (column 1) and the actual series used (column 2) for 1870 to 1914 is given in Table

Table 8.21
Value Indexes 1913=1.00

Year	Construction Input Price	Dwelling Unit Construction Value	Year	Construction Input Price	Dwelling Unit Construction Value
1870	0.6187	0.6187	1895	0.6284	0.7200
1871	0.6531	0.6531	1896	0.6301	0.6900
1872	0.7074	0.7074	1897	0.5985	0.6500
1873	0.7298	0.7298	1898	0.6088	0.6600
1874	0.7228	0.7228	1899	0.6287	0.6800
1875	0.6975	0.6975	1900	0.6809	0.7000
1876	0.6618	0.6618	1901	0.6806	0.7000
1877	0.6404	0.6404	1902	0.7108	0.7000
1878	0.6135	0.6135	1903	0.7580	0.7300
1879	0.5910	0.5910	1904	0.7823	0.7600
1880	0.6043	0.6043	1905	0.7892	0.7892
1881	0.6375	0.6400	1906	0.8295	0.8295
1882	0.6717	0.6500	1907	0.8620	0.8620
1883	0.6604	0.6800	1908	0.9129	0.9129
1884	0.6427	0.6500	1909	0.9045	0.9045
1885	0.6194	0.6200	1910	0.9042	0.9042
1886	0.6192	0.6900	1911	0.9462	0.9462
1887	0.6490	0.7700	1912	0.9651	0.9651
1888	0.6651	0.7900	1913	1.0000	1.0000
1889	0.6691	0.8000	1914	0.9638	0.9638
1890	0.6767	0.8000			
1891	0.6584	0.7800			
1892	0.6665	0.7600			
1893	0.6521	0.7700			
1894	0.6471	0.7500			

8.21.

We use the value of Quebec rural units, rather than Quebec town or city units, because the data apparently refer to structures and a large proportion of residential structures in Quebec cities and towns would be duplexes and triplexes whereas rural units would be predominately single unit dwellings. Table 8.22 shows that Quebec rural average unit values are probably much better as an index to current dollar value than the residential construction price index.

The proportion of the value of starts in year t assumed to be put in place in year t, *viz.* 0.85, is that used in Steele (1972, p.168); the remaining construction attributed to year t was the proportion 0.15 of starts in year t-1. Firestone suggests that one-third completion in t were

Table 8.22
Indicators of Average Unit Values, 1914-1926, Canada

Year	Average Construction Cost Per Dwelling Unit, 1-3 Unit Buildings (dollars)	Average Value, Starts Basis, Quebec Rural Houses (dollars)	Residential Construction Price Index, 1913=99.6
1914		979	96.0
1915		1,077	94.0
1916		1,215	102.9
1917		1,199	122.5
1918		1,253	140.0
1919		1,463	165.0
1920		1,812	201.7
1921	4,407	1,661	177.8
1922	4,635	1,670	161.8
1923	4,549	1,769	166.2
1924	4,031	1,588	162.5
1925	4,146	1,646	159.2
1926	4,206	1,648	157.2

Sources: Column 1:   Steele, 1972, Table A3.4, p.221
           Column 2:   Quebec Department of Municipal Affairs, Trade and Commerce, Bu-
                       reau of Statistics, *Municipal Statistics*. Average values computed from
                       this source are put on a starts basis by weighting year t's value 0.786
                       and t+1 by 0.214.
           Column 3:   Steele, 1964, Table A6.

started in (t-1) and two-thirds of the value of these dwellings was put in place in t, implying a carry-over of roughly 0.22, against our 0.15. Regressing Quebec Municipal Statistics completions on Quebec contract awards suggests that Firestone is too high (see results reported in Steele, 1972, p.107). The "under construction" data in the decennial Censuses, 1871 to 1901, however, suggest that Firestone in not *much* too high. These Censuses were taken about April 1, so that probably not more than 15 percent of the years starts could have been started by then, and yet units under construction are quite consistently equal to about one-half the previous year's starts (Steele, 1976, Table 8, p.25).

Farm Housing

The average value of farm units is assumed to be 0.45 times the value of nonfarm units until 1890, and starting in 1891, 0.3 times the value of nonfarm units. We note that in 1941 the ratio of the value of farm units to nonfarm is 0.46. We use the ratio of 0.3 for the period after 1891 because most farm units started from then until 1920 were prairie units and these were much smaller, and lower in quality than eastern farm units.

Construction of New Dwelling Units, 1913 Dollars

The current dollar value is deflated by the residential construction price index (Steele, 1974, Table A.6).

Alterations and Additions

These estimates were made by graphic extrapolation. As a first approximation, the 1913 dollar value of alterations and additions in 1926 (Steele, 1972, Table A3.1, p.218) was extrapolated back for Census years, on the basis of the number of dwelling units in the stock. Then the value of construction of new units was graphed. Using the initial estimates of alterations and additions in Census years as a quite flexible anchor, final estimates were derived by a graphical extra-polations back from 1926, based on the assumption that alterations and additions move with construction of new units, but show much less amplitude. This is the relationship indicated by data for later years, and the data of Table 8.23 for Toronto indicate that it held in at least some locations during some years of our period.

Table 8.23
Residential Alterations and Additions, City of Toronto

Year	Thousands of Current Dollars	As a Percentage of New Residential Construction Expenditure
1891	255	9.4
1892	138	10.9
1893	68	14.7
1894	86	31.2
1895	59	27.1
1896	56	22.7
1897	75	20.7
1898	n.a.	
1899	n.a.	
1900	88	11.5
1901	108	7.2
1902	111	5.0
1903	152	6.2
1904	135	4.0

Source: *City Council Minutes*, Toronto

Notes to Part B

1   Saywell, John T., *Housing Canadians: Essays on the History of Residential Construction in Canada*, Discussion Paper No. 24, February 1975.

2   This conclusion, from work in Canadian data after 1920, is substantiated by U.S. studies of earlier years. Gottlieb's disdain for building materials-based estimates (1964, pp.2-4) is so great he does not depict them along with other available estimates in his final assessment (p.83).

3   Some of these alternative series of estimates are included in the appendix tables for readers whose conclusions about the relative merits of various assumptions are different from the author's.

4   Table 8.10A indicates that Firestone's characterization of the problem — "On examination it was clear that Census enumerators did not make a clear distinction between buildings ... and dwellings." (1951, p.378) — is misleading.

5   Saywell's study (referred to above) contains many contemporary comments on the great housing squeeze.

6   This occupied dwelling adjustment is much smaller than Pickett's, especially for 1921; he derived his dwelling estimate by assuming households per dwelling unit declined linearly from 1901 to 1931.

7   Wickens used a rate of 3.3 percent for the twenties in the U.S. and assumed rates of 2.8, 2.8, and 2.5 for the 10s, 00s and 90s respectively, arguing that demolitions for redevelopment were not important before the 1920s. (Wickens, 1941, pp.75, 54, 55).

8   Of course this raises the question as to whether the vacant units we include in the stock in 1891 should be included at all. For our purposes — computing decade starts — it does not matter, of course, whether we remove many of the vacant units from the 1891 stock (at the same time increasing our loss rate for the 80s and reducing it for the 90s) or leave our treatment as is.

9   Gottlieb found rates substantially higher than this for Ohio (1964, p.37).

10   These rates should be set in the context of our urban estimates for the 1920s and 1930s, at 2.5 and 6.4 percent, respectively (Steele, 1972, Tables 6.4 and 6.7). Our estimates are substantially higher than Wickens for 1890-1929 in the U.S.; Grebler, Blank and Winnick, however, comment: "It is likely that Wickens' estimates of structural conversions are much too low ..." (1956, p.330).

11   For instance, Pickett assumes essentially, that imports slightly led housebuilding (1963, p.46) but it seems quite plausible to suppose that suppliers did not order until after sales rose — so that imports would follow sales.

12   Shared by Gottlieb (1964, pp. 2-5). He ignores such series in constructing his decade annual indexes (see esp. p.67).

13   Details are available in worksheets and notes prepared by Helen and Kenneth Buckley and located in Files 42, 47 and 114 of the Buckley Files at the Saskatchewan Archives in Saskatoon. The deflated unweighted sums were converted to index form and chained at dates the sample changed. (Kenneth Buckley was incorrect in reporting that Hamilton was included from 1890 (1955, p.122); Hamilton was added in 1891 (and so the index reflects Hamilton activity in 1892)). By 1905 the index reflects 20 cities. We use for 1912 the number 1033.7, a correction arising from a correction in the price index used (File 114, note dated June, 1963).

14   This is sometimes ignored by investigators who go to enormous lengths to correct for annexations, which are well documented while giving short shrift to the fringe building problem (see for instance, Blank, 1954).

15   The percentage changes in urban population due to rural-urban reclassification was 17.8, 8.2, 13.6 and 19.5 and 4.7 respectively, for the five decades after 1870 (Stone, 1967, Table 5.1, p.84). The *Toronto Yearbook* records large annexations in early 1884 and again in early 1888 (the first two in 1888 representing increases in land area of well over 10 percent), quiescence in the 90s, followed by even more important annexations at the beginning and end of 1909, and at the end of 1912 (*Toronto Yearbook*, 1918, p.7). As for Montreal, from 1883 to 1914 it annexed 27 municipalities with a population at the time of union of 124,000. Most of this population was acquired in 1905 and 1910 (Leacock, 1942, p.231-232). Comparing percentage changes in building in these two cities in annexation years, we find no evidence that annexations substantially distorted the building pattern.

16   Except for 1920, based on reports in the City of Toronto Minutes, and on totals computed by J.T. Saywell from building permits kept in the City of Toronto Archives. For 1920, *Annual Report* of the City of Toronto Department of Buildings.

17   The Quebec data used are residential buildings constructed (adjusted to a dwelling units started basis), as reported to the Quebec Government and published in Quebec *Municipal Statistics*. Further details of the construction of the residential index are given in the appendix, Tables A3 and A4.

18   See Table 8.4, above.

19   Regressions run over 1921-1930 produced results which were substantially the same.

20   The evidence is a survey of civil service families reported in Greenway (1941, Table 32, p.172).

21   *Encyclopedia Canadiana*, 1958, Volume V, p.63. This would have resulted in large imports in the fiscal year ending March 31, 1918. Pickett's index for 1917 would include 0.7 of fiscal year 1918 (1963, p.46).

22   Blank's estimation involved stratifying the U.S. into 36 urban classes and one rural nonfarm class (1954, pp.35, 45-48). His blow-up ratios from urban to all nonfarm were 1.77, 1.53, 1.37, 1.42, for the decades 90s to 20s respectively (1954, p.48); this suggests his estimates may fall by something like 15 percent too much in 1900, 11 percent too much in 1910 and 4 percent too little in 1920. Blank ignored the well-justified if somewhat arbitrary adjustment made by Wickens for the late 20s and early 30s to correct for the

assumption of r (n,t) constant over a decade (Wickens, 1941, p.41).

23   We note that the average annual rate of change is centred at *end* of the last year of decade (n-1) (e.g. end of 1880) not the middle of the first year of decade n. The smoothing indicated by this expression applies from 1881 to 1910 except in the case of the farm index.

In the case of the farm index, the estimation is divided into two parts because of the use of the farm mortgage series until 1891 and Buckley's farm estimates thereafter. For 1890 and earlier the $\hat{g}$ used is that derived from the $\hat{r}$ for the 1880s and the $\hat{r}$ for the 1870s. The smoothing equation is used only from 1901 to 1910.

24   The farm index used the $\hat{r}$ for 1896 as the base $\hat{r}$ for the 1891-1921 period.

25   If any one of the five decade sums were different by more than five percent we multiplied all $\hat{r}$ (n)s by the ratio of the Census-derived decade starts to the decade sums of our annual estimates. One would expect large differences in these latter two numbers whenever a value for $\hat{r}$ (n) deviated from the trend. For instance the $\hat{r}$ (n) for the urban mortgage series for the 1890s is below its value for the 1880s and 1910s. As a result, the initial mid-1890s value for $\hat{r}$ (n,t) was approximately equal to $\hat{r}$ (n) but $\hat{r}$ (n,t) was higher than $\hat{r}$ (n) for other years in the decade. Thus the average value of $\hat{r}$ (n,t) for the 1890s was higher than $\hat{r}$ (n) and so of course, the decade sum of annual estimates was higher than the Census-derived decade sum. Thus iteration was required.

Every distributor required at least two iterations (i.e. one iteration in addition to the estimation using the raw $\hat{r}$ (n)); the largest number of iterations was required by the residential distributor — four iterations, except when using the quasi-Pickett decade estimates, in which case three were required.

26   The relative stability of the glass index ratios is interesting in view of the fact that they are ratios to *non*farm starts while window glass would be used for all starts. The stability is partly explained by the much lower value per unit of farm dwellings — and so presumably, the much lesser quantity of window glass per unit.

27   The 1911 under construction count is not very useful because the Census was taken at the beginning of June in that year. Most houses started in 1910 would have been completed before then and many houses actually under construction would have been missed by enumerators because of the difficulty in noticing houses just barely started.

28   His Census-derived decade estimate is 219 thousand instead of 172 thousand, because of an adding error. Also, while his false decade estimate gives an average value for $\hat{r}$ (n,t) over the 70s of 0.167, he uses for 1872 and 1873 a value of $\hat{r}$ (n,t) of 0.5 (Pickett, 1963, Table IV, p.47).

29   This pattern also appears in Firestone's series (1958, Table 90, p.299), which uses construction materials as a distributor. We have already commented, above, on the part the Halifax Explosion played in yielding the very high 1917 figure.

30   Pickett added 94 thousand units to the Census occupied dwelling count of 1,764 thousand (Pickett, 1963, Table I, p.41 and *1941 Census*, Volume V, Table I, p.3); we add only 41 thousand units. Pickett took vacancies at 77 thousand units (1963, Table I, p.41); we took

them at only 41 thousand units.

31   City of Ottawa, *Annual Report of the Assessment Commissioner for 1921*, p.56.

32   Computed from *1891 Census*, Volume I, Table II and *1901 Census*, Volume IV, Table XVII. For purposes of computing the net change the number of "houses" of six rooms or more in 1891 was multiplied by the ratio of total occupied dwellings to "houses" (i.e. occupied dwellings excluding temporary). This yields a lower percentage of dwellings with six or more rooms than the unadjusted data; on the other hand, we have left the data uncorrected for slight upward bias caused by the fact that the 1901 data are for families, not dwellings. The material of construction data show an enormous drop in the percentage of dwellings constructed of wood but we suspect that part of this drop is due to problems in the 1901 Census definition of "other" materials of construction.

33   Buckley did not have residential data for any of these years and had no Toronto data at all for 1890 (1955, p.122).

34   The resulting Toronto figure is 55 percent of that reported. This is a substantially smaller cut than made by Buckley. Buckley also cut 1892 and we have not. The Hamilton data we used is given in Buckley File 47, Saskatchewan Archives, Saskatoon.

35   The number of instruments registered in Winnipeg reached great heights in 1881 and 1882 and then fell back so much as to suggest a collapse of the property boom (Buckley, 1955, Table O); the building of the Canadian Pacific Railway apparently raised hopes which were not realized.

Bibliography — Residential Rents

Bangs, R.G., (1945) *National Income-Real Estate: Estimated Net Rentals, Dwelling (excluding rural-farm), Stores and Office Buildings*, (processed, Statistics Canada (then Dominion Bureau of Statistics), Ottawa. The date of 1945 is a guess);

Buckley, K.A.H., (1955) *Capital Formation in Canada, 1986-1930*, (Toronto: University of Toronto Press);

Censuses of Canada: Department of Agriculture, (1893) *Census of Canada, 1890-91* Vol. I (Ottawa: Queen's Printer);

The Census Office, (1906) *Fourth Census of Canada*, 1901, Vol. IV (Ottawa: King's Printer);

Dominion Bureau of Statistics, (1927) *Sixth Census of Canada, 1921* Vol. III (Ottawa: King's Printer); and DBS (1935,36), *Seventh Census of Canada, 1931*, Vols. V, VIII (Ottawa: King's Printer) and DBS (1949), *Eighth Census of Canada, 1941, Housing*, Vol. IX (Ottawa: King's Printer);

Canada, Royal Commission on the Relations of Labour and Capital in Canada, (1889) *Report* (RCRLC) (Ottawa: Queen's Printer);

Canada, Board of Inquiry into Cost of Living in Canada, (1915) *Report* (Ottawa: King's Printer);

Canada, Department of Labour, (1917) *Wholesale Prices, Canada, 1916* (Ottawa: King's Printer);

Firestone, O.J., (1958) *Canada's Economic Development, 1867-1953*, (London: Bowes and Bowes);

Grebler, L.D., M. Blank and L. Winnick, (1956) *Capital Formation in Residential Real Estate* (Princeton: National Bureau of Economic Research);

Greenway, H.F., (1941) *Housing in Canada* (Census Monograph No.8, *Seventh Census of Canada*, 1931) (Ottawa: King's Printer);

Mavor, James, (1910) *Papers* (in the Robarts Library Archives University of Toronto. The date is a guess);

MacGregor, D.C., J.B. Rutherford, G.E. Britness and J.J. Deutch, (1939) *National Income*, App. 4 of the Royal Commission on Dominion Provincial Relations (Ottawa: King's Printer);

Ontario Bureau of Industries, *Annual Report* for 1886, 1887, 1888, 1889 (Toronto: Ontario Department of Agriculture);

Pickett, J., (1961) *Residential Capital Formation in Canada, 1871-1921* (with Appendix) (Glasgow: Royal College of Science and Technology, mimeo, 1961);

Rymes, T.K., (1967) *Fixed Capital Flows and Stocks, Manufacturing, Canada 1926-1960, Methodology*, Dominion Bureau of Statistics (Ottawa: Queen's Printer);

Steele, M.L., (1972) *Dwelling Starts in Canada, 1921-1940* (Toronto: unpublished Ph.D dissertation, University of Toronto); and (1976) *Housing Starts in Canada, 1868-1920* (Guelph: processed);

Stone, L.O., (1967) *Urban Development in Canada* (1961 Census Monograph) (Ottawa: Queen's Printer);

Urquhart, M.C. and K.A.H Buckley, (1965) *Historical Statistics of Canada* (HSC) (Toronto: Macmillian of Canada);

Wickens, D.L., (1941) *Residential Real Estate* (New York: National Bureau of Economic Research).

Additional Bibliography — Residential Construction

(see also Bibliography for Residential Rents)

Blank, D.M., *The Volume of Residential Construction, 1889-1950* (New York: National Bureau of Economic Research);

Buckley, K.A.H., (1963) *Population, Labour Force and Economic Growth.* (Banff Business Policies Conference on Canadian Economic Survival);

Censuses of Canada: see the bibliography of Chapter 2 for the evolution of the census office: *Census of Canada, 1870-71* (Vols. I, III); *Census of Canada, 1880-81* (Vol. I); *Census of Canada, 1890-91* (Vols. I, II); *Fourth Census of Canada, 1901* (Vol. IV); *Sixth Census of Canada, 1921* (Vols. III, V); *Seventh Census of Canada, 1931* (Administrative Report and Vol. V); *Eighth Census of Canada, 1941* (Vol. V);

Central Mortgage and Housing Corporation, *Canadian Housing Statistics* (CHS) (Ottawa, 1972, 1973); *Housing in Canada* (Ottawa, various quarters.);

City of Ottawa, *Annual Report* of the Assessment Commissioner for 1921 (Ottawa, 1922);

City of Toronto: *Annual Report* of the Department of Buildings, 1920; *Minutes* of the City Council (Toronto, various years); *Report of the Housing Commission* (Toronto: 1918);

Dominion Bureau of Statistics (now Statistics Canada), *Canada Year Book* (CYB) (various years) and *Canadian Statistical Review* (CSR) (June, 1969 and August, 1973);

Easterbrook, W.T., (1938) *Farm Credit in Canada* (Toronto: University of Toronto Press);

Encyclopedia Canadiana (Ottawa: Canadiana Co., 1958);

Firestone, O.J., *Canada's Economic Development, 1867-1953* (London: Bowes and Bowes, 1958) and *Residential Real Estate in Canada* (Toronto: University of Toronto Press, 1951);

Gottlieb, M., (1964) *Estimates of Residential Building, United States, 1840-1939* (New York: National Bureau of Economic Research);

Leacock, S., (1942) *Montreal, Seaport and City* (Garden City, New York: Doubleday, Doran and Co.);

Neufeld, E.P., (1972) *The Financial System of Canada* (Toronto: MacMillan of Canada);

Nicolls, J.P., (1954) *Real Estate Values in Vancouver* (Vancouver);

Pickett, J., (1963) "Residential Capital Formation in Canada, 1871-1921", *Canadian Journal of Economics and Political Science*, XXIX;

Quebec, Department of Municipal Affairs, Trade and Commerce, Bureau of Statistics, *Municipal Statistics* (Quebec: King's Printer, various years);

Saywell, John T., *Housing Canadians: Essays on the History of Residential Construction in Canada* (Economic Council of Canada Discussion Paper No. 24, February, 1975);

Steele, M.L., *Estimates of New Residential Construction, 1941-1950* (Ottawa: mimeo, 1969); *Residential Construction in Canada, 1967-1920* (Guelph: processed, 1974);

Toronto Municipal Intelligence Bureau, *Toronto Year Book*, (Toronto, 1918);

United States Department of Commerce, Bureau of the Census, *Historical Statistics of the United States, Colonial Times to 1957* (Washington, D.C.: 1960).

Table A1
Estimated Nonfarm and Farm Dwelling Starts, 1867-1921
(thousands of units)

Year	Farm	Non-farm	Total	Year	Farm	Non-farm	Total
1867	n.a.	5.9	n.a.	1897	4.2	11.8	16.0
1868	2.3	11.3	13.6	1898	5.9	13.1	19.0
1869	4.2	7.8	12.0	1899	7.8	12.9	20.7
1870	6.2	11.3	17.6	1900	7.1	10.0	17.1
1871	7.4	16.7	24.0	1901	8.4	11.6	20.1
1872	3.7	11.5	15.2	1902	12.8	12.8	25.5
1873	5.7	12.8	18.5	1903	16.6	16.8	33.5
1874	10.7	13.5	24.2	1904	20.2	20.9	41.1
1875	8.1	12.7	20.9	1905	24.6	27.3	51.9
1876	9.9	9.5	19.4	1906	17.9	33.2	51.1
1877	11.0	7.0	18.0	1907	19.0	31.6	50.5
1878	9.5	4.9	14.5	1908	16.6	25.6	42.2
1879	9.7	5.1	14.8	1909	23.0	37.1	60.1
1880	11.4	5.7	17.0	1910	30.2	48.7	78.9
1881	9.1	4.9	14.0	1911	13.5	57.7	71.2
1882	7.8	3.6	11.4	1912	7.5	68.9	76.4
1883	5.0	3.3	8.2	1913	6.5	57.6	64.1
1884	6.1	4.9	11.1	1914	6.1	38.2	44.4
1885	6.3	6.6	12.9	1915	5.6	15.9	21.5
1886	5.9	9.6	15.5	1916	7.9	15.1	23.0
1887	4.2	13.7	17.9	1917	10.4	13.3	23.7
1888	5.2	16.1	21.3	1918	11.2	12.6	23.8
1889	4.5	17.5	22.0	1919	7.7	23.6	31.3
1890	4.1	16.1	20.2	1920	7.9	24.1	32.0
1891	2.5	19.5	22.0	1921	5.1	28.3	33.5
1892	5.0	17.5	22.6				
1893	5.3	12.0	17.4				
1894	3.7	8.4	12.0				
1895	4.0	7.7	11.7				
1896	3.4	9.0	12.4				

Notes

1. These estimates are based on the favoured Census-derived decade estimates (see Table 8.12). The nonfarm series is the "favoured" series, computed using a changing weighted average of the series shown in Table A2. For further explanation, see text.

2. The annual nonfarm estimates are much more firmly based than the annual farm estimates. Error in these latter may be very large.

Table A2
Alternative Estimates of Nonfarm Dwelling Starts, 1867-1921
(thousands of units)

Year	Using Favoured Census-Derived Decade Estimates and, Using as Distributor			
	Buckley Urban	Residential	Urban Mortgage	Pickett Glass
1867	5.7	5.9	n.a.	n.a.
1868	11.0	11.3	n.a.	n.a.
1869	9.7	9.8	1.7	n.a.
1870	11.6	11.8	10.0	n.a.
1871	19.9	20.2	5.9	10.3
1872	13.3	13.6	5.4	11.0
1873	14.5	13.2	11.8	12.7
1874	14.8	15.1	8.6	12.6
1875	12.5	12.7	12.8	11.1
1876	7.7	7.9	14.3	8.1
1877	5.5	5.8	10.7	6.1
1878	3.9	4.0	7.7	7.9
1879	3.7	3.9	8.8	9.4
1880	3.1	3.2	12.9	9.9
1881	3.7	3.8	8.4	11.8
1882	3.3	3.5	4.0	10.4
1883	3.7	3.5	2.6	7.6
1884	4.5	4.1	7.5	8.0
1885	6.0	6.3	7.4	9.8
1886	9.8	9.3	10.3	10.9
1887	17.1	14.0	12.6	10.8
1888	15.7	17.4	12.2	9.6
1889	17.8	18.0	16.3	9.7
1890	16.6	17.7	11.2	9.9
1891	16.2	22.0	12.0	9.5
1892	15.3	19.4	12.0	13.5
1893	14.3	13.4	8.1	11.8
1894	9.6	8.2	8.9	10.9
1895	9.8	6.3	11.8	10.5
1896	7.6	7.1	14.8	10.7
1897	8.6	10.0	17.1	11.2
1898	11.8	13.1	13.1	13.0
1899	13.4	12.2	15.1	15.8
1900	11.3	9.1	12.8	16.2
1901	12.8	12.1	8.9	15.4
1902	13.6	14.1	9.7	20.4
1903	18.2	14.5	16.3	23.9
1904	22.5	17.7	20.9	23.3
1905	28.8	27.2	24.4	27.3

Table A2 (continued)

Year	Buckley Urban	Residential	Urban Mortgage	Pickett Glass
1906	34.1	34.8	29.7	33.6
1907	31.4	32.4	31.1	28.9
1908	23.6	28.3	26.9	26.2
1909	36.1	37.5	38.7	29.7
1910	46.4	48.5	53.6	36.7
1911	60.1	53.8	56.7	43.5
1912	77.0	52.1	69.4	52.6
1913	60.3	46.4	63.4	49.8
1914	38.0	40.6	36.4	40.7
1915	13.2	18.6	8.6	23.8
1916	14.4	15.8	16.4	22.6
1917	10.4	16.3	23.1	27.2
1918	9.7	15.6	1.3	20.5
1919	17.1	30.0	6.1	17.6
1920	17.9	30.3	36.0	22.5
1921	20.0	36.7	25.8	11.1

Note: These estimates use annual distributors given in Table A3 and the favoured Census-derived decade estimates given in Table 8.12. For explanation for estimation procedure, see text, Section 4.

Table A3
Annual Distributor Indexes, Farm and Nonfarm, 1867-1921

		Alternative Nonfarm Distributors			
	Farm Index (1)	Buckley Urban Index (2)	Residential Index (3)	Urban Mortgage [a] (4) (millions of	Pickett Glass (5) (thousands of
Year	(1900=524)	(1900=100)	(1864=100)	1913 dollars)	1900 dollars)
1867	n.a.	28.0	27.6	n.a.	n.a.
1868	21	55.3	54.1	n.a.	n.a.
1869	44	49.7	48.1	0.04	n.a.
1870	72	61.1	59.2	0.27	n.a.
1871	95	107.5	104.0	0.18	45.6
1872	52	73.8	71.4	0.19	57.7
1873	91	82.5	71.0	0.48	79.3
1874	191	86.2	83.4	0.41	92.9
1875	161	74.2	71.8	0.70	96.9
1876	221	46.9	45.4	0.90	84.0
1877	272	34.4	34.2	0.78	75.3

Table A3   (continued)

		Alternative Nonfarm Distributors			
Year	Farm Index (1) (1900=524)	Buckley Urban Index (2) (1900=100)	Residential Index (3) (1864=100)	Urban Mortgage [a] (4) (millions of 1913 dollars)	Pickett Glass (5) (thousands of 1900 dollars)
1878	264	25.1	24.2	0.65	115.5
1879	299	24.3	24.0	0.85	162.2
1880	391	21.2	20.5	1.44	203.3
1881	347	25.2	24.3	1.07	282.2
1882	331	23.4	22.7	0.59	285.5
1883	238	26.4	22.6	0.44	234.1
1884	326	32.2	26.3	1.41	267.6
1885	373	43.5	39.7	1.56	354.7
1886	392	70.9	57.0	2.39	411.9
1887	310	123.2	82.4	3.24	418.2
1888	429	112.2	96.9	3.44	375.7
1889	412	125.6	94.2	4.99	371.3
1890	420	115.3	86.3	3.73	367.7
1891	281	111.1	100.9	4.26	338.8
1892	372	104.1	84.7	4.51	462.8
1893	385	97.5	56.7	3.20	388.6
1894	261	66.2	34.6	3.65	346.2
1895	281	68.7	26.7	4.97	323.9
1896	235	55.2	31.1	6.36	320.4
1897	287	64.1	46.3	7.37	326.2
1898	392	92.7	64.8	5.63	372.3
1899	509	110.7	66.4	6.38	442.5
1900	457	100.0	55.3	5.29	445.5
1901	535	120.3	83.4	3.57	416.8
1902	803	136.5	108.5	3.81	543.8
1903	1038	192.7	122.9	6.27	628.1
1904	1254	249.5	164.4	7.91	607.1
1905	1528	332.8	273.9	9.10	706.7
1906	1116	409.4	376.6	10.95	864.9
1907	1188	388.2	372.9	11.38	740.1
1908	1051	299.0	342.7	9.81	672.2
1909	1476	467.2	474.2	14.14	761.9
1910	1965	608.3	634.7	19.63	945.2
1911	894	797.4	724.6	20.87	1124.1
1912	509	1033.0	722.2	25.66	1363.5
1913	450	817.7	662.4	23.57	1298.2
1914	431	520.8	596.2	13.62	1064.7
1915	398	183.5	281.0	3.22	624.7

Table A3   (continued)

| | Farm Index (1) | Buckley Urban Index (2) | Residential Index (3) | Urban Mortgage [a] (4) (millions of | Pickett Glass (5) (thousands of |
				Alternative Nonfarm Distributors	
Year	(1900=524)	(1900=100)	(1864=100)	1913 dollars)	1900 dollars)
1916	575	201.6	246.5	6.21	596.4
1917	770	147.0	260.6	8.76	719.9
1918	849	138.9	257.0	0.49	545.9
1919	594	248.8	509.9	2.34	470.4
1920	620	262.1	530.3	13.87	604.2
1921	411	296.5	659.8	10.01	298.2

a These data are very poor before 1877.

Notes by Column

(1)   1868-1891: Table A5, Column (1)
1892-1921: Table A5, Column (2) linked to Table A5, Column (1) at 1891.

(2)   Buckley, 1955 Table O, p.140 except for 1912. The 1912 figure is taken from correction dated June, 63 in Buckley File 114, Saskatoon Archives.

(3)   This weights percentage changes from Table A4, Columns (1), (2), (3), (4) as follows:
1867-1882: 1, 0, 0, 0
1883-1914: 0.5, 0.5, 0, 0
1915-1921: 0, 0.4, 0.2, 0.4

(4)   Estimated value of mortgage loans by insurance companies on dwellings started in Canada, in 1913 "units". (See explanation of AVI.)
The estimator is

$$\frac{((0.8 \ \Delta \ MAI(t) + 0.2 \ \Delta MAI(t+1)) + 0.55 \ MAI(t-1))}{AVI(t)}$$

where MAI(t) = mortgage loans outstanding at the end of year t on Canadian real estate, of federally registered life companies (assessment and non-assessment) and of fire insurance companies, in millions of dollars.

and AVI(t) = construction price index (Table A6, Column (3) times 0.01) for 1868-1914; at 1914 to this is linked the average value of Quebec rural dwellings (Table A4, Column (5)). The weights 0.8 and 0.2 in the first part of the expression are to adjust ΔMAI to a starts basis.

Source of mortgage asset data: Company reports in *Report* of the Superintendent of Insurance, Sessional Papers of the House of Commons. For the years 1868 to 1875, and to a much lesser extent, to 1877, the companies reported haphazardly, so that we estimated assets in these years on the basis of a scanty and changing group of companies. All asset values for 1873 were interpolated. The huge mortgage assets of Union Mutual, which were reported only for the years ending 1870, 71 and 72, were omitted.

(5)   Window glass consumption in Canada from Pickett, 1963, Table IV, p.47, for 1872 and later years. The 1871 value was extrapolated using data in Pickett, 1961, Appendix C.

Table A4
Components of Residential Index, 1865 to 1921

Year	Montreal Dwelling Starts (1) (number)	Toronto Residential Index (2)	Quebec Dwelling Starts City (3) (number)	Town and Rural (4)	Average Value, Quebec Rural Starts (5) (current dollars)
1865	510				
1866	355				
1867	455				
1868	893				
1869	794				
1870	977				
1871	1717				
1872	1179				
1873	1173	n.a.			
1874	1377				
1875	1186				
1876	750				
1877	565				
1878	400				
1879	397				
1880	339				
1881	402		n.a.	n.a.	n.a.
1882	374	299			
1883	421	260			
1884	461	320			
1885	475	636			
1886	1060	408			
1887	1725	515			
1888	1533	754			
1889	1757	602			
1890	1676	530			
1891	1334	816			
1892	1123	683			
1893	1086	254			
1894	671	153			
1895	489	125			
1896	594	139			
1897	836	218			
1898	669	436			
1899	606	499			
1900	522	402			
1901	544	793			
1902	641	1128			
1903	784	1176			
1904	1078	1528			

Table A4 (continued)

Year	Montreal Dwelling Starts (1)	Toronto Residential Index (2)	Quebec Dwelling Starts		Average Value, Quebec Rural Starts (5)
			City (3)	Town and Rural (4)	
	(number)		(number)		(current dollars)
1905	1908	2386			
1906	2243	3758			
1907	2383	3450			
1908	2211	3140	n.a.	n.a.	n.a.
1909	3051	4357			
1910	4754	4874			
1911	5551	5438			
1912	5271	5676			
1913	4942	5090			
1914	4901	3920	5876	4643	979
1915		832	2381	3543	1077
1916		657	2195	3341	1215
1917		926	2408	2287	1199
1918		1097	1763	2091	1253
1919	n.a.	2568	4517	2800	1463
1920		2184	4398	3369	1812
1921		2621	8133	3662	1661

Notes by Column

(1)   Index put on basis, 1910=4, 873 the number of permits for new houses, 1913 (The City of Toronto, *Report of the Housing Commission*, 1918).

Index is the following converted to index form:

1882-1910: value of residential permits deflated by CNPI (see Table A6); 1890-97, 1900-04: reports in City Council *Minutes*, Toronto. Our 1891 figure is only 55 percent of that given, partly because there is some reason to believe many of the permits lapsed (Buckley, 1955, p.123), but more important, because the spectacular rise in the reported figure for Toronto is unrepresentative of the country as a whole; 1882, 1888-1890, 1898, 1906-1910: J.T. Saywell's computations directly from individual permits; 1883, 1885-1887: estimates based on Saywell's part-year totals; 1884 and 1899: estimated using global permits; 1905: estimated using "new residences", 1906 (*Annual Report* of the Assessment Commissioner) and using deflated 1904 average permit value; 1910-1921: number of residential permits; 1910-1917: permits for new houses from The City of Toronto, *Report of the Housing Commission*, 1918; 1918-1921: estimated using "new residences" in (t+1).

(2)   Annual reports of new building (City of Montreal Archives). For 1883 and earlier, estimated using 1.62 as the ratio of "familles" to "maisons".

(3), (4)   Estimated as 0.7861 QC(t) + 0.214 QC(t+1) where QC is the value of dwelling houses completed, as reported in Quebec *Municipal Statistics* divided by the estimated value per unit. This estimated value for cities and towns is twice the rural value per unit given in column (5). Reported city and town numbers were not used because units reported are buildings not dwelling units, and there are signs that the number of dwelling units per building varied substantially.

(5)   Estimated as 0.7861 RA(t) + 0.214 RA(t+1) where RA is the average value of dwelling houses completed, as reported in Quebec *Municipal Statistics*.

Table A5
Components of the Farm Index, 1867 to 1921

Year	Farm Mortgage (1) (millions of 1913 dollars)	Buckley Prairie Farm (2)	Buckley Other Farm (3)
		(dwelling units)	
1867	n.a.		
1868	84		
1869	171		
1870	280		
1871	370		
1872	204		
1873	354		
1874	745		
1875	630		
1876	860		
1877	1060		
1878	1028	n.a.	n.a.
1879	1165		
1880	1525		
1881	1353		
1882	1292		
1883	926		
1884	1270		
1885	1452		
1886	1530		
1887	1210		
1888	1673		
1889	1606		
1890	1639		
1891	1094	2.5	1.8
1892	1324	3.5	2.2
1893	1247	3.8	2.1
1894	1649	2.6	1.4
1895	905	2.9	1.4
1896	861	2.5	1.1
1897	497	3.0	1.4
1898	990	4.0	2.0
1899	1058	5.5	2.3
1900	1042	5.0	2.0
1901	1128	6.5	1.7
1902	1511	9.4	2.9
1903	1343	12.4	3.5
1904	1835	15.4	3.8
1905	2476	19.2	4.2

Table A5   (continued)

Year	Farm Mortgage (1) (millions of 1913 dollars)	Buckley Prairie Farm (2)	Buckley Other Farm (3)
		(dwelling units)	
1906	1772	12.2	4.9
1907	1816	12.9	5.3
1908	1886	11.7	4.4
1909	3202	16.7	5.9
1910	3603	23.6	6.5
1911	3230	9.5	4.2
1912		5.0	2.8
1913		4.3	2.6
1914		4.4	2.2
1915		4.4	1.7
1916		7.2	1.6
1917	n.a.	9.9	1.9
1918		11.1	1.9
1919		7.3	1.8
1920		7.2	2.3
1921		5.1	1.2

Notes by Column

(1)   Estimated value of mortgage loans by building societies and loan companies on dwellings started in Canada in 1913 dollars. The estimator is

$$((0.8\ \Delta MAB(t) + 0.2\ \Delta MAB(t+1)) + 0.055\ MAB(t-1))/CNPI(t)$$

where $MAB(t)$ = mortgage loans outstanding at the end of the year t on Canadian real estate, of loan companies and building societies

and $CNPI(t)$ = construction price index (Table A6, column (3) times 0.01).

The ratios 0.8 and 0.2 in the first part of the estimator are to adjust MAB to a starts basis.

Source of mortgage asset data: *Canada Year Book*, various years. This series is adjusted in 1880 because MAB for 1880 is so great it likely reflects takeovers or the purchase of outstanding mortgages; the calculated value for 1880 was replaced by a value assuming that 1880 percentage increase was equal to the percentage increase (30.9) in the real value of the wheat crop (using the wholesale price index as deflator).

(2), (3)   Except for 1891-1895 prairie farm, sources are "Buckley Revised Series Prairie Farm" (with note "used in July 54") plus Buckley other farm (labelled just "Farm") both in File 69, Saskatchewan Archives, Saskatoon. For 1891-95 prairie farm, Buckley's 1896 estimate is carried back, roughly on the basis of the real value of the wheat crop.

Table A6
Components of Residential Construction Input Price Index, 1967 to 1921

Year	Wage Index (1) (1913=99.0)	Residential Construction Materials Index (2) (1913=100)	Residential Construction Input Price Index (CNPI) (3) (1913=99.6)
1867		68.0	59.3
1868	n.a.	68.6	59.8
1869		70.3	61.3
1870		70.7	61.7
1871	48.8	74.6	65.1
1872	53.1	80.7	70.5
1873	53.1	84.3	72.7
1874	53.8	82.8	72.0
1875	51.7	80.0	69.5
1876	51.7	74.3	65.9
1877	51.7	70.9	63.8
1878	51.7	66.7	61.1
1879	51.7	63.1	58.9
1880	51.7	65.2	60.2
1881	51.7	70.5	63.5
1882	55.4	73.7	66.9
1883	52.1	73.9	65.8
1884	52.9	70.6	64.0
1885	51.4	67.8	61.7
1886	53.4	66.6	61.7
1887	57.3	69.0	64.7
1888	57.9	71.2	66.3
1889	57.7	72.0	66.7
1890	57.4	73.3	67.4
1891	58.1	70.0	65.6
1892	58.8	70.9	66.4
1893	56.4	70.0	65.0
1894	55.3	69.9	64.5
1895	55.4	66.9	62.6
1896	56.3	66.6	62.8
1897	55.7	62.0	59.6
1898	56.4	63.2	60.7
1899	55.4	66.9	62.6
1900	55.8	74.9	67.9
1901	59.8	72.6	67.8
1902	63.8	74.9	70.8
1903	66.6	80.8	75.5
1904	69.1	83.2	78.0
1905	72.2	82.4	78.6

Table A6 (continued)

Year	Wage Index (1) (1913=99.0)	Residential Construction Materials Index (2) (1913=100)	Residential Construction Input Price Index (CNPI) (3) (1913=99.6)
1906	76.0	86.6	82.7
1907	79.4	89.7	85.9
1908	80.6	97.0	91.0
1909	82.2	94.8	90.1
1910	85.9	92.6	90.1
1911	89.3	97.2	94.3
1912	94.9	96.9	96.2
1913	99.0	100.0	99.6
1914	99.9	93.8	96.0
1915	100.2	90.3	94.0
1916	101.5	103.8	102.9
1917	109.0	130.5	122.5
1918	124.8	150.3	140.9
1919	146.6	175.9	165.0
1920	179.0	215.0	201.7
1921	168.7	183.2	177.8

Notes by Column

(1)   1901-1921: construction wage index (HSC, Series D8) converted to base 1913 = 99.0

1871-1900: construction wage index constructed using a weighted average of backward percentage changes. (i.e. ((t-1) − t)/t)100) of various series yielding an index reflecting these series as follows:

1900 back to 1894:	0.25(a) + 0.75(b)
1893 back to 1891:	0.5(a) + 0.5(b)
1890 back to 1889:	0.75(a) + 0.25(b)
1887 back to 1884:	0.5(a) + 0.5(c)
1883 back to 1871:	(a)

Series (a) was constructed back to 1881 using wages reported by immigration agents for carpenters and labourers (HSC, Series D198, D199, D204, D205). Within occupation, percentage changes by cities were averaged, and then the simple average of the percentage changes in the two occupations was obtained. The percentage change for Winnipeg between 1882 and 1883 was omitted because of its enormous size. The series before 1881 is a rougher and more arbitrary one, constructed also from immigration agents' data (HSC, Series D189 and D192).

Series (b) was constructed using the unweighted average of percentage changes in construction wage rates in the Ottawa area and in the Toronto area (HSC, Series D487 and D488).

Series (c) was constructed using the unweighted average of percentage changes of wage per hour of Ontario carpenters and Ontario labourers. (HSC, Series D168, D176, D177).

(2)   1890-1921: price index of building and construction materials (HSC, Series J68) converted to base 1913=100.

1867-1889: unweighted average of price index of wood, wood products and paper (HSC, Series J39 put in base 1913=100) and wholesale price index excluding gold (HSC, Series J34 put in base 1913=100). This was linked to the earlier series at 1890.

Table A6 (continued)

(3)   1871-1921: 0.37 (wage index) + 0.63 (materials index). (This is about the same as assuming weights of 0.42 and 0.58 respectively, if the index were on the basis 1935-39=100.)

1867-1870: materials index linked at 1871 to the above construction index.

Table A3.1

Value of New Residential Construction Put in Place, 1922-1940
(millions of current dollars)

Year	Dwellings in New Buildings	Alterations and Additions	Total
	(1)	(2)	(3)
1922	158.1	22.8	180.9
1923	153.4	22.5	176.0
1924	142.4	21.6	164.0
1925	146.4	21.7	168.2
1926	161.9	22.3	184.2
1927	182.2	22.8	205.0
1928	198.7	23.4	222.1
1929	193.5	24.4	217.9
1930	146.2	21.5	167.7
1931	122.6	19.4	142.0
1932	55.9	9.2	65.1
1933	37.3	7.6	44.9
1934	45.8	12.7	58.5
1935	54.0	11.9	66.0
1936	62.5	11.7	74.2
1937	81.1	16.5	97.7
1938	82.8	15.8	98.6
1939	95.6	16.0	111.5
1940	98.7	14.6	113.4

Note: The percentage error in column 2 is probably very substantial.

Source: Marion Steele (1972)

Table A3.2
Number of Dwelling Units Started in New Buildings,
by Type, 1921-1940
(thousands of dwelling units)

	One-to-Three Unit Buildings			Four-or-More Unit Buildings	In Commercial Buildings	Grand Total
	Urban	Rural	Sub-Total			
	(1)	(2)	(3)	(4)	(5)	(6)
1921	17.4	12.7	30.1	1.0	2.8	33.9
1922	22.6	16.5	39.1	1.4	2.9	43.5
1923	20.5	14.9	35.4	2.8	2.6	40.8
1924	21.2	15.4	36.0	3.2	2.4	42.3
1925	21.2	15.4	36.7	4.3	2.5	43.4
1926	22.1	16.1	38.2	8.0	3.1	49.4
1927	23.5	17.1	40.6	11.4	3.6	55.6
1928	22.8	16.6	39.3	12.5	2.4	54.2
1929	24.9	18.1	43.1	6.3	2.1	51.4
1930	20.1	14.6	34.7	5.2	1.4	41.3
1931	17.2	12.5	29.7	6.7	1.6	38.0
1932	8.8	6.4	15.1	0.8	0.9	16.8
1933	8.4	6.1	14.6	1.0	0.5	16.1
1934	10.0	7.3	17.2	0.9	1.2	19.4
1935	11.4	8.3	19.7	1.6	0.9	22.2
1936	13.4	9.8	23.2	2.0	0.5	25.7
1937	18.0	13.1	31.0	2.6	0.9	34.6
1938	18.3	13.3	31.7	3.6	1.4	36.6
1939	21.6	15.7	37.3	4.4	0.6	42.2
1940	20.5	15.0	35.5	4.0	0.4	39.9

Note: The percentage error in Column 5 is probably very substantial

Sources: Marion Steele (1972)

Table A3.4
Average Construction Cost, Apartments and Urban
Dwellings in One-to-Three Unit Buildings Started,
1921-1940, in Current and Constant Dollars

	Apartments		Urban Dwellings in One-to-Three Unit Buildings	
	(current dollars)	(constant (1949) dollars)	(current dollars)	(constant (1949) dollars)
	(1)	(2)	(3)	(4)
1921	3497	6107	4407	7697
1922	3181	6109	4635	8900
1923	3269	6115	4549	8509
1924	3194	6105	4031	7706
1925	3131	6108	4146	8089
1926	2742	5418	4205	8308
1927	2383	4690	4421	8701
1928	3087	5936	4724	9085
1929	3783	6960	4482	8244
1930	3101	5854	4074	7690
1931	2540	5140	3994	8081
1932	2112	4665	3281	7248
1933	928	2142	2868	6623
1934	1841	4124	3051	6835
1935	2146	4834	3054	6878
1936	2093	4579	3046	6666
1937	2355	4806	2946	6013
1938	2290	4770	2705	5636
1939	2231	4609	2806	5798
1940	2232	4333	3023	5869

Source: Steele, 1972

Table A3.5
Estimates of Residential Capital Stocks and Flows

	Stock End-Year (1) (millions of 1961 dollars)	Stock End-Year (2)	Depreciation (3)	Demolitions and Abandonments (4)	Fire Damage (5)	Subtotal (3)+(4) +(5) (6)	Gross Capital Formation (7)	Net Capital Formation (8)
					(millions of current dollars)			
1921	9637	3966	n.a.	n.a.	16	n.a.	n.a.	n.a.
1922	9896	3929	58	5	16	79	181	102
1923	10150	4040	61	5	8	74	176	102
1924	10380	4048	61	5	7	73	164	91
1925	10623	4074	61	5	8	74	168	94
1926	10907	4161	62	5	8	76	184	108
1927	11242	4345	64	5	8	77	205	128
1928	11600	4646	68	6	9	82	222	140
1929	11910	4824	73	6	11	91	218	127
1930	12104	4666	73	6	12	91	168	77
1931	12255	4363	68	4	14	86	142	56
1932	12209	4066	63	4	14	81	65	-16
1933	12120	4000	60	4	10	74	45	-29
1934	12073	4050	61	4	10	75	59	-16
1935	12051	4091	61	4	8	73	66	-7
1936	12050	4290	63	4	8	74	74	0
1937	12101	4423	67	4	8	79	98	19
1938	12163	4415	66	4	6	76	99	23
1939	12259	4603	67	4	6	77	112	35
1940	12340	5022	72	4	6	82	113	31

Steele, 1972. Gross capital formation excludes government and defence expenditures on housing, real estate commissions on existing real estate and land. Depreciation rate (applied to constant dollar values) assumed to be 1.5 percent. All estimates except those in column 5 were computed in constant dollars and then converted to current dollars.

Chapter 9. Gross Domestic Product and Gross Domestic Expenditure on Goods and Services, Government and Education

M.C. URQUHART with participation

of DUNCAN MCDOUGALL

Duncan McDougall prepared the estimates of wages and salaries and of outlay on goods and services for the federal and provincial governments for 1910, 1900, 1890, 1880 and 1870.

The material of this chapter is presented separately for 5 individual components as follows: government of Canada; provincial government; municipal government; public education; universities. They are dealt with in order.

GOVERNMENT OF CANADA

The estimates for federal government wages and salaries, gross domestic product and expenditures on goods and services cover all ordinary activities of government but do not include operations of the public utility kind: they do not include operations of government-owned railway or telecommunication systems; they do include the full activities of the post office and of canals.

1. Wages and Salaries

(a) Base Years

Six years of the period were, in effect, base years, namely, 1870, 1880, 1890, 1900, 1910 and 1926: the five base years from 1870 to 1910 inclusive were chosen because they corresponded with years covered by the census; the year 1926 was chosen because it was the first year covered by the official national accounts.

The basic sources of data were for 1870 the Public Accounts report, for 1880, 1890, 1900 and 1910, the reports of the auditor general of Canada and for 1926 Statcan, *National Income and Expenditure Accounts 1926-1974*, Volume I (Catalogue 13-531). The public accounts and auditor general reports for the fiscal year ending in the year following the year of record were used for the year of record. For example, the data recorded for 1870 are those of the fiscal year 1870-71.

The auditor general's Reports and the Public Accounts give expenditure in great detail and record virtually all wage and salary payments as distinct items of payment — a negligible amount of estimation of wages and salaries from more comprehensive aggregates was involved. Wages and salaries for 1910 (fiscal 1910-11) were obtained in great detail from the auditor general's report for the fiscal year ending March 31, 1911. It was possible to obtain wages and salaries with the same degree of comprehensiveness with a lesser though still substantial amount of detail from the auditor general's reports for 1880 (1880-81), 1890 (1890-91) and 1900 (1900-01) and from the public accounts for 1870 (1870-71). The recorded wages and salaries paid by the Government of Canada for the operation of railways were removed from the government accounts since they were also included in the section on transportation. We have then for the decadal years from 1870 to 1910 the following Canadian government wage and salary payments.

Government of Canada Wage and Salary Payments
(thousands of dollars)

	1870	1880	1890	1900	1910
Total Government of Canada wage and salary payments	3,877.6	6,803.8	11,165.9	15,887.4	32,574.4
Less: railway operating wages and salaries	157.3	555.1	2,227.0	3,616.5	7,083.2
Less: census	122.7				
Government of Canada wage and salary bill for project	3,597.6	6,284.7	8,938.9	12,270.9	25,491.2

The wage and salary bill for 1926 was obtained from the *National Income and Expenditure Accounts 1926-1974*, Table 49, p.68. Wages and salaries of $64 million on ordinary account, $7 million for military services and $1 million on capital account gave a total of $72 million dollars.

(b) Interbase Years

Wages and salaries between pairs of the base years noted above were obtained by use of an interpolator that was basically related to government expenditure on goods and services. The interpolation was done as follows.

The starting point was total expenditure chargeable to the consolidated fund which included what might be called federal government current account expenditure (*Canada Year Book 1932* (CYB), p.711). It did not include items charged to capital account, railway subsidies, war and demobilization expenditure, nor small miscellaneous charges. From the foregoing expenditure were subtracted the payment of interest on the public debt and subsidies to the provinces; canal capital expenditures were then added to yield the interpolating series based on adjusted government current account expenditures. Canal capital expenditures were included since the federal government carried out much canal capital formation by its own labour force. The source for all of these series was CYB, p.711 ff.

The ratio of federal government payment of wages and salaries to this interpolating series was then calculated for the base years. The ratios were as follows. (In 1870 military wages paid in connection with the Red River Rebellion were excluded in the calculations of the ratio, since they were a non-recurrent special expenditure.)

Ratio of Government of Canada
Wages and Salaries to
Adjusted Government Expenditure

Year	Ratio	Year	Ratio
1870	0.4326	1900	0.3581
1880	0.3780	1910	0.3722
1890	0.3703	1926	0.3758

These ratios were then interpolated linearly between each succeeding pair of base years and the resultant ratios were multiplied by the interpolating expenditure series to yield government wage and salaries for ongoing government operations. Wartime and demobilization expenditure for World War I were not included in the foregoing government expenditure. Therefore, for the years 1914 to 1919 inclusive, military pay and allowances, civilian wages in the militia department, and pay of censors by the militia department were added to foregoing estimates of wages paid by civilian departments. (The military pay and allowances etc. were obtained year by year from the public accounts of Canada for each of the fiscal years ending March 31, 1915 through March 31, 1921; these accounts can be found as sessional paper number 2 in each of the sessional papers for 1916 to 1921.) The amounts of these wartime wages and salaries paid through the militia department were:

Fiscal Year	Amount (thousands of dollars)	Fiscal Year	Amount (thousands of dollars)
1914-15	25,563	1918-19	254,496
1915-16	101,916	1919-20	82,136
1916-17	188,795	1920-21	10,129
1917-18	211,009		

2. Gross Domestic Product

In the official accounts for Canada for the years 1926 to 1939, wages and salaries in the public administration and defence sector averaged 0.783 of gross domestic product in this sector with little variation from year to year (Statcan, *National Income and Expenditure Accounts 1926-1974*, Volume I, Tables 28 and 29, Page 38). It was assumed that this ratio prevailed steadily throughout the period 1870 to 1926 with the exception of the wartime years. (The simple calculation was just to divide the wage and salary bill by the ratio 0.783 to obtain gross domestic product.) In the wartime years, it was the civilian departments' wages and salaries that were taken as the fixed ratio 0.783 of gross domestic product; wages and salaries of the militia department were then added, without any mark-up for non-wage product, to obtain overall gross domestic product in the wartime years.

3. Government of Canada Purchases of Goods and Services

Government of Canada purchases of goods and services include all purchases of newly produced goods and services, both current and capital account. They were calculated as follows.

(i)   The beginning step was to obtain total budgetary expenditure (from *Historical Statistics of Canada* (HSC), Series G42). This expenditure includes all items, both current and capital account, that involve the purchase of newly produced goods and services and more besides. From this total the following non-commodity expenditures are subtracted.

(ii)   Interest on the public debt (from *Public Accounts 1918-19*, p.72 for 1870 to 1918; Public Accounts for subsequent years).

(iii)   Subsidies to provinces (*Public Accounts 1918-19*, p.76 for 1870 to 1918; *Public Accounts*, annual for subsequent years).

(iv)   Railway operating expenditure (*Public Accounts*, annual, expenditures of Canadian government under the heading "Collection of Revenue").

(v)   Pensions (*Public Accounts, 1918-19*, p.76 for 1870 to 1918; *Public Accounts* annual, for subsequent years).

(vi)   Railway subsidies (*Public Accounts, 1926-27*, p.44 for all years).

(vii)   Mail subsidies and steamship subventions (*Public Accounts 1918-19*, p.75 for 1870 to 1918; *Public Accounts* annual, for subsequent years).

(viii)   Indian annuities. These were calculated at 13 percent of the expenditures for Indian affairs. This proportion was obtained from the 1910-11 distribution of expenditure on Indian affairs. (Source of expenditures on Indian affairs, *Public Accounts, 1917-18*, p.74 for 1870 to 1918; *Public Accounts* annual, for subsequent years).

(ix)   Railway capital expenditure (*Public Accounts 1918-19*, pp. 90-91 for 1870 to 1918; *Public Accounts*, annual, for subsequent years).

(x)   Provincial debt — very small and in only six years, all before 1900 (*Public Accounts 1918-19* p.90 for all relevant years).

(xi)   Overseas war expenditures, applicable only to years 1916 to 1919 (individual *Public Accounts* for 1916-17, 1917-18, 1918-19, 1919-20).

The subtraction of these entries in items (ii) to (xi) from item (i) gave us:

(xii)   Federal government expenditure on goods and services as a remainder.

An Evaluation of the Data

(i) Wage and Salary Payments

Potentially, the public sector estimates, especially for the government of Canada and for the provincial governments, can be the most accurate of all estimates. Such is the case since there has been an annual publication of public accounts for all of these governments and also auditors reports. Especially in the case of the Government of Canada for all but the early years there are the annual public accounts and an annual, very detailed auditor general's report. In these documents, especially the latter, wage and salary payments are presented in great detail as separate items of expenditure. Similarly, expenditure on goods and services can be obtained with a high degree of precision from these two reports. However, the amount of time involved in going through the accounts of a single year to obtain the necessary information is quite large. And the cost of going through the accounts for each of 57 years would have been very large indeed. In the circumstances, we followed the strategy of trying to get good wage and salary estimates for base years and then devising interpolators. Having done this it behoves us to try to see how well the interpolators work. That is why we need an evaluation — on this occasion an evaluation of the Federal Government estimates.

Federal Government Wages and Salaries
($000,000)

	Project	Dominion Bureau of Statistics	Ratio of Project to DBS
1919	153	326	0.47
1919 adjusted	(153)	(180)	(0.85)
1920	91	118	0.69
1920 adjusted	(91)	(113)	(0.81)
1921	77	93	0.83
1922	70	86	0.81
1923	68	86	0.79
1924	69	88	0.78
1925	71	94	0.76
1926	72	96	0.75

The feature of the estimation that is the most encouraging is the relative constancy of the ratio of federal government wages and salaries to the interpolator. They are almost identical in 1880, 1890, 1910 and 1926; the ratio is only slightly different from these years in 1900; even in 1870 it is not so far different from that of 1880 to seem unlikely in a new country.

There is another set of data against which we can check. During the 1920s and the 1930s the Dominion Bureau of Statistics (DBS) did work on national income estimates, much of it never published. These estimates covered years from 1919 to the late thirties. Among them was a series on Government of Canada wages and salaries. The methods of estimation were not described in any detail but there is a likelihood that some use was made of the public accounts in their preparation. (I knew the person who had prepared the estimates and I believe he would have made use of the public accounts.) A comparison of the two series appear in the preceding table.

The DBS salaries are higher than the project salaries (and in 1926 higher than the current official figure). The difference in level may be accounted for by DBS including utilities such as the railways, which we have excluded since they are covered in the transportation sector. Whatever the cause of the difference in level the trend of the two series is clearly much the same for 1926 to 1921 and the apparent divergences of trend for 1920 and 1919 are readily explained by use of the demobilization data. The relevant demobilization expenses are as follows.

Demobilization of Veterans, Personal Income Payments
(thousands of dollars)

	1919	1920	1921
Pay and allowances	67,733	8,010	327
Separation allowance	9,716	450	83
War service gratuity	136,033	4,608	295
Civilian employees	4,652	1,669	772
Censors	34	–	–

Source: the *Public Accounts* for 1919-20, 1920-21, 1921-22.

DBS has obviously included war service gratuities as a part of wage and salary income. We deemed it inappropriate to include these gratuities, which for many veterans covered service for several years, in any one year. We have in effect left them out of wages and salaries (although they are implicitly included in government expenditures on goods and services) and so in the bracketed figures for 1919 and 1920 we have omitted them from the DBS wage and salary payments. At the same time, we put in special figures for wage and salary payments for 1914 to 1920. The properly adjusted figures for 1919 and 1920 are shown in the bracketed figures for each of these years. Once this adjustment is made the two series for these years follow the same trend just as they did for 1921 to 1926. I find these results most encouraging in supporting the validity of our interpolation process in general.

(ii) Gross Domestic Product

Some question must arise about the correctness of our assumption that labour income comprised 78.3 percent of gross domestic product throughout the period 1870 to 1926. There is not much to be said about this matter. In the official accounts the non-wage component of gross domestic product is simply depreciation of government held depreciable assets. We just did not have the resources to try to estimate the size of real capital assets historically, and so there would be two matters affecting how the course of depreciation would move from year to year relative to the movements in wages and salaries. On one hand, it seems likely that the amount of depreciable assets held by the federal government relative to the number of workers employed (excluding railway property) would increase with the passing of time: this influence, taken by itself, would tend to increase the amount of depreciation relative to the wage bill. On the other hand, wage ratios have tended to rise relative to the price of commodities, including depreciable assets: that influence would tend to make depreciation costs fall relative to the wage bill. Whether or not these two influences were offsetting is open to question. It does seem that in the economy at large they have been over quite long periods of time. In the absence of information to the contrary, we have assumed that the same was true of all of the public sector.

(iii) Government Expenditure on Goods and Services

These expenditures based as they are on calculations derived directly from the national accounts should be quite good for each year. Our figure for 1926 is $40 million higher than that in the national accounts. This is mainly because we did not remove canal expenditure to transportation as the official statistics have probably done: this item accounted for $20 million. Our figure for 1910 at 61.6 million dollars is very close to McDougall's estimates for 1910 for labour income plus professional services and contingencies at 59.0 million dollars, if we take out the railways which is in conformity with our practice. This series is quite consistent, I believe, throughout the time span.

THE PROVINCIAL GOVERNMENTS

The techniques of estimation of similar sets of data for provincial governments were much like those used for the Government of Canada and will not be elaborated again here. Basically, they involved obtaining data in detail for certain base years and interpolating by use of clearly related series for intervening years. The following descriptions of the acquisition of provincial data, province by province, is therefore terse.

1. Ontario

The base years for which detailed reckonings from the public accounts of wages and salaries and expenditures on goods and services were made were 1871, 1880, 1890, 1900, 1910 and 1920. The data were obtained from Ontario public accounts for the most closely corresponding fiscal years: fiscal years ended December 31 for 1870, 1880, 1890 and 1900 and October 31 for 1910 and 1920. The years 1918 and 1924 also had special treatment as noted below.

Wages and Salaries

The wage and salary data include all wages and salaries including colonization roads and capital expenditures. The interpolator for the period 1871 to 1910 is "ordinary expenditures" (current account expenditure) of Ontario from CYB 1932, p.735. The ratio for 1880 of wages and salaries to ordinary expenditure for interpolation purposes was the ratio of the 1880 wages and salaries figure to the average expenditure for the five years 1878-1882. This was done because railway grants were unusually low in 1880 and 1881 thus causing an anomaly. For 1881 we did use the actual ratio of 1880 by itself.

For 1918 and 1924 the individual department categories of wages and salaries were projected from 1920 on the basis of the total expenditure for each individual category, obtained from public accounts — it was assumed the proportion of wages and salaries to total expenditure for each category was the same in 1918 and 1924 as in 1920. (Election expenses in 1920 were omitted in calculating the ratios for projection. They should have been added back in in 1920 but unfortunately were not. The election wage and salary expenses were $447,308 and extra contingencies were $149,103. These election expenses were included in statutory expenditure.)

For the interpolations for 1910 to 1926, the total provincial wage and salary payments (and all expenditures) were divided into three categories: ordinary wages and salaries (by far the largest amount); statutory wages and salaries; special warrant wages and salaries. In the years between 1910 and 1918, 1918 and 1920, 1920 and 1924 in three categories: the ordinary wages and salaries were interpolated by the series on ordinary expenditure (CYB 1932, p.735); the statutory wages and salaries by total statutory expenditure; and the special warrants wages and salaries by special warrants expenditure. (These last two items are obtained from the public accounts — in our work we have some detail on expenditure for every province for every year.)

The resulting ratio of wages and salaries to total expenditure then became as follows.

Ratios of Wages and Salaries to
Total Expenditure by Category

	1910	1918	1920	1924
Ordinary account	0.3102	0.2464	0.2503	0.1955
Statutory	0.0345	0.0592	0.0592	0.0592
Special warrants	0.2313	0.0654	0.0654	0.0654

(The statutory and special warrants components were each given a constant value for 1918 and 1924 as for 1920.)

A different treatment was required for 1925 and 1926. In 1925 the Ontario accounts underwent such a major change that it as not possible to estimate them as had been done in previous years; a new method was devised. In 1924 (and also in 1921) the statutory had substantial capital items in highways and northern development. There was, in addition, also all the interest and debt charges in here so that the ratio of salaries and wages to the total was small. However, if we separate out the capital items among the statutory the ratio of wages and salaries to total expenditure on the capital goods component was 0.3068. Taking this state of affairs into account, we project the 1924 expenditures to 1925 and 1926 on the basis of the above ratio of wages and salaries to capital expenditure and the ratio of all remaining wage and salary payments to ordinary expenditure (CYB 1932, p.735).

Provincial Expenditures on Goods and Services (Contingencies)

The expenditures on goods and services other than wages and salaries were obtained in exactly the same manner as the expenditure on wages and salaries. We have called this expenditure on goods and services other than wages and salaries "contingencies".

The sum of the wage and salary expenditures and the non-wage and salary expenditure gives us the government expenditure on goods and services.

Gross Domestic Product

The GDP was obtained for all provinces together.

2. Prince Edward Island

The estimates for this province were not done in the same detail as for other provinces since the amounts involved were quite small. Sources of government expenditure were the public accounts.

Wages and Salaries

The base years for wages and salaries were 1880, 1890, 1902 and 1910. The fiscal year endings were December 31 for 1880, 1890 and 1900 and April 30 for 1910.

Wage and salary payments were obtained from the P.E.I. public accounts. The 1900 accounts were not available so I did the wages and salaries for 1902.

Schoolteachers salaries were paid by the province and they had to be removed since they belonged in public education. Some imputation of wages and salaries from larger totals of expenditure had to be done for some of the public works and mental institutions for the years before 1910 from the 1910 ratios.

Interpolation and extrapolation of all wages and salaries was done on the basis of the movements of ordinary expenditures (CYB 1932, p.734) which in P.E.I.'s case includes expenditures on capital account (CYB 1932, p.734, fn. 2).

The ratios of wages and salaries to expenditures were as follows.

Ratio of Wages and Salaries to Total Expenditure

Year	1870	1880	1890	1902	1910	1926
Ratio	(0.3881)	0.3881	0.3599	0.2736	0.3430	(0.3430)

The 1880 ratio was used for all years back to 1870; the 1910 ratio was used for all years from 1910 to 1926.

Contingencies (Expenditures on goods and services excluding wages, etc.)

These expenditures on goods and services other than wages and salaries have the following ratios to total expenditures. They were obtained from the public accounts.

Ratios of Expenditures on Contingencies

Year	1870	1880	1890	1902	1910	1926
Ratio	(0.1910)	0.1910	0.1751	(0.2019)	0.2019	(0.2019)

The basic ratios were obtained for the years 1880, 1890 and 1910. The 1910 ratios were used for all years from 1900 to 1926. The 1880 ratios were used for 1870 to 1880. The ratios were interpolated on a straight line basis between 1880 and 1890 and between 1890 and 1900.

Gross Domestic Product

GDP was obtained as a lump with all other provinces.

Evaluation of Data

A separate tabulation for 1926 from the public accounts for that year yielded a figure of $269,414 for wages and salaries versus our projection from 1910 of $259,347 and a figure of $178,323 for contingencies versus our figure of $152,659. These figures are remarkably close I think. The reason that the recalculated contingencies are a bit higher than the projected ones may be that I did not take some transfers (e.g. in cases of ferries) out of larger totals when they were present in small amount.

3. New Brunswick

The estimates for this province were not based on as many years as most other provinces. The main reason for this state of affairs were that the wage and salary bills for 1890 and 1900 had to be adjusted substantially and such adjustment took much time. Along with that was the fact that the ratios of corrected wages, and of contingencies, to the interpolators were very steady for the three years 1890, 1900 and 1910. The base years, then, for New Brunswick became 1890, 1900 and 1910. The fiscal year endings were December 31 for 1890 and October 31 for 1900 and 1910.

Wages and Salaries

1870 to 1910. Wages and salaries for 1890, 1900 and 1910 were obtained from N.B. public accounts supplemented by information from separate reports for various departments

(McDougall plus adjustments). Schoolteachers salaries were removed. The interpolator was total ordinary plus capital expenditure less interest payments on public debt. (Ordinary and capital were included together until 1908 and came from CYB 1932, p.734.) For 1909 and 1910 capital expenditures (from Public Accounts) had to be added to the CYB figures.

The ratios of wages and salaries to the interpolator used then were:

Year	1870	1880	1890	1900	1910
Ratio	0.2683	0.2683	0.2683	0.2796	0.2857

The 1890 ratios were used for 1870 to 1890. The ratios for 1891 to 1899 and 1901 to 1909 were linearly interpolated between 1890 and 1900 and between 1900 and 1910 respectively.

1910 to 1926. The 1910 figures were the sole base year for this period. The 1910 wages and salaries were divided into expenditure on ordinary account and expenditure on capital account. Each of these separate components was then extrapolated to 1926, the first on the basis of ordinary expenditures (CYB 1932, p.734) and the second on the basis of capital expenditure (Public Accounts). The extrapolation was done as usual by multiplying the proportion of wages in 1910 in each case by the extrapolator. The ratio of ordinary wages and salaries to ordinary expenditure was 0.3250. The ratio of wages and salaries in capital goods was 0.0836.

Contingencies (Expenditure on goods and services other than wages and salaries)

For 1870 to 1910. The procedure for contingencies was exactly similar to that for wages and salaries. The ratios of contingencies to aggregate expenditure in base years 1870 to 1910 were:

Year	1870	1880	1890	1900	1910
Ratio	0.3622	0.3622	0.3622	0.3442	0.3558

As usual the 1870 to 1890 figures all used the 1890 ratios and the ratios were interpolated linearly.

For 1910 to 1926 the 1910 ratios were used. The ratios were: Ordinary contingencies to ordinary expenditures 0.2991; Capital contingencies to capital expenditures 0.7024.

Gross Expenditure on Goods and Services

This item for every year was the sum of the expenditures on wages and salaries and the expenditures on contingencies (non-wage and salary goods and services).

Gross Domestic Product

Once wages and salaries were known the GDP was obtained for all provinces together.

4. Nova Scotia

We had both wages and salaries and contingencies for most base years right from 1870 onward. However, our method for 1870 to 1910 differed slightly from that for 1910 to 1926 so we deal with these two periods separately.

Wages and Salaries 1870 to 1910

Wages and Salaries, 1870 to 1910 were taken from tabulations from public accounts in base years. Teachers salaries were removed. Without question the coverage of wages and salaries increased over the years, first, because certain items (e.g. crown prosecutions) had wages and salaries but were entirely recorded as contingencies in earlier years; second, because certain services were added, e.g. hospitals, technical school.

The early worksheets, especially to 1890 were not good. However, time prevented us from redoing these. Even 1900 should have some added. The separation out of wages was fairly good in 1910. The ratios show something of what I say.

The base years, for which wages and salaries were taken from the public accounts were 1870, 1880, 1890, 1900, 1910. Interpolation was done between these years by use of total ordinary expenditures (CYB 1932 p.734). Interest was a sufficiently constant proportion that it did not need to be subtracted. The actual interpolation was done by obtaining wages and salaries as a proportion of total expenditures in these base years, doing a linear interpolation of these ratios between adjacent base years and then multiplying the corresponding ordinary expenditure by these ratios.

The ratios of wages and salaries to ordinary expenditures in the base years were:

Year	1870	1880	1890	1900	1910
Ratio	0.0941	0.1126	0.1198	0.1512	0.1709

(My guess is that much of the increase in these ratios as time passed is based on better estimation as well as government absorbing new expenditures.)

Wages and Salaries 1910 to 1926

The base years were 1910 and 1920 when data were taken directly from the public accounts. Estimates for 1926 were obtained by projecting from 1920 on a department by department basis using ordinary expenditure for the projections — there were no wages and salaries in the capital account expenditures.

The resulting ratios of total wages and salaries to total ordinary expenditure for the key years were:

Year	1910	1920	1926
Ratio	0.1709	0.1941	0.1548

A linear interpolation of these ratios was made and the resultant ratios were multiplied by the ordinary expenditures to obtain the estimates of wages and salaries.

A subsequent check of the wages and salaries directly from the public accounts for 1926 yielded a figure of $968,526 for total wages and salaries compared with the figure that we got by projection from 1920 of $979,599. The projection method in the large was good despite being not good for individual items. The divergences of the projections from the actuals were pretty well offsetting.

Contingencies 1870 to 1910

The contingencies were done at the same time and in almost the same way as the estimates of wages and salaries were done. The exception was 1880. The data from the tabulations were quite inadequate to make an estimate for that year: that being the case we made the 1880 ratio of contingencies to ordinary expenditure the same as the 1890 ratio.

The ratios of contingencies to ordinary expenditures then were:

Year	1870	1880	1890	1900	1910
Ratio	0.3828	0.3693	0.3693	0.4109	0.4072

The contingencies were better covered in the earlier years than the wages and salaries. They include capital as well as ordinary expenditures.

Contingencies 1910 to 1926

For 1910 to 1926 the contingencies were divided into ordinary and capital expenditure. The contingencies on ordinary expenditure were interpolated on the basis of ordinary expenditure of the government (CYB 1932, p.734). The contingencies on capital account were extrapolated on the basis of expenditure on capital account (Public Accounts).

The ratios were as follows:

	1910	1920	1926
Current account	0.3774	0.2803	0.2301
Capital account	0.9671	0.3419	0.3419

The current ratios were interpolated linearly. The capital ratios were different however: from 1910 to 1918 a ratio of 0.9671 was used for each year — the capital expenditure was small at this time; for 1920 to 1926 the ratio 0.3419 was used for each year based on the 1920 data when the capital expenditure was much larger; the year 1919 which was at the transition was arbitrarily put at 0.6545 (half way between 0.3419 and 0.9671).

The 1926 contingency figure checks out reasonably well with the figure we got from the later special tabulation.

5. Quebec

The Quebec figures were done with much care since they were a fairly large part of the total of provincial expenditure for all Canada. As with other provinces they were done separately for two periods, 1870 to 1910 and 1910 to 1926.

Period 1870 to 1909

Wages and Salaries

The method was roughly the same as for other provinces: the wages and salaries were obtained directly from the public accounts for base years. They were then interpolated between base years using a measure of government expenditure on goods and services as a interpolator.

The base fiscal years, which were determined partly by the availability of the books in our library, were 1870-71, 1880-81, 1888-89, 1900-01, 1909-10. The fiscal year ended June 30. We took these fiscal years as representing the calendar year in which the fiscal year began.

The main source of data, as usual, was the public accounts of the Province of Quebec. For a large part of the expenditure the wages and salaries were given separately in these accounts and could be obtained from there. However, there were several items for which wages and salaries were not available in the public accounts. These voids were of two kinds:

(i) Certain items, i.e. wages, were not available for any year. These included lunatic asylums, police reformatories and reformatory and industrial salaries, school inspectors' salaries and normal school salaries. The school inspector salaries and normal school salaries were obtained from Department of Education Reports. The asylum wages and salaries and reformatory and industrial wages were obtained by assuming that wage and salary outlay bore approximately the same relationship to total outlay on goods and services as was the case in each of these groups in Ontario in 1900; this meant that the ratio of salaries to total expenditures on goods and services that was used was 0.45 (0.4567 in Ontario) for reformatories and industrial schools and was 0.30 (0.3179 in Ontario) for asylums. The totals on goods and services in each case were obtainable from the public accounts, supplemented in some cases by the official gazette. In 1870-71 the total expenditure on normal schools was broken into salaries and contingencies in the same proportions as in 1880-81.

(ii) Items where wages and salaries were available in some base years but not in others and where some estimation might be necessary follow:

> 1870-71   Indemnities of members of legislative council and of Assembly.
>   Share of sheriffs contingencies — made same as 1909-10.
>   Payments to petty jurors.
>
> 1880-81   Indemnities, legislative council and assembly.
>   Share of prothonotaries salary in total prothonotary expenditure
>   — based on use of 1900-01 ratios.
>   Share of sheriffs contingencies — same as 1909-10.
>   A number of quite small items.
>
> 1888-89   Share of prothonotaries salaries — use 1901 ratio.
>   Share of sheriffs contingencies — 1909-10 ratio.
>   A number of quite small items.

1900-01	Clerk of the legislative account — as in 1910. Share of Sheriffs' contingencies — as in 1909-10. Election expenses.
1909-10	no change.

Wages and salaries for other years were obtained by interpolation. Since there were practically no wage and salary payments in the capital account — nearly all done on contract — it was thought proper to use an adjusted measure of ordinary expenditure as an interpolator. This adjusted measure was obtained as follows.

Total expenditures were obtained from the public accounts of Quebec year by year including capital expenditures. From them were subtracted total debt charges and special expenditures, such as trust funds, expenditures on railways, repayment of temporary loans, and expenditures charged to capital (usually small). This gave a series to which wages and salaries were related. The relationship for the base years are given in the following table (note: the series obtained from public accounts yearly gives a series very close to CYB 1932, p.734 less public debt charges).

Base Year Ratios and Quantities

	1870-71	1880-81	1888-89	1900-01	1909-10
Wages and salaries ($)	582,495	766,536	1,001,574	1,217,214	1,785,663
Expenditure adjusted ($)	1,559,895	1,896,082	2,518,925	2,943,113	4,355,461
Ratio: wages to expenditure	0.3734	0.4043	0.3976	0.4136	0.4100
Ratio: contingencies to expenditure	0.2607	0.3288	0.3564	0.3474	0.3554

These ratios were interpolated linearly and then multiplied by the adjusted expenditure for the year to give wages and salaries for non-base years.

Contingencies

Ordinary contingencies were obtained in the same manner as ordinary wages and salaries. However, while wages and salaries in capital expenditure were so small as to be treated with ordinary wages and salaries, that was not true of capital expenditure on contingencies. The latter was irregular but could be quite substantial. Most capital expenditure was done on a contract basis and hence was all contingency. It was obtained on a year to year basis and added to ordinary contingencies.

Period 1909 to 1926

This period was done in four sections.

(i) Ordinary account — by far the major part was for both wages and salaries and contingences.

(ii) Capital account
      (a) major projects other than roads
      (b) roads (good roads)
      (c) trust funds

Wages and Salaries

The anchor years were 1909 (1909-10), 1920 (1920-21) and to some extent 1926. The basic data for these base years are:

	1909-10	1920-21	1926-27
Ordinary account wages and salaries ($)	1,772,161	4,317,641	7,694,834
Ordinary expenditure less public debt charges ($)	4,502,626	12,257,068	23,419,208
Ratio: W & S to expenditures	0.3936	0.3523	0.3286
Ratio: contingencies to ordinary expenditure	0.3425	0.3624	0.3525
Total expenditure major projects ex. roads ($)	724,439	465,609	1,161,808
Ratio: W & S to expenditures	0.0027	0.0205	0.0205
Ratio: contingencies to expenditure	0.9973	0.7079	0.7079
Total expenditures – good roads ($)	—	5,081,844	1,505,890
Ratio: W & S to expenditures	N.A.	0.0617	0.0617
Ratio: contingencies to expenditures	N.A.	0.1338	0.1338
Trust Funds			
Total expenditure ($)	17,000	643,135	1,052,036
Ratio: W & S to total expenditures	0.0	0.0317	0.0317
Ratio: contingencies to total expenditures	1.0	0.1115	0.1115

The actual wages and salaries in 1909-10 and 1920-21 were taken from the public accounts in a great deal of detail for all four sections. The 1920 figures were projected to 1926 by assuming that the ratio of wages and salaries and of contingencies to total expenditure for 19 separate categories were the same in 1926 as in 1920. (The 1926 total expenditures were, of course, from the public accounts). These 1920 ratios, especially for the big items, were not greatly different from those of 1910.

The interpolators were as follows:

(i) for ordinary account — total ordinary expenditure (CYB 1932, p.734) less public debt expenses (Quebec Statistical Yearbook). The CYB ordinary expenditures less the public debt costs exclude all those special items that we took out of our total expenditure 1870 to 1910.

(ii) For capital account (a) major products expenditure, (b) good roads expenditure, (c) trust funds expenditure, were all available, year by year, from the public accounts or from the

Statistical Year Book of the Province.

It will be noted that for capital account items for each of the three items taken separately we used the same ratios in 1926 as in 1920 — done just by assumption. Similarly for roads, where we did not have figures for 1909-10 we used the same ratios as in 1920 for all years back to 1912-13 at which time the roads item began. For all other categories between 1909 and 1920 the ratios were linearly interpolated before being multiplied by the relevant total.

Expenditures on goods and services are the sum of wages and salaries and contingencies.

GDP is obtained at the level of all provinces together as a multiple of wages and salaries.

6. Manitoba

As usual the estimates were prepared separately for the two time periods, 1873 to 1910 and 1910 to 1926.

Period 1873 to 1910

Wages and Salaries

The base years were 1878, 1890, 1900 and 1910. The year 1878 was dictated by the availability of the accounts (in French) for that year and not for 1880.

Ratios of Wages and Salaries to Interpolators
and the Interpolator Itself, Base Years

	1878	1890	1900	1910
Wages and salaries ($)	41,073	186,198	257,148	898,933
Ordinary expenditures ($)	107,926	708,302	1,085,405	3,234,941
Ratio: wages and salaries to ordinary expenditures	0.3806	0.2629	0.2369	0.2779
Ratio: contingencies to ordinary expenditures	0.2549	0.2549	0.3586	0.3565

Note: The actual wages in 1900 were $264,194 and in 1910 were $939,659; these differ from the amounts in the table used for calculating ratios by the amounts of the election expenses which were episodic.

The material came from the public accounts. McDougall's figures for 1890, 1900 and 1910 were used (some adjustments). I prepared 1878 from a French version. Telephones had to be removed from McDougall's figures for 1900 and 1910.

The interpolators for the years between the base years and the extrapolation to 1873 was ordinary expenditure of the province (CYB 1932, p.735). The ratios of wages and salaries to the interpolator were calculated for base years; for intervening years the ratios were obtained by straight line interpolation between adjacent base years; for 1873 to 1877 the 1878 ratio was used. The actual wages and salaries for non-base years were then obtained by multiplying the ratios of the wage and salary payments to the interpolator by the interpolator.

The values of the ratios, of both wages and salaries and contingencies, to the interpolators are given in the preceding table.

Contingencies

These were obtained in the same manner as the wages and salaries except that we did not have a contingency ratio for 1878; the contingency ratio for 1890 was used as the ratio for all years prior to 1890.

Total Expenditure on Goods and Services

These were the sum of the wages and salaries and the contingencies.

Period 1910 to 1926

From 1910 onward the expenditures on wages and salaries and on contingencies were calculated separately for ordinary account and capital account.

Wages and Salaries, Expenditures etc.
1910 to 1926

	1910	1920	1926
Ordinary account			
ordinary expenditure – adjusted	2,127,185	6,555,291	6,580,762
Elections	40,726	86,559	
Wages and salaries	864,294	2,292,077	2,271,998
Ratio: wages and salaries to total	0.4063	0.3497	0.3452
Ratio: contingencies to total	0.3423	0.3305	0.2112
Capital account			
Total relevant capital expend.	650,096	3,354,278	1,045,067
Capital account wages and salaries	30,002	388,197	147,349
Ratio: cap. acct. wages and salaries			
to total capital outlay	0.0461	0.11573	0.1410
Ratio: contingencies to cap. exp.	0.7862	0.5528	0.7407

Note: current account wage ratios were based on current account wages excluding election outlays.

Wages and Salaries

Base years were 1910, 1920 and 1926 (a full base year). Data were obtained from the public accounts. For years between base years, interpolations of ordinary wages were made on the base of ordinary expenditures (CYB 1932, p.735) less telephone expenditures and public debt charges. These latter expenditures were obtained from the public accounts of Manitoba year by year, found in Journals and Sessional papers of Manitoba. Interpolations of capital wages and salaries were made on the base of real capital expenditure (from public accounts year by year).

The relevant base year data are found in the preceding table.

Contingencies

Contingencies were done like 1910-26 wages and salaries.

Total Expenditure on Goods and Services

Total expenditure on goods and services equals expenditure on wages and salaries plus expenditures on contingencies current plus capital.

Note: we did not have public debt charges for 1922, 1923 and 1925. We estimated them by linear interpolation.

7. Saskatchewan

These estimates were done in the same way for the entire period. Base years were 1910 and 1920; 1926 was a semi base year (explained below).

Except for 1905 and 1906, the estimates were made in accordance with three sectors of expenditure: ordinary (current account), capital (public works, building) and capital (public improvements, roads).

Wages and Salaries

Wages and salaries for the two base years, 1910 and 1920, were obtained from the public accounts in a good deal of detail. The 1926 ordinary wages and salaries were projected from 1920 on the basis of 20 categories of expenditure — the 1920 ratio of wages and salaries to total expenditure for each category was multiplied by the total expenditure for that category in 1926 to give a wage for that category in 1926. The total ordinary wage bill was the simple sum of each category wage bill.

Interpolations (and extrapolations) were done on a different basis for each of the three large sectors of the economy.

The interpolator for ordinary wages and salaries was the total ordinary expenditures (all years available in the *Public Accounts 1920-21*, pp. 26-27 and *Public Accounts 1926-27* p.22) less all public debt charges and, where relevant, less railways and telephones, loans to supplementary revenue fund, King's Printer advances, public works warehouse, telephone stores and transactions under the farm loans act. Wages and salaries in 1910, 1920 and 1926 were taken as a proportion of adjusted ordinary expenditure in each year. These ratios were then linearly interpolated, the 1910 ratio being used for 1905 to 1909, and then multiplied by the adjusted ordinary expenditure to get the adjusted wages and salaries.

The interpolator (and extrapolator) for the public buildings capital expenditure was just this single item taken from the public accounts. The wage ratios were interpolated linearly from 1910 to 1920; the 1910 ratio was used for 1905 to 1909; the 1920 ratio was used for 1921 to 1926. The public improvements (roads) capital item was handled just like the capital account public buildings except that the interpolator (extrapolator) was the capital item "public improvements" in the capital accounts.

Contingencies

The contingencies were handled exactly like the wages and salaries.

Total Expenditure on Goods and Services

Total expenditures on goods and services is obtained as the sum of wages and salaries and contingencies.

The ratios and the quantities involved in the base years are shown in the following table.

Base Year Ratios and Quantities

	1910	1920	1926
Ordinary account:			
Wages and salaries, current account ($)	787,517	2,509,494	2,262,206
Adjusted ordinary expenditure ($)	2,201,406	8,970,561	9,498,650
Ratio: wages and salaries to ordinary expenditure	0.3555	0.2797	0.2382
Ratio: contingencies to ordinary expenditure	0.2772	0.3109	0.2844
Capital account: Public Works (Bldgs.)			
Wages and salaries ($)	26,461	40,389	
Total expenditure on goods and services ($)	1,355,128	2,724,521	377,097
Ratio: W & S to expenditure	0.0195	0.0148	(0.0148)
Ratio: contingencies to expenditures	0.9012	0.8569	(0.8569)
Capital account: Improvements (Roads)			
Wages and salaries ($)	15,175	43,090	
Total real expenditure ($)	*146,868	**595,992	1,431,499
Ratio: W & S to total real expenditure	0.1033	0.0723	(0.0723)
Ratio: contingencies to total expenditures	0.8967	0.0789	(0.0789)

* steel bridges   ** in this year large transfers to municipalities

8. Alberta

The preparation of the Alberta estimates was (descriptively) quite straight forward. The base years were 1910 and 1920 and full information from the public accounts was obtained for these years. There was both an income account and a capital account.

Wages and Salaries 1905-26

Wages and salaries were obtained in detail from the public accounts for these years. Telephones, a provincial operation in Alberta, were excluded. The current account and capital accounts were clearly separated.

The interpolator and extrapolator for the wages and salaries on income (current) account was a series called "expenditure" on the Income Account of the Province of Alberta (obtained in its entirety from the Province of Alberta *Public Accounts, 1926*, p.16) less interest on the provincial debt, obtained year by year from the Alberta public accounts. Wages and salaries in each of 1910 and 1920 on income account were taken as a ratio to the interpolator for that year; the 1910 ratio was assumed to apply to all years before 1910 and was multiplied by the interpolator for each year 1905 to 1909 to obtain an estimate for each year; for years 1921 to 1926 it was assumed that the 1921 ratio applied; for years 1911 to 1919 the ratios were obtained by straight line interpolation between the 1910 and 1920 ratios.

The interpolator in the capital accounts was total capital account expenditure (excluding purely financial items). This expenditure was obtained year by year from the public accounts. The number of items varied from year to year but, at its most extensive grouping, it included capital accounts expenditures on public works, agriculture and statistics, miscellaneous, education, municipal affairs, general administrative functions, dairy and poultry industry, public health.

Base Year Ratios and Quantities

	1910	1920
Income (Current) Account.		
Wages and salaries, current account ($)	1,010,121	3,089,332
Current account expenditure ($)	3,403,587	6,975,945
Ratio: wages and salaries to expenditure	0.2968	0.4429
Ratio: contingencies to expenditure	0.3016	0.2736
Capital Account.		
Wages and salaries, capital account ($)	227,013	474,833
Capital account expenditure ($)	1,149,219	2,707,941
Ratio: wages and salaries to expenditure	0.1975	0.1753
Ratio: contingencies to expenditure	0.7193	0.4756

Note: In 1920, there was, in addition to the above items, a special expenditure of $2,083,134 for drought relief containing a wage and salary component of only $21,862 but a contingency component of $1,486,690 — purchase of seed grain, etc. There were much smaller but irregular amounts for drought relief in some later years, but they were treated on an *ad hoc* basis on their own.

The capital account ratios of wages and salaries to relevant capital account expenditure (interpolator) were calculated from the data for both in each of 1910 and 1920. The procedure for obtaining other years for capital account expenditure on wages and salaries were exactly like the income account procedures.

Contingencies

Contingencies were obtained in an exactly parallel manner to wages and salaries.

Government Expenditures on Goods and Services

These were the sum of wages and salaries and contingencies.
    The quantities and ratios of 1910 and 1920 are in the preceding table.

9. British Columbia

B.C. was done differently in each of three periods as follows: (i) 1871 to 1910, (ii) 1910 to 1917, (iii) 1918 to 1921. We deal with each of these in turn.

1871 to 1910 (actually to 1909 since 1910 belongs to the 1910 to 1917 period)

The base years were 1880 (1880-81), 1890 (1890-91), 1900 (1900-01) and 1910 (1910-11). The economy was divided into three parts: (a) ordinary expenditure excluding public works; (b) public works, works and buildings; (c) roads, streets, bridges including surveys. They were not called current and capital accounts but I have treated them in that way.

Wages and Salaries and Contingencies

Wages and salaries and contingencies, separately, were obtained for each of the above three divisions from the public accounts for the base years but needed quite a bit of work to get teams and men in the right place in every year.
    The interpolators were: (a) British Columbia total expenditures *excluding* all public works expenditure; (b) public works expenditure on buildings, and (c) public works expenditure on roads and streets and surveys obtained as follows: for 1871 to 1885-86, Sessional Papers of B.C. 1903, p.D21, Table 1; for 1886-87 to 1901-02 from Sessional Papers 1912, p.C21, Table 2; for 1902-23 to 1910-11, *ibid* p.C23, Table C3 (railway payments were excluded).
    In this period there was not a separate capital account. The public works division included both capital and current account expenditure for public works.
    For all division the ratios of the wages and salaries and of contingency to the interpolator for 1880 were used back to 1871 and multiplied by the relevant interpolators.
    For years between the base years the interpolators ratios were interpolated on a straight line basis and then multiplied by the interpolators.
    The ratios of wages and salaries and contingencies to the interpolator for each division were:

	1880	1890	1900	1910
Ordinary account ex. public works				
Wages and salaries ($)	101,812	246,427	511,094	1,290,236
Interpolator ($)	277,543	660,028	1,533,182	3,570,247
Ratio: W & S to interpolator	0.3668	0.3734	0.3334	0.361
Ratio: contingencies to interpolator	0.2409	0.2420	0.2033	0.2216
Public Works — Buildings, etc.				
Wages and salaries ($)	0	5,331	24,483	91,239
Interpolator ($)	12,009	123,262	203,162	1,078,595
Ratio: W & S to interpolator	0	0.0432	0.1205	0.0846
Ratio: contingencies to interpolator	1.0	0.8890	0.8504	0.7041
Public Works — Roads and Surveys				
Wages and salaries ($)	49,568	123,048	331,294	2,048,829
Interpolator ($)	74,133	210,567	551,475	3,545,964
Ratio: W & S to interpolator	0.6686	0.5844	0.6007	0.5778
Ratio: contingencies to interpolator	0.3314	0.3748	0.3993	0.3962

1910 to 1917

The method for this period was much like that for 1870 to 1910. The public accounts were presented in the same way until 1917-18; the break in the format of the public accounts came with 1918 (1918-19).

Ordinary Wages and Salaries and Contingencies

In 1920-21, public works had been divided into an income (current) account and a capital account and the former part was included with the current account in that year, which was one of our base years. We removed the public works income account expenditure from current expenditure in 1920-21 and then got the expenditure on wages and salaries and on contingencies, current account, from the public accounts for 1920-21. This gave us an exact counterpart of what we had had in the non-public works sector of the economy before 1910.

We took ratios of wages and salaries and contingencies to current account expenditures less the public works current account expenditure for 1920 (1920-21) and then did a linear interpolation of these ratios between 1910 and 1920 to get the ratios for 1911 to 1917. These ratios were multiplied by the interpolator, total expenditure less all public works expenditure, to obtain estimates for 1911 to 1917. The interpolator series for 1910 to 1917 was from *B.C. Public Accounts* 1922-23, Appendix II, p.A399 (a long series).

Public Works — Buildings etc.

The ratios used for all years from 1910-17 were the 1910 ratios for both wages and salaries and contingencies.

The ratio contingencies in 1910 is higher for this 1910-17 series than for the 1870 to 1910 series. This is because I shifted expenditure on school buildings (McDougall) from "transfers" to "contingencies" thus raising the contingency ratio from 0.7041 to 0.8660 (N.B. to make it consistent with 1900-01). The 1901 to 1910 figures for contingencies in this division only should have been changed to reflect this change in 1910. (Incidentally, this change makes the 1910 contingency ratio almost the same as the 1900 contingency ratio which is 0.8504. This change should be made sometime for greater accuracy although not affecting interpolators in any way.)

These ratios are close to the 1921 ratios.

Public Works — Roads, Streets, etc.

The ratios used were the 1910 ratios. The interpolator was the same as for 1870 to 1910 (from 1922-23 *Public Accounts* — see above).

The ratios to interpolators for 1910 to 1917 were:

(i)   Ordinary account excluding public works

	1910	1920
Ratio wages and salaries to interpolator	0.3619	0.2707
Ratio contingencies to interpolator	0.2216	0.2356

(ii)   Public works building: ratios for all years 1910-1917

Wages and salaries	0.0846
Contingencies	0.8660

(iii) Public works: roads, streets, bridges, etc. ratios for all years 1910-17 were:

Wages and salaries	0.5778
Contingencies	0.3965

1918 to 1926

The public accounts become divided into current account, capital account chargeable to income and capital account statutory. We estimate in accordance with each of these divisions.

Current Account

Wages and salaries and contingencies — 1920-21 and 1926, to a lesser extent, were base years — were obtained in detail from the public accounts for 1920-21. Estimates for 1926 were made in general by assuming that the ratios of wages and salaries and contingencies separately to total expenditures would be the same in 1926 as in 1920, department by department. The exception to this way of estimating 1926 items was for legislation, the Prime Minister's office and Department of Fisheries where wages and salaries and contingencies were estimated directly from the public accounts.

The total wages and salaries and contingencies (current account) for each of 1920 and 1926 were taken as ratios of total current account expenditure less public debt charges. The ratios were interpolated linearly between 1920 and 1926 and the 1920 ratios were used for 1918 and 1919. The source of this interpolator was *Public Accounts B.C. 1922-23*, p. A336 and *Public Accounts 1926-27*, p. L316.

Capital Account — Chargeable to Income

The 1920 ratios of wages and salaries and contingencies to the interpolator for that year were used for all years from 1918 to 1926. The interpolator was the total expenditure on buildings, roads and other properties chargeable to income (i.e. real expenditure only and excludes transfers).

Capital Account — Statutory

The ratios of wages and salaries and contingencies to *real* statutory capital account expenditures in 1920 were applied to the interpolator for all other years. The interpolator was total *real* statutory capital account expenditures; it excluded transfers such as settlements to railways, land settlement board funds.

The interpolator was extracted from the public accounts year by year.

Soldier settlement items which were in the capital account were done separately year by year from the public accounts for both wages and salaries and contingences.

The relevant ratios for this period are:

Ratios to Interpolators

Current account	1920	1926
Wages & Salaries	0.4035	0.4043
Contingencies	0.3023	0.3022

Capital Account — Chargeable to income	
Wages & Salaries	0.1303 for all years
Contingencies	0.7620 for all years

Capital Account — Statutory excluding soldiers settlement	
Wages & salaries	0.3999 for all years *
Contingencies	0.6480 for all years *

* Note: these add to more than unity — the federal government made payments not included in the interpolator.

Soldiers Settlement

Both wages and salaries and contingencies were obtained directly from the public accounts year by year.

Government Expenditure on Goods and Services

These items are the sum of wages and salaries and contingencies.

Gross Domestic Product: All Provinces

Gross domestic product was derived from wages and salaries for all provinces taken together as a group. The procedure followed was exactly the same as in the case of the Government of Canada and a description of it will not be repeated here. Wages and salaries were presumed to bear a ratio of 0.783 to gross domestic product throughout. It should be added that this ratio was obtained from official data for all governments in the period 1926 to 1939. It is therefore appropriate that the mark-up on wages for provincial governments matches that of the federal government.

MUNICIPAL GOVERNMENT

The municipal government data cover the ordinary operations of municipalities, excluding education (the public schools) and excluding municipal public utility services such as water, gas, electricity and public transportation. We have as usual to describe the basis of our estimates of wages and salaries, gross domestic product, and municipal expenditures on goods and services.

1. Wages and Salaries of Municipal Employees

Basic Years, 1910 and 1926

There are two basic years in which wage data are available.

(a) 1910. Wages and salaries were collected in the 1911 population census and tabulated by an industrial classification that gives us municipal employees by province. The data were obtained from the microfilm tape of these data, from Film Roll 11006. Data at the level of regions, e.g. Montreal City were also available.

These data give numbers employed who report time and wages and a smallish number of employees who did not report time or wages. We included only the reported wages and did not impute a wage to those not reporting wages which, of course, we could have done easily. Where checks were possible, as with the schoolteacher data, the reported wages for those actually giving time and wages matched quite well with the alternative source data. It seems possible, although there is no way of being sure, that those employees who did not give time and wages were casual employees or had been employed part of the year only.

These 1910 wages and salaries were obtained from the source for each province. The 1910 municipal wage bills, excluding education, were as follows (in thousands of dollars):

P.E.I.	40.8	P.Q.	5,638.7	Sask.	755.9
N.S.	593.2	Ontario	7,315.2	Alberta	1,644.1
N.B.	434.2	Manitoba	1,854.7	B.C.	4,033.5

(b) 1926. The official national accounts report wages and salaries for municipal employees, including teachers, in 1926 as a single figure for all Canada. We have our own estimate for teachers salaries in 1926 (see education tables) and if we subtract these from the national accounts figure for municipal including educational salaries we obtain a figure of $63 million dollars for wages and salaries of non-educational employees.

The Rowell-Sirois data

Another set of municipal data had been prepared for the years 1913, 1921 and 1926 for the Royal Commission on Dominion-Provincial Relations, the Rowell-Sirois Commission. These data included tax revenues under various headings that were not particularly useful for us since municipal property taxes included school taxes. There were also various categories of expenditure which were more useful since we could use the sum of two categories, expenditures on "Streets and Roads" and on "All Other Expenditures", both current account, as a measure of municipal non-educational expenditure on goods and services.

There were municipal data of various degrees of relevance from provincial government documents throughout the period. These data were such that it became most practical to estimate wages and salaries, gross domestic product and municipal expenditure on goods and services in different ways for each of three periods, 1870 to 1910, 1910 to 1913, and 1913 to 1926.

The reasons for having one period begin in 1913 were, first, that this was the earliest Rowell-Sirois year, second, that the form of reporting of Ontario municipal statistics underwent a change at about this time causing some discontinuity in the data, and third, that Quebec began to collect comprehensive municipal statistics with the establishment of the Quebec Bureau of Statistics in 1914. (Prior to 1914 there were substantial quantities of data for Quebec reported in *Municipal Statistics* in the Quebec Sessional Papers but there is a gap in the data at a critical time in 1912 and the expenditure figures include both current account and capital account jointly.) In turn, the reasons for having 1910 to 1913 as a separate period was to try to estimate municipal wages and salaries in 1913 by extrapolating the 1910 census measures to 1913, province by province; and the best available data for doing the extrapolation from 1910 to 1913 differed from those available from 1913 to 1926. The best data available for the 1870 to 1910 estimate differed again from those for the later periods.

We deal with the individual periods in the order 1910 to 1913, 1870 to 1910 and 1913 to 1926.

1910 to 1913

The rate of changes (increases) over the period 1910 to 1913 was higher than in any other period. City expenditures in Toronto and Montreal and municipal expenditures in the western provinces rose especially rapidly. In addition, there were the problems of data noted above. In these circumstances, it appeared best to extrapolate wages and salaries from 1910 to 1913, province by province, using schoolteachers salaries as the extrapolators and that is what was done. Municipal salaries were extrapolated strictly in proportion to schoolteachers salaries.

That there would be a considerable correspondence between movements in expenditures on schools and on municipal services is quite sure. However, in a period of such rapid municipal expansion as the 1910-13 period, it is quite possible that the growth in municipal employment exceeded that in the schools. Nevertheless, we can get some comfort from another check that can be made. The ratio of the total municipal wages and salaries in 1913, for all provinces together, to total municipal expenditure on goods and services as given in the Rowell-Sirois data is 0.6549. The corresponding ratio for 1926, our other anchor year for wages and salaries, is 0.6675. (We do not have data on municipal salaries by province in 1926 — hence we only made the comparison in the aggregate.)

The estimates for 1911 and 1912 were also made province by province, by extrapolating from 1910 on the basis of the schoolteachers salary bills.

Schoolteachers salaries are from our own section on education.

1870 to 1910

The salaries of municipal employees were carried back from 1910 to 1870 as follows:

(i) Municipal salaries bills for each of the provinces, P.E.I., N.S., N.B., Manitoba, Saskatchewan, Alberta and British Columbia were extrapolated backward from 1910 strictly in proportion to the movements in teachers salaries for each province separately. (The evidence for Ontario suggest a not unreasonable correspondence between teachers salaries and municipal non-educational expenditures on goods and services.).

The teachers salaries came from our section on education: they are available on an annual basis.

(ii) Ontario municipal salaries were projected backward to 1870 on the basis of Ontario non-educational municipal expenditure on goods and services. These expenditures included capital expenditures on streets and roads and on municipal buildings since capital and current expenditures were not separated for these items; they excluded expenditures on water and electricity works and also interest on loans and support for the poor. The sources of data were:

Period	Source
1901 – 1910	Report of Bureau of Industries, Ontario Sessional Papers (1912) Vol. XLIV, Part XI, Paper No. 44
1894 – 1900	Report of Bureau of Industries, Ontario Sessional Papers (1905) Vol. XXXVII, Part VII, Paper No. 28
1886 – 1893	Report of Bureau of Industries, Ontario Sessional Papers (1896) Vol. XXVIII, Part VII, Paper No. 36
1878	Ontario Sessional Papers (1880) Vol. XII, Part IV, Paper No. 58
1866 – 1868	Ontario Sessional Papers (1870-71) Vol. III, Part I, Paper No. 1.
1879 – 1885	Linear interpolation between 1878 and 1886
1870 – 1877	Linear interpolation between 1868 and 1878

The resulting series along with teachers salaries in Ontario are given in Table 9.1.

Table 9.1
Ontario: Municipal and Educational Wages and Salaries
(in thousands of dollars)

Year	Municipal Wages and Salaries	School Teachers Wages and Salaries
1870	1,416	1,370
1871	1,466	1,348
1872	1,517	1,559
1873	1,568	1,735
1874	1,618	1,879
1875	1,669	2,001
1876	1,720	2,097
1877	1,770	2,320
1878	1,821	2,305
1879	1,874	2,389
1880	1,928	2,438
1881	1,981	2,439
1882	2,034	2,482
1883	2,087	2,568
1884	2,140	2,674
1885	2,193	2,721
1886	2,247	2,796
1887	2,300	2,788
1888	2,777	2,875
1889	3,132	2,934
1890	3,096	3,077
1891	3,541	3,167
1892	2,933	3,228
1893	2,906	3,301
1894	2,791	3,400
1895	2,685	3,514
1896	2,705	3,550
1897	2,919	3,422
1898	2,918	3,450
1899	2,871	3,483
1900	3,019	3,517
1901	3,465	3,594
1902	3,651	3,748
1903	4,053	3,884
1904	4,518	4,097
1905	4,748	4,338
1906	5,292	4,600
1907	6,144	4,977
1908	6,374	5,508
1909	6,502	5,954
1910	7,315	6,358

As a check on what the estimate of wages would have been in earlier years had the expenditure on streets and roads and on public buildings been excluded additionally from municipal expenditures in the extrapolation from 1910, I present the following comparison.

Year	Municipal Wages, Project ($000)	Municipal Wages, Alternative Estimate ($000)
1886	2,247	2,188
1890	3,096	2,875
1896	2,705	3,181
1899	2,871	2,807
1900	3,019	2,932
1901	3,465	3,830
1902	3,651	3,857
1905	4,748	4,650
1906	5,292	5,059
1909	6,502	6,576
1910	7,315	7,315

The alternative estimate is based on extrapolation of the 1910 wage bill by non-educational municipal expenditures less expenditures on water and electricity, on streets, roads and bridges, on public buildings, on interest on loans and on welfare. It will be seen in comparing the alternative estimates that the levels over time of the two estimates are very much the same even though there are some variations in the short term movements.

(iii) Quebec municipal salaries were obtained in two parts. Municipal salaries for Montreal were extrapolated backward from 1910 on the basis of Montreal's municipal revenues. Municipal salaries for the rest of the province of Quebec were extrapolated backward from 1910 on the basis of schoolteachers salaries for the entire province. The method used was determined by the availability of data. There were reports with municipal data for the municipalities of Quebec before 1910 but they were not sufficiently complete in geographical coverage or in the kinds of financial data that were available to be useful for our purposes.

However, the city of Montreal published a very good statement of municipal financial affairs annually. Available for the project were the annual reports of the city for 1870, 1877, 1877-78, 1878-79, 1881, 1882, 1890, 1900, 1910, 1913, 1920, 1926. Total revenues (not including borrowed funds, of course) were available on an annual basis for every year in these reports. However, these revenues included school taxes, water rates and interest receipts among other things.

For Montreal we used, as an extrapolator of the 1910 municipal wage bill, obtained from the 1911 census microfilm data on wages earned in 1910, Montreal city revenues from real estate taxes (excluding school taxes) plus business and personal taxes, plus police licenses, plus market licenses but excluding water rates, interest receipts, percentage on street railway, etc. (The school taxes were shown as an expenditure and were deducted from the overall real estate taxes.)

We used then as extrapolators Montreal City revenues obtained from Montreal city reports as follows:

Montreal City
Selected Revenues *
(dollars)

Year	
1870	496,042
1877	1,005,869
1880	962,029
1887	1,148,618
1890	1,355,203
1891	1,420,382
1900	1,892,813
1910	3,912,137

* Revenues from real estate taxes, business and personal taxes, licenses, and markets less the amount of school taxes.

Revenues for intervening years were obtained by linear interpolation between the nearest adjacent years. This meant rather long interpolations between 1891 and 1900, and 1900 and 1910. However, the individual yearly reports given long runs of annual revenues from various sources, such as real estate taxes, business and personal taxes, licences and market revenues — for example, the 1913 report has annual data of this sort from 1885 to 1913. These data suggest that linear interpolation does not do any violence to the underlying data. (These runs of data themselves could have been used as the interpolators. The reason that we did not do this is that we did not have annual data on the size of the school taxes which were deducted from total real estate taxes to obtain that part of local taxes that was available for general municipal purposes.)

For the rest of Quebec, we used schoolteachers salaries in all Quebec for the extrapolator of the 1910 data on wages and salaries obtained in the census. A partial judgement of the appropriateness of this procedure may be made from the Ontario data. It is noticeable from it that schoolteachers and municipal wages and salaries moved pretty much in step from 1870 to 1900 but that the growth rate of municipal taxes was higher than that of teachers salaries from 1900 to 1910. The higher municipal growth rate from 1900 onward would be concentrated in the cities. The use of teachers salaries as an extrapolator for the Province of Quebec outside Montreal may then be not inappropriate.

The two components of municipal wages and salaries in Quebec then are as follows:

	1870	1880	1890	1900	1910
Montreal municipal wages and salaries ($000)	461	895	1,261	1,762	3,642
Rest of Quebec municipal wages and salaries ($000)	385	686	866	1,083	1,997
Total ($000)	846	1,581	2,127	2,845	5,639

1913 to 1926

The salaries for municipal employees were developed for this period as follows.

Municipal employee salaries were available, by means already described, for 1913 on a province by province basis; they were available in 1926 as an aggregate for Canada.

(i) Ontario: estimate was available for 1913 (*Supra*). An estimate for 1926 was made by assuming that wages and salaries were the same proportion of provincial current expenditure on goods and services as in 1913. (Proportion in 1913 was 0.6120.) Current expenditures on goods and services in 1913 and in 1926 were available from the Rowell-Sirois categories "Streets and Roads" and "All Other" current expenditure.

Ontario municipal wages and salaries were then interpolated between 1913 and 1926 by use of data for total real estate taxes levied for municipal purposes, that is exclusive of school taxes. These data were available on an annual basis from 1913 to 1926. The ratio of municipal wages and salaries to real estate taxes for municipal purposes was 0.3975 in 1913 and 0.3825 in 1926. This ratio was interpolated on a straight line basis between 1913 and 1926. The resultant ratios were then multiplied by the real estate taxes in each year to yield municipal wages and salaries. A check of the reasonableness of the 1921 figure was possible by comparing it to the Rowell-Sirois figure for expenditure on goods and services in 1921. The ratio of wages and salaries to expenditure on goods and services in 1921 at 0.6019 compares with the corresponding ratio in 1913 of 0.6120.

Municipal real estate taxes in Ontario for municipal (i.e. non-educational) purposes were obtained from Ontario Bureau of Municipal Affairs, *Municipal Statistics*, annual beginning in 1917 but covering data from 1916 onward and Ontario Department of Agriculture, Bureau of Industries, *Municipal Bulletins*, No. 9 and No. 10 for 1913 to 1915.

Year	Ontario Municipal Taxes ($000)
1913	23,133
1914	26,221
1915	32,478
1916	34,295
1917	38,134
1918	44,302
1919	43,608
1920	48,396
1921	55,765
1922	58,453
1923	59,984
1924	62,476
1925	64,859
1926	68,058

(ii) Province of Quebec: Municipal wages and salaries were already available for 1913 (*Supra*). For 1926, municipal wages and salaries were assumed to be the same proportion of Quebec's municipal expenditure on goods and services (Rowell-Sirois municipal expenditures on "Streets and Roads" and "All Other" current expenditures) as in 1913: this proportion was 0.7693. The interpolator between 1913 and 1926 was "ordinary" payments (excluding education) of Quebec municipalities. These data were available from the Quebec Statistical Year Book for 1915 to 1926. Since other available data did not give a reliable figure for 1913, the 1913 figure for ordinary expenditure was obtained by chaining the 1913 figure for such expenditure to the 1926 figure by the ratio of Rowell-Sirois "All Other" expenditure in 1913 to that in 1926. (It had been meant to use "All Other" plus "Streets and Roads" as the chaining measure but by error the "Streets and Roads" were omitted. Fortunately, since ratios are involved the chaining factor used was almost what it would have been if correctly measured.) The 1914 figure for Quebec municipal "ordinary" payments was interpolated half way between the 1913 and 1915 figures.

The ratio of municipal wages and salaries as calculated to "ordinary" municipal payments was 0.3043 in 1926 and 0.3003 in 1913. This ratio was interpolated linearly for intervening years and then multiplied by the corresponding figures for "ordinary" payments to obtain municipal wages and salaries year by year. It yielded a figure for wages and salaries in 1921 that was 0.9071 of the Rowell-Sirois figure for expenditure on "Streets and Roads" and "All Other" current compared with 0.7693 for the same ratio in 1913.

Sources of Data: "ordinary" payments from 1915 to 1926 came from *Municipal Statistics* which was prepared by the Statistical Year Book of Quebec and published annually as a separate report and in the Quebec Sessional Papers; the data were also given in abbreviated form in the Quebec Statistical Year Book. This Year Book was established in 1914 and given explicit government authority to collect municipal statistics and the means of compelling the annual submission of reports. Its data became comprehensive only with 1915. The sources of 1913 and 1914 have been described already.

Year	Quebec Ordinary Expenditures ($000)
1913	23,701
1914	26,340
1915	28,979
1916	29,501
1917	28,646
1918	31,750
1919	37,593
1920	43,016
1921	48,763
1922	45,888
1923	43,332
1924	47,261
1925	49,257
1926	50,820

(iii) British Columbia: municipal wages and salaries in 1913 were already available (*Supra*). Wages and salaries for 1921 and for 1926 were assumed to be the same proportion of Rowell-Sirois municipal expenditure on goods and services (expenditure on "Streets and

Roads" and "All Other" current) as in 1913. Wages and salaries of teachers were used as the interpolators between 1913 and 1921 and between 1921 and 1926.

It might be noted that the B.C. municipal wage bill was very high in 1913. This may have been a consequence of B.C. municipalities doing much of their own construction work but this point is not clear. What is clear is that B.C. current account expenditure on "Streets and Roads" and "All Other" only increased from $5,725 thousand in 1913 to $7,517 thousand in 1921 and then declined to $6,640 thousand in 1926.

(iv) All other provinces (P.E.I., N.S., N.B., Man., Sask., Alta.): 1913 municipal salaries and wages were already available (*Supra*). (By mistake the 1913 figure for Saskatchewan was put at $1,710.7 thousand in 1913 rather than $1,293.1 thousand — recalculation would have been costly for the small change in the total of the six provinces it would have involved — and in fact the Saskatchewan figure in 1910 seemed unreasonably low in light of the number of gainfully occupied: I suspect that the figure of $1,710.7 thousand in 1913 came from arbitrarily rounding up the Saskatchewan wages figure in 1910 to $1,000 thousand.)

The 1926 salaries and wages for this group were calculated as a residual between total municipal salaries (supra) in 1926 and those for P.Q., Ontario, and B.C.

Salaries for this group of provinces were interpolated between 1913 and 1926 using teachers salaries of the group as an interpolator.

A comparison of the provincial distribution of resultant wage and salary bills with 1931 census data follows.

Distribution of Municipal Wages and Salaries
(percentage of total)

	Project 1926	Census of Canada June 1, 1930 to May 30, 1931
Quebec	24.6	28.3
Ontario	41.4	41.1
British Columbia	8.6	10.2
All other provinces	25.4	20.4
Canada	100.0	100.0

2. Gross Domestic Product

Municipal gross domestic product was obtained at an aggregate basis throughout the whole period by multiplying municipal wages and salaries by 1.25. This latter number was derived from the national accounts of Canada for the national accounts industry "public administration and defence" for the years 1926 to 1939 (the actual average was 1.277).

3. Municipal Expenditures on Goods and Services

Current Account

(a) Municipal Expenditure 1913 to 1926

For this period the expenditures were calculated separately for Ontario, Quebec, British Columbia and all other provinces as a group. Expenditures for 1913 and 1926 were obtained from the Rowell-Sirois data (outlay on "Streets and Roads" and "All Other" current).

The interpolator for Ontario was Ontario real estate taxes (excluding school taxes). The ratio of expenditure on goods and services to municipal taxes was 0.6495 in 1913 and 0.6249 in 1926. For interpolation this ratio was linearly interpolated from 1913 to 1926 and then multiplied by the amount of the municipal real estate tax.

The Quebec interpolator was total ordinary municipal payments, excluding education, as described above in the calculation of Quebec municipal wages. The procedure was exactly like that for Ontario. The ratio of expenditure on goods and services to total ordinary municipal payments excluding education was 0.3903 in 1913 and 0.3955 in 1926.

The British Columbia interpolation between 1913 and 1926 was done separately for two periods *viz.*, from 1913 to 1921 and 1921 to 1926. The interpolator was schoolteachers salaries. The ratio of expenditures on goods and services from Rowell-Sirois data, to schoolteachers salaries was 5.9015 in 1913, 1.7303 in 1921, and 1.7710 in 1926. The method of interpolation for each period was like that for Ontario.

The interpolators of all other provinces (P.E.I., N.S., N.B., Man., Sask., Alta.,) as a group was schoolteachers salaries for the group. The ratios of expenditure on goods and services in this group to schoolteachers salaries were 2.02 in 1913 and 1.15 in 1926. However, the actual ratios of expenditures on goods and services to teachers salaries used, in this case, were 2.0 for 1914 to 1919 and 1.1 for 1920 to 1925. Interpolation was then done as in the case of Ontario.

The municipal expenditures on goods and services for each group in the two terminal years were:

Municipal Expenditures on Goods and Services, Current Account
(thousands of dollars)

	1913	1926
Ontario	15,025	42,532
Quebec	9,250	20,100
British Columbia	5,725	6,640
All other provinces	14,824	25,109

(b) Municipal Expenditure 1870 to 1913

Municipal non-educational expenditures for 1870 to 1912 were calculated as a constant proportion of municipal salaries, the calculations being done at the level of the aggregate for all provinces together. The ratio of municipal non-educational expenditure on goods and services in the aggregate to municipal wages and salaries in the aggregate in 1913 was 1.527. The countrywide wage bill for each year from 1870 to 1912 was multiplied by this ratio to obtain expenditure on goods and services in each year.

Capital Account

Capital account expenditures on goods and services of municipalities for all Canada for all years from 1971 onward were obtained from the detailed estimates of Statistics Canada in its preparation of capital stock estimates by the perpetual inventory method. The source was the printout of the detailed perpetual inventory estimates by Statcan of capital formation from 1871 onward (the Maclist document described in the chapter on construction and investment).

These capital account expenditures were large as shown by the following table.

Capital Account Expenditures on Goods and Services,
Municipalities, Selected Years
(thousands of dollars)

Year	Current Account Expenditure	Capital Account Expenditure
1871	4,382	533
1880	6,823	2,667
1890	10,549	2,400
1900	13,840	5,100
1910	34,068	18,300
1913	44,824	38,100
1920	69,998	34,100
1926	94,381	25,000

PUBLIC EDUCATION

The category "public education" includes primary school, typically grades 1 to 8, and high school, typically grades 9 to 12 or 13; it does not include universities, trade schools, or normal schools.

The base data from which GDP in public education are derived are wages and salaries paid to teachers. These salaries and wages provide by far the most clearly identifiable available data for the period. In addition, they are by far the largest component of GDP in education. Once this component is obtained, total GDP is obtained as a constant multiple of schoolteachers salaries. The rationale for this latter procedure will be explained later; but first, the mode of estimation of teachers wages and salaries will be described.

Estimation of Teachers Wages and Salaries

Under the British North America Act, jurisdiction over education lies with the provinces. In nearly all cases the delivery of educational services was administered by local school boards but they were responsible to a provincial department of education and had to provide information about their operations to these departments. In each province, the provincial department of education issued an annual report containing much statistical information about the school system. These reports were the ultimate source of the educational data.

In consequence of the foregoing circumstances, the wage and salary estimates were obtained on a province by province basis and to a description of these sources, by province, we now turn. To begin, information giving the earliest year for which comprehensive data on teachers wage and salaries were available follows.

Earliest Year of Comprehensive Salary Data

Province	Year
Alberta	1905 (Previously with N.W.T.)
British Columbia	1873
Manitoba	1884
New Brunswick	1876
Nova Scotia	1879
Ontario	1870
Prince Edward Island	1880
Quebec	1892
Saskatchewan	1906 (Previously with N.W.T.)
North West Territories	1896

Basis of Estimation of School Teachers Salaries, by Province

(i) Ontario

Education data are obtained throughout the period from the annual reports of the Minister of Education from 1876 onward and prior to 1876 from the annual reports of the Chief Superintendent of Education. They are quite comprehensive.

Teachers salaries are available in these reports in aggregate (and on average) by three main groups and one very small group as follows: the public schools, the term used for elementary non-religious schools; high schools and collegiate — the latter is really another name for a high school; the Roman Catholic separate schools which are the publicly assisted Roman Catholic Schools; publicly assisted Protestant schools, a very small group.

A statement giving aggregate teachers salaries was given for each of these groups in every report. Two anomalies should be noted. First, from 1870 to 1887, the statistics for the publicly supported Roman Catholic schools are included with those for the public schools (in 1887, the two are segregated in the public schools table); the Roman Catholic school statistics are then also given separately. For these years the two should not be added. From 1887 onward, the public school data exclude the Roman Catholic separate school data: therefore the data for each must be added together along with the high schools and Protestant separate schools to obtain a total. Second, from 1886 onward, there are very small salary bills given for Protestant separate school teachers. It is not clear whether or not some of these separate schools are included in the public school data but, in any event, the amounts are so small as not to matter.

The Ontario data are quite complete and I know of no reason to question their accuracy. Until 1890 the Ontario salaries account for at least half of countrywide salaries.

(ii) Quebec

Data are obtained from annual reports of the Department of Public Instruction of the Province of Quebec. Data derived from this source also appear in Quebec *Statistical Year Book*, first issued in 1914 and Quebec *Educational Statistics* which begin with 1915.

The Quebec data are distinctive in two ways. First, "primary" education, the equivalent of "elementary" education, was divided into three categories: (1) "elementary", the first four years; (2) model schools, the 5th and 6th years approximately; and (3) academies, the 7th and 8th and possibly the 9th year. Secondary education, the equivalent of high schools elsewhere, was given in "classical colleges" which were essentially operated by the Catholic church. "Superior" educational institutions included the universities, the normal schools and certain specified professional or trade schools. The data of the latter group are not included in "public" education but are in that of the general government.

Second, the institutions in which the teaching was done were, in the main, religiously oriented. Roman Catholic schools were by far the largest group; Protestant schools were a much smaller group; and there were a small number of independent schools. A large proportion of the Catholic schools and the Protestant schools received public financial support, both from local grants and provincial grants. These schools were said to be "under control" and had to abide by regulations of the Provincial Board of Public Instruction.

Data concerning the schools "under control" were obtained by the Department in the course of its administrative procedure. Data for the independent schools were obtained by school inspectors of the Department as a matter of information.

In the Roman Catholic schools the teaching staff was made up partly of lay personnel and partly of clergy or members of the Catholic orders. The lay personnel tended to be more characteristic of the "elementary" grades and the religious personnel more characteristic of the "model school" and "academy" grades. The classical colleges were almost entirely taught by male clergy.

The nature of the data on teachers salaries was such that a considerable amount of estimation within the project was involved. From 1892 to 1926 the numbers of teachers were reported according to the following classification.

	Lay Teachers		Religious Order Teachers	
	M	F	M	F
R.C. Elementary school				
R.C. Model schools and academies				
R.C. Classical colleges			M = Male	
Protestant Elementary			F = Female	
Protestant Model schools and academies				

In the tabulations that were made those teachers in independent schools were assigned to the appropriate category in the foregoing chart. Numbers of teachers for each category and by sex were available annually from 1892 to 1926.

In this period, 1892 onward, salaries of lay teachers only were obtained and given in the form of averages in each annual report. These salaries of lay teachers were in four categories: lay male elementary teachers; lay female elementary teachers; lay male teachers in model schools and academies; lay female teachers in model schools and academies. In the calculation of total provincial teachers salaries, it was assumed that religious teachers received the same salary as those in the corresponding category of lay teacher. In addition, it was assumed that the male religious teachers in the classical colleges, for whom there was no lay counterpart, received the same salaries as teachers in the model schools and academies: there is support for this last practice in light of the fact that average salaries for male teachers in Quebec were reported to be slightly higher than those of professors in the 1911 wage earner data collected with the census; classical college teachers were dubbed professors in the Quebec Department of Education reports.

What little information there is about the average salaries of religious teachers comes from the individual reports of school inspectors who reported such in a very small number of cases. One such report by inspector J.B. Demers, which gives data on lay and religious salaries for 1885-86, 1905-06 and 1910-11 (Annual Report of Quebec Department of Public Instruction 1910-11), suggests that salaries of religious teachers were below those of their lay counterpart in some cases and above in others. This evidence is not very extensive, however. Perhaps it may be best to think of the salaries attributed to the religious teachers as an imputation.

There are very, very few useful data for the salaries of any group, lay or religious, before 1892. Given this circumstance the teachers salaries for Quebec were projected backward from 1892 to 1870 by using Ontario teachers salary bill as an extrapolator: it was assumed that the ratio of Quebec teachers salaries to Ontario teachers salaries was the same for each year from 1870 to 1891 as in 1892.

The result must admittedly be an approximation. Between 1870 and 1892 the number of students enrolled increased about 17 percent in Ontario and about 26 percent in Quebec (data from HSC, Table V1-20.). Unfortunately HSC does not give the total number of teachers in Quebec at this time. However, the report of the department of Public Instruction for 1912 shows that the number of lay and religious teachers in the school system increased by nearly 100 percent between 1868 and 1888 while data from HSC show that the number of teachers in the school system in Ontario increased by just short of 80 percent between 1870 and 1890.

Information for average salaries in Ontario indicates that salaries for particular types of teachers increased between 1880 and 1890 but that average salaries for all elementary teachers together changed little because the proportion of female to male teachers in Ontario moved from just over equality in 1880 to approximately two female teachers to each male in 1890 and salaries of female teachers were considerably below those of males. Some gleaning of change in Quebec comes from the reports of one inspector, a Mr. Gay, who reported average salaries of males and females for the county of Pontiac and the western half of the county of Ottawa between 1875 and 1894. His reports show some increase in the salary of each type of teacher between 1880 and 1890. In the case of Quebec, female teachers already outnumbered male teachers by about 9 to 2 in 1880 and by only slightly more than 9 to 2 in 1890. It seems likely that the average salary of all teachers together rose modestly in Quebec in this period. Hence, the use of Ontario teachers salaries as an extrapolator may lead to some overstatement of the bill for Quebec teachers in the pre 1890 period. Our data on Quebec salary rates in the pre 1892 period are, however, very sketchy and indeed the count of teachers and students is subject to some variation, especially in Quebec where the reporting of "independent" schools is not consistent from year to year.

Quebec teachers salaries accounted for about 25 percent of countrywide salaries in the early 1890s.

(iii) All Other Provinces

Data for all other provinces came from annual reports of department of education for the provinces.

Alberta

Teachers salaries in the aggregate were reported annually in reports of the Education Department from 1905 onward. Prior to 1905 Alberta was included in the North West Territories. The Alberta data report salaries of officials as well as those of teachers.

British Columbia

Teachers salaries were available on aggregate basis for 1873, 1874 and from 1877 onward. Extrapolation from 1873 to 1870 was done in proportion to Ontario salaries. Ontario salaries were also used for interpolators between 1874 and 1877. The project did not have a report for 1895: it was estimated by linear interpolation between 1894 and 1896. Administrative salaries were also given.

Manitoba

Teachers salaries were reported in aggregate from 1884 onward. Teachers salaries before 1884 were done on a per capita basis using Ontario's per capita education expenditure as an extrapolator: Manitoba's per capita education expenditure in 1891 was projected to 1881 and 1871 on the basis of Ontario per capita educational expenditure. Educational expenditure on teachers salaries per capita was interpolated between census years on a straight line basis and total schoolteachers salaries were then calculated for years 1871 and 1881. Total teachers salaries were interpolated linearly between 1881 and 1884, between 1871 and 1881 and were extrapolated from 1871 to 1870 by assuming that the change between each of these last years were equal to the average change for 1871 to 1881. Manitoba's school board administrative salaries are given separately.

New Brunswick

Teachers salaries were obtained from *Annual Reports of Schools of New Brunswick* by *the Chief Superintendent of Education* (found in Journals of the Legislative Assembly of New Brunswick) for the years 1876, 1882, 1888 to 1918, 1920 and 1927. Teachers salaries were extrapolated from 1876 to 1870 on the basis of the movements in Ontario salaries. Interpolations between 1876 and 1882, 1882 and 1888, 1918 and 1920, and 1920 to 1927 were made on the basis of Ontario salaries. Numbers of teachers and average salaries were given in the source and aggregates were calculated.

Nova Scotia

Teachers salaries were obtained from the *Annual Report of the Superintendent of Education of Nova Scotia* (found in Journals of the Legislative Assembly) for the years 1879 to 1921, 1924 to 1926. Teachers salaries were extrapolated from 1879 to 1870 in proportion to the year to year movements in the Ontario salary bill and were interpolated between 1921 and 1924 on the basis of Ontario salaries. Numbers of teachers and average salaries were given in the source and aggregates were calculated from these data.

Prince Edward Island

Teachers salaries were obtained from *Annual Report of the Public Schools of the Province of Prince Edward Island* each year (in Journal of the Legislative Assembly): for the years 1880 to 1926 they were available as aggregates. The aggregate of teachers salaries for Prince Edward Island was extrapolated from 1880 to 1870 on the basis of the aggregate for Ontario teachers: it was assumed that P.E.I. aggregate salaries remained a constant proportion of Ontario's aggregate salaries.

Saskatchewan

Teachers salaries were obtained from the *Annual Report of the Department of Education* of the Province of Saskatchewan as aggregates for all years from 1906 onward. Teachers salaries for September 1 to December 31, 1905 are included with the North-West Territories. (The provinces of Alberta and Saskatchewan became operative at September 1, 1905.) Officials salaries are shown separately.

North-West Territories

Teachers salaries for the old North-West Territories were obtained from the *Report of the Council of Public Instruction of the North-West Territories of Canada 1896* changing at the end to *Statistical Report of the Department of Education of the North-West Territories, 1904-05* for the years 1896, 1898 to 1900, 1902, 1904-05. Salaries for 1897, 1901 and 1903 were estimated by straight line interpolation between adjoining years.

Salaries before 1896 were extrapolated back to earlier years in two steps. First, the average cost of teachers salaries per capita was extrapolated back to earlier years on the basis of the costs of Ontario teachers salary per capita. Second, total teachers salaries were then calculated for each census year. A linear extrapolation was then made between each of 1871 and 1881, 1881 and 1891, and 1891 and 1896. The 1871 to 1881 series was linearly extrapolated back to 1870.

(Note: This procedure gives too high a figure for early years. We should extrapolate back to 1886 on the basis of the number of teachers which we have from the source books. That would give us only about $35,000 in 1886. The population is not a good extrapolator on account of vagaries in the count of Indians).

Gross Domestic Product: Public Education

Estimation of total gross domestic product in public education was calculated as a constant mark up of teachers salaries.

The estimates of this mark up were prepared from data of the official national accounts in Statistics Canada *National Income and Expenditure Accounts, Volume 1, The Annual Estimates 1926-1974* Tables 43 and 49. Separate data were not available for schools but there were data for local government expenditure of which the schools formed a very large part. It was assumed that the data for local government were representative of schools. Gross domestic product of government comprised salaries plus depreciation on physical assets. For the years 1926 to 1940, all wages and salaries comprised just slightly over 80 percent of GDP of local government and capital consumption allowances slightly under 20 percent of GDP; there was little year to year variation throughout these years. It was assumed that GDP was equal to 1.25 times wages and salaries. Within the school system, data, especially for the western provinces and Quebec from as early as 1900 and 1890, indicate that school board administrative salaries tended to approximate 5 percent of teachers salaries. Total salaries were thus 1.05 times teachers salaries and if GDP was calculated at 1.25 times total salaries it meant that GDP was equal to 1.31 times teachers salaries (1.31 = 1.05 x 1.25). The best that could be done to see whether capital consumption allowances relative to wages, before 1926, might approximate the post 1926 ratios was to examine the level of physical assets of school boards relative to teachers salaries, data which were available quite early in reports on the schools. The ratios of physical assets relative to teachers salaries tended to be higher in city schools than in country schools; at the same time rates of depreciation on country schools were undoubtedly higher than those of city schools since the latter tended to be constructed of more durable materials. Whether or not the two variations were offsetting can only be a matter of conjecture. It was assumed that they were and that depreciation charges relative to teachers salaries were the same for both. If this assumption was justified the trend from country school to city school growth would not change the ratios of depreciation charges. Inspection of ratios of physical asset values relative to teachers salaries through time for each of town and country schools suggests that there were not big trend changes within each group.

Public School Purchases of Goods and Services

Current Expenditures

Estimates of public school current account purchases of goods and services were, like GDP, calculated as a constant proportion of teachers wages and salaries. A starting point for school board gross current account purchases of goods and services is GDP of the public schools itself, made up as it is of payments of wages and salaries and depreciation of physical assets. There were, in addition, expenses for plant operation and caretaking, fuel, insurances, repairs, supplies, stationery, etc., library costs for library books, maps and apparatus. Sporadic data for Ontario, Quebec and the prairie provinces on these items suggest that plant operating and fuel and caretaking amounted to 20-21 percent of teachers salaries, repairs to 5 percent of teachers salaries and other items to 5 percent of teachers salaries. In the event, it was assumed that the purchases of goods and services beyond the items included in GDP amounted to 31 percent of teachers salaries. Consequently, public school purchases of goods and services were calculated at 1.61 times teachers salaries.

Such information as there is seems to imply that there is little, if any, trend in the relationship of most of these expenditures to teachers salaries. As an exception within provinces, there may have been some upward trend in caretaking, cleaning and like expenses relative to teachers salaries. For instance, one room country schools had limited janitorial service while city and town schools had a more developed service. The growth of the urban schools relative to country schools then probably meant a relative increase in caretaking and janitorial services. However, if we take education on a countrywide basis, it would only be with World War I that the urbanizing effect became important. Until then the growth of country schools in the west would help to offset the urbanization of central Canada. Hence, it is not at all certain that on a countrywide basis expenses for caretaking and janitorial service do have a substantial trend.

Capital Expenditures

Capital expenditures were obtained from Statistics Canada by way of the printout of detail that lies behind the estimates of fixed capital stocks and flows which were prepared on a perpetual inventory basis (Maclist).

A Comparison of Departments of Education and Decennial Census Salary Data for School Teachers for 1910

In the census of persons of 1911, taken on June 1, 1911, many useful data on the work behaviour of the population were obtained. The occupation of every gainfully occupied person was obtained. For persons employed on wage or salary information was sought and, for the most part, obtained on the number of weeks worked and on the amount of earnings — there were always some persons reported as being wage-earners for whom time worked and earnings were not recorded. These data were tabulated in great detail. A census volume giving the numbers occupied, classified by industry, occupation and region, was published but the wage and salary data were not published at the time of the 1911 census and, indeed, were only given in highly aggregative and very brief form in the 1931 census volume on earnings. The data are available in detail on microfilm obtainable from the census division of Statistics Canada.

The departments of education schoolteacher salary data and the census data can be checked one against the other and since the departments of education data should be quite accurate the check should give some indication of how reliable the census data are. There is some question about the year to which the census earnings apply and hence about the departments of education year to which the census data should be comparable. The earnings volume of the 1921 census describes the 1911 census earnings data as covering the year ending May 31, 1911. However, the 1911 census forms on which the earnings data for each individual were obtained, states specifically that it is the earnings for 1910 that are wanted and one reference in the 1911 instructions to enumerators also states that the earnings for 1910 are to be obtained. In what follows, we compare the departments of education salary data for 1910 with the census data; in addition, we give departments of education data for the year ending June 30, 1911, should the reader wish to make that comparison also.

To make the desired comparisons, one must know the year covered by the statistical data for each of the departments of education. In their reports for 1910 and 1911 the various departments reported their year ending, for statistical purposes, as given below.

Departments of education salaries for calendar 1910 were calculated from the simple averages of teachers salaries in school years ending in 1910 and 1911 for P.E.I., N.S., N.B., P.Q., and B.C. and for the school years ending December 31, 1910 for Ontario, Manitoba, Saskatchewan, and Alberta. The alternative departments of education data for the year ending June 30, 1911, for the reader's own use, were calculated from the data for the school year ending in 1911 for P.E.I., N.S., N.B., P.Q. and B.C., and averages of school years ending December

Date of Ending of School Reporting Year For Statistical Purposes

Province	Date
P.E.I.	September 30
N.S.	July 31
N.B.	June 30
P.Q.	June 30
Ont.	December 31
Man.	December 31
Sask.	December 31
Alta.	December 31
B.C.	June 30

Table 9.2
Schoolteachers Earnings, Departments of
Education and Census for 1910

	Department of Education		Census Employee Data		
Province	Estimated Earnings For Calendar 1910 (dollars)	Alternative Estimates For Year Ending June 30, 1911 (dollars)	Number Reporting Earnings	Earnings Reported (dollars)	Numbers Not Reporting Earnings
P.E.I	131,755	131,853	514	132,400	192
N.S.	814,459	838,013	2,694	890,900	696
N.B.	654,933	659,775	2,068	698,700	270
P.Q.	3,640,210	3,700,780	7,604	2,136,400	5,185
Ont.	6,357,902	6,556,873	11,439	6,564,600	1,688
Man.	1,327,010	1,382,630	2,208	1,356,900	552
Sask.	1,208,651	1,253,788	1,517	934,600	627
Alta.	908,045	1,026,314	1,427	936,700	322
B.C.	909,991	986,001	1,244	947,700	316
Canada	15,952,956	16,535,027	30,715	14,598,200	9,848

Source: Departments of education data from annual reports of departments of education; census data from census microfilm. Note: the "earnings reported" are the earnings of those actually reporting earnings.

31, 1910 and December 31, 1911 for Ontario, Manitoba, Saskatchewan and Alberta.

Table 9.2 gives comparisons of numbers of school teachers and total earnings from the departments of education data and from the census data.

The census data for earnings of those teachers reporting salaries and the departments of education data for earnings for 1910 correspond reasonably well except for Quebec and Saskatchewan. The reason for the divergence in Quebec is very clear. It will be noted that, in the census data, the number of teachers not reporting earnings is very large, 5,185 souls, relative to the number of teachers reporting earnings. These teachers not reporting salaries would be clerics of the Catholic church and members of the religious orders engaged in teaching. The Department of Education of Quebec reported 1,986 male teachers in religious bodies and 3,736 female teachers in religious bodies in the school year 1910-11: these teachers were imputed an income in the data of this product in the first column; most of them must have reported their occupation as teaching but gave no salary in the case of the census. The case of Saskatchewan is much harder to explain. The number of teachers reporting time and wages in the census, at 1,517, is well short of the numbers engaged in teaching as reported by the Department of Education. The best count of the number teaching at one time is, perhaps, the number of classrooms in operation which was reported by the Department of Education at 2,207 in 1910: the actual numbers of teachers reported by the Department as teaching in 1910 was 2,672 but the latter is a gross number and not the net number teaching at any one time. Before dealing further with Saskatchewan we should look at the relative numbers of teachers reported by the departments of education and the census for each province. These data follow in Table 9.3.

It is evident from Table 9.3 that the numbers reporting earnings in the census roughly matched the numbers given by the departments of education in the provinces of P.E.I., N.S., N.B., Ontario and B.C.; they fell short of the departments of education by large numbers for P.Q. and Saskatchewan and by smaller numbers for Manitoba and Alberta. We have already dealt with the major part of the explanation for Quebec; we might just add that it is possible that some clerics who were teachers may have reported themselves as clerics rather than teachers which could account for the overall number reported in the occupation in the census being less than the number reported by the Department.

The explanation of the shortfall of census numbers in the prairie provinces must be different: religious personnel among teachers were unimportant. The explanations must lie in the fact that many schools, at that time, were not open for a full year, that some teachers were relatively short term visitors from the east who might have left the province before census time and that, more generally, many persons moved into and out of the teaching profession each year. There is also the possibility that the census was less well taken in the prairie provinces than elsewhere but I am not aware of any evidence that such was the case. The fact that many schools were open less than a full year, which was approximately 200 school days, is shown by Table 9.4 from the Saskatchewan Department of Education report for 1910.

Separate data show that the schools that were open less than a full year were predominately rural schools in which there would be only one teacher. Similarly, the Department of Education of Alberta, in its report for 1910 records that 1,414 teachers were employed in schools that were open for the full year and 803 teachers were in schools that were open only part of the year. Some evidence of the turnover of teaching staff may be gleaned from the facts that the Saskatchewan Department of Education reported 2,672 teachers employed some time in 1910 while there were only 2,207 operating classrooms; Manitoba Department of Education reported 2,774 teachers employed in 1910 but only 2,227 classrooms; similarly the Alberta Department of Education report for 1910 records that while there were 2,217 teachers employed at some time in 1910 the total number employed at any one time did not exceed 1,610 teachers and that consequently "there were 607 schools or rooms that changed teachers during the year". In the Saskatchewan and especially in the Alberta reports much reference is made to the fact that large numbers of teachers came from Britain and other Canadian provinces. In Saskatchewan, in

Table 9.3
Numbers of Teachers Reported by the Department of
Education and the 1911 Census

	Department of Education Data Number Employed During Year	Number of Wage Earners Reporting Wages	Number of Wage Earners Not Reporting Wages	Total Number Reported as Wage Earners	Total Number Reporting Occup- ation
P.E.I. (1910-11)	591	514	192	706	714
N.S. (1910-11)	2,799	2,694	696	3,390	3,423
N.B. (1910-11)	1,991	2,068	270	2,338	2,386
P.Q. (1910-11)	13,481	7,604	5,185	12,789	13,048
Ont. 1910	11,372	11,439	1,699	13,127	14,166
Man. 1910	2,774	2,208	552	2,760	2,836
Sask. 1910	2,672	1,517	627	2,144	2,171
Alta. 1910	2,217	1,427	322	1,749	1,834
B.C. 1910-11	1,179	1,244	316	1,560	1,708

Source: Column 1, annual department of education reports of individual provinces: for the year ending in mid 1911 for P.E.I., N.B., N.S., P.Q. and B.C.; for years ending December 31, 1910 for Ontario, Manitoba, Saskatchewan and Alberta. Columns 2 to 4, from census tapes on employee earnings and wages. Column 5, from *1911 Census*, Volume VI, *Occupations*.

1910, out of the total of 2,672 teachers reported, 541 held provisional certificates, good for eight months and 837 held third class certificates that were not permanent certificates; Alberta and B.C. reported like situations. The Alberta annual reports also refer to the large numbers that left teaching for other fields. School inspectors in the western provinces also wrote of the problem of obtaining and keeping good teachers. The Department of Education reports do not provide information about the numbers of visiting teachers from other provinces so we can not add more about that. It must have been all of these circumstances that led to the discrepancies of the census data from the Department of Education data, especially for Saskatchewan and to a lesser degree for Alberta and even Manitoba.

Table 9.4
Length of School Year, Saskatchewan 1910

Length of School Year	Number of Schools Open
Less than 20 days	5
Between 20 and 50 days	33
Between 51 and 100 days	179
Between 101 and 150 days	566
Between 151 and 200 days	576
More than 200 days	553

Source: Saskatchewan, Department of Education, *Annual Report, 1910*

On the whole then, except when there are unusual circumstances the census data correspond quite well with data from the Department of Education reports. Might one be correct in assuming that unusual circumstances of the sort found for Quebec, Saskatchewan and Alberta in the case of schoolteachers are not apt to be found in other occupations? If so, may one not draw the inference that the census data are quite reliable as a source of income data in the wage-earning occupations?

UNIVERSITIES

The method used to estimate university salaries and wages and university gross domestic product was determined by the limitations of the available data. The first limitation was imposed by the paucity of available data for all universities. The only available information covering all universities was the total numbers of undergraduate students in the years 1871-72, 1881-82, 1891-92, 1901-02, 1911-12, 1920-21 and 1925-26: the estimates for 1871-72 to 1911-12 were presented by Robin S. Harris in his *A History of Higher Education in Canada, 1663-1960* (U. of T. Press, 1976); the estimates for 1920-21 and 1925-26 were prepared by Statistics Canada and appear in Statcan, *Historical Compendium of Educational Statistics from Confederation to 1975*, Catalogue No. 81-568, in which, incidentally, the Robin Harris figures are also reproduced. The second limitation was imposed by the fact that until 1920-21, the reasonably accessible financial data were limited to those of the University of Toronto: they were available in reports to the Legislature of Ontario and appear in the sessional papers of Ontario; these reports include numbers of students in the University of Toronto (as well as the financial data) from 1880-81 onward.

Given the above limitations the general methodology was the following. University of Toronto reports for 1880-81, 1891-92, 1901-02, 1911-12 and 1920-21 were used to obtain costs per undergraduate student of all salaries plus the separately given items here called "contingencies" which make up the remainder of current account expenditure. Whilst the financial data were available in the University of Toronto reports (Sessional Paper 31, 1877) for 1871-72 the number of undergraduates was not presented; the cost per student in 1871-72 was assumed to be the same as for 1880-81. The same costs per student were then multiplied by the total numbers of undergraduates, countrywide, to obtain total current account university costs for salaries and contingencies separately for 1871, 1880, 1891, 1911 and 1920. Total salary costs and contingency costs were then interpolated on a straight line basis between the foregoing years and 1870 was obtained by linear extrapolation.

A different procedure was used for estimation for years 1921-26. Statcan in Catalogue No. 81-586 provided estimates of total current account expenditures of all universities in 1920-21 and 1925-26. The Statcan estimate for 1920-21 was quite close to the estimate obtained in the alternative way — the Statcan total current account cost figure for 1920-21 was $8,975,000 while the project estimate, based on costs per undergraduate student at Toronto and the total number of undergraduates in the country was $9,321,519. Given this close correspondence, the Statcan figure for total current account expenditures in 1925-26 was accepted and was divided between salaries and contingencies in the same proportions as in 1920-21. Salaries and contingencies were interpolated linearly between 1920-21 and 1925-26 and extrapolated to 1926-27 on the same linear basis.

The relevant basic data are given in Table 9.5.

Table 9.5
University Costs, Selected Years
(All expenditure figures in dollars)

Year	1871-72	1880-81	1891-92	1901-02	1911-12	1920-21	1925-26
University of Toronto:							
Undergraduate							
Students (no.)	n.a.	400	647	1,398	3,275	4,547	
Aggregate Salaries	(35,091)	40,898	79,767	162,090	527,377	1,123,983	
Contingencies [1]	(23,828)	23,668	29,717	63,109	294,340	737,926	
Total Current							
Expenditure [2]	(58,919)	64,566	109,484	225,196	821,717	1,861,909	
Expenditure per Student:							
Salaries	(102)	102	123	116	161	247	
Contingencies [1]	(59)	59	46	45	90	162	
Total Expenditure [2]	(161)	161	169	161	251	409	
All Canadian Universities:							
Students (no.)	1,590	3,006	5,112	6,641	12,891	22,791	
Total Salaries	162,180	306,612	628,776	770,356	2,075,451	5,629,377	(6,820,560)
Contingencies [1]	93,810	177,354	235,152	298,845	1,160,190	3,692,142	(4,473,440)
Total Expenditure [2]	255,990	483,966	863,928	1,069,201	3,235,641	9,321,519	11,294,000
Gross Domestic							
Product	202,725	383,265	785,970	962,945	2,594,314	7,036,721	8,525,700

1.   Contingencies are expenditure on goods and services other than wages and salaries.
2.   Total expenditures are the sum of wages and salaries and contingencies.

Note: U. of T. data were not available for 1881-82; data for 1880-81 were used.

Sources: Census of Canada for total number of students. University of Toronto reports in Sessional Papers of Ontario. Statistics Canada, *Historical Compendium of Educational Statistics from Confederation to 1975*, Catalogue No. 81-568 for total expenditure on goods and services in 1925-26.

Gross Domestic Product

The above wages and salaries include non-academic as well as academic salaries. To obtain gross domestic product the wages and salaries were multiplied by 1.25. This yields the same multiple as that used in the case of the public schools. There may be some question about the use of the same ratio as for the schools but there is some supporting evidence for this procedure. This evidence lies in the fact that for 1880-21, 1911-12 and 1920-21 the University of Toronto ratio of "contingencies" to salaries is much like that of the public schools. At the same time, one should note that the same U. of T. ratios for 1891-92 and 1901-02 are somewhat lower than in the other years.

Bibliography of Sources Cited in Chapter 9

Major sources:

Government of Canada, *Public Accounts*, annual, and Auditor-General's *Reports*.

All Provinces, *Public Accounts*, annual.

All Provinces, *Reports* of Ministry of Education or like bodies, mostly annual.

Statistics Canada, *National Income and Expenditure Accounts, 1926-1974*, Volume I.

Statistics Canada, *Historical Compendium of Educational Statistics from Confederation to 1975*.

Dominion Bureau of Statistics, *Canada Year Book*, 1932.

Ontario Bureau of Industries, *Municipal Statistics*, and previously in Sessional Papers, published in various ways.

City of Montreal, annual financial statements.

Province of Quebec, *Statistical Year Book*, 1914 onward.

Census of Canada, 1911 Census, microfilmed data on occupations, wages and salaries.

Maclist, printout of data on capital formation of background material behind capital stock estimates.

Historical Statistics of Canada (HSC), see bibliography of Chapter 2.

Harris, Robin S., *A History of Higher Education in Canada, 1663-1960*, (University of Toronto Press, 1976).

Canada, Royal Commission on Dominion-Provincial Relations, *Report* and Appendices, 1939.

Supplementary Tables

Provincial Government: Tables 9.6 – 9.7
Public Education: Table 9.8

Table 9.6

Wages and Salaries, Provincial Governments, by Province, 1870-1926
(thousands of dollars)

Year	Prince Edward Island	Nova Scotia	New Brunswick	Quebec	Ontario	Manitoba	Saskatchewan	Alberta	British Columbia
1870	133	50	124	582	353				
1871	157	57	117	594	406				41
1872	196	62	149	638	502				196
1873	155	60	145	707	711	52			162
1874	171	68	158	762	901	46			298
1875	153	73	182	786	849	50			297
1876	137	68	153	776	749	35			374
1877	128	63	168	800	753	35			313
1878	129	74	164	735	708	41			184
1879	121	55	157	741	726	56			182
1880	99	57	155	766	692	66			151
1881	100	56	149	826	709	79			195
1882	98	64	152	855	736	79			269
1883	102	62	234	857	732	127			242
1884	105	66	152	778	814	161			257
1885	99	72	137	829	775	143			302
1886	113	76	144	913	816	135			295
1887	106	78	154	991	890	152			308
1888	102	79	146	1001	918	142			311
1889	95	85	143	1087	1192	160			333
1890	110	85	147	1130	1022	186			374
1891	107	85	154	1249	1118	172			548
1892	89	103	154	1010	1123	214			529
1893	99	83	162	986	1107	203			561
1894	92	114	152	1036	1115	176			704
1895	100	112	155	1035	1119	176			543
1896	91	118	160	1288	1130	188			564
1897	96	121	167	1136	1176	190			692
1898	91	123	166	1057	1235	202			793
1899	81	126	174	1191	1215	232			679

Table 9.6 (continued)
(thousands of dollars)

Year	Prince Edward Island	Nova Scotia	New Brunswick	Quebec	Ontario	Manitoba	Saskatchewan	Alberta	British Columbia
1900	88	141	186	1217	1337	265			866
1901	88	166	216	1217	1342	238			1006
1902	88	168	200	1221	1437	305			1175
1903	92	184	191	1319	1609	314			995
1904	103	184	206	1415	1725	322			853
1905	100	209	203	1538	1758	359	42	47	881
1906	81	224	203	1412	2178	411	485	420	1073
1907	109	253	221	1570	2488	484	765	666	1398
1908	122	271	230	1852	2745	683	949	764	1485
1909	122	279	384	1774	2890	753	711	978	2636
1910	131	294	2068	2822	935	824	1237	3432	
1911	136	310	403	2417	3142	1066	935	1186	4332
1912	180	321	390	2671	3117	1302	1274	1439	5668
1913	154	346	434	3020	3325	1463	1651	1721	5772
1914	152	378	469	3068	3594	1547	1480	1719	4070
1915	175	378	457	3099	3901	1581	1252	1732	3541
1916	155	397	430	3033	3708	1464	1197	1776	3173
1917	167	438	552	3602	5321	1631	1522	2144	2734
1918	166	487	642	3834	5108	1732	1770	2653	3499
1919	224	629	810	4330	6886	2055	1889	3224	4468
1920	238	877	1177	4895	10045	3237	2862	4465	643
1922	235	867	887	6053	13554	3093	2613	4402	6856
1923	270	912	1081	6282	14523	2841	2366	3789	7602
1924	245	936	1071	6786	13479	2472	2278	3585	7530
1925	255	963	1149	7077	14670	2439	2468	3781	7570
1926	259	979	1103	7844	14274	2419	2371	3940	6711

Table 9.7

Expenditures on Goods and Services, Provincial Governments, by Province, 1870-1926
(thousands of dollars)

Year	Prince Edward Island	Nova Scotia	New Brunswick	Quebec	Ontario	Manitoba	Saskatchewan	Alberta	British Columbia
1870	199	256	292	1070					
1871	235	286	276	1077	935				68
1872	293	305	352	1139	1148				332
1873	232	291	240	1292	1614	52			278
1874	256	323	371	1374	2035	46			494
1875	228	342	428	1460	1907	50			509
1876	204	313	361	1499	1671	36			621
1877	192	282	395	1628	1670	35			531
1878	193	330	386	1459	1563	68			309
1879	181	242	369	1469	1594	94			298
1880	149	243	365	1492	1436	113			254
1881	150	238	352	1649	1482	137			330
1882	147	275	357	1630	1623	138			452
1883	153	261	550	1752	1622	226			421
1884	157	277	359	1677	1812	289			483
1885	148	301	322	1723	1734	259			575
1886	168	319	340	2108	1832	249			525
1887	158	323	362	2396	2009	284			549
1888	152	325	344	2187	2081	271			583
1889	142	348	336	2611	2714	310			685
1890	163	347	347	2952	2338	366			723
1891	161	343	360	2880	2508	349			991
1892	136	414	358	2134	2474	444			1057
1893	153	328	376	2237	2395	431			1088
1894	145	447	350	2089	2372	383			1399
1895	158	436	355	1986	2341	392			1169
1896	146	455	364	2571	2325	430			1102
1897	156	461	378	2156	2384	446			1433
1898	150	465	375	1986	2464	485			1511
1899	136	472	390	2202	2389	571			1194

Table 9.7 (continued)
(thousands of dollars)

Year	Prince Edward Island	Nova Scotia	New Brunswick	Quebec	Ontario	Manitoba	Saskatchewan	Alberta	British Columbia
1900	151	526	415	2263	2592	653			1571
1901	152	613	484	2264	2593	592			1777
1902	154	614	447	2320	2765	752			2088
1903	158	667	427	2489	3084	766			1726
1904	175	660	462	2674	3297	777			1467
1905	167	743	454	2915	3344	859	75	101	1489
1906	134	786	455	2696	4127	973	863	955	1935
1907	179	882	497	2964	4695	1136	1639	1660	2618
1908	199	934	516	3692	5160	1588	2683	1926	2812
1909	196	953	862	4055	4990	1735	2033	2526	4911
1910	208	997	820	4318	5645	2174	1963	3090	6563
1911	217	1117	972	5075	6333	3042	1907	3159	8670
1912	287	1173	873	5825	6322	3566	2162	3904	11745
1913	245	1270	1231	6734	6747	4457	3001	4254	12180
1914	242	1512	1442	7230	7325	4682	2192	4050	8165
1915	278	1662	1164	6624	7979	3824	1619	3718	6366
1916	246	1687	1089	6466	7594	3794	1286	3600	5823
1917	265	1547	1593	7460	10835	3819	1672	4292	5088
1918	263	1597	1738	8371	10488	4350	1927	4860	6530
1919	357	2173	2759	9650	14352	5045	2832	6098	8439
1920	360	3197	3326	10184	20523	6787	5170	8269	12432
1921	378	3283	4417	10889	21856	8730	5354	8677	12449
1922	374	3305	3125	13550	29576	7719	5523	8985	13195
1923	430	3462	3597	15851	30817	6432	3477	6898	14648
1925	406	3683	3495	16178	31103	4713	3300	7145	15027
1926	412	3772	3384	17241	30152	4583	3137	7526	12581

Table 9.8

Teachers Salaries, Public Education, by Province, 1870-1926
(current dollars)

Year	Prince Edward Island	Nova Scotia	New Brunswick	Quebec	Ontario
1870	54,938	248,916	230,918	690,600	1,369,573
1871	54,058	244,921	227,237	679,991	1,347,731
1872	62,548	283,347	262,889	786,646	1,559,230
1873	69,590	315,259	292,477	875,227	1,734,788
1874	75,360	341,440	316,771	947,851	1,878,840
1875	80,260	363,627	337,350	1,009,402	2,008,879
1876	83,400	377,868	350,566	1,048,970	2,097,249
1877	93,063	421,633	380,798	1,170,444	2,320,010
1878	92,437	418,811	368,579	1,162,628	2,304,519
1879	95,831	434,181	372,658	1,205,290	2,389,085
1880	97,807	418,724	371,252	1,230,203	2,438,360
1881	97,341	434,014	362,776	1,230,529	2,439,097
1882	98,477	431,146	360,951	1,252,349	2,482,408
1883	102,284	456,624	370,904	1,295,662	2,568,206
1884	105,930	370,728	383,743	1,349,234	2,674,419
1885	111,355	489,158	388,090	1,373,008	2,721,481
1886	113,332	506,532	396,299	1,410,459	2,795,753
1887	111,172	408,047	392,906	1,406,389	2,787,613
1888	108,710	501,726	403,004	1,450,354	2,874,877
1889	108,220	502,758	405,838	1,479,989	2,933,701
1890	111,509	503,380	417,053	1,552,450	3,077,141
1891	111,579	523,989	416,065	1,598,043	3,167,475
1892	114,146	525,104	429,973	1,628,330	3,227,635
1893	116,460	416,101	437,437	1,529,315	3,301,234
1894	120,874	555,849	439,490	1,823,311	3,399,741
1895	120,896	576,004	450,350	1,688,930	3,514,294
1896	122,991	572,776	475,548	1,878,808	3,549,796
1897	126,851	590,308	481,161	1,987,261	3,422,183
1898	122,744	597,843	476,276	1,904,202	3,449,878
1899	123,262	595,687	486,364	1,943,819	3,483,341

Table 9.8 (continued)

(current dollars)

Year	Prince Edward Island	Nova Scotia	New Brunswick	Quebec	Ontario
1900	124,423	608,656	483,090	1,946,410	3,517,466
1901	122,730	600,274	463,701	2,122,194	3,593,832
1902	123,188	611,058	478,000	2,155,621	3,748,285
1903	120,874	612,496	477,805	2,283,882	3,884,102
1904	121,863	478,286	490,996	2,775,539	4,096,999
1905	123,385	665,329	552,592	2,611,241	4,338,346
1906	98,702	689,807	538,305	2,687,286	4,600,165
1907	125,366	717,931	553,984	2,763,330	4,976,568
1908	126,835	759,369	573,640	3,184,195	5,508,199
1909	132,306	771,526	626,645	3,306,070	5,954,379
1910	131,656	790,905	650,090	3,579,640	6,357,902
1911	131,853	838,013	659,775	3,700,780	6,755,843
1912	155,123	859,266	681,731	4,898,012	7,347,197
1913	142,955	900,715	697,303	4,517,653	7,992,724
1914	144,925	943,621	737,810	5,005,395	8,685,521
1915	149,781	969,720	774,747	5,429,206	9,092,834
1916	155,718	1,024,717	798,029	5,228,841	9,445,008
1917	159,751	1,058,353	830,464	5,540,322	9,959,877
1918	159,414	1,118,804	880,844	6,941,248	10,672,130
1919	177,680	1,214,041	979,343	7,633,923	11,962,001
1920	225,226	1,456,290	1,248,302	7,937,724	15,348,960
1921	287,807	1,832,059	1,374,782	9,502,805	18,094,119
1922	322,625	1,973,052	1,402,566	11,067,886	19,665,348
1923	343,953	2,082,651	1,406,911	11,923,603	20,927,605
1924	328,975	2,157,238	1,388,824	12,218,411	21,834,306
1925	330,228	2,150,488	1,362,552	12,693,219	22,566,947
1926	328,108	2,238,357	1,309,371	13,521,635	22,777,666

Table 9.8 (continued)

Teachers Salaries, Public Education, by Province, 1870-1926
(current dollars)

Year	Manitoba	Saskatchewan	Alberta	Northwest Territories	British Columbia
1870	16,742	(see N.W.T.)		29,337	15,765
1871	23,114			31,853	15,513
1872	29,486			34,369	17,947
1873	35,858			36,886	19,968
1874	42,230			39,402	22,220
1875	48,602			41,918	26,587
1876	54,974			44,435	30,254
1877	61,346			46,951	36,315
1878	67,718			49,467	39,732
1879	74,090			51,983	36,892
1880	80,462			54,500	40,215
1881	86,834			57,016	41,169
1882	101,015			63,146	49,642
1883	115,195			69,276	44,457
1884	129,376			75,406	50,763
1885	150,789			81,536	62,204
1886	168,042			87,666	70,337
1887	181,042			93,795	78,572
1888	198,882			99,925	88,287
1889	206,813			106,055	106,455
1890	200,929			112,185	122,002
1891	251,719			118,315	136,943
1892	291,329			129,173	182,819
1893	317,119			140,031	215,128
1894	359,076			150,890	199,545
1895	378,656			161,748	192,772
1896	441,185			172,606	185,998
1897	445,204			179,432	200,637
1898	465,371			186,258	233,361
1899	508,896			204,929	241,030

Table 9.8 (continued)

(current dollars)

Year	Manitoba	Saskatchewan	Alberta	Northwest Territories	British Columbia
1900	561,091			234,976	277,965
1901	582,325			278,061	395,248
1902	625,829			321,145	366,607
1903	697,996			420,896	404,032
1904	785,100			520,646	436,553
1905	840,354		308,473	359,379	456,695
1906	910,086	471,735	386,107		559,357
1907	1,009,224	585,593	497,745		515,857
1908	1,103,990	831,841	592,227		601,542
1909	1,203,232	1,044,010	758,815		688,805
1910	1,327,010	*1,208,651	908,045		833,980
1911	1,452,630	1,298,924	1,144,583		986,001
1912	1,593,742	**1,691,097	1,411,200		720,690
1913	1,734,853	2,190,870	1,672,525		970,100
1914	1,861,809	2,739,477	2,050,697		1,085,340
1915	2,066,440	2,975,261	2,244,963		2,578,097
1916	2,195,226	3,131,762	2,421,404		1,928,524
1917	2,314,005	3,494,632	2,620,085		1,957,515
1918	2,382,840	4,041,026	2,860,352		2,369,530
1919	2,648,229	5,048,460	3,560,318		2,709,784
1920	3,296,035	6,266,364	4,371,508		3,394,115
1921	4,335,529	7,273,198	5,213,011		4,344,419
1922	5,016,903	7,223,117	5,428,826		4,807,160
1923	5,018,809	7,166,970	5,411,486		4,896,385
1924	4,849,712	7,279,859	5,443,247		3,616,370
1925	4,838,723	7,288,108	5,477,156		3,622,624
1926	4,914,087	7,438,093	5,640,218		3,749,410

*   By error, in making the sum for all Canada, the entry for this number was $1,280,651.

**   By error, in making the sum for all Canada, the entry for this number was $1,596,616.

Chapter 10. Wholesale and Retail Trade; Community, Business and Personal Services

M.C. URQUHART

Gross Domestic Product at Factor Cost in Trade and Services

These two service groups are handled together since common elements are involved in their estimation. Entries for gross domestic product in these groups are given in the tables only for decennial census years and for 1926; estimates for inter-census years and for 1921 to 1925 enter the aggregate national gross domestic product by the procedure of calculating the ratio of the aggregate gross domestic product to gross domestic product less these two groups for census years and 1926, interpolating these ratios linearly between census years and to 1926, and multiplying the gross domestic product excluding these two groups for inter-census years and 1921 to 1925 by these calculated ratios.

A detailed presentation of all source material would be inordinately bulky. However, enough information is provided for the interested researcher to check the material presented herein and to form a judgement of its accuracy, albeit with a good deal of search effort.

The methodology involved the estimation of labour income from the basic sources in census years and then inferring gross domestic product from the labour income: the latter comprised by far predominant part of gross domestic product in these industries as will be seen shortly. The estimates for 1926 are the official material. While the censuses were taken first in 1871 and then every ten years thereafter, the income data belong to the preceding calendar year.

The census year estimates of labour income are obtained by multiplication of numbers occupied in the industries that fall into these two groups by a measure of per unit labour income: these estimates are made at the ultimate level of detail obtainable from the census information. The occupation of each member of the working population was obtained in every census; wage earnings were also obtained for individuals in the working population, employed on wages, in the censuses of 1900, 1910 and 1920. (The same data were available in the 1931 census and some use was made of them. In addition, the 1931 census had a classification of gainfully occupied persons that was specifically labelled "Gainfully occupied, 10 years of age and over by industry, selected occupations and sex for Canada and the provinces". The "selected" non-agricultural occupations were quite comprehensive.)

Information on the activities covered in these two groups, the nature of the material available, and the estimation process will be described in substantial detail for 1910; since similar categories were covered in other census years it is not necessary to deal with them in the same detail but each census year will be dealt with separately. The reason for starting with 1910 is that, for that year, the information available is given in more detail and in a more directly usable form than the other years.

In 1910 occupational and wage-earner data were collected and tabulated in great detail. Self-employed persons and wage-earners were clearly identified separately. It was most important that the so-called occupational classification was, in fact, almost like an industrial classification and could be very readily made to conform with the 1948 standard industrial classification which was the basis of the project's classification of manufacturers. Such a classification meant that persons in occupations of a general nature are assigned to the industry in which they work. For instance, general labourers are distributed among mining, manufacturing (several division), construction (several divisions), transportation and so on; stenographers and typists were one of the few occupations that had an unassigned group (see below).

The occupational data for 1910 were published in a volume of the 1911 census: none of the wage-earner data for 1910 of the 1911 census was published. However, the wage-earner data had been tabulated in great detail, at the time of the census, in manuscript form of several thousand pages. These wage-earner data had been placed on microfilm of which the project obtained its own copies; in addition, not all of the occupational data tabulations had been published and the full tabulations of them were also obtained on microfilm.

Since gross domestic product estimates for the wholesale and retail trade group and the community, business and personal service group were essentially to be derived from estimates of labour income, including an imputed income for the self-employed, it was important that there be a clear demarcation between those persons engaged in these industry groups and those persons performing somewhat like functions but who were attached to other industries and whose productive contribution had been covered in these other industries. Accordingly, a complete assignment of the entire labour force to the industries of the project, that was both exclusive and exhaustive was done. It was possible to match the occupational data to the project's industry grouping quite accurately, owing to the so-called occupational distribution of the labour force being essentially an industrial distribution. Exceptions to there being a complete industrial distribution occurred in the case of typists and stenographers for whom there was a single n.o.s. (not otherwise specified) category, in addition to some specific assignments to particular industries.

Without being exhaustive, the following listings indicate the type of service actively covered in each of the main groups.

1. Trade, Wholesale and Retail

These two categories, so named, were elaborated in great detail by type of wholesale or retail business. Insignificant numbers of "pharmacists" and "purchasing agents n.s." were included; more importantly, 218 males and 1,767 females in the typing and stenographic category were assigned to this group.

2. Community, Business and Personal Services

This group included several subordinate categories as follows:

(a)   Business and Professional Service
        Accountancy — accountants
        Advertising — bill posters
        Engineering and scientific services
            electrical engineers
            civil engineers, etc.
            geologists
            architects
            draftsmen
            metallurgists and assayers
        Law — lawyers and notaries
            clerks and stenographers
            law students

(b)   Health and Welfare
        Physicians and surgeons
        Dentists
        Oculists
        Trained nurses
        Veterinary surgeons
        Bacteriologists
        Hospital and asylum workers
        Charitable institution workers
        Office employees

(c)   Religion
        Clergymen
        Church workers
        Missionaries
        Salvation Army workers
        Sextons
        Janitors (estimated)

(d)   Other Community or Public Service
        Authors
        Journalists, editors, reporters
        Painters and artists
        Designers and sculptors
        Naturalists

(e)   Recreation
        Theatres and theatrical services
            actors
            various theatrical employees

showmen n.s.
theatre and playhouse employees
Other recreation
athletic pursuits
musicians and teachers of music

(f)   Personal and Domestic Service n.e.s.
Barbers, hairdressers
Hotel and saloon keepers
Restaurant workers
Domestic service
chauffeurs
housekeepers
servants, n.s.
coach and livery
Other domestic service
charworkers
bootblacks
porters
watchmen
cooks
janitors
other domestic and personal
Custom and repair
laundries and laundry workers
undertakers
Photographers (from professional)

Labour Income 1910-11

In order to give some dimensions to order of size of these groups, the numbers engaged and labour income in 1910 in wage form or imputed, by the above groupings, is given in the next succeeding table.

Two points of elaboration may be helpful.

First, while a large proportion of the typists and stenographers were assigned to the particular industries in which they were employed under the designation "office employees" and while a special specific allocation was made to law, there were 1,603 males and 9,754 females assigned the designation "Stenographers and typists n.o.s.". It is not clear to which industries these persons should be assigned despite the fact that they are classified with the general group designation "professional". Our best guess was that they were probably employed pretty much across the board with perhaps some emphasis on the financial sector. In any event, the proportions of these particularly designated persons assigned to wholesale and retail trade were the same as the proportions assigned to retail and wholesale trade for 1930-31 in the 1931 census: in that census there was a complete assignment of stenographers and typists by industry in the numbers in total of 3,531 males and 64,993 females in the stenography and typing occupational category.

Second, the wage-earner data collected in the census applied only to persons employed on

Service Sector	Numbers Engaged	Total Labour Income ($000)
Wholesale and retail trade	247,435	163,556
Community, business and personal services		
Business and professional services	16,090	20,632
Health and welfare	34,466	27,363
Religion	13,747	11,028
Other community services	2,194	3,140
Recreation	8,514	5,097
Personal and domestic services n.e.s.	188,998	66,364
Total community, business and personal services	264,009	133,624

wage or salary. In addition, to the wage-earners for whom wages were reported there were smallish numbers of wage-earners for whom wages had not been reported and, much more important for these two groups, quite large numbers of self-employed persons for whom no income was reported. From the wage-earner data, average earnings per worker could be calculated for each of the classes for whom wage-earners were reported separately. There were separate data for males and females.

The numbers of gainfully occupied males and females employed which included all wage-earners plus the self-employed (own accounts) were then matched as nearly as possible with the average wage earnings of the comparable categories for whom wages were reported.

The way in which the data for three retail trade categories were available may illustrate the nature of the procedures.

Data are given for male wage earners and male gainfully occupied in each of three categories, *viz.* (1) Clothing, men's furnishing; (2) Coal and wood yards; (3) Dry goods.

(1) Male workers in men's clothing stores 1910-11

(a) Wage earners

Category of Worker	Number of Wage Earners:		Average Earnings of Wage Earners Reporting Earnings ($)
	With Wages Reported	Wages Not Reported	
Managers and superintendents	114	23	1,395
Salesmen and buyers	1,436	147	705
Office employees	49	3	867
Messengers	47	2	483

(b) Gainfully occupied

Category of Worker	Number Gainfully Occupied	Average Earnings ($)	Total Labour Income ($)
Managers, superintendents and salesmen	1,759	756	1,329,804
Office employees	55	867	47,685
Messengers and labourers	48	483	23,184
Own accounts	1,261	*(756)	953,316
Total	3,123		$2,353,989

* The own accounts were assigned an average labour earnings equal to a weighted average of the average earnings of wage earners in the managers and superintendents and the salesmen categories.

(2)   Male workers, coal and wood stores 1910-11

(a) Wage earners

Category of Worker	Number of Wage Earners:		Average Earnings of Wage Earners Reporting Earnings ($)
	With Wages Reported	Wages Not Reported	
Managers and superintendents	254	17	1,076
Inspectors	4	0	750
Salesmen	537	55	730
Office employees	189	10	814
Carters and labourers	2,349	145	518

(b) Gainfully occupied

Category of Worker	Number Gainfully Occupied	Average Earnings ($)	Total Labour Income ($)
Managers, superintendents, inspectors, salesmen	878	841	738,398
Office employees	204	814	166,056
Carters and labourers	2,505	518	1,297,590
Own accounts	1,203	*841	1,011,723
Total	4,790		$3,213,767

(3)   Male workers, dry goods 1910-11

(a) Wage earners

| | Number of Wage Earners: | | Average Earnings of Wage Earners |
| | With Wages | Wages Not | Reporting Earnings |
Category of Worker	Reported	Reported	($)
Managers and superintendents	488	45	1,550
Salesmen and buyers	6,675	629	696
Office employees	369	31	771
Messengers	482	35	737

(b) Gainfully occupied

| | Number Gainfully | Average Earnings | Total Labour Income |
Category of Worker	Occupied	($)	($)
Salesmen and buyers	1,568	*745	1,168,160
Skilled employees	6,647	*745	4,952,015
Office employees	408	771	314,568
Messengers and labourers	427	737	314,699
Own accounts	2,945	*745	2,194,025
Total	11,995		8,943,467

* These average earnings are weighted averages of wage earners in the managers and superintendents and the salesmen categories.

Some check on the propriety of the incomes implied for valuing the services of the self-employed can be made by use of data from the official national accounts. (I hope this is not just a case of the blind following the blind.)

In retail trade, for 1910, the project estimate, from census material, was that labour income of the self-employed, excluding the allocated stenographers and typists, was 41.43 million dollars out of a total labour income including the self-employed of 119.90 million dollars yielding a ratio of labour income of self-employed to all labour income in retail trade of 0.3455. The official national accounts report labour income and property income separately for incorporated business and a single figure for all income of unincorporated business. If one divides the aggregate income of unincorporated business into labour income and property income in the same proportions as recorded for the corporate sector a comparison of the resulting income for the self-employed with total labour income including wage-earners and self-employed, one gets the following ratios for 1926 to 1930.

Ratio of Labour Income of
Self-Employed to Total
Labour Income, Retail Trade

Year	Ratio
1926	0.3418
1927	0.3514
1928	0.3582
1929	0.3650
1930	0.3298

These results are, at least, not disturbing and, at most, reassuring.

The same calculations done in the same way for wholesale trade yield a different picture.

For the project a labour income of the self employed of 12.05 million dollars out of a total labour income for wholesale trade of 42.59 million dollars yield a ratio of self employed labour income to total labour income of 0.2830.

The comparable ratios derived from the national accounts for 1926 to 1930 were much lower as follows.

Ratio of Labour Income of
Self-Employed to Total
Labour Income, Retail Trade

Year	Ratio
1926	0.0952
1927	0.0970
1928	0.0979
1929	0.0974
1930	0.0943

The wholesale trade comparisons seem to imply either that the 1910 estimates are much too high or that there was a great decline in the proportion of own accounts in the total labour utilization in the wholesale trade industry between 1910 and the late 1920s. The latter interpretation is supported if a simple count of the number of own accounts in the labour force in wholesale trade in 1910 is compared with a similar count for the labour force for 1930-31 as obtained in the census of 1931. The proportions of self-employed in the total labour complement in wholesale trade in 1930-31 was of a much, much smaller order than in 1910-11. In contrast, there were not great changes in these proportions of numbers engaged in retail trade between 1910-11 and 1930-31.

One final comparison is to consider wholesale and retail trade together. For these two trade groups together the ratio of labour income of the self-employed to total labour income for all gainfully occupied persons in 1910-11 was 0.3292. The ratios derived from the official national accounts were as follows.

Ratios of Labour Income of
Self-Employed to Total Labour
Income, Wholesale and Retail Trade

Year	Ratio
1926	0.2643
1927	0.2752
1928	0.2825
1929	0.2891
1930	0.2595

Sources: for these immediately preceding data: Data for 1910-11 prepared for this project from microfilm identified above. Data from official national accounts: DBS *National Income and Expenditure Accounts, Vol. 1, The Annual Estimates 1926-1974*, Tables 28 to 31.

It was mentioned above that the salaries and wages of the stenographers and typists who were specially assigned to trade from the undistributed group given in the source were not included in the data from which these calculations for 1910-11 were made. The reason for the exclusion is that from the way the original unassigned group was presented in the source it was difficult to make much judgement of its characteristics. And, in any event, the labour income of these stenographers assigned to trade was less than one million dollars.

A valuation of labour for own accounts was made differently for different occupational categories as follows.

For wholesale and retail trade the unit labour income of own accounts was obtained as the weighted sum of unit labour income for managers and superintendents and salesmen supplemented in some cases by data from other categories of wage earners.

For various categories in the community and personal service group two main alternative procedures were used. For many categories, such as personal and domestic service, broken into many subcategories and tabulated separately for males and females, all gainfully occupied were attributed an average labour income equal to the average labour income of the employees on wages or salary: included here were categories like barbering and hairdressing; hotels and lodging houses; restaurant, cafe, tavern workers; private domestic services, etc. Account was taken of weeks employed of wage-earners.

In the case of own accounts in the main professions a different procedure was used. In the 1940s and 1950 DBS did studies by general questionnaire of some professions. Among these were:

DBS *Survey of Incomes in the Legal Profession in Canada, 1946 to 1948*.

DBS *Survey of Incomes in the Medical Profession in Canada, 1939 and 1944 to 1946*.

DBS *Survey of Incomes in the Profession of Dentistry for Canada, 1941-44*.

From these reports it was possible to get ratios of labour earnings for those persons in independent professional practice to those professional persons engaged on salary or wage. These ratios for the three above groups were as follows.

Ratios of Unit Labour Income of Professionals in
Independent Professional Practice to Professionals
on Wage or Salary, from DBS Survey Data

Profession	Ratio
Law	1.0733
Medicine	1.2195
Dentistry	1.0603

The unit labour income of the self-employed in each of these three professions for 1910-11 was obtained by multiplying the average unit labour income of those persons employed on wage or salary by the ratios of income from independent practice to income from full time salary.

For occupations like engineering, architecture and the like there were large numbers on salary or wage in 1910-11 and the self-employed persons were attributed the same labour income as the full-time person on wage or salary.

Labour Income 1920-21

Numbers Engaged and Labour Income,
Selected Private Service Sectors, 1920-21

Service Sector	Numbers Gainfully Occupied	Total Labour Income ($000)
Wholesale and retail trade	313,355	351,546
Community, business and personal services		
Business and professional services	21,702	38,920
Health and welfare	62,931	66,435
Religion	15,430	29,690
Other community services	4,552	6,786
Recreation	15,633	17,886
Personal and domestic services n.e.s.	207,524	113,202
Total community, business and personal services	327,772	272,920

The data on labour income in 1920-21 obtained in the census of 1921 were derived from two sources as follows: the occupational data came from DBS *Census of Canada 1921* Vol. IV *Occupations*; the wage earner data were obtained from microfilm tapes on which extensive unpublished tabulations of wage and salary data were recorded. The published wage-earner data covering only centers having 20,000 or more person were not comprehensive and hence the need for the tapes resulted.

The dimensions of the two groups are illustrated by the preceding information on numbers engaged and labour incomes.

There was a good deal of similarity between the available data in 1921 and those of the census of 1911 at a somewhat less detailed level than was basically available in the 1911 census and with somewhat different industry grouping. There was a classification of the gainfully occupied that was quite like an industrial classification and a very much similar classification of workers on wages with numbers employed and the total wage bill. The latter permitted the calculation of an average wage or salary at a level of substantial detail. In the gainfully occupied data, labourers, clerks and office employees were assigned to particular occupational-industrial groups; there were relatively small numbers assigned to unspecified industries, 129,681 persons in all, of whom 91,511 were labourers n.o.s., these labourers undoubtedly being largely assignable to the construction industry, and 33,644 were office clerks n.o.s. who were probably quite widely assignable. The wage earner data were classified both on the occupational-industrial basis and an industrial-occupational basis: in a few instances resort to the latter classification yielded information not available in the other classification.

In the regrouping of some of the 1920-21 occupational-industrial assignments to match the 1911 assignments, use was made of the very detailed assignments of occupation by industry in the 1931 census: the data of the 1931 census supplemented the data of the 1911 census in making these reassignments.

As usual, there were large numbers of own-accounts in the wholesale and retail industries. These own accounts were assigned a labour income per person based on the average labour income of the wage earners in each of wholesale and retail trade separately, and for males and females separately, in the wage earner classes (i) salesmen, (ii) inspectors, samplers, gaugers, (iii) managers and superintendents, (iv) agents, canvassers and collectors.

The various categories of the community, business and personal service group in the source were not separated in the individual categories of the numbers of gainfully occupied persons in exactly the same manner as in 1910-11: various regrouping of the categories was required. This reassignment was done on the basis of the 1911 census assignments, the assignments of McInnis in his industrial classification for 1921 based on the DBS standard industrial classification of 1948, and, in a few instances, on the basis of the 1931 census classification.

Such further problems as there were for 1920-21 were handled in much the same way as for 1910-11. Accordingly, further elaboration of the 1920-21 estimating procedure will not be helpful.

Note: it is to be noted that the number of weeks employed was collected in this census: there was not a significant amount of shortfall in weeks worked in the year below what might be expected for holiday time for these categories of trade and community, personal and business service.

Labour Income 1900

The data for 1900, derived from the census of 1901, were obtained from two bulletins of the Census and Statistics Office of Canada: Census of Canada, 1901, Bulletin I: *Wage-Earners by Occupation*; Bulletin XI: *Occupations of the People*.

The first bulletin gives number of wage earners by occupation and the labour earnings of those wage earners for whom wages were reported. The second bulletin gives the number of gainfully occupied persons classified by occupation.

Again to give dimensions to the figures, the figures on numbers of gainfully occupied and labour income for 1900 are presented forthwith.

Numbers Engaged and Labour Income
Selected Private Service Sectors, 1900-01

Service Sector	Numbers Gainfully Occupied	Total Labour Income ($000)
Wholesale and retail trade	123,507	52,443
Community, business and personal services		
Business and professional services	12,313	9,900
Health and welfare	20,287	12,074
Religion	19,585	8,835
Other community services	2,870	1,717
Recreation	5,985	2,358
Personal and domestic services, n.e.s.	162,008	36,139
Total community, business and personal services	223,048	71,023

It is to be noted that the category "Religion" includes 7,623 nuns who were labelled "teachers" with total salaries of $1,875,258.

The occupational classifications of both wage earners and the gainfully occupied did have elements of industrial groupings in it but still required a good deal of reassignment of workers in order to match the industrial classification of 1911 and the comparably matched classification of 1921. The task then became one of reassignment of gainfully occupied persons as reported for 1901 into the industrial classification that matches the 1910-11 classification and then assigning a labour income to these gainfully occupied persons. The following material just deals with the problems of achieving these goals. These problems are best dealt with under a number of separate headings.

Point 1. The labourers, for the most part, were not assigned to specific industrial groups with which we are dealing on the basis of the 1931 complete industrial assignment: the same proportion of the labourers was assigned to an industry as was assigned in 1931.

Point 2. Office employees, which for 1901 comprised (i) stenographers and typists, (ii) office and other clerks and (iii) bookkeepers, were distributed among industrial groupings, and hence to the groups now being dealt with in the same proportions as they were assigned among industrial groups in the 1910-11 distribution.

Point 3. The problem of assignment of gainfully occupied persons from the occupational classification of the 1901 census to an industrial classification comparable to 1910-11 was quite similar to the problem of reassignment of gainfully occupied persons in 1920-21. Therefore the reassignment of 1920-21 was used as a guide in the reassignment of the 1900-01 gainfully occupied persons to industrial groupings.   It will be remembered that the reassignment for 1920-21 had been helped by use of the 1931 occupation by industry classification.

Point 4. In an industrial classification a great many occupations may be represented in a single industry and as a counterpart the members of some occupations are dispersed among different industries: for instance, there are cooks in lumber camps; many industries have accountants; many industries have telephone operators; wholesale trade may have coopers; and so on.   The reassignment of the gainfully occupied in 1900-01 to the industry groups and categories that we are dealing with here could only be done for the main occupations assignable to an industry.   Once this main reassignment was done it was then necessary to add to each industry category a number of gainfully occupied persons that would represent all of the minor occupations that appear in an industry.   This assignment of minor numbers of persons in particular occupations to an industry characterized, in the main, by other occupations was done by assigning persons in minor occupations to major industries on the basis of the proportions from these minor occupations that appeared in the major industries in 1931.   The persons from these minor occupations were, of course, assigned the labour income received by persons in those occupations in 1900-01.

The size of this adjustment of labour income for minor occupations based on the 1931 census data is shown by the following data.

Ratio of Minor Occupation Labour Income to Total Occupation Labour Income, 1900-01 Adjustment

Industry Category	Male	Female
Retail trade	0.0665	0.0305
Wholesale trade	0.0630	0.0969
Business and professional services	0.1054	0.0161
Health and welfare	0.0810	0.1109
Religion	0.0253	0.1272
Other community services	0.0509	0.0694
Recreation	0.1138	0.0658
Personal and domestic services n.e.s.	0.1299	0.0381

Point 5. Own accounts were calculated as the difference between total gainfully occupied for a group or category and the total number of wage earners for that group of category.   Labour income for own accounts was calculated by the same method as that used in 1911.

Point 6. The data on number of wage earners and their labour income was given in much finer subdivisions of wage earners than was the case for the gainfully occupied persons.   Hence, several categories of wage earners might match up with one category of gainfully occupied persons.   Sometimes the matching was easy; sometimes the matching was quite difficult.

Labour Income 1890

The census of persons of 1891 obtained data on the occupation of everyone among the gainfully occupied; unlike later censuses it did not obtain wage earner data from individuals. Consequently, labour income of those industrial groups being covered here had to be obtained from other sources. The main sources of data on labour income in 1890-91 then became:

Census of Canada 1901, Vol. III, *Census of Manufactures*;
Census of Canada 1891, Vol. III, *Census of Manufactures*;
Census of Canada 1891, Vol. II for "occupations";
Census of Canada 1891, Vol. IV, Data on comparison of manufacturers wages 1880
    and 1890;
Government of Ontario, *Report of the Ontario the Bureau of Industries 1899*, in
    Sessional Papers of Ontario 1890, Vol. 22, Part 7.

Other source material such as that in later censuses was also used.

The figures on gainfully occupied and labour income in 1890-91 follow.

Numbers Engaged and Labour Income
Selected Private Service Sectors, 1890-91

Service Sector	Numbers Gainfully Employed	Total Labour Income ($000)
Wholesale and retail trade	103,422	42,442
Community, business and personal services		
Business and professional services	8,857	7,479
Health and welfare	10,871	7,686
Religion	12,063	6,995
Other community services	2,194	1,280
Recreation	4,100	1,731
Personal and domestic services, n.e.s.	139,973	28,959
Total community, business and personal services	178,058	54,130

The problem of reassigning gainfully occupied persons as given in the data on occupations in the census to the industrial classes with which we are dealing was much like that of 1900. Insofar as the problems were similar, the procedures of estimation were similar and there is no point in repeating the description of what was done here: it appears in the write up on the 1900-01 data. There were, however, a few new problems with which we now deal.

In a number of cases occupational categories reported separately in later censuses were grouped together in 1891. For example, lawyers and notaries were reported together as one figure for each of male and female gainfully occupied. The numbers were split between lawyers and notaries in the same proportions as in the 1901 census when lawyers and notaries were reported separately. Similarly, bookkeepers and accountants were reported as one number in 1891. They were divided into bookkeepers and accountants in the same proportions as in 1901 when they were reported separately. Likewise, clerks and copyists, reported together in 1891, were separated between bank clerks and office and other clerks in the 1901 ratios. Furthermore, "porters and helpers (in stores, etc.)" from the 1891 census were divided in the 1901 ratios into personnel in the trade category and personnel in the domestic and personal service category. Yet again, "watchmen, policemen and detectives" in 1891 were separated into watchmen (assigned to the domestic and personal service category) and policemen and detectives (who are mostly public employees). Finally, there are other similar cases but complete elaboration is probably not fruitful: the principles of division may be seen. In some cases, the divisions described immediately above were to enable assignment of an individual group to particular industrial categories; in other cases, the divisions were among occupations within an industry and thus the assignment of different labour incomes to the different occupational groups.

On the matter of the assignment of occupational groups to "industries" we finish by repeating the statement in the write-up on 1901 that some occupations appear in several industries and some industries involve the employment of persons of many occupations. The method of assignments of relevant occupational groups to particular industries in 1891 was done, with only rare exception, on the basis of the proportional assignments in 1901. In exceptional cases resort was had to the splendid assignments of 1931 (on which many of the assignments of 1901 itself had been made).

Next, the assignment of labour income to the gainfully occupied persons must be dealt with. Unfortunately, censuses before 1901 did not elicit wage earner information in the general population. Therefore, one had to have resort to other sources for such information. Fortunately, there were a number of sets of other wage data that made comparisons between labour income in 1890 and 1900. Equally fortunately, the decade comparisons derived from different sources were quite consistent one with the other.

There were a number of sources of wage data. Perhaps the most important single source of wage data relevant to 1890 was that collected by the Ontario Bureau of Industries (OBI) (administered by the Ontario Department of Agriculture). OBI collected data annually for several thousand persons from employers and employees beginning with 1884 and carrying through for 1889 (after which year, unfortunately, the collection of such data ended). For 1889 data were collected from 549 employers covering 17,328 workers for weekly wages and from 3,814 workers (3,529 males and 285 females), the latter collected by 22 special agents and covering hours of work per week, days worked in the year, yearly wages and for comparative purposes with company reports, weekly wages. This is a large sample of employees. The data collected directly from the individuals were the most useful since they had yearly wages by occupation.

Another useful source was provided by the census of manufacturers in which numbers employed and wage bills were available by industrial detail for both 1890 and 1900.

A third source on civil service salaries was available in the reports of the auditor general.

Schoolteachers salaries, by type of school, were available annually for Ontario. They were used for comparative purposes only since the data for education were not included in the groups being dealt with here.

Much use was made of the OBI data for Ontario: it was necessary to adapt the Ontario wages to obtain wages for all Canada since Ontario wages were the highest among the provinces (with a few exceptions such as male school teachers in Quebec).

Various sources are cited in HSC, along with reproduction of some data.

It may be stated at the outset that the inference from all data is that there was not much change in annual labour earnings between 1890 and 1900.

Various techniques were used to derive the 1890 labour income estimates from data of the above sources.

First, the employment and labour income data of the census of manufacturers were used to see how 1890 compared with 1900. A direct comparison of average labour income would not have been of value since the two censuses of manufacturers differed in a number of respects such as: the census of 1900 covered, in the main, only businesses with five or more employees while that of 1890 covered businesses of any number of employees; certain hand-trades, e.g. blacksmiths, which were included in the census of 1890 were not included in the census of 1900; the census of 1900 explicitly included self employed on salary while it is not clear that such workers were included in 1890. In order to try to eliminate the effects of such differences in trying to make use of the 1900 data the following use was made of the 1900 data.

The purpose of the exercise is to estimate how much the OBI labour earnings for Ontario for 1889, which we take as being the equivalent of 1890, should be adjusted to make them applicable to all Canada. One could compare the average labour income per unit of labour for Ontario, from the 1890-91 census of manufactures, with the average labour income for all Canada for 1890-91 from the same census to get an adjustment factor to extrapolate from the Ontario figures to the figures for all Canada — in fact, average census of manufactures labour income for Ontario in 1890-91 was $299 and for all Canada $272. The differential exhibited overstates the extent to which Ontario labour income per worker exceeds the comparable Canadian labour income in other occupations than manufacturing, since labour income per worker is higher in large establishments than small establishments and Ontario had a considerably higher proportion of large establishments than the rest of the country. The 1900 retabulation of the 1890 data yielded the following averages for all Canada.

Average Labour Earnings 1890 in Manufacturing,
1900 tabulations, all Canada

	Works Employing Less Than 5 Persons	Works Employing 5 or More Employees	All Works
Number of employees	97,562	272,025	369,595
Average earnings	$ 217	$ 291	$ 272

There is not a comparable tabulation for Ontario for 1890.

The 1900 census of manufactures covered (with few exceptions) only establishments with five or more employees, yielding the following results.

Average Labour Earnings, 1900, in
Manufacturing Establishments Employing
5 Persons or More, Wage Labour Only

	Ontario	Canada
Number of persons employed	142,330	300,026
Average earnings	$ 307	$ 292

If the average earnings for all workers in manufacturing for establishments of all sizes in Ontario in 1890 of $299 (as noted above) was projected to all Canada on the basis of the ratio of

Canada unit labour earnings, 1900 ÷ Ontario unit labour earnings, 1900 = 292 ÷ 307

the unit labour income for all Canada in manufacturing would have been (292 ÷ 307) x 299 = $284. It seems reasonable to attribute the shortfall of the actual average unit labour earnings in 1890 for all Canada of $272 — $12 below the projected $284 — to the fact that Ontario's proportion of establishments of five or more employees was substantially higher than the Canadian average. Consequently, it seems appropriate to transform the Ontario OBI wage data for 1889 to the Canada levels on the basis of the ratio of unit Canadian labour earnings in manufacturing in 1900 (for establishments with five or more employees) to similar earnings in Ontario. This would mean multiplying the OBI annual unit labour earnings by the ratio of 292 to 307, or 0.951. (In fact, in the project, the OBI estimates were multiplied by 0.958 which was the ratio of the actual average unit labour earnings for all Canada of $272 to the projected unit labour earnings of $284 which ratio presumably measures Ontario's higher unit wages attributable to largeness of scale. However, whatever the reason for what was done the result is practically the same.)

Note that the unit labour earnings that are being developed are those for trade and service activities for much of which scale is not important.

One other point to be noted from the above data is that the unit labour earnings for all Canada for establishments with five or more employees, as they are measured here, are $291 for 1890 and $292 for 1900 (wage earners only for 1900). The 1900 figures do not include salaried workers. If they and the salaried self employed are included, the all Canada average for 1900 becomes $329 (See Census of Canada 1901, Vol. III, *Manufactures*, Table XIX as well as Tables VIII and II). The correct unbiased relationship of unit labour earnings in 1900 to similar earnings in 1890 is somewhere between $329 to $291 and $292 to $291. The reason that the ratio of the unit labour earnings of $329 for all workers in 1900 is biased upward in the comparison with 1890 is that all self-employed persons on salary (and perhaps even some with an imputed earning) are included in 1900 and it is doubtful whether many (if any) proprietors were included in 1890: the proprietors on salary had considerably above average labour earnings. In addition, it was asserted at the time the census was taken that a number of very small activities that were scarcely even manufacturing had been included.

The average labour earnings for all reported persons in the census of manufactures 1880, 1890 and 1900 have also been calculated when establishments are classified by size of sales. The following are the results.

Average Labour Earnings of All
Reported Persons, By Size of
Establishment Sales, 1881, 1891, 1901
(average earnings in dollars)

Number of Persons in 1901	Establishments By Value of Production	1900	1890	1880
206,331	$50,000 and over	364	337	287
38,814	$25,000 to under $50,000	345	316	265
34,968	$12,000 to under $25,000	320	300	253
56,400	$2,000 to under $12,000	230	249	223
7,522	Under $2,000	87	148	138
344,035	All establishments	329	272	233

It can been seen that there are anomalies for the small companies in 1900, which are no doubt related to the restriction of coverage to establishments employing five persons or more.

With the above background, we now examine the way in which the unit labour earnings were determined for each of the service categories with which we are dealing.

Retail and Wholesale Trade

It was necessary to calculate an average unit labour earnings for each of the occupations in wholesale and retail trade.

From the Ontario OBI reports estimates have been made for unit earnings for Canada in 1890 for the following trade related occupations as now given.

Occupation	Males (16 yrs and older)	Females (16 yrs and older)
	(dollars per annum)	
Salesman	397	221
Bookkeeper	587	282
Office clerk	370	
Deliveryman	*322	
Teamster	*345	
Labourer (general)	283	
Agent	517	

* average of two = 334

These unit labour values were used to estimate aggregate labour income for the occupations to which they applied. In addition, average earnings in 1890, in occupations for which no direct estimate was available in 1890, were inferred from 1900 average earnings for these occupations by attributing a change in unit labour earnings between 1900 and 1890 of the same proportion as the change in labour earnings in closely related occupations for which we have unit labour earnings available for both 1890 and 1900. For instance, average earnings of male salesmen were $397 in 1890 compared with $409 in 1900; it was assumed that the average earnings of retail merchants changed in the same proportion between 1900, for which year we have a reported figure, and 1890 yielding unit labour earnings of $449 for retail merchants in 1890 as compared with $463 in 1900. Thus, changes in labour earnings of salesmen between 1900 and 1890 were used to derive changes in other salesmen-related occupations for whom a direct figure was not available from the OBI data, such as for males in the occupations of auctioneers, hucksters and peddlers, brokers etc. The same principles were followed by using average earnings for bookkeepers, office clerks etc. which were available for both 1900 and 1890 to project the 1900 earnings of related occupations to 1890 if there were no OBI figures for 1890. In this way, the unit labour earnings for the principal occupations in trade in 1890 were obtained; there were minor variations from this procedure in one or two cases but the numbers involved were so small a description of these variations is not warranted.

Finally, there were the additions to be made for the numbers of other personnel not specific to trade. The numbers assigned to trade were based on the 1901 ratios (in turn largely based on 1931). The unit labour earnings were weighted averages of the unit earnings of those persons whose occupations were trade oriented, calculated as described above, for males and females separately and likewise for retail and wholesale trade separately.

The ratios of supplementary personnel to total personnel were as follows.

Ratio of Supplementary Personnel to Total Personnel

Occupation	Males	Females
Retail trade	0.0668	0.0305
Wholesale trade	0.0630	0.0966

Community, Business and Personal Service — Unit Labour Income

Wherever possible, the same techniques as in trade were used. However, unit labour earnings could not be obtained in this manner for many occupations. Where such was the case, the 1890 unit labour earnings for males were calculated as being three percent less than the 1900 earnings, i.e. they were assigned a value equal to 0.97 times the unit labour earnings in 1900. This ratio for 1890 of 0.97 of 1900 unit labour values for males was derived from several sources, such as: salesmen's earnings 1890 were 0.97 salesmen's earnings in 1900 (see work on trade above); schoolteachers salaries, available from provincial education department reports, showed very little change between 1890 and 1900; construction wage rates in the Ottawa and Toronto areas are consistent with the above (HSC 1st edition, Series D485-488); wages of selected occupations as reported by immigration agents in Montreal are also consistent with the above (HSC Series D196-207); auditor general reports of Canada provide similar data for accountants; Ontario Bureau of Industries annual reports on farm labour show practically no change in unit labour earnings 1890 to 1900.

The 1890 unit labour earnings for females were taken as equal to the 1900 earnings, in those cases where there was not a direct OBI figure for 1890, an arrangement justified in the same manner as for males.

The evidence for little change in occupational unit labour earnings between 1890 and 1900 is very strong. It is supported by similar evidence, based on a wider range of data, for the United States. (See *U.S. Historical Statistics, Colonial Times to the Present*, Series D683-926).

Labour Income 1880

The census of persons in 1881, in common with other decennial censuses, obtained the occupation of every gainfully occupied person; wage or labour earnings were not collected in this personal census.

The main source of data for assignment of persons by occupation was the Census of 1881, Vol. II, Table XIII, *Occupations of the People*.

The unit labour earnings were derived from a variety of sources which will be given as the exposition proceeds.

The numbers employed and total labour income in the various groups follow.

Numbers Engaged and Labour
Income, Selected Private Sectors, 1880

Service Sector	Numbers Gainfully Occupied	Total Labour Income ($000)
Wholesale and retail trade	72,317	25,580,408
Community, business and personal services		
Business and professional services	8,600	5,596,806
Health and welfare	8,447	5,448,472
Religion	13,406	5,341,612
Other community services	653	273,712
Recreation	768	208,325
Personal and domestic services	83,526	14,336,177
Total community, business and personal services	115,400	31,205,104

The numbers of gainfully occupied persons in the groups and categories considered here are derived from the table giving the occupations of the working population in the reports on the census of 1881. They are allocated among different "industrial" categories in a manner similar to that used for 1901 — there is little to be gained from a repetition of a description of the process. However, an important difference in 1881 is that the gainful occupations of persons are not given separately for males and females: hence, the allocation of occupations to industrial groupings and the evaluation of unit labour income requires adaptations of procedures.

The main adaptation, insofar as 1890-91 data are used in making inferences about the 1880-81 data, and they are used extensively, is to put the males and females together in 1890-91 and then make inferences from the combined data for the 1880-81 situation. The allocation of gainfully occupied to industrial categories thus becomes a matter of allocating males and females jointly.

Unit Labour Incomes — The Derivation

The unit labour incomes assigned for 1880-81 to each of the categories of activities under consideration at present were made equal to 85 percent of the same category of activities in 1890-91. Now, no doubt unit labour earnings for some occupations would be less than 85 percent of the 1890-91 level and some would be more. But the best estimate is that on the average unit labour earnings increased 17 percent between 1880 and 1890 (that is 1880 figures were 85 percent of 1890 figures) and the overstatements resulting from use of this figure would, more or less, be balanced by understatements.

The basis of choice of estimation of 1880 unit labour costs at 85 percent of 1890 costs are the following:

(i) The census of manufactures data for 1880 and 1890 covered manufacturing concerns of all sizes in both cases. Those censuses are, probably, more nearly comparable, one with the other, than either census is with 1900.

From the data given above, in the examination of 1890 data, the following ratios of 1880 unit labour earnings to 1890 labour earnings are derived.

1880 Unit Labour Earning in Manufacturing as a Proportion
of 1890 Unit Labour Earnings for Various Class Sizes

Number of Gainfully Occupied 1880	Size of Establishment By Value of Product ($)	Ratios of 1880 Unit Labour Earnings to 1890 Unit Earnings
53,501	Under 2,000	0.9342
68,208	2,000 to 11,999	0.8956
27,273	12,000 to 24,999	0.8433
22,386	25,000 to 49,999	0.8386
83,526	50,000 and over	0.8516
254,894	All sizes	0.8566

(ii) Ontario teachers salaries show similar changes. One has to be careful in interpreting these data since there was some upgrading of certificate qualifications between 1880 and 1890. However, one might expect the teachers in cities and towns to be more representative of what happened in the occupations under consideration than the teachers in counties.

Ratio of Average Salaries of Teachers in Publicly Supported
Schools in 1880 to Similar Averages 1890 in Ontario

	Ratio
Male teachers, cities	0.8491
Female teachers, cities	0.8286
Male teachers, towns	0.8650
Female teachers, towns	0.8649
Male teachers, counties	0.9820
Female teachers, counties	0.9060

Source of Data: *Report of the Ontario Department of Education,*
Ontario Sessional Papers 1892, *Paper No. 11*, pp. xvi to xvii.

(iii) Immigration reports

The immigration office reports are inconclusive since the do not include data for 1880 and only for Hamilton in 1881. Much of the increase in wage rates in this decade appears to have taken place in these early years for which few data are available.

(iv) The U.S. data are more informative. Before the presentation of the data a word should be given about the relevance of the U.S. data. During the 1880s both Canada and the United States were on the gold standard, which would tend to lead to prices and wages moving together. In addition, U.S. wages changed very little in the 1890s just as Canadian wages changed little. It is in the light of these facts that the U.S. wages are used for support of the Canadian data.

Two principal sets of data are available for the U.S. First, average monthly earnings, with board, of farm labourers in all of the United States increased from $11.70 in the 1880 to $13.93 in 1890 — as a proportion 1880 average earnings were 0.8399 of the 1890 earnings (*U.S. Historical Statistics, Colonial Times to 1970*, Series D705). Second, average annual earnings of non-farm employees in the United States increased from $386 in 1880 to $475 in 1890 — as a proportion 1880 earnings were 0.8126 of 1890 earnings (*U.S. Historical Statistics*, Series D735.)

To repeat, the unit labour earnings for 1880 were calculated at 0.85 of the unit labour earnings in 1890.

Total wages and salaries, as usual, were the product of numbers of persons engaged and unit labour earnings.

Labour Income 1870

The census of persons in 1871 obtained the occupation of every gainfully occupied person and published data on the occupational distribution of the population. These data were the principal source for calculating the industrial distribution of the labour force into the groups that are being dealt with here (Census of 1871, Vol. II, Table XIII, *Occupations of the People*).

The data on wages came from a quite limited number of sources, noted below. But first, the numbers employed and total labour earnings, as recorded in the income statistics calculated herein, are given for the groups involved in this section of our work.

Numbers Employed and Total Labour Income, Selected Private Sectors, 1870

Service Sector	Numbers Gainfully Occupied	Total Labour Income ($000)
Wholesale and retail trade	51,710	16,940,747
Community, business and personal services		
Business and professional services	9,832	5,503,475
Health and welfare	6,106	3,888,833
Religion	8,469	3,254,359
Other community services	641	249,865
Recreation	452	113,664
Personal services, n.e.s.	66,363	10,528,395
Total community, business and personal services	91,863	23,538,591

The method of allocation of gainfully occupied persons from the occupational to an industrial basis was quite similar to that used for 1880-81. There is nothing to be gained by further elaboration.

The method of attributing a labour income to those persons had both similarities to and differences from the method used in 1880-81.

The census of manufactures was the principal data source for a comparison of 1870-71 unit labour earnings with those of 1880-81. Unit labour earnings could be calculated for industrial groups for both years from the separate data for the numbers employed and the total labour bill. The numbers employed were broken down, by industry, into adult males, adult females, boys and girls: fortunately, the proportions of each in particular industries did not seem to vary greatly between 1870-71 and 1880-81. The labour costs were not broken down in like fashion but are just given as one figure for an industry category as a whole. The calculations of the ratio of 1870-71 unit wages to the 1880-81 unit wages were made for 22 different industries: these ratios varied all the way from values greater than one for three industries to values less than 0.9 for five industries; the remainder clustered with values between 0.9 and 1.0. The actual average figure for all industries appeared to be as good a ratio as any of the ratio of 1870-71 unit wages to 1880-81 unit wages. That figure was 0.93.

The census of manufactures data provide the principal measure available of unit labour earnings in 1870-71 compared with 1880-81. Two other sources of less reliable data are available in wages reported by immigration agencies and school teacher salaries in Ontario. Both of these sources suggest some increase in unit labour earnings between 1870-71 and 1880-81. The immigration agency data are not very precise; the Ontario school teacher data may be more reliable, but there are questions about them. The ratios of 1880 teachers salaries to 1870 salaries follow.

Ratio of Average Salaries of Teachers in Common Schools in
1870 to Similar Averages in 1880, in Ontario

Number of Teachers 1870	Sex and Location of Teachers	Ratio
66	Males, cities	0.8035
187	Females, cities	0.7130
118	Males, towns	0.8546
222	Females, towns	0.8828
2,845	Males, counties	0.6806
1,893	Females, counties	0.7759
84	Males, villages	no separate data in 1880
110	Females, villages	no separate data in 1880

Source: Ontario Sessional Papers, 1871-72, *Paper No. 3, Report of the Minister of Education.*

It is hard to tell what to make of the school teacher data. It is of interest that the counties, which support such a high number of the teachers and show the largest proportional increase between 1870 and 1880, showed much the smallest proportional increase between 1880 and 1890. It should be noted that the data for 1870 include Roman Catholic Schools; the data for 1880 may also but teachers in Roman Catholic separate schools in 1872 numbered 254 according to the Report of the Department of Education for 1900, while 592 teachers are designated as Roman Catholic in the Department of Education report for 1870.

Robert Olley systematized the reports of wages in the construction industry made by the immigration agents. It must be regarded as notional rather than being precise. Such as it is, however, it yielded the following results as Olley calculates them. (Robert Edward Olley, *Construction Wage Rates in Ontario 1864-1903.* M.A. thesis, Queen's University, 1961.)

The reasons for choosing the years herein shown are these. First, the immigration agent reports between 1866 and 1871 did not contain useful material: 1866 has been included because, as can be seen, wages rose significantly between 1866 and 1871 and it is possible that wages rose from 1870, our first year, to 1871. Second, 1873 is included because it was a peak year in the boom after 1870. Third, data are lacking for 1880 and so data for 1881 are given; 1883 is included because again there was some upward movement from 1881 to 1883.

The movement of these construction wage rates corresponds much more closely with the unit labour earnings of the census of manufactures than with the school teachers salaries.

U.S. wage data did not appear to be of comparative usefulness since U.S. wages were still much inflated from the Civil War and the U.S. had not yet returned to the gold standard.

From the foregoing, the most relevant and precise estimate appeared to be that obtained from the census of manufactures. Accordingly, calculations of 1870-71 trade and service unit labour earnings were that they were 0.93 of the 1880-81 earnings, which is equivalent to unit labour earnings increasing 7.5 percent between 1870 and 1880.

The final procedures, then, for calculation of aggregate labour income in the trade and service sectors being dealt with at this point were the following.

Olley's Measures of Daily Wage Rates in Dollars Per Day in Ontario
in the Construction Trades Based on Immigration Agent Reports

Year	Brick-layers and Masons	Carpenters	Labourers	Painters	Plasterers	Stone-Cutters
1866	1.77	1.32	—	1.28	1.39	1.74
1871	2.25	1.63	1.25	1.38	1.63	2.13
1873	2.85	1.50	1.40	1.56	1.76	2.75
1881	2.21	1.68	1.21	1.50	1.82	2.68
1883	2.60	1.85	1.35	1.50	1.69	2.68

Source: Olley, documented above.

As in 1880 the occupational distribution of gainfully occupied persons was done for men and women together as they were not given separately by sex in the census. The unit labour earnings were then calculated, occupation by occupation, by multiplying the 1880 unit labour values by 0.93. These occupational unit labour values were then multiplied by the numbers in each occupation as assigned to particular industries. Some occupations were assigned to only one industrial group; some occupations were assigned to a number of occupational groups in the same proportions as used in immediately successive censuses. In addition, additions to particular industrial groups were made by adding the widely common supplementary activities for each industry in the same proportion as in 1880 and valuing the services of these supplementary workers at a common unit value equal to 0.93 of the 1880 values.

It is apparent that unit labour values for various occupations would not have varied in the same proportion between 1870 and 1880 and that the procedure followed herein does violence to this fact: some unit labour earnings would have varied more than the average and some less. However, it will be noted also that a distinct unit labour costs was retained in 1870 for each occupation. Thus, the occupational weighting (by numbers) in 1870 is by the numbers in the occupation as derived from the 1871 census.

Gross Domestic Product at Factor Cost

The data on non-labour income in these sectors for the period 1870 to 1926 are so limited that it is not possible to derive direct estimates of such income. The best that can be done is to compare non-labour income with labour income in the early years of the official estimates. Owing to the effects of the depression of the 1930s and the wartime years of the 1940s, which may be expected to be atypical years, the investigations herein were limited to the relationship between labour income and gross domestic product for the years 1926 to 1930 — inclusion of even the latter year may be questionable.

The relevant quantitative data are taken from the official national accounts of Canada. The industrial distribution of income is given in four tables: gross domestic product at factor cost; wages, salaries and supplementary labour income of persons on wage or salary; profits (in the incorporated sector) and other investment income; net income of unincorporated business, industry rent.

From the foregoing, an estimate of labour income by industry was obtained by attributing the same proportion of net income in unincorporated business to labour income as was true of the corporate sector and adding it to the wage and salary bill actually given separately for these industries.

The labour income and gross domestic product for each of wholesale trade, retail trade and community business and personal service, for 1926 to 1930 follow.

Labour Income and GDP at Factor Cost
(values in millions of dollars)

Year:	1926	1927	1928	1929	1930
Wholesale trade					
Labour income	126	134	143	154	159
GDP at factor cost	164	187	195	197	*267
Ratio: labour income to GDP	0.7683	0.7166	0.7333	0.7817	0.5955
Retail trade					
Labour income	275	313	349	389	373
GDP at factor cost	370	409	453	476	476
Ratio: labour income to GDP	0.7432	0.7653	0.7704	0.8172	0.7836
Community, business and personal services					
Labour income	545	568	603	645	630
GDP at factor cost	695	626	673	719	702
Ratio: labour income to GDP	0.9144	0.9073	0.8960	0.8971	0.8974

* The 1930 figure for GDP at factor cost is suspect: it implies a very large capital consumption allowance.

These ratios perhaps overstate the labour income (by a relatively small amount) because an undetermined number of the workers on wage and salary would be employed in the non-corporate sector. Hence, the ratio of the total wage bill of all persons on wage or salary to profits and other investment income might overstate labour's share in unincorporated business. However, this result is not necessarily true since some of the investment income would have belonged to persons in unincorporated businesses.

It is perhaps worth noting that in the post World War II period the ratio of labour income to GDP in wholesale trade was considerably lower than in the 1920s; on the other hand, the share of labour income to GDP in retail trade was actually higher than in the 1920s in several years.

In any event, the decision was made to treat labour income as being a proportion 0.80 of gross domestic product at factor cost in both wholesale and retail trade and as being a proportion 0.90 of labour income in all the community, business and personal service sectors. The rationale of the choice of the last ratio is quite clear from the above data for 1926 to 1930. The rationale of choice of the former ratio (i.e. the ratio for trade) is a little less clear: the initial decision had been to use a ratio of 0.75 for the labour income share of GDP in trade; unfortunately, the reason for making that share 0.80 rather than 0.75 was not recorded in full but I believe that the decision was influenced by Sydney Smith's data on national income which had estimates of entrepreneurial withdrawals in trade (DBS *Monthly Review of Business Statistics*, November, 1943). His entrepreneurial withdrawals plus wages and salaries in trade averaged about 0.80 of GDP for 1926 to 1930. Smith's wages and entrepreneurial withdrawals are from the cited document. A gross domestic product for the Smith data was obtained by adding to his net income originating the implicit figures for capital consumption allowances from the official data. The resultant ratio of wages and salaries plus entrepreneurial withdrawals in trade (note the suspect 1930 figure) are:

	Ratio		Ratio		Ratio
1926	0.7697	1928	0.8307	1930	0.7116
1927	0.8129	1929	0.8537		

The results of all of the foregoing calculations for GDP in these sectors follows.

Labour Income and Gross Domestic Product
at Factor Cost, Selected Years
(value sums in millions of dollars)

	1870	1880	1890	1900	1910	1920	1926
Wholesale and retail trade							
Labour income	16.9	25.6	42.4	52.4	163.6	351.5	—
GDP	21.2	32.0	53.1	65.6	204.4	439.4	534.0
Community, business and personal services							
Labour income	23.8	31.2	54.1	71.0	133.6	272.9	—
GDP	26.5	36.9	60.1	84.5	148.4	303.2	506.0

Bibliography of Sources Cited in Chapter 10

Census of Canada: the data from every census gave occupations and, after 1900, also employment and earnings: 1871, Vol. II; 1881, Vol II; 1891, Vol. II; 1901, Bulletin I and Bulletin IX; 1911, Vol. 6 and DBS census microfilm; 1921, Vol. 4 and DBS microfilm; 1931, Vols. 5 and 7.

DBS, *Census of Manufactures*, from Censuses of Canada for 1870-71, 1880-81, 1890-91, 1900-01.

DBS, *Canada Year Book*, especially for 1932.

DBS, *Survey of Incomes in the Legal Profession in Canada, 1946 to 1948*.

DBS, *Survey of Incomes in the Medical Profession in Canada, 1939 and 1944 to 1946*.

DBS, *Survey of Incomes in the Profession of Dentistry for Canada, 1941-44*.

Statistics Canada, *National Income and Expenditure Accounts, 1926-1974*, Volume I.

Statistics Canada, *Historical Compendium of Educational Statistics from Confederation to 1975*.

Government of Canada, *Public Accounts*, annual throughout, and Auditor-General's *Report*.

Government of Canada, Royal Commission on Dominion-Provincial Relations (the Rowell-Sirois Commission) *Report* and Appendices.

All Provincial Governments, *Public Accounts* or like documents, annual.

Province of Ontario, Ontario Bureau of Industries, *Reports*, annual.

Province of Ontario, Bureau of Municipal Statistics, annual, beginning in 1917.

Province of Ontario, Minister of Education and predecessors, *Annual Report*, from 1870 onward.

Province of Quebec, Bureau of Statistics, *Municipal Statistics*, annual beginning in 1914.

Province of Quebec, *Statistical Year Book*, annual from 1914.

Province of Quebec, Department of Public Instruction, *Annual Report*, from 1892.

Province of British Columbia, Education Agencies, *Annual Report*, beginning in 1877, and earlier sporadic reports.

All Other Provinces, Education Departments, *Annual Reports*.

City of Montreal, *Annual Report on Municipal Finance*.

Historical Statistics of Canada (see citation in Chapter 2).

Harris, Robin S., *A History of Higher Education in Canada, 1663-1960* (University of Toronto Press, 1976).

Chapter 11. Balance of International Payments, 1870–1925

A.M. SINCLAIR

Introduction

The balance of payments estimates for 1870-1925 are based on much previous research in the area, especially the work by Viner, Knox and Hartland relating to various current account items.[1] New estimates have been made of capital inflows plus related outflows of interest and dividend payments. These new estimates are based on a variety of secondary sources that reported on contemporary financial flows, including the *Investors Monthly Manual*, the *Economist*, the *Statist* and the *Canadian Gazette* for details on capital inflows and on these sources plus various *Poor's* and *Moody's Manuals* for direct investment estimates and related interest dividend outflows. The *Monetary Times* and various federal and provincial Sessional Papers and Provincial Accounts were used.

Capital Account Entries

The indispensable source on capital inflows is the *Investors Monthly Manual* (IMM) (and later the *Economist*), which provides a comprehensive and detailed listing of bonds and stocks issued in London on a monthly basis. The IMM provides information on issues, type of issue (bond, equipment bond, income bond, share, etc.), nominal yield, issue price, maturity date, date of issue, new capital created and calls on new capital created. As an example, the IMM records an issue in January of 1872 at par of £229,500 in Grand Trunk Railway second equipment mortgage bonds, with a nominal yield of six percent and a maturity date in 1919. In this case the new capital created is £229,500, but the calls were spread out over two calendar years. Calls of 20

---

[1] The Canadian balance of payments prior to 1926 has been studied in detail by three scholars: Jacob Viner (*Canada's Balance of International Indebtedness 1900-1913*, Harvard University Press, 1924), F.A. Knox (in two works, the earliest contained in H. Marshall, F.A. Southard and K.W. Taylor (*Canadian American Industry*, Yale University Press, 1936), and the latest being *Dominion Monetary Policy 1929-1934*, Ottawa, 1939) and Penelope Hartland (*The Canadian Balance of Payments Since 1868*, NBER, New York, circa 1954).

percent of the capital created were payable in January, April, July and September of 1872 and in January of 1873. For balance of payments purposes the call figures are the relevant ones for two reasons: they are more accurate in indicating the timing of cash transactions, as shown in the example given, and in many cases (not the one illustrated), capital was created but never called.

All call entries in each issue of the IMM with an obvious Canadian "destination" were identified and are included in the capital inflow estimates. The number of new issues per year varies enormously, from six in 1876 (Grand Trunk, Toronto -2 issues, Quebec Province, Canadian Government and the St. Lawrence and Ottawa Railroad) to 65 in 1897 (many being Klondyke issues where a reasonable estimate of the cash flow proceeding to Canada as a result of the call is zero). (The IMM data also allow for the calculation of interest payments from Canada to London, and they are used, as will be explained later on, where other and better sources are not available). The IMM data is considerable and detailed, but it is not complete. It is supplemented by data on new issues contained in the *Statist* and the *Canadian Gazette*. These sources do not give separate information on capital created and on calls, but only the former. Generally these additional sources add little: the *Canadian Gazette* records a municipal issue by London, Ontario of £31,000 in 1873 not recorded in the IMM, for example, and the *Statist* records a £100,000 share issue by the Scottish Ontario and Manitoba Land Co. Ltd. in 1880 not recorded in the IMM. After 1920 the IMM ceased publication but the *Economist* recorded some of the same information, and it is used in place of the IMM, again supplemented by the *Statist* and the *Canadian Gazette*.

The IMM, *Statist* and *Canadian Gazette* contain little record of direct investment in Canada. Major data sources on direct investment include D. Patterson (on British direct investment), the *Monetary Times* and *Poor's* and *Moody's Manuals*. A detailed examination of the *Monetary Times* was undertaken, despite the general poor quality of the information recorded, since it appears to be the only available published source for the early period in particular. A typical *Monetary Times* entry in the March 26, 1910 issue records the formation of the Spitzer Brothers and Co. firm in Toronto by three Spitzers from New York with a capital of $40,000. However, unlike other uses of this data, estimates have been made of the Canadian contribution to the total capital issued, which of course is not a capital inflow, by adjusting the capital estimation downward in proportion to the number of Canadian owners listed in the *Monetary Times*.

Capital outflows are not estimated directly but are calculated as a residual and incorporate the errors and omissions term.

Current Account Items

Interest and Dividend Payments

Previous estimates of interest and dividend payments have tended to be very crude. For example, Viner's calculations of interest and dividend payments are "mechanical" and almost certainly subject to great error. Briefly, he uses weighted averages of current interest rates to calculate the return on the estimated outstanding stock of Canadian assets held by non-residents, which stock is in turn estimated by using the residual from the current account estimates. (Viner's direct estimate of the capital inflow and outflow is used only as a rough check on the residual estimate).

A more meaningful result is produced by calculating, for each year, the interest and dividends paid on *each* bond and quoted stock held abroad (in practice this means "issued abroad" for most securities, since apart from the CPR and a few other cases there is little or no information on trade in outstanding securities). Much of the raw information is, as noted, included in published sources including *The Investors Monthly Manual*, the *Economist*, the *Statist* and the *Canadian Gazette*.

In addition, the various provincial Public Accounts are useful sources of information on provincial issues, especially on "sinking funds" which have to be considered before estimating the actual flow of interest payments abroad. (Sinking funds were often but not always held in London, usually in the form of purchases of the bond issue for which the fund was set up. No evidence suggests that municipal governments established similar sinking funds on their foreign liabilities). Interest on federal debt payable abroad is calculated using the various Sessional Papers. Municipal payments are calculated from the British financial press data, supplemented by Viner and Cleona Lewis for municipal issues in the U.S.

Railroad issues are complex, owing to the number of mergers of lines and to the interrelations between lines in Canada and those in the U.S. Mergers often result in the bonds of one company being in effect retired with new issues of the acquiring company taking their place. Canadian railways owned, leased and had trackage rights in the U.S., and U.S. railways had the same relationship *vis-à-vis* Canada. *Poor's Manual* for various years is used to sort out on an issue by issue basis for each railroad the actual external flow of funds generated in each year, in so far as this can be established. For the major lines, the information base on bonds and stocks is very complete, the main problem arising through payments akin to rent for lines leased abroad, where there are some gaps.

Dividend payments on direct investment in Canada are estimated from two sources: Patterson and various *Poor's Manuals*. Patterson is used to estimate dividends paid by U.K. companies in Canada up to 1900. *Poor's Manuals* (later *Poor's* and *Moody's Manuals*) are published for various sectors, the most useful ones for direct investment in Canada from the U.S. being those for Industrials and for Utilities. The Manuals contain information on every U.S. company of any size in a detailed accounting and descriptive form. For select years only these Manuals were examined in detail to locate U.S. companies with Canadian interest. Dividend payments were estimated by two basic procedures: an estimate of the size of the Canadian facilities in relation to total company size, prorating profits (and hence dividend outflow) on this basis, and an estimate of the percent of the Canadian facilities of U.S. firms owned by Canadian shareholders, estimated in terms of the proportion of Canadian directors to the total number of directors of the company. Intervening years were estimated by interpolation.

Adjusted Exports and Imports

Trade of Canada and predecessor volumes (annual) reported in the Canadian Sessional Papers for various years were used as the source of export and import data. Exports and imports are adjusted to exclude and include various items, and in addition, fiscal year estimates were changed to calendar year estimates on the assumption of an equal distribution over months (up to and including 1900 the fiscal year ended 30 June, thereafter 31 March).

Basically, "imports for consumption" are reduced by excluding coin and bullion (included separately under gold), settlers effects (no financial implications) and miscellaneous and non-commercial items. "Total exports" are reduced by excluding coin and bullion (included under gold), settlers effects, gold bearing quartz (included under gold), and exports of foreign produce other than coin and bullion.

Gold

Figures for gold are calculated from recorded imports or exports and unrecorded imports or exports as given in Hartland, Viner and Knox, plus reports of gold bearing quartz as given in Sessional Papers.

Freight

Freight receipts for 1870 to 1890 are simply estimated as two percent of adjusted exports, following Viner who used two percent of his exports figure. Viner and Knox are used for subsequent years. For *freight payments*, Hartland is used (Viner made some arithmetical errors which are corrected by Hartland) plus Knox. (All Knox numbers are from Marshall, Southard and Taylor.)

Tourism

Hartland's numbers are used for 1870-1925.

Migrants Capital, Non-Commercial Remittances and Insurance

Hartland is used to 1890, then Viner and Knox.

Bibliography of Sources Cited in Chapter 11

Knox, F.A. (in H. Marshall, F.A. Southard and K.W. Taylor, *Canadian American Industry*, Yale University Press, 1936).

Knox, F.A., *Dominion Monetary Policy 1929-1934* (Royal Commission on Dominion-Provincial Relations, 1939).

Hartland, Penelope, *The Canadian Balance of Payments Since 1868*, National Bureau of Economic Research, 1954.

Viner, Jacob, *Canada's Balance of International Indebtedness, 1900-1913*, Harvard University Press, 1924.

DBS and predecessors, *Trade of Canada* annual. 1939 and 1944 to 1946.

News Publications

   Canadian Gazette, 1883 to 1912
   Economist
   Investors Monthly Manual
   Poor's and Moody's Manuals
   Monetary Times
   Statist

Chapter 12. Miscellaneous Items: Royalties; Indirect Taxes; Gross Capital Formation

M.C. URQUHART

ROYALTIES

Gross Domestic Product at Factor Cost From Royalties

Provincial governments, in particular, and the Federal Government, to a lesser extent, received considerable amounts of revenue from natural resources. These revenues are commonly called royalties and that is the term used here for all such revenue. As these royalties comprise rents for the use of resources in which the relevant government may have some rights they are a part of income produced within an economy. At the same time, they have been charged, ordinarily, as an expense by the business using the resources and consequently are not reflected in the income attributable to the industries using the resources. Hence, they have not been included elsewhere as a part of the national income.

In this project, these royalties were classified as originating from three sources, *viz.*, resources of the forest, the mine and the fishery. Their payment could take a variety of forms: for instance, in the case of the forest, they might take the form of timber dues, timber licenses, timber leases, ground rents, timber bonuses and so forth.

The basic sources of data for this project's figures are, in every case but one, government documents. The exception was the use of estimates of mineral royalties for Nova Scotia for the years 1902 to 1926 from *Canadian Fiscal Facts*, a publication of the Canadian Tax Foundation in 1957; this work had many other data for other provinces and for Canada but it was felt that the royalty data therein were not as comprehensive as was desired. The government source data were most commonly found in the public accounts of the relevant governments. Such was true in the cases of British Columbia, Alberta, Saskatchewan, New Brunswick and Nova Scotia: sometimes long series could be found in one report. Data for Ontario came from the annual reports of the Department of Crown Lands which in turn became the Department of Lands, Forests and Mines and, then, the Department of Lands and Forests. Data for Quebec were obtained from the Report of the Minister of Lands and Forests in the Quebec Sessional Papers and most especially from the Report for 1928. Federal Government data for forestry and minerals were obtained from the Report of the Department of the Interior for 1927-28, which had the complete run of data — mineral royalties were estimated at 88 per cent of the item "hay, coal, mining fees, stone quarries, export tax on gold, etc."; federal data for the fisheries came from the Report of the Department of Marine and Fisheries, which also had long runs in the 1927-28 report.

There were not any revenues from resource royalties for Manitoba or Prince Edward Island in the period covered in this project.

INDIRECT TAXES LESS SUBSIDIES
ALL GOVERNMENTS

Indirect taxes are levied by all levels of Government, federal, provincial and municipal. The two largest single items among these taxes are customs duties, collected by the federal government, and property taxes, collected by municipal bodies. The type of subsidy that is a counterpart to the indirect taxes is relatively small and enters only into the calculation of the federal government position.

The basic procedure followed to obtain the single series involved essentially four steps. First, a series for federal government indirect taxes was obtained from an accessible source: the level of this series was such that the 1926 entry in the series was slightly below the official national accounts measure of indirect taxes for 1926. Second, a series for provincial government indirect taxes was obtained by summing such series for individual provinces: this series, from its construction, had the same value for indirect taxes in 1926 as the official national accounts. Third, a similar series for the sum of property taxes of municipalities in Canada was derived: this series was at a level where the 1926 value of property taxes was the same as the similar value in the national accounts; municipal property taxes comprised by far the largest item of municipal indirect taxes, in fact more than 88 percent of such taxes in the official national accounts for 1926. Fourth, the above three series were added together to obtain a single series of all indirect taxes for 1870 to 1926: owing to the nature of the construction of this series, the entry in 1926 was between five and six percent below the entry in the national accounts in 1926 for all indirect taxes less subsidies; accordingly the whole series was raised in a proportion (about 6 percent) that made the 1926 value the same as that in the national accounts.

The method of calculation of the series for each level of government now follows.

1. Government of Canada

(a) Indirect taxes for each year, 1870 to 1926, are taken from HSC, Series G12. This series was prepared by the Comptroller of the Treasury of the Government of Canada from Public Accounts of Canada.

(b) Subsidies for each year, 1870 to 1926 were obtained from the public accounts of Canada (or auditor-general's reports). They include railway subsidies and rail and steamship subsidies.

(c) The subsidies were subtracted from the indirect taxes to yield the desired federal series.

2. Provincial Governments

The material on which the estimates for provincial governments were based came originally from provincial public accounts. Fortunately, from these accounts, the Canadian Tax Foundation had published annual data on various individual taxes for each province from 1901 onward in *Canadian Fiscal Facts, 1957*: these data, supplemented by some additional material for Ontario and Quebec taken directly from the public accounts of each, provided the basis for the estimates for 1901 to 1926. For the period prior to 1901 the estimates were based on tax data for Ontario, Quebec and British Columbia taken directly from their respective public accounts. Somewhat more detail of what was done in each of these two periods follows.

(a) 1901 to 1926

(i) For 1913 to 1926 the data used for a series for each province came entirely from *Fiscal Facts*. In addition to the usual indirect taxes such as business taxes, amusement taxes, liquor control revenues and the like, incomes from resources were included in these series. The latter, insofar as they are royalties, are not indirect taxes but are a part of national resource rentals collected by the province: their inclusion did not create a problem since the series that was obtained from the sum for all provinces of the aforementioned receipts was used as an extrapolator of the official figure of indirect provincial taxes for 1926 given in Statcan, *National Income and Expenditure Accounts, 1926-1974*; in addition, the movement of the series with resource revenues included was very similar to that with resource revenues excluded. A check on the reliability of this extrapolator from 1926 for 1921 and 1913 by use of estimates prepared for the Rowell-Sirois Royal Commission (*Report of the Royal Commission on Dominion-Provincial Relations, Volume III, Documentation*) showed that, as one would expect, the calculations of indirect taxes by the method used here gave practically the same results for 1921 and 1913 as those set forth in the Rowell-Sirois estimates made from the public accounts. It is worth noting that the item in the extrapolator series for 1926 was equivalent to more than 92 percent of the national accounts figure for 1926.

(ii) For 1901 to 1913 the data from *Fiscal Facts* were supplemented by additional data for Ontario and Quebec to yield the extrapolator from 1913 to 1901. For some reason *Fiscal Facts* did not cover considerable amounts collected by each of these provinces in the form of licenses, law stamps, registration stamps and Algoma taxes in Ontario. Estimates for these items for those years were obtained from the public accounts for each of these provinces and were added to the series obtained from *Fiscal Facts*. This augmented series was linked at 1913 to the series for 1913 to 1926.

(b) 1870 to 1901

The extrapolator from 1901 to 1870 was comprised of the sum of indirect taxes for British Columbia, Ontario and Quebec as obtained from each provinces public accounts; the relevant items for these three provinces together accounted for slightly over 88 percent of the sum for all provinces of such items in 1901. This sum of indirect tax items for the three provinces was linked to that for all provinces at 1901.

The items taken from the public accounts for each of the three provinces for 1871 to 1901 were as follows.

British Columbia: law stamps, timber royalty and licenses, mining receipts general, licenses, real property tax, wild land tax, mineral tax, registry fees.

Ontario: licenses, law stamps, Algoma taxes, woods and forests.

Quebec: stumpage ground rents and bonuses, corporation taxes, registration stamps, licenses of hotels shops etc., law stamps.

A check on four years to show whether the inclusion of some timber royalties would have produced biases in the series led to the following results.

Index of Sum of Indirect Taxes in B.C., Ontario and Quebec, 1900=100, on Alternative Basis

	1870	1876	1886	1901
Sum of all items including forest revenue	23	29	42	100
Sum of items excluding forestry revenue	17	29	42	100

Special sources included, *inter alia*, *Quebec Statistical Yearbook*, 1914, p.257; *Quebec Sessional Papers, 1894, Sessional Paper 3, Public Accounts*; *British Columbia, Sessional Papers, 1903*, Public Accounts July 1, 1901 to June 30, 1902; *British Columbia Sessional Papers 1911*, Public Accounts.

Only a portion (seven sixteenths) of the motor vehicle licenses that corresponded to business use was included.

The official national accounts figure for provincial indirect taxes for 1926 was about eight percent larger than the figure for 1926 obtained in these calculations of provincial indirect taxes: there is always a matter of judgement of what is included in indirect taxes. To make the series calculated herein consistent with the national accounts level the whole series was multiplied by 1.08.

3. Municipal Governments (local government)

The property tax, including the component for education, is by far the largest source of municipal revenue: the national accounts, for calendar year 1926 record municipal property tax revenues at 219 million dollars out of total local government indirect tax revenues of 247 million dollars. Estimates of the real property tax revenues of municipal governments were used as a proxy for the movement of municipal government indirect tax revenues. The estimates for each year 1870 to 1926 were made on a province by province basis and then aggregated to give a national total.

Fortunately, *The Report: The Royal Commission on Dominion-Provincial Relations, Book III, Documentation*, Table 18 (p.52) records real property tax revenue of municipalities for each province for each of the years 1913, 1921 and 1926: these data were used for these years. The further steps then involved interpolating the estimates for each province between 1921 and 1926 and between 1913 and 1921 and extrapolating the estimates from 1913 back to 1870 for each province. The main sources of the annual data were public reports and records. In addition, *Canadian Fiscal Facts* published data on taxes levied for twelve major cities for most of the years from 1906 onwards.

A description, in detail, of the procedures used in making the estimates for each province would be bulky beyond usefulness. However enough description to provide the main procedure for replication follows.

All Provinces: Municipal Real Property Taxes

For all provinces the municipal real property taxes were taken from the Rowell-Sirois Royal Commission Report for 1913, 1921 and 1926. The official national accounts used the Rowell-Sirois data for the real property component of indirect taxes in 1926. (Statcan, *National Income and Expenditure Accounts 1926-1974*, p.64)

Prince Edward Island: Municipal

> The data for 1913, 1921 and 1926 are from the Rowell-Sirois report.
> For years 1922 to 1925: straight line interpolation between 1921 and 1926 was used.
> For years 1914 to 1920: straight line interpolation between 1913 and 1921 was used.
> Data for years 1870 to 1912 were extrapolated from 1913 on the basis of province wide

total of wages and salaries of municipalities for which the origin is described in the section of this document on municipal government.

Nova Scotia: Municipal

> The municipal property taxes for 1913, 1921 and 1926 were Rowell-Sirois estimates.

(i) For 1922 to 1925, 1914 to 1920 and 1909 to 1912 the municipal real estate taxes as reported in the Journal of the House of Assembly, *Statistics of Incorporated Cities, Towns and Municipalities* were used to interpolate between or extrapolate before the Rowell-Sirois values. The statistics are reported separately for each of rural municipal districts, towns and cities but were available for all three municipal units alike.

(ii) Prior to 1909:

> (a) Rural municipalities tax collections were not reported before 1909 but assessed values were available for 1880 to 1888 (Nova Scotia Journals, Appendix 14) and for 1909 from *Statistics of Incorporated Cities, Towns and Municipalities*. Assessed values for years 1889 to 1908 were obtained by linear interpolation between 1888 and 1909. (These interpolations checked reasonably with assessed values for 1889 and 1892 which were also attainable from official documents, but were assessed for "income" as well as property taxes).
> Real estate tax rate for 1909 for rural municipalities was obtained by dividing the taxes levied by the assessed value to yield a tax rate of $0.98 tax per $100 assessment (a tax rate of 9.8 mills). This real estate rate projected back to 1899, on the basis of the movements of the "town" tax rate (see below), was placed at $0.875 per $100 assessed valued in 1899. An examination of data in the Halifax Archives yielded a property tax of $0.37 per $100 assessment for East Hants in 1888 and the same value was used for all years 1880 to 1889; for years between 1890 and 1898 the property tax rate was obtained by linear interpolation between 1889 and 1899.
> The value of property tax for 1880 to 1907 was them obtained as the product of assessed

values of property and property tax rates.

There were no rural municipalities before 1880.

(b) For towns, the taxes collected were published for 1899 to 1909 (and beyond) in House of Assembly, *Statistics of Incorporated Towns*. For 1880 to 1899 extrapolation was done by a series derived from multiplication of assessed values by property tax rates. Assessed values were available from *Statistics of Incorporated Towns*, reports for 1880 to 1889, 1892 and 1899; tax rates for 1899, simply the quotient of sum of taxes of all towns to the sum of assessed values for all towns, was $1.71 per $100 assessment. In the absence of other information, the tax rates for Halifax of $1.20 per $100 assessment in 1880 and $1.09 per $100 in 1890 were used and values for intervening years were determined by linear interpolation. Total property taxes were obtained as the product of assessed values and rates.

For 1870 to 1880 the taxation of towns was extrapolated on the basis of the movement of Halifax taxes.

(c) The cities were Halifax for all years and Sydney from 1903 to 1926.

Halifax taxes were obtained directly from N.S. Journals, *Statistics of Incorporated Cities, Towns and Municipalities* for 1918 to 1926. For other years the Halifax property taxes came from Annual Reports of the Treasurer of the City of Halifax for the years 1914, 1911, 1910, 1903, 1891, 1881, 1880 and 1872.

Sydney was classified as a town before 1903 and a city thereafter: before 1903 it was left with the towns. For 1918 to 1926 its property taxes came from the same source as for Halifax. For 1917 to 1909 its property taxes were extrapolated backward from 1918 on the basis of municipal expenditure of incorporated towns: this gave about the same data as would have been obtained by using City of Halifax's taxes as an extrapolator. Sydney's property taxes, published with those of the towns until 1902, were available for 1902; the estimates for the years 1903 to 1908 were obtained by linear interpolation between 1902 and 1909.

The sum of city, town and rural municipality property taxes from 1909 back to 1876 were then used to extrapolate the figure for 1909 which in turn had been an extrapolation of the 1913 Rowell-Sirois level for all Nova Scotia.

New Brunswick: Municipal

The data for 1913, 1921 and 1926 are Rowell-Sirois data.

Estimates for 1922 to 1925 and 1914 to 1920 were obtained by using taxes levied in St. John, available in *Fiscal Facts*, as interpolator between the Rowell-Sirois data of 1921 and 1926 and of 1913 and 1921; the St. John taxes were at least one-half of all real estate taxes in these years.

For years 1870 to 1912 estimates of wages and salaries of teachers were used as an extrapolator of the 1913 property tax estimate. The way in which teachers' salaries were estimated is described in the section on education.

Quebec: Municipal

The data for 1913, 1921 and 1926 are Rowell-Sirois data.

The interpolator and extrapolator for all years was the revenue of the City of Montreal from real estate taxes, business taxes and income from licences. These data were available for every year from treasurers' reports of the City of Montreal. The average ratio of all Quebec Municipal property taxes to the above Montreal taxes for the years 1913, 1921 and 1926 was 2.03 with slight variations among years. The estimates for all years but 1913, 1921 and 1926 were then obtained by multiplying the Montreal revenues, described above by the factor 2.03. (The result would have been practically the same if only Montreal property taxes had been used except that the multiplying factor would have been larger.)

Ontario: Municipal

The data for 1913, 1921 and 1926 are Rowell-Sirois data.

The interpolators and extrapolators for every year were Ontario Municipal property tax including the school tax. These data were obtained from the following sources.

Data for 1915 to 1926 came from reports of the Ontario Bureau of Municipal Affairs, *Municipal Statistics*, found in the Ontario Sessional Papers.

Data for 1886 to 1915 came from reports of the Ontario Bureau of Industries, especially the report for 1912, also found in Ontario Sessional Papers.

Data for 1868, 1877 and 1878 came from *Municipal Returns for Ontario* in Sessional Papers of Ontario for 1870, 1879 and 1880. Estimates for years 1870 to 1876 and 1879 to 1885 were obtained by straight line interpolation between 1868 and 1877 and between 1878 and 1886.

Manitoba: Municipal

The data for 1913, 1921 and 1926 are Rowell-Sirois data.

Total municipal taxes for all Manitoba were obtained from the reports of the Department of the Municipal Commissioner for the years 1905 to 1914, 1919 and 1921 to 1926 found in the Manitoba Sessional Papers; in addition the same information was available for 1918 in the report of the Assessment and Taxation Commission, 1919. Tax receipts of the city of Winnipeg were available for all years from reports of the City of Winnipeg.

An estimate of total taxes for all municipalities in Manitoba for 1920 was made by chaining 1920 from 1921 by use of Winnipeg tax data; similarly Winnipeg city tax data were used to interpolate for all Manitoba municipalities for the years between 1914 and 1918.

The municipal tax figure obtained from the foregoing sources for all Manitoba for 1926 was the same as the Rowell-Sirois figure; for 1921 it was slightly above the Rowell-Sirois figure; for 1913 the Rowell-Sirois figure for Manitoba was 11 percent above the figure obtained from the reports of the Department of the Municipal Commission. Therefore from the estimates made from the data from the Department of the Municipal Commissioner, Manitoba were raised by the following factors:

Year	Multiplication Factor	Year	Multiplication Factor
1905-12	1.11	1916	1.05
1913	1.11	1917	1.03
1914	1.09	1918	1.02
1915	1.07	1919	1.01
		1920	1.00

For 1885 to 1905 Winnipeg city taxes were used as the extrapolator. In 1905 the Winnipeg taxes amounted to 0.46159 of all municipal taxes in Manitoba and it was assumed that that was the appropriate proportion right back to 1885.

From 1885 back to 1870 municipal wage and salary payments were used as the extrapolator. The derivation of this series has been dealt with in the description of the section on gross domestic product in government.

Especially important reports for Winnipeg are the Municipal Reports for the City of Winnipeg for 1924, 1902-03 and 1897-98.

Saskatchewan: Municipal

The data for 1913, 1921 and 1926 are from the Rowell-Sirois report.

Municipal taxes for all Saskatchewan municipalities were available from Annual Reports of the Department of Municipal Affairs for Saskatchewan for the years 1913, 1917, 1922, 1923, 1924, 1925, 1926. For years between 1913 and 1917 and between 1917 and 1922 an estimate was made by linear interpolation. These Saskatchewan data were then used to interpolate the Rowell-Sirois data. For Rowell-Sirois years the ratio of the data from Saskatchewan Department reports to the Rowell-Sirois data are:

Ratio of Municipal Taxes
From Department Reports to
Rowell-Sirois Data

1913	0.4841
1921	0.8115
1926	0.6786

These ratios were interpolated linearly between the adjacent years and the Departmental report data for intervening years were adjusted in proportion to these ratios to obtain data for all years on a Rowell-Sirois basis.

For years 1900 to 1913, R.H. Coats in *Report of the Board of Inquiry into Cost of Living, Vol. III,* pp.334 and 993, presents indexes of municipal tax rates and municipal assessments for individual provinces for years 1900, 1905, 1910 and 1913. These rates for Saskatchewan were compounded to yield an index of actual municipal taxes for Saskatchewan for years 1900, 1905, 1910, 1913; indexes of municipal taxes for intervening years were obtained by linear interpolation. The whole series was then used to extrapolate the 1913 figure of municipal taxes back as far as 1900.

The extrapolator from 1900 back to 1879 annually was schoolteachers and municipal salaries the derivation of which is described in the sections on gross domestic product in education on government.

Alberta: Municipal

The data for 1913, 1921 and 1926 are from the Rowell-Sirois report.

Estimates for years between 1921 and 1926 were obtained by using the sum of Edmonton and Calgary taxes, obtained from *Canadian Fiscal Facts,* p.215, as an interpolator: these two cities accounted for 50.13 per cent of municipal taxes in 1921 and 33.08 per cent in 1926.

Estimates for years between 1913 and 1921 were obtained by using Edmonton municipal taxes only, from *Canadian Fiscal Facts*: Edmonton accounted for 24.82 percent of all municipal tax revenues in 1921 and 35.43 percent in 1913.

Extrapolation for Alberta back to 1892 was made on the basis of Edmonton municipal taxes which were assumed to amount to 35.43 percent of the Alberta total for every year 1892 to 1913. Edmonton municipal taxes were obtained from *Canadian Fiscal Facts* as far back as 1906; Edmonton taxes from 1892 to 1905 were obtained by M.C. Urquhart from annual reports of the City of Edmonton in the Legislative Library of the Province of Alberta. The report for the year ending December 31, 1916 is particularly valuable.

There are no data for Alberta municipalities before 1892.

British Columbia: Municipal

The data for 1913, 1921 and 1926 are from the Rowell-Sirois report.

Interpolation for years between 1921 and 1926 was by B.C. municipal taxes obtained in B.C. Sessional Papers Vol. I, 1927: these B.C. taxes for 1926 were 0.9946 of the Rowell-Sirois figure and for 1921 were 1.0893 of the Rowell-Sirois figure.

Between 1913 and 1921 the interpolator was the sum of the Vancouver and Victoria municipal taxes obtained from *Canadian Fiscal Facts*, p.215: these two cities together accounted for a proportion 0.5436 in 1921 and 0.5080 in 1913.

The extrapolator from 1913 back to 1906 was also the sum of Vancouver and Victoria municipal taxes from *Fiscal Facts*: it was assumed that the ratio of these cities' municipal taxes to all B.C. municipal taxes was 0.5080, the same as in 1913.

The extrapolator from 1906 back to 1870 was the sum of municipal and schoolteachers salaries, the derivation of which has been described already in the sections on education and government: the ratio of these two salary items together to estimated municipal property taxes in 1906 was 1.6239 and it was assumed that this ratio held constant back to 1870.

The levels of the entries for 1926 in each of the foregoing series and the like entries in the national accounts for indirect taxes are as follows.

	Entry in Above Project Series	Entry in the National Accounts
	(millions of dollars)	
Federal government	291	300
Provincial government	82	80
Municipal governments	219	247
All governments	592	627

It should be pointed out that the official national accounts include in indirect taxes of provinces in 1926 the amount of 18 million dollars for resource royalties and similar levies on resources. This project treats these resource royalties as a part of factor income accruing to governments (as have the official accounts from 1947 onward). However, the project estimate of indirect taxes of provinces exclusive of resource royalties remains at 80 million dollars because the official accounts appear to have omitted some items that, arguably, are appropriately concluded. The basis of this judgement derives from the following table.

Alternative Estimates of Provincial
Indirect Taxes in 1926
(millions of dollars)

Item	Official Estimate	*Fiscal Facts*
Amusement tax	5	4.9
Corporation tax (not on profits)	12	11.9
Gasoline tax	6	6.5
Motor vehicle licenses	7	15.9
Other licenses permits and fees	6	10.3
Miscellaneous taxes on		
natural resources	16	21.3
Real property tax	8	9.5
Profits on liquor commissions	15	16.4
Miscellaneous	5	2.3
	80	99.0
Less: True royalty	–	9.6
Non-business motor licenses	–	9.0
Remainder	80	80.4

Sources: The official estimates are from Statcan: *National Income and Expenditure Accounts 1926-1974* Vol. I, Table 46; the *Fiscal Facts* data are from Canadian Tax Foundation, *Canadian Fiscal Facts*, Table 47.

The true royalty component of the official miscellaneous taxes on natural resources was estimated from the way in which this component changed in the official accounts when Statcan transferred the assignment of resource royalties from indirect taxes to government factor income. The relevant data show the change that took place in the item "miscellaneous taxes on natural resources" when the reassignment occurred with data for 1947, the first year for which the change has been made, and 1948.

The relevant data, in millions of dollars, are given in the next following table.

These presumed royalties approximate 60 per cent of the miscellaneous taxes and royalties of line (1) and it was assumed that the same proportion held true in 1926 and hence the estimate for true royalties in 1926 of 9.6 million dollars in the entry for national resource items in 1926.

Likewise in 1926 the non-business motor licenses were calculated as the difference between the figure for all motor licenses of *Fiscal Facts* and the official figure of business motor vehicle licenses.

The project extrapolator series total for indirect taxes of all governments in 1926 of 591,695 thousand dollars was the proportion 0.94369 of the official total of 627 million dollars. The extrapolator total then was divided by 0.94369 throughout to provide the estimate of indirect

		1947	1948
(1)	Miscellaneous taxes on natural resources, royalties included	39	47
(2)	Miscellaneous taxes on natural resources, royalties excluded	16	18
(3)	Presumed royalties (1) − (2)	23	29

Source:

Line (1)   DBS.: *National Accounts Income and Expenditure, 1926-1956*, Table 40.
Line (2)   Statcan: *National Income and Expenditure Accounts 1926-1974*, Table 46.

taxes of all governments.

An idea of how the large item of municipal real property taxes was distributed among provinces may be gleaned from the distribution of the project municipal property taxes for 1926.

Municipal Real Property Taxes, 1926, by Province
(thousands of dollars)

Prince Edward Island	251
Nova Scotia	5,618
New Brunswick	3,725
Quebec	45,575
Ontario	91,271
Manitoba	17,540
Saskatchewan	19,995
Alberta	19,977
British Columbia	14,688
All provinces	218,640

GROSS INVESTMENT EXPENDITURE
CAPITAL FORMATION IN DURABLE PHYSICAL ASSETS

Gross investment expenditure or, alternatively, gross capital formation covers herein only outlay on durable physical assets used for production, such as buildings and structures and machinery and equipment. Even on this restricted basis it does not cover improvements of farm land such as clearing and breaking. It covers residential buildings but does not include consumer equipment such as automobiles.

Such a measure of capital formation leaves out much capital formation, such as investment in livestock herds and inventories of all kinds wherever located and all investment in human training and education and the acquisition of knowledge.

Building and Engineering Construction

A description of the way in which expenditures on building and engineering construction were estimated has been given already in the section on the estimation of income in the construction industry.   There remains to be described estimates of capital formation in machinery and equipment.

Machinery and Equipment

Capital formation in plant and equipment from 1896 to 1925 was prepared by Statistics Canada in the making of its capital stock estimates for 1926 and following years by the perpetual inventory method. All of the project data obtained from this source were taken from Maclist. The general method employed was presumably the same as for construction and has been described already in connection with it.

For the years from 1870 to 1895 estimates of machinery and equipment expenditure were prepared within this project. The estimates were prepared separately for agriculture, railroads, manufacturing, shipping and water transport, schools, government and a residual sector.   The general method used to make estimates on a sector by sector basis for this period was to multiply the average ratio of expenditure on machinery and equipment to expenditure on construction for the years 1896 to 1900 by the expenditure on construction for the years 1870 to 1895 to obtain an estimate of expenditure on machinery and equipment in these years; but there were some amendments to the procedure in particular industries.

The sectors for which the standard (general) method described in the preceding paragraph were used were manufacturing, schools and government. The average ratios for 1896 to 1900 of expenditures on machinery and equipment to expenditures on construction for these industries were all based on data from Maclist. They are as follows:

Manufacturing	1.5547
Schools	0.1519
Governments	0.2101

The sectors for which slight variations from the standard procedure were used were railroads and the residual sector. For the railways the ratio of equipment and machinery to construction used for the extrapolation was the average for the 10 years from 1896 to 1905: the actual ratio was 0.3159. The longer period was used in the railroad case because there is considerable variation in individual year ratios between periods of slow railway expansion and periods of more rapid growth and it was felt desirable to have years representative of both phases of railway growth. For the residual sector, the ratio of machinery and equipment to construction used for extrapolation was the four year average of the ratios for the years 1896 to 1899: the actual ratio was 0.6025. The reason that the ratio for 1900 was omitted from this average was that there was a clear discrete break in the level of the ratios between 1896-1899 and 1900. The data from which the ratios were calculated were all from Maclist.

The sectors for which fairly extensive variation from the standard procedure were used were agriculture and water transport (shipping). For agriculture, the procedure was different for each of three periods. For extrapolation to years 1891-1895, the average ratio of expenditures on machinery and equipment to expenditures on non-residential construction, obtained from

Maclist, was multiplied by the non-residential construction expenditure for 1891-1895. For earlier years the starting point was from estimates of farm expenditure on machinery and equipment for 1890, 1880 and 1870 calculated by Professor R.F.J. Barnett from production data in the decennial censuses of manufacturers and external trade data (Robert F.J. Barnett, *Canada's Manufacturing Development and Foreign Trade 1870-1915*; unpublished manuscript). For each of 1880 and 1890, the ratio of Barnett's estimate of expenditure on machinery to non-residential construction in agriculture (from Maclist) was calculated, a linear interpolation of these ratios was then made for 1881 to 1889, and the resulting ratios were multiplied by agricultural non-residential construction expenditure to obtain estimates of agricultural machinery and equipment purchases. Since the estimated non-residential construction expenditures from Maclist only went back to 1876, the machinery and equipment estimates for 1876 to 1879 were obtained by multiplying the non-residential construction figures by the ratio of machinery and equipment to non-residential construction in 1880. The estimates for the machinery and equipment expenditure for 1871-1875 were obtained by straight line interpolation between 1876 and 1870. The machinery and equipment figures for 1870, 1880 and 1890 were Barnett's as cited above; all other basic data came from Maclist. The basic ratios of machinery and equipment expenditures to non-residential construction expenditures were as follows: average 1896-1900, 1.8830; 1890, 2.2922; 1880, 0.9386.

Water transport (shipping) equipment was obtained in two ways. The data for 1891 to 1895 came directly from Maclist; the figure for 1891 was used also for 1890. Barnett had made

Barnett's Estimates of Capital Formation in Agriculture and Shipping
(all monetary values in millions of dollars)

Agriculture

	Machinery and Equipment (1900$)	Price Index, Iron and Steel 1900=100	Machinery and Equipment (current dollars)
1870	2,039	125.8	2.565
1880	3,239	127.5	4.130
1890	6,926	105.9	7.335

Water Transport

	Machinery and Equipment, Including Ships (1900$)	Price Index 1900=100	Machinery and Equipment, Including Shipping (current dollars)
1870	4,171	95.8	3,996
1880	3,582	104.9	3,758
1890	3,673	98.5	3.618

estimates for water transport for 1870, 1880 and 1890 by the method used for the estimation of agricultural equipment. His estimates were used to chain the 1890 figure back to 1880 and 1870. The estimates for the years 1871-1879 and 1881 to 1889 were obtained by linear interpolation between 1870 and 1880 and between 1880 and 1890 respectively.

The Barnett data, referred to above, were given in the original in 1900 dollars. They were converted to current dollar values by use of Barnett's own price indices. The relevant material is given in the immediately preceding table.

The 1890 value of water transport machinery and equipment, extrapolated from the 1891 Maclist value was 1.3 million dollars. The Maclist category obviously contained less than the Barnett category.

Checks for Reliability

The most important check is a comparison of the project (Maclist) estimates and Buckley's estimates for 1896 to 1930. The data are given in Table 12.1.

The variations of the ratios of Table 12.1 are disquieting. A comparison of the components of the project estimates on the one hand and the Buckley estimates on the other for each of the periods 1926-30 and 1906-10 throws some light on the variation between those two periods. It has been impossible to match the Maclist and Buckley categories precisely; the correspondences are sufficiently good for the derivation of useful inferences from the data. The comparisons are shown in Table 12.2.

It is at once apparent that practically all of the excess of the Buckley aggregate over that of Maclist in both periods is accounted for by the railway and other land transport group and the water transport group. Since the expenditures of railways on equipment were almost the same

Table 12.1
Comparison of Project and Buckley Investment
Expenditures on All Machinery and Equipment,
Quinquennial Totals, 1896 to 1930.
(millions of dollars)

Quinquennium	Project (Maclist)	Buckley	Ratio: Project to Buckley
1896 – 1900	192	187	1.03
1901 – 1905	441	380	1.16
1906 – 1910	696	586	1.19
1911 – 1915	1,079	412	1.18
1916 – 1920	1,301	1,322	0.98
1921 – 1925	1,178	1,211	0.97
1926 – 1930	*1,866	2,097	0.87

* The figure given in the official national accounts is 1,859.

Sources: Project, Maclist.
            Buckley, *Capital Formation in Canada.*

in Buckley and Maclist, the excess of Buckley over Maclist in the railway and other group transport group is accounted for by differences in outlay on automobiles, buses and trucks. Now, while part of the Maclist outlay on automobiles and trucks is included in such industries as manufacturing, construction and trade (but not agriculture where the item, automobiles and trucks is already transferred) it seems nevertheless apparent that Buckley's estimates for automobiles and trucks substantially exceeds those of Maclist. Buckley assumed that 20 percent of all passenger vehicles sales was for business use. Similarly, Buckley's estimates of investment in ships and boats substantially exceeds anything that can be identified for this item in 1926-30. In addition, to water transport proper, we know that Maclist includes 11 million dollars for boats in the fisheries group but that accounts for only a small part of the difference. The facts are that the Maclist estimates in 1926-30 included substantially less in the way of expenditures on

Table 12.2
Comparison of Maclist and Buckley Estimates of Investment
in Plant and Equipment, by Component, 1926-30 and 1906-10.
(millions of dollars)

	Quinquennium 1926 – 30		Quinquennium 1906 – 10	
	Maclist	Buckley	Maclist	Buckley
Agriculture, Farm machinery only	314	339	149	149
Railways, other ground and air transport (incld. vehicles in agriculture) (221.0 +111.4 + 20.9)	353	516	97	132
Manufacturing, mining, electric light and power and construction	726	716	271	152
Water transport	18	113	5	26
All other (incld. trade, service, gov't, forestry, fisheries and water systems)	385	413	138	127
Total	1,796	2,097	660	586

Source: Maclist; Buckley, C.F.I.C., Table D.

Note: The industry classifications are as given in Maclist. The part of the expenditure on trucks and cars which Maclist included under agriculture was transferred to railway, other transport etc. The Buckley data are from his five classifications: (1) Farm Machinery, etc.; (2) Industrial, Electrical and Mining Machinery etc.; (3) Railway Rolling Stock and Other Land Vehicles; (4) Ships and Boats; (5) Office and Store, Professional and Miscellaneous Machinery and Equipment.

automobiles and ships and boats than did Buckley. These two categories were relatively much smaller before 1926-27 and indeed, the automotive group is unimportant before World War I.

The data for 1906-10 show that most of the excess of the Maclist estimates over the Buckley estimates is accounted for by the manufacturing *et al* group. The components of this group for 1906-10 were as follows:

Manufacturing	206.2 $mm
Mining	19.4 $mm
Electric light and power	16.1 $mm
Construction	29.2 $mm

Consequently, most of the difference must be accounted for by manufacturing.

The differences in manufacturing in the early period are explained by the fact that Buckley used flow expenditure entirely (production plus imports less exports) for his estimates while Maclist used recorded stocks of capital in decennial and quinquennial censuses to estimate net changes in the value of capital stock between censuses and, by extension, through use of assumptions about length of life of capital stock items, to estimate gross flows between censuses.

Now for 1896-1900 the Maclist and Buckley estimates are almost the same. This factor provides us with some reassurance since the estimates for the period before 1896 were based on the ratios of machinery and equipment to construction in 1896-1900. In addition, the expenditures on manufacturing *et al* were $80 million in Maclist and $84 million in Buckley.

Finally, there is the matter of the derivation of the estimates before 1896. The main question that arises is the appropriateness, for several industries, of estimating machinery and equipment outlays by assuming they were in the same proportion to construction as the average for the period 1896 to 1900 or thereabouts: one might wonder whether machinery and equipment expenditures might not have increased over time relative to construction outlays.

The data on this matter provide conflicting evidence. On one hand, for manufacturing as a whole between 1890 and 1900, the first census years for which a breakdown of fixed capital into buildings and machinery is available, the ratio of machinery to buildings increased from 1.32 in 1890 to 1.51 in 1900. On the other hand the like ratio for 1915, the next year for which a full breakdown of fixed capital was available was 0.79. It seems likely that a good deal of variation may have been caused by variation in census-taking methods. In any event, the Statcan estimates of construction expenditure for 1870 to 1890 were based on assumptions that implied that the rates of increase in the net capital stock of machinery equipment in these decades were about the same as the rates of increase in the net capital stock of buildings and structures. Constancy in the ratio of expenditure on machinery and equipment to that on construction would be consistent with this Statcan process; it might still be questioned whether the 1896-1900 ratio was the appropriate one.

The two other relatively large categories of expenditure on machinery and equipment, those of agriculture and railways, require little comment. The case of the railways has been dealt with already in the chapter on construction. The method of estimation for agriculture did not use the ratio method but rather is tied to levels of purchases of agricultural machinery and equipment in census years. The census year estimates should therefore be reasonably reliable.

Bibliography of Sources Cited in Chapter 12

Sources for Royalties:

Canada, Department of the Interior, *Report*, 1927-28.

Canada, Department of Marine and Fisheries, annual *Reports*, especially 1927-28.

Ontario, Department of Crown Lands and successor Departments, *Reports*, annual.

Quebec, Minister of Lands and Forests, annual *Reports* and especially for 1928.

Alberta, British Columbia, New Brunswick, Nova Scotia, Saskatchewan; *Public Accounts* of each government, annual.

Indirect Taxes Less Subsidies

Canada and all provinces: *Public Accounts*.

Royal Commission on Dominion-Provincial Relations *Report, Book III, Documentation*, 1939.

Statistics Canada, *National Income and Expenditure Accounts, 1926-1974*, Volume I.

Canada, *Report of* Board of Inquiry Into the Cost of Living, Volume III (1915).

Provincial and Municipal data: *Reports* of Departments of Municipal Affairs, Department Bureaus and *Financial Reports* of Cities of Halifax, Montreal, Winnipeg, and Edmonton.

Canadian Tax Foundation, *Canadian Fiscal Facts*, 1957.

Barnett, Robert F.J., *Canada's Manufacturing Development and Foreign Trade 1870-1915* (unpublished memorandum).

Maclist, a set of unpublished data from Statcan (see the bibliography to Chapter 5).

Supplementary Tables

Resource Royalties: Tables 12.3 and 12.4

General Comment

The sum of all royalty revenues allocated to provinces and the Dominion in the second of the following tables may not coincide with the sum of the countrywide estimates for forestry, mining and the fisheries in the first of these tables owing to the absence of data for particular provinces for particular years. In such cases of lack of data, estimates for missing data were made for the industry totals but were not made for the entries for individual provinces. Entries of N.A. have been made in the provincial tables where the data were absent.

By error, forestry revenues in B.C. were not included in industry totals in 1886 to 1890 but they were small indeed as follows in thousands of dollars: 1886 – 3; 1887 – 7; 1888 – 15; 1889 – 25; 1890 – 25. Additionally, forestry revenues were not available for Ontario in 1891 and 1911 at the time the aggregate data were first prepared (Sessional papers were not available); the actual forestry revenues for Ontario were obtained later as follows in thousands of dollars: 1984 – 1,023; 1911 – 1,711. The availability of these later figures showed that our original aggregate estimates were somewhat too high but not by enough to warrant making changes with all the revision that involves.

Bases of Royalties by Province

British Columbia:	Revenues were from mining only 1871-1879; revenues from forestry started in 1880 and comprised the largest share of the total from 1907 onward; revenues from fishing started in 1909.
Alberta:	Revenues were from mining.
Saskatchewan:	Revenues were from forestry.
Ontario:	Revenues from forestry only 1876-97. Revenues from forestry comprised by far the greater share of the total throughout the period except for two years.
Quebec:	Revenues were from forestry.
New Brunswick:	Revenues from fishing started in 1883; revenues from forestry comprised by far the greatest share of the total throughout the period.
Nova Scotia:	Revenues were from mining.

Table 12.3

Public Revenue from Resource Royalties, by Industry
(thousands of dollars)

Fiscal Year Ending	Forestry	Mining	Fisheries	Total Revenue
1870	915	(100)	12	1,027
1871	* 1,000	110	11	1,120
1872	1,550	159	10	1,718
1873	* 1,300	137	14	1,451
1874	* 1,100	115	15	1,229
1875	780	75	14	868
1876	958	68	13	1,040
1877	899	85	14	999
1878	723	67	18	807
1879	789	53	19	862
1880	1,239	77	25	1,340
1881	1,735	112	24	1,871
1882	1,842	118	21	1,982
1883	1,527	(113)	24	1,663
1884	1,242	109	30	1,379
1885	1,328	125	29	1,483
1886	1,509	137	30	1,675
1887	1,810	158	53	2,021
1888	2,508	166	65	2,739
1889	2,123	187	78	2,388
1890	1,812	189	78	2,080
1891	* 2,300	193	71	2,564
1892	3,340	188	121	3,649
1893	2,898	207	89	3,193
1894	1,973	276	104	2,353
1895	2,084	300	97	2,481
1896	1,865	360	116	2,341
1897	2,636	1,074	122	3,833
1898	2,281	1,474	94	3,849
1899	2,589	1,464	97	4,150

Table 12.3 (continued)

Fiscal Year Ending	Forestry	Mining	Fisheries	Total Revenue
1900	3,017	1,626	97	4,740
1901	3,033	1,514	87	4,634
1902	3,366	1,422	90	4,878
1903	4,350	1,427	109	5,886
1904	4,969	1,227	103	6,300
1905	4,330	1,262	111	5,702
1906	4,163	1,444	70	5,677
1907	4,201	2,775	106	7,082
1908	5,598	1,570	98	7,267
1909	4,552	2,141	124	6,816
1910	6,109	2,395	148	8,653
1911	* 6,700	(2,323)	195	9,218
1912	6,799	2,251	153	9,202
1913	7,176	2,534	167	9,877
1914	6,935	2,777	162	9,874
1915	5,966	1,649	162	7,776
1916	5,412	1,850	152	7,415
1917	5,911	1,958	179	8,048
1918	6,775	2,004	190	8,969
1919	8,957	2,251	404	11,612
1920	11,108	2,610	363	14,081
1921	* 12,300	2,386	292	14,978
1922	11,267	2,170	354	13,790
1923	10,733	2,213	229	13,175
1924	13,489	2,136	202	15,827
1925	14,738	1,999	237	16,974
1926	14,910	2,849	250	18,009

* For these years data on forestry for at least one province were missing and estimation was necessary.

For bracketed figures in mining royalties data for at least one province were missing and estimation was necessary.

Table 12.4
Public Revenue from Resource Royalties, by Province
1870-1926
(thousands of dollars)

Fiscal Year	British Columbia	Alberta	Saskatchewan	Ontario	Quebec	New Brunswick	Nova Scotia	Dominion
1870	N.A.			428	406	21	72	74
71	8 (1)			488	448	N.A.	67	87
72	8			972	519	46	83	91
73	5			N.A.	528	N.A.	101	109
74	8			519	533	N.A.	91	96
75	7			294	387	47	62	71
76	8			438	392	55	60	88
77	7			427	351	57	77	69
78	9			285	315	99	57	43
79	3 (1)			332	343	63	49	72
1880	7			501	544	127	70	93
81	6			840	669	127	102	128
82	5			894	685	137	109	152
83	4			506	661	179	N.A.	206
84	8			465	530	131	101	147
85	5			604	529	107	119	119
86	12			716	583	126	127	116
87	14			991	599	117	149	159
88	23			1,316	959	130	154	171
89	35			1,079	806	145	169	181
1890	35			916	646	138	171	198
91	54			N.A.	624	111	174	189
92	59			2,175	889	126	166	234
93	46			1,757	829	207	175	178
94	69			981	772	107	243	181
95	108			853	951	150	252	167
96	137			813	782	141	274	193
97	284			1,327	911	176	270	865
98	299			985	894	146	278	1,248
99	309			1,097	1,113	176	319	1,137

Table 12.4. (continued)

Fiscal Year	British Columbia	Alberta	Saskatchewan	Ontario	Quebec	New Brunswick	Nova Scotia	Dominion
1900	368			1,284	1,234	164	413	1,276
01	451			1,566	1,055	188	438	936
02	472			1,417	1,242	168	487	1,092
03	601			2,373	1,167	187	619	939
04	675			2,697	1,380	275	585	687
05	801			2,130	1,266	235	614	657
06	996			2,151	1,018	271	613	627
07	1,640			2,772	978	287	602	804
08	2,682			2,133	906	304	661	580
09	2,248 (2)			1,703	1,034	355	605	871
1910	2,790			2,523	1,127	445	596	1,172
11	3,020			N.A.	1,533	480	633	1,142
12	2,827			2,377	1,510	454	774	1,260
13	3,151			2,340	1,589	705	839	1,253
14	3,056			1,841	1,737	673	748	1,819
15	2,252			1,669	1,684	549	716	906
16	2,062			1,430	1,568	490	805	1,058
17	2,459	7		1,796	1,413	496	724	1,153
18	2,529	139	12	1,874	2,024	663	641	1,088
19	2,951	211	8	2,764	2,604	751	607	1,716
1920	2,683	284	5	3,884	3,035	1,442	656	2,092
21	3,465	278	4	N.A.	3,692	1,182	606	1,850
22	2,915	285	6	4,347	3,148	720	530	1,840
23	3,333	250	2	2,469	3,778	982	712	1,648
24	3,424	197	2	4,280	4,321	1,195	728	1,681
25	3,496	254	2	4,707	5,219	981	348	1,965
26	3,750	277	4	4,253	5,757	966	682	2,320

Footnotes: (1) 6 months only
              (2) 9 months only.

Index

714